Morning & Evening

365-DAY DEVOTIONAL

Charles Spurgeon

WHITAKER
HOUSE

Publisher's note:
In this completely new edition from Whitaker House, we have lightly edited the unabridged original text for the modern reader. Words, expressions, and sentence structure have been updated for clarity and readability, while retaining the entirety of Spurgeon's original writings.

All Scripture quotations are taken from the King James Version (KJV) of the Holy Bible.

MORNING AND EVENING
Revised and Updated Edition

ISBN-13: 978-0-88368-749-9
Printed in the United States of America
© 1997, 2002 by Whitaker House

Whitaker House
1030 Hunt Valley Circle
New Kensington, PA 15068
www.whitakerhouse.com

Library of Congress Cataloging-in-Publication Data
Spurgeon, C. H. (Charles Haddon), 1834–1892.
 Morning and evening / Charles Haddon Spurgeon.
    p. cm.
Rev. ed. of: Morning & evening. ©1997.
 ISBN 0-88368-749-6 (pbk.)
 1. Devotional calendars—Baptists. I. Spurgeon, C. H. (Charles Haddon), 1834–1892.
Morning and evening daily devotions. II. Title.
 BV4811 .S6669 2002
 242'.2—dc21

                          2001008421

10 11 12 13 14 15 16 **ШJ** 24 23 22 21 20 19 18

CONTENTS

PREFACE TO
MORNING BY MORNING

Poets have delighted to sing of the morning as "Mother of the Dews, sowing the earth with orient pearl." Many saints, rising from their beds at the first blush of dawn, have found the poetry of nature to be the reality of grace as they have felt the dews of heaven refreshing their spirits. Hence, morning devotions have always been dear to enlightened, heaven-loving souls, and it has been their practice never to see the face of dawn until they have first seen the face of God. The breath of morn redolent with the smell of flowers is incense offered by earth to her Creator, and people should never let the dead earth excel them in praising their God.

Those alive with the Spirit tune their hearts to sing just as birds salute the radiant mercy that reveals itself in the east. The first fresh hour of every morning should be dedicated to the Lord, whose mercy gladdens it with golden light. The eye of day opens its lids and, in so doing, opens the eyes of hosts of heaven-protected slumberers. It is fitting that those eyes should first look up to the great Father of Lights, the Fount and Source of all the good upon which the sunlight gleams. It promises for us a day of grace when we begin our day with God; the sanctifying influence of the season spent in heavenly places influences each succeeding hour.

Morning devotions anchor the soul, so that it will not very readily drift far away from God during the day. They perfume the heart so that it smells fragrant with piety until nightfall; they hold up the soul's garments so that it is less apt to stumble; they feed all their power so that the soul is not permitted to faint.

The morning is the gate of the day and should be well-guarded with prayer. It is one end of the thread on which the day's actions are strung and should be well-knit with devotion. If we felt the majesty of life more, we would be more careful of its mornings. He who rushes from his bed to his business and does not wait to worship is as foolish as if he had not put on his clothes or washed his face. He is as unwise as one who dashes into battle without being armed. Let us bathe in the softly flowing river of communion with God before the heat of the wilderness and the burden of the way begin to oppress us.

In writing these short reflections on certain passages of Scripture, I wanted to assist the believer in his private meditations. A child may sometimes console a desolate heart that might not otherwise have been cheered. Even a flower smiling upward from the ground may turn our thoughts heavenward. It is my hope that, by the Holy Spirit's grace, as the reader turns, morning by morning, to read a simple page, he will hear in it a still small voice that will speak the Word of God to his soul.

The mind wearies of one thing; therefore, I have endeavored to use variety in presenting these devotionals. I have tried to change the style constantly—sometimes exhorting, then solioquizing, then conversing. I have used the first, second, and third persons, and both the singular and the plural—all with the desire of avoiding sameness and dullness.

The subject matter, also, I hope, is wide in its range, and not altogether without a dash of freshness. Readers of my sermons may recognize thoughts and expressions that they have encountered before; but much is, to me at least, as far as anything can be when it deals with the common theme of salvation, new and original. I have written out of my own heart, and most of the portions are remembrances of words that were refreshing in my own experience; therefore, I hope that these daily meditations will be refreshing to the reader as well. In fact, I know they will be if the Spirit of God rests on them.

My ambition has led me to hope that this little volume may also enrich the worship of families where God's altar burns in the morning. We know that it has been the custom in some households to read Mason, Hawker, Bogatsky, Smith, or Jay, and without wishing to usurp the place of any of these, this devotional aspires to a position among them. My happiness will overflow if this book becomes a blessing to Christian households. Family worship is, beyond measure, important both for the present and succeeding generations, and I would consider it a great honor to be, in part, a chaplain in the houses of my friends.

I have written no prayers because I think that a prayer is good for nothing if it is not written on the heart by the Holy Spirit and made to gush forth still warm from the soul. I would as soon think of printing a model for our children to use in addressing their parents as draw up a prayer to be offered to our Father who is in heaven. It has been said in defense of forms, "Better to go on crutches than not at all," but it is my firm conviction that those who truly *go* in the sense of worshipping aright might, with a little effort and an earnest cry to the Holy Spirit for assistance, go much better on their own legs than using some wearisome aid.

If there is not time to read both the morning devotional and a portion from Scripture, I earnestly request that this book would be set aside, for it would be a sore affliction to me to know that any family read the Word of God less on my account. I have had it in my heart to inspire my friends to search their Bibles more than ever; therefore, I have culled passages out of corners and nooks of Scripture, so that curiosity might lead the reader to search for their context. I would be disappointed indeed if, after all, I frustrated my own purpose by diverting one moment of time to the perusal of my remarks that should have been given to searching the Word of God itself.

I also hope that preachers may sometimes glean a text and suggestions for a sermon from one of these daily thoughts. Certainly they are free to do so if they can. The ideas are not ours but are common property. Tossed about by cares and worried by business, men's minds are not always in a condition on Saturday evening to leave their earthly concerns behind and begin a line of meditation. But once their thoughts take wing, the very events of the week can even help their flight. Perhaps we may lift some heart upward, and, if so, God be praised. Possibly a hint given here may serve as a match to set fire to a preacher's soul, and that heart ablaze may warm and gladden hundreds. Amen, and the Lord our God says so, too.

Hoping for a favorable reception for this present work, I have already written a volume of the same size and character for evening reading.[1] Meanwhile, with many prayers for heaven's blessing upon this labor of love, and with earnest requests for the prayers of the faithful, this work is humbly dedicated to the honor of the triune Jehovah, and respectfully presented to the Christian church.

—*C. H. Spurgeon*

---

1. *Evening by Evening* is available from Whitaker House. *Morning and Evening*, a compilation of Spurgeon's morning and evening devotionals in one volume, is also available.

PREFACE TO
EVENING BY EVENING

When the noise and turmoil of the day are over, it is sweet to commune with God. The cool and calm of evening agree most delightfully with prayer and praise. The hours of the declining sun are like quiet alleys in the garden of time wherein man may find his Maker waiting to commune with him, even as of old the Lord God walked with Adam in Paradise in the cool of the day.

It is fitting that we should set apart a peaceful season before the day has quite ended, a season of thanksgiving for abounding grace, of repentance for multiplied follies, of self-examination for insinuating evils. To leap from day to day like a mad hunter beating the bushes is an omen of being delivered over to destruction. But the solemn pause, the deliberate consideration—these are means of grace and signs of an indwelling life. The ocean tide stays awhile at ebb before it resolves to flood again; the moon sometimes lingers at its fullest size. There are distinct hedges in nature set between the seasons—even the strike of the bell is a little warning that men should not remove landmarks; instead, they should frequently examine the boundaries in their lives and keep up with due interval and solemnity the remembrance of the passing of days and months and years. Each evening it would be well to traverse the boundaries of the day and take note of all that it has brought and all that it has seen.

The drops of the night come from the same Fount as the dew of the morning. He who met Abraham at the break of day communed with Isaac in the field at evening. He who opens the doors of the day with the hand of mercy draws the curtains of the night around His people. By His shining presence, He makes the *"outgoings of the morning and evening to*

11

rejoice" (Ps. 65:8). A promise at dawn and a sure word at sunset crown the brow of day with light and sandal its feet with love. To breakfast with Jesus and to dine with Him also is to enjoy the days of heaven on earth.

It is dangerous to fall asleep before the head is leaned on Jesus' bosom. When divine love puts its finger on weary eyelids, it is brave sleeping; but so that the Lord's beloved may have such sleep given to him, it is necessary that he should make a near approach to the throne and unburden his soul before the great Preserver of men. To enter into the blaze of Jehovah's presence by way of the atoning blood is the sure method of refining ourselves of earthly dross and renewing the soul after exhausting service.

The reading of the Word and prayer are as gates of precious stones to admit us into the presence of the august Majesty. He is most blessed who most frequently swings those gates on their sapphire hinges. When the stars are revealed and all the hosts of heaven walk in golden glory, then surely that is the time when the solemn temple is lit up and the worshipper is invited to enter. If one hour can be endowed with a sacredness above the others, it must be the hour when the Lord looses the cords of Orion and leads forth the Bear and its cubs. (See Job 38:31–32.) Then voices from worlds afar call us to contemplation and adoration, and the stillness of the lower world prepares an oratory for the devout soul. He surely never prays at all who does not end the day as all men wish to end their lives—in prayer.

In many households the gathering of the family for evening prayer is easier than the morning opportunity, and in all the tents of our Israel, the evening sacrifice should be solemnly remembered. Before we take refuge underneath the wings of the Eternal, let us entreat Him to deliver us from the terror by night and give us safe dwelling in His secret place. It is blessed work to set the night watchmen in their posts by supplication, and then to commit ourselves without fear to the embraces of divine love.

Having had the seal of our Master's blessing set upon our former volume, entitled *Morning by Morning,* we have felt encouraged to give our best attention to the present series of brief meditations, and I send them forth with importunate prayer for a blessing to rest on every reader. May the Father's smile be their benediction. I have striven to keep out of the common track; hence, I have used unusual texts and have brought forward neglected subjects. The vice of many religious works is their dullness—from this I have tried to be free: my friends must judge how successful I have been. I have drawn much of my subject matter out of my own experience, and I have always felt assured that a truth that has been sanctified to our own good will not be without an anointing for others. If I may lead one heart upward that otherwise would have drooped, or sow in a single mind a holy purpose that otherwise never would have been conceived, I will be grateful. May the Lord send us such results in thousands of instances, and His will be all the praise. The longer I live, the more deeply I am conscious that the Holy Spirit alone can make truth profitable to the heart; therefore, in earnest prayer, I commit this volume and its companion to His care.

—*C. H. Spurgeon*

They did eat of the fruit of the land of Canaan that year.
—Joshua 5:12

Israel's weary wanderings were over, and the promised rest was attained. No more moving tents, fiery serpents, fierce Amalekites, and howling wildernesses. The Israelites came to the land that flowed with milk and honey, and they ate the old corn of the land. Perhaps this year, beloved Christian reader, this may be your case or mine. The prospect is joyful, and, if faith is actively exercised, it will yield pure delight. To be with Jesus in the rest that remains for the people of God is a cheering hope indeed, and to expect this glory so soon is a double bliss. Unbelief shudders at the Jordan, which still rolls between us and the good land, but let us rest assured that we have already experienced more ills than death at its worst can cause us. Let us banish every fearful thought and rejoice with exceeding great joy in the prospect that this year we will begin to *"ever be with the Lord"* (1 Thess. 4:17). Many will this year remain on earth to do service for their Lord. If this is our lot, there is no reason that the New Year's text should not still be true. *"We which have believed do enter into rest"* (Heb. 4:3). The Holy Spirit is the guarantee of our inheritance. He gives us "glory begun below." Those who are in heaven are secure; likewise, we on earth are kept safe in Christ Jesus. There, they triumph over their enemies; here, we have victories, too. Celestial spirits enjoy communion with their Lord; this privilege is not denied to us. They rest in His love; we have perfect peace in Him. They sing His praise; it is our privilege to bless Him, too. We will this year gather celestial fruits on earthly ground, where faith and hope have made the desert like the garden of the Lord. In the past, man ate angels' food; why not now? Oh, for grace to feed on Jesus and to eat of the fruit of the land of Canaan this year!

JANUARY 1

Evening

We will be glad and rejoice in thee.
—Song of Solomon 1:4

"*We will be glad and rejoice in thee.*" We will not open the gates of the year to the dolorous notes of the trombone, but to the sweet strains of the harp of joy and the grand sounds of the cymbals of gladness. "*O come, let us sing unto the LORD: let us make a joyful noise to the rock of our salvation*" (Ps. 95:1). We, the called and faithful and chosen, will drive away our griefs and set up our banners of confidence in the name of God. Let others lament over their troubles; we who have the sweetening tree to cast into Marah's bitter pool (see Exodus 15:23) will magnify the Lord with joy. Eternal Spirit, our precious Comforter, we, who are the temples in which You dwell, will never cease from adoring and blessing the name of Jesus. "*We will*"—we are resolved about it. Jesus must have the crown of our hearts' delight. We will not dishonor our Bridegroom by mourning in His presence. We are ordained to be the minstrels of the skies; let us rehearse our everlasting anthem before we sing it in the halls of the New Jerusalem. "*We will be glad and rejoice.*" These words have one sense: double joy, blessing upon blessing. Does there need to be any limit to our rejoicing in the Lord? Do not men of grace find their Lord to be precious even now? What better fragrance do they have in heaven itself? "*We will be glad and rejoice in thee.*" That last word is the meat in the dish, the kernel of the nut, the soul of the text. What blessings are laid up in Jesus! What rivers of infinite bliss have their source, yes, and every drop of their fullness, in Him! Since, O sweet Lord Jesus, You are the present portion of Your people, favor us this year with such a sense of Your preciousness that, from its first to its last day, we may be glad and rejoice in You. Let January open with joy in the Lord, and December close with gladness in Jesus.

JANUARY 2

Morning

Continue in prayer.
—Colossians 4:2

It is interesting to notice how large a portion of Scripture is occupied with the subject of prayer, either in furnishing examples, enforcing precepts, or pronouncing promises. We scarcely open the Bible before we read, *"Then began men to call upon the name of the LORD"* (Gen. 4:26), and just as we are about to close the volume, the *"Amen"* (Rev. 22:21) of an earnest supplication meets our ear. Instances are plentiful. Here we find a wrestling Jacob, there a Daniel who prayed three times a day, and a David who with all his heart called on his God. On the mountain we see Elijah, and in the dungeon Paul and Silas. We have multitudes of commands and myriads of promises. What do these examples teach us but the sacred importance and necessity of prayer? We may be certain that whatever God has made prominent in His Word, He intended to be conspicuous in our lives. If He has said much about prayer, it is because He knows we have much need of it. So deep are our needs that, until we are in heaven, we must not cease to pray. Do you have no needs? Then I fear you do not know your own poverty. Do you have no need to ask God for mercy? Then may the Lord's mercy show you your misery! A prayerless soul is a Christless soul. Prayer is the lisping of the believing infant, the shout of the fighting believer, the requiem of the dying saint falling asleep in Jesus. It is the breath, the watchword, the comfort, the strength, the honor of a Christian. If you are a child of God, you will seek your Father's face and live in your Father's love. Pray that this year you may be holy, humble, zealous, and patient. Have closer communion with Christ, and enter more often into the banqueting-house of His love. Pray that you may be an example and a blessing to others, and that you may live more to the glory of your Master. The motto for this year must be *"Continue in prayer."*

JANUARY 2
Evening

Let the people renew their strength.
—Isaiah 41:1

All things on earth need to be renewed. No created thing continues by itself. *"Thou renewest the face of the earth"* (Ps. 104:30) was the psalmist's utterance. Even the trees, which do not wear themselves out with care or shorten their lives with labor, must drink of the rain of heaven and draw from the hidden treasures of the soil. The cedars of Lebanon, which God has planted, live only because, day by day, they are full of sap freshly drawn from the earth. Neither can man's life be sustained without renewal from God. As it is necessary to prevent the wasting away of the body by frequent meals, so we must restore the hungry soul by listening to the preached Word or by feeding on the Book of God or the soul-fattening table of the ordinances. How depressed are our graces when means are neglected! What poor starvelings some saints are who live without the diligent use of the Word of God and secret prayer! If our piety can live without God, it is not of divine creating; it is but a dream. For if God had begotten it, it would wait on Him as the flowers wait on the dew. Without constant restoration, we are not ready for the perpetual assaults of hell or the stern afflictions of heaven or even the conflicts within. When the whirlwind is loosed, woe to the tree that has not sucked up fresh sap and grasped the rock with many intertwined roots. When tempests arise, woe to the mariners who have not strengthened their masts, cast their anchors, or sought a haven. If we allow the good to grow weaker, the evil will surely gather strength and struggle desperately for mastery over us; and so, perhaps, a painful desolation and a lamentable disgrace may follow. Let us draw near to the footstool of divine mercy in humble entreaty. Then we will realize the fulfillment of the promise, *"They that wait upon the LORD shall renew their strength"* (Isa. 40:31).

I will preserve thee, and give thee
for a covenant of the people.
—Isaiah 49:8

Jesus Christ is Himself the sum and substance of the covenant, and as one of its gifts, He is the property of every believer. Believer, can you estimate what you have received in Christ? *"In him dwelleth all the fulness of the Godhead bodily"* (Col. 2:9). Consider the word *God* and its infinity, and then, meditate on Christ, the perfect Man, and all His beauty; for all that Christ, as God and Man, ever had, or can have, is yours. Out of pure, free favor, it passed over to you to be your personal property forever. Our blessed Jesus, as God, is omniscient, omnipresent, and omnipotent. Will it not console you to know that all these great and glorious attributes are altogether yours? Has He power? That power is yours to support and strengthen you, to overcome your enemies, and to preserve you even to the end. Has He love? Well, there is not a drop of love in His heart that is not yours; you may dive into the immense ocean of His love, and you may say of it all, "It is mine." Has He justice? It may seem a stern attribute, but even that is yours, for He will, by His justice, see to it that all that is promised to you in the covenant of grace will be most certainly secured to you. And all that He has as perfect Man is yours. As a perfect Man, Christ received the Father's delight. He stood accepted by the Most High. Believer, God's acceptance of Christ is your acceptance; for do you not know that the love that the Father set on a perfect Christ, He sets on you now? For all that Christ did is yours. That perfect righteousness that Jesus brought about, when through His stainless life He kept the law and made it honorable, is yours and is imputed to you. Christ is in the covenant.

My God, I am yours—what a comfort divine!
What a blessing to know that the Savior is mine!
In the heavenly Lamb thrice happy I am,
And my heart it does dance at the sound of His name.

JANUARY 3
Evening

The voice of one crying in the wilderness, Prepare ye the way of the Lord, make his paths straight.
—Luke 3:4

The voice crying in the wilderness demanded a way for the Lord to be prepared, a way prepared in the wilderness. I would be attentive to the Master's proclamation and give Him a road into my heart, built, by gracious operations, through the desert of my nature. The four directives in Isaiah 40, from which today's text comes (v. 3), must have my serious attention: *"Every valley shall be exalted"* (v. 4). Low and groveling thoughts of God must be given up, doubting and despairing must be removed, and self-seeking and carnal delights must be forsaken. Across these deep valleys, a glorious causeway of grace must be raised. *"Every mountain and hill shall be made low"* (v. 4). Proud creature-sufficiency and boastful self-righteousness must be leveled to make a highway for the King of Kings. Divine fellowship is never granted to haughty, high-minded sinners. The Lord shows respect to the lowly and visits the contrite in heart, but the arrogant are an abomination to Him. My soul, beseech the Holy Spirit to set you right in this respect. *"The crooked shall be made straight"* (v. 4). The wavering heart must have a straight path of decision for God and holiness marked out for it. Double-minded men are strangers to the God of truth. My soul, take heed that you are honest and true in all things, as in the sight of the heart-searching God. *"The rough places* [shall be made] *plain"* (v. 4). Stumbling blocks of sin must be removed, and thorns and briers of rebellion must be uprooted. So great a Visitor must not find miry ways and stony places when He comes to honor His favored ones with His company. Oh, that this evening the Lord would find in my heart a highway made ready by His grace, so that He may make a triumphal progression through the utmost boundaries of my soul, from the beginning of this year even to the end of it.

Grow in grace, and in the knowledge of our Lord
and Saviour Jesus Christ.
—2 Peter 3:18

Grow in grace"—not in one grace only, but in all grace. Grow in that root-grace, *faith.* Believe the promises more firmly than you have before. Let faith increase in fullness, constancy, and simplicity. Grow also in *love.* Ask that your love may become extended, more intense, more practical, influencing every thought, word, and deed. Grow likewise in *humility.* Seek to lie very low, and know more of your own nothingness. As you grow downward in humility, seek also to grow upward—having nearer approaches to God in prayer and more intimate fellowship with Jesus. May God the Holy Spirit enable you to *"grow...in the knowledge of our Lord and Saviour."* He who does not grow in the knowledge of Jesus refuses to be blessed. To know Him is *"life eternal"* (John 17:3), and to advance in the knowledge of Him is to increase in happiness. He who does not long to know more of Christ knows nothing of Him yet. Whoever has sipped this wine will thirst for more, for although Christ satisfies, yet it is such a satisfaction that the appetite is not satiated, but whetted. If you know the love of Jesus, then, *"as the hart panteth after the water brooks"* (Ps. 42:1), so will you pant after deeper depths of His love. If you do not desire to know Him better, then you do not love Him, for love always cries, "Nearer, nearer." Absence from Christ is hell, but the presence of Jesus is heaven. Do not rest content, then, without an increasing acquaintance with Jesus. Seek to know more of Him in His divine nature, in His human relationship, in His finished work, in His death, in His resurrection, in His present glorious intercession, and in His future royal advent. Abide close to the cross, and search the mystery of His wounds. An increase of love for Jesus, and a more perfect apprehension of His love for us, is one of the best tests of growth in grace.

JANUARY 4

Evening

And Joseph knew his brethren, but they knew not him.
—Genesis 42:8

This morning our prayer went forth for growth in grace and in the knowledge of our Lord Jesus; it may be well tonight to consider a related topic, namely, our heavenly Joseph's knowledge of us. This knowledge was most blessedly perfect long before we had the slightest knowledge of Him. *"Thine eyes did see my substance, yet being unperfect; and in thy book all my members were written,...when as yet there was none of them"* (Ps. 139:16). Before we existed in the world, we existed in His heart. When we were enemies to Him, He knew us, with our misery, our foolishness, and our wickedness. When we wept bitterly in despairing repentance and viewed Him as only a judge and a ruler, He viewed us as His well-beloved brethren, and His heart yearned toward us. He never mistook His chosen, but always beheld them as objects of His infinite affection. *"The Lord knoweth them that are his"* (2 Tim. 2:19) is as true of the prodigals who are feeding swine as of the children who sit at the table. But, alas, we did not know our Royal Brother, and out of this ignorance grew a host of sins. We withheld our hearts from Him and allowed Him no entrance to our love. We mistrusted Him and gave no credit to His words. We rebelled against Him and paid Him no loving homage. The *"Sun of righteousness"* (Mal. 4:2) shone forth, and we could not see Him. Heaven came down to earth, and earth perceived it not. Let God be praised, for those days are over for us; yet even now we know but little of Jesus compared with what He knows of us. We have but begun to study Him, but He knows us completely. It is a blessed circumstance that the ignorance is not on His side, for then it would be a hopeless case for us. He will not say to us, *"I never knew you"* (Matt. 7:23). He will confess our names in the day of His appearing; meanwhile, He will manifest Himself to us as He does not to the world.

JANUARY 5

*And God saw the light, that it was good: and God
divided the light from the darkness.*
—Genesis 1:4

Light might well be good, since it sprang from that command of goodness, *"Let there be light"* (Gen. 1:3). We who enjoy it should be more grateful for it than we are and see more of God *in* it and *by* it. *Physical* light was said by Solomon to be sweet, but *gospel* light is infinitely more precious, for it reveals eternal things and ministers to our immortal natures. When the Holy Spirit gives us spiritual light and opens our eyes to behold *"the glory of God in the face of Jesus Christ"* (2 Cor. 4:6), then we also behold sin in its true colors, and ourselves in our real position. We see the Most Holy God as He reveals Himself, the plan of mercy as He offers it, and the world to come as the Word describes it. Spiritual light has many beams and prismatic colors, but whether they are knowledge, joy, holiness, or life, they are all divinely good. If the light received is thus good, what must the essential Light be, and how glorious must the place where He reveals Himself be! O Lord, since light is so good, give us more of it, and more of Yourself, the true Light. No sooner is there a good thing in the world than a division is necessary. Light and darkness have no communion. God has divided them; let us not mistake them. Sons of light must not have fellowship with deeds, doctrines, or deceits of darkness. The children of the day must be sober, honest, and bold in their Lord's work, leaving the works of darkness to those who will dwell in it forever. Our churches should by discipline divide the light from the darkness, and we should by our distinct separation from the world do the same. In our judgments, actions, relationships, teaching, and listening, we must discern between the precious and the vile, and maintain the great distinction that the Lord made on the world's first day. O Lord Jesus, be our Light throughout the whole of this day, for Your light is the light of men.

JANUARY 5
Evening

And God saw the light.
—Genesis 1:4

This morning we noticed the goodness of the light, and the Lord's dividing it from the darkness. We now note the special eye that the Lord had for the light: *"God saw the light."* He looked at it with satisfaction, gazed on it with pleasure, and saw that it *"was good"* (Gen. 1:4). If the Lord has given you light, dear reader, He looks on that light with special interest, not only because it is dear to Him as His own handiwork, but also because it is like Himself, for *"God is light"* (1 John 1:5). It is pleasant to the believer to know that God's eye is thus tenderly observant of that work of grace that He has begun in him. He never loses sight of the treasure that He has placed in our earthen vessels. Sometimes we cannot see the light, but God always sees the light, and that is much better than our seeing it. Better for the judge to see my innocence than for me to think I see it. It is very comfortable for me to know that I am one of God's people; but whether I know it or not, if the Lord knows it, I am still safe. This is the foundation: *"The Lord knoweth them that are his"* (2 Tim. 2:19). You may be sighing and groaning because of inbred sin and mourning over your darkness, yet the Lord sees light in your heart, for He has put it there. All the cloudiness and gloom of your soul cannot conceal your light from His gracious eye. You may have sunk low in despondency and even despair, but if your soul has any longing toward Christ, and if you are seeking to rest in His finished work, God sees the light. He not only sees it, but also preserves it in you. *"I the LORD do keep it"* (Isa. 27:3). This is a precious thought to those who, after anxious watching and guarding of themselves, feel their own powerlessness to keep themselves. The light thus preserved by God's grace He will one day develop into the splendor of noonday and the fullness of glory. The light within is the dawn of the eternal day.

JANUARY 6

Morning

Casting all your care upon him; for he careth for you.
—1 Peter 5:7

It is a happy way of soothing sorrow when we can feel that He cares for us. Christian, do not dishonor your faith by always wearing a brow of care. Come and cast your burden on your Lord. You are staggering beneath a weight that your Father would not feel. What seems to be a crushing burden to you would be like a little dust on the scale to Him. Nothing is so sweet as to "Lie passive in God's hands, and know no will but His." O child of suffering, be patient. God has not passed you over in His loving care. He who is the feeder of sparrows will also furnish you with what you need. Do not sit down in despair. Hope on, and hope ever. Take up the arms of faith against a sea of trouble, and your fight of faith will yet end your distresses. There is One who cares for you. His eye is fixed on you, His heart beats with pity for your sorrow, and His omnipotent hand will yet bring you the needed help. The darkest cloud will scatter itself in showers of mercy. The blackest gloom will give place to the morning. If you are one of His family, He will bind up your wounds and heal your broken heart. Do not doubt His grace because of your tribulation, but believe that He loves you as much in seasons of trouble as in times of happiness. What a serene and quiet life might you lead if you would leave providing to the God of divine care! With a little oil in the cruse and a handful of meal in the barrel, Elijah outlived the famine, and you will do the same. If God cares for you, why do you need to worry? Can you trust Him for your soul, and not for your body? He has never refused to bear your burdens; He has never fainted under their weight. Come, then, soul; be done with fretful care, and leave all your concerns in the hands of a gracious God.

Now the hand of the LORD was upon me in the evening.
—Ezekiel 33:22

In the way of judgment, this may be the case, and, if so, it is mine to consider the reason for such a visitation and to bear the rod and Him who has appointed it. I am not the only one who is chastened in the night season; let me cheerfully submit to the affliction and carefully endeavor to be profited by it. But the hand of the Lord may also be felt in another manner—strengthening the soul and lifting the spirit up toward eternal things. Oh, that I may in this sense feel the Lord dealing with me! A sense of the divine presence and indwelling bears the soul toward heaven as on the wings of eagles. At such times we are full to the brim with spiritual joy, and we forget the cares and sorrows of earth. The invisible is near, and the visible loses its power over us. The servant-body waits at the foot of the hill, and the master-spirit worships on the summit in the presence of the Lord. Oh, that a hallowed season of divine communion may be granted to me this evening! The Lord knows that I need it very greatly. My graces languish, my corruptions rage, my faith is weak, and my devotion is cold; all these are reasons why His healing hand should be laid upon me. His hand can cool the heat of my burning brow and stop the tumult of my palpitating heart. The glorious right hand that molded the world can create my mind anew. The unwearied hand that bears up the earth's huge pillars can sustain my spirit. The loving hand that encloses all the saints can cherish me. And the mighty hand that breaks the enemy in pieces can subdue my sins. Why should I not feel that hand touching me this evening? Come, my soul. Address your God with the potent plea that Jesus' hands were pierced for your redemption, and you will surely feel that same hand on you that once touched Daniel and drew him to his knees so that he might see visions of God.

For to me to live is Christ.
—Philippians 1:21

The believer did not always live for Christ. He began to do so when God the Holy Spirit convinced him of sin, and when by grace he was brought to see the dying Savior making a propitiation for his guilt. From the moment of the new and celestial birth, the believer begins to live for Christ. Jesus is to believers the *"one pearl of great price"* (Matt. 13:46), for whom we are willing to part with all that we have. He has so completely won our love that it beats alone for Him. To His glory we would live, and in defense of His Gospel we would die. He is the pattern of our life and the model after which we would sculpture our character. Paul's words mean more than most men think. Many would say that Paul's words imply that the aim and end of his life was Christ, but rather, his life itself was Jesus! In the words of an ancient saint, he did "eat and drink and sleep eternal life." Jesus was his very breath, the soul of his soul, the heart of his heart, the life of his life. Can you say, as a professing Christian, that you live up to this ideal? Can you honestly say that for you *"to live is Christ"*? Are you doing your work for Christ, or are you working toward self-aggrandizement and for family advantage? Do you ask, "Is that a base reason?" For the Christian it is. He professes to live for Christ. How can he live for another purpose without committing spiritual adultery? Many carry out this principle in some measure, but who would dare to say that he has lived wholly for Christ as the apostle did? Yet this alone is the true life of a Christian—its source, its sustenance, its fashion, its end. It is all gathered up in one word: *Jesus.* Lord, accept me. I present myself, praying to live only in You and for You. Let me be as the bullock that stands between the plough and the altar. Let my motto be: "Ready for work or for sacrifice."

My sister, my spouse.
—Song of Solomon 4:12

Observe the sweet titles with which the heavenly Solomon addresses His bride, the church, with intense affection: "'*My sister*'—one near to Me by ties of nature, partaker of the same sympathies. '*My spouse*'—nearest and dearest, united to Me by the tenderest bonds of love; My sweet companion, part of My own self. '*My sister*' by My incarnation, which makes Me bone of your bone and flesh of your flesh. '*My spouse*' by heavenly betrothal, in which I have attached you to Myself in righteousness. '*My sister*,' whom I knew of old, and over whom I watched from her earliest infancy. '*My spouse*,' taken from among the daughters, embraced by arms of love, and betrothed to Me forever." See how true it is that our royal Kinsman is not ashamed of us, for He dwells with manifest delight on this twofold relationship. We have the word "*my*" twice in our text, as if Christ dwelt with rapture on His possession of His church. His "*delights were with the sons of men*" (Prov. 8:31), because those sons of men were His own chosen ones. He, the Shepherd, sought the sheep, because they were His sheep. He has gone about "*to seek and to save that which was lost*" (Luke 19:10), because what was lost was His long before it was lost to itself or lost to Him. The church is the exclusive portion of her Lord; no one else may claim a partnership or pretend to share her love. Jesus, Your church delights to have it so! Let every believing soul drink solace out of these wells. Soul, Christ is near to you in ties of relationship. Christ is dear to you in bonds of marriage union, and you are dear to Him! Behold, He grasps both of your hands with both of His own, saying, "*My sister, my spouse*." Note the two sacred anchors by which your Lord secures such a double hold of you that He neither can nor will ever let you go. O beloved, do not be slow to return the hallowed flame of His love.

The iniquity of the holy things.
—Exodus 28:38

What a veil is lifted by these words, and what a disclosure is made! It will be humbling and profitable for us to pause awhile and see this sad sight. The iniquities of our public worship—its hypocrisy, formality, luke-warmness, irreverence, wandering of heart, and forgetfulness of God—what a full measure we have there! Our work for the Lord—its rivalry, self-ishness, carelessness, slackness, and unbelief—what a mass of defilement is there! Our private devotions—their laxity, coldness, neglect, sleepiness, and vanity—what a mountain of dead earth is there! If we looked more carefully, we would find this *"iniquity of the holy things"* to be far greater than appears at first sight. Dr. Payson, writing to his brother, said, "My parish, as well as my heart, very much resembles the garden of the slug-gard. What is worse is that I find many of my desires for the improvement of both proceed either from pride, vanity, or laziness. I look at the weeds that overspread my garden and breathe out an earnest wish that they were eradicated. But why? What prompts the wish? It may be that I may walk out and say to myself, 'In what fine order is my garden kept!' This is pride. Or it may be that my neighbors may look over the wall and say, 'How finely your garden flourishes!' This is vanity. Or I may wish for the destruction of the weeds because I am weary of pulling them up. This is laziness." Even our desires after holiness may be polluted by wrong motives. Under the greenest sods, worms hide themselves. We do not need to look long to dis-cover them. How cheering is the thought that when the high priest bore the *"iniquity of the holy things,"* he wore on his brow the words, "HOLINESS TO THE LORD" (Exod. 28:36). Even so, while Jesus bears our sin, He pres-ents before His Father's face not our lack of holiness, but His own holiness. Oh, for grace to view our Great High Priest with the eyes of faith!

Thy love is better than wine.
—Song of Solomon 1:2

Nothing gives the believer as much joy as fellowship with Christ. He has enjoyment, as others have, in the common mercies of life. He can be glad both in God's gifts and God's works; but in all of these separately, yes, and in all of them added together, he does not find such substantial delight as in the matchless person of his Lord Jesus. The believer has wine that no vineyard on earth ever yielded; he has bread that all the cornfields of Egypt could never bring forth. Where can such sweetness be found as we have tasted in communion with our Beloved? In our judgment, the joys of earth are little better than husks for swine compared with Jesus, the heavenly Manna. We would rather have one mouthful of Christ's love and a sip of His fellowship than a whole world full of carnal delights. What is the chaff compared with the wheat? What is the sparkling artificial gem compared with the true diamond? What is a dream compared with the glorious reality? What is earth's greatest enjoyment compared with our Lord Jesus in His most despised estate? If you know anything of the inner life, you will confess that our highest, purest, and most enduring joys must be the fruit of the Tree of Life, which is in the midst of the Paradise of God. No spring yields such sweet water as that well of God that was dug with the soldier's spear. (See John 19:34.) All earthly bliss is *"of the earth, earthy"* (1 Cor. 15:47), but the comforts of Christ's presence are like Himself, heavenly. We can review our communion with Jesus and find no regrets of emptiness therein; no dregs are in this wine, no dead flies in this ointment. The joy of the Lord is solid and enduring. Vanity has not looked on it, but discretion and prudence testify that it abides the test of years and is, in time and eternity, worthy to be called the only true delight. For nourishment, consolation, exhilaration, and refreshment, no wine can rival the love of Jesus. Let us drink to the full this evening.

I…will be their God.
—Jeremiah 31:33

Christian, here in this promise is all you need. In order to be happy, you need something that will satisfy you; is this not enough? If you can pour this promise into your cup, will you not say with David, "My cup runs over. (See Psalm 23:5.) I have more than my heart could wish for"? When His promise to be your God is fulfilled, are you not a possessor of all things? Desire is as insatiable as death, but He who fills *"all in all"* (Eph. 1:23) can fill it. Who can measure the capacity of our wishes? But the immeasurable wealth of God can more than overflow it. I ask you if you are not complete when God is yours? Do you need anything but God? Is not His all-sufficiency enough to satisfy you, if all else should fail? But you need more than quiet satisfaction; you desire rapturous delight. Come, soul; here is music fit for heaven in this your portion, for God is the Maker of heaven. Not all the music played by sweet instruments or drawn from strings can yield such melody as this sweet promise, *"I…will be their God."* Here is a deep sea of bliss, a shoreless ocean of delight. Come and bathe your spirit in it. Swim for an age, and you will find no shore; dive throughout eternity, and you will find no bottom. *"I…will be their God."* If this does not make your eyes sparkle and your heart beat high with bliss, then assuredly your soul is not in a healthy state. But you need more than present delights—you crave something concerning which you may exercise hope. What more can you hope for than the fulfillment of this great promise, *"I…will be their God"?* This is the masterpiece of all the promises. Its enjoyment makes a heaven below and will make a heaven above. Dwell in the light of your Lord, and let your soul always be ravished with His love. Extract all the *"marrow and fatness"* (Ps. 63:5) that this portion yields to you. Live up to your privileges, and rejoice with unspeakable joy.

JANUARY 9
Evening

Serve the LORD with gladness.
—Psalm 100:2

Delight in divine service is a token of acceptance. Those who serve God with a sad countenance, because they do what is unpleasant to them, are not serving Him at all; they bring the form of homage, but the life is absent. Our God requires no slaves to grace His throne. He is the Lord of the empire of love, and He would have His servants dressed in the uniform of joy. The angels of God serve Him with songs, not with groans. A murmur or a sigh would be mutiny in their ranks. Obedience that is not voluntary is disobedience, for the Lord looks at the heart, and if He sees that we serve Him from force, and not because we love Him, He will reject our offering. Service coupled with cheerfulness is heart-service and, therefore, true. Take away joyful willingness from the Christian, and you have removed the test of his sincerity. If a man is driven to battle, he is no patriot; but he who marches into the fray with flashing eye and beaming face, singing, "It is sweet to die for one's country," proves himself to be sincere in his patriotism. Cheerfulness is the support of our strength; in the joy of the Lord we are strong. It acts as the remover of difficulties. It is to our service what oil is to the wheels of a railroad car. Without oil the axle soon grows hot, and accidents occur; if there is not a holy cheerfulness to oil our wheels, our spirits will be clogged with weariness. The man who is cheerful in his service to God proves that obedience is his element; he can sing,

Make me to walk in Your commands,
'Tis a delightful road.

Reader, let me put this question to you: Do you *"serve the LORD with gladness"*? Let us show the people of the world, who think our religion is slavery, that to us it is a delight and a joy! Let our gladness proclaim that we serve a good Master.

There is laid up for me a crown of righteousness.
—2 Timothy 4:8

Doubting one, you have often said, "I fear I will never enter heaven." Fear not! All the people of God will enter there. I love the quaint saying of a dying man, who exclaimed, "I have no fear of going home. I have sent all before me. God's finger is on the latch of my door, and I am ready for Him to enter." "But," said one, "are you not afraid lest you should miss your inheritance?" "No," said he, "there is one crown in heaven that the angel Gabriel could not wear; it will fit no head but mine. There is one throne in heaven that Paul the apostle could not fill; it was made for me, and I will have it." O Christian, what a joyous thought! Your portion is secure; *"there remaineth...a rest"* (Heb. 4:9). "But cannot I forfeit it?" No, it is titled in your name. If I am a child of God, I will not lose it. It is mine as securely as if I were there possessing it now. Come with me, believer, and let us sit on the top of Nebo and view the bountiful land, even Canaan. Do you see that little river of death glistening in the sunlight? Do you see the pinnacles of the eternal city across it? Do you observe the pleasant country and all its joyous inhabitants? Know, then, that if you could fly across, you would see written on one of its many mansions, "This remains for such a one; it is preserved for him only. He will be caught up to dwell forever with God." Poor doubting one, see the fair inheritance; it is yours. If you believe in the Lord Jesus, if you have repented of sin, if you have been renewed in heart, you are one of the Lord's people, and there is a place reserved for you, a crown laid up for you, a harp especially provided for you. No one else will have your portion. It is reserved in heaven for you, and you will have it before long, for there will be no vacant thrones in glory when all the chosen are gathered in.

In my flesh shall I see God.
—Job 19:26

Note the subject of Job's devout anticipation: "I will see God." He does not say, "I will see the saints"— though, doubtless, that will be untold happiness— but "I will see God." It is not, "I will see the pearly gates; I will behold the walls of jasper; I will gaze upon the crowns of gold," but "I will see God." This is the sum and substance of heaven; this is the joyful hope of all believers. By faith, it is their delight to see Him now in the ordinances. They love to behold Him in communion and in prayer; but there in heaven they will have open and unclouded vision, and seeing *"him as he is"* (1 John 3:2), they will be made completely like Him. Likeness to God—what more can we wish for? A sight of God—what can we desire that is better? Some read the passage, *"In my flesh shall I see God,"* and find there an allusion to Christ as the *"Word…made flesh"* (John 14:1) and that glorious beholding of Him that will be the splendor of the latter days. Whether this is so or not, it is certain that Christ will be the object of our eternal vision; we will never wish for any joy beyond that of seeing Him. Do not think that this will be a narrow sphere for the mind to dwell in. It is but one source of delight, yet that source is infinite. All His attributes will be subjects for contemplation, and as He is infinite in each aspect, there is no fear of exhausting them. His works, His gifts, His love for us, and His glory in all His purposes and in all His actions—these will make a theme that will be ever new. The patriarch looked forward to this sight of God as a personal enjoyment. *"Whom…mine eyes shall behold, and not another"* (Job 19:27). Consider the reality of heaven's bliss; think what heaven will be to you. *"Thine eyes shall see the king in his beauty"* (Isa. 33:17). All earthly brightness fades and darkens as we gaze on it, but here is a brightness that can never dim, a glory that can never fade: I will see God.

These have no root.
—Luke 8:13

My soul, examine yourself this morning in the light of today's text. You have received the Word with joy. Your feelings have been stirred, and a lively impression has been made. But remember: to receive the Word in your ears is one thing; to receive Jesus into your very soul is quite another. Superficial feeling is often joined to inward hardness of heart, and a lively impression of the Word is not always a lasting one. In the parable of the sower, the seed in one case fell on ground having a rocky bottom, covered over with a thin layer of earth. When the seed began to take root, its downward growth was hindered by the hard stone; therefore, it spent its strength in pushing its green shoot aloft as high as it could; but, having no inward moisture derived from root nourishment, it withered away. Is this my case? Have I been making a fair show in the flesh without having a corresponding inner life? Good growth takes place upward and downward at the same time. Am I rooted in sincere fidelity and love for Jesus? If my heart remains hardened and unfertilized by grace, the good seed may germinate for a season, but it must ultimately wither, for it cannot flourish on a rocky, unbroken, unsanctified heart. Let me dread a godliness as rapid in growth and as lacking in endurance as Jonah's gourd. Let me count the cost of being a follower of Jesus. Above all, let me feel the energy of His Holy Spirit, and then, I will possess an abiding and enduring seed in my soul. If my mind remains as stubborn as it was by nature, the sun of trial will scorch, and my hard heart will help to cast the heat the more terribly on the ill-covered seed. My faith will soon die, and my despair will be terrible; therefore, O heavenly Sower, plough me first, and then, cast the truth into me. Let me yield a bounteous harvest for You.

I have prayed for thee, that thy faith fail not.
—Luke 22:32

How encouraging is the thought of the Redeemer's never-ceasing intercession for us. When we pray, He pleads for us; and when we are not praying, He is advocating our cause, and by His supplications shielding us from unseen dangers. Notice the word of comfort addressed to Peter: *"Simon, Simon, behold, Satan hath desired to have you, that he may sift you as wheat: but…"* (Luke 22:31–32). But what? "But go and pray for yourself"? That would be good advice, but that is not what is written. Neither did our Lord say, "But I will keep you watchful, and so you will be preserved." That, too, would be a great blessing. But no, He said, *"I have prayed for thee, that thy faith fail not."* We know little of what we owe to our Savior's prayers. When we reach the hilltops of heaven and look back on all the ways in which the Lord our God has led us, how we will praise Him who, before the eternal throne, undid the mischief that Satan was doing on earth! How we will thank Him because He never withheld His peace, but day and night He pointed to the wounds on His hands and carried our names on His breastplate! Even before Satan had begun to tempt, Jesus had forestalled him and entered a plea in heaven. Mercy outruns malice. Note that He did not say, "Satan hath sifted you; therefore, I will pray," but He said, *"Satan hath desired to have you."* He checked Satan even in his very desire and nipped it in the bud. He did not say, "But I have desired to pray for you." No, He said, *"'I have prayed for thee.'* I have done it already. I have gone to court and entered a counterplea even before an accusation is made." O Jesus, what a comfort it is that You have pleaded our cause against our unseen enemies, disarmed their mines, and unmasked their ambushes. This is a matter for joy, gratitude, hope, and confidence.

Ye are Christ's.
—1 Corinthians 3:23

You are Christ's. You are His by donation, for the Father gave you to the Son. You are His through the purchase of His blood, for He paid the price for your redemption. You are His by dedication, for you have consecrated yourself to Him. You are His by relation, for you are named by His name, and made one of His brothers and joint heirs. Labor in practical ways to show the world that you are the servant, the friend, the bride of Jesus. When tempted to sin, reply, "I cannot do this great wickedness, for I am Christ's." Immortal principles forbid the friend of Christ to sin. When wealth is before you to be won by sin, say that you are Christ's, and do not touch it. Are you exposed to difficulties and dangers? Stand fast in the evil day, remembering that you are Christ's. Are you placed where others are sitting down idly, doing nothing? Rise to the work with all your powers; and when the sweat stands on your brow, and you are tempted to loiter, cry, "No, I cannot stop, for I am Christ's. If I were not purchased by blood, I might be like *'Issachar...couching down between two burdens'* (Gen. 49:14); but I am Christ's and cannot loiter." When the siren song of pleasure would tempt you from the path of right, reply, "Your music cannot charm me; I am Christ's." When the cause of God provides you with opportunities, give your goods and yourself away, for you are Christ's. Never contradict your profession of faith. Always be one whose manners are Christian, whose speech is like the Nazarene, whose conduct and conversation are so characteristic of heaven that all who see you may know that you are the Savior's, recognizing in you His features of love and His countenance of holiness. "I am a Roman!" was of old a reason for integrity; far more, then, let this be your argument for holiness: "I am Christ's!"

I have yet to speak on God's behalf.
—Job 36:2

We should not court publicity for our virtue or fame for our zeal; but, at the same time, it is a sin to be always seeking to hide that which God has bestowed on us for the good of others. A Christian is not to be a village in a valley, but a *"city that is set on an hill"* (Matt. 5:14). He or she is not to be a candle *"under a bushel"* (v. 15), but a candle in a candlestick, giving light to all. Retirement may be lovely in its season, and to hide oneself is no doubt modest, but the hiding of Christ in us can never be justified, and the keeping back of truth that is precious to ourselves is a sin against others and an offense against God. If you are of a nervous temperament and a retiring disposition, take care that you do not indulge this trembling propensity too much, lest you should be useless to the church. Seek, in the name of Him who was not ashamed of you, to do what you can to tell others what Christ has told you. If you cannot speak with trumpet tongue, use the still small voice. If the pulpit cannot be your tribune, if the press may not carry on its wings your words, yet say with Peter and John, *"Silver and gold have I none; but such as I have give I thee"* (Acts 3:6). Talk to the Samaritan woman by Sychar's well, if you cannot preach a sermon on the mountain. Utter the praises of Jesus in a small group, if not among the whole congregation; in the field, if not at a busy intersection; in the midst of your own household, if you cannot speak of Him in the midst of the great family of humankind. From the hidden springs within, let sweetly flowing rivulets of testimony flow forth, giving drink to every passerby. Do not hide your talent. Trade with it, and you will bring in good interest to your Lord and Master. To speak for God will be refreshing to ourselves, cheering to saints, useful to sinners, and honoring to the Savior. Lord, unloose all your children's tongues.

Jehoshaphat made ships of Tharshish to go to Ophir for gold: but they went not; for the ships were broken at Eziongeber.
—1 Kings 22:48

Solomon's ships had returned in safety, but Jehoshaphat's vessels never reached the land of gold. Providence prospers one and frustrates the desires of another, in the same business and at the same spot, yet the Great Ruler is as good and wise at one time as another. May we have grace today, in the remembrance of this text, to bless the Lord for ships broken at Eziongeber, as well as for vessels freighted with temporal blessings. Let us not envy the more successful or murmur at our losses as though we were singularly and specially tried. Like Jehoshaphat, we may be precious in the Lord's sight, although our schemes end in disappointment. The secret cause of Jehoshaphat's loss is well worthy of notice, for it is the root of much of the suffering of the Lord's people; it was his alliance with a sinful family, his fellowship with sinners. In 2 Chronicles 20:37, we are told that the Lord sent a prophet to declare, *"Because thou hast joined thyself with Ahaziah, the Lord hath broken thy works."* This was a fatherly chastisement, which appears to have been blessed to him, for in the verse that follows this morning's text, we find him refusing to allow his servants to sail in the same vessels with those of the wicked king. Would to God that Jehoshaphat's experience might be a warning to the rest of the Lord's people to avoid being *"unequally yoked together with unbelievers"* (2 Cor. 6:14)! A life of misery is usually the lot of those who are united in marriage, or in any other way of their own choosing, with the people of the world. Oh, for such love for Jesus that, like Him, we may be *"holy, harmless, undefiled, separate from sinners"* (Heb. 7:26); for if it is not so with us, we may expect to hear it often said, "The Lord has broken your works."

The iron did swim.
—2 Kings 6:6

The ax head seemed hopelessly lost. Since it was borrowed, the honor of the prophetic band was likely to be imperiled, and thus the name of their God would be compromised. Contrary to all expectation, the ax head was made to mount from the depth of the stream and to swim, for things impossible with men are possible with God. Just a few years ago, I knew of a Christian who was called to undertake a work far exceeding his strength. It appeared so difficult as to involve absurdity in the mere idea of attempting it. Yet he was called to do it, and his faith rose with the occasion. God honored his faith, unlooked-for aid was sent, and *"the iron did swim."* Another of the Lord's family was in grievous financial straits. He would have been able to meet all claims, and much more, if he could have realized a certain portion of his estate, but he was overtaken by a sudden financial constraint. In vain he sought for the help of friends, but faith led him to the unfailing Helper; remarkably, the trouble was averted, his footsteps were enlarged, and *"the iron did swim."* A third had a sorrowful case of depravity to deal with. He had taught, reproved, warned, invited, and interceded, but all in vain. At first, the carnal spirit of Old Adam was too strong for this reformer's prayerful influence; the stubborn spirit of the sinner would not relent. Then came an agony of prayer, and before long, a blessed answer was sent from heaven. The hard heart was broken; *"the iron did swim."* Beloved reader, what is your desperate circumstance? What heavy matter do you have in hand this evening? Bring it forth. The God of the prophets lives and lives to help His saints. He will not allow you to lack any good thing. Believe in the Lord of Hosts! Pleading the name of Jesus, approach Him, and the iron will swim; you, too, will see the hand of God working marvels for His people. *"According to your faith be it unto you"* (Matt. 9:29), and yet again the iron will swim.

Mighty to save.
—Isaiah 63:1

We understand the words *"to save"* to mean the whole of the great work of salvation, from the first holy desire onward to complete sanctification. The words are *multum in parvo*—much in little. Indeed, here is all mercy in one word. Christ is not only *"mighty to save"* those who repent, but He is also able to make people repent. He will carry those to heaven who believe; but He is, moreover, mighty to give people new hearts and to work faith in them. He is mighty to make the one who hates holiness love it, and to constrain the despiser of His name to bend the knee before Him. This is not all the meaning, for the divine power is equally seen in the work that follows. The life of a believer is a series of miracles brought about by the mighty God. The bush burns, but it is not consumed. He is mighty enough to keep His people holy after He has made them so, and to preserve them in His fear and love until He consummates their spiritual existence in heaven. Christ's might does not lie in making a believer and then leaving him to shift for himself, but He who begins the *"good work in you will perform it until the day of Jesus Christ"* (Phil. 1:6). He who imparts the first germ of life in the dead soul prolongs the divine existence and strengthens it, until it bursts asunder every bond of sin, and the soul leaps from earth, perfected in glory. Believer, here is encouragement. Are you praying for some loved one? Oh, do not give up your prayers, for Christ is *"mighty to save."* You are powerless to reclaim the rebel, but your Lord is almighty. Lay hold of His mighty arm and rouse it to put forth its strength. Does your own case trouble you? Fear not, for His strength is sufficient for you. Whether to begin with others or to carry on the work in you, Jesus is *"mighty to save."* The best proof lies in the fact that He has saved *you*. What a thousand mercies that you have not found Him mighty to destroy!

JANUARY 14
Evening

Beginning to sink, [Peter] cried, saying, Lord, save me.
—Matthew 14:30

Sinking times are praying times with the Lord's servants. Peter neglected prayer when starting on his daring journey; but when he began to sink, his danger made him a suppliant, and his cry, though late, was not too late. In our hours of bodily pain and mental anguish, we find ourselves as naturally driven to prayer as a shipwreck is driven upon the shore by the waves. The fox hurries to its hole for protection; the bird flies to the wood for shelter; even so the tried believer hastens to the mercy seat for safety. Heaven's great harbor of refuge is "All-prayer"; thousands of weather-beaten vessels have found a haven there, and the moment a storm comes on, it is wise for us to make for it with all sail. Short prayers are long enough. There were only three words in the petition that Peter gasped out, but they were sufficient for his purpose. Not length but strength is desirable. A sense of need is a mighty teacher of brevity. If our prayers had less of the tail feathers of pride and more wing, they would be all the better. Verbiage is to devotion as chaff is to wheat. Precious things lie in small spaces, and all that is real prayer in many a long address might have been uttered in a petition as short as that of Peter's. Our extremities are the Lord's opportunities. Immediately, a keen sense of danger forces an anxious cry from us that the ear of Jesus hears, and with Him, ear and heart go together, and the hand does not long linger. At the last moment we appeal to our Master, but His swift hand makes up for our delays by instant, effective action. Are we nearly engulfed by the boisterous waters of affliction? Let us then lift up our souls to our Savior, and we may rest assured that He will not allow us to perish. When we can do nothing, Jesus can do all things; let us enlist His powerful aid on our side, and all will be well.

Do as thou hast said.
—2 Samuel 7:25

God's promises were never meant to be thrown aside as wastepaper. He intended that they should be used. God's gold is not miser's money, but is minted to be traded with. Nothing pleases our Lord better than to see His promises put in circulation. He loves to see His children bring them up to Him, and say, "Lord, do as You have said." We glorify God when we plead His promises. Do you think that God will be any the poorer for giving you the riches He has promised? Do you dream that He will be any the less holy for giving holiness to you? Do you imagine that He will be any the less pure for washing you from your sins? *"Come now, and let us reason together, saith the* Lord: *though your sins be as scarlet, they shall be as white as snow; though they be red like crimson, they shall be as wool"* (Isa. 1:18). Faith lays hold of the promise of pardon; it does not delay, saying, "This is a precious promise, but I wonder if it is true?" Instead, it goes straight to the throne with it and pleads, "Lord, here is the promise. Do as You have said." Our Lord replies, *"Be it unto thee even as thou wilt"* (Matt. 15:28). When a Christian grasps a promise, if he does not take it to God, he dishonors Him; but when he hastens to the throne of grace and cries, "Lord, I have nothing to recommend me but this: You have said it," then his desire will be granted. Our heavenly Banker delights to cash His own notes. Never let the promise rust. Draw the word of promise out of its scabbard, and use it with holy violence. Do not think that God will be troubled by your persistence in reminding Him of His promises. He loves to hear the loud outcries of needy souls. It is His delight to bestow favors. He is more ready to hear than you are to ask. The sun is not weary of shining or the fountain of flowing. It is God's nature to keep His promises; therefore, go at once to the throne with the words, "Do as You have said."

But I give myself unto prayer.
—Psalm 109:4

Lying tongues were busy against the reputation of David, but he did not defend himself; he moved the case into a higher court and pleaded before the great King Himself. Prayer is the safest method of replying to words of hatred. The psalmist did not pray in a coldhearted manner; he gave himself to the exercise—threw his whole soul and heart into it—straining every sinew and muscle, as Jacob did when wrestling with the angel. In this way, and only in this way, will any of us speed to the throne of grace. As a shadow has no power because there is no substance in it, even so the supplication in which a man's proper self is not thoroughly present in agonizing earnestness and vehement desire is utterly ineffective, for it lacks that which would give it force. "Fervent prayer," said an old churchman, "like a cannon planted at the gates of heaven, makes them fly open." The common fault with most of us is our readiness to yield to distractions. Our thoughts go roving here and there, and we make little progress toward our desired end. Like mercury, our minds will not hold together, but they roll off this way and that. How great an evil this is! It injures us, and what is worse, it insults our God. What would we think of a petitioner, if, while having an audience with a prince, he played with a feather or tried to catch a fly? Continuance and perseverance are intended in the expression of our text. David did not cry once and then relapse into silence; his holy clamor continued until it brought down the blessing. Prayer must not be our accidental work, but our daily business, our habit, and vocation. As artists give themselves to their models and poets to their classical pursuits, so we must addict ourselves to prayer. We must be immersed in prayer as in our element, and so *"pray without ceasing"* (1 Thess. 5:17). Lord, teach us to pray so that we may be more and more prevalent in supplication.

I will help thee, saith the LORD.
—Isaiah 41:14

Let us hear the Lord Jesus speak these words to each one of us: "I will help you. It is but a small thing for Me, your God, to help you. Consider what I have done already. What! not help you? Why, I bought you with My blood. What! not help you? I have died for you; and if I have done the greater, will I not do the lesser? Help you! It is the least thing I will ever do for you. I have done more and will do more. Before the world began, I chose you. I made the covenant for you. I laid aside My glory and became a man for you. I gave up My life for you, and if I did all of this, I will surely help you now! In helping you, I am giving you what I have bought for you already. If you had need of a thousand times as much help, I would give it to you. You require little compared with what I am ready to give. It is much for you to need, but it is nothing for me to bestow. Help you? Do not fear! If there were an ant at the door of your granary asking for help, it would not ruin you to give him a handful of your wheat; you are nothing but a tiny insect at the door of My all-sufficiency. I will help you." O my soul, is this not enough? Do you need more strength than the omnipotence of the united Trinity? Do you need more wisdom than exists in the Father, more love than displays itself in the Son, or more power than is manifest in the influences of the Spirit? Bring your empty pitcher here! Surely this well will fill it. Hurry, gather up your needs, and bring them here—your emptiness, your sorrows, your deficiencies. Behold, this river of God is full for your supply. What can you desire besides? Go forth, my soul, in this your might. The eternal God is your Helper!

Fear not, I am with thee;
Oh, be not dismay'd!
For I am thy God;
I will still give thee aid.

JANUARY 16
Evening

Messiah [shall] *be cut off, but not for himself.*
—Daniel 9:26

Blessed be His name, there was no cause of death in Him. Neither original nor actual sin had defiled Him; therefore, death had no claim on Him. No man could have taken His life from Him justly, for He had done no man wrong. No man could have even struck Him down by force unless He had been pleased to yield Himself to die. But one sins and another suffers. Justice was offended by us, but it found its satisfaction in Him. Rivers of tears, mountains of offerings, seas of the blood of bullocks, and hills of frankincense could not have accomplished the removal of sin. But Jesus was cut off for us, and the cause of wrath was cut off at once, for sin was put away forever. Herein is wisdom, whereby substitution, the sure and speedy way of atonement, was devised! Herein is condescension, which brought Messiah, the Prince, to wear a crown of thorns and to die on the cross! Herein is love, which led the Redeemer to lay down His life for His enemies! It is not enough, however, to admire the spectacle of the innocent bleeding for the guilty; we must make sure of our interest in it. The special purpose of the Messiah's death was the salvation of His church. Have we a part and a lot among those for whom He gave His life as a ransom? Did the Lord Jesus stand as our Representative? Are we healed by His stripes? It would be a terrible thing indeed if we would come short of a portion in His sacrifice; it would be better for us if we had never been born. Solemn as the question is, it is a joyful circumstance that it is one that may be answered clearly and without mistake. To all who believe on Him, the Lord Jesus is a present Savior, and upon them all the blood of reconciliation has been sprinkled. Let all who trust in the merit of Messiah's death be joyful at every remembrance of Him, and let their holy gratitude lead them to the fullest consecration to His cause.

JANUARY 17

Morning

And I looked, and, lo, a Lamb stood on the mount Sion.
—Revelation 14:1

The apostle John was privileged to look within the gates of heaven, and in describing what he saw, he began by saying, *"I looked, and, lo, a Lamb."* This teaches us that the chief objective of contemplation in the heavenly state is *"the Lamb of God, which taketh away the sin of the world"* (John 1:29). Nothing else attracted the apostle's attention as much as the person of that divine Being, who has redeemed us by His blood. He is the theme of the songs of all glorified spirits and holy angels. Christian, here is joy for you; you have looked, and you have seen the Lamb. Through your tears, your eyes have seen the Lamb of God taking away your sins. Rejoice, then. In a little while, when your tears will have been wiped from your eyes, you will see the same Lamb exalted on His throne. It is the joy of your heart to hold daily fellowship with Jesus. You will have the same joy to a higher degree in heaven. You will enjoy the constant vision of His presence. You will dwell with Him forever. *"I looked, and, lo, a Lamb."* Why, that Lamb is heaven itself, for as good Rutherford said, "Heaven and Christ are the same thing." To be with Christ is to be in heaven, and to be in heaven is to be with Christ. A prisoner of the Lord very sweetly wrote in one of his glowing letters, "O my Lord Jesus Christ, if I could be in heaven without You, it would be a hell; and if I could be in hell, and have You still, it would be a heaven to me, for You are all the heaven I need." It is true, is it not, Christian? Does not your soul say so?

> Not all the harps above
>   Can make a heavenly place,
> If God His residence remove,
>   Or but conceal His face.

All you need to be blessed, supremely blessed, is *"to be with Christ"* (Phil. 1:23).

*And it came to pass in an eveningtide, that David arose from off his
bed, and walked upon the roof of the king's house.*
—2 Samuel 11:2

At that hour of night, David saw Bathsheba. We are never out of the
reach of temptation. Both at home and abroad, we are liable to meet with
allurements to evil; the morning opens with peril, and the shades of evening find us still in jeopardy. They are well kept whom God keeps, but woe
to those who go forth into the world, or even dare to walk unarmed around
their own house. Those who think they are secure are more exposed to
danger than any others. The armor-bearer of sin is self-confidence. David
should have been engaged in fighting the Lord's battles; instead, he tarried
at Jerusalem and gave himself up to luxurious repose, for he arose from
his bed in the evening. Idleness and luxury are the devil's jackals, and they
find him abundant prey. In stagnant waters noxious creatures swarm, and
neglected soil soon yields a dense tangle of weeds and briars. Oh, for the
constraining love of Jesus to keep us active and useful! When I see the king
of Israel sluggishly leaving his couch at the close of the day and falling at
once into temptation, let me take warning and set holy watchfulness to
guard my door. Is it possible that the king had mounted his housetop for
retirement and devotion? If so, what a caution is given to us to consider
no place, however secret, a sanctuary from sin! Because our hearts are so
like a tinderbox and sparks are so plentiful, we need to use all diligence in
all places to prevent a blaze. Satan can climb housetops and enter prayer
closets. Even if we could shut out that foul fiend, our own corruptions are
enough to work our ruin unless grace prevents it. Reader, beware of evening temptations. Do not be secure. The sun is down, but sin is up. We
need a watchman for the night as well as a guardian for the day. O blessed
Spirit, keep us from all evil this night. Amen.

There remaineth therefore a rest to the people of God.
—Hebrews 4:9

How different will be the state of the believer in heaven from what it is here! Here he is born to toil and suffer weariness, but in the land of the immortal, fatigue is never known. Anxious to serve his Master, he now finds his strength unequal to his zeal. His constant cry is, "Help me to serve You, O my God." If he is thoroughly active, he will have much labor; not too much for his will, but more than enough for his power, so that he will cry out, "I am not wearied *of* the labor, but I am wearied *in* it." Ah, Christian, the hot day of weariness does not last forever. The sun is nearing the horizon. It will rise again, with a brighter day than you have ever seen, on a land where they serve God day and night, and yet rest from their labors. Here, rest is but partial; there, it is perfect. Here, the Christian is always unsettled; he feels that he has not yet attained. There, all are at rest; they have attained the summit of the mountain. They have ascended to the bosom of their God. They cannot go any higher. Ah, toil-worn laborer, only envision when you will rest forever! Can you imagine it? It is a rest eternal, a rest that *"remaineth."* Here, my best joys bear *mortal* on their brow, my fair flowers fade, my delicious cups are drained to the dregs, my sweetest birds fall before Death's arrows, my most pleasant days are shadowed into nights, and the flood tides of my bliss subside into ebbs of sorrow; but there, everything is immortal. The harp remains unrusted, the crown unwithered, the eye undimmed, the voice unfaltering, and the heart unwavering. The immortal being is wholly absorbed in infinite delight. Happy day, when mortality will *"be swallowed up of life"* (2 Cor. 5:4), and the eternal Sabbath will begin!

JANUARY 18

Evening

He expounded unto them in all the scriptures
the things concerning himself.
—Luke 24:27

The two disciples on the road to Emmaus had a most profitable journey. Their companion and teacher was the best of tutors, their interpreter one of a thousand, *"in whom are hid all the treasures of wisdom and knowledge"* (Col. 2:3). The Lord Jesus condescended to become a preacher of the Gospel, and He was not ashamed to exercise His calling before an audience of two persons; neither does He now refuse to become the teacher of even one. Let us court the company of so excellent an Instructor, for until He is *"made unto us wisdom"* (1 Cor. 1:30), we will never be *"wise unto salvation"* (2 Tim. 3:15). This unrivalled Tutor used as His textbook the Best of Books. Although able to reveal fresh truth, He preferred to expound the old. He knew by His omniscience what was the most instructive way of teaching, and by turning immediately to Moses and the prophets, He showed us that the surest road to wisdom is not speculating, reasoning, or reading human books, but meditating on the Word of God. The readiest way to be spiritually rich in heavenly knowledge is to dig in this mine of diamonds, to gather pearls from this heavenly sea. When Jesus Himself sought to enrich others, He dug in the quarry of Holy Scripture. The favored pair were led to consider the best of subjects, for Jesus *"expounded…the things concerning himself."* Here the diamond cut the diamond, and what could be more admirable? The Master of the house unlocked His own doors, conducted the guests to His table, and placed His own delicacies on it. He who hid the treasure in the field guided the searchers to it Himself. Our Lord would naturally discourse upon the sweetest of topics, and He could find none sweeter than His own person and work. With an eye to these truths, we should always search the Word. Oh, for grace to study the Bible with Jesus as both our Teacher and our Lesson!

JANUARY 19

Morning

I sought him, but I found him not.
—Song of Solomon 3:1

Tell me where you lost the company of Christ, and I will tell you the most likely place to find Him. Have you lost Christ by refraining from prayer? Then it is there you must seek and find Him. Did you lose Christ by sinning? You will find Christ in no other way but by giving up sin and seeking, by the Holy Spirit, to mortify the member in which the lust dwells. Did you lose Christ by neglecting the Scriptures? You must find Christ in the Scriptures. It is a true saying, "Look for a thing where you dropped it; it is there." So look for Christ where you lost Him, for He has not gone away. But it is hard work to go back for Christ. Bunyan tells us that the pilgrim found the piece of the road back to the Arbor of Ease, where he had lost his roll, the hardest he had ever traveled. Twenty miles onward is easier to go than one mile backward for lost evidence. Take care, then, when you find your Master, to cling closely to Him. But how is it that you have lost Him? One would have thought you would never have parted with such a precious Friend, whose presence is so sweet, whose words are so comforting, and whose company is so dear to you! How is it that you did not watch Him every moment for fear of losing sight of Him? Yet, since you have let Him go, what a mercy that you are seeking Him, even though you mournfully groan, *"Oh that I knew where I might find him!"* (Job 23:3). Go on seeking, for it is dangerous to be without your Lord. Without Christ, you are like a sheep without its shepherd; like a tree without water at its roots; like a withered leaf in a tempest—not bound to the tree that gives it life. Seek Him with your whole heart, and He will be found by you. Give yourself thoroughly to the search, and truly, to your joy and gladness, you will yet discover Him.

Then opened he their understanding, that they might
understand the scriptures.
—Luke 24:45

Jesus, whom we viewed last evening as opening Scripture, we see here opening the understanding of the two on the road to Emmaus. In the first work of opening the Scriptures, Jesus has many fellow laborers, but in the second, opening a person's understanding, He stands alone. Many can bring the Scriptures to the mind, but the Lord alone can prepare the mind to receive the Scriptures. Our Lord Jesus differs from all other teachers. They reach the ear, but He instructs the heart; they deal with the outward letter, but He imparts an inward taste for the truth, by which we perceive its savor and spirit. The most uneducated men become mature scholars in the school of grace when the Lord Jesus by His Holy Spirit unfolds the mysteries of the kingdom to them and grants the divine anointing by which they are enabled to behold the invisible. We are blessed if we have had our understanding cleared and strengthened by the Master! How many men of profound learning are ignorant of eternal things! They know the killing letter of revelation, but its killing spirit they cannot discern. They have a veil over their hearts that the eyes of carnal reason cannot penetrate. Such was our case a little time ago. We who now see were once utterly blind. Truth was to us as beauty in the dark, a thing unnoticed and neglected. Had it not been for the love of Jesus, we would have remained to this moment in utter ignorance, for without His gracious opening of our understanding, we could no more have attained spiritual knowledge than an infant can climb the pyramids or an ostrich can fly up to the stars. Jesus' college is the only one in which God's truth can really be learned; other schools may teach us what is to be believed, but Christ's alone can show us how to believe it. Let us sit at the feet of Jesus and, by earnest prayer, call in His blessed aid, so that our dull wits may grow brighter and our feeble understanding may receive heavenly things.

Abel was a keeper of sheep.
—Genesis 4:2

As a shepherd, Abel sanctified his work to the glory of God and offered a sacrifice of blood on his altar. The Lord respected Abel and his offering. This early type of Christ is exceedingly clear and distinct. Like the first streak of light that tinges the East at sunrise, it does not reveal everything, but it clearly manifests the great fact that the sun is coming. As we see Abel, a shepherd and yet a priest, offering a sweet-smelling sacrifice unto God, we discern our Lord, who brings before His Father a sacrifice to which Jehovah ever has respect. Abel was hated by his brother—hated without a cause; even so was the Savior. The natural and carnal man hated the accepted man, in whom the Spirit of grace was found, and did not rest until his blood had been shed. Abel fell and sprinkled his altar and sacrifice with his own blood; therein sets forth the Lord Jesus slain by the enmity of man, while serving as a Priest before the Lord. *"The good shepherd giveth his life for the sheep"* (John 10:11). Let us weep over Him as we view Him slain by the hatred of mankind, staining the horns of His altar with His own blood. Abel's blood speaks. The Lord said to Cain, *"The voice of thy brother's blood crieth unto me from the ground"* (Gen. 4:10). The blood of Jesus has a mighty tongue, and the import of its prevailing cry is not vengeance, but mercy. It is precious beyond all preciousness to stand at the altar of our Good Shepherd—to see Him bleeding there as the slaughtered Priest, and then to hear His blood speaking peace to all His flock, peace in our consciences, peace between Jew and Gentile, peace between man and his offended Maker, peace down all the ages of eternity for blood-washed men. Abel was the first shepherd in order of time, but our hearts will ever place Jesus first in order of excellence. Great Keeper of the sheep, we the people of Your pasture bless You with our whole hearts when we see You slain for us.

Turn away mine eyes from beholding vanity;
and quicken thou me in thy way.
—Psalm 119:37

There are various kinds of vanity. The cap and bells of the fool, the mirth of the world, the dance, the lyre, and the cup of the indulgent—all these things men know to be vanities. They display their proper name and title prominently. Far more treacherous are those equally conceited things, *"the cares of this world, and the deceitfulness of riches"* (Mark 4:19). A person may follow vanity as much in his business as an actor seeks it in the theater. If he is spending his life in amassing wealth, he passes his days in a vain show. Unless we follow Christ and make God the great purpose of our lives, we differ only in appearance from the most frivolous. It is clear that there is much need of the first prayer of our text, *"Turn away mine eyes from beholding vanity."* In the second prayer, *"Quicken thou me in thy way,"* the psalmist confessed that he was dull, heavy, lethargic, all but dead. Perhaps, dear reader, you feel the same. We are so sluggish that the best motives cannot quicken us, apart from the Lord Himself. What! Will not hell quicken me? Will I think of sinners perishing, and yet not be awakened? Will not heaven quicken me? Can I think of the reward that awaits the righteous and yet be cold? Will not death quicken me? Can I think of dying and standing before my God yet be slothful in my Master's service? Will not Christ's love constrain me? Can I think of His dear wounds, can I sit at the foot of His cross and not be stirred with fervency and zeal? It seems so! No mere consideration can quicken us to zeal, but God Himself must do it; hence, the cry, *"Quicken **thou** me"* (emphasis added). The psalmist breathed out his whole soul in vehement pleadings; his body and his soul united in prayer. *"Turn away mine eyes,"* says the body. *"Quicken thou me,"* cries the soul. This is an appropriate prayer for every day. O Lord, hear it in my case this night.

And so all Israel shall be saved.
—Romans 11:26

When Moses sang at the Red Sea, it was his joy to know that all the Israelites were safe. Not a drop of spray fell from that solid wall of water until the last of God's chosen ones had safely planted his foot on the other side of the flood. That done, immediately the waters dissolved into their proper place again, but not until then. Part of that song was, *"Thou in thy mercy hast led forth the people which thou hast redeemed"* (Exod. 15:13). In the last time, when the elect will sing *"the song of the Lamb"* and *"of Moses the servant of God"* (Rev. 15:3). This will be the boast of Jesus: *"Of them which thou gavest me have I lost none"* (John 18:9). In heaven there will not be a vacant throne.

> For all the chosen race
>   Shall meet around the throne,
> Shall bless the conduct of His grace,
>   And make His glories known.

As many as God has chosen, as many as Christ has redeemed, as many as the Spirit has called, as many as believe in Jesus—all these will safely cross the dividing sea. We are not all safely landed yet. "Part of the host have crossed the flood, and part are crossing now." The vanguard of the army has already reached the shore. We are marching through the depths. We are, on this day, following hard after our Leader into the heart of the sea. Let us be of good cheer. The rear guard will soon be where the vanguard already is; the last of the chosen ones will soon have crossed the sea, and then, when all are secure, the song of triumph will be heard. But, oh, if one were absent—if one of His chosen family were to be cast away—it would make an everlasting discord in the song of the redeemed and cut the strings of the harps of paradise, so that music could never be extorted from them again.

*He was sore athirst, and called on the Lord, and said,
Thou hast given this great deliverance into the hand of thy servant:
and now shall I die for thirst?*
—Judges 15:18

Samson was thirsty and ready to die. The difficulty was totally different from any that the hero had met before. Merely to get thirst assuaged is not nearly as great a matter as to be delivered from a thousand Philistines! But when the thirst was upon him, Samson felt that this little present difficulty was more weighty than the great past difficulty out of which he had been so wonderfully delivered. It is very common for God's people, after they have enjoyed a great deliverance, to find a little trouble too much for them. Samson slew a thousand Philistines and piled them up in heaps—then he fainted for a little water! Jacob wrestled with God at Peniel and overcame Omnipotence itself, and then went limping on his hip! It is strange that there must be a shrinking of the sinew whenever we win the day. It is as if the Lord must teach us our littleness, our nothingness, in order to keep us within bounds. Samson boasted very loudly when he said, "I [have] *slain a thousand men*" (Judg. 15:16). His boastful throat soon grew hoarse with thirst, and he resorted to prayer. God has many ways of humbling His people. Dear child of God, if after receiving great mercy you are laid very low, your case is not an unusual one. When David had mounted the throne of Israel, he said, "*I am this day weak, though anointed king*" (2 Sam. 3:39). You must expect to feel weakest when you are enjoying your greatest triumph. If God has won for you great deliverances in the past, your present difficulty is only like Samson's thirst, and the Lord will not let you faint or allow your enemies to triumph over you. The road of sorrow is the road to heaven, but there are wells of refreshing water all along the route. So, tried ones, cheer your hearts with Samson's words, and rest assured that God will deliver you before long.

Son of man, What is the vine tree more than any tree, or than
a branch which is among the trees of the forest?
—Ezekiel 15:2

These words are for the humbling of God's people. They are called God's vine, but what are they by nature more than others? They, by God's goodness, have become fruitful, having been planted in a good soil. The Lord has trained them upon the walls of the sanctuary, and they bring forth fruit to His glory; but what are they without their God? What are they without the continual influence of the Spirit producing fruitfulness in them? Believer, learn to reject pride, seeing that you have no ground for it. Whatever you are, you have nothing to make you proud. The more you have, the more you are in debt to God; and you should not be proud of that which makes you a debtor. Consider your origin; look back to what you were. Consider what you would have been had it not been for divine grace. Look on yourself as you are now. Does not your conscience reproach you? Do not your thousand wanderings stand before you and tell you that you are unworthy to be called His child? And if He has made you anything, are you not taught thereby that it is grace that has changed you? Great believer, you would have been a great sinner if God had not transformed you. O you who are valiant for truth, you would have been as valiant for error if grace had not laid hold of you. Therefore, be not proud, though you have a large estate, that is, a wide domain of grace. Once, you did not have a single thing to call your own except your sin and misery. Oh, strange infatuation, that you, who have borrowed everything, would think of exalting yourself! You are a poor pensioner dependent on the bounty of your Savior; you are one who has a life that dies without fresh streams of life from Jesus, and yet you are still proud! Shame on you, O lowly heart!

Doth Job fear God for nought?
—Job 1:9

This was the wicked question of Satan concerning Job, that upright man of old. Sadly, there are many people today about whom it might be asked with legitimacy, for they love God after a fashion because He prospers them. But if things were to go badly for them, they would give up all their boasted faith in God. If they can clearly see that since the time of their supposed conversion they have enjoyed prosperity, then they will love God in their poor carnal way; but if they endure adversity, they rebel against the Lord. Their love is the love of the table, not of the Host; a love of the cupboard, not of the Master of the house. As for the true Christian, he expects to have his reward in the next life and to endure hardness in this life. The promise of the old covenant is adversity. Remember Christ's words, *"Every branch in me that beareth not fruit he taketh away: and every branch that beareth fruit..."* (John 15:2). What happens to a branch that does bear fruit? *"He purgeth it, that it may bring forth more fruit"* (v. 2). If you bring forth fruit, you will have to endure affliction. "Alas" you say, "that is a terrible prospect!" But this affliction works out such precious results that the Christian who is the subject of it must learn to rejoice in tribulations, because as his tribulations abound, so his consolations abound by Christ Jesus. Rest assured, if you are a child of God, you will be no stranger to the rod. Sooner or later, every bar of gold must pass through the fire. Do not fear, but rather rejoice that fruitful times are in store for you, for in them you will be weaned from earth and made ready for heaven. You will be delivered from clinging to the present and caused to long for those eternal things that are so soon to be revealed to you. When you feel that you would gladly serve God without the promise of any benefits in this life, you will then rejoice in the infinite reward of the future.

I have exalted one chosen out of the people.
—Psalm 89:19

Why was Christ *"chosen out of the people"*? Speak, my heart, for heart-thoughts are best. Was it not that He might be able to be our Brother in the blessed tie of kindred blood? Oh, what relationship there is between Christ and the believer! The believer can say, "I have a Brother in heaven. I may be poor, but I have a Brother who is rich and is a King. Will He permit me to be in need while He is on His throne? Oh, no! He loves me; He is my Brother." Believer, wear this blessed thought like a diamond necklace around the neck of your memory. As a golden ring, put it on the finger of remembrance and use it as the King's own seal, stamping the petitions of your faith with the confidence of success. He is a *"brother...born for adversity"* (Prov. 17:17); treat Him as such. Christ was also *"chosen out of the people"* so that He might know our needs and sympathize with us. He *"was in all points tempted like as we are, yet without sin"* (Heb. 4:15). In all our sorrows, we have His sympathy. Temptation, pain, disappointment, weakness, weariness, poverty—He knows them all, for He has felt them all. Remember this, Christian, and let it comfort you. However difficult and painful your road may be, it is marked by the footsteps of your Savior. Even when you reach the dark valley of the shadow of death and the deep waters of the swelling Jordan, you will find His footprints there. In all places, wherever we go, He has been our forerunner; each burden we have to carry has once been laid on the shoulders of Immanuel.

His way was much rougher and darker than mine.
Did Christ, my Lord, suffer, and shall I repine?

Take courage! Royal feet have left a bloodred track on the road and consecrated the thorny path forever.

JANUARY 23
Evening

We will remember thy love more than wine.
—Song of Solomon 1:4

Jesus will not let His people forget His love. If all the love they have enjoyed should be forgotten, He will visit them with fresh love. "Do you forget My Cross?" He asks. "I will cause you to remember it, for at My Table I will manifest Myself anew to you. Do you forget what I did for you in the council chamber of eternity? I will remind you of it, for you will need a counselor and will find Me ready at your call." Mothers do not let their children forget them. If a boy has gone to Australia and does not write home, his mother writes, "Has John forgotten his mother?" Then a sweet letter comes back, which proves that the gentle reminder was not in vain. So is it with Jesus. He says to us, "Remember Me," and our response is, "'*We will remember thy love.*' We will remember Your love and its matchless history. It is as ancient as '*the glory which* [You] *had with* [the Father] *before the world was*' (John 17:5). O Jesus, we remember Your eternal love when You became our Surety and espoused us as Your betrothed. We remember the love that suggested the sacrifice of Yourself, the love that, until the fullness of time, mused over that sacrifice. We long for the hour of which in the volume of the Book it was written of You, '*Lo, I come*' (Heb. 10:7). We remember Your love, O Jesus, as it was manifested to us in Your holy life, from the manger of Bethlehem to the Garden of Gethsemane. We track You from the cradle to the grave—for every word and deed of Yours was love—and we rejoice in Your love, which death did not exhaust, Your love that shone resplendent in Your resurrection. We remember that burning fire of love that will never let You hold Your peace until Your chosen ones are all safely housed, until Zion is glorified, and Jerusalem is settled on her everlasting foundations of light and love in heaven."

Surely he shall deliver thee from the snare of the fowler.
—Psalm 91:3

God delivers His people *"from the snare of the fowler"* in two senses: *from* and *out of.* First, He delivers them *from* the snare; He does not let them enter it. Second, if they should be caught in it, He delivers them *out of* it. The first promise is the most precious to some; the second is the best to others. *"He shall deliver thee from the snare."* How? Trouble is often the means whereby God delivers us. God knows that our backsliding will soon end in our destruction, and, in mercy, He sends the rod. We say, "Lord, why is this happening?"—not knowing that our trouble has been the means of delivering us from far greater evil. Many have been thus saved from ruin by their sorrows and their crosses; these have frightened the birds from the net. At other times, God keeps His people from the snare of the fowler by giving them great spiritual strength, so that when they are tempted to do evil they say, *"How then can I do this great wickedness, and sin against God?"* (Gen. 39:9). But what a blessed thing it is that, if the believer does, in an evil hour, come into the net, God will bring him out of it! O backslider, you may be cast down, but do not despair. Wanderer though you have been, hear what your Redeemer says: "Return, O backsliding children; I will have mercy on you." But you say you cannot return, for you are a captive. Then listen to the promise: *"Surely he shall deliver thee from the snare of the fowler."* You will yet be brought out of all evil into which you have fallen; and though you will never cease to repent of your ways, He who has loved you will not cast you away. He will receive you and give you joy and gladness, so *"that the bones which [He has] broken may rejoice"* (Ps. 51:8). No bird of paradise will die in the fowler's net.

Martha was cumbered about much serving.
—Luke 10:40

Martha's fault was not that she served, for the condition of a servant well becomes every Christian. "I serve" should be the motto of all the princes of the royal family of heaven. Nor was it her fault that she had *"much serving."* We cannot do too much. Let us do all that we possibly can. Let head and heart and hands be engaged in the Master's service. It was no fault of hers that she was busy preparing a feast for the Master. Happy Martha, to have an opportunity of entertaining so blessed a Guest, and happy, too, to have the spirit to throw her whole soul so heartily into the engagement. Her fault was that she grew *"cumbered about much serving,"* so that she forgot Him and only remembered the service. She allowed service to override communion, and so she presented one duty stained with the blood of another. We ought to be Martha and Mary in one: we should do much service and have much communion at the same time. For this we need great grace. It is easier to serve than to commune. Joshua never grew weary in fighting with the Amalekites; but Moses, on the top of the mountain in prayer, needed two helpers to sustain his hands. The more spiritual the exercise, the sooner we tire in it. The choicest fruits are the hardest to grow; the most heavenly graces are the most difficult to cultivate. Beloved, while we do not neglect external things, which are good enough in themselves, we also ought to see to it that we enjoy living, personal fellowship with Jesus. See to it that sitting at the Savior's feet is not neglected, even though it may be under the seeming purpose of doing Him service. The first thing for our soul's health, the first thing for His glory, and the first thing for our own usefulness is to keep ourselves in perpetual communion with the Lord Jesus and to see that the vital spirituality of our religion is maintained over and above everything else in the world.

JANUARY 25

Morning

I will mention the lovingkindnesses of the LORD, and the praises of the LORD, according to all that the LORD hath bestowed on us.
—Isaiah 63:7

Can you not do this? Are there no mercies that you have experienced? Even though you are gloomy now, can you forget that blessed hour when Jesus met you and said, "Come unto Me"? Can you not remember that rapturous moment when He snapped your fetters, dashed your chains to the earth, and said, "I came to break your bonds and set you free"? Or if you have let the love of your relationship with Christ grow cold, there must surely be some precious milestone along the road of life not quite grown over with moss, on which you can read a happy memorial of His mercy toward you. What? Did you never have a sickness like the one from which you are suffering now, and did He not restore you? Were you never poor before, and did He not supply your needs? Were you never in dire straits before, and did He not deliver you? Arise! Go to the river of your experience and pull up a few bulrushes; plait them into an ark, wherein your infant-faith may float safely on the stream. Do not forget what your God has done for you; leaf through your book of memories, and consider the days of old. Can you not remember the times of refreshing? Have you forgotten the mountaintop experiences? Have you never been helped in your times of need? I know you have. Go back, then, a little way to the choice mercies of yesterday; though all may be dark now, light up the lamps of the past. They will glitter through the darkness, and you will trust in the Lord *"until the day break, and the shadows flee away"* (Song 2:17). *"Remember, O LORD, thy tender mercies and thy lovingkindnesses; for they have been ever of old"* (Ps. 25:6)

Do we then make void the law through faith?
God forbid: yea, we establish the law.
—Romans 3:31

When the believer is adopted into the Lord's family, his relationship to Old Adam and the law ceases at once; but then he is under a new rule and a new covenant. Believer, you are God's child. It is your first duty to obey your heavenly Father. You have nothing to do with a servile spirit: you are not a slave but a child. And now, inasmuch as you are a beloved child, you are bound to obey your Father's faintest wish, the least intimation of His will. Does He bid you to fulfill a sacred ordinance? It is at your peril that you neglect it, for you will be disobeying your Father. Does He command you to seek the image of Jesus? Is it not your joy to do so? Does Jesus tell you, *"Be ye therefore perfect, even as your Father which is in heaven is perfect"* (Matt. 5:48)? Then not because the law commands, but because your Savior directs, you will labor to be perfect in holiness. Does He bid His saints to love one another? Do it, not because the law says, *"Love thy neighbour"* (Lev. 19:18), but because Jesus says, *"If ye love me, keep my commandments"* (John 14:15). This is the commandment that He has given to you, *"That ye love one another"* (John 13:34). Are you told to give to the poor? Do it, not because charity is a burden that you dare not shirk, but because Jesus teaches, *"Give to every man that asketh of thee"* (Luke 6:30). Does the Word say, "Love God with all your heart"? (See Deuteronomy 6:5.) Look at the commandment and reply, "Ah, commandment, Christ has fulfilled you already. I have no need, therefore, to fulfill you for my salvation, but I rejoice to yield obedience to you because God is my Father now, and He has a claim on me that I would not dispute." May the Holy Spirit make your heart obedient to the constraining power of Christ's love, so that your prayer may be, *"Make me to go in the path of thy commandments; for therein do I delight"* (Ps. 119:35). Grace is the mother and nurse of holiness, and not the apologist of sin.

Your heavenly Father.
—Matthew 6:26

God's people are doubly His children: they are His by creation and by adoption in Christ. Hence they are privileged to call Him, *"Our Father which art in heaven"* (Luke 11:2). *Father*—oh, what a precious word that is! Here is authority: *"If then I be a father, where is mine honour?"* (Mal. 1:6). Here is affection mingled with authority. This kind of authority does not provoke rebellion. If you are children, where is your obedience? This kind of required obedience is most cheerfully given: it would not be withheld even if it could be. The obedience that God's children yield to Him must be loving obedience. Do not approach the service of God as slaves do their taskmaster's toil, but follow His commands, because that is your Father's way. Yield your bodies *"as instruments of righteousness"* (Rom. 6:13), because righteousness is your Father's will, and His will should be the will of His child. Father!—here is a kingly attribute so sweetly veiled in love that the King's crown is forgotten in the King's face, and His scepter becomes not a rod of iron, but a silver scepter of mercy; the scepter indeed seems to be forgotten in the tender hand of Him who wields it. Father!—here is honor and love. How great is a father's love for his children! What friendship cannot do and mere benevolence will not attempt, a father's heart and hand must do for his children. They are his offspring, and he must bless them; they are his children, and he must show himself strong in their defense. If an earthly father watches over his children with unceasing love and care, how much more does our heavenly Father? "Abba, Father!" He who can say this, has uttered better music than cherubim or seraphim can reach. There is heaven in the depth of that word—*Father!* There is all I can ask, all my necessities can demand, and all my wishes can desire. I have all in all now and throughout eternity when I can say, "Father."

All they that heard it wondered at those things.
—Luke 2:18

We must not cease to wonder at the great marvels of our God. It would be very difficult to draw a line between holy wonder and real worship, for when the soul is overwhelmed with the majesty of God's glory, though it may not express itself in song or even utter its voice with bowed head in humble prayer, yet it silently adores. Our incarnate God is to be worshipped as "the Wonderful." That God should consider His fallen creature, man, and, instead of sweeping him away with the *"besom [broom] of destruction"* (Isa. 14:23), should Himself undertake to be man's Redeemer and to pay his ransom price, is, indeed, marvelous! But to each believer redemption is most marvelous as he views it in relation to himself. It is a miracle of grace, indeed, that Jesus would forsake the thrones and royalties above to suffer a shameful death below *for you.* Let your soul lose itself in wonder, for wonder is, in this way, a very practical emotion. Holy wonder will lead you to grateful worship and heartfelt thanksgiving. It will cause within you godly watchfulness. You will be afraid to sin against such a love as this. Feeling the presence of the mighty God in the gift of His dear Son, you will *"put off thy shoes from off thy feet, for the place whereon thou standest is holy ground"* (Exod. 3:5). You will be moved at the same time to glorious hope. If Jesus has done such marvelous things on your behalf, you will feel that heaven itself is not too great for your expectation. Who can be astonished at anything, when he has once been astonished at the manger and the Cross? What is left that is wonderful after one has seen the Savior? Dear reader, it may be that, from the quietness and solitude of your life, you are scarcely able to imitate the shepherds of Bethlehem, who told what they had seen and heard, but you can, at least, fill up the circle of the worshippers before the throne by wondering at what God has done.

And of his fulness have all we received.
—John 1:16

These words tell us that there is a fullness in Christ. There is a fullness of essential deity and a fullness of perfect manhood, for *"in him dwelleth all the fulness of the Godhead bodily"* (Col. 2:9). There is a fullness of atoning efficacy in His blood, for *"the blood of Jesus Christ his Son cleanseth us from all sin"* (1 John 1:7). There is a fullness of justifying righteousness in His life, for *"there is therefore now no condemnation to them which are in Christ Jesus"* (Rom. 8:1). There is a fullness of divine prevalence in His plea, for *"he is able also to save them to the uttermost that come unto God by him, seeing he ever liveth to make intercession for them"* (Heb. 7:25). There is a fullness of victory in His death, for through death He destroyed *"him that had the power of death, that is, the devil"* (Heb. 2:14). There is a fullness of efficacy in His resurrection from the dead, for by it we are *"begotten…again unto a lively hope"* (1 Pet. 1:3). There is a fullness of triumph in His ascension, for when He *"ascended on high, [He] led captivity captive…[and] received gifts for men"* (Ps. 68:18). (See also, Ephesians 4:8.) There is a fullness of blessings of every sort and shape: a fullness of grace to pardon, of grace to regenerate, of grace to sanctify, of grace to preserve, and of grace to perfect. There is a fullness at all times: a fullness of comfort in affliction, a fullness of guidance in prosperity. There is a fullness of every divine attribute: of wisdom, of power, of love. This fullness of blessings is impossible to survey, much less to explore. *"It pleased the Father that in him should all fulness dwell"* (Col. 1:19). Oh, what a fullness this must be of which all receive! Fullness, indeed, there must be when the stream is always flowing, and yet the well springs up as free, as rich, as full as ever. Come, believer, and find all your needs supplied. Ask largely, and you will receive largely, for this fullness is inexhaustible; it is stored up where all the needy may reach it—in Jesus, Immanuel, *"God with us"* (Matt. 1:23).

> *But Mary kept all these things,*
> *and pondered them in her heart.*
> —Luke 2:19

This blessed woman exercised three powers of her being: her *memory*— she *"kept all these things"*; her *affections*—she *"kept...them in her heart"*; and her *intellect*— she *"pondered them."* Memory, affection, and understanding were all exercised about the things that she had heard. Beloved, remember what you have heard of your Lord Jesus and what He has done for you. Make your heart the golden pot of manna to preserve the memorial of the heavenly Bread on which you have fed in days gone by. Let your memory treasure up everything about Christ that you have either felt, known, or believed, and then let your fond affections hold Him fast forevermore. Love the person of your Lord! Bring forth the alabaster box of your heart, even though it may be broken, and let all the precious ointment of your affection come streaming on His pierced feet. Let your intellect be exercised concerning the Lord Jesus. Meditate on what you read. Do not stop at the surface; dive into the depths. Do not be like the swallow that touches the brook with its wing, but be like the fish that penetrates the lowest wave. Abide with your Lord. Do not let Him be to you as a wayfaring man, who tarries for a night; but constrain Him, saying, *"Abide with us: for... the day is far spent"* (Luke 24:29). Hold Him, and do not let Him go. The word *ponder* means "to weigh." Make ready the balances of judgment. Oh, but where are the scales that can weigh the Lord Christ? He *"weighed the mountains in scales"* (v. 12)—in what scales shall we weigh *Him*? *"He taketh up the isles as a very little thing"* (Isa. 40:15)—who will take *Him* up? Even so, if your understanding cannot comprehend, let your affections do so. If your spirit cannot encompass the Lord Jesus in the grasp of understanding, let it embrace Him in the arms of affection.

Perfect in Christ Jesus.
—Colossians 1:28

Do you not feel in your own soul that perfection is not in you? Does not every day teach you that? Every tear that trickles from your eyes weeps "imperfection"; every harsh word that proceeds from your lips mutters "imperfection." You have too frequently had a view of your own heart to dream for a moment of any perfection in yourself. But amid this sad consciousness of imperfection, here is comfort for you—you are *"perfect in Christ Jesus."* In God's sight, you are *"complete in Him"* (Col. 2:10); even now you are *"accepted in the beloved"* (Eph. 1:6). But there is a second perfection, yet to be realized, which is sure to all the seed. Is it not delightful to look forward to the time when every stain of sin will be removed from the believer, and he will be presented faultless before the throne, *"not having spot, or wrinkle, or any such thing"* (Eph. 5:27)? The church of Christ, then, will be so pure that not even the eye of Omniscience will see a spot or blemish in her; she will be so holy and so glorious that Hart did not go beyond the truth when he said, "With my Savior's garments on, holy as the Holy One." Then we will know, taste, and feel the happiness of this vast but short sentence, "Complete in Christ." Not until then will we fully comprehend the heights and depths of the salvation of Jesus. Does not your heart leap for joy at the thought of it? Black as you are, you will be white one day; filthy as you are, you will be clean. Oh, this is a marvelous salvation! Christ takes a worm and transforms it into an angel; Christ takes a black and deformed thing and makes it clean and matchless in His glory, peerless in His beauty, and fit to be the companion of seraphim. O my soul, stand and admire this blessed truth of perfection in Christ.

*And the shepherds returned, glorifying and praising God for all the
things that they had heard and seen, as it was told unto them.*
—Luke 2:20

What was the subject of the shepherds' praise? They praised God
for what they had *"heard,"* for the *"good tidings of great joy"* (Luke 2:10)
that a Savior had been born unto them. Let us imitate them. Let us also
raise a song of thanksgiving that we have heard of Jesus and His salvation.
Moreover, they praised God for what they had *"seen."* That is the sweetest
music—what we have experienced, what we have felt within, what we have
made our own: *"The things which* [we] *have made touching the king"* (Ps.
45:1). It is not enough to hear about Jesus; mere hearing may tune the harp,
but the fingers of living faith must create the music. If you have seen Jesus
with the God-giving sight of faith, allow no cobwebs to linger among the
harpstrings. Awake your psaltery and harp and loudly praise His sovereign
grace. One point for which they praised God was the agreement between
what they had heard and what they had seen. Observe the last part of the
sentence: *"As it was told unto them."* Have you not found the Gospel to be
in yourself just what the Bible said it would be? Jesus said He would give
you rest—have you not enjoyed the sweetest peace in Him? He said you
would have joy, comfort, and life through believing in Him—have you not
received all these? Are His ways not *"ways of pleasantness"* (Prov. 3:17) and
His paths not paths of peace (v. 17)? Surely, you can say with the queen
of Sheba, *"The half was not told me"* (1 Kings 10:7). I have found Christ
sweeter than His servants ever said He was. I looked on His likeness as they
painted it, but it was a crude portrait compared with Himself; for the King
in His beauty outshines all imaginable loveliness. Surely, what we have seen
not only keeps pace with, but far exceeds what we have heard. Let us, then,
glorify and praise God for a Savior so precious and so satisfying.

JANUARY 29

Morning

The things which are not seen.
—2 Corinthians 4:18

In our Christian pilgrimage, it is a good thing, for the most part, to be looking forward. Forward lies the crown, and onward is the goal. Whether it is for hope, for joy, for consolation, or for the inspiring of our love, the future must, after all, be the grand object of the eyes of faith. Looking into the future, we see sin cast out; the body of sin and death destroyed; the soul made perfect, and fit to be a partaker *"of the inheritance of the saints in light"* (Col. 1:12). Looking further yet, the believer's enlightened eyes can see death's river passed, the gloomy stream forded, and the hills of light attained on which stands the celestial city. He sees himself enter within the pearly gates, hailed as more than conqueror, crowned by the hand of Christ, embraced in the arms of Jesus, glorified with Him, and made to sit together with Him on His throne, even as He has overcome and has sat down with the Father on His throne. The thought of this future may well relieve the darkness of the past and the gloom of the present. The joys of heaven will surely compensate for the sorrows of earth. Hush, hush, my doubts! Death is but a narrow stream, and you will soon have forded it. Time, how short—eternity, how long! Death, how brief—immortality, how endless! The road is so short! I will soon be there.

> When the world my heart is rending
> With its heaviest storm of care,
> My glad thoughts to heaven ascending
> Find a refuge from despair.
> Faith's bright vision shall sustain me
> Till life's pilgrimage is past;
> Fears may vex and troubles pain me,
> I shall reach my home at last.

The dove came in to him in the evening.
—Genesis 8:11

Blessed be the Lord for another day of mercy, even though I am now weary from its labor. I lift my song of gratitude to the Preserver of men. The dove found no rest outside the ark so it returned to it, and my soul has learned more than ever, this day, that there is no satisfaction to be found in earthly things—God alone can give rest to my spirit. As to my business, my possessions, my family, my accomplishments, these are all well enough in their way, but they cannot fulfill the desires of my immortal nature. *"Return unto thy rest, O my soul; for the Lord hath dealt bountifully with thee"* (Ps. 116:7). It was at the still hour, when the gates of the day were closing, that with weary wing the dove came back to its master. O Lord, enable me this evening thus to return to Jesus. The dove could not endure to spend a night hovering over the restless waste; neither can I bear to be even for another hour away from Jesus, the Rest of my heart, the Home of my spirit. The bird did not merely alight on the roof of the ark; it *"came in to him."* Even so would my longing spirit look into the secrets of the Lord, pierce to the interior of truth, enter into that which is *"within the veil"* (Heb. 6:19), and reach to my Beloved. To Jesus I must come. Short of the nearest and dearest communion with Him, my panting spirit cannot stand firm. Blessed Lord Jesus, be with me, reveal Yourself, and abide with me all night, so that, when I awake, I may still be with You. I note that the dove brought in its mouth an olive branch that it had plucked off, a memorial of the past day and a prophecy of the future. Have I no pleasing record to bring home, no pledge and earnest of lovingkindness yet to come? Yes, my Lord, I present You my grateful acknowledgments for tender mercies that have been *"new every morning"* (Lam. 3:23) and fresh every evening. Now, I pray You, put forth Your hand and take Your dove in to Yourself.

*When thou hearest the sound of a going in the tops of the mulberry
trees,...then thou shalt bestir thyself.*
—2 Samuel 5:24

The members of Christ's church should be very prayerful, always seeking the anointing of the Holy One to rest on their hearts, that the kingdom of Christ may come, and that His *"will be done in earth, as it is in heaven"* (Matt. 6:10). But there are times when God seems especially to favor Zion; such seasons ought to be to them like *"the sound of a going in the tops of the mulberry trees."* We ought, then, to be doubly prayerful, doubly earnest, wrestling more at the throne than we have been inclined to do. Action should then be prompt and vigorous. The tide is flowing; let us pull manfully for the shore. Oh, for Pentecostal outpourings and Pentecostal labors! Christian, in yourself there are times when you hear the sound of marching among the mulberry trees. You have a special power in prayer; the Spirit of God gives you joy and gladness; the Scripture is open to you; the promises are applied; you walk in the light of God's countenance; you have wonderful freedom and liberty in devotion and more closeness of communion with Christ than was your custom. Now, at such joyous periods when you hear the *"sound of a going in the tops of the mulberry trees,"* is the time to rouse yourself. Now is the time to get rid of any evil habits, while God the Spirit is helping your weaknesses. Spread your sail; but remember what you sometimes sing—"I can only spread the sail; Thou! Thou! must breathe the auspicious gale." However, be sure you have the sail up. Do not miss the gale by being unprepared for it. Seek God's help, so that you may be more earnest in duty when you are made more strong in faith; that you may be more constant in prayer when you have more liberty at the throne; that you may be more holy in your conversation while you live more closely to Christ.

JANUARY 30
Evening

In whom also we have obtained an inheritance.
—Ephesians 1:11

When Jesus gave Himself for us, He gave us all the rights and privileges that are in Him. Although, as eternal God, He has essential rights to which no creature may venture to claim, as Jesus, the Mediator, the federal Head of the covenant of grace, He now has no heritage apart from us. All the glorious consequences of His obedience unto death are the joint riches of all who are in Him and on whose behalf He accomplished the divine will. Note that He entered into glory, but not for Himself alone, for it is written, *"Whither the forerunner is for us entered"* (Heb. 6:20, emphasis added). Does He stand in the presence of God? He appears *"in the presence of God for us"* (Heb. 9:24, emphasis added). Consider this, believer: you have no right to heaven in yourself; your right lies in Christ. If you are pardoned, it is through His blood. If you are justified, it is through His righteousness. If you are sanctified, it is because you are in Jesus, *"who of God is made unto [you] ...sanctification"* (1 Cor. 1:30). If you will be kept from falling, it will be because you are preserved in Christ Jesus; and if you are perfected at the last, it will be because you are *"complete in him"* (Col. 2:10). Thus Jesus is magnified, for all is in Him and by Him. The inheritance is made certain to us, for it is obtained in Him, and each blessing is sweeter—even heaven itself the brighter—because it is Jesus our Beloved *"in whom also we have obtained"* all. Where is the person who can estimate our divine portion? Weigh the riches of Christ and His treasure; then try to count the treasures that belong to the saints. Reach the bottom of Christ's sea of joy; then hope to understand the bliss *"which God hath prepared for them that love him"* (1 Cor. 2:9). Hurdle the boundaries of Christ's possessions; then dream of a limit to the fair inheritance of the elect. *"All things are yours;... ye are Christ's; and Christ is God's"* (1 Cor. 3:21, 23).

JANUARY 31
Morning

THE LORD OUR RIGHTEOUSNESS.
—Jeremiah 23:6

It will always give a Christian the greatest calm, quiet, ease, and peace to think of the perfect righteousness of Christ. How often are the saints of God downcast and sad! I do not think they should be. I do not think they would be if they could always see their perfection in Christ. Some are always talking about corruption, the depravity of the heart, and the innate evil of the soul. These things are quite true, but why not go a little further and remember that we are *"perfect in Christ Jesus"* (Col. 1:28)? It is no wonder that those who are dwelling on their own corruption should wear such downcast looks; but surely, if we call to mind that *"Christ Jesus… is made unto us…righteousness"* (1 Cor. 1:30), we will be of good cheer. Even though distresses afflict me and Satan assaults me; even though there may be many things to be experienced before I get to heaven, these things are done for me in the covenant of divine grace. Nothing is lacking in my Lord! Christ has done it all! On the cross, He said, *"It is finished"* (John 19:30), and if it is finished, then I am complete in Him and can *"rejoice with joy unspeakable and full of glory"* (1 Pet. 1:8). *"Not having mine own righteousness, which is of the law, but that which is through the faith of Christ, the righteousness which is of God by faith"* (Phil. 3:9). You will not find on this side of heaven a holier people than those who receive into their hearts the doctrine of Christ's righteousness. When the believer says, "I live in Christ alone. I rest solely on Him for salvation; and I believe that, however unworthy, I am still saved in Jesus," then there rises up as a motive of gratitude these thoughts: "Will I not live for Christ? Will I not love Him and serve Him, seeing that I am saved by His merits?" *"The love of Christ constraineth us… that they which live should not henceforth live unto themselves, but unto him which died for them"* (2 Cor. 5:14–15). If we are saved by imputed righteousness, we will greatly value imparted righteousness.

Then Ahimaaz ran by the way of the plain, and overran Cushi.
—2 Samuel 18:23

Running is not everything. The path that we select is also significant. A swift foot over hill and down dale will not keep pace with a slower traveler who is on level ground. How is it with my spiritual journey? Am I laboring up the hill of my own works and down into the ravines of my own humiliations and resolutions, or do I run by the unobstructed way of "believe and live"? (See John 20:31.) How blessed it is to wait on the Lord by faith! The soul runs without weariness and walks without fainting when it operates in faith. Christ Jesus is the way of life, and He is a plain way, a pleasant way, a way suitable for the tottering feet and feeble knees of trembling sinners. Am I on His path, or am I hunting after another track, such as one that false religions or philosophy may promise me? I read of *"the way of holiness"* in which *"the wayfaring men, though fools, shall not err"* (Isa. 35:8). Have I been delivered from proud reason and been brought as a little child to rest in Jesus' love and blood? If so, by God's grace I will outrun the strongest runner who chooses any other path. This truth I may remember to my profit in my daily cares and needs. It will be my wisest course to go at once to my God and not to wander in a roundabout manner to this friend and that. He knows my needs and can relieve them. To whom should I go but to Himself by the direct appeal of prayer and the plain argument of the promise? "Straightforward makes the best runner." I will not confer with the servants but hasten to their master. In reading this passage, it strikes me that if men vie with each other over common matters, and one outruns the other, I ought to be in solemn earnestness to run in such a way that I may obtain the prize. Lord, help me to *"gird up the loins of [my] mind"* (1 Pet. 1:13). May *"I press toward the mark for the prize of the high calling of God in Christ Jesus"* (Phil. 3:14).

FEBRUARY 1

Morning

They shall sing in the ways of the LORD.
—Psalm 138:5

Christians begin to *"sing in the ways of the LORD"* when they first lose their burdens at the foot of the Cross. Not even the songs of the angels seem as sweet as the first song of rapture that gushes from the inmost soul of the forgiven child of God. You know how John Bunyan described it. He said that when poor Pilgrim lost his burden at the Cross, he gave three great leaps and went on his way singing,

> Blest Cross! blest Sepulchre! blest rather be
> The Man that there was put to shame for me!

Believer, do you remember the day when your fetters fell off? Do you remember the place where Jesus met you and said, "'*I have loved* [you] *with an everlasting love'* (Jer. 31:3). *'I have blotted out, as a thick cloud,* [your] *transgressions, and, as a cloud* [your] *sins'* (Isa. 44:22). They will not be mentioned against you forevermore." Oh, what a sweet season it is when Jesus takes away the pain of sin! When the Lord first pardoned my sin, I was so joyous that I could scarcely refrain from dancing. I thought on my way home from the house where I had been set at liberty that I must tell the stones in the street the story of my deliverance. My soul was so full of joy that I wanted to tell every snowflake that was falling from heaven of the wondrous love of Jesus, who had blotted out the sins of one of the chief of rebels. But it is not only at the beginning of the Christian life that believers have reason for song; as long as they live, they discover reasons to sing in the ways of the Lord, and their experience of His constant lovingkindness leads them to say, "*I will bless the LORD at all times: his praise shall continually be in my mouth*" (Ps. 34:1). See to it, friend, that you magnify the Lord this day.

> Long as we tread this desert land,
> New mercies shall new songs demand.

Thy love to me was wonderful.
—2 Samuel 1:26

Come, dear readers, and let each one of us speak for himself of the wonderful love, not of Jonathan, but of Jesus. We will not relate what we have been told, but the things that we have tasted and handled of the love of Christ. Your love for me, O Jesus, was wonderful when I was a stranger wandering far from You, fulfilling the desires of the flesh and of the mind. Your love restrained me from committing the *"sin unto death"* (Rom. 6:16) and withheld me from self-destruction. Your love held back the ax when Justice said, "Cut it down! Why trouble the ground with it?" Your love drew me into the wilderness, stripped me there, and made me feel the guilt of my sin and the burden of my iniquity. Your love spoke gently to me when I was very dismayed: *"Come unto me…and I will give you rest"* (Matt. 11:28). Oh, how matchless was Your love when, in a moment, You washed my sins away and made my polluted soul, which was crimson with the blood of my birth and black with the grime of my transgressions, to be white as the driven snow and pure as the finest wool. How You showed me Your love when You whispered in my ears, "I am yours and you are Mine." Your words were so kind when You said, *"The Father himself loveth you"* (John 16:27). And sweet the moments, surpassing sweet, when You declared to me *"the love of the Spirit"* (Rom. 15:30). My soul will never forget those times of fellowship where You have unveiled Yourself to me. Did Moses have his cleft in the rock, where he saw the train, the back, of his God? We, too, have had our clefts in the rock where we have seen the full splendor of the Godhead in the person of Christ. Did David remember the tracks of the wild goat, the land of Jordan, and the heights of Hermon? We, too, can remember places that are dear to our memories, equal to these in blessedness. Precious Lord Jesus, give us a fresh portion of Your wondrous love with which to begin the month. Amen.

FEBRUARY 2

Morning

Without shedding of blood is no remission.
—Hebrews 9:22

This is the voice of unalterable truth. In none of the Jewish ceremonies were sins, even typically, removed without the shedding of blood. In no case, by no means, can sin be pardoned without atonement. It is clear, then, that there is no hope for me apart from Christ; for there is no other shedding of blood than His that is worth a thought as an atonement for sin. Am I, then, believing in Him? Is the blood of His atonement truly applied to my soul? All men are equal as to their need of Him. Even if we are moral, generous, amiable, or patriotic, the rule will not be altered to make an exception for us. Sin will yield to nothing less potent than the blood of Him whom God has set forth as a propitiation. What a blessing that there is the one way of pardon! Why should we seek another? Persons of merely formal religion cannot understand how we can rejoice that all our sins are forgiven for Christ's sake. Their works, prayers, and ceremonies give them very little comfort. It is good that they are uneasy, for they are neglecting the one great salvation and endeavoring to get remission without blood. My soul, take the time to consider that the justice of God is obligated to punish sin. See that punishment executed on your Lord Jesus and fall down in humble joy. Kiss the dear feet of Him whose blood has made atonement for you. It is in vain when the conscience is aroused to fly to feelings and evidences for comfort: we learned this habit in the Egypt of our legal bondage. The only restorative for a guilty conscience is a sight of Jesus suffering on the cross. *"The blood is the life"* (Deut. 12:23) says the Levitical law, and let us rest assured that it is the life of faith and joy and every other holy grace.

> Oh, how sweet to view the flowing
> Of my Savior's precious blood;
> With divine assurance knowing
> He has made my peace with God.

And these are ancient things.
—1 Chronicles 4:22

These things are not as ancient as those precious things that delight our souls. Let us for a moment recall them, recounting them as misers delight in calculating the worth of their gold. The sovereign choice of the Father, by which He elected us to eternal life, before *"the earth was"* (Prov. 8:23), is a matter of vast antiquity, since no date can be conceived for it in the mind of man. We were *"chosen…in him before the foundation of the world"* (Eph. 1:4). Everlasting love went with the choice, for it was not a mere act of divine will by which we were set apart, but divine affection was also involved. The Father loved us in and from the beginning. Here is a theme for daily contemplation. The eternal purpose to redeem us from our foreseen ruin, to cleanse and sanctify us, and, at last, to glorify us was of infinite antiquity; it runs side by side with immutable love and absolute sovereignty. The covenant is always described as being everlasting, and Jesus, the second party in it, was actively involved from the start. He struck hands in sacred suretyship long before the first of the stars began to shine, and it was in Him that the elect were ordained to eternal life. Thus in the divine purpose a most blessed covenant union was established between the Son of God and His elect people, which will remain as the foundation of their safety when time will be no more. Is it not well to be conversant with these ancient things? Is it not shameful that they should be so much neglected and even rejected by the majority of believers? If they knew more of their own sin, would they not be more ready to adore His amazing grace? Let us both admire and adore Him tonight, as we sing,

> A monument of grace,
>   A sinner saved by blood!
> The streams of love I trace
>   Up to the Fountain, God;
> And in His sacred bosom see
>   Eternal thoughts of love to me.

FEBRUARY 3
Morning

Therefore, brethren, we are debtors.
—Romans 8:12

As God's creatures, we are all debtors to Him: to obey Him with all our bodies, souls, and strength. Having broken His commandments, as we all have, we are debtors to His justice, and we owe to Him a vast amount that we are not able to pay. But, of the Christian, it can be said that he does not owe God's justice anything, for Christ has paid the debt His people owed. For this reason, the believer owes even more to love. I am a debtor to God's grace and forgiving mercy; but I am no debtor to His justice, for He will never accuse me of a debt that has already been paid. Christ said, *"It is finished"* (John 19:30), and by that He meant that whatever His people owed was wiped away forever from the book of remembrance. Christ, to the uttermost, has satisfied divine justice. The account is settled. The handwriting is nailed to the cross. The receipt is given, and we are debtors to God's justice no longer. But then, because we are not debtors to our Lord in that sense, we become debtors to God ten times more than we would have been otherwise. Christian, pause and ponder for a moment. What a debtor you are to divine sovereignty! How much you owe to His unbiased love, for He gave His own Son that He might die for you. Consider how much you owe to His forgiving grace that, after ten thousand affronts, He loves you as infinitely as ever. Consider what you owe to His power: how He has raised you from your death in sin; how He has preserved your spiritual life; how He has kept you from falling; and how, though a thousand enemies have beset your path, you have been able to continue on your way. Consider what you owe to His immutability: though you have changed a thousand times, He has not changed once. You are as deep in debt as you can be to every attribute of God. To God you owe yourself, and all you have. Yield yourself as a *"living sacrifice"*; it is but your *"reasonable service"* (Rom. 12:1).

FEBRUARY 3

Evening

Tell me…where thou feedest, where thou
makest thy flock to rest at noon.
—Song of Solomon 1:7

These words express the desire of the believer to follow Christ and his longing for present communion with Him. Where do You feed Your flock? In Your house? I will go, if I may find You there. In private prayer? Then I will pray without ceasing. In the Word? Then I will read it diligently. In Your commandments? Then I will walk in them with all my heart. Tell me where You feed, for wherever You stand as the Shepherd, there will I lie down as a sheep; for none but You can supply my need. I cannot be satisfied to be apart from You. My soul hungers and thirsts for the refreshment of Your presence. "Where do You make Your flock to rest at noon?" For whether it is at dawn or at noon, my only rest must be where You are and Your beloved flock. My soul's rest must be a grace-given rest, and it can be found only in You. Where is the shadow of that rock? Why should I not repose underneath it? *"Why should I be as one that turneth aside by the flocks of thy companions?"* (Song 1:7). You have companions—why should I not be one? Satan tells me that I am unworthy, but I always was unworthy. Yet You have long loved me; therefore, my unworthiness cannot be a barrier to my having fellowship with You now. It is true I am weak in faith and prone to fall, but my very feebleness is the reason why I should always be where You feed Your flock, so that I may be strengthened and preserved in safety beside the still waters. Why should I turn away from You? There is no reason why I should, but there are a thousand reasons why I should not, for Jesus beckons me to come. If He withdrew Himself a little, it was only to make me prize His presence more. Now that I am grieved and distressed at being away from Him, He will lead me once again to that sheltered nook where the lambs of His fold are shielded from the burning sun.

The love of the LORD.
—Hosea 3:1

Believer, look back through all your experiences and think of the ways in which the Lord your God has led you in the wilderness—how He has fed and clothed you every day; how He has tolerated your bad manners, put up with all your grumbling and all your longings after Egypt's pots of meat; how He has opened the rock to supply you, and fed you with manna from heaven. Think of how His grace has been sufficient for you in all your troubles—how His blood has been a pardon for you in all your sins, how His rod and His staff have comforted you. When you have thus looked back on the love of the Lord, then let faith survey His love in the future, for remember that Christ's covenant and blood have something more in them than the past. He who has loved you and pardoned you will never cease to love and pardon. He is Alpha, and He will be Omega also. He is first, and He will be last. Therefore, remember, when you pass through the *"valley of the shadow of death"* (Ps. 23:4), you need fear no evil, for He is with you. When you stand in the cold floods of the Jordan, you do not need to fear, for death cannot separate you from His love. When you come into the mysteries of eternity, you do not need to tremble, *"for I am persuaded, that neither death, nor life, nor angels, nor principalities, nor powers, nor things present, nor things to come, nor height, nor depth, nor any other creature, shall be able to separate us from the love of God, which is in Christ Jesus our Lord"* (Rom. 8:38–39). Now, soul, is your love not refreshed? Does this Scripture not make you love Jesus? Does a flight through the unlimited plains of heavenly love not inflame your heart and compel you to delight yourself in the Lord your God? Surely as we meditate on *"the love of the LORD,"* our hearts burn within us, and we long to love Him more.

Your refuge from the avenger of blood.
—Joshua 20:3

It is said that in the land of Canaan, cities of refuge were set up so that any man might reach one of them within half a day at the most. Likewise, the word of our salvation is near to us. Jesus is a present Savior, and the distance to Him is short. It requires only a simple renunciation of our own merit and a laying hold of Jesus to be our all in all. With regard to the roads leading to the cities of refuge, we are told that they were carefully preserved. Every river was bridged and every obstruction removed, so that the man who fled might find an easy passage to safety. Once a year the elders went along the roads and saw to their order, so that nothing might impede the flight of anyone or cause him, through delay, to be overtaken and slain. How graciously do the promises of the Gospel remove stumbling blocks from our paths! Wherever there were hidden roads or turns, there were signs placed, with this inscription on them: "To the city of refuge!" This is a picture of the road to Christ Jesus. It is no roundabout road of the law. It does not involve obeying endless rules; it is a straight road: "Believe and live." (See John 20:31.) It is a road so hard that no self-righteous man can ever tread it, but so easy that every sinner, who knows himself to be a sinner, may by it find his way to heaven. No sooner did the manslayer reach the outskirts of the city than he was safe. It was not necessary for him to pass far within the walls, for the suburbs themselves were sufficient protection. Learn that if you touch just the hem of Christ's garment, you will be made whole; if you will only lay hold on him with "*faith as a grain of mustard seed*" (Matt. 17:20), you will be safe.

A little genuine grace ensures
The death of all our sins.

Do not waste any time. Do not loiter by the way, for "*the avenger of blood*" is swift of foot; it may be that he is at your heels on this quiet, evening hour.

The Father sent the Son to be the Saviour of the world.
—1 John 4:14

It is a sweet thought that Jesus Christ did not come forth without His Father's permission, authority, consent, and assistance. He was sent by the Father so that He might be the Savior of men. We are too apt to forget that, while there are distinctions as to the persons in the Trinity, there are no distinctions of honor. We too frequently ascribe the honor of our salvation, or at least the depths of its benevolence, more to Jesus Christ than to the Father. This is a very great mistake. What if Jesus came? Did not His Father send Him? If He spoke wondrously, did not His Father pour grace into His lips so that He might be an able minister of the new covenant? He who knows the Father, the Son, and the Holy Spirit, as he should know them, never sets one before another in his love. He sees them at Bethlehem, at Gethsemane, and on Calvary, all equally engaged in the work of salvation. O Christian, have you put your confidence in the Man Christ Jesus? Have you placed your reliance solely on Him? Are you united with Him? Then believe that you are united with the God of heaven. Since to the Man Christ Jesus you are brother, and hold closest fellowship, you are linked thereby with God the Eternal, and *"the Ancient of days"* (Dan. 7:9, 13, 22) is your Father and your Friend. Did you ever consider the depth of love that was in the heart of Jehovah, when God the Father equipped His Son for the great enterprise of mercy? If not, make this your day's meditation. The Father sent Him! Contemplate that subject. Think about how Jesus works what the Father wills. In the wounds of the dying Savior, see the love of the great I Am. Let every thought of Jesus also be connected with the Eternal, ever blessed God, for *"it pleased the LORD to bruise him; he hath put him to grief"* (Isa. 53:10).

FEBRUARY 5

Evening

At that time Jesus answered.
—Matthew 11:25

This is an unusual way in which to begin a verse—*"At that time Jesus answered."* If you look at the context, you will notice that no one had asked Him a question and that He was not in conversation with any human being. Yet it is written, *"Jesus answered and said, I thank thee, O Father"* (Matt. 11:25). When a man answers, he answers a person who has been speaking to him. Who, then, had spoken to Christ? His Father. Yet there is no record of it. This should teach us that Jesus had constant fellowship with His Father; God spoke to His heart so often, so continually, that it was not a circumstance uncommon enough to be recorded. It was the habit and life of Jesus to talk with God. Even as Jesus was, in this world, so are we; let us, therefore, learn the lesson that this simple statement concerning Him teaches us. May we likewise have silent fellowship with the Father, so that often we may answer Him. Though the world does not know to whom we speak, may we be responsive to that secret voice unheard by any other ear, which our own ears, opened by the Spirit of God, recognize with joy. God has spoken to us; let us speak to God—either to set our seal that God is true and faithful to His promise, to confess the sin of which the Spirit of God has convicted us, to acknowledge the mercy that God's providence has given, or to express assent to the great truths that God the Holy Spirit has opened to our understanding. What a privilege is intimate communion with the Father of our spirits! It is a secret hidden from the world, a joy with which even the dearest friend cannot share. If we would hear the whispers of God's love, our ears must be purged and ready to listen to His voice. This very evening may our hearts be in such a state so that, when God speaks to us, we, like Jesus, may be prepared at once to answer Him.

FEBRUARY 6

Praying always.
—Ephesians 6:18

What multitudes of prayers we have said from the first moment when we learned to pray. Our first prayer was a prayer for ourselves; we asked that God would have mercy on us and blot out our sins. He heard us. But when He had blotted out our sins like a cloud, then we had more prayers for ourselves. We have had to pray for sanctifying grace, for constraining and restraining grace. We have been led to crave a fresh assurance of faith, the comfortable application of the promise, deliverance in the hour of temptation, strength in the time of duty, and help in the day of trial. We have been compelled to go to God for our souls, as constant beggars asking for everything. Bear witness, children of God: you have never been able to get anything for your souls elsewhere. All the bread your soul has eaten has come down from heaven, and all the water of which it has drunk has flowed from the living Rock—Christ Jesus the Lord. Your soul has never grown rich in itself; it has always been a pensioner on the daily bounty of God; hence, your prayers have ascended to heaven for a range of spiritual mercies all but infinite. Your needs were innumerable; therefore, the supplies have been infinitely great. Your prayers have been as varied as the mercies have been countless. Do you not have cause to say, *"I love the LORD, because he hath heard my voice and my supplications"* (Ps. 116:1)? For as your prayers have been many, so also have been God's answers to them. He has heard you in the day of trouble, has strengthened and helped you, even when you have dishonored Him by trembling and doubting at the mercy seat. Remember this, and let it fill your heart with gratitude to God, who has thus graciously heard your poor weak prayers. *"Bless the LORD, O my soul, and forget not all his benefits"* (Ps. 103:2).

FEBRUARY 6

Evening

Pray one for another.
—James 5:16

As an encouragement to offer intercessory prayer cheerfully, remember that such prayer is the sweetest God ever hears, for the prayer of Christ is of this same character. In all the incense that our Great High Priest now puts into the golden censer, there is not a single grain for Himself. His intercession must be the most acceptable of all supplications—and the more our prayer is like Christ's, the sweeter it will be. Thus while petitions for ourselves will be accepted, our pleadings for others, having in them more of the fruits of the Spirit—more love, more faith, more brotherly kindness—will be, through the precious merits of Jesus, the sweetest offering that we can present to God, the very fat of our sacrifice. Remember, also, that intercessory prayer is exceedingly prevalent. What wonders it has brought about! The Word of God teems with its marvelous deeds. Believer, you have a mighty engine in your hand; use it well, and use it constantly. Use it with faith, and you will surely be a benefactor to your brethren. When you have the King's ear, speak to Him for the suffering members of His body. When you are favored to draw very near to His throne, and the King says to you, *"Whatsoever ye shall ask the Father in my name, he will give it you"* (John 16:23), let your petitions be, not for yourself alone, but for the many who need His aid. If you have grace at all and you are not an intercessor, that grace must be as small as a grain of mustard seed. You have just enough grace to float your soul clear from the quicksand, but you have no deep floods of grace. Otherwise, you would carry in your joyous boat a weighty cargo of the needs of others, and you would bring back from your Lord rich blessings, which without you they might not have obtained.

Oh, let my hands forget their skill,
My tongue be silent, cold, and still,
This bounding heart forget to beat,
If I forget the mercy seat!

FEBRUARY 7

Morning

Arise ye, and depart.
—Micah 2:10

The hour is approaching when the message will come to us, as it comes to all—"Arise, and leave the home in which you have dwelled. Leave the city in which you have done your business. Leave your family and friends. Arise, and take your last journey." And what do we know of the journey? What do we know of the country to which we are bound? We have read a little about it, and some has been revealed to us by the Spirit, but how little we know of the realms of the future! We know that there is a black and stormy river called Death. God bids us cross it, promising to be with us. And, after death, what comes? What wondrous world will open to our astonished sight? What scene of glory will be unfolded to our view? No traveler has ever returned to tell. But we know enough of the heavenly land to make us welcome with joy and gladness our summons there. The journey of death may be dark, but we may go forth on it fearlessly, knowing that God is with us as we walk through the gloomy valley; therefore, we need fear no evil. We will be departing from all we have known and loved here, but we will be going to our Father's house—to our Father's home, where Jesus is—to that royal *"city which hath foundations, whose builder and maker is God"* (Heb. 11:10). This will be our last removal, to dwell forever with Him whom we love, in the midst of His people, in the presence of God. Christian, meditate much on heaven. It will help you to press on and to forget the toil of the way. This vale of tears is but the pathway to the better country. This world of woe is but the stepping-stone to a world of bliss.

> Prepare us, Lord, by grace divine,
>   For Thy bright courts on high;
> Then bid our spirits rise,
>   And join the chorus of the sky.

FEBRUARY 7
Evening

And they heard a great voice from heaven
saying unto them, Come up hither.
—Revelation 11:12

Without considering these words in their prophetic connection, let us regard them as the invitation of our great Forerunner to His sanctified people. In due time, every believer will hear *"a great voice from heaven,"* saying, *"Come up hither."* To the saints, this should be the subject of joyful anticipation. Instead of dreading the time when we will leave this world to go to the Father, we should be panting for the hour of our emancipation. Our song should be,

> My heart is with Him on His throne,
> And ill can brook delay;
> Each moment listening for the voice,
> "Rise up and come away."

We are not called down to the grave, but up to the skies. Our heaven-born spirits should long for their native air, yet the celestial summons should be the object of patient waiting. Our God knows best when to bid us, *"Come up hither."* We must not wish to hasten the period of our departure. I know that strong love will make us cry,

> O Lord of Hosts, the waves divide,
> And land us all in heaven.

But patience must have her perfect work. God ordains with accurate wisdom the most fitting time for the redeemed to abide below. Surely, if there could be regrets in heaven, the saints might mourn that they did not live longer here to do more good. Oh, for more sheaves for my Lord's garner— more jewels for His crown! But how, unless there is more work? It is true that living so briefly, our sins are fewer; but oh, when we are fully serving God and He is giving us precious seed to scatter and to reap a hundredfold, we would even say it is well for us to remain where we are. Whether our Master says "go" or "stay," let us be equally well pleased as long as He continues to bless us with His presence.

FEBRUARY 8

Morning

Thou shalt call his name Jesus.
—Matthew 1:21

When a person is dear, everything connected with him becomes dear for his sake. Thus, so precious is the person of the Lord Jesus in the estimation of all true believers that everything about Him they consider to be inestimable—beyond all price. *"All thy garments smell of myrrh, and aloes, and cassia"* (Ps. 45:8), said David, as if the very clothing of the Savior were so sweetened by His person that he could not but love it. Certainly, every spot where that hallowed foot has trod, every word that those blessed lips have uttered, or any thought that His loving Word has revealed is precious to us beyond all price. And this is true of the names of Christ; they are all sweet in the believer's ear. Whether He is called the Husband of the church, her Bridegroom, her Friend; whether He is named *"the Lamb slain from the foundation of the world"* (Rev. 13:8), the King, the Prophet, or the Priest; every title of our Master—Shiloh, Immanuel, Wonderful, the Mighty Counselor—every name is like the honeycomb dripping with honey, and luscious are the drops that fall from it. But if there is one name sweeter than another in the believer's ear, it is the name of *Jesus.* Jesus! His name moves the harps of heaven to melody. If there is one name more charming, more precious than another, it is the name *Jesus,* the life of all our joys. It is woven into the very foundation of our psalmody. Many of our hymns begin with it, and scarcely any that are good for anything end without it. It is the sum total of all delights. It is the music with which the bells of heaven ring; a song in a word; an ocean for comprehension, although a drop for brevity; a matchless oratorio in two syllables; a gathering up of the hallelujahs of eternity in five letters.

Jesus, I love Thy charming name,
  'Tis music to mine ear.

FEBRUARY 8
Evening

He shall save his people from their sins.
—Matthew 1:21

Many persons, when asked what they mean by salvation, will reply, "Being saved from hell and taken to heaven." This is one result of salvation, but it is not one tenth of what is contained in that blessing. It is true that our Lord Jesus Christ redeems all His people from the wrath to come. He saves them from the fearful condemnation that their sins have brought upon them, but His triumph is far more complete than this. He saves His people "*from their sins.*" Oh, sweet deliverance from our worst foes! Where Christ works a saving work, He casts Satan from his throne and will not let him be master any longer. No man is a true Christian if sin reigns in his mortal body. Sin will be in us; it will never be utterly expelled until the spirit enters glory, but it will never have dominion. There will be a striving for dominion—a lusting against the new law and the new spirit that God has implanted—but sin will never get the upper hand so as to be absolute monarch of our natures. Christ will be the Master of the heart, and sin must be mortified. The Lion of the tribe of Judah will prevail, and the dragon will be cast out. Believer, is sin subdued in you? If your life is unholy, your heart is unchanged; and if your heart is unchanged, you are an unsaved person. If the Savior has not sanctified you, renewed you, given you a hatred of sin and a love of holiness, He has done nothing in you of a saving character. Grace that does not make a man better than others is a worthless counterfeit. Christ saves His people, not *in* their sins, but *from* them. Without "*holiness,...no man shall see the Lord*" (Heb. 12:14). "*Let every one that nameth the name of Christ depart from iniquity*" (2 Tim. 2:19). If we are not saved from sin, how will we hope to be counted among His people? Lord, save me now from all evil and enable me to honor my Savior.

David inquired of the L<small>ORD</small>.
—2 Samuel 5:23

When David made this inquiry, he had just fought the Philistines and gained a signal victory. The Philistines had come up in great hosts, but, by the help of God, David had easily put them to flight. Note, however, that when they came a second time, David did not go up to fight them without inquiring of the Lord. Once he had been victorious, and he might have said, as many have in other cases, "I will be victorious again; I may rest quite sure that, if I have conquered once, I will triumph yet again. Why should I bother to seek the Lord's direction?" Not so, David. He had gained one battle by the strength of the Lord; he would not venture on another until he had ensured the same. He inquired, "Should I go up against them?" He waited until God's sign was given. Learn from David to take no step without God. Christian, if you would know the path of duty, take God for your compass; if you would steer your ship through the dark billows, put the tiller into the hand of the Almighty. Many rocks might be escaped, if we would let our Father take the helm; many shoals or quicksand we might well avoid, if we would leave to His sovereign will to choose and to command. The Puritan said, "As sure as ever a Christian carves for himself, he'll cut his own fingers"; this is a great truth. Said another old clergyman, "He who goes before the cloud of God's providence goes on a fool's errand"; and so he does. We must mark God's providence leading us; and if providence tarries, tarry until providence comes. He who goes before providence will be very glad to run back again. *"I will instruct thee and teach thee in the way which thou shalt go"* (Ps. 32:8) is God's promise to His people. Let us, then, take all our perplexities to Him, and say, "Lord, what would You have me to do?" Do not leave your room this morning without inquiring of the Lord.

Lead us not into temptation;
but deliver us from evil [or, the evil one].
—Luke 11:4

What we are taught to seek or shun in prayer, we should equally pursue or avoid in action. Therefore, we should avoid temptation earnestly, seeking to walk guardedly in the path of obedience, so that we may never tempt the devil to tempt us. We are not to enter the thicket in search of the lion. Dearly might we pay for such presumption. A lion may cross our paths or leap on us from the thicket, but we have nothing to do with hunting it. He who meets with a lion, even though he wins the day, will find it a stern struggle. Let the Christian pray that he may be spared from the encounter. Our Savior, who experienced what temptation meant, thus earnestly admonished His disciples: *"Pray that ye enter not into temptation"* (Luke 22:40). But no matter what we do, we will be tempted; hence the prayer *"deliver us from evil."* God had one Son without sin; but He has no son without temptation. The natural *"man is born unto trouble, as the sparks fly upward,"* (Job 5:7), and the Christian man is born to temptation just as certainly. We must always be on watch against Satan, because, like a thief, he gives no warning of his approach. Believers who have had experience in the ways of Satan know that there are certain seasons when he will most probably make an attack, just as at certain seasons bleak winds may be expected. Thus the Christian is put on a double guard by fear of danger, and the danger is averted by preparing to meet it. Prevention is better than cure: it is better to be so well armed that the devil will not attack you than to endure the perils of the fight, even though you come off a conqueror. Pray this evening first that you may not be tempted, and next that if temptation is permitted, you may be delivered from the evil one.

FEBRUARY 10

I know how to abound.
—Philippians 4:12

Many who know *"how to be abased"* (Phil. 4:12) have not learned *"how to abound."* On top of a pinnacle, their heads grow dizzy, and they are ready to fall. The Christian more often disgraces his profession of faith in prosperity than in adversity. It is a dangerous thing to be prosperous. The crucible of adversity is a less severe trial to the Christian than the refinery of prosperity. Oh, what leanness of soul and neglect of spiritual things have been brought on through the very mercies and bounties of God! Yet this does not need to happen, for the apostle Paul said that he knew how to abound. When he had much, he knew how to use it. Abundant grace enabled him to bear abundant prosperity. When he had a full sail, he was loaded with much ballast and so floated safely. More than human skill is needed to carry an overflowing cup of mortal joy with a steady hand, yet Paul had learned that skill, for he declared, *"In all things I am instructed both to be full and to be hungry"* (Phil. 4:12). It is a divine lesson to know how to be full, for the Israelites were full once, but while the meat was yet in their mouths, the wrath of God came on them. Many have asked for mercies so that they might satisfy their own hearts' lusts. When we have much of God's providential mercies, it often happens that we have but little of God's grace and little gratitude for the bounties we have received. We are full and we forget God. Satisfied with earth, we are content to do without heaven. Rest assured that it is harder to know how to be full than it is to know how to be hungry, so desperate is the tendency of human nature to pride and forgetfulness of God. Take care that you ask in your prayers that God would teach you how to be full.

> Let not the gifts Thy love bestows
> Estrange our hearts from Thee.

FEBRUARY 10

Evening

I have blotted out, as a thick cloud, thy transgressions, and, as a cloud, thy sins: return unto me; for I have redeemed thee.
—Isaiah 44:22

Carefully observe the instructive comparison made here: our sins are like a cloud. As clouds are of many shapes and shades, so are our transgressions. As clouds obscure the light of the sun and darken the landscape below, so do our sins hide from us the light of Jehovah's face and cause us to sit in the shadow of death. They are earthborn things and rise from the miry places of our nature. When so collected that their measure is full, they threaten us with storm and tempest. Sadly, unlike clouds, our sins do not yield any beneficial showers; rather, they threaten to deluge us with a fiery flood of destruction. O black clouds of sin, how can it be fair weather with our souls while you remain? Let our joyful eyes dwell on the notable act of divine mercy—blotting out. God Himself appears on the scene, and in divine graciousness, instead of manifesting His anger, He reveals His grace. At once and forever, He effectively removes the mischief, not by blowing away the cloud, but by blotting it out from existence once and for all. No sin remains against the justified man; the great transaction of the Cross has eternally removed his transgressions from him. On Calvary's summit the great deed, by which the sin of all the chosen was forever put away, was completely and effectively performed. Practically, let us obey the gracious command, *"Return unto me."* Why should pardoned sinners live at a distance from their God? If we have been forgiven of all our sins, let no fear keep us from the boldest access to our Lord. Let us regret any backslidings, but let us not persevere in them. To the greatest possible nearness of communion with the Lord, let us, in the power of the Holy Spirit, strive mightily to return. O Lord, this night restore us!

And they took knowledge of them, that they had been with Jesus.
—Acts 4:13

A Christian should be a striking likeness of Jesus Christ. You have read accounts of the life of Christ that have been beautifully and eloquently written, but the best life of Christ is His living biography, written out in the words and actions of His people. If we were what we profess to be, and what we should be, we would be pictures of Christ. We would have such a striking likeness to Him that the world would not have to say, "Well, there seems to be somewhat of a likeness to Christ." Instead, when they saw us, they would exclaim, "He has been with Jesus! He has been taught of Him. He is like Him and has caught the very idea of the holy Man of Nazareth. He works it out in his life and everyday actions." A Christian should model Christ's boldness. Never blush to own your faith. Your profession will never disgrace you; take care that you never disgrace it. Be like Jesus, very valiant for your God. Imitate Him in your loving spirit. Think kindly, speak kindly, and do kindly, so that men may say of you, "He has been with Jesus." Imitate Jesus in His holiness. Was He zealous for His Master? So be you; always go about doing good. Do not waste time; it is too precious. Was He self-denying, never looking to His own interests? Be the same. Was He devout? Be fervent in your prayers. Did He defer to His Father's will? So submit yourselves to Him. Was He patient? So learn to endure. Best of all, as the highest portraiture of Jesus, try to forgive your enemies, as He did; let those sublime words of your Master, *"Father, forgive them; for they know not what they do"* (Luke 23:34), always ring in your ears. Forgive, as you hope to be forgiven. Heap coals of fire on the head of your enemy by your kindness to him. Good for evil, remember, is Godlike. Be Godlike, then. In all ways and by all means, live so that all may say of you, "He has been with Jesus."

FEBRUARY 11
Evening

Thou hast left thy first love.
—Revelation 2:4

We will always remember that best and brightest of hours when we first saw the Lord. We lost our burdens, received His promises, rejoiced in full salvation, and went on our way in peace. It was springtime in the soul. The winter was past. The mutterings of Sinai's thunders were hushed, and the flashings of its lightning were no more perceived. God and man were reconciled; the law threatened no vengeance, and justice demanded no punishment. Then the flowers appeared in our hearts. Hope, love, peace, and patience sprang from the sod. The hyacinth of repentance, the snowdrop of pure holiness, the crocus of golden faith, the daffodil of early love—all arrayed the garden of the soul. The *"time of the singing of birds"* (Song 2:12) came, and we rejoiced with thanksgiving. We magnified the holy name of our forgiving God, and our resolve was, "Lord, I am Yours, wholly Yours. All I am and all I have, I would devote to You. You have bought me with Your blood; let me spend myself and be spent in Your service. In life and in death, let me be consecrated to You." How have we kept this resolve? Our first love burned with a holy flame of devotion to Jesus; is it the same now? Might not Jesus well say to us, *"I have somewhat against thee, because thou hast left thy first love"* (Rev. 2:4)? Alas, we have done but little for our Master's glory! Our winter has lasted all too long. We are as cold as ice when we should feel a summer's glow and bloom with sacred flowers. We give God pennies when He deserves dollars. No, He deserves our hearts' blood to be invested in the service of His church and of His truth. Will we continue to do so? Lord, after You have so richly blessed us, will we be ungrateful and become indifferent to Your good cause and work? Quicken us so that we may return to our first love and do our first works! Sun of Righteousness, send us a refreshing spring.

For as the sufferings of Christ abound in us, so our consolation
also aboundeth by Christ.
—2 Corinthians 1:5

Consider this blessed proportion. The Ruler of providence bears a pair of scales: on one side, He puts His people's trials; on the other, He puts their consolations. When the scale of trial is nearly empty, you will always find the scale of consolation in nearly the same condition; likewise, when the scale of trials is full, you will find the scale of consolation just as heavy. When the black clouds gather most, the light is the more brightly revealed to us. When the night lowers and the tempest is coming on, the heavenly Captain is always closest to His crew. It is a blessed thing that when we are most cast down, we are most lifted up by the consolations of the Spirit. Trials make more room for consolation. Great hearts can be made only by great troubles. The spade of trouble digs the reservoir of comfort deeper and makes more room for consolation. God comes into our hearts and finds them full. He begins to break our comforts and to make our hearts empty, so that there is more room for grace. The humbler a man lies, the more true comfort he will always have, because he will be more fit to receive it. Another reason we are often happiest in our troubles is that then we have the closest dealings with God. When the barn is full, man can live without God. When the purse is bursting with gold, we try to do without as much prayer. But take our resources away, and we need God. Cleanse the idols out of the house, and then, we are compelled to honor Jehovah. *"Out of the depths have I cried unto thee, O Lord"* (Ps. 130:1). There is no cry as good as the one that comes from the bottom of the mountains—no prayer half as hearty as one that comes from the depths of the soul. Hence, deep trials and afflictions bring us to God, and we are happier; for nearness to God is happiness. Come, troubled believer, do not fret over your heavy troubles, for they are the heralds of weighty mercies.

FEBRUARY 12

Evening

He shall give you another Comforter,
that he may abide with you for ever.
—John 14:16

Our great Father revealed Himself to believers of old before the coming of His Son. He was known to Abraham, Isaac, and Jacob as God Almighty. Then Jesus came, and the ever-blessed Son in His own proper person was the delight of His people's eyes. At the time of the Redeemer's ascension, the Holy Spirit became the Head of the present dispensation, and His power was gloriously manifested in and after Pentecost. He remains at this hour the present Immanuel—God with us, dwelling in and with His people, quickening, guiding, and ruling in their midst. Is His presence recognized as it ought to be? We cannot control His working. He is most sovereign in all His operations, but are we sufficiently anxious to obtain His help or sufficiently watchful lest we provoke Him to withdraw His aid? Without Him we can do nothing, but by His almighty energy, the most extraordinary results can be produced. Everything depends on His manifesting or concealing His power. Do we always look up to Him both for our inner lives and our outward service with the respectful dependence that is fitting? Do we not too often run before His call and act independently of His aid? Let us humble ourselves this evening for past failures, and now entreat the heavenly dew to rest upon us, the sacred oil to anoint us, and the celestial flame to burn within us. The Holy Spirit is no temporary gift; He abides with the saints. We have but to seek Him aright, and He will be found by us. He is jealous, but He is compassionate. If He leaves in anger, He returns in mercy. Gracious and tender, He does not weary of us, but He waits to be merciful still.

> Sin has been hammering my soul
> Unto a hardness, void of love.
> Let grace work, too, and o'er my soul
> Drop from above.

FEBRUARY 13

Morning

Behold, what manner of love the Father hath bestowed upon us, that we should be called the sons of God: therefore the world knoweth us not, because it knew him not. Beloved, now are we the sons of God.
—1 John 3:1–2

Behold, what manner of love the Father hath bestowed upon us." Consider who we were, and what we feel ourselves to be even now when corruption is powerful in us, and you will wonder at our adoption. Yet we are called *"the sons of God."* What a significant relationship is that of a son, and what privileges it brings! What care and tenderness the son expects from his father, and what love the father feels toward the son! But all that, and more than that, we now have through Christ. As for the temporary drawback of suffering with the Elder Brother, this we accept as an honor: *"Therefore the world knoweth us not, because it knew him not."* We are content to be unknown with Him in His humiliation, for we are to be exalted with Him. *"Beloved, now are we the sons of God."* That is easy to read, but it is not so easy to feel. How is it with your heart this morning? Are you in the lowest depths of sorrow? Does corruption rise within your spirit and grace seem like a poor spark trampled underfoot? Does your faith almost fail you? Fear not! It is neither your graces nor your feelings on which you are to live: you must live simply by faith on Christ. With all these things against us, *"now"*—in the very depths of our sorrow, wherever we may be—*"now,"* as much in the valley as on the mountain, *"Beloved, now are we the sons of God."* "Ah, but," you say, "see how I am clothed! My graces are not bright; my righteousness does not shine with apparent glory." But read the next part: *"It doth not yet appear what we shall be: but we know that, when he shall appear, we shall be like him"* (1 John 3:2). The Holy Spirit will purify our minds, and divine power will refine our bodies; then we will *"see him as he is"* (v. 2).

FEBRUARY 13
Evening

There is therefore now no condemnation.
—Romans 8:1

Come, my soul, think of this: By believing in Jesus, you are actually and effectively cleared from guilt. You are released from your prison. No longer chained like a slave, you are delivered from the bondage of the law. You are freed from sin and can walk as a freeman. Your Savior's blood has obtained your full pardon. Now, you have the right to approach your Father's throne. No flames of vengeance and no fiery swords are there to scare you. Justice cannot smite the innocent. Your disabilities are taken away. You were once unable to see your Father's face; you can see it now. You could not speak with Him, but now you have access with boldness. Once the fear of hell was upon you. But you have no fear of it now, for how can there be punishment for the guiltless? He who believes is not condemned and cannot be punished. And more than all, the privileges you might have enjoyed, if you had never sinned, are yours now that you are justified. All the blessings that you would have had if you had kept the law, and more, are yours, because Christ has kept it for you. All the love and the acceptance that perfect obedience could have obtained from God belong to you, because Christ was perfectly obedient on your behalf. He has imputed all His merits to your account so that you might be exceedingly rich through Him, who for your sake became exceedingly poor. Oh, how great the debt of love and gratitude you owe to your Savior!

> A debtor to mercy alone,
>> Of covenant mercy I sing;
> Nor fear with Your righteousness on,
>> My person and offerings to bring:
> The terrors of law and of God,
>> With me can have nothing to do;
> My Savior's obedience and blood
>> Hide all my transgressions from view.

FEBRUARY 14

And his allowance was a continual allowance given him of the king, a
daily rate for every day, all the days of his life.
—2 Kings 25:30

Jehoiachin was not sent away from the king's palace with a store to last him for months, but his provision was given to him as a daily pension. Herein he well depicts the happy position of all the Lord's people. A daily portion is all that a person really needs. We do not need tomorrow's supplies; that day has not yet dawned, and its needs are as yet unborn. The thirst that we may suffer in the month of June does not need to be quenched in February, for we do not feel it yet. If we have enough for each day as the days arrive, we will never know need. Sufficient for the day is all that we can enjoy. We cannot eat, drink, or wear more than the day's supply of food and clothing. The surplus gives us the care of storing it and the anxiety of watching against a thief. One walking stick helps a traveler, but a bundle of sticks is a heavy burden. Enough is not only as good as a feast, but is all that the truest glutton can enjoy. This is all that we should expect; a craving for more than this is ingratitude. When our Father does not give us more, we should be content with our daily allowance. Jehoiachin's case is ours. We have a sure portion, a portion given to us by the King. It is a gracious and a perpetual portion. Here is surely ground for thankfulness. Beloved Christian, in matters of grace, you need a daily supply. You have no store of strength. Day by day, you must seek help from above. It is a very sweet assurance that a daily portion is provided for you. In the Word, through the ministry, by meditation, in prayer, and in waiting on God, you will receive renewed strength. In Jesus, all necessary things are laid up for you. Then enjoy your ongoing allowance. Never go hungry while the daily bread of grace is on the table of mercy.

She was healed immediately.
—Luke 8:47

One of the most touching and teaching of the Savior's miracles is before us tonight. The woman was very ignorant. She imagined that virtue came out of Christ by a law of necessity, without His knowledge or direct will. Moreover, she was a stranger to the generosity of Jesus' character, or she would not have gone behind Him to steal the cure that He was so ready to give. Misery should always place itself right in the face of mercy. Had she known the love of Jesus' heart, she would have said, "I have but to put myself where He can see me. Then His omniscience will reveal my situation to Him, and His love will work my cure immediately." We admire her faith, but we marvel at her ignorance. After she had obtained the cure, she rejoiced with trembling. She was glad that the divine virtue had worked a miracle in her, but she feared lest Christ might retract the blessing and cancel the grant of His grace. Little did she comprehend the fullness of His love! We do not have as clear a view of Him as we could wish. We do not know the heights and depths of His love, but we know with certainty that He is too good to withdraw from a trembling soul the gift that it has been able to obtain. But here is the marvel of it: little as her knowledge was, her faith, because it was real faith, saved her, and saved her at once. There was no tedious delay—faith's miracle was instantaneous. If we have faith as a grain of mustard seed, salvation is our present and eternal possession. If, in the list of the Lord's children, we are written as the weakest of the family, yet, being heirs through faith, no power, human or devilish, can eject us from salvation. Even if we do not dare to lean our heads on His bosom as John did, yet we can venture into the crowd behind Him and touch the hem of His garment, and we will be made whole. Courage, timid one! Your faith has saved you. Go in peace. *"Being justified by faith, we have peace with God"* (Rom. 5:1).

FEBRUARY 15

Morning

To him be glory both now and for ever.
—2 Peter 3:18

Heaven will be full of the ceaseless praises of Jesus. Eternity—your unnumbered years will speed their everlasting course, but forever and forever, *"to him be glory."* Is He not a *"priest for ever after the order of Melchisedec"* (Heb. 5:6)? *"To him be glory."* Is He not King forever?—*"King of kings, and Lord of lords"* (1 Tim. 6:15), *"the everlasting Father"* (Isa. 9:6)? *"To him be glory...for ever."* Never will His praises cease. What was bought with blood deserves to last while immortality endures. The glory of the Cross must never be eclipsed; the luster of the grave and of the Resurrection must never be dimmed. O Jesus, You will be praised forever! As long as immortal spirits live—as long as the Father's throne endures—forever, forever, unto You will be glory. Believer, you are anticipating the time when you will join the saints above in ascribing all glory to Jesus, but are you glorifying Him now? The apostle's words were, *"To him be glory both now and for ever."* Will you not this day make them your prayer? "Lord, help me to glorify You. I am poor; help me to glorify You by being content. I am sick; help me to give You honor by being patient. I have talents; help me to extol You by spending them for You. I have time, Lord; help me to redeem it, so that I may serve You. I have a heart to feel, Lord; let that heart feel no love but Yours and glow with no flame but affection for You. I have a head to think, Lord; help me to think *of* You and *for* You. You have put me in this world for something, Lord; show me what that is, and help me to work out the purpose of my life. I cannot do much, but as the widow put in her two mites, which were all her living, so, Lord, I cast my time and eternity into Your treasury. I am all Yours. Take me, and enable me to glorify You now in all that I say, in all that I do, and with all that I have."

Whereby they have made thee glad.
—Psalm 45:8

Who are the ones who are privileged to make the Savior glad? His church—His people. But is it possible? He makes us glad, but how can we make Him glad? By our love. We think our love is so cold and so faint; indeed, we must sorrowfully confess it to be, but it is very sweet to Christ. Hear His own eulogy of that love in the golden Song of Solomon: *"How fair is thy love, my sister, my spouse! how much better is thy love than wine!"* (Song 4:10). See, loving heart, how He delights in you. When you lean your head on His bosom, you not only receive, but also give Him joy. When you gaze with love on His all-glorious face, you not only obtain comfort, but also impart delight. Our praise, too, gives Him joy—not the song of the lips alone, but the melody of the heart's deep gratitude. Our gifts, too, are very pleasant to Him. He loves to see us lay our time, our talents, and our substance upon the altar, not for the value of what we give, but for the sake of the motive from which the gift springs. To Him, the lowly offerings of His saints are more acceptable than the thousands of offerings of gold and silver. Holiness is like frankincense and myrrh to Him. Forgive your enemy, and you make Christ glad. Distribute of your substance to the poor, and He rejoices. Be the means of saving souls, and you give Him the opportunity to see the fruit of His soul's labors. Proclaim His Gospel, and you are a sweet aroma to Him. Go among the ignorant and lift up the Cross, and you have given Him honor. It is in your power even now to break the alabaster box and pour the precious oil of joy upon His head, as did the woman of old, whose memorial is told to this day wherever the Gospel is preached. Will you be backward then? Will you not perfume your beloved Lord with the myrrh, aloes, and cinnamon of your heart's praise? Yes, ivory palaces, you will hear the songs of the saints!

FEBRUARY 16
Morning

I have learned, in whatsoever state I am, therewith to be content.
—Philippians 4:11

These words show us that contentment is not a natural human inclination. Covetousness, discontentment, and complaining are as natural to man as weeds are to the soil. We need not sow thistles and brambles; they come up naturally enough, because they are indigenous to earth. Similarly, we do not need to teach men to complain; they complain fast enough without any education. But the precious things of the earth must be cultivated. If we would have wheat, we must plough and sow. If we want flowers, we must plant and care for a garden. Now, contentment is one of the flowers of heaven, and if we would have it, it must be cultivated. It will not grow in us by nature. It is the new nature alone that can produce it, and even then we must be especially careful and watchful that we maintain and cultivate the grace that God has sown in us. Paul said, *"I have learned…to be content."* This statement implies that he did not know how to be content at one time. It cost him some pains to arrive at the mystery of that great truth. No doubt he sometimes thought he had learned the lesson, and then broke down. And when at last he had attained it, and could say, *"I have learned, in whatsoever state I am, therewith to be content,"* he was an old gray-headed man, on the borders of the grave—a poor prisoner shut up in Nero's dungeon in Rome. We might well be willing to endure Paul's infirmities and share the cold dungeon with him, if we, too, might by any means attain his good position. Do not indulge the notion that you can be contented with learning, or learn without discipline. It is not a power that may be exercised naturally, but a science to be acquired gradually. We know this from experience. Brother, hush that grumbling, natural though it be, and continue to be a diligent pupil in the College of Contentment.

Thy good spirit.
—Nehemiah 9:20

Common, too common, is the sin of forgetting the Holy Spirit. This is folly and ingratitude. He deserves our best, for He is good, supremely good. As God, He is good essentially. He shares in the threefold ascription of *"Holy, holy, holy"* (Isa. 6:3; Rev. 4:8), which ascends to the triune Jehovah. He is purity, truth, and grace. He is good benevolently, tenderly bearing with our waywardness and striving with our rebellious wills. He quickens us from our death in sin, and then He trains us for the skies as a loving nurse fosters her child. How generous, forgiving, and tender is this patient Spirit of God! He is good operatively. All His works are good in the most eminent degree. He suggests good thoughts, prompts good actions, reveals good truths, applies good promises, assists in good attainments, and leads to good results. There is no spiritual good in all the world of which He is not the author and sustainer; heaven itself will owe the perfect character of its redeemed inhabitants to His work. He is good officially. Whether as Comforter, Instructor, Guide, Sanctifier, Quickener, or Intercessor, He fulfills His office well, and each work is laden with the highest good to the church of God. Those who yield to His influences become good, those who obey His impulses do good, and those who live under His power receive good. Let us then act toward so good a person according to the dictates of gratitude. Let us revere and adore Him, *"who is over all, God blessed for ever"* (Rom. 9:5). Let us recognize His power and admit our need of Him by waiting on Him in all our holy enterprises. Let us hourly seek His aid and never grieve Him. And let us praise Him whenever any opportunity to do so arises. The church will never prosper until more reverently it believes in the Holy Spirit. He is so good and kind that it is sad indeed that He should be grieved by slights and neglect.

FEBRUARY 17

Morning

Isaac dwelt by the well Lahairoi.
—Genesis 25:11

Hagar had once found deliverance there at the well, and Ishmael had drunk from the water so graciously revealed by the God who lives and sees the sons of men. But Isaac's visit to the well was not a casual visit, such as worldlings pay to the Lord in times of need, when it serves their turn. They cry to Him in trouble, but forsake Him in prosperity. Isaac, however, *dwelt* there, and made the well of the living and all-seeing God his constant source of supply. The usual tenor of a man's life, the dwelling of his soul, is the true test of his state. Perhaps the providential visitation experienced by Hagar struck Isaac's mind and led him to revere the place. Its mystical name endeared it to him. His frequent musings by its brim at eventide made him familiar with the well. His meeting Rebekah there had made his spirit feel at home near the spot, but, best of all, the fact that he there enjoyed fellowship with the living God had made him select that hallowed ground for his dwelling. Let us learn to live in the presence of the living God. Let us pray to the Holy Spirit that this day, and every other day, we may feel, *"Thou God seest me"* (Gen. 16:13). May the Lord Jehovah be as a well to us, delightful, comforting, unfailing, springing up unto eternal life. The bottle of the creature cracks and dries up, but the well of the Creator never fails. Happy is he who dwells at the well and thus has abundant and constant supplies near at hand. The Lord has been a sure helper to others: His name is Shaddai, God All-sufficient. Our hearts have often had most delightful communion with Him. Through Him our soul has found her glorious Husband, the Lord Jesus. This day, *"in him we live, and move, and have our being"* (Acts 17:28). Let us, then, dwell in closest fellowship with Him. Glorious Lord, constrain us that we may never leave You, but dwell by the well of the living God.

FEBRUARY 17
Evening

Whereas the LORD was there.
—Ezekiel 35:10

Edom's princes saw the whole country left desolate, and they counted upon its easy conquest. But there was one great difficulty in their way that was quite unknown to them: *"The LORD was there."* In His presence lay the special security of the chosen land. Whatever may be the schemes and devices of the enemies of God's people, there is still the same effective barrier to thwart their plans. The saints belong to God, and He is in the midst of them. He will protect His own. What comfort this assurance provides for us in our troubles and spiritual conflicts! We are constantly opposed yet perpetually preserved! How often Satan shoots his arrows against our faith, but our faith defies the power of hell's fiery darts. They are not only turned aside, but they are quenched upon its shield, for *"the LORD is there."* Our good works are the subjects of Satan's attacks. A saint never yet had a virtue or a grace that was not the target for hellish bullets. Whether it was a bright and sparkling hope, a warm and fervent love, an all-enduring patience, or a zeal flaming like coals of fire, the old enemy of everything that is good has tried to destroy it. The only reason why anything virtuous or lovely survives in us is this: *"The LORD is there."* If the Lord is with us through life, we do not need to fear for our dying confidence; for when we come to die, we will find that *"the LORD is there."* Where the billows are the most tempestuous and the water is the coldest, we will feel the bottom and know that it is secure. When time is passing away, our feet will stand upon the Rock of Ages. Beloved, from the first of a Christian's life to the last, the only reason why he does not perish is that *"the LORD is there."* When the God of everlasting love changes or leaves His elect to perish, then may the church of God be destroyed; but not until then, because it is written, JEHOVAH SHAMMAH, *"The LORD is there."*

Show me wherefore thou contendest with me.
—Job 10:2

Perhaps, O tried soul, the Lord is doing this to develop your graces. Some of your graces would never be discovered if it were not for your trials. Do you not know that your faith never looks so grand in summer weather as it does in winter? Love is too often like a glowworm, showing but little light unless it is in the midst of surrounding darkness. Hope itself is like a star—not to be seen in the sunshine of prosperity and only to be discovered in the night of adversity. Afflictions are often the black foils in which God sets the jewels of His children's graces, to make them shine the better. It was but a little while ago that on your knees you were saying, "Lord, I fear I have no faith. Let me know that I have faith." Were you not really, though perhaps unconsciously, praying for trials—for how can you know that you have faith until your faith is exercised? Depend on it: God often sends us trials so that our graces may be discovered, and so that we may be certified of their existence. Besides, it is not merely discovery. Real growth in grace is the result of sanctified trials. God often takes away our comforts and our privileges in order to make us better Christians. He trains His soldiers not in tents of ease and luxury, but by turning them out and sending them on forced marches and into hard service. He makes them ford through streams, swim through rivers, climb mountains, and walk many long miles with heavy knapsacks of sorrow on their backs. Well, Christian, may not this account for the troubles through which you are passing? Is not the Lord bringing out your graces and making them grow? Is this not the reason that He is contending with you?

> Trials make the promise sweet;
>   Trials give new life to prayer;
> Trials bring me to His feet,
>   Lay me low, and keep me there.

Father, I have sinned.
—Luke 15:18

It is quite certain that those whom Christ has washed in His precious blood do not need to make a confession of sin as culprits or criminals before God the Judge. Christ has forever taken away all their sins in a legal sense, so that they no longer stand where they can be condemned, but they are once and for all *"accepted in the beloved"* (Eph. 1:6). But having become children, and offending as children, should they not every day go before their heavenly Father and confess their sin and acknowledge their iniquity in that character? Nature teaches that it is the duty of erring children to make a confession to their earthly father, and the grace of God in the heart teaches us that we, as Christians, owe the same duty to our heavenly Father. We daily offend and should not rest without daily pardon. Suppose that my trespasses against my Father are not at once taken to Him to be washed away by the cleansing power of the Lord Jesus; what will be the consequence? If I have not sought forgiveness and been cleansed from these offenses against my Father, I will feel at a distance from Him. I will doubt His love for me. I will tremble in His presence, and I will be afraid to pray to Him. I will become like the Prodigal, who, although he was his father's child, was still far away from his father. But if, with a child's sorrow at offending so gracious and loving a Parent, I go to Him and tell Him all, and I do not rest until I realize that I am forgiven, then I will feel a holy love toward my Father. I will go through my Christian life not only as saved, but also as one enjoying present peace in God through Jesus Christ my Lord. There is a wide distinction between confessing sin as a culprit and confessing sin as a child. The Father's heart is the place for penitent confessions. We have been cleansed once and for all, but, as children of God, our feet still need to be washed from the defilement of our daily walk.

Thus saith the Lord God; I will yet for this be inquired of by the house of Israel, to do it for them.
—Ezekiel 36:37

Prayer is the forerunner of mercy. Turn to sacred history, and you will find that scarcely ever did a great mercy come to this world unheralded by supplication. You have found this true in your own personal experience. God has given you many unsolicited favors, but still great prayer has always been the prelude of great mercy with you. When you first found peace through the blood of the Cross, you had been praying much, and earnestly interceding with God that He would remove your doubts and deliver you from your distresses. Your assurance was the result of prayer. When at any time you have had high and rapturous joys, you have been obliged to look on them as answers to your prayers. When you have had great deliverance out of painful trouble and mighty help in great danger, you have been able to say, *"I sought the Lord, and he heard me, and delivered me from all my fears"* (Ps. 34:4). Prayer is always the preface to blessing. It goes before the blessing as the blessing's shadow. When the sunlight of God's mercies rises on our needs, it casts the shadow of prayer far down on the plain. When God piles up a hill of mercies, He Himself shines behind them, and He casts on our spirits the shadow of prayer, so that we may rest assured. If we are much in prayer, our pleadings are the shadows of mercy. Prayer is thus connected with the blessing to show us the value of it. If we had the blessings without asking for them, we would think them common things; but prayer makes our mercies more precious than diamonds. The things we ask for are precious, but we do not realize their preciousness until we have sought for them earnestly.

Prayer makes the darken'd cloud withdraw;
    Prayer climbs the ladder Jacob saw;
Gives exercise to faith and love;
    Brings every blessing from above.

[Andrew] *first findeth his own brother Simon.*
—John 1:41

This case is an excellent example of what happens when spiritual life is vital. As soon as a man has found Christ, he begins to find others. I will not believe that you have tasted of the honey of the Gospel if you can eat it all yourself. True grace puts an end to all spiritual monopoly. Andrew first found his own brother Simon and then others. Relationship has a very strong demand upon our initial individual efforts. Andrew did well to begin with Simon. I do not doubt that there are some Christians giving away tracts at other people's houses who would do well to give away a tract at their own. Likewise, I wonder whether there are not some who are engaged in works of ministry abroad who are neglecting their special sphere of usefulness at home. You may or may not be called to evangelize people in a particular locality, but certainly you are called to see after your own household, your own relatives, and your acquaintances. Let your religion begin at home. Many tradesmen export their best commodities—the Christian should not. All his conversation everywhere should carry the best aroma; but let him pay special care to put forth the sweetest fruit of spiritual life and testimony among his own family. When Andrew went to find his brother, he could not have imagined how eminent Simon would become. Simon Peter was worth ten Andrews as far as we can gather from sacred history, yet Andrew was instrumental in bringing him to Jesus. You may be very deficient in talent yourself, yet you may be the means of drawing to Christ one who will become prominent in grace and service. Dear friend, little do you know the possibilities that are in you. You may merely speak a word to a child, and in that child there may be slumbering a noble heart that will stir the Christian church in years to come. Andrew had only two talents, but he found Peter. Go and do likewise.

God…comforteth those that are cast down.
—2 Corinthians 7:6

Who comforts like God? Go to some poor, distressed child of God and tell him sweet promises; whisper in his ear choice words of comfort. He is like a deaf adder; he does not listen to the voice of the charmer. He is drinking from the well of bitterness, and comfort him as you may, it will be only a note or two of mournful resignation that you will get from him. You will bring forth no psalms of praise, no hallelujahs, no joyful sonnets. But let God come to His child. Let Him lift up his face, and the mourner's eyes glisten with hope. Do you not hear him sing—

'Tis paradise, if Thou art here;
If Thou depart, 'tis hell?

You could not have cheered him, but the Lord has done it. He is *"the God of all comfort"* (2 Cor. 1:3). There is no balm in Gilead, but there is balm in God. There is no physician among the creatures, but the Creator is Jehovah-Rophi, *"the LORD that healeth thee"* (Exod. 15:26). It is marvelous how one sweet word of God will make whole songs for Christians. One word of God is like a piece of gold, and the Christian is the goldbeater; he can hammer that promise out for whole weeks. So, then, poor Christian, you do not need to sit down in despair. Go to the Comforter, and ask Him to give you consolation. You are a poor, dry well. You have heard it said that when a pump is dry, you must pour water down it first of all, and then you will get water. So, Christian, when you are dry, go to God. Ask Him to shed abroad His joy in your heart, and then, your joy will be full. Do not go to earthly acquaintances, for you will find them Job's comforters after all; but go first and foremost to your *"God, [who] comforteth those that are cast down,"* and you will soon say, "In the multitude of my thoughts within me, Your comforts delight my soul."

Then was Jesus led up of the Spirit into the wilderness
to be tempted of the devil.
—Matthew 4:1

A holy character does not avert temptation: Jesus was tempted. When Satan tempts us, his sparks fall upon kindling. In Christ's case, however, it was like striking sparks on water. Yet the enemy continued his evil work. Now, if the devil goes on striking when there is no result, how much more will he do it when he knows what flammable stuff our hearts are made of. Though you become greatly sanctified by the Holy Spirit, expect that the great dog of hell will still bark at you. In the company of men, we expect to be tempted; but even seclusion will not guard us from the same trial. Jesus Christ was led away from human society into the wilderness and was tempted by the devil. Solitude has its charms and its benefits and may be useful in checking the lust of the eye and the pride of life, but the devil will follow us into the most lovely retreats. Do not suppose that it is only the worldly-minded who have dreadful thoughts and blasphemous temptations, for even spiritually-minded persons endure the same. We may suffer the darkest temptation in the holiest place. The utmost consecration of spirit will not insure you against satanic temptation. Christ was consecrated through and through. It was His meat and drink to do the will of Him who sent Him, yet He was tempted! Your heart may glow with an angelic flame of love for Jesus, yet the devil will try to bring you down to Laodicean lukewarmness. If you tell me when God permits a Christian to lay aside his armor, I will tell you when Satan gives up temptation. Like the old knights in wartime, we must sleep with helmet and breastplate buckled on, for the arch-deceiver will seize our first unguarded hour to make us his prey. May the Lord keep us watchful in all seasons and give us a final escape from the jaw of the lion and the paw of the bear.

FEBRUARY 21

Morning

He hath said.
—Hebrews 13:5

If we can only grasp these words by faith, we have an all-conquering weapon in our hand. What doubt will not be slain by this two-edged sword? What fear is there that will not fall smitten with a deadly wound before this arrow from the bow of God's covenant? Will not the distresses of life and the pangs of death; will not the corruption within, and the snares without; will not the trials from above, and the temptations from beneath all seem but light afflictions, when we can hide ourselves beneath the bulwark of *"he hath said"*? Yes, whether for delight in our silence, or for strength in our conflict, *"he hath said"* must be our daily resort. And this may teach us the extreme value of searching the Scriptures. There may be a promise in the Word that would exactly fit your case, but you may not know of it; therefore, you miss its comfort. You are like prisoners in a dungeon, and there may be one key in the bunch that would unlock the door. You might be set free; but if you will not look for it, you may remain a prisoner still, though liberty is so near at hand. There may be a potent medicine in the great pharmacopoeia of Scripture, yet you may continue to be sick unless you examine and search the Scriptures to discover what *"he hath said."* Besides reading the Bible, should you not store your memories richly with the promises of God? You can remember the sayings of great men; you treasure up the verses of renowned poets; should you not be profound in your knowledge of the words of God, so that you may be able to quote them readily when you would solve a difficulty or overthrow a doubt? Since *"he hath said"* is the source of all wisdom and the fountain of all comfort, let it dwell in you richly, as *"a well of water springing up into everlasting life"* (John 4:14). Then you will grow healthy, strong, and happy in the divine life.

FEBRUARY 21
Evening

Understandest thou what thou readest?
—Acts 8:30

If we sought to have a more intelligent understanding of the Word of God, we would be better teachers of others and less likely to be carried about by *"every wind of doctrine"* (Eph. 4:14). Only the Holy Spirit, the Author of the Scriptures, can enlighten us properly to understand them; therefore, we should constantly pray for His teaching and His guidance into all truth. When the prophet Daniel needed to interpret Nebuchadnezzar's dream, what did he do? He earnestly prayed that God would open up the vision. The apostle John, in his vision at Patmos, saw a book sealed with seven seals that no one was found worthy to open or even to look upon. The book was later opened by the Lion of the tribe of Judah, who had prevailed to open it; but it is written first, *"I wept much"* (Rev. 5:4). The tears of John were his liquid prayers. As far as he was concerned, they were the sacred keys by which the folded book was opened. If, for your own benefit and the benefit of others, you desire to be *"filled with the knowledge of [God's] will in all wisdom and spiritual understanding"* (Col. 1:9), remember that prayer is your best means of study. Like Daniel, you will understand the dream and its interpretation when you have sought God. Like John, you will see the seven seals of precious truth loosed after you have wept much. Stones are not broken except by an earnest use of the hammer. The one who desires to break the stones must go down on his knees. Use the hammer of diligence, and let the knee of prayer be exercised. There is not a stony doctrine in revelation that is useful for you to understand that will not fly into pieces under the exercise of prayer and faith. You may force your way through anything with the leverage of prayer. Thoughts and arguments are like the steel wedges that give a hold upon truth; but prayer is the lever that forces open the iron chest of sacred mystery so that we may obtain the treasure hidden within.

FEBRUARY 22

Morning

His bow abode in strength, and the arms of his hands were made
strong by the hands of the mighty God of Jacob.
—Genesis 49:24

The strength that God gives to His Josephs is real strength. It is not a boasted valor; fiction; or a thing of which men talk, but that ends in smoke; it is true, divine strength. How did Joseph stand against temptation? Because God gave him aid. There is nothing that we can do without the power of God. All true strength comes from *"the mighty God of Jacob."* Notice in what a blessedly familiar way God gives this strength to Joseph: *"The arms of his hands were made strong by the hands of the mighty God of Jacob."* Thus God is represented as putting His hands on Joseph's hands, placing His arms on Joseph's arms. As a father teaches his children, so the Lord teaches them who fear Him. He puts His arms on them. Marvelous condescension! God Almighty, eternal, omnipotent, stoops from His throne and lays His hands on the child's hand, stretching His arm on the arm of Joseph so that he may be made strong! This strength was also covenant strength, for it is ascribed to *"the mighty God of Jacob."* Now, wherever you read of the God of Jacob in the Bible, you should remember the covenant with Jacob. Christians love to think of God's covenant. All the power, all the grace, all the blessings, all the mercies, all the comforts, and all the things we have flow to us from the Source, through the covenant. If there were no covenant, then we would fail indeed; for all grace proceeds from it, as light and heat proceed from the sun. No angels ascend or descend, save on that ladder that Jacob saw, at the top of which stood a covenant God. Christian, it may be that the archers have sorely grieved you, shot at you, and wounded you, but still your bow abides in strength; be sure, then, to ascribe all the glory to Jacob's God.

The LORD is slow to anger, and great in power.
—Nahum 1:3

Jehovah *"is slow to anger."* When mercy comes into the world, it drives winged steeds; the axles of its chariot wheels are red-hot with speed. But when wrath goes forth, it toils on with sluggish footsteps, for God takes no pleasure in the sinner's death. God's rod of mercy is always in His outstretched hands. His sword of justice is in its sheath, held down by the pierced hand of love that bled for the sins of men. *"The LORD is slow to anger"* because He is great in power. He is truly great in power who has power over himself. When God's power restrains Himself, then it is power indeed: the power that binds omnipotence surpasses omnipotence. A man who has a strong mind can bear to be insulted for a long time, and he resents the wrong only when a sense of right demands his action. The weak mind is irritated by little things, but the strong mind bears irritation like a rock that does not move, even though a thousand breakers dash upon it and cast their pitiful malice in spray upon its summit. God sees His enemies, yet He does not rouse Himself to action, but holds in His anger. If He were less divine than He is, long before this, He would have sent forth the whole of His thunders and emptied the magazines of heaven. Long before this, He would have blasted the earth with the wondrous fires of its lower regions, and man would have been utterly destroyed. But the greatness of His power brings us mercy. Dear reader, what is your state of mind this evening? Can you by humble faith look to Jesus and say, "My Substitute, You are my rock and my trust"? Then, beloved, do not be afraid of God's power. If by faith you have fled to Christ for refuge, the power of God no longer needs to terrify you any more than the shield and sword of the warrior terrifies those whom he loves. Instead, rejoice that He who is *"great in power"* is your Father and Friend.

I will never leave thee, nor forsake thee.
—Hebrews 13:5

No promise is of private interpretation. Whatever God has said to any one saint, He has said to all. When He opens a well for one, it is that all may drink. When He opens the granary door to give out food, there may be one starving man who is the occasion of its being opened, but all hungry saints may come and feed, too. Whether He gave the word to Abraham or to Moses does not matter, believer; He has given it to you as one of the covenanted seed. There is not a high blessing too lofty for you, nor a wide mercy too extensive for you. Lift up your eyes to the north and to the south, to the east and to the west, for all this is yours. Climb to Pisgah's top, and view the utmost limit of the divine promise, for the land is all your own. There is not a brook of living water of which you may not drink. If the land flows with milk and honey, eat the honey and drink the milk, for both are yours. Be bold to believe, for He has said, *"I will never leave thee, nor forsake thee."* In this promise, God gives to His people everything. *"I will never leave thee."* Then no attribute of God can cease to be engaged for us. Is He mighty? He will show Himself strong on the behalf of those who trust Him. Is He love? Then with lovingkindness will He have mercy on us. Whatever attributes may compose the character of deity, every one of them to its fullest extent will be engaged on our side. To sum it up, there is nothing you can lack, nothing you can ask for, nothing you can need in time or in eternity, nothing living, nothing dying, nothing in this world, nothing in the next world, nothing now, nothing at the Resurrection morning, nothing in heaven that is not contained in this text: *"I will never leave thee, nor forsake thee."*

Take up the cross, and follow me.
—Mark 10:21

You are not to construct your own cross, although unbelief is a master carpenter at cross-making. Neither are you permitted to choose your own cross, although self-will would gladly be lord and master. But your cross is prepared and appointed for you by divine love, and you are to accept it cheerfully. You are to take up the cross as your chosen badge and burden, not stand around complaining about it. This night Jesus invites you to submit your shoulder to His easy yoke. Do not kick at it in petulance, trample on it in pride, fall under it in despair, or run away from it in fear. Take it up like a true follower of Jesus. Jesus was a cross-bearer; He leads the way in the path of sorrow. Surely you could not desire a better guide! And if He carried a cross, what nobler burden would you desire? The *Via Crucis* is the way of safety; do not fear to tread its thorny paths. Beloved, the cross is not made of feathers or lined with velvet. It is heavy and galling to disobedient shoulders, but it is not an iron cross, though your fears have painted it with iron colors. It is a wooden cross, and a man can carry it, for the Man of Sorrows first bore the load. Take up your cross, and by the power of the Spirit of God, you will soon be so in love with it that, like Moses, you would not exchange *"the reproach of Christ* [for all] *the treasures in Egypt"* (Heb. 11:26). Remember that Jesus carried it, and it will smell sweetly; remember that soon it will be followed by the crown, and the thought of the coming weight of glory will greatly lighten the present heaviness of trouble. May the Lord help you to bow your spirit in submission to the divine will before you fall asleep this night so that waking with tomorrow's sun, you may go forth to the day's cross with the holy and submissive spirit that becomes a follower of the Crucified One.

I will cause the shower to come down in his season;
there shall be showers of blessing.
—Ezekiel 34:26

Here is sovereign, divine mercy: "I will give them showers in their season." For who can say, "I will give them showers," except God? There is only one voice that can speak to the clouds and bid them to rain. Who sends down the rain upon the earth? Who scatters the showers upon the green herbs? Do not I, the Lord? So grace is the gift of God and is not created by man. It is also needed grace. What would the ground do without showers? You may break the clods; you may sow your seeds, but what can you do without the rain? As absolutely necessary is the divine blessing. In vain you labor, until God gives the plenteous shower and sends salvation down. Then it is plenteous grace. "I will send them showers." It does not say, "I will send them drops," but *"showers."* So it is with grace. If God gives a blessing, He usually gives it in such a measure that there is not room enough to receive it. Plenteous grace! Oh, we need plenteous grace to keep us humble, to make us prayerful, to make us holy; we need plenteous grace to make us zealous, to preserve us through this life, and at last to land us in heaven. We cannot do without saturating showers of grace. It is also seasonable grace. *"I will cause the shower to come down in his season."* What is your season this morning? Is it the season of drought? Then that is the season for showers. Is it a season of great heaviness and black clouds? Then that is the season for showers. *"As thy days, so shall thy strength be"* (Deut. 33:25). And here is a varied blessing. "I will give you *'showers'* of blessing." The word *"showers"* is in the plural. God will send all kinds of blessings. All God's blessings go together, like links in a golden chain. If He gives converting grace, He will also give comforting grace. He will send *"showers of blessing."* Look up today, O parched plant, and open your leaves and flowers for a heavenly watering.

FEBRUARY 24

Evening

O LORD of hosts, how long wilt thou not have mercy
on Jerusalem?...And the LORD answered the angel...
with good words and comfortable words.
—Zechariah 1:12–13

What a sweet answer to an anxious inquiry! This night let us rejoice in it. O Zion, there are good things in store for you. Your time of travail will soon be over. Your children will be brought forth, and your captivity will end. Patiently bear the rod for a season, and in the darkness still trust in God, for His love burns toward you. God loves the church with a love too deep for human imagination. He loves her with all His infinite heart; therefore, let her sons be of good courage. She cannot be far from prosperity to whom God speaks *"good words and comfortable words."* The prophet goes on to tell us what these comfortable words are: *"I am jealous for Jerusalem and for Zion with a great jealousy"* (Zech. 1:14). The Lord loves His church so much that He cannot bear that she would go astray to others; when she has done so, He cannot bear that she would suffer too much or too heavily. He will not have His enemies afflict her. He is displeased with them because they increase her misery. When God seems to have left His church, His heart is still warm toward her. History shows us that whenever God uses a rod to chasten His servants, He always breaks it afterward, as if He loathed the rod that gave His children pain. *"Like as a father pitieth his children, so the LORD pitieth them that fear him"* (Ps. 103:13). God has not forgotten us because He chastens us; His correction is no evidence of a lack of love. If this is true of His church collectively, it is also true of each individual member. You may fear that the Lord has passed you by, but that is not so. He who counts the stars and calls them by their names is in no danger of forgetting His own children. He knows your situation as thoroughly as if you were the only creature He ever made or the only saint He ever loved. Approach Him, and be at peace.

FEBRUARY 25
Morning

The wrath to come.
—Matthew 3:7

It is pleasant to pass over a country after a storm has spent itself, to smell the freshness of the herbs after the rain has passed away, and to note the drops while they glisten like purest diamonds in the sunlight. That is the position of a Christian. He is going through a land where the storm has spent itself on his Savior's head, and if there are a few drops of sorrow falling, they come from clouds of mercy, and Jesus cheers him by the assurance that they are not for his destruction. But how terrible it is to witness the approach of a tempest; to see the forewarnings of a storm; to mark the birds of heaven as they droop their wings; to see the cattle as they lay their heads low in terror; to discern the face of the sky as it grows black; to look at the sun that does not shine and the angry and frowning heavens! How terrible to await the dread advance of a hurricane—such as occurs, sometimes, in the tropics—to wait in terrible apprehension until the wind rushes forth in fury, tearing up trees from their roots, forcing rocks from their pedestals, and hurling down all the dwelling places of man! And yet, sinner, this is your present position. No hot drops have as yet fallen, but a shower of fire is coming. No terrible winds howl around you, but God's tempest is gathering its dread artillery. As yet, the floods are dammed up by mercy, but the floodgates will soon be opened. The thunderbolts of God are yet in His storehouse, but lo, the tempest hastens, and how awful will that moment be when God, robed in vengeance, will march forth in fury! Where, where, where, O sinner, will you hide your head, or where will you flee? O that the hand of mercy may now lead you to Christ! He is freely set before you in the Gospel. His riven side is the rock of shelter. You know your need of Him. Believe in Him, cast yourself on Him, and then, the fury will be gone forever.

*But Jonah rose up to flee unto Tarshish from the presence of the
Lord, and went down to Joppa.*
—Jonah 1:3

Instead of going to Nineveh to preach the Word as God commanded him, Jonah disliked the work and went to Joppa to escape from it. There are occasions when God's servants shrink from duty. But what is the consequence? What did Jonah lose by his conduct? He lost the presence and comfortable enjoyment of God's love. When we serve our Lord Jesus as believers should, our God is with us. Though we have the whole world against us, if we have God with us, what does it matter? But the moment we turn back and seek our own desires, we are at sea without a pilot. Then may we bitterly lament and groan, "O my God, where have You gone? How could I have been so foolish as to shun Your service and thus lose all the brightness of Your face? This price is too high. Let me return to my allegiance so that I may rejoice in Your presence." Jonah also lost all peace of mind. Sin soon destroys a believer's comfort. Sin is like the poisonous mulberry tree, from whose leaves distill deadly drops that destroy the life of joy and peace. Jonah lost everything on which he might have drawn comfort in any other situation. He could not plead the promise of divine protection, for he was not in God's will. He could not say, "Lord, I met with these difficulties in the course of my duty; therefore, help me through them." He was reaping his own deeds; he was filled with his own ways. Christian, do not act like Jonah, unless you wish to have all the waves and the billows rolling over your head. In the long run, you will find that it is far harder to shun the work and will of God than to yield yourself to it immediately. Jonah lost his time, for he had to go to Tarshish after all. It is hard to contend with God. Let us yield ourselves to Him right now.

Salvation is of the LORD.
—Jonah 2:9

Salvation is the work of God. It is He alone who quickens the soul "*dead in trespasses and sins*" (Eph. 2:1), and it is He also who maintains the soul in its spiritual life. He is both "*Alpha and Omega, the beginning and the ending*" (Rev. 1:8). "*Salvation is of the LORD.*" If I am prayerful, God makes me prayerful. If I have graces, they are God's gifts to me. If I hold on in a consistent life, it is because He upholds me with His hand. I do nothing whatever toward my own preservation, except what God Himself first does in me. Whatever I have, all my goodness is of the Lord alone. Wherein I sin, that is my own; but wherein I act uprightly, that is of God, wholly and completely. If I have repulsed a spiritual enemy, the Lord's strength fortified my arm. Do I live a consecrated life before men? It is not I, but Christ who lives in me. Am I sanctified? I did not cleanse myself; God's Holy Spirit sanctifies me. Am I weaned from the world? I am weaned by God's chastisements sanctified to my good. Do I grow in knowledge? The great Instructor teaches me. All my jewels were fashioned by heavenly art. I find in God all that I need, but I find in myself nothing but sin and misery. "*He only is my rock and my salvation*" (Ps. 62:2, 6). Do I feed on the Word? That Word would be no food for me unless the Lord made it food for my soul and helped me to feed on it. Do I live on the manna that comes down from heaven? What is that manna but Jesus Christ Himself incarnate, whose body and whose blood I eat and drink? Am I continually receiving fresh increase of strength? Where do I gather my might? My help comes from heaven's hills. Without Jesus, I can do nothing. As a branch cannot bring forth fruit unless it "*abide[s] in the vine*" (John 15:4), no more can I, unless I abide in Him. What Jonah learned in the great deep, let me learn this morning in my place of prayer: "*Salvation is of the LORD.*"

FEBRUARY 26
Evening

Behold, if the leprosy have covered all his flesh,
he shall pronounce him clean that hath the plague.
—Leviticus 13:13

Although this regulation appears to be strange, there was wisdom in it. The outward manifestation of the disease proved that the leper's constitution was sound. It may be well for us to see the symbolic meaning of so unusual a rule. We, too, are lepers and may apply the law of the leper to ourselves. When a man sees himself to be altogether lost and ruined, covered with the defilement of sin, and in no part free from pollution; when he disclaims all righteousness of his own and pleads guilty before the Lord, then he is clean through the blood of Jesus and the grace of God. Hidden, unfelt, unconfessed iniquity is the true leprosy; but when sin is seen and felt, it has received its deathblow, and the Lord looks with eyes of mercy on the afflicted soul. Nothing is more deadly than self-righteousness or more hopeful than repentance. We must confess that we are sinful, for no confession short of this will be the whole truth. If the Holy Spirit is at work in us, convicting us of sin, there will be no difficulty about making such an acknowledgment—it will spring spontaneously from our lips. What comfort the text gives to truly awakened sinners: the very circumstance that so grievously discouraged them is here turned into a sign of a hopeful condition! Stripping comes before clothing; digging out the foundation is the first thing in building—and a thorough sense of sin is one of the earliest works of grace. Poor, leprous sinner, take heart from the text, and come as you are to Jesus.

> For let our debts be what they may,
>   However great or small,
> As soon as we have nought to pay,
>   Our Lord forgives us all.
> 'Tis perfect poverty alone
>   That sets the soul at large:
> While we can call one mite our own,
>   We have no full discharge.

FEBRUARY 27
Morning

*Thou hast made the LORD, which is my refuge,
even the most High, thy habitation.*
—Psalm 91:9

The Israelites in the wilderness were continually exposed to change. Whenever the pillar halted its motion, the tents were pitched. But tomorrow, before the morning sun had risen, the trumpet sounded, the ark was in motion, and the fiery, cloudy pillar was leading the way through the narrow gorges of the mountain, up the hillside, or along the arid waste of the wilderness. They had scarcely time to rest a little before they heard the sound of "Away! This is not your rest; you must still be journeying onward toward Canaan!" They never stayed in one place very long. Even wells and palm trees could not detain them, yet they had an abiding home in their God. His cloudy pillar was the supporting beam for their tents; its flame by night, their household fire. They must go onward from place to place, continually changing, never having time to settle and to say, "Now we are secure; in this place we will dwell." "Yet," said Moses, "though we are always changing, Lord, You have *'been our dwelling place in all generations'* (Ps. 90:1)." The Christian knows no change with regard to God. He may be rich today and poor tomorrow; he may be sickly today and well tomorrow; he may be in happiness today and distressed tomorrow, but there is no change with regard to his relationship to God. If He loved me yesterday, He loves me today. My unmoving mansion of rest is my blessed Lord. Let prospects be blighted; let hopes be blasted; let joy be withered; and let mildew destroy everything. I have lost nothing of what I have in God. He is *"my strong habitation, whereunto I may continually resort"* (Ps. 71:3). I am a pilgrim in the world, but at home in my God. In the earth I wander, but in God I dwell in a quiet habitation.

FEBRUARY 27

Evening

Whose goings forth have been from of old, from everlasting.
—Micah 5:2

The Lord Jesus represented His people before the throne long before they appeared on the stage of time. It was *"from everlasting"* that He signed the covenant with His Father that He would pay blood for blood, suffering for suffering, agony for agony, and death for death on behalf of His people. It was *"from everlasting"* that He gave Himself up without murmuring a word. From the crown of His head to the soles of His feet, He sweat great drops of blood. He was spat upon, pierced, mocked, torn asunder, and crushed beneath the pains of death. His offering Himself as our Surety was *"from everlasting."* Pause, my soul, and wonder! You have been loved by Jesus *"from everlasting."* Not only when you were born into the world did Christ love you, but His *"delights were with the sons of men"* (Prov. 8:31) before there were any sons of men! He thought of them often; from everlasting to everlasting He had set His affection upon them. Has He planned so long for your salvation, my soul, not to accomplish it? Has He *"from everlasting"* been going forth to save you, and will He lose you now? What? Has He carried you in His hand, as His precious jewel, and will He now let you slip away between His fingers? Did He choose you before the mountains were brought forth or the channels of the deep were dug, and will He reject you now? Impossible! I am sure He would not have loved you so long if He was not a changeless Lover. If He could grow weary of you, He would have been tired of you long before now. If He had not loved you with a love as deep as hell and as strong as death, He would have turned from you long ago. Oh, joy above all joys, to know that you are His everlasting and inalienable inheritance, given to Him by His Father before the earth ever was! Everlasting love will be the pillow for your head tonight.

My expectation is from him.
—Psalm 62:5

It is the believer's privilege to use this language. If he is looking for anything from the world, it is a poor *"expectation"* indeed. But if he looks to God for the supply of his needs, whether in temporal or spiritual blessings, his expectation will not be a vain one. Constantly, he may draw from the bank of faith and have his needs supplied out of the riches of God's lovingkindness. I know this: I would rather have God for my banker than all the Rothschilds. My Lord never fails to honor His promises. When we bring them to His throne, He never sends them back unanswered. Therefore, I will wait only at His door, for He always opens it with the hand of lavish grace. At this hour I will try Him anew. But we have expectations beyond this life. We will die soon, and then, our *"expectation is from him."* Do we not expect that when we lie on the bed of sickness He will send angels to carry us to His bosom? We believe that when the pulse is faint and the heart beats heavily, some angelic messenger will stand and look with loving eyes on us and whisper, "Sister spirit, come away!" As we approach the heavenly gate, we expect to hear the welcome invitation, *"Come, ye blessed of my Father, inherit the kingdom prepared for you from the foundation of the world"* (Matt. 25:34). We are expecting harps of gold and crowns of glory; we are hoping soon to be among the multitude of shining ones before the throne. We are looking forward and longing for the time when we will be like our glorious Lord, for *"we shall see him as he is"* (1 John 3:2). Then, if these are your expectations, O my soul, live for God. Live with the desire and resolve to glorify Him from whom come all your supplies, and of whose grace in your election, redemption, and calling, it is that you have any *"expectation"* of coming glory.

*The barrel of meal wasted not, neither did the cruse of oil fail,
according to the word of the LORD, which he spake by Elijah.*
—1 Kings 17:16

See the faithfulness of divine love. Observe that this woman had daily needs. She had to feed herself and her son during a time of famine; now, in addition, the prophet Elijah needed to be fed. But though the need was three times as great, the meal did not run out, for she had a constant supply. Each day she went to the barrel, but each day the amount in it remained the same. You, dear reader, also have daily needs. Because they come so frequently, you are inclined to fear that the barrel of meal will one day be empty, and the jar of oil will fail you. Rest assured that, according to the Word of God, this will not be the case. Each day, though it brings its troubles, will also bring its help. Though you would live to outnumber the years of Methuselah, and your needs would be as numerous as the sands of the seashore, God's grace and mercy will last through all your necessities, and you will never know a real lack. For three long years during this widow's lifetime, the heavens never saw a cloud, and the stars never wept a holy tear of dew upon the wicked earth. Famine, desolation, and death made the land a howling wilderness, but this woman was never hungry; she was always joyful in abundance. So will it be for you. You will see the sinner's hope perish, for he trusts in his own strength. You will see the proud Pharisee's confidence waver, for he builds his hope on the sand. You will even see your own schemes blasted and withered, but you will find that your place of defense will be in the Rock of your salvation. Your bread will be given to you, and your water supply will be secure. It is better to have God for your guardian than to own the Bank of England. You might spend the wealth of the Indies, but you can never exhaust the infinite riches of God.

With lovingkindness have I drawn thee.
—Jeremiah 31:3

The thunders of the law and the terrors of judgment are all used to bring us to Christ, but the final victory is effected by lovingkindness. The Prodigal Son set out for his father's house from a sense of need, but his father saw him a great way off and ran to meet him. The last steps he took toward his father's house were with his father's kiss still warm on his cheek and the welcome still musical in his ears.

> Law and terrors do but harden
>   All the while they work alone;
> But a sense of blood-bought pardon
>   Will dissolve a heart of stone.

The Master came one night to the door and knocked with the iron hand of the law. The door shook and trembled on its hinges, but the man piled every piece of furniture that he could find against the door. He said, "I will not admit the Man." The Master turned away, but by and by He came back, and with His own soft hand, using mostly that part where the nails had penetrated, He knocked again—oh, so softly and tenderly. This time the door did not shake, but, strange to say, it opened, and there on his knees the once unwilling host was found rejoicing to receive his guest. "Come in; come in. You have knocked in a way that has moved my heart for You. I could not think of Your pierced hand leaving its blood mark on my door, and of Your going away homeless. I yield, I yield; Your love has won my heart." So, in every case, lovingkindness wins the day. What Moses with the tablets of stone could never do, Christ does with His pierced hand. Such is the doctrine of effectual calling. Is this my experience? Can I say, "He drew me, and I followed on, glad to confess the voice divine?" If so, may He continue to draw me, until at last I sit down at the Marriage Supper of the Lamb.

FEBRUARY 29

Evening

*Now we have received...the spirit which is of God; that we might
know the things that are freely given to us of God.*
—1 Corinthians 2:12

Dear reader, have you received the Spirit of God, the Holy Spirit, in your soul? The necessity of the work of the Holy Spirit in the heart may be clearly seen from this fact: all that has been done by God the Father and by God the Son will be of no value to us unless the Spirit reveals these things to our souls. What effect does the doctrine of election have on any man until the Spirit of God enters into him? Election is a dead letter in my consciousness until the Spirit of God calls me *"out of darkness into his marvellous light"* (1 Pet. 2:9). Then, through my calling, I see my election, and knowing myself to be called by God, I know I have been chosen in the eternal purpose. A covenant was made with the Lord Jesus Christ by His Father; but of what good is that covenant to us until the Holy Spirit brings us its blessings and opens our hearts to receive them? There hang the blessings on the nail—Christ Jesus—but being short of stature, we cannot reach them. The Spirit of God takes them down and hands them to us, and thus they become actually ours. Covenant blessings in themselves are like the manna in the skies, far out of mortal reach; but the Spirit of God opens the windows of heaven and scatters the living bread around the camp of the spiritual Israel. Christ's finished work is like wine stored in the wine vat; through unbelief we can neither draw nor drink. The Holy Spirit dips our hearts into this precious wine, and then we drink; but without the Spirit, we are as truly dead in sin as though the Father never had elected us, and as though the Son had never bought us with His blood. The Holy Spirit is absolutely necessary to our well-being. Let us walk lovingly toward Him and tremble at the thought of grieving Him.

MARCH 1

Morning

Awake, O north wind; and come, thou south; blow upon my garden,
that the spices thereof may flow out.
—Song of Solomon 4:16

Anything is better than the dead calm of indifference. Our souls may wisely desire the north wind of trouble if that alone can be sanctified to the drawing forth of the perfume of our graces. As long as it cannot be said, *"The LORD was not in the wind"* (1 Kings 19:11), we will not shrink from the wintriest blast that ever blew on plants of grace. Did not the spouse in this verse humbly submit herself to the reproofs of her Beloved? Did she not entreat Him to send forth His grace in some form and make no stipulation as to the particular manner in which it should come? Did she not, like ourselves, become so utterly weary of deadness and unholy calm that she sighed for any visitation that would brace her to action? Yet she desired the warm south wind of comfort, too, the smiles of divine love, the joy of the Redeemer's presence. These are often mightily effective in arousing our sluggish life. She desired either one or the other, or both, so that she might be able to delight her Beloved with the spices of her garden. She could not endure to be unprofitable, nor can we. How cheering a thought that Jesus can find comfort in our poor feeble graces. Can it be? It seems far too good to be true. Well may we court trial or even death itself if we will thereby be aided to make Immanuel's heart glad. Oh, that our hearts were crushed to atoms if only by such bruising our sweet Lord Jesus could be glorified. Graces unexercised are as sweet perfumes slumbering in the cups of flowers. The wisdom of the great Husbandman overrules diverse and opposite causes to produce the one desired result. He makes both affliction and consolation draw forth the grateful fragrances of faith, love, patience, hope, resignation, joy, and the other fair flowers of the garden. May we know, by sweet experience, what this means.

MARCH 1

Evening

He is precious.
—1 Peter 2:7

As all the rivers run into the sea, so all delights center on our Beloved. The glance of His eyes outshines the sun. The beauty of His face is fairer than the choicest flowers. No fragrance is like the breath of His mouth. Gems of the earth and pearls from the sea are worthless things when compared to His preciousness. Peter told us that Jesus is precious, but he did not and could not tell us how precious, nor could any of us compute the value of God's unspeakable gift. Words cannot express the preciousness of the Lord Jesus to His people or fully tell how essential He is to their satisfaction and happiness. Believer, have you not found in the midst of plenty a sore famine if your Lord has been absent? The sun was shining, but Christ had hidden Himself, and all the world was black to you; or it was night, and since the *"bright and morning star"* (Rev. 22:16) was gone, no other star could yield so much as a ray of light to you. What a howling wilderness this world is without our Lord! If He hides Himself from us, the flowers of our garden wither. Our pleasant fruits decay, the birds suspend their songs, and a tempest overturns our hopes. All earth's candles cannot make daylight if the Sun of Righteousness is eclipsed. He is the Soul of our souls, the Light of our light, the Life of our lives. Dear reader, what would you do in the world without Him, when you wake up and look ahead to the day's battle? What would you do at night, when you come home jaded and weary, if there were no door of fellowship between you and Christ? Blessed is His name! He will not allow us to try our lot without Him, for Jesus never forsakes His own. Yet let the thought of what life would be without Him enhance His preciousness.

All the Israelites went down to the Philistines, to sharpen every man his share, and his coulter, and his ax, and his mattock.
—1 Samuel 13:20

We are engaged in a great war with the Philistines of evil. Every weapon within our reach must be used. Preaching, teaching, praying, giving—all must be brought into action, and talents that have been thought too humble for service must now be employed. Coulter, ax, and mattock may all be useful in slaying Philistines. Rough tools may deal hard blows, and killing need not be elegantly done, as long as it is done effectively. Each moment of time, in season or out of season; each fragment of ability, educated or untutored; each opportunity, favorable or unfavorable, must be used, for our foes are many and our force but meager. Most of our tools need to be sharpened. We need quickness of perception, tact, energy, promptness—in a word, complete adaptation—for the Lord's work. Practical common sense is a very scarce thing among the conductors of Christian enterprises. We might learn from our enemies if we would, and so make the Philistines sharpen our weapons. This morning let us note enough to sharpen our zeal during this day by the aid of the Holy Spirit. Observe the energy of the papists, how they compass sea and land to make one proselyte. Are they to monopolize all the earnestness? Mark the heathen devotees, what tortures they endure in the service of their idols. Are they alone to exhibit patience and self-sacrifice? Observe the prince of darkness, how persevering he is in his endeavors, how unabashed in his attempts, how daring in his plans, how thoughtful in his plots, how energetic in all! The devils are united as one man in their infamous rebellion, while we believers in Jesus are divided in our service of God and scarcely ever work with unanimity. O that from Satan's infernal industry we may learn to go about like Good Samaritans, seeking whom we may bless!

Unto me, who am less than the least of all saints, is this grace given, that I
should preach among the Gentiles the unsearchable riches of Christ.
—Ephesians 3:8

The apostle Paul felt it was a great privilege to be allowed to preach the Gospel. He did not look on his calling as a drudgery, but he fulfilled it with intense delight. Yet while Paul was thankful for his calling, his success in it greatly humbled him. The fuller a vessel becomes, the deeper it sinks in the water. Idlers may indulge a fond conceit of their abilities, because they are untried; but the earnest worker soon learns his own weakness. If you seek humility, try hard work. If you would know your nothingness, attempt some great thing for Jesus. If you would feel how utterly powerless you are apart from the living God, attempt the great work of proclaiming *"the unsearchable riches of Christ,"* and you will know, as you never knew before, what a weak, unworthy thing you are. Although the apostle thus knew and confessed his weakness, he was never perplexed as to the subject of his ministry. From his first sermon to his last, Paul preached Christ, and nothing but Christ. He lifted up the cross and extolled the Son of God who bled thereon. Follow his example in all your personal efforts to spread the glad tidings of salvation, and let "Christ and Him crucified" (see 1 Corinthians 2:2) be your ever-recurring theme. The Christian should be like those lovely spring flowers that, when the sun is shining, open their golden cups, as if to say, "Fill us with your beams!" but when the sun is hidden behind a cloud, they close their cups and droop their heads. Likewise, the Christian should feel the sweet influence of Jesus. Jesus must be his sun, and he must be the flower that yields itself to the Sun of Righteousness. Oh, to speak of Christ alone is the subject that is both *"seed to the sower, and bread to the eater"* (Isa. 55:10). This is the live coal for the lips of the speaker and the master key to the heart of the hearer.

MARCH 3

Morning

I have chosen thee in the furnace of affliction.
—Isaiah 48:10

Comfort yourself, tried believer, with this thought: God said, *"I have chosen thee in the furnace of affliction."* Does not the word come like a soft shower, assuaging the fury of the flame? Is it not an asbestos armor, against which the heat has no power? Let affliction come. God has chosen me! Poverty, you may stride in at my door, but God is in the house already, and He has chosen me. Sickness, you may intrude, but I have a balsam ready—God has chosen me. Whatever befalls me in this vale of tears, I know that He has *"chosen"* me. If, believer, you require still greater comfort, remember that you have the Son of Man with you in the furnace. In that silent room of yours, there sits by your side One whom you have not seen, but whom you love; and often when you do not know it, He makes your bed in your affliction and smoothes your pillow for you. You are in poverty, but in that lovely house of yours, the Lord of life and glory is a frequent visitor. He loves to come into these desolate places so that He may visit you. Your Friend sticks closely to you. You cannot see Him, but you may feel the pressure of His hands. Do you not hear His voice? Even in the valley of the shadow of death He says, *"Fear thou not; for I am with thee: be not dismayed; for I am thy God"* (Isa. 41:10). Remember that noble speech of Caesar: "Fear not, thou carriest Caesar and all his fortune." Fear not, Christian; Jesus is with you. In all your fiery trials, His presence is both your comfort and safety. He will never leave one whom He has chosen for His own. *"Fear…not, for I am with thee"* is His sure word of promise to His chosen ones in the *"furnace of affliction."* Will you not, then, take fast hold of Christ, and say,

> Through floods and flames, if Jesus lead,
>   I'll follow where He goes?

MARCH 3
Evening

He saw the Spirit of God descending like a dove.
—Matthew 3:16

As the Spirit of God descended on the Lord Jesus, the Head, so He also, in part, descends on the members of Christ's body, the church. His descent is to us after the same fashion as that in which it fell upon our Lord. There is often an exceptional rapidity about it. Before we are completely aware of what is happening, we are impelled onward and heavenward beyond all expectation. Yet it is not done with earthly haste, for the wings of the dove are as soft as they are swift. Quietness seems to be essential to many spiritual operations. The Lord is in the still small voice; and, like the dew, His grace is distilled in silence. The dove has always been the chosen symbol of purity, and the Holy Spirit is holiness itself. Where He comes, everything that is pure, lovely, and of good report abounds, and sin and uncleanness depart. Peace also reigns where the holy Dove comes with power. He bears the olive branch that shows that the waters of divine wrath are assuaged. Gentleness is a sure sign of the sacred Dove's transforming power; hearts touched by His benign influence are meek and lowly from that point on. Harmlessness follows as a matter of course. Eagles and ravens may hunt their prey; the turtledove can endure wrong, but it cannot inflict it. We must be harmless as doves. The dove is a fitting picture of love; its voice is full of affection. Thus, the soul visited by the blessed Spirit abounds in love for God, in love for other Christians, and in love for sinners. Above all, it abounds in love for Jesus. The brooding of the Spirit of God on *"the face of the deep"* (Gen. 1:2) first produced order and life. In our hearts, He causes and fosters new life and light. Blessed Spirit, as You rested on our dear Redeemer, even so rest on us from this time forward and forever.

My grace is sufficient for thee.
—2 Corinthians 12:9

If none of God's saints were poor and tried, we would not know half so well the consolations of divine grace. When we find the wanderer who has nowhere to lay his head, who yet can say, "Still I will trust in the Lord"; when we see the pauper starving on bread and water, who still glories in Jesus; when we see the bereaved widow overwhelmed in affliction, who yet has faith in Christ, oh, what honor it reflects on the Gospel. God's grace is illustrated and magnified in the poverty and trials of believers. Saints bear up under every discouragement, believing *"that all things work together for [their] good"* (Rom. 8:28), and that out of apparent evils a real blessing will ultimately spring—that their God will either deliver them speedily or most assuredly support them in the trouble, as long as He is pleased to keep them in it. This patience of the saints proves the power of divine grace. There is a lighthouse out at sea. It is a calm night; I cannot tell whether the edifice is firm. The tempest must rage about it, and then, I will know whether it will stand. So it is with the Spirit's work. If it were not on many occasions surrounded with tempestuous waters, we would not know that it was true and strong; if the winds did not blow on it, we would not know how firm and secure it was. The masterpieces of God are those who stand steadfast and unmovable in the midst of difficulties—"Calm mid the bewildering cry, confident of victory." He who would glorify his God must set his account on meeting with many trials. No man can be illustrious before the Lord unless his conflicts are many. If yours, then, is a much tried path, rejoice in it, because you will all the better show forth the all-sufficient grace of God. As for His failing you, never dream of it—hate the thought. The God who has been sufficient until now should be trusted to the end.

MARCH 4

Evening

They shall be abundantly satisfied with the fatness of thy house.
—Psalm 36:8

The queen of Sheba was amazed at the sumptuousness of Solomon's table. She was overwhelmed when she saw the provision of a single day. She marveled equally at the number of servants who feasted at the royal table. But what is this compared with the hospitality of the God of grace? Hundreds of thousands of His people are fed daily; hungry and thirsty, they bring large appetites with them to the banquet, but not one of them leaves unsatisfied. There is enough for each, enough for all, enough forevermore. Though the host that feeds at Jehovah's table is as countless as the stars of heaven, each one receives his portion of meat. Think how much grace one saint requires, so much that nothing but the Infinite One could supply him for one day; yet the Lord spreads His table, not for one, but for many saints; not for one day, but for many years; not for many years only, but for generation after generation. Observe the full feasting spoken of in the text. The guests at mercy's banquet are satisfied—no, they are *"abundantly satisfied."* They are filled not with ordinary fare, but with *"fatness,"* the unique abundance of God's own house. Such feasting is guaranteed by a faithful promise to all those children of men who put their trust under the shadow of Jehovah's wings. I once thought that if I could just get the leftover meat at God's back door of grace, I would be satisfied—like the woman who said, *"The dogs eat of the crumbs which fall from their masters' table"* (Matt. 15:27). But no child of God is ever served with scraps and leftovers. Like Mephibosheth, they all eat from the king's own table. In matters of grace, we all have Benjamin's portion; we all have many times more than we could have expected. Although our needs are great, we are often amazed at the marvelous abundance of grace that God gives to us to enjoy.

MARCH 5

Morning

Let us not sleep, as do others.
—1 Thessalonians 5:6

There are many ways of promoting Christian wakefulness. Among the rest, let me strongly advise Christians to converse together concerning the ways of the Lord. Christian and Hopeful, as they journeyed toward the Celestial City, said to themselves, "To prevent drowsiness in this place, let us fall into good discourse." Christian inquired, "Brother, where shall we begin?" Hopeful answered, "Where God began with us." Then Christian sang this song:

> When saints do sleepy grow, let them come hither,
>   And hear how these two pilgrims talk together;
> Yea, let them learn of them, in any wise,
>   Thus to keep open their drowsy, slumb'ring eyes.
> Saints' fellowship, if it be managed well,
>   Keeps them awake, and that in spite of hell.

Christians who isolate themselves and walk alone are very liable to grow drowsy. Keep Christian company, and you will be kept wakeful by it and refreshed and encouraged to make quicker progress on the road to heaven. But as you take *"sweet counsel"* (Ps. 55:14) in the ways of God, take care that the theme of your conversation is the Lord Jesus. Let your eyes be constantly looking to Him; let your heart be full of Him; let your lips speak of His worth. Friend, live near the cross, and you will not sleep. Impress on yourself a deep sense of the value of the place to which you are going. If you remember that you are going to heaven, you will not sleep on the road. If you think that hell is behind you, and the devil is pursuing you, you will not loiter. Christian, will you sleep while the pearly gates are open, the songs of angels are waiting for you to join them, and a crown of gold is ready for your brow? In holy fellowship continue to *"watch and pray, that ye enter not into temptation"* (Matt. 26:41).

Say unto my soul, I am thy salvation.
—Psalm 35:3

What does this sweet prayer teach me? It will be my evening's petition, but first let it serve as an instructive meditation. The text informs me that David had his doubts; otherwise, why would he pray, *"Say unto my soul, I am thy salvation,"* if he were not sometimes plagued with doubts and fears? Let me, then, be encouraged, for I am not the only saint who has to complain of weakness of faith. If David doubted, I do not need to conclude that I am not a Christian because I have doubts. The text reminds me that David was not content while he had doubts and fears. Instead, he went immediately to the mercy seat to pray for assurance, which he valued as much as fine gold. I, too, must seek an abiding sense of my acceptance in the Beloved. I must have no joy when His love is not shed abroad in my soul. When my Bridegroom is gone from me, my soul must and will fast. I also learn that David knew where to obtain full assurance. He went to his God in prayer, crying, *"Say unto my soul, I am thy salvation."* I must spend much time alone with God if I expect to have a clear sense of Jesus' love. If my prayers cease, my eye of faith will grow dim. Much in prayer, much in heaven; slow in prayer, slow in progress. I notice that David would not be satisfied unless his assurance had a divine source. *"Say unto my soul."* Lord, please speak to me! Nothing short of a divine testimony in the soul will ever satisfy the true Christian. Moreover, David could not rest unless his assurance had a vivid personality about it. *"Say unto my soul, I am thy salvation."* Lord, if You say this to all the saints, it would mean nothing, unless You said it to me. Lord, I have sinned; I do not deserve Your smile. I hardly dare to ask, but oh, say to my soul, even to my soul, *"I am thy salvation."* Let me have a present, personal, unfailing, indisputable sense that I am Yours and that You are mine.

MARCH 6

Morning

Ye must be born again.
—John 3:7

Regeneration is a subject that lies at the very basis of salvation, and we should be very diligent to take heed that we really are *"born again,"* for there are many who imagine they are, who are not. Be assured that the name of a Christian is not the nature of a Christian; and that being born in a Christian land and being recognized as professing the Christian religion is of no avail whatever unless there is something more added to it—being born again is a matter so mysterious that human words cannot describe it. *"The wind bloweth where it listeth, and thou hearest the sound thereof, but canst not tell whence it cometh, and whither it goeth: so is every one that is born of the Spirit"* (John 3:8). Nevertheless, it is a change that is known and felt: known by works of holiness and felt by a gracious experience. This great work is supernatural. It is not an operation that a man performs for himself. A new principle is infused, which works in the heart, renews the soul, and affects the entire man. It is not a change of my name, but a renewal of my nature, so that I am not the person I used to be, but a *"new creature"* (2 Cor. 5:17) in Christ Jesus. To wash and dress a corpse is a far different thing from making it alive. Man can do the one, but God alone can do the other. If you have, then, been born again, your acknowledgment will be, "O Lord Jesus, the everlasting Father, You are my spiritual Parent. Unless Your Spirit had breathed into me the breath of a new, holy, spiritual life, I would have been to this day *'dead in trespasses and sins'* (Eph. 2:1). My heavenly life is wholly derived from You, and from You alone. My *'life is hid with Christ in God'* (Col. 3:3). It is no longer I who live, but Christ who lives in me (Gal. 2:20)." May the Lord enable us to be well assured on this vital point, for to be unregenerate is to be unsaved, unpardoned, without God, and without hope.

Before destruction the heart of man is haughty.
—Proverbs 18:12

It is an old, familiar saying that "coming events cast their shadows before them." The writer of Proverbs teaches us that a haughty heart is the prophetic prelude to evil. Pride forecasts destruction even more reliably than a change of mercury in the barometer predicts rain. When men have ridden the high horse, destruction has always overtaken them. Let David's aching heart show that there is an eclipse of a man's glory when he focuses on his own greatness. (See 2 Samuel 24:10.) Nebuchadnezzar, the mighty builder of Babylon, was reduced to creeping on the earth, devouring grass like an ox, until his nails had grown like birds' claws and his hair like eagles' feathers. (See Daniel 4:33.) Pride turned the boaster into a beast, just as once before it had made an angel into a devil. God hates haughty looks and never fails to bring them down. All the arrows of God are aimed at proud hearts. Christian, is your heart haughty this evening? For pride can get into the Christian's heart as well as into the sinner's; it can delude him into dreaming that he is *"rich, and increased with goods, and* [in] *need of nothing"* (Rev. 3:17). Are you glorying in your grace or your talents? Are you proud of yourself because you have a holy expression and sweet experiences? If so, then, take note, reader: destruction is coming to you also. Your flaunting poppies of self-conceit will be pulled up by the roots, your mushroom graces will wither in the burning heat, and your self-sufficiency will become as straw for the dunghill. If we forget to live at the foot of the cross in deepest lowliness of spirit, God will not forget to make us suffer under His rod. Destruction will come to you, O self-exalted believer. The destruction of your joys and of your comforts will come, even though there can be no destruction of your soul. Therefore, *"he that glorieth, let him glory in the Lord"* (1 Cor. 1:31).

Have faith in God.
—Mark 11:22

Faith is the foot of the soul by which it can march along the road of the commandments. Love can make the feet move more swiftly, but faith is the foot that carries the soul. Faith is the oil that enables the wheels of holy devotion and of earnest piety to move well. Without faith the wheels are taken from the chariot, and we drag heavily. With faith I can do all things; without faith I neither have the inclination nor the power to do anything in the service of God. If you would find the men who serve God the best, you must look for the men of the most faith. Little faith will save a man, but little faith cannot do great things for God. Bunyan's Little-faith could not have fought Apollyon; it needed Christian to do that. Poor Little-faith could not have slain Giant Despair; it required Great-heart's arm to knock that monster down. Little-faith will go to heaven most certainly, but it often has to hide itself in a nutshell, and it frequently loses all but its jewels. Little-faith says, "It is a rough road, beset with sharp thorns, and full of dangers; I am afraid to go"; but Great-faith remembers the promise, *"Thy shoes shall be iron and brass; and as thy days, so shall thy strength be"* (Deut. 33:25), and so she boldly ventures. Despondent, Little-faith mingles her tears with the flood; but Great-faith sings, *"When thou passest through the waters, I will be with thee; and through the rivers, they shall not overflow thee"* (Isa. 43:2), and she fords the stream at once. Do you want to be comfortable and happy? Do you enjoy religion? Do you want to have the religion of cheerfulness and not that of gloom? Then *"have faith in God."* If you love darkness and are satisfied to dwell in gloom and misery, then be content with little faith; but if you love the sunshine and would sing songs of rejoicing, covet earnestly this best gift: great faith.

It is better to trust in the LORD than to put confidence in man.
—Psalm 118:8

Undoubtedly, the reader has been tried with the temptation to rely on things that are seen, instead of resting alone on the invisible God. Christians often look to man for help and counsel and mar the noble simplicity of their reliance on their God. Does this evening's portion meet the eye of a child of God who is anxious about earthly concerns? Then I would reason with him for a while. You say that you trust in Jesus, and only in Jesus, for your salvation. Then why are you troubled? "Because of my great care," you answer. Is it not written, *"Cast thy burden upon the LORD"* (Ps. 55:22)? Does Scripture not also say, *"Be careful for nothing; but in every thing by prayer and supplication with thanksgiving let your requests be made known unto God"* (Phil. 4:6)? Can you not trust God for your material needs? "Oh, I wish I could," you say. If you cannot trust God for earthly needs, how can you dare to trust Him for spiritual needs? Can you trust Him for your soul's redemption and not rely on Him for a few lesser mercies? Is God not enough for your needs, or is His all-sufficiency too limited? Do you need another eye besides the One who sees every secret thing? Is His heart faint? Is His arm weary? If so, then seek another God; but if He is infinite, omnipotent, faithful, true, and all-wise, why do you waste your time seeking another confidence? Why do you comb the earth to find another foundation, when God is strong enough to bear all the weight that you can ever build upon Him? Christian, just as you would not dilute your wine with water, do not alloy the gold of your faith with the dross of human confidence. Wait only on God, and let your hope come from Him. Do not covet Jonah's gourd, but rest in Jonah's God. Let the sandy foundations of earthly trust be the choice of fools; but like the one who foresees the storm, build your house upon the Rock of Ages.

We must through much tribulation
enter into the kingdom of God.
—Acts 14:22

God's people have their trials. It was never designed by God, when He chose His people, that they should be an untried people. They were chosen in the "*furnace of affliction*" (Isa. 48:10). They were never chosen for worldly peace and earthly joy. Freedom from sickness and the pains of mortality were never promised to them; but when their Lord drew up the charter of privileges, He included chastisements among the things to which they would inevitably be heirs. Trials are a part of our lot; they were predestinated for us in Christ's last legacy. As surely as the stars are fashioned by His hands and their orbits fixed by Him, our trials are allotted to us. He has ordained their season and their place, their intensity and the effect they will have on us. Good men must never expect to escape troubles. If they do, they will be disappointed, for none of their predecessors has been without them. Mark the patience of Job. Remember Abraham, for he had his trials, and by his faith under them, he became the "Father of the faithful." Note well the biographies of all the patriarchs, prophets, apostles, and martyrs, and you will discover none of those whom God made vessels of mercy who were not made to pass through the fire of affliction. It is ordained of old that the cross of trouble should be engraved on every vessel of mercy, as the royal mark whereby the King's vessels of honor are distinguished. But although tribulation is thus the path of God's children, they have the comfort of knowing that their Master has traversed it before them. They have His presence and sympathy to cheer them, His grace to support them, and His example to teach them how to endure. And when they reach the kingdom, it will more than make amends for the "*much tribulation*" through which they passed to enter it.

MARCH 8

Evening

She called his name Benoni [son of sorrow]: but his father called him
Benjamin [son of my right hand].
—Genesis 35:18

To every matter there is a bright as well as a dark side. Rachel was overwhelmed with the sorrow of her difficult childbirth, which led to her death; Jacob, though weeping at the loss of his wife, could see the mercy of the child's birth. It is well for us if, while the flesh mourns over trials, our faith triumphs in divine steadfastness. Samson's lion yielded honey, and so will our adversities, if we look at them in the right way. The stormy sea feeds multitudes with its fish; the wild forest blooms with beautiful flowers; the stormy wind sweeps away the pestilence, and the biting frost loosens the soil. Dark clouds distill bright drops, and black earth grows colorful flowers. A vein of good is to be found in every mine of evil. Sad hearts have an unusual ability to discover the most disadvantageous point of view from which to gaze upon a trial. If there were only one swamp in the world, they would soon be up to their necks in it; and if there were only one lion in the desert, they would hear it roar. We all have a little tendency to act this way. We are likely, at times, to cry as Jacob did, *"All these things are against me"* (Gen. 42:36). Faith's way of walking is to cast all care upon the Lord and then to anticipate good results from the worst calamities. Like Gideon's men, faith does not fret over the broken pitcher but rejoices that the lamp blazes forth all the more. Out of the rough oyster shell of difficulty, faith extracts the rare pearl of honor; from the deep ocean caves of distress, it uplifts the priceless coral of experience. When the flood of prosperity ebbs, faith finds treasures hidden in the sand; and when the sun of delight goes down, faith turns her telescope of hope to the starry promises of heaven. When death itself appears, faith points to the light of resurrection beyond the grave, thus making our dying Benoni to be our living Benjamin.

MARCH 9

Morning

Yea, he is altogether lovely.
—Song of Solomon 5:16

The superlative beauty of Jesus is all-attracting. It is not so much to be admired as to be loved. He is more than pleasant and fair; He is lovely. Surely the people of God can fully justify the use of this golden word, for He is the object of their warmest love, a love founded on the intrinsic excellence of His person, the complete perfection of His charms. O disciples of Jesus, look to your Master's lips and say, "Are they not most sweet?" Do not His words cause your hearts to burn within you as He talks with you by the way? Worshippers of Immanuel, look up to His head of much fine gold, and tell me, are not His thoughts precious to you? Is not your adoration sweetened with affection as you humbly bow before that countenance, which *"is as Lebanon, excellent as the cedars"* (Song 5:15)? Is there not a charm in His every feature, and is not His whole person fragrant with such a savor of His good ointments, that therefore the virgins love Him? Is there one member of His glorious body that is not attractive?—one portion of His person that is not a fresh lodestone to our souls?—one office that is not a strong cord to bind your heart? Our love is not as a seal set on His heart of love alone. It is fastened on His arm of power also. Nor is there a single part of Him on which it does not fix itself. We anoint His whole person with the sweet spikenard of our fervent love. His whole life we would imitate; His whole character we would copy. In all other beings we see some lack; in Him there is all perfection. Even the best of His favored saints have had blots on their garments and wrinkles on their brows. He is nothing but loveliness. All earthly suns have their spots. The fair world itself has its wilderness. We cannot love the whole of the loveliest thing, but Christ Jesus is gold without alloy, light without darkness, glory without cloud—*"Yea, he is altogether lovely."*

MARCH 9

Evening

Abide in me.
—John 15:4

Communion with Christ is a certain cure for every ill. Whether it is bitter sorrow or excessive pleasure, close fellowship with the Lord Jesus will remove the pain from the one and the imbalance from the other. Live near to Jesus, Christian, and it is matter of secondary importance whether you reside on the mountain of honor or in the valley of humiliation. Living near to Jesus, you are covered with the wings of God; underneath you are the *"everlasting arms"* (Deut. 33:27). Let nothing keep you from that hallowed fellowship, which is the choice privilege of a soul wedded to the Lord. Do not be content with an interview now and then, but always seek to retain His company. Only in His presence will you find either comfort or safety. Jesus should not be a friend who calls upon us now and then, but One with whom we walk continuously. Do you have a difficult road before you? O traveler to heaven, see that you do not go without your Guide. Do you have to pass through the fiery furnace? Do not enter it unless, like Shadrach, Meshach, and Abednego, you have the Son of God as your Companion. Do you have to battle the Jericho of your own sins? Then do not attempt the warfare until, like Joshua, you have seen the Captain of the Lord's host with His sword drawn in His hand. Are you called to meet the Esau of your many temptations? Do not meet him until at Jabbok's brook you have laid hold on the angel and have prevailed. In every case, in every condition, you will need Jesus. When the iron gates of death open, you will need Him most of all. Keep close to your soul's Husband. Lean your head on His breast, and ask to be refreshed with the spiced wine of His pomegranate. Then you will be found by Him at the end, without *"spot, or wrinkle, or any such thing"* (Eph. 5:27). Since you have lived with Him and lived in Him here, you will abide with Him forever.

In my prosperity I said, I shall never be moved.
—Psalm 30:6

Moab...*settled on his lees, and hath not been emptied from vessel to vessel"* (Jer. 48:11). Give a man wealth. Let his ships bring home continually rich freights, and let the winds and waves appear to be his servants to bear his vessels across the bosom of the mighty deep. Let his lands yield abundantly, and let the weather be propitious to his crops. Let uninterrupted success attend him. Let him stand among men as a successful merchant. Let him enjoy continued health, and allow him with braced nerve and brilliant eye to march through the world and live happily. Give him a buoyant spirit. Let him have a song perpetually on his lips. Let his eyes ever sparkle with joy— and the natural consequence of such an easy state to any man, even if he is the best Christian who has ever lived, will be presumption. Even David said, *"I shall never be moved,"* and we are not better than David, nor half so good. Brother, beware of the smooth places of the way. If you are treading them, or if the way is rough, thank God for it. If God would always rock us in the cradle of prosperity; if we were always dandled on the knees of fortune; if we did not have some stain on the alabaster pillar; if there were not a few clouds in the sky; if we did not have some bitter drops in the wine of this life, we would become intoxicated with pleasure. We would dream we stand and stand we would, but it would be on a pinnacle. Like a man asleep on the mast, each moment we would be in jeopardy. We bless God, then, for our afflictions. We thank Him for our ups and downs. We extol His name for losses of property, for we feel that had He not chastened us thus, we might have become too secure. Continued worldly prosperity is a fiery trial.

> Afflictions, though they seem severe,
>   In mercy oft are sent.

MARCH 10

Evening

Man…is of few days, and full of trouble.
—Job 14:1

Before we fall asleep, it may be of great service to us to remember the truth of this evening's text; it could lead to our being set free from earthly things. There is nothing very pleasant in recalling that we are not immune to adversity, but it may humble us and prevent our boasting like the psalmist in our morning's portion, *"In my prosperity I said, I shall never be moved"* (Ps. 30:6). It may keep us from sinking our roots too deeply into this soil from which we are so soon to be transplanted into the heavenly garden. Let us recall the frail claim we hold on our earthly blessings. If we would remember that all the trees of the earth are marked for the woodsman's ax, we would not be so ready to build our nests in them. We should love with the love that expects death and that counts on separations. Our dear relatives are but loaned to us, and the hour when we must return them to the Lender's hand may be even at the door. The same is certainly true of our worldly goods. Do not riches take wings and fly away? Our health is equally precarious. As frail flowers of the field, we must not think that we will bloom forever. There is a time appointed for weakness and sickness when we will have to glorify God by our suffering and not by earnest activity. There is no single point at which we can hope to escape from the sharp arrows of affliction; out of our few days, there is not one secure from sorrow. Man's life is a cask full of bitter wine; he who looks for joy in it had better seek for honey in an ocean of brine. Beloved reader, do not *"set your affection on things…on the earth"* (Col. 3:2), but seek those things that are above. Here the moth devours, and *"thieves break through and steal"* (Matt. 6:19), but there all joys are perpetual and eternal. The path of trouble is the way home. Lord, make this thought a pillow for many weary heads!

Sin…exceeding sinful.
—Romans 7:13

Beware of frivolous thoughts of sin. At the time of conversion, the conscience is so tender that we are afraid of the slightest sin. Young converts have a holy timidity, a godly fear lest they should offend God. But alas! Very soon the fine bloom on these first ripe fruits is removed by the rough handling of the surrounding world. The sensitive plant of young piety turns into a willow in later life; it grows too pliant, too easily yielding. By degrees men become familiar with sin. The ear in which the cannon has been booming will not notice slight sounds. At first a little sin startles us; but soon, we say, "Is it not a little one?" Then there comes a larger one, and then another, until by degrees we begin to regard sin as but a little transgression. Then follows an unholy presumption: "We have not fallen into open sin. True, we tripped a little, but we stood upright on the whole. We may have uttered one unholy word, but most of our conversation has been consistent." So we excuse sin. We throw a cloak over it and call it by dainty names. Christian, beware of thinking lightly of sin. Take heed lest you fall little by little. Sin, a little thing? Is it not a poison? Who knows its deadliness? Sin, a little thing? Do not the little foxes spoil the grapes (Song 2:15)? Does not the tiny coral insect build a rock that wrecks a navy? Do not little strokes fell lofty oaks? Will not droplets of water eventually wear away stones? Sin, a little thing? It circled the Redeemer's head with thorns and pierced His heart! It made Him suffer anguish, bitterness, and woe. If you could weigh the least sin on the scales of eternity, you would fly from it as from a serpent and abhor the least appearance of evil. Look on all sin as that which crucified the Savior, and you will see it to be *"exceeding sinful."*

Thou shalt be called, Sought out.
—Isaiah 62:12

The surpassing grace of God is seen very clearly in that we were not only sought, but *"sought out."* Men seek for something that has been lost on the floor of the house, but in such a situation, there is only seeking, not seeking out. The loss is more perplexing and the search more persevering when a thing is sought out. We were mingled with the mire. It is as if we were like some precious piece of gold that had fallen into a sewer. Men gather together to carefully inspect the mass of abominable filth, and they continue to stir and rake and search among the heap until the treasure is found. Or, to use another example, we were lost in a maze. We wandered here and there, and when mercy came after us with the Gospel, it did not find us at the first coming. It had to search for us and seek us out, for like lost sheep, we were so desperately lost. We had wandered into a strange country, and it did not seem possible that even the Good Shepherd would be able to follow our devious wanderings. Glory be to unconquerable grace: we were sought out! No gloom could hide us; no filthiness could conceal us. We were found and brought home. Glory be to infinite love: God the Holy Spirit restored us! If the lives of some of God's people could be written, they would fill us with holy astonishment. Strange and marvelous are the ways that God used in their cases to find His own. Blessed be His name! He never relinquishes the search until the chosen are sought out. They are not a people sought today and cast away tomorrow. Almightiness and wisdom combined will make no failures. They will be called, *"Sought out."* That any should be sought out is matchless grace, but that we should be sought out is grace beyond degree! We can find no reason for it but God's own sovereign love. We can only lift up our hearts in wonder and praise the Lord that this night we wear the name *"Sought out."*

Thou shalt love thy neighbour.
—Matthew 5:43

Love your neighbor. Perhaps he rolls in riches, and you are poor, living in your little cottage side by side with his lordly mansion. Every day you see his estates, his fine linen, and his sumptuous banquets. God has given him these gifts. Do not covet his wealth, and think no cruel thoughts concerning him. Be content with your own lot, if you cannot better it. Do not look on your neighbor and wish that he were as you. Love him, and then you will not envy him. Perhaps, on the other hand, you are rich, and the poor live near you. Do not be too proud to call them your neighbor. Accept your responsibility to love them. The world calls them your inferiors. In what are they inferior? They are far more your equals than your inferiors, for God has made *"of one blood all nations of men for to dwell on all the face of the earth"* (Acts 17:26). It is your coat that is better than theirs, but you are by no means better than they. They are men, and what are you more than that? Take heed that you love your neighbor even though he is in rags or has sunken in the depths of poverty. But, perhaps, you say, "I cannot love my neighbors, because, for all I do for them, they return ingratitude and contempt." That leaves more room for the heroism of love. Would you be a featherweight warrior, instead of bearing the rough fight of love? He who dares the most will win the most. If your path of love is rough, tread it boldly, still loving your neighbors through thick and thin. *"Heap coals of fire on* [their heads]" (Rom. 12:20), and if they are hard to please, do not seek to please them, but to please your Master. Remember, if they spurn your love, your Master has not spurned it, and your actions are as acceptable to Him as if they had been acceptable to them. Love your neighbor, for, in so doing, you are following the footsteps of Christ.

MARCH 12

Evening

To whom belongest thou?
—1 Samuel 30:13

No neutrality can exist in Christianity. We are either ranked under the banner of Prince Immanuel to serve and fight His battles, or we are followers of the black prince, Satan. *"To whom belongest thou?"* Reader, let me assist you in your response. Have you been born again? If you have, you belong to Christ, but without the new birth, you cannot be His. In whom do you trust? Those who believe in Jesus are the sons of God. Whose work are you doing? You are sure to serve your master, for he whom you serve is admittedly your lord. What company do you keep? If you belong to Jesus, you will fraternize with those who wear the sign of the Cross. As the saying goes, Birds of a feather flock together. What is your conversation? Is it heavenly, or is it earthly? What have you learned of your Master? Servants learn much from their masters to whom they are apprenticed. If you have served your time with Jesus, it will be said of you, as it was of Peter and John, *"They took knowledge of them, that they had been with Jesus"* (Acts 4:13). We press the question, *"To whom belongest thou?"* Answer honestly before you give sleep to your eyes. If you are not Christ's, you are in a hard service. Run away from your cruel master! Enter into the service of the Lord of Love, and you will enjoy a life of blessedness. If you are Christ's, let me advise you to do four things. You belong to Jesus; therefore, *obey Him.* Let His Word be your law; let His wish be your will. Since you belong to the Beloved, *love Him.* Let your heart embrace Him; let your whole soul be filled with Him. Because you belong to the Son of God, *trust Him.* Do not rest anywhere but on Him. You belong to the King of Kings, so *be decided for Him.* Do not waver in your loyalty. Although you are not branded outwardly, live your life so that all will know to whom you belong.

Why sit we here until we die?
—2 Kings 7:3

Dear reader, this little book was mainly intended for the edification of believers, but if you are yet unsaved, my heart yearns over you. I would gladly say a word that may be blessed to you. Open your Bible and read the story of the lepers. Notice their position, which was much the same as yours. If you remain where you are, you will perish; if you go to Jesus, you can only die. Nothing ventured, nothing gained is the old proverb, and in your case the venture is no great one. If you sit still in despair, no one can pity you when your ruin comes; but if you die with mercy sought, if such a thing were possible, you would be the object of universal sympathy. No one will escape who refuses to look to Jesus. You know that some are saved who believe in Him, for certain of your own acquaintances have received mercy. Then why not you? The Ninevites said, *"Who can tell?"* (Jonah 3:9). Act on the same hope, and try the Lord's mercy. To perish is so awful that if there were but a straw to catch at, the instinct of self-preservation would lead you to stretch out your hand. We have thus been talking to you on your own unbelieving ground. We would now assure you, as from the Lord, that if you seek Him, you will find Him. Jesus casts out no one who comes to Him. You will not perish if you trust Him; on the contrary, you will find treasure far richer than the poor lepers gathered in Syria's deserted camp. May the Holy Spirit embolden you to go at once, and you will not believe in vain. When you are saved yourself, tell the good news to others. Do not hold your peace. Tell the church first, and unite with them in fellowship. Let the minister be informed of your discovery, and then proclaim the good news in every place. May the Lord save you before the sun goes down today.

Then he put forth his hand, and took her, and pulled her
in unto him into the ark.
—Genesis 8:9

Worn out from her wanderings, the dove finally returns to the ark as her only resting place. How heavily she flies—she will drop—she will never reach the ark! But she struggles on. Noah has been watching for the dove all day long, and he is ready to receive her. She has just enough strength to reach the edge of the ark. She can hardly alight upon it. She is ready to drop when Noah puts forth his hand and pulls her in to him. Notice these words: *"pulled her in unto him."* She did not fly right in herself, for she was too fearful or too weary to do so. She flew as far as she could, and then he reached out his hand and pulled her in to safety. This act of mercy was shown to the wandering dove; she was not scolded for her wanderings. Just as she was, she was pulled into the ark. So you, seeking sinner, with all your sin, will be received. *Only return*—these are God's two gracious words. What? Nothing else? No, "only return." The dove had no olive branch in her mouth this time. She had nothing at all but herself and her wanderings. But the message is still "only return." She does return, and Noah pulls her in. Fly, wanderer; fly, fainting one, dove as you are. Although you think you are black as the raven with the mire of sin, fly back, back to the Savior. Every moment you wait only increases your misery. Your attempts to plume yourself and make yourself fit for Jesus are all vanity. Come to Him just as you are. *"Return, thou backsliding Israel"* (Jer. 3:12). God does not say, "Return, thou repenting Israel" (though undoubtedly there is such an invitation), but He says, *"thou backsliding"* one. As a backslider with all your backslidings, return, return, return! Jesus is waiting for you! He will stretch forth His hand and pull you in. He will pull you in to Himself, your heart's true home.

Let him that thinketh he standeth take heed lest he fall.
—1 Corinthians 10:12

It is a curious fact that there is such a thing as being proud of grace. A man says, "I have great faith; I will not fall. Poor, Little-faith may, but I never will." "I have fervent love," says another. "I can stand; there is no danger of my going astray." He who boasts of grace has little grace of which to boast. Some who do this imagine that their graces can keep them, knowing not that the stream must flow constantly from the fountainhead, or else the brook will soon be dry. If a continuous stream of oil does not come to the lamp, though it burns brightly today, it will smoke tomorrow, and its scent will be noxious. Take heed that you do not glory in your graces, but let all your glorying and confidence be in Christ and His strength, for only then can you be kept from falling. Pray much. Spend longer times in holy adoration. Read the Scriptures more earnestly and constantly. Watch your lives more carefully. Live nearer to God. Take the best examples for your pattern. Let your conversation be holy. Let your hearts be perfumed with affection for men's souls. Live in such a way that men will know that you have been with Jesus and have learned of Him. When that happy day will come, when He whom you love will say, "Come up higher," may it be your happiness to hear Him say, "[You] *have fought a good fight,* [you] *have finished* [your] *course,* [you] *have kept the faith: henceforth there is laid up for* [you] *a crown of righteousness*" (2 Tim. 4:7–8). On, Christian, with care and caution! On, with holy fear and trembling! On, with faith and confidence in Jesus alone, and let your constant petition be, *"Uphold me according unto thy word"* (Ps. 119:116). He is able, and He alone, *"to keep you from falling, and to present you faultless before the presence of his glory with exceeding joy"* (Jude 24).

I will take heed to my ways.
—Psalm 39:1

Fellow pilgrim, do not say in your heart, "I will go here and there, and I will not sin," for you are never so far from the danger of sinning as to boast of security. The road is very muddy; it will be hard to pick your path so as not to soil your garments. This world is full of corruption; you will need to watch often if, in handling it, you are to keep yourself clean. At every turn in the road, there is a thief ready to rob you of your jewels. There is a temptation in every blessing and a snare in every joy. If you ever reach heaven, it will be a miracle of divine grace to be ascribed entirely to your Father's power. Be on your guard. When a man carries an explosive in his hands, he should be careful not to go near an open flame. You, too, must take care that you do not enter into temptation. Even your daily activities are sharp tools; you must watch how you handle them. There is nothing in this world to foster a Christian's faith, but everything tries to destroy it. How quick you should be to look to God so that He may keep you! Your prayer should be, "Hold me up, and I will be safe." Having prayed, you must also watch; guard every thought, word, and action with holy jealousy. Do not expose yourselves unnecessarily to danger, but if you are called to go where the darts are flying, never venture forth without your shield. If even once the devil finds you without protection, he will rejoice that his hour of triumph has come, and he will soon make you fall down wounded by his arrows. Though you cannot be slain, you can be wounded. Be sober; be vigilant. Danger may come in the hour when everything seems to be the most secure. Therefore, take heed to your ways, and pray diligently. No one ever fell into error through being too watchful. May the Holy Spirit guide us in all our ways so that we may always please the Lord.

Be strong in the grace that is in Christ Jesus.
—2 Timothy 2:1

Christ has grace without measure in Himself, but He has not retained it for Himself. As the reservoir empties itself into the pipes, so has Christ emptied out His grace for His people. *"Of his fulness have all we received, and grace for grace"* (John 1:16). He seems only to have in order to dispense to us. He stands like the fountain, always flowing, but only running in order to supply the empty pitchers and the thirsty lips that draw near to it. Like a tree, He bears sweet fruit, not to hang on boughs, but to be gathered by those who have need. Grace, whether its work is to pardon, to cleanse, to preserve, to strengthen, to enlighten, to quicken, or to restore, is ever to be had from Him freely and without price. Nor is there one form of the work of grace that He has not bestowed on His people. As the blood of the body, though flowing from the heart, belongs equally to every member, so the influences of grace are the inheritance of every saint united to the Lamb. Herein there is a sweet communion between Christ and His church, inasmuch as they both receive the same grace. Christ is the Head on which the oil is first poured, but the same oil runs to the very skirts of the garments, so that the humblest saint has an unction of the same costly moisture as that which fell on the Head. This is true communion when the sap of grace flows from the stem to the branch, and when it is perceived that the stem itself is sustained by the very nourishment that feeds the branch. As we day by day receive grace from Jesus, and more constantly recognize it as coming from Him, we will behold Him in communion with us, and enjoy communion with Him. Let us make daily use of our riches and ever go to Him as to our own Lord in covenant, taking from Him the supply of all we need with as much boldness as men take money from their own pockets.

He did it with all his heart, and prospered.
—2 Chronicles 31:21

This is no unusual occurrence; it is the general rule of the moral universe that men who do their work with all their hearts prosper, while those who go to their labor leaving half their hearts behind are almost certain to fail. God does not give harvests to idle men except harvests of thistles. Neither is He pleased to send wealth to those who will not dig in the field to find its hidden treasure. It is universally acknowledged that if a man desires to prosper, he must be diligent in business. It is the same in religion as it is in other things. If you want to prosper in your work for Jesus, let it be heart-work, and let it be done with all your heart. Put as much force, energy, heartiness, and sincerity into Christ's work as you do into your business, for His cause deserves far more. The Holy Spirit helps our infirmities, but He does not encourage our idleness; He loves active believers. Who are the most useful people in the Christian church? Those who do what they undertake for God with all their hearts. Who are the most successful Sunday school teachers? The most talented? No, they are the most zealous; workers whose hearts are on fire are the ones who see their Lord riding forth prosperously in the majesty of His salvation. (See Psalm 45:4.) Wholeheartedness shows itself in perseverance. There may be failure at first, but the diligent worker will say, "It is the Lord's work, and it must be done. My Lord has commanded me to do it, and in His strength, I will accomplish it." Christian, are you serving your Master with all your heart? Remember the earnestness of Jesus! Think what heart-work was His! He could say, *"The zeal of thine house hath eaten me up"* (John 2:17). When He sweat great drops of blood, it was no light burden He had to carry on those blessed shoulders; when He poured out His heart, it was no weak effort He was making for the salvation of His people. After Jesus gave Himself so passionately, can we afford to be lukewarm?

I am a stranger with thee.
—Psalm 39:12

O Lord, I am a stranger *with* You, but not *to* You. All my natural alienation from You, Your grace has effectively removed. Now, in fellowship with You, I walk through this sinful world as a pilgrim in a foreign country. Lord, You are a stranger in Your own world. Man forgets You, dishonors You, sets up new laws and alien customs, and does not know You. When Your dear Son came to His own, His own did not receive Him (John 1:11). *"He was in the world, and the world was made by him, and the world knew him not"* (v. 10). Never was a foreigner considered as questionable a character as much as Your beloved Son was among His own people. It is no surprise, then, if I who live the life of Jesus am a stranger here below. Lord, I would not be a citizen where Jesus was an alien. His pierced hand has loosened the cords that once bound my soul to earth, and now I find myself a stranger in the land. Among those with whom I dwell, my speech seems to these an outlandish tongue, my manners unusual, and my actions strange. A barbarian would be more at home among genteel society than I could ever be among the company of sinners. But here is the sweetness of my lot: I am a stranger along with You. You are my fellow sufferer, my fellow pilgrim. Oh, what joy to be in such blessed society! My heart burns within me by the way when You speak to me, and though I am a sojourner, I am far more blessed than those who sit on thrones or dwell in their comfortable houses.

> To me remains nor place, nor time:
>   My country is in every clime;
> I can be calm and free from care
>   On any shore, since God is there.
> While place we seek, or place we shun,
>   The soul finds happiness in none:
> But with a God to guide our way,
>   'Tis equal joy to go or stay.

MARCH 16
Evening

Keep back thy servant also from presumptuous sins.
—Psalm 19:13

Such was the prayer of David, the *"man after [God's] own heart"* (Acts 13:22). If holy David needed to pray this way, how much more do we, babes in grace, need to do so! It is as if he said, "Keep me back, or I will rush headlong over the precipice of sin." Our evil natures, like an ill-tempered horse, are prone to run away. May the grace of God put the bridle on them and hold them in, so that we do not rush into mischief. What might the best of us not do if it were not for the boundaries that the Lord sets upon us both in providence and in grace? The psalmist's prayer is directed against the worst form of sin—that which is done with deliberation and willfulness. Even the holiest need to be "kept back" from the vilest transgressions. It is a solemn thing to find the apostle Paul warning saints against the most loathsome sins. *"Mortify therefore your members which are upon the earth; fornication, uncleanness, inordinate affection, evil concupiscence, and covetousness, which is idolatry"* (Col. 3:5). What! Do saints need to be warned against such sins as these? Yes, they do. The whitest robes, unless their purity is preserved by divine grace, will be defiled by the blackest spots. Experienced Christian, do not boast in your experience; you will trip if you look away from Him who *"is able to keep you from falling"* (Jude 24). You whose love is fervent, whose faith is constant, whose hopes are bright, do not say, "We will never sin." Instead, cry, *"Lead us not into temptation"* (Matt. 6:13). There is enough kindling in the heart of the best of men to light a fire that will burn to the lowest hell, unless God quenches the sparks as they fall. Who would have dreamed that righteous Lot could have been found drunken and committing uncleanness? Hazael said, *"Is thy servant a dog, that he should do this great thing?"* (2 Kings 8:13). We are very likely to ask the same self-righteous question. May infinite wisdom cure us of the foolishness of self-confidence.

MARCH 17

Morning

Remember the poor.
—Galatians 2:10

Why does God allow so many of His children to be poor? He could make them all rich if He pleased. He could lay bags of gold at their doors and send them a large annual income. He could scatter round their houses an abundance of provisions, as once He made the quails lie in heaps round the camp of Israel and rained bread out of heaven to feed them. There is no need for them to be poor, except that He sees it to be best. *"The cattle upon a thousand hills"* (Ps. 50:10) are His. He could supply them. He could make the richest, the greatest, and the mightiest bring all their power and riches to the feet of His children, for the hearts of all men are in His control. But He does not choose to do so; instead, He allows them to experience need. He allows them to suffer in poverty and obscurity. Why is this? There are many reasons: one is to give us, who are favored with enough, an opportunity of showing our love for Jesus. We show our love for Christ when we sing of Him and when we pray to Him, but if there were no sons of need in the world, we would lose the sweet privilege of demonstrating our love by charitably ministering to His poorer brethren. He has ordained that thus we should prove that our love stands not only in word, but also in deed and in truth. If we truly love Christ, we will care for those who are loved by Him. Those who are dear to Him will be dear to us. Let us, then, look on it not as a duty but as a privilege to relieve the poor of the Lord's flock—remembering the words of the Lord Jesus, *"Inasmuch as ye have done it unto one of the least of these my brethren, ye have done it unto me"* (Matt. 25:40). Surely this assurance is sweet enough, and this motive strong enough to lead us to help others with a willing hand and a loving heart—remembering that all we do for His people is graciously accepted by Christ as done to Himself.

*Blessed are the peacemakers: for they shall be called
the children of God.*
—Matthew 5:9

This is the seventh of the beatitudes, and seven represented the number of perfection among the Hebrews. It may be that the Savior placed the blessing of the peacemaker seventh on the list because that person most nearly approaches the perfect man in Christ Jesus. He who would have perfect blessedness, as far as it can be enjoyed on earth, must attain to this seventh benediction and become a peacemaker. There is a significance also in the position of the text. The verse that precedes it speaks of the blessedness of *"the pure in heart: for they shall see God"* (Matt. 5:8). It is important to understand that we are to be first pure, then peaceable. Our peaceable nature is never to be an acceptance of sin or a permissiveness of evil. We must set our faces like flints against everything that is contrary to God and His holiness. Once purity in our souls is a settled matter, we can go on to peaceableness. No less than the preceding verse does the verse that follows seem to have been put there on purpose. However peaceable we may be in this world, we will be misrepresented and misunderstood. That should not surprise us, considering that the Prince of Peace, by His very peacefulness, brought fire upon the earth. He Himself, though He loved mankind and did no wrong, was *"despised and rejected of men; a man of sorrows, and acquainted with grief"* (Isa. 53:3). Lest, therefore, the peaceable in heart should be surprised when they meet with enemies, it is added in the following verse, *"Blessed are they which are persecuted for righteousness' sake: for theirs is the kingdom of heaven"* (Matt. 5:10). Thus, the peacemakers are not only pronounced to be blessed, but they are surrounded with blessings. Lord, give us grace to climb to this seventh beatitude! Purify our minds that we may be first pure, then peaceable. Fortify our souls so that our peaceableness may not lead us into cowardice or despair when, for Your sake, we are persecuted.

MARCH 18

Morning

Ye are all the children of God by faith in Christ Jesus.
—Galatians 3:26

The fatherhood of God is common to all His children. Ah! Little-faith, you have often said, "Oh that I had the courage of Great-heart, that I could wield his sword and be as valiant as he! But, alas, I stumble at every straw, and a shadow makes me afraid." Listen, Little-faith. Great-heart is God's child, and you are God's child, too; Great-heart is not one bit more God's child than you are. Peter and Paul, the highly favored apostles, were of the family of the Most High, and so are you also. The weak Christian is as much a child of God as the strong one.

> This cov'nant stands secure,
> Though earth's old pillars bow;
> The strong, the feeble, and the weak,
> Are one in Jesus now.

All the names are in the same family register. One may have more grace than another, but God our heavenly Father has the same tender heart toward all. One may do more mighty works, and may bring more glory to his Father, but he whose name is the least in the kingdom of heaven is as much the child of God as he who stands among the King's mighty men. Let this cheer and comfort us, when we draw near to God and say, "Our Father." Yet while we are comforted by knowing this, let us not rest contented with weak faith, but ask, like the apostles, to have it increased. However feeble our faith may be, if it is real faith in Christ, we will reach heaven at last; but we will not honor our Master much on our pilgrimage, neither will we abound in joy and peace. If then you desire to live for Christ's glory and be happy in His service, seek to be filled with the spirit of adoption more and more completely, until *"perfect love casteth out fear"* (1 John 4:18).

As the Father hath loved me, so have I loved you.
—John 15:9

As the Father loves the Son, in the same manner Jesus loves His people. What is divine love like? God loved Jesus without beginning, and, in the same way, Jesus loves His people. *"I have loved thee with an everlasting love"* (Jer. 31:3). You can trace the beginning of human affection; you can easily find the beginning of your love for Christ, but His love for us is a stream whose source is hidden in eternity. God the Father loves Jesus without any change. Christian, be comforted in knowing that there is no change in Christ's love for those who rest in Him. Yesterday you may have been on the mountaintop, and you said, "He loves me!" Today you may be in the valley of humiliation, but He loves you still the same. On the high elevations, you heard His voice, which spoke so sweetly with the musical sounds of love; now, at sea level or even in the sea, when all His waves and billows roll over you, His heart is faithful to His ancient choice. The Father loves the Son without any end, and this is how the Son loves His people. Believer, you do not need to fear the loosing of the silver cord, for His love for you will never cease. Rest confident that even down to the grave, Christ will go with you, and that up again from it, He will be your Guide to the celestial hills. Moreover, the Father loves the Son without any measure, and the Son bestows that same immeasurable love on His chosen ones. The whole heart of Christ is dedicated to His people. He *"loved [us], and gave himself for [us]"* (Gal. 2:20). His is a love that surpasses knowledge. We have indeed an immutable Savior, a precious Savior, one who loves without measure, without change, without beginning, and without end, even as the Father loves Him! There is much food here for those who know how to digest it. May the Holy Spirit lead us into its marrow and fatness.

Strong in faith.
—Romans 4:20

Christian, take good care of your faith, for remember, faith is the only way whereby you can obtain blessings. If we ask blessings from God, nothing can bring them down but faith. Prayer cannot draw down answers from God's throne unless it is the earnest prayer of the man who believes. Faith is the angelic messenger between the soul and the Lord Jesus in glory. If that angel is withdrawn, we can neither send up prayer, nor receive the answers. Faith is the telegraphic wire that links earth and heaven—on which God's messages of love fly so fast that before we call He answers, and while we are yet speaking He hears us. But if that telegraphic wire of faith be snapped, how can we receive the promise? Am I in trouble? I can obtain help for trouble by faith. Am I beaten about by the enemy? My soul on her dear Refuge leans by faith. But take faith away, and in vain I call to God. There is no road between my soul and heaven. In the deepest wintertime, faith is a road on which the horses of prayer may travel—yes, and all the better for the biting frost. But blockade the road, and how can we communicate with the great King? Faith links me with divinity. Faith clothes me with the power of God. Faith engages on my side the omnipotence of Jehovah. Faith ensures every attribute of God in my defense. It helps me to defy the hosts of hell. It makes me march triumphant over the necks of my enemies. But without faith how can I receive anything of the Lord? Do not let him who wavers—who is *"like a wave of the sea"* (James 1:6)—expect that he will receive anything of God (v. 7)! O, then, Christian, watch your faith well. With it you can win all things, however poor you are, but without it you can obtain nothing. If you can believe, *"all things are possible to him that believeth"* (Mark 9:23).

MARCH 19

And she did eat, and was sufficed, and left.
—Ruth 2:14

Whenever we are privileged to eat of the bread that Jesus gives, we are, like Ruth, satisfied with the full and sweet meal. When Jesus is the Host, no guest leaves the table hungry. Our heads are satisfied with the precious truth that Christ reveals. Our hearts are content with Jesus, as the altogether lovely object of affection. Our hopes are satisfied, for whom have we in heaven but Jesus? Our desires are satiated, for what can we wish for more than to know Christ and to *"be found in him"* (Phil. 3:9)? Jesus fills our consciences until they are at perfect peace, our judgment with persuasion of the certainty of His teachings, our memories with recollections of what He has done, and our imaginations with the prospects of what He is yet to do. As Ruth was *"sufficed, and left,"* so it is with us. We have drunk deeply of Christ, and we have thought that we could take in all of Him; but when we have done our best, we have had to leave a vast remainder. We have sat at the table of the Lord's love, and said, "Nothing but the infinite can ever satisfy me. I am such a great sinner that I must have infinite merit to wash my sin away." But we have had our sins cleansed and found that there was merit to spare; we have had our hunger relieved at the feast of sacred love and found that there was an abundance of spiritual food remaining. Certain sweet things in the Word of God we have not enjoyed yet, and we are obliged to leave for a while; for we are like the disciples to whom Jesus said, *"I have yet many things to say unto you, but ye cannot bear them now"* (John 16:12). Yes, there are graces to which we have not attained, places of fellowship nearer to Christ that we have not reached, and heights of communion that our feet have not climbed. At every banquet of love there are many baskets of fragments left. Let us praise the generosity of our glorious heavenly Boaz.

MARCH 20

Morning

My beloved.
—Song of Solomon 2:8

In her most joyous moments, the ancient church was accustomed to give this golden name, *"beloved,"* to the Anointed of the Lord. When the time of the singing of birds was come and the voice of the turtledove was heard in her land, her love note was sweeter than either, as she sang, *"My beloved is mine, and I am his: he feedeth among the lilies"* (Song 2:16). Ever in her song of songs, she calls Him by that delightful name, *"my beloved"*! Even in the long winter, when idolatry had withered the garden of the Lord, her prophets found space to lay aside the burden of the Lord for a little season, and to say, as Isaiah did, *"Now will I sing to my wellbeloved a song of my beloved touching his vineyard"* (Isa. 5:1). Though the saints had never seen His face, though as yet He was not made flesh, nor had dwelt among us, nor had man beheld His glory, yet He was *"the consolation of Israel"* (Luke 2:25), the hope and joy of all the chosen, the *"beloved"* of all those who were upright before the Most High. We, in the summer days of the church, are also inclined to speak of Christ as the best beloved of our soul and to feel that He is very precious, *"the chiefest among ten thousand"* (Song 5:10), and *"altogether lovely"* (v. 16). So true is it that the church loves Jesus, and claims Him as her beloved, that the apostle dared to defy the whole universe to separate her from the love of Christ. He declared that neither persecution, distress, affliction, peril, nor the sword has been able to do it; he joyously boasted, *"In all these things we are more than conquerors through him that loved us"* (Rom. 8:37). Oh, that we knew more of You, ever precious One!

> My sole possession is Your love;
>> In earth beneath or heaven above,
>> I have no other store;
>> And though with fervent suit I pray,
> And importune You day by day,
>> I ask You nothing more.

Husbands, love your wives, even as Christ also loved the church.
—Ephesians 5:25

What a golden example Christ gives to His disciples! Few teachers could venture to say, "If you want to practice my teaching, imitate my life." But since the life of Jesus is the exact transcript of perfect virtue, He can point to Himself as the paragon of holiness, as well as the teacher of it. The Christian should take nothing short of Christ for his model. Under no circumstances should we be content unless we reflect the grace that was in Him. The Christian husband is to look at the portrait of Christ Jesus, and he is to paint his life according to that copy. The true Christian is to be a husband in the same way that Christ was to His church. The love of a husband is special. The Lord Jesus cherishes the church and has a special affection for her that is set upon her above the rest of mankind: *"I pray for them: I pray not for the world"* (John 17:9). The church is the favorite of heaven and the treasure of Christ, the crown of His head, the bracelet of His arm, the breastplate of His heart, the very center and core of His love. A husband should love his wife with a constant love, for thus Jesus loves His church. He does not vary in His affection. He may change in His display of affection, but the affection itself is still the same. A husband should love his wife with an enduring love, for nothing *"shall be able to separate us from the love of God, which is in Christ Jesus our Lord"* (Rom. 8:39). A true husband loves his wife with a hearty love that is fervent and intense. It is not mere lip service. Beloved, what more could Christ have done to prove His love than He has done? Jesus has a delighted love toward His spouse. He prizes her affection and delights in her with sweet satisfaction. Believer, you are amazed by Jesus' love. You admire it, but are you imitating it? In your domestic relationships is the rule and measure of your love to be *"even as Christ also loved the church"*?

Ye shall be scattered, every man to his own,
and shall leave me alone.
—John 16:32

Few had fellowship with the sorrows of Gethsemane. The majority of the disciples were not sufficiently advanced in grace to be admitted to behold the mysteries of His *"agony"* (Luke 22:44). Occupied with the Passover Feast at their own houses, they represent the many who live on the letter, but are mere babes as to the spirit of the Gospel. To the Twelve, no, to eleven only, was the privilege given to enter Gethsemane and see this great sight. Out of the eleven, eight were left at a distance; they had fellowship, but not of that intimate sort to which men greatly beloved are admitted. Only three highly favored ones could approach the veil of our Lord's mysterious sorrow. Within that veil, even these must not intrude; a stone's throw distance must be left between. He must tread *"the winepress alone"* (Isa. 63:3), and of the people there must be none with Him. Peter and the two sons of Zebedee represent the few eminent, experienced saints who may be written down as "Fathers." Having done business on great waters, they can, in some degree, measure the huge Atlantic waves of their Redeemer's passion. To some selected spirits it is given, for the good of others, and to strengthen them for future, special, and tremendous conflict, to enter the inner circle and hear the pleadings of the suffering High Priest. They have fellowship with Him in His sufferings and are made conformable unto His death (Phil. 3:10). Yet even these cannot penetrate the secret places of the Savior's woe. "Thine unknown sufferings" is the remarkable expression of the Greek liturgy. There was an inner room in our Master's grief, shut out from human knowledge and fellowship. There Jesus was left alone. Here Jesus was more than ever an *"unspeakable gift"* (2 Cor. 9:15). Was not Watts right when he penned, "And all the unknown joys He gives were bought with agonies unknown"?

Canst thou bind the sweet influences of Pleiades,
or loose the bands of Orion?
—Job 38:31

If we are inclined to boast of our abilities, the grandeur of nature may soon show us how puny we are. We cannot move the least of all the twinkling stars or quench even one of the beams of the morning. We speak of power, but the heavens laugh us to scorn. When the Pleiades, a magnificent cluster of stars, shine forth in the spring with new joy, we cannot restrain their influences, and when Orion reigns aloft, and the year is bound in winter's fetters, we cannot relax the icy bands. The seasons revolve according to divine appointment. The whole race of men cannot change their schedule. Lord, what is man? In the spiritual, as in the natural world, man's power is limited on all sides. When the Holy Spirit sheds abroad His delights in the soul, nothing can take away that joy. All the cunning and malice of men are ineffective in halting the life-giving power of the Comforter. When He deigns to visit a church and revive it, the most inveterate enemies cannot resist the good work; they may ridicule it, but they can no more restrain it than they can push back the spring when the Pleiades rule the hour. God wills it, and so it must be. On the other hand, if the Lord in sovereignty or in justice binds up a man so that his soul is in bondage, who can give him liberty? God alone can remove the winter of spiritual death from an individual or a people. He looses the bands of Orion, and no one but He can do that. What a blessing it is that He can do it! Oh, that He would perform the wonder tonight! Lord, end my winter, and let my spring begin. In spite of all my desires to do so, I cannot raise my soul out of her death and dullness, but all things are possible with You. I need celestial influences, the clear shinings of Your love, the beams of Your grace, the light of Your countenance—these are the Pleiades to me. I suffer from sin and temptation—these are my wintry signs, my terrible Orion. Lord, work wonders in me and for me. Amen.

He went a little farther, and fell on his face, and prayed.
—Matthew 26:39

There are several instructive features in our Savior's prayer in His hour of trial. It was lonely prayer. He withdrew even from His three favored disciples. Believer, be much in solitary prayer, especially in times of trial. Family prayer, social prayer, and prayer in the church will not suffice. These are very precious, but the best spice will smoke in your censer in your private devotions, where no ear hears but God's. It was humble prayer. Luke said Jesus knelt, but Matthew said He "*fell on his face.*" Where, then, must be your place, humble servant of the great Master? What dust and ashes should cover your head! Humility gives us good foothold in prayer. There is no hope of prevalence with God unless we abase ourselves so that He may exalt us in due time. It was filial prayer. Jesus cried, "*Abba, Father*" (Mark 14:36). You will find it a stronghold in the day of trial to plead your adoption. You have no rights as a subject, for you have forfeited them by your treason; but nothing can forfeit a child's right to a father's protection. Do not be afraid to say, "My Father, hear my cry." Observe that it was persevering prayer. He prayed three times. Do not stop praying until you prevail. Be like the importunate widow, whose continual coming earned what her first supplication could not win. "*Continue in prayer, and watch in the same with thanksgiving*" (Col. 4:2). Last, it was the prayer of resignation. "*Nevertheless not as I will, but as thou wilt*" (Matt. 26:39). Yield, and God yields. Let it be as God wills, and God will determine for the best. Be content to leave your prayer in His hands, who knows when to give, how to give, what to give, and what to withhold. So pleading earnestly, importunately, yet with humility and resignation, you will surely prevail.

Father, I will that they also, whom thou hast given me,
be with me where I am.
—John 17:24

Death, why do you touch the tree whose spreading branches offer rest from weariness? Why do you snatch away the excellent of the earth, in whom is all our delight? If you must use your ax, use it on the trees that yield no fruit; then we might thank you. But why do you fell the good cedars of Lebanon? Oh, hold back your ax, and spare the righteous. But no, it must not be. Death smites the best of our friends; the most generous, the most prayerful, the holiest, the most devoted must die. Why? Because Jesus prayed, *"Father, I will that they also, whom thou hast given me, be with me where I am"* (John 17:24). It is His prayer that bears them on eagles' wings to heaven. Every time a believer mounts from this earth to paradise, it is an answer to Christ's prayer. A good old saint remarked, "Many times Jesus and His people pull against one another in prayer. You bend your knee in prayer and say, 'Father, I desire that Your saint would be here with me where I am.' Christ says, *'Father, I will that they also, whom thou hast given me, be with me where I am.'"* Thus the disciple is at cross-purposes with his Lord. The soul cannot be in both places; the beloved one cannot be with Christ and with you, too. Now, which pleader will win the day? If you had your choice, if the King stepped from His throne and said, "Here are two supplicants praying in opposition to one another; which one should be answered?" Oh, I am sure, though it would be agony, you would jump to your feet and say, "Jesus, not my will, but Yours be done." You would give up your prayer for your loved one's life if you realized the thoughts that Christ was praying in the opposite direction: *"Father, I will that they also, whom thou hast given me, be with me where I am."* Lord, You may have them. By faith we let them go.

MARCH 23
Morning

His sweat was as it were great drops of blood
falling down to the ground.
—Luke 22:44

The mental pressure arising from our Lord's struggle with temptation so forced His frame to an unnatural excitement that His pores sent forth great drops of blood that fell down to the ground. This proves how tremendous the weight of sin must have been when it was able to crush the Savior so that He sweat great drops of blood! This demonstrates the mighty power of His love. It is a very apt observation of old Isaac Ambrose that the gum that oozes from the tree without cutting is always the best. This precious camphor tree yielded the sweetest spices when it was wounded under the knotty whips, and when it was pierced by the nails on the cross; but see, it gives forth its best spice when there is no whip, no nail, no wound. This sets forth the voluntary nature of Christ's sufferings, since, without a lance, the blood flowed freely. No need to put on the leech or apply the knife; it flowed spontaneously. No need for the rulers to cry, *"Spring up, O well"* (Num. 21:17); of itself it flows in crimson torrents. If men suffer great pain of mind, apparently the blood rushes to the heart. The cheeks are pale; a fainting fit comes on; the blood has gone inward as if to nourish the inner man while passing through its trial. But see our Savior in His agony. He is so utterly oblivious of self that instead of His agony driving His blood to the heart to nourish Himself, it drives it outward to bedew the earth. The agony of Christ, inasmuch as it pours Him out upon the ground, depicts the fullness of the offering that He made for men. Do we not perceive how intense must have been the wrestling through which He passed, and will we not hear its voice to us? *"Ye have not yet resisted unto blood, striving against sin"* (Heb. 12:4). Behold the great Apostle and High Priest of our profession, and sweat even to blood rather than yield to the great tempter of your soul.

MARCH 23

Evening

I tell you that, if these should hold their peace,
the stones would immediately cry out.
—Luke 19:40

But could the stones cry out? They most certainly could if He who opens the mouth of the dumb commanded them to lift up their voice. If they were able to speak, they would have much to testify in praise of Him who created them by the word of His power. They could extol the wisdom and power of their Maker who called them into being. Will we not speak well of Him who made us new creatures and out of stones raised up children of Abraham? The old rocks could tell of chaos and order and of the handiwork of God in successive stages of Creation's drama. Cannot we talk of God's decrees, of God's great work in ancient times, and all that He did for His church in the days of old? If the stones were to speak, they could tell of their breaker who took them from the quarry and made them fit for the temple. Cannot we tell of our glorious Breaker, who broke our hearts with the hammer of His Word so that He might build us into His temple? If the stones could cry out, they would magnify their builder, who polished them and fashioned them into a palace. Will we not talk of our Architect and Builder, who has put us in our places in the temple of the living God? If the stones could cry out, they might have a long, long story to tell by way of a memorial. A great stone has often been set up as a memorial before the Lord. We, too, can testify of the great things God has done for us. They are our Ebenezers, our stones of help and pillars of remembrance. The broken stones of the law cry out against us, but Christ Himself, who has rolled away the stone from the door of the tomb, speaks for us. Stones might well cry out, but we will not let them. We will hush their noise with ours. All our days, we will break forth into sacred song and bless the majesty of the Most High, glorifying Him who is called *"the shepherd, the stone of Israel"* (Gen. 49:24).

MARCH 24

Morning

[Jesus] *was heard in that he feared.*
—Hebrews 5:7

Did this fear arise from the infernal suggestion that He was utterly forsaken? There may be sterner trials than this, but surely it is one of the worst to be utterly forsaken! "See," said Satan, "You have no friends anywhere! Your Father has shut up His compassionate heart against You. Not an angel in His courts will stretch out a hand to help You. All heaven is alienated from You; You are left alone. See the companions with whom You have taken sweet counsel; what are they worth? Son of Mary, see there Your brother James. See there Your beloved disciple John and Your bold apostle Peter. How the cowards sleep when You are in Your sufferings! You have no friends left in heaven or earth. All hell is against You. I have stirred up my infernal den. I have sent my command throughout all regions, summoning every prince of darkness to set on You this night. We will spare no arrows; we will use all our infernal might to overwhelm You. What will You do, O solitary One?" It may be that this was the temptation. I think it was, because the appearance of an angel unto Him, strengthening Him, removed that fear. He *"was heard in that he feared."* He was alone no more, but heaven was with Him. It may be that this is the reason for His coming three times to His disciples. As Hart put it,

> Backward and forward thrice He ran,
>   As if He sought some help from man.

He would see for Himself whether it was really true that all men had forsaken Him. He found them all asleep; but perhaps He gained some faint comfort from the thought that they were sleeping, not from treachery, but from sorrow. Their spirits indeed were willing, but their flesh was weak. (See Matthew 26:41.) At any rate, He *"was heard in that he feared."* Jesus was heard in His deepest woe; my soul, you will be heard also.

In that hour Jesus rejoiced in spirit.
—Luke 10:21

The Savior was *"a man of sorrows"* (Isa. 53:3), but every thoughtful mind has discovered the fact that down deep in His innermost soul, He carried an inexhaustible treasury of refined and heavenly joy. Of all the human race, there was never a man who had a deeper, purer, or more abiding peace than our Lord Jesus Christ. He was *"anointed...with the oil of gladness above* [His] *fellows"* (Ps. 45:7). His vast benevolence must, from the very nature of things, have afforded Him the deepest possible delight, for benevolence is joy. There were a few remarkable seasons when this joy manifested itself. *"In that hour Jesus rejoiced in spirit, and said, I thank thee, O Father, Lord of heaven and earth"* (Luke 10:21). Christ had His songs, even though darkness surrounded Him and though His face was marred and His countenance had lost the glow of earthly happiness. Sometimes, it was still lit up with a matchless splendor of unparalleled satisfaction, as He thought about the final reward and in the midst of the congregation sang His praise to God. In this, the Lord Jesus is a blessed picture of His church on earth. At this hour the church expects to walk along a thorny road in sympathy with her Lord. Through much tribulation, she is forcing her way to the crown. To bear the cross is her calling, and to be scorned and counted a stranger by her mother's children is her lot; yet the church has a deep well of joy, of which none can drink but her own children. There are stores of wine, oil, and corn hidden in the midst of our Jerusalem, on which the saints of God are evermore sustained and nurtured. Sometimes, as in our Savior's case, we have our seasons of intense delight, for *"there is a river, the streams whereof shall make glad the city of God"* (Ps. 46:4). Exiles though we are, we still rejoice in our King; yes, in Him we exceedingly rejoice, while in His name we set up our banners.

Betrayest thou the Son of man with a kiss?
—Luke 22:48

The kisses of an enemy are deceitful. Let me be on my guard when the world puts on a loving face, for it will, if possible, betray me as it did my Master—with a kiss. Whenever a man is about to attack religion, he usually professes very great reverence for it. Let me beware of the sleek-faced hypocrisy that is the armor-bearer to heresy and infidelity. Knowing the deceptiveness of unrighteousness, let me be wise as a serpent to detect and avoid the designs of the enemy. The *"young man void of understanding"* (Prov. 7:7) was led astray by the kiss of the strange woman. May my soul be so graciously instructed all this day that the *"much fair speech"* (v. 21) of the world may have no effect on me. Holy Spirit, let me not, a poor frail son of man, be betrayed with a kiss! But what if I would be guilty of the same accursed sin as Judas, that *"son of perdition"* (John 17:12)? I have been baptized into the name of the Lord Jesus; I am a member of His visible church; I sit at the Communion table—all these are like so many kisses from my lips. Am I sincere in them? If not, I am a base traitor. Do I live in the world as carelessly as others do and yet make a profession of being a follower of Jesus? If so, I expose religion to ridicule and lead men to speak evil of the holy name by which I am called. Surely if I act thus inconsistently, I am a Judas, and it would be better for me if I *"had never been born"* (Mark 14:21). Dare I hope that I am clear in this matter? Then, O Lord, keep me so. O Lord, make me sincere and true. Preserve me from every false way. Never let me betray my Savior. I love You, Jesus, and though I often grieve You, yet I desire to abide faithful even to death. O God, forbid that I would be a high-soaring professor of faith, and then fall at last into the lake of fire because I betrayed my Master with a kiss.

The Son of man.
—John 3:13

How constantly our Master used the title, the *"Son of man"*! If He had chosen, He could have always spoken of Himself as the Son of God, *"Wonderful, Counsellor, The mighty God, The everlasting Father, The Prince of Peace"* (Isa. 9:6). But behold the lowliness of Jesus! He prefers to call Himself the *"Son of man."* Let us learn a lesson of humility from our Savior. Let us never court great titles or proud degrees. There is here, however, a far sweeter thought. Jesus loved mankind so much that He delighted to honor it; since it is a high honor, indeed, the greatest dignity of mankind, that Jesus is the Son of Man. He desires to display this name so that He may, as it were, hang royal stars upon the breast of humanity and show forth the love of God to Abraham's seed. *"Son of man"*—whenever He said those words, He placed a halo around the head of Adam's children. Yet there is perhaps a more precious thought that remains. Jesus Christ called Himself the *"Son of man"* in order to express His oneness and sympathy with His people. He thus reminds us that He is the One whom we may approach without fear. We may take all our griefs and troubles to Him, for, as a Man, He knows them by experience. In that He Himself has suffered as the *"Son of man,"* He is able to help and to comfort us. All hail, blessed Jesus! Inasmuch as You are forever using the sweet name that acknowledges that You are a Brother and a close relative, it is to us a dear token of Your grace, Your humility, and Your love.

> Oh, see how Jesus trusts Himself
> Unto our childish love,
> As though by His free ways with us
> Our earnestness to prove!
> His sacred name a common word
> On earth He loves to hear;
> There is no majesty in Him
> Which love may not come near.

*Jesus answered, I have told you that I am he: if therefore
ye seek me, let these go their way.*
—John 18:8

Mark, my soul, the care that Jesus manifested toward the sheep of His hand, even in His hour of trial! The ruling passion is strong in death. He resigns Himself to the enemy, but He interposes a word of power to set His disciples free. As for Himself, *"as a sheep before her shearers is dumb"* (Isa. 53:7), He does not open His mouth; but for His disciples' sake, He speaks with almighty energy. Herein is love, constant, self-forgetting, faithful love. But is there not far more here than is to be found on the surface? Have we not the very soul and spirit of the Atonement in these words? The Good Shepherd lays down His *"life for the sheep"* (John 10:11) and pleads that they must go free. The Surety is bound, and justice demands that those for whom He stands a substitute should go their way. In the midst of Egypt's bondage, that voice rings as a word of power, *"Let these go their way."* (See also Exodus 9:1.) Out of the slavery of sin and Satan, the redeemed must come. In every cell of the dungeons of Despair, the sound is echoed, *"Let these go their way,"* and forth come Despondency and Much-afraid. Satan hears the well-known voice and lifts his foot from the neck of the fallen; Death hears it, and the grave opens her gates to let the dead arise. Their way is one of progress, holiness, triumph, and glory, and none will dare to keep them from it. *"No lion shall be there, nor any ravenous beast shall go up thereon"* (Isa. 35:9). The Hind of the morning has drawn the cruel hunters upon Himself, and now the most timid roes and deer of the field may graze in perfect peace among the lilies. The thundercloud has burst over the Cross of Calvary, and the pilgrims of Zion will never be smitten by the bolts of vengeance. Come, my heart, rejoice in the immunity that your Redeemer has secured for you. Bless His name all the day, every day.

MARCH 26

Evening

When he cometh in the glory of his Father with the holy angels.
—Mark 8:38

If we have been partakers with Jesus in His shame, we will share in the radiance that will surround Him when He appears again in glory. Are you, beloved one, with Christ Jesus? Does a vital union knit you together with Him? Then you are today with Him in His shame. You have taken up His cross and gone with Him outside *"the camp, bearing his reproach"* (Heb. 13:13). Without a doubt, you will be with Him when the cross is exchanged for the crown. But judge yourself this evening. For if you are not with Him by being born again, neither will you be with Him when He comes in His glory. If you back away from the dark, painful side of communion with Him, you will not understand its bright, happy period, when the King will come again, *"and all the holy angels with him"* (Matt. 25:31). What! Are angels with Him? And yet He did not take up the angels; He took up the seed of Abraham. Are the holy angels with Him? Come, my soul; if you are indeed His own beloved, you cannot be far from Him. If His friends and His neighbors are called together to see His glory, what are you doing if you are married to Him? Will you be distant from Him? Though it is a Day of Judgment, yet you cannot be far from that heart which, having admitted angels into intimacy, has admitted you into union. Has He not said to you, *"I will betroth thee unto me in righteousness, and in judgment, and in lovingkindness"* (Hosea 2:19)? Have not His own lips said, *"I am married unto you"* (Jer. 3:14)? He delights in you. If the angels, who are but friends and neighbors, will be with Him, it is abundantly certain that His own beloved, in whom is all His delight, will be near Him and sit at His right hand. Here is a morning star of hope for you; it is of such exceeding brilliance that it may well light up the darkest and most desolate experience.

MARCH 27
Morning

Then all the disciples forsook him, and fled.
—Matthew 26:56

He never deserted His disciples, but they, in cowardly fear of their lives, fled from Him in the very beginning of His sufferings. This is but one instructive example of the frailty of all believers, if left to themselves. They are but sheep at best, and they flee when the wolf comes. They had all been warned of the danger and had promised to die rather than to leave their Master, yet they were seized with sudden panic and took to their heels. It may be that I, at the opening of this day, have prepared my mind to bear a trial for the Lord's sake, and I imagine myself to be certain to exhibit perfect fidelity; but let me be very vigilant of myself, lest having the same evil heart of unbelief, I would depart from my Lord as the apostles did. It is one thing to make a promise and quite another to carry it out. It would have been to their eternal honor to have stood at Jesus' side; instead, they fled from honor. May I be kept from imitating them! Where else could they have been so safe as near their Master, who could presently call for twelve legions of angels? They fled from their true safety. O God, let me not play the fool also. Divine grace can make the coward brave. The smoking flax can flame forth like fire on the altar when the Lord wills it. These very apostles who were timid as rabbits grew to be bold as lions after the Spirit had descended on them. Even so, the Holy Spirit can make my fearful spirit brave to confess my Lord and witness for His truth. What anguish must have filled the Savior as He saw His friends so faithless! This was one bitter ingredient in His cup, but that cup is drained dry; do not let me put another drop in it. If I forsake my Lord, I will crucify Him afresh, and subject Him to *"open shame"* (Heb. 6:6). Keep me, O blessed Spirit, from an end so shameful.

And she said, Truth, Lord: yet the dogs eat of the crumbs
which fall from their masters' table.
—Matthew 15:27

This woman gained comfort in her misery by thinking great thoughts of Christ. The Master had talked about the children's bread. "Now," she reasoned, "since You are the Master of the table of grace, I know that You are a generous Host. There is sure to be abundance of bread on Your table. There will be more than enough food for the children—enough that there will be crumbs to throw on the floor for the dogs. The children will still have plenty even though the dogs are fed." She thought of Jesus as One who had such an abundance to give that all she needed would be just a crumb in comparison. Remember that what she really wanted was to have the devil cast out of her daughter. It was a very great thing to her, but she had such high esteem of Christ that she said, "It is nothing to Him; it is but a crumb for Christ to give. My sins are many, but it is nothing for Jesus to take them all away. The weight of my guilt presses me down as a giant's foot crushes a worm, but it is no more than a grain of dust to Him. He has already borne its curse *'in his own body on the tree'* (1 Pet. 2:24). It will be a small thing for Him to give me full remission, although it will be an infinite blessing for me to receive it." The woman opened her soul's mouth very wide, expecting great things of Jesus, and He filled it with His love. Dear reader, do the same. She confessed what Christ laid at her door, but she laid hold of Him and drew arguments even out of His hard words. She believed great things of Him, and thus she persuaded Him. She won the victory by believing in Him. Her case is an example of prevailing faith. If we would conquer like her, we must imitate her tactics. This is the royal road to comfort. Great thoughts of your sin alone will drive you to despair, but great thoughts of Christ will pilot you into the haven of peace.

The love of Christ, which passeth knowledge.
—Ephesians 3:19

The love of Christ, in its sweetness, its fullness, its greatness, its faithfulness, passes all human comprehension. Where will language be found that will describe His matchless, unparalleled love toward the children of men? It is so vast and boundless that, as the swallow but skims the water and does not dive into its depths, so all descriptive words but touch the surface, while depths immeasurable lie beneath. Well might the poet say, "O love, thou fathomless abyss!" for this love of Christ is indeed measureless and fathomless; none can attain unto it. Before we can have any right idea of the love of Jesus, we must understand His previous glory in its height of majesty and His incarnation on the earth in all its depths of shame. But who can tell us the majesty of Christ? When He was enthroned in the highest heavens, He was very God of very God. By Him were the heavens made, and all the hosts thereof. His own almighty arm upheld the spheres. The praises of cherubim and seraphim perpetually surrounded Him; the full chorus of the hallelujahs of the universe unceasingly flowed to the foot of His throne. He reigned supreme above all His creatures, God over all, blessed forever (Rom. 9:5). Who can tell His height of glory then? And who, on the other hand, can tell how low He descended? To be a Man was something, to be a Man of Sorrows was far more. To bleed, die, and suffer—these were much for Him who was the Son of God; but to suffer such unparalleled agony—to endure a death of shame and desertion by His Father—this is a depth of condescending love that the most inspired mind must utterly fail to fathom. Herein is love! Truly it is love that *"passeth knowledge."* Oh, let this love fill our hearts with adoring gratitude and lead us to practical manifestations of its power.

I will accept you with your sweet savour.
—Ezekiel 20:41

The merits of our great Redeemer are a sweet savor to the Most High. Whether we speak of the active or passive righteousness of Christ, there is an equal fragrance. There was a sweet aroma in His active life by which He honored the law of God. He made every precept glitter like a precious jewel in the pure setting of His own person. In His passive obedience, with unmurmuring submission, He endured hunger and thirst, cold and nakedness. He sweat great drops of blood in Gethsemane, gave His back to the smiters, and His cheeks to those who plucked out His hair. Then He was nailed to the cruel cross so that He might suffer the wrath of God on our behalf. These things are sweet before the Most High. Because of the way that He lived and the way that He died, because of His substitutionary sufferings and His vicarious obedience, the Lord our God accepts us. What a preciousness there is in Him to overcome our lack of preciousness! What a sweet fragrance to remove our bad aroma! What a cleansing power in His blood to take away sin such as ours! What glory in His righteousness to make such unacceptable creatures be *"accepted in the beloved"* (Eph. 1:6)! Believer, how sure and unchanging our acceptance must be since it is in Him! Never doubt your acceptance in Jesus. You cannot be accepted without Christ; but when you have received His merit, you cannot be unaccepted. Despite all your doubts, fears, and sins, Jehovah's gracious eye never looks on you in anger. Although He sees sin in you, in yourself, when He looks at you through Christ, He sees no sin. You are always accepted in Christ and are always blessed and dear to the Father's heart. Therefore, lift up a song, and as you see the smoking incense of the merit of the Savior rising before the sapphire throne, let the incense of your praise rise also.

Though he were a Son, yet learned he obedience
by the things which he suffered.
—Hebrews 5:8

We are told that the Captain of our salvation was made perfect through suffering; therefore, we who are sinful, and who are far from being perfect, must not wonder if we are called to pass through suffering, too. Will the Head be crowned with thorns, and will the other members of the body be rocked on the dainty lap of ease? Must Christ pass through seas of His own blood to win the crown, and are we to walk to heaven in silver slippers that stay dry? No, our Master's experience teaches us that suffering is necessary, and the true-born child of God must not, would not, escape it if he could. But there is one very comforting thought in the fact of Christ's *"being made perfect"* (Heb. 5:9) *"by the things which he suffered."* It is that He can have complete sympathy with us. He is not *"an high priest which cannot be touched with the feeling of our infirmities"* (Heb. 4:15). In this sympathy of Christ we find a sustaining power. One of the early martyrs said, "I can bear it all, for Jesus suffered, and He suffers in me now. He sympathizes with me, and this makes me strong." Believer, lay hold of this thought in all times of agony. Let the thought of Jesus strengthen you as you follow in His steps. Find a sweet support in His sympathy. Remember that to suffer is an honorable thing; to suffer for Christ is glory. The apostles rejoiced that they were counted worthy to do this. Just so far as the Lord will give us grace to suffer *for* Christ, to suffer *with* Christ, just so far does He honor us. The jewels of a Christian are his afflictions. The regalia of the kings whom God has anointed are their troubles, their sorrows, and their grief. Let us not, therefore, shun being honored. Let us not turn aside from being exalted. Grief exalt us, and troubles lift us up. *"If we suffer, we shall also reign with him"* (2 Tim. 2:12).

I called him, but he gave me no answer.
—Song of Solomon 5:6

Prayer sometimes waits like a petitioner at the gate until the King comes forth to fill the heart with the blessings that it seeks. The Lord, when He has given great faith, has been known to try it by long delays. He has permitted His servants' voices to echo in their ears as from a brazen sky. They have knocked at the golden gate, but it has remained immovable, as though it were rusted on its hinges. Like Jeremiah, they have cried, "*Thou hast covered thyself with a cloud, that our prayer should not pass through*" (Lam. 3:44). Thus have true saints continued for a long time in patient waiting without receiving a reply. This was not because their prayers were not intense or because they were unaccepted; it was because God who is a Sovereign gives according to His own pleasure. If it pleases Him for our patience to be exercised, He will do as He desires with His own! Beggars must not be choosers regarding the time, place, or form of their answers. But we must be careful not to mistake delays in prayer as denials. God's long-dated bills will be punctually honored. We must not allow Satan to shake our confidence in the God of truth by pointing to our unanswered prayers. Unanswered petitions are not unheard. God keeps a file for our prayers; they are not blown away by the wind but are treasured in the King's archives. There is a registry in the court of heaven in which every prayer is recorded. Tried believer, your Lord has a tear-bottle in which the costly drops of sacred grief are stored and a book in which your holy groanings are numbered. In due time, your suit will prevail. Can you not be content to wait a little? Will not your Lord's time be better than your time? Soon He will appear, to your soul's joy, and make you put away the sackcloth and ashes of long waiting. He will clothe you with the scarlet and fine linen of your heart's desire.

He was numbered with the transgressors.
—Isaiah 53:12

Why did Jesus permit Himself to be included with sinners? This wonderful condescension was justified by many powerful reasons. In such a character He could better become their Advocate. In some trials there is an identification of the counselor with the client. They cannot be looked upon in the eyes of the law as separate from one another. Now, when the sinner is brought to the bar, Jesus appears there Himself. He stands to answer the accusation. He points to His side, His hands, His feet, and He challenges Justice to bring anything against the sinners whom He represents. He pleads His blood, and pleads so triumphantly, being numbered with them and having a part with them, that the Judge proclaims, "Let them go their way. *'Deliver* [them] *from going down to the pit:* [He has] *found a ransom'* (Job 33:24)." Our Lord Jesus was numbered with the transgressors in order that they might feel their hearts drawn toward Him. Who can be afraid of one who is written in the same list with us? Surely we may come boldly to Him and confess our guilt. He who is numbered with us cannot condemn us. Was He not put down in the transgressor's list that we might be written in the red roll of the saints? He was holy, and written among the holy; we were guilty, and numbered among the guilty. He transferred His name from the holy list to this black indictment, and our names were taken from the indictment and written in the roll of acceptance, for there is a complete transfer made between Jesus and His people. All our estate of misery and sin Jesus has taken, and all that Jesus has comes to us. His righteousness, His blood, and everything that He has He gives to us as our dowry. Rejoice, believer, in your union to Him who was numbered among the transgressors. Prove that you are truly saved by being manifestly numbered with those who are *"new creature[s]"* (2 Cor. 5:17) in Him.

Let us search and try our ways, and turn again to the LORD.
—Lamentations 3:40

The spouse who loves her absent husband longs for his return. A protracted separation from her spouse causes a partial death to her spirit. It is the same with souls who love the Savior. They must see His face. They cannot bear that He should be away and not be in fellowship with them. A disapproving glance or an uplifted finger is grievous to loving children who never want to offend their tender father; they are happy only when they see his smile. Beloved, it was the same with you at one time. A Scripture, a correction, a touch of the rod of affliction, and you went to your Father's feet, crying, "Show me why You are angry with me." Is it so now? Are you content to follow Jesus from a distance? Can you contemplate ending your communion with Christ without alarm? Can you bear to have your Beloved walking contrary to you because you are walking contrary to Him? Have your sins separated you and your God, and is your heart at rest? Let me warn you in kindness: it is a grievous thing when we can live contentedly without the present enjoyment of the Savior's face. Let us realize what an evil thing it is to have little love for our own dying Savior, little joy in our precious Jesus, little fellowship with the Beloved! Hold a true Lent in your souls, while you sorrow over your hardness of heart. But do not stop with sorrow! Remember where you first received salvation. Go at once to the cross. There, and only there, can your spirit be made alive. No matter how hard, how unfeeling, how dead we may have become, let us go again in all our rags and poverty and defilement of our natural condition. Let us clasp that cross and look into His eyes. Let us bathe in that fountain filled with blood. Then we will have our first love restored to us. Once again we will experience the simplicity of our faith and the tenderness of our hearts.

With his stripes we are healed.
—Isaiah 53:5

Pilate delivered our Lord to the Roman officers to be scourged. The Roman scourge was a most dreadful instrument of torture. It was made of the sinews of oxen. Sharp bones were intertwined here and there among the sinews, so that every time the lash came down, pieces of bone inflicted fearful lacerations and tore the flesh from the bone. The Savior was, no doubt, bound to the column, and thus beaten. He had been beaten before, but this beating by the Roman soldiers was probably the severest of His flagellations. My soul, stand here and weep over His poor stricken body. Believer in Jesus, can you gaze on Him without tears, as He stands before you the image of agonizing love? He is at once fair as the lily for innocence and red as the rose with the crimson of His own blood. As we feel the sure and blessed healing that His stripes have worked in us, do not our hearts melt at once with love and grief? If ever we have loved our Lord Jesus, surely we must feel that affection glowing now within our hearts.

> See how the patient Jesus stands,
>> Insulted in His lowest case!
> Sinners have bound the Almighty's hands,
>> And spit in their Creator's face.
> With thorns His temples gor'd and gash'd
>> Send streams of blood from every part;
> His back's with knotted scourges lash'd.
>> But sharper scourges tear His heart.

We would gladly go to our rooms and weep; but since our business calls us away, we will first pray for our Beloved to print the image of His bleeding self on the tablets of our hearts throughout the day. At nightfall, we will return to commune with Him, and grieve that our sin should have cost Him so much.

And Rizpah the daughter of Aiah took sackcloth, and spread it for
her upon the rock, from the beginning of harvest until water dropped
upon them out of heaven, and suffered neither the birds of the air to
rest on them by day, nor the beasts of the field by night.
—2 Samuel 21:10

If the love of a woman for her slain sons could make her continue her mournful vigil for so long a period, will we grow weary of considering the sufferings of our blessed Lord? Rizpah drove away the birds of prey, and will we not chase from our meditations those worldly and sinful thoughts that defile both our minds and the sacred themes on which we are focused? Away, birds of evil! Leave the sacrifice alone! Unsheltered and alone, Rizpah bore the heat of summer, the night dews, and the rain. Sleep was chased from her weeping eyes: her heart was too full for slumber. Behold how she loved her children! Will Rizpah's example endure, or will we begin to complain at the first little inconvenience or trial? Are we such cowards that we cannot bear to suffer with our Lord? Showing unusual courage, she chased away even the wild beasts. Will we not be ready to encounter every foe for Jesus' sake? Her children were slain by hands other than hers, yet she wept and watched. What should we do who have by our sins crucified our Lord? Our obligations are boundless; our love should be fervent and our repentance thorough. To watch with Jesus should be our business, to protect His honor our occupation, to abide by His cross our solace. Those ghastly corpses might well have frightened Rizpah, especially at night, but in our Lord, at whose cross we are sitting, there is nothing revolting, but everything attractive. Never was living beauty so enchanting as in our dying Savior. Jesus, we will watch with You. Graciously reveal Yourself to us. Then we will not sit in sackcloth, but in a royal pavilion.

Let him kiss me with the kisses of his mouth.
—Song of Solomon 1:2

For several days we have been dwelling on the Savior's passion, and for some little time to come we will linger there. In beginning a new month, let us seek the same desires after our Lord as those that glowed in the heart of the elect spouse. See how she leaps at once to Him; there are no prefatory words; she does not even mention His name; she is in the heart of her theme at once, for she speaks of Him who was the only *"him"* in the world to her. How bold is her love! It was great condescension that permitted the weeping penitent to anoint His feet with spikenard. It was rich love that allowed the gentle Mary to sit at His feet and learn of Him. But here, love, strong, fervent love, aspires to higher tokens of regard and closer signs of fellowship. Esther trembled in the presence of Ahasuerus, but the spouse in joyful liberty of perfect love knows no fear. If we have received the same free spirit, we also may ask the same. By *"kisses"* we suppose to be intended those varied manifestations of affection by which the believer is made to enjoy the love of Jesus. The kiss of reconciliation we enjoyed at our conversion, and it was sweet as honey dripping from the comb. The kiss of acceptance is still warm on our brow, as we know that He has accepted our persons and our works through rich grace. The kiss of daily, present communion is what we pant after to be repeated day after day, until it is changed into the kiss of reception, which removes the soul from earth, and the kiss of consummation, which fills it with the joy of heaven. Faith is our walk, but fellowship intensely felt is our rest. Faith is the road, but communion with Jesus is the well from which the pilgrim drinks. O Lover of our souls, do not be a stranger to us; let the lips of Your blessing meet the lips of our asking. Let the lips of Your fullness touch the lips of our need, and immediately, we will feel the healing effect of Your kiss.

APRIL 1

Evening

It is time to seek the LORD.
—Hosea 10:12

This month of April is said to derive its name from the Latin verb *aperio*, which means to open. All the buds and blossoms are now opening, and we have arrived at the gates of the flowery season. Reader, if you are yet unsaved, may your heart, in accord with the universal awakening of nature, be opened to receive the Lord. Every blossoming flower warns you that *"it is time to seek the LORD."* Do not be out of tune with nature, but let your heart bud and bloom with holy desires. Do you tell me that the warm blood of youth leaps in your veins? Then I entreat you, give your vigor to the Lord. It was my unspeakable happiness to be called in early youth, and I could gladly praise the Lord for it every day. Salvation is priceless; let it come when it may, but oh, an early salvation has a double value in it. Young men and women, since you may perish before you reach your prime, now is the time to seek the Lord. You who are experiencing the first signs of aging, quicken your pace. That hollow cough and hectic flush are warnings that you must not take lightly. It is indeed *"time to seek the LORD."* Did I observe a little gray mingled with your once luxurious, dark tresses? Years are swiftly passing, and death is drawing nearer with its hasty march. Let each return of spring inspire you to set your house in order. Dear reader, if you are now advanced in age, let me entreat and implore you to delay no longer. There is a day of grace for you now—be thankful for that, but it is a limited season and grows shorter every time the clock ticks. Here in your silent room, on this first night of another month, I speak to you as best I can by paper and ink. From my inmost soul, as God's servant, I lay before you this warning, *"It is time to seek the LORD."* Do not neglect that work. It may be your last call from destruction, the final syllable from the lips of grace.

He answered him to never a word.
—Matthew 27:14

He was never slow of speech when He could bless the sons of men, but He would not say a single word for Himself. *"Never man spake like this man"* (John 7:46), and never was any man silent like Him. Was this singular silence the indication of His perfect self-sacrifice? Did it show that He would not utter a word to stop the slaughter of His sacred person, which He had dedicated as an offering for us? Had He so entirely surrendered Himself that He would not interfere in His own behalf, even in the minutest degree, but be bound and slain a submissive, uncomplaining victim? Was this silence a type of the defenselessness of sin? Nothing can be said to lessen or excuse human guilt; therefore, He who bore its whole weight stood speechless before His judge. Is not patient silence the best reply to a contentious world? Calm endurance answers some questions infinitely more conclusively than the loftiest eloquence. The best apologists for Christianity in the early days were its martyrs. The anvil breaks a host of hammers by quietly bearing their blows. Did not the silent Lamb of God furnish us with a grand example of wisdom? Where every word was occasion for new blasphemy, it was the line of duty to afford no fuel for the flame of sin. The ambiguous and the false, the unworthy and the contemptible, will before long overthrow and destroy themselves; therefore, the true can afford to be quiet and find silence to be their wisdom. Evidently our Lord, by His silence, furnished a remarkable fulfillment of prophecy. A long defense of Himself would have been contrary to Isaiah's prediction. *"He is brought as a lamb to the slaughter, and as a sheep before her shearers is dumb, so he openeth not his mouth"* (Isa. 53:7). By His quiet, He conclusively proved Himself to be the true Lamb of God. As such we salute Him this morning. Be with us, Jesus, and in the silence of our hearts, let us hear the voice of Your love.

He shall see his seed, he shall prolong his days, and the pleasure
of the LORD shall prosper in his hand.
—Isaiah 53:10

All you who love the Lord, plead for the speedy fulfillment of the promise of today's text. It is easy work to pray when our desires are grounded in and based on God's own promise. How can He who gave the Word refuse to keep it? Unchangeable truth cannot demean itself by a lie, and eternal faithfulness cannot degrade itself by neglect. God must bless His Son; His covenant binds Him to it. What the Spirit prompts us to ask from Jesus is that which God decrees to give to Him. Whenever you are praying for the kingdom of Christ, let your eyes behold the dawning of the blessed day that is drawing near, when the Crucified One will receive His crown in the place where men rejected Him. Be encouraged, you who prayerfully work and toil for Christ with little apparent success. It will not always be so. Better times are ahead for you. Your eyes cannot see the blissful future. Borrow the telescope of faith, wipe the misty breath of your doubts from the glass, look through it, and see the coming glory. Reader, do you make this your constant prayer? Remember that the same Christ who told us to say, *"Give us this day our daily bread"* (Matt. 6:11), first gave us this petition: *"Hallowed be thy name. Thy kingdom come. Thy will be done in earth, as it is in heaven"* (vv. 9–10). Do not let your prayers be all about your own sins, your own needs, your own imperfections, or your own trials. Instead, let them climb the starry ladder and reach Christ Himself. Then, as you draw near to the blood-sprinkled mercy seat, offer this prayer continually: "Lord, extend the kingdom of Your dear Son." Such a petition, fervently presented, will elevate the spirit of all your devotions. Remember that you prove the sincerity of your prayer by working to promote the Lord's glory.

They took Jesus, and led him away.
—John 19:16

He had been in agony all night. After spending the early morning at the hall of Caiaphas, He had been hurried from Caiaphas to Pilate, from Pilate to Herod, and from Herod back again to Pilate. He had, therefore, but little strength left, and yet neither refreshment nor rest were permitted Him. They were eager for His blood, so they led Him out to die, bearing the weight of the cross. O heartbreaking procession! Well may the daughters of peace weep. My soul, weep also. What do we learn here as we see our blessed Lord led forth? Do we not perceive that truth that was foreshadowed by the scapegoat? Did not the high priest bring the scapegoat and put both his hands on its head, confessing the sins of the people, so that those sins might be laid on the goat and be removed from the people? Then the man selected to lead the goat took it into the wilderness, and it carried away the sins of the people, so that if they were sought for, they could not be found. Now we see Jesus brought before the priests and rulers, who pronounce Him guilty. God Himself places the blame for our sins on Him: "The Lord *hath laid on him the iniquity of us all*" (Isa. 53:6); "*He hath made him to be sin for us*" (2 Cor. 5:21). As the substitute for our guilt, bearing our sin—represented by the cross—on His shoulders, the great Scapegoat was led away by the appointed officers of justice. Beloved, can you feel assured that He carried *your* sin? As you look at the cross on His shoulders, does it represent *your* sin? There is one way by which you can tell whether He carried your sin or not. Have you laid your hand on His head, confessed your sin, and trusted in Him? Then your sin no longer lies on you; it has all been transferred by blessed imputation to Christ, and He bears it on His shoulder as a load heavier than the cross. Do not let the picture vanish until you have rejoiced in your own deliverance and adored the loving Redeemer on whom your iniquities were laid.

APRIL 3
Evening

All we like sheep have gone astray; we have turned every one to his own way; and the LORD hath laid on him the iniquity of us all.
—Isaiah 53:6

This confession of sin is common to all the elect people of God. We have all fallen; therefore, in common chorus, from the first who entered heaven to the last who will enter there, we can all say, *"All we like sheep have gone astray."* The confession, while unanimous, is also unique and individual: *"We have turned every one to his own way."* There is a particular sinfulness about every person. All are sinful, but each one has some special aggravation not found in others. It is the mark of genuine repentance that it naturally associates itself with other penitents, but it also takes up a position of individuality. *"We have turned every one to his own way"* is a confession that each person has sinned against light in a way unique to himself or sinned with an intensity that he does not perceive in others. This confession is also unreserved. There is not a word to detract from its force or a syllable by way of excuse. The confession is a giving up of all pleas of self-righteousness. It is the declaration of those who are consciously guilty—guilty with severity, guilty without excuse. They stand with their weapons of rebellion broken in pieces and cry, *"All we like sheep have gone astray; we have turned every one to his own way."* Yet we hear no mournful wailing attending this confession of sin, for the next sentence makes it almost a song: *"The LORD hath laid on him the iniquity of us all."* It is the most grievous sentence of the three, but it overflows with comfort. It is strange that where misery was con-centrated, mercy reigned; where sorrow reached her climax, weary souls find rest. The bruised Savior is the Healer of bruised hearts. See how the lowliest repentance gives place to assured confidence through simply gazing at Christ on the cross!

For he hath made him to be sin for us, who knew no sin; that we
might be made the righteousness of God in him.
—2 Corinthians 5:21

Mourning Christian, why do you weep? Are you mourning over your own corruption? Look to your perfect Lord, and remember, you are complete in Him. In God's sight, you are as perfect as if you had never sinned; no, more than that, the Lord our Righteousness has put a divine garment on you, so that you have more than the righteousness of man—you have the righteousness of God! Oh, you who are mourning by reason of inbred sin and depravity, remember, none of your sins can condemn you. You have learned to hate sin, but you have also learned to know that your sin is not yours: it was laid on Christ's head. Your standing is not in yourself: it is in Christ. Your acceptance is not in yourself, but in your Lord. You are as much accepted by God today, with all your sinfulness, as you will be when you stand before His throne, free from all corruption.

Oh, I beseech you, lay hold of this precious thought of perfection in Christ! For you are *"complete in him"* (Col. 2:10). With your Savior's garment on, you are holy as the Holy One is holy. *"Who is he that condemneth? It is Christ that died, yea rather, that is risen again, who is even at the right hand of God, who also maketh intercession for us"* (Rom. 8:34). Christian, let your heart rejoice, for you are *"accepted in the beloved"* (Eph. 1:6). What do you have to fear? Let your face always wear a smile. Live close to your Master. Live in the suburbs of the Celestial City. Soon, when your time comes, you will rise up where your Jesus sits and reign at His right hand. All this will occur because the divine Lord was made *"to be sin for us, who knew no sin; that we might be made the righteousness of God in him."*

APRIL 4

Evening

Come ye, and let us go up to the mountain of the LORD.
—Isaiah 2:3

It is exceedingly beneficial to our souls to rise above this present evil world to something nobler and better. The cares of this world and the deceitfulness of riches are likely to choke everything that is good within us and cause us to grow fretful, despondent, and perhaps proud and carnal. It is good for us to cut down these thorns and briers, for heavenly seed sown among them is not likely to yield a harvest. Where will we find a better sickle with which to cut them down than communion with God and the things of the kingdom? In the valleys of Switzerland, many of the inhabitants become sickly because the air is close and stagnant; but up yonder, on the mountains, you find a hardy race, who breathe the clear, fresh air as it blows from the virgin snows of the Alpine summits. It would be good if those who live in the valley could frequently leave their homes among the marshes and the fever mists and inhale the bracing mountain air. It is to such an exploit of climbing that I invite you this evening. May the Spirit of God assist us to leave the mists of fear and the fevers of anxiety and all the ills that gather in this valley of earth. Let us ascend the mountains of anticipated joy and blessedness. May God the Holy Spirit cut the cords that keep us here below and assist us to climb! Too often, we sit like chained eagles fastened to the rock. Unlike the eagle, though, we begin to love our chain and would, perhaps, if it really came to the test, loathe to have it snapped. May God grant us grace so that, if we cannot escape from the chains of our flesh, He would enable our spirits to be set free. Leaving our fleshly bodies behind, like Abraham left behind his servants when he was called to offer Isaac as a sacrifice, may our souls reach the top of the mountain. May we there enjoy communion with the Most High.

On him they laid the cross, that he might bear it after Jesus.
—Luke 23:26

We see in Simon's carrying the cross a picture of the work of the church throughout all generations; she is the cross-bearer for Jesus. Mark, then, Christian: Jesus does not suffer so as to exclude your suffering. He bears a cross, not that you may escape it, but that you may endure it. Christ exempts you from sin, but not from sorrow. Remember that, and expect to suffer. But let us comfort ourselves with this thought: that in our case, as in Simon's, it is not *our* cross, but *Christ's* cross that we carry. When you are molested for your piety or when your religion brings the trial of cruel ridicule on you, then remember that it is not *your* cross, but it is *Christ's* cross. How delightful it is to carry the cross of our Lord Jesus! You carry the cross after Him. You have blessed company; your path is marked with the footprints of your Lord. The mark of His bloodred shoulder is on that heavy burden. It is *His* cross, and He goes before you as a shepherd goes before his sheep. Take up your cross daily, and follow Him. Do not forget, also, that you bear this cross in partnership. It is the opinion of some that Simon carried only one end of the cross, and not the whole of it. That is very possible; Christ may have carried the heavier part, against the transverse beam, and Simon may have borne the lighter end. Certainly it is so with you. You carry only the light end of the cross; Christ bore the heavier end. And remember that although Simon had to bear the cross for a very little while, it gave him lasting honor. Even so the cross we carry is only for a little while at most, and then, we will receive the crown, the glory. Surely we should love the cross, and, instead of shrinking from it, count it very costly, when it works out for us *"a far more exceeding and eternal weight of glory"* (2 Cor. 4:17).

Before honour is humility.
—Proverbs 15:33

Humiliation of soul always brings a blessing with it. If we empty our hearts of self, God will fill them with His love. He who desires close communion with Christ should remember the word of the Lord, *"To this man will I look, even to him that is poor and of a contrite spirit, and trembleth at my word"* (Isa. 66:2). If you would climb to heaven, stoop. Do we not say of Jesus, "He descended so that He might ascend"? So must you. You must grow downward so that you may grow upward, for the sweetest fellowship with heaven is to be had by humble souls, and by them alone. God will deny no blessing to a thoroughly humbled spirit. *"Blessed are the poor in spirit: for theirs is the kingdom of heaven"* (Matt. 5:3), which includes all of its riches and treasures. The whole treasury of God will be given as a gift to the soul that is humble enough to be able to receive it without growing proud because of it. God blesses us all up to the full measure and extremity that it is safe for Him to do so. If you do not receive a blessing, it is because it is not safe for you to have one. If our heavenly Father were to let your unhumbled spirit win a victory in His holy war, you would steal the crown for yourself; meeting with a new enemy, you would fall a victim. So you are kept low for your own safety. When a man is sincerely humble and never ventures to touch as much as a grain of the praise, there is scarcely any limit to what God will do for him. Humility makes us ready to be blessed by the God of all grace and equips us to deal efficiently with our fellowmen. True humility is a flower that will adorn any garden. This is a sauce with which you may season every dish of life, and you will find an improvement in every case. Whether it is in prayer or praise or in work or suffering, the genuine salt of humility cannot be used in excess.

Let us go forth therefore unto him without the camp.
—Hebrews 13:13

Jesus, bearing His cross, went forth to suffer without the gate. The Christian's reason for leaving the camp of the world's sin and religion is not that he loves to be an individual, but because Jesus did so, and the disciple must follow his Master. Christ was *"not of the world"* (John 17:14). His life and His testimony were a constant protest against conformity with the world. Never did such overflowing affection for men exist as you find in Him, but still He was separate from sinners. Likewise, Christ's people must *"go forth...unto him."* They must take their position *"without the camp,"* as witness-bearers for the truth. They must be prepared to tread the straight and narrow path. They must have bold, unflinching, lionlike hearts, loving Christ first, and His truth next, and Christ and His truth above all the world. Jesus would have His people *"go forth...without the camp"* for their own sanctification. You cannot grow in grace to any great degree while you are conformed to the world. The life of separation may be a path of sorrow, but it is the highway of safety. And though the separated life may cost you many pangs and make every day a battle, yet it is a happy life after all. No joy can excel that of the soldier of Christ. Jesus reveals Himself so graciously and gives such sweet refreshment that the warrior feels more calm and peace in his daily strife than others feel in their hours of rest. The highway of holiness is the highway of communion. It is thus that we will hope to win the crown if we are enabled by divine grace faithfully to follow Christ *"without the camp."* The crown of glory will follow the cross of separation. A moment's shame will be well recompensed by eternal honor; a little while of witness-bearing will seem nothing when we are forever *"with the Lord"* (1 Thess. 4:17).

In the name of the Lord I will destroy them.
—Psalm 118:12

Our Lord Jesus, by His death, did not purchase a right to only a part of us, but to our entire being. In His crucifixion and death, He contemplated our entire sanctification—spirit, soul, and body—so that in this triple kingdom, He Himself might reign supreme without a rival. It is the business of the newborn nature that God has given to the regenerated to assert the rights of the Lord Jesus Christ. My soul, since you are a child of God, you must conquer each part of yourself that is not submitted to Christ; you must surrender all your powers and passions to the silver scepter of Jesus' gracious reign. You must never be satisfied until He who is King by purchase becomes King by gracious coronation and reigns supreme in your life. Seeing then that sin has no right to any part of us, we go about a good and lawful warfare when we seek, in the name of God, to drive it out. My body, you are a member of Christ. Will you tolerate your subjection to the prince of darkness? My soul, Christ has suffered for your sins and redeemed you with His most precious blood. Will you permit your memory to become a storehouse of evil or your passions to be firebrands of iniquity? Will you surrender your judgment to be perverted by error or your will to be chained by sin? No, my soul, you are Christ's, and sin has no right to you. Be courageous concerning this, Christian! Do not be discouraged as though your spiritual enemies could never be destroyed. You are able to overcome them, though not in your own strength; the weakest of them would be too much for you in that. But you can and will overcome them through the blood of the Lamb. Do not ask, "How will I banish them, for they are greater and mightier than I?" but go to the strong for strength, wait humbly on God, and the mighty God of Jacob will surely come to your rescue. Then you will sing of victory through His grace.

O ye sons of men, how long will ye turn my glory into shame?
—Psalm 4:2

An instructive writer has made a sad list of the honors that the blinded people of Israel awarded to their long-expected King. First, they gave Him a procession of honor, in which Roman legionaries, Jewish priests, men, and women took part, He Himself bearing His cross. This is the triumph that the world awards to Him who comes to overthrow man's direst foes. Derisive shouts are His only acclamations and cruel taunts His only tributes of praise. Next, they presented Him with the wine of honor. Instead of a golden cup of generous wine, they offered Him the criminal's stupefying death-draught, which He refused because He would preserve an uninjured taste wherewith to taste of death. Afterward, when He cried, *"I thirst"* (John 19:28), they gave Him vinegar mixed with gall, thrust to His mouth on a sponge. Oh, wretched, detestable inhospitality to the King's Son. Third, He was provided with a guard of honor, who showed their esteem of Him by gambling over His garments, which they had seized as their booty. Such was the bodyguard of the adored of heaven—a quartet of brutal gamblers. Then a throne of honor was found for Him on the bloody tree; no easier place of rest would rebellious men yield to their faithful Lord. The cross was, in fact, the full expression of the world's feeling toward Him. "There," they seemed to say, "Son of God, this is the manner in which God Himself should be treated, could we reach Him." Finally, the title of honor was nominally "King of the Jews," but that the blinded nation distinctly repudiated, and really called Him "King of thieves," by preferring Barabbas, and by placing Jesus in the place of highest shame between two thieves. His glory was thus in all things turned into shame by the sons of men, but it will yet gladden the eyes of saints and angels, world without end.

Deliver me from bloodguiltiness, O God, thou God of my salvation:
and my tongue shall sing aloud of thy righteousness.
—Psalm 51:14

In this solemn confession, it is pleasing to observe that David plainly named his sin. He did not call it manslaughter or speak of it as an indiscretion by which an unfortunate accident occurred to a worthy man, but he called it by its true name, bloodguiltiness. He did not actually kill the husband of Bathsheba, but he planned in his heart that Uriah should be slain; therefore, he stood before the Lord as a murderer. Learn in confession to be honest with God. Do not give fair names to foul sins; call them what you will, they will smell no sweeter. See your sins as God sees them; with all openness of heart, acknowledge their real character. Observe that David was evidently oppressed with the heinousness of his sin. It is easy to use words, but it is harder to feel their meaning. The Fifty-first Psalm is the portrait of a contrite spirit. Let us seek to have the same brokenness of heart; for however excellent our words may be, if our hearts are not conscious that we are deserving of hell because of our sins, we cannot expect to find forgiveness. Our text has in it an earnest prayer that is addressed to the God of salvation. It is His prerogative to forgive; it is His very name and nature to save those who seek His face. Better still, the text calls Him the "*God of my salvation*" (emphasis added). Yes, blessed is His name! While I am continuing to go to Him through Jesus' blood, I can rejoice in the "*God of my salvation.*" The psalmist ended with a commendable vow: if God would deliver him, he would sing—no, more than that, he would "*sing aloud.*" Who can sing in any other style in the face of such great mercy! But notice the subject of the song: God's righteousness. We must sing of the finished work of a precious Savior; and he who knows the most of forgiving love will sing the loudest.

If they do these things in a green tree, what shall be done in the dry?
—Luke 23:31

Among other interpretations of this suggestive question, the following is full of teaching: "If Christ, the innocent Substitute for sinners, suffered as He did, what will be done when the sinner himself—the dry tree—falls into the hands of an angry God?" When God saw Jesus in the sinner's place, He did not spare Him; and when He finds the unregenerate without Christ, He will not spare them. O sinner, Jesus was led away by His enemies; so will you be dragged away by fiends to the place appointed for you. Jesus was deserted by God; and if He, who was only a sinner because He carried our sins, was deserted, how much more will you be? *"Eloi, Eloi, lama sabachthani"* (Mark 15:34)—what an awful shriek! But what will your cry be when you will say, "O God! O God! why have You forsaken me?" and the answer will come back, *"Ye have set at nought all my counsel, and would none of my reproof: I also will laugh at your calamity; I will mock when your fear cometh"* (Prov. 1:25–26). If God *"spared not his own Son"* (Rom. 8:32), how much less will He spare you! What whips of burning wire will be yours when your conscience smites you with all its terrors? You richest, merriest, most self-righteous sinners—who would want to stand in your place when God will say, "Awake, O sword, against the man who rejected Me; smite him, and let him feel the pain forever"? Jesus was spit on; sinner, what shame will be yours! We cannot sum up in one word all the mass of sorrows that met on the head of Jesus who died for us; therefore, it is impossible for us to tell you what streams, what oceans of grief, must roll over your spirit if you die as you are now. You may die so; you may die now. By the agonies of Christ, by His wounds and by His blood, do not bring on yourselves the wrath to come! Trust in the Son of God, and you will never die.

I will fear no evil: for thou art with me.
—Psalm 23:4

How independent of outward circumstances the Holy Spirit can make the Christian! What a bright light may shine within us when it is all dark without! How firm, how happy, how calm, how peaceful we may be, when the world shakes to and fro and the pillars of the earth are removed! Even death itself, with all its terrible influences, has no power to suspend the music of a Christian's heart. Instead, it makes that music become sweeter, clearer, and more heavenly, until the last kind act that death can do is to let the earthly strain melt into the heavenly chorus, the earthly joy into eternal bliss! Let us have confidence, then, in the blessed Spirit's power to comfort us. Dear reader, are you facing poverty? Do not fear; the divine Spirit can give you, in your need, a greater abundance than the rich have in their wealth. You do not know what joys may be stored up for you in the cottage around which grace will plant the roses of content. Are you conscious of a growing failure of your bodily powers? Do you expect to suffer long nights of languishing and days of pain? Oh, do not be sad! That bed may become a throne to you. Little do you know how every pang that shoots through your body may be a refining fire to consume your dross—a beam of glory to light up the secret parts of your soul. Are your eyes growing dim? Jesus will be your light. Do your ears fail you? Jesus' name will be your soul's best music, and His person your dear delight. Socrates said, "Philosophers can be happy without music." Christians can be happier than philosophers when all outward causes of rejoicing are withdrawn. In You, my God, my heart will triumph, come what may of troubles without! By Your power, O blessed Spirit, my heart will be exceedingly glad, though all things fail me here below.

There followed him a great company of people, and of women,
which also bewailed and lamented him.
—Luke 23:27

Amid the mob that hounded the Redeemer to His doom, there were some gracious souls whose bitter anguish sought expression in wailing and crying. What fit music to accompany that march of woe! When my soul can, in imagination, see the Savior bearing His cross to Calvary, it joins the godly women and weeps with them; for, indeed, there is true cause for grief, a cause that lies deeper than those mourning women thought. They bewailed innocence maltreated, goodness persecuted, love bleeding, meekness about to die; but my heart has a deeper and more bitter cause to mourn. My sins were the scourges that lacerated those blessed shoulders and crowned with thorns those bleeding brows. My sins cried, "Crucify Him! Crucify Him!" and laid the cross on His gracious shoulders. His being led forth to die is sorrow enough for one eternity, but my having been His murderer is more, infinitely more, grief than one poor fountain of tears can express. Why those women loved and wept is not hard to guess, but they could not have had greater reasons for love and grief than my heart has. Nain's widow saw her son restored, but I myself have been raised to newness of life. Peter's wife's mother was cured of the fever, but I have been cured of the greater plague of sin. Out of Mary Magdalene seven devils were cast, but a whole legion have been cast out of me. Mary and Martha were favored with visits, but He dwells with me. His mother bare His body, but He has formed in me the hope of glory. In nothing behind the holy women in debt, let me not be behind them in gratitude or sorrow.

> Love and grief my heart dividing,
>   With my tears His feet I'll lave—
> Constant still in heart abiding,
>   Weep for Him who died to save.

Thy gentleness hath made me great.
—Psalm 18:35

These words may be translated, "Thy goodness hath made me great." David gratefully ascribed all his personal greatness not to his own goodness but to the goodness of God. "Thy providence" is another reading, and providence is nothing more than goodness in action. Goodness is the bud, and providence is the flower; goodness is the seed, and providence is the harvest. Some render it, "Thy help," which is another word for providence. Providence is the firm ally of the saints, aiding them in the service of their Lord. Two other renderings are, "Thy humility" and "Thy condescension hath made me great." The word *condescension* combines the ideas mentioned so far, including that of humility. The verse means that God's humbling of Himself is the cause of our being made great. We are so little that if God would manifest His greatness without reaching out to us in love, we would be trampled under His feet. But God, who must stoop to view the skies and bow to see what angels do, lowers His eyes even further to look at the lowly and contrite and make them great. There are yet other translations. For instance, the Septuagint reads, "Thy discipline"—His fatherly correction—"hath made me great." The Chaldee paraphrase reads, "Thy word hath increased me." The idea remains the same. David ascribed all his own greatness to the loving goodness of his Father in heaven. May this sentiment be echoed in our hearts this evening while we cast our crowns at Jesus' feet and cry, "*Thy gentleness hath made me great.*" How marvelous our experience of God's gentleness has been! How gentle are His corrections! How gentle His forbearance! How gentle His teachings! How gentle His entreaties! Meditate on this theme, believer. Let gratitude be awakened, let humility be deepened, and let love be rekindled before you fall asleep tonight.

The place, which is called Calvary.
—Luke 23:33

The hill of comfort is the hill of Calvary; the house of consolation is built with the wood of the cross; the temple of heavenly blessing is founded on the shattered rock—split open by the spear that pierced His side. No scene in sacred history ever gladdens the soul as Calvary's tragedy does.

> Is it not strange, the darkest hour
>   That ever dawned on sinful earth
> Should touch the heart with softer power
>   For comfort than an angel's mirth?
> That to the cross the mourner's eye should turn
>   Sooner than where the stars of Bethlehem burn?

Light springs from the midday-midnight of Golgotha, and every herb of the field blooms sweetly beneath the shadow of the once accursed tree. In that place of thirst, grace has dug a fountain that ever gushes with waters pure as crystal, each drop capable of alleviating the woes of mankind. You who have had your seasons of conflict will confess that it was not at Olivet that you ever found comfort, not on the hill of Sinai, nor on Tabor; but Gethsemane, Gabbatha, and Golgotha have been a means of comfort to you. The bitter herbs of Gethsemane have often taken away the bitterness of your life, the scourge of Gabbatha has often scourged away your cares, and the groans of Calvary yield us comfort rare and rich. We never would have known Christ's love in all its heights and depths if He had not died; nor could we guess the Father's deep affection if He had not given His Son to die. The common mercies we enjoy all sing of love, just as the seashell, when we put it to our ears, whispers of the deep sea from whence it came; but if we desire to hear the ocean itself, we must not look at everyday blessings, but at the transactions of the Crucifixion. He who desires to know love, let him retire to Calvary and see the Man of Sorrows die.

For there stood by me this night the angel of God.
—Acts 27:23

Storms and long darkness, coupled with imminent risk of shipwreck, had brought the crew of the vessel into a sad situation. One man alone among them remained perfectly calm, and, by his word, the rest were reassured. Paul was the only man who had heart enough to say, *"Sirs, be of good cheer"* (Acts 27:25). Veteran Roman soldiers and brave old mariners were on board, yet their poor Jewish prisoner had more spirit than they had combined. He had a secret Friend who kept his courage up. The Lord Jesus dispatched a heavenly messenger to whisper words of consolation in the ear of His faithful servant; therefore, Paul wore a shining countenance and spoke like a man at ease. If we fear the Lord, we may look for timely interventions when our circumstances are at their worst. Angels are not kept from us by storms or hindered by darkness. They do not consider it a humiliation to visit the poorest of the heavenly family. If angels' visits are few and far between during ordinary times, they are frequent in our storm-tossed nights. Friends may abandon us when we are under pressure, but our encounters with the inhabitants of the angelic world will be more abundant. In the strength of their encouraging words, brought to us from the throne by way of Jacob's ladder, we will be strong to do great things for God. Dear reader, is this an hour of distress for you? Then ask for special help. Jesus is the Angel of the covenant, and if His presence is earnestly sought, it will not be denied. Those who, like Paul, have had the angel of God standing by them throughout a night of storm, when anchors would no longer hold and rocks were close at hand, remember what that presence brings in heart-cheer.

O angel of my God, be near,
　Amid the darkness, hush my fear;
Loud roars the wild tempestuous sea,
　Your presence, Lord, shall comfort me.

I am poured out like water, and all my bones are out of joint.
—Psalm 22:14

Did earth or heaven ever behold a sadder spectacle of woe? In soul and body, our Lord felt Himself to be weak as water poured on the ground. The placing of the cross in its socket had shaken Him with great violence, had strained all the ligaments, pained every nerve, and more or less dislocated all His bones. Burdened with His own weight, the majestic Sufferer felt the strain increasing every moment of those six long hours. His sense of faintness and general weakness were overpowering, while to His own consciousness He became nothing but a mass of misery and swooning sickness. When Daniel saw the great vision, he thus described his sensations, *"There remained no strength in me: for my comeliness was turned in me into corruption, and I retained no strength"* (Dan. 10:8). How much more faint must have been our greater Prophet when He saw the dread vision of the wrath of God and felt it in His own soul! To us, sensations such as our Lord endured would have been unbearable, and kind unconsciousness would have come to our rescue; but in His case, He was wounded and felt the sword; He drained the cup and tasted every drop.

> O King of Grief! (a title strange, yet true
>   To Thee of all kings only due,)
> O King of Wounds! how shall I grieve for Thee,
>   Who in all grief preventest me!

As we kneel before our now ascended Savior's throne, let us remember well the way by which He prepared it as a throne of grace for us. Let us in spirit drink of His cup, so that we may be strengthened for our hour of heaviness whenever it may come. In His natural body every member suffered, and so must it be in the spiritual. But as out of all His grief and woes His body came forth uninjured to glory and power, even so will His spiritual body come through the furnace with not so much as the smell of fire on it.

Look upon mine affliction and my pain; and forgive all my sins.
—Psalm 25:18

It is well for us when prayers about our sorrows are linked with pleas concerning our sins—when, being under God's hand, we are not wholly absorbed with our pain, but remember our offenses against God. It is well, also, to take both sorrow and sin to the same place. It was to God that David carried his sorrow, and it was to God that David confessed his sin. Notice that we must take our sorrows to God. You may give even your little sorrows to God, for He counts the hairs of your head; your great sorrows you may commit to Him, for He holds the ocean in the hollow of His hand. Go to Him, whatever your present trouble may be, and you will find Him willing and able to relieve you. But we must take our sins to God, too. We must carry them to the cross so that the blood may fall upon them, to purge away their guilt and to destroy their defiling power. The special lesson of the text is this: in the right spirit, we are to go to the Lord with our sorrows and our sins. Note that all David asked concerning his sorrow was, *"Look upon mine affliction and my pain."* But the next petition is vastly more precise, definite, decided, plain: *"Forgive all my sins."* Many sufferers would have put it, "Remove my affliction and my pain, and look at my sins." But David did not say this. He cried, "Lord, as for my affliction and my pain, I will not dictate to Your wisdom. Lord, look at them. I will leave them to You. I would be glad to have my pain removed, but do as You desire. But as for my sins, Lord, I know what I want to happen to them. I must have them forgiven; I cannot endure to lie under their curse for a moment longer." A Christian considers sorrow to be lighter on the scale than sin; he can bear it if his troubles continue, but he cannot support the burden of his transgressions.

My heart is like wax; it is melted in the midst of my bowels.
—Psalm 22:14

Our blessed Lord experienced a terrible sinking and melting of soul. *"The spirit of a man will sustain his infirmity; but a wounded spirit who can bear?"* (Prov. 18:14). Deep depression of spirit is the most grievous of all trials; all else is as nothing. Well might the suffering Savior cry to His God, *"Be not far from me"* (Ps. 71:12), for above all other seasons a man needs his God when his heart is melted within him because of heaviness. Believer, come near the cross this morning and humbly adore the King of Glory as having once been brought far lower, in mental distress and inward anguish, than anyone among us; and mark His fitness to become a faithful High Priest, who can *"be touched with the feeling of our infirmities"* (Heb. 4:15). Especially let those of us whose sadness springs directly from the withdrawal of a present sense of our Father's love enter into near and intimate communion with Jesus. Let us not give way to despair, since through this dark room the Master has passed before us. Our souls may sometimes long and faint, and thirst even to anguish, to behold the light of the Lord's countenance. At such times let us sustain ourselves with the sweet fact of the sympathy of our great High Priest. Our drops of sorrow may well be forgotten in the ocean of His grief, but how high should our love rise! Come in, O strong and deep love of Jesus, like the sea at the flood in spring tides. Cover all my powers, drown all my sins, wash out all my cares, lift up my earthbound soul, and float it right up to my Lord's feet. There let me lie, a poor broken shell, washed up by His love, having no virtue or value, only venturing to whisper to Him that if He will put His ear to me, He will hear within my heart faint echoes of the vast waves of His own love that have brought me where it is my delight to lie, even at His feet forever.

APRIL 12

Evening

The king's garden.
—Nehemiah 3:15

The mention of the king's garden by Nehemiah brings to mind the Paradise that the King of Kings prepared for Adam. Sin had utterly ruined that fair abode of all delights and had driven out the children of men to till the ground, which yielded thorns and briers to them. My soul, remember the Fall, for it was your fall. Weep much because the Lord of love was so shamefully mistreated by the head of the human race, of which you are a member, as undeserving as any. Behold how dragons and demons dwell on this fair earth, which once was a garden of delights. See yonder another King's garden, which the King waters with His bloody sweat. It is Gethsemane, whose bitter herbs are far sweeter to renewed souls than even Eden's luscious fruits. There the mischief of the serpent in the first Garden was undone. There the curse was lifted from the earth and borne by the woman's promised Seed. My soul, think much about the agony and the passion; resort to the Garden of the olive press and view your great Redeemer rescuing you from your lost estate. This is the Garden of Gardens indeed, wherein the soul may see the guilt of sin and the power of love, two sights that surpass all others. Is there no other King's garden? Yes, my heart, you are, or should be. How do the flowers flourish? Do any choice fruits appear? Does the King walk within and rest in the arbor of your spirit? Be sure that the plants are trimmed and watered and the mischievous foxes hunted out. Come, Lord, and let the heavenly wind blow at Your coming so that the spices of Your garden may flow abroad. Nor must I forget the King's garden of the church. O Lord, send prosperity to it. Rebuild her walls, nourish her plants, ripen her fruits, and from the huge wilderness, reclaim the barren waste and make of it a King's garden.

A bundle of myrrh is my wellbeloved unto me.
—Song of Solomon 1:13

Myrrh may well be chosen to serve as a type of Jesus because of its preciousness, its perfume, and its pleasantness; its healing, preserving, and disinfecting qualities; and its connection with sacrifice. But why is He compared to *"a bundle of myrrh"*? First, for plenty. He is not a drop of it, but a barrelful. He is not a sprig or flower of it, but a whole bundle. There is enough in Christ for all my needs; let me not be slow to avail myself of Him. Our *"wellbeloved"* is compared to a bundle also for variety: for there is in Christ not only the one thing that is necessary, but *"in him dwelleth all the fulness of the Godhead bodily"* (Col. 2:9). Everything necessary is in Him. Take Jesus in His different characters, and you will see a marvelous variety: Prophet, Priest, King, Husband, Friend, Shepherd. Consider Him in His life, death, resurrection, ascension, and second advent; view Him in His virtue, gentleness, courage, self-denial, love, faithfulness, truth, righteousness. Everywhere He is a bundle of preciousness. He is *"a bundle of myrrh"* for preservation—not loose myrrh tied up, but myrrh to be stored in a container. We must value Him as our best treasure. We must prize His words and His laws. We must keep our thoughts of Him and knowledge of Him as under lock and key, lest the devil would steal anything from us. Moreover, Jesus is *"a bundle of myrrh"* for His unique qualities. The symbol suggests the idea of distinguishing, discriminating grace. From before the foundation of the world, He was set apart for His people; and He gives forth His perfume only to those who understand how to enter into communion with Him, to have close dealings with Him. Oh, blessed people whom the Lord has admitted into His secrets, and for whom He sets Himself apart. Oh, choice and happy are those who are thus made to say, *"A bundle of myrrh is my wellbeloved unto me."*

APRIL 13

Evening

*And he shall put his hand upon the head of the burnt offering; and it
shall be accepted for him to make atonement for him.*
—Leviticus 1:4

Our Lord's being made sin for us is shown here by the very significant
transfer of sin to the bullock, which was made by the elders of the people.
The laying of the hand was not a mere touch of contact, for in other places
of Scripture the original word for *"put"* has the meaning of leaning heavily,
as in the expression, *"Thy wrath lieth hard upon me"* (Ps. 88:7). Surely this is
the very essence and nature of faith, which not only brings us into contact
with the great Substitute, but also teaches us to lean on Him with all the
burden of our guilt. Jehovah placed on the head of the Substitute all the
offenses of His covenant people, but each one of the chosen is brought personally to ratify this solemn covenant act, when by grace he is enabled by
faith to lay his hand upon the head of the *"Lamb slain from the foundation
of the world"* (Rev. 13:8). Believer, do you remember that rapturous day
when you first obtained pardon through Jesus, the Sin-bearer? Can you not
make glad confession and join with the writer in saying, "My soul recalls its
day of deliverance with delight. Laden with guilt and full of fear, I saw my
Savior as my Substitute, and I laid my hand on Him. Oh, how timidly I did
so at first, but then my courage grew, and confidence was confirmed until I
leaned my soul entirely on Him. Now it is my unceasing joy to know that
my sins are no longer counted against me, but they are laid on Him. Jesus,
like the good Samaritan, has said of all my future sinfulness, like the debts
of the wounded traveler, 'Charge that to My account'"? Blessed discovery!
Eternal solace of a grateful heart!

> My numerous sins transferr'd to Him,
>   Shall never more be found,
> Lost in His blood's atoning stream,
>   Where every crime is drown'd!

All they that see me laugh me to scorn: they shoot out the lip,
they shake the head.
—Psalm 22:7

Mockery was a great ingredient in our Lord's woe. Judas mocked Him in the garden; the chief priests and scribes laughed Him to scorn; Herod considered Him to be insignificant; the servants and the soldiers jeered at Him and brutally insulted Him; Pilate and his guards ridiculed His royalty; and on the tree all sorts of horrid jests and hideous taunts were hurled at Him. Ridicule is always hard to bear, but when we are in intense pain, it is so heartless, so cruel, that it cuts us to the quick. Imagine the Savior crucified, racked with anguish far beyond all human comprehension, and then, picture that motley multitude, all wagging their heads or thrusting out their lips in bitter contempt of one poor suffering victim! Surely there must have been something more in the Crucified One than they could see; otherwise, such a great and mixed crowd would not unanimously have honored Him with such contempt. Was it not evil confessing, in the very moment of its greatest apparent triumph, that after all it could do no more than mock at that victorious goodness that was then reigning on the cross? O Jesus, *"despised and rejected of men"* (Isa. 53:3), how could You die for men who treated you so horribly? Herein is amazing love, divine love, yes, love beyond measure. We, too, have despised You in the days of our unregeneracy, and even since our new birth, we have set the world high in our hearts. Yet You bled to heal our wounds and died to give us life. Oh, that we could set You on a glorious high throne in all men's hearts! We would ring out Your praises over land and sea until men would as universally adore You as once they unanimously rejected You.

Thy creatures wrong You, O sovereign Good!
Thou are not loved, because not understood:
This grieves me most, that vain pursuits beguile
Ungrateful men, regardless of Thy smile.

APRIL 14

Evening

Say ye to the righteous, that it shall be well with him.
—Isaiah 3:10

It is always well with the righteous! If the prophet had said, "Say ye to the righteous, that it is well with him in his prosperity," we would have been thankful for so great a blessing, for prosperity can also bring danger. It is a gift from heaven to be secured from the enticements of wealth. If it had been written, "It is well with him when under persecution," we would have been thankful for so sustaining an assurance, for persecution is hard to bear. But when no time is mentioned, all time is included. God's *shalls* must be understood always in their largest sense. From the beginning to the end of the year, from the first gathering of evening shadows until the daystar shines, in all conditions and under all circumstances, it will be well with the righteous. It is so well with him that we could not imagine it to be better, for he is well fed; he feeds upon the flesh and blood of Jesus. He is well clothed; he wears the imputed righteousness of Christ. He is well housed; he dwells in God. He is well married; his soul is joined in the bonds of marriage union to Christ. He is well provided for; the Lord is his Shepherd. He is well endowed; heaven is his inheritance. It is well with the righteous—well upon divine authority. The mouth of God speaks the comforting assurance. Beloved, if God declares that all is well, ten thousand devils may declare it to be ill, but we laugh them all to scorn. Blessed be God for a faith that enables us to believe God when the creatures contradict Him! It is, says the Word, at all times well with you, righteous one; then, beloved, if you cannot see it, believe in God's Word instead of your sight. Yes, believe it on divine authority more confidently than if your eyes and your feelings told it to you. Whom God blesses is blessed indeed, and what His lips declare is a truth that is steadfast and sure.

My God, my God, why hast thou forsaken me?
—Psalm 22:1

We here behold the Savior in the depth of His sorrows. No other place so well shows the grief of Christ as Calvary, and no other moment at Calvary is so full of agony as that in which His cry rends the air—*"My God, my God, why hast thou forsaken me?"* At this moment physical weakness was united with acute mental torture from the shame and ignominy through which He had to pass. He suffered spiritual agony surpassing all expression, resulting from the departure of His Father's presence, unbearably heightening His grief. This was the black midnight of His horror. It was then that He descended into the abyss of suffering. No man can enter into the full meaning of these words. Some of us think at times that we could cry, "My God, my God, why have You forsaken me?" There are seasons when the brightness of our Father's smile is eclipsed by clouds and darkness, but let us remember that God never really forsakes us. It is only an illusory forsaking with us, but in Christ's case, it was a real forsaking. We grieve at a little withdrawal of our Father's love; but the real turning away of God's face from His Son, who will calculate how deep the agony that it caused Him? In our case, our cry is often dictated by unbelief. In His case, it was the utterance of a dreadful fact, for God had really turned away from Him for a season. O poor, distressed soul, who once lived in the sunshine of God's face, but are now in darkness, remember that He has not really forsaken you. God in the clouds is as much our God as when He shines forth in all the luster of His grace. But since even the thought that He has forsaken us gives us agony, what must the woe of the Savior have been when He exclaimed, *"My God, my God, why hast thou forsaken me?"*

Lift them up for ever.
—Psalm 28:9

God's people need lifting up. They are very heavy by nature. They have no wings, or, if they have, they are like the dove of old that lay among the pots; and they need divine grace to make them mount on wings covered with silver and feathers of yellow gold. By nature *"sparks fly upward"* (Job 5:7), but the sinful souls of men fall downward. O Lord, *"lift them up for ever"!* David himself said, *"Unto thee, O Lord, do I lift up my soul"* (Ps. 25:1), and he here felt the necessity that other men's souls should be lifted up as well as his own. When you ask this blessing for yourself, do not forget to seek it for others. There are three ways in which God's people need to be lifted up. They need to be elevated in character. Lift them up, O Lord; do not permit Your people to be like the world's people. The world lies in the wicked one; lift them out of it. The world's people are looking after silver and gold, seeking their own pleasures and the gratification of their lusts; but, Lord, lift Your people up above all this. Keep them from being "muckrakers," as John Bunyan called the man who was always scraping after gold. Set their hearts upon their risen Lord and their heavenly heritage. Moreover, believers need to be prospered in conflict. In battle, if they seem to fall, O Lord, be pleased to give them the victory. If the enemy's foot is upon their necks for a moment, help them to grasp the sword of the Spirit and eventually win the battle. Lord, lift up Your children's spirits in the day of conflict. Do not let them sit in the dust, mourning forever. Do not allow the adversary to vex them sorely and make them fret. But if they have been persecuted like Hannah (see 1 Samuel 1:2–20), let them sing of the mercy of a delivering God. We may also ask our Lord to lift them up on the Last Day. Lift them up by taking them home, lift their bodies from the tomb, and raise their souls to Your eternal kingdom in glory.

The precious blood of Christ.
—1 Peter 1:19

Standing at the foot of the cross, we see, falling from His hands, feet, and side, crimson streams of precious blood. It is precious because of its redeeming and atoning efficacy. By it, the sins of Christ's people are atoned for. They are redeemed from under the law. They are reconciled to God and made one with Him. Christ's blood is also precious in its cleansing power; it *"cleanseth us from all sin"* (1 John 1:7). *"Though your sins be as scarlet, they shall be as white as snow"* (Isa. 1:18). Through Jesus' blood there is not a spot left on any believer; no wrinkle or any such thing remains. His precious blood, which makes us clean, removes the stains of abundant iniquity and permits us to stand *"accepted in the beloved"* (Eph. 1:6), notwithstanding the many ways in which we have rebelled against our God. The blood of Christ is likewise precious in its preserving power. Under the sprinkled blood, we are safe from the destroying angel. Remember it is God's seeing the blood that is the true reason for our being spared. Here is comfort for us when the eye of faith is dim, for God's eye is still the same. The blood of Christ is precious also in its sanctifying influence. The same blood that justifies by taking away sin, in its after-action, quickens the new nature and leads it onward to subdue sin and to carry out the commands of God. There is no motive for holiness so great as that which streams from the veins of Jesus. And precious, unspeakably precious, is this blood, because it has an overcoming power. It is written, *"They overcame…by the blood of the Lamb"* (Rev. 12:11). How could they do otherwise? He who fights with the precious blood of Jesus fights with a weapon that cannot know defeat. The blood of Jesus! Sin dies at its presence, death ceases to be death, and heaven's gates are opened. The blood of Jesus! We will march on, conquering and to conquer, as long as we trust its power!

And [Moses'] hands were steady until the going down of the sun.
—Exodus 17:12

The prayer of Moses was so mighty that everyone depended on it. The petitions of Moses defeated the enemy more than the fighting of Joshua. Yet both were needed. In the soul's conflict, force and fervor, decision and devotion, valor and vehemence must join their forces, and all will be well. You must wrestle with your sin, but the major part of the wrestling must be done alone in private with God. Prayers like Moses' hold up the token of the covenant before the Lord. The rod was the symbol of God's working with Moses, the symbol of God's government in Israel. Learn, O interceding saint, to hold up the promise and the oath of God before Him. The Lord cannot deny His own declarations. Hold up the rod of promise, and you will have what you will. When Moses grew weary, his friends assisted him. At any time your prayer weakens, let faith support one hand and holy hope uplift the other. Then prayer seating itself upon the Stone of Israel, the Rock of our salvation, will persevere and prevail. Beware of faintness in devotion; if Moses felt it, who can escape? It is far easier to fight with sin in public than to pray against it in private. It is said that Joshua never grew weary in the fighting, but Moses did grow weary in the praying. The more spiritual an exercise, the more difficult it is for flesh and blood to maintain it. Let us cry, then, for special strength, and may the Spirit of God, who helps our infirmities, as He helped Moses, enable us like him to continue with our hands steady *"until the going down of the sun."* May we remain steadfast until the evening of life is over, until we come to the rising of a better sun, in the land where prayer is swallowed up in praise.

Ye are come...to the blood of sprinkling, that speaketh
better things than that of Abel.
—Hebrews 12:22, 24

Reader, have you come *"to the blood of sprinkling"*? The question is not whether you have come to a knowledge of doctrine, an observance of ceremonies, or to a certain form of experience, but have you come to the blood of Jesus? The blood of Jesus is the life of all vital godliness. If you have truly come to Jesus, we know how you came—the Holy Spirit sweetly brought you there. You came to the blood of sprinkling with no merits of your own. Guilty, lost, and helpless, you came to take that blood, and that blood alone, as your everlasting hope. You came to the cross of Christ with a trembling and an aching heart, and oh, what a precious sound it was to you to hear the voice of the blood of Jesus! The dripping of His blood is as the music of heaven to the penitent sons of earth. We are full of sin, but the Savior bids us lift our eyes to Him. As we gaze on His streaming wounds, each drop of blood, as it falls, cries, "It is finished! I have made an end of sin, and I have brought in everlasting righteousness." Oh, sweet language of the precious blood of Jesus! If you have come to that blood once, you will come to it constantly. Your life will be one of *"looking unto Jesus"* (Heb. 12:2). Your whole conduct will be epitomized in this phrase: *"To whom coming"* (1 Pet. 2:4). Not to whom I *have* come, but to whom I am *always* coming. If you have ever come to the blood of sprinkling, you will feel your need of coming to it every day. He who does not desire to wash in it every day has never washed in it at all. The believer always feels it to be his joy and privilege that there is still a fountain opened. Past experiences are doubtful food for Christians; a present coming to Christ alone can give us joy and comfort. This morning let us sprinkle our doorposts fresh with blood, and then, feast on the Lamb, assured that the destroying angel must pass us by.

We would see Jesus.
—John 12:21

The constant cry of the world is, "Who will show us any good?" People seek satisfaction in earthly comforts, enjoyments, and riches. But the convicted sinner knows of only one good: *"Oh that I knew where I might find him!"* (Job 23:3). When a person is truly awakened to feel his guilt, if you could pour the gold of India at his feet, he would say, "Take it away. I want to find Him!" It is a blessed thing for a man when he has brought his desires into focus so that they all center on one object. When he has fifty different desires, his heart resembles a pool of stagnant water, spread out into a marsh, breeding disease and pestilence. But when all his desires are brought into one channel, his heart becomes like a river of pure water, flowing swiftly to fertilize the fields. Happy is he who has one desire, if that one desire is set on Christ, even though it may not yet have been realized. If Jesus is the soul's desire, it is a blessed sign of divine work within. Such a man will never be content with mere laws. He will say, "I want Christ; I must have Him. Rules are of no use to me; I need Him! Do not offer me these. You offer me the empty pitcher, while I am dying of thirst. Give me water, or I will die. Jesus is my soul's desire. I would see Jesus!" Is this your condition, my reader, at this moment? Do you have but one desire, and is it Christ? Then you are not far from the kingdom of heaven. Have you but one wish in your heart, and that one wish is that you would be washed from all your sins in Jesus' blood? Can you really say, "I would give all I have to be a Christian. I would give up everything I have and hope for, if I could only feel that I have an interest in Christ"? Then, despite all your fears, be of good cheer. The Lord loves you, and you will come out into daylight soon. Rejoice *"in the liberty wherewith Christ hath made us free"* (Gal. 5:1).

APRIL 18

Morning

She bound the scarlet line in the window.
—Joshua 2:21

Rahab depended for her preservation on the promise of the spies, whom she considered to be the representatives of the God of Israel. Her faith was simple and firm, but it was very obedient. To tie the scarlet line in the window was a very trivial act in itself, but she dared not run the risk of omitting it. Come, my soul, is there not a lesson here for you? Have you been attentive to all of your Lord's will, even though some of His commands might seem nonessential? Have you observed in His own way the two ordinances of the believers' baptism and the Lord's Supper? Neglecting these sacraments points to much unloving disobedience in your heart. From now on, in all things, be blameless, even to the tying of a thread, if that is what you are commanded to do. This act of Rahab sets forth a yet more solemn lesson. Have I implicitly trusted in the precious blood of Jesus? Have I tied the scarlet cord, as with a Gordian knot in my window, so that my trust can never be removed? Or can I look out toward the Dead Sea of my sins, or the Jerusalem of my hopes, without seeing the blood, and seeing all things in connection with its blessed power? If it hangs from the window, the passerby can see a cord of so conspicuous a color; likewise, it will be well for me if my life makes the power of the Atonement conspicuous to all onlookers. What is there to be ashamed of? Let men or devils gaze if they will; the blood is my boast and my song. My soul, there is One who will see that scarlet line, even when from weakness of faith you cannot see it yourself; Jehovah, the Avenger, will see it and pass over you. Jericho's walls fell flat. Rahab's house was on the wall, and yet it stood unmoved. My nature is built into the wall of humanity, yet when destruction destroys the race, I will be secure. My soul, tie the scarlet thread in the window afresh, and rest in peace.

And thou saidst, I will surely do thee good.
—Genesis 32:12

When Jacob was on the other side of the brook Jabbok, and Esau was coming toward him with armed men, Jacob earnestly sought God's protection. As his primary argument, Jacob pleaded, *"And thou saidst, I will surely do thee good."* Oh, the force of that plea! He was holding God to His word: *"Thou saidst."* The attribute of God's faithfulness is a splendid horn of the altar on which to lay hold, but the promise is a mightier anchor still because it contains something more: *"Thou saidst, I will surely do thee good."* Has God said it, and will He not do it? *"Let God be true, but every man a liar"* (Rom. 3:4). Will God be untrue? Will He not keep His word? Will not every word that comes from His lips stand fast and be fulfilled? Solomon, at the opening of the temple, used this same mighty plea. He asked God to remember the word that He had spoken to his father David and to bless that place. When a man gives a promissory note, his honor is pledged. He signs his name, and he must pay the debt when the time comes; otherwise, he loses credit. It will never be said that God dishonors His bills. The reputation of the Most High has never been impeached and never will be. He is punctual to the moment: He is never before His time, but He is never behind it. Search God's Word through, and compare it with the experience of God's people. You will find the two agree from the first to the last. Many patriarchs have said with Joshua, *"Not one thing hath failed of all the good things which the LORD your God spake concerning you; all are come to pass"* (Josh. 23:14). If you have a divine promise, you do not need to plead it with an *if*; you may claim it with certainty. The Lord meant to fulfill the promise, or He would not have given it. God does not give His words merely to quiet us and to keep us hopeful for a while, with the intention of putting us off in the end. When He speaks, it is because He means to do as He has said.

APRIL 19

Morning

Behold, the veil of the temple was rent in twain
from the top to the bottom.
—Matthew 27:51

No lowly miracle was performed in the rending of so strong and thick a veil. It was not intended merely as a display of power; many lessons were taught to us in this act. The old law of ordinances was put away, and like worn-out clothes, it was torn and laid aside. When Jesus died, the sacrifices were all finished, because all were fulfilled in Him; therefore, the place of their presentation was marked with an obvious token of decay. The torn veil also revealed all the hidden things of the old dispensation: the mercy seat could now be seen, and the glory of God gleamed forth above it. By the death of our Lord Jesus, we have a clear revelation of God, for He was *"not as Moses, which put a veil over his face"* (2 Cor. 3:13). Life and immortality are now brought to light, and things that have been hidden since the foundation of the world are manifest in Him. The annual ceremony of atonement was thus abolished. The atoning blood, which was once every year sprinkled within the veil, was now offered once for all by the great High Priest, and, therefore, the place of the symbolic rite was broken up. No blood of bullocks or of lambs is needed now, for Jesus has entered within the veil with His own blood. Hence access to God is now permitted and is the privilege of every believer in Christ Jesus. There is no small space laid open through which we may peer at the mercy seat, but the tear reaches from the top to the bottom. We may come with boldness to the throne of heavenly grace (Heb. 4:16). Would we be wrong to say that the opening of the Holy of Holies in this marvelous manner by our Lord's dying cry was a foreshadowing of the opening of the gates of paradise to all the saints by virtue of the Passion? Our bleeding Lord has the key of heaven; He opens it and no man shuts it. Let us enter in with Him into the heavenly places and sit with Him there until our common enemies will be made His footstool.

APRIL 19

Evening

The Amen.
—Revelation 3:14

The word *"Amen"* solemnly confirms that which went before. Jesus is the great Confirmer. The Amen in all His promises is forever unchanging. Sinner, I would comfort you with this reflection. Jesus Christ said, *"Come unto me, all ye that labour and are heavy laden, and I will give you rest"* (Matt. 11:28). If you come to Him, He will say "Amen" in your soul; His promise will be true to you. Jesus fulfilled the words of the prophet, *"A bruised reed shall he not break"* (Isa. 42:3). O poor, broken, bruised heart, if you come to Him, He will say "Amen" to you, and that will be as true in your soul as in hundreds of cases in years past. Christian, is it not comforting to you also that there is not a word that has gone out of the Savior's lips that He has ever retracted? The words of Jesus will stand when heaven and earth pass away. If you take hold of but half a promise, you will find it to be true. Beware of him whom Bunyan called "Clip-promise," who destroys much of the comfort of God's Word. He does not doubt the promise, but he clips the edge of it. He suggests that the promise will not all be fulfilled, only a part of it. But Jesus is *"yea, and…Amen"* (2 Cor. 1:20) in all His offices. He was a Priest to pardon and cleanse once, and He is Amen as Priest still. He was a King to rule and reign for His people and to defend them with His mighty arm, and He is an Amen King, the same still. He was a Prophet of old to foretell good things to come, and His lips are sweet and drip with honey still. He is an Amen Prophet. He is Amen as to the merit of His blood, and He is Amen as to His righteousness. That sacred robe will remain fair and glorious although nature will decay. He is Amen in every single title that He bears; your Husband, never seeking a divorce; your Friend, sticking closer than a brother; your Shepherd, with you in death's dark vale. He is your help and your deliverer; your castle and your high tower; the horn of your strength, your confidence, your joy, your all in all, and in everything, your *"yea, and…Amen."*

That through death he might destroy him
that had the power of death.
—Hebrews 2:14

O child of God, death has lost its sting, because the devil's power over it is destroyed. Then cease to fear dying. Ask grace from God the Holy Spirit that by an intimate knowledge and a firm belief of your Redeemer's death, you may be strengthened for that dread hour. Living near the Cross of Calvary allows you to think of death with pleasure and welcome it, when it comes, with intense delight. It is sweet to die in the Lord; it is a covenant blessing to sleep in Jesus. Death is no longer banishment; it is a return from exile, a going home to the many mansions where the loved ones already dwell. The distance between glorified spirits in heaven and militant saints on earth seems great; but it is not so. We are not far from home—a moment will bring us there. The sail is spread; the soul is launched on the deep. How long will its voyage be? How many wearying winds must beat upon the sail before it will be reefed in the port of peace? How long will that soul be tossed on the waves before it comes to that sea that knows no storm? Listen to the answer, *"Absent from the body, and…present with the Lord"* (2 Cor. 5:8). The ship has just departed, but it is already at its haven. It spread its sail, and it was there. Like that ship of old, on the Lake of Galilee, a storm had tossed it, but when Jesus walked on the sea to them and said, *"It is I; be not afraid"* (John 6:20), immediately the ship came to land. Do not think that a long period intervenes between the instant of death and the eternity of glory. When the eyes close on earth, they open in heaven. The horses of fire are not on the road even for an instant. Then, O child of God, what is there for you to fear in death, seeing that, through the death of your Lord, its curse and sting are destroyed? Now it is but a Jacob's ladder whose foot is in the dark grave, but whose top reaches to everlasting glory.

Fight the LORD's battles.
—1 Samuel 18:17

The sacramental host of God's elect is warring still on earth, and Jesus Christ is the Captain of their salvation. He has said, *"Lo, I am with you alway, even unto the end of the world"* (Matt. 28:20). Listen to the shouts of war! Now let the people of God stand fast in their ranks, and let no man's heart fail him. It is true that just now in England the battle is turned against us, and unless the Lord Jesus lifts His sword, we do not know what may become of the church of God in this land. But let us be of good courage and act like men. There never was a day when Protestantism seemed to tremble more in the scales than now that a fierce effort is being made to restore the antichrist to his ancient seat. We greatly need a bold voice and a strong hand to preach and publish the old Gospel for which martyrs bled and confessors died. The Savior is, by His Spirit, still on earth; let this truth encourage us. He is always in the midst of the fight; therefore, the results of the battle are not in doubt. And as the conflict rages, what a sweet satisfaction it is to know that the Lord Jesus, in His office as our great Intercessor, is powerfully interceding for His people! O anxious gazer, do not look so much at the battle below, for there you will be enshrouded in smoke and amazed with garments rolled in blood. Instead, lift your eyes yonder where the Savior lives and pleads, for while He intercedes, the cause of God is safe. Let us fight as if it all depended on us, but let us look up and know that it all depends on Him. Now, by the lilies of Christian purity, by the roses of the Savior's atonement, and *"by the roes, and by the hinds of the field"* (Song 2:7), we charge you who are lovers of Jesus to do valiantly in the holy war, for truth and righteousness, for the kingdom and crown jewels of your Master. Onward! *"For the battle is not yours, but God's"* (2 Chron. 20:15).

I know that my redeemer liveth.
—Job 19:25

The essence of Job's comfort lies in that little word *"my"*—*"my redeemer"*—and in the fact that the Redeemer lives. Oh, to take hold of the living Christ! We must belong to Him before we can enjoy Him. What good is gold in the mine to me? It is gold in my purse that will satisfy my needs; then I can purchase the bread that I need. Of what use would be a Redeemer who does not redeem me or an Avenger who will not stand up for me? Do not rest content until by faith you can say, "Yes, I cast myself on my living Lord, and He is mine." It may be that you hold Him with a weak grip. You half think it presumption to say, "He lives as *my* Redeemer," yet remember: if you have a faith that is only the size of a grain of mustard seed, that little faith entitles you to say it. But there is also another word here, indicative of Job's strong confidence: "I *know*." To say "I hope so," or "I trust so" is easy, and there are thousands in the fold of Jesus who hardly ever get much further. But to reach the essence of consolation, you must say, "I know." *Ifs*, *buts*, and *perhaps*es are sure murderers of peace and comfort. Doubts are dreary things in times of sorrow. Like wasps, they sting the soul! If I have any suspicion that Christ is not mine, then there is vinegar mingled with the gall of death; but if I know that Jesus lives for me, then darkness is not dark. Even the night is light about me. Surely if Job, in those ages before the Incarnation and Advent of Christ, could say, "*I know*," we should not speak less positively. God forbid that our confidence should be presumption. Let us see that our evidences are right, lest we build on an ungrounded hope. Then let us not be satisfied with the mere foundation, for it is from the upper rooms that we get the widest view. A living Redeemer, truly mine, is joy unspeakable.

Who is even at the right hand of God.
—Romans 8:34

He who was once despised and rejected of men now occupies the honorable position of a beloved and honored Son. The right hand of God is the place of majesty and favor. Our Lord Jesus is His people's Representative. When He died for them, they had rest; He rose again for them, and they had liberty; when He sat down at His Father's right hand, they had favor, honor, and dignity. The raising and elevation of Christ is the elevation, the acceptance, and enshrinement, the glorifying of all His people, for He is their Head and Representative. This sitting at the right hand of God, then, is to be viewed as the acceptance of the person of the Surety, the reception of the Representative, and therefore, the acceptance of our souls. O believer, see in this your sure freedom from condemnation. *"Who is he that condemneth?"* (Rom. 8:34). Who will condemn those who are in Jesus at the right hand of God? The right hand is the place of power. Christ at the right hand of God has all power in heaven and in earth. Who will fight against the people who have such power vested in their Captain? O my soul, what can destroy you if Omnipotence is your helper? If the shield of the Almighty covers you, what sword can smite you? Rest secure. If Jesus is your all-prevailing King and has trampled your enemies underneath His feet; if sin, death, and hell are all vanquished by Him; and if you are represented in Him, by no possibility can you be destroyed.

Jesus' tremendous name
    Puts all our foes to flight:
Jesus, the meek, the angry Lamb,
    A Lion is in fight.

By all hell's host withstood;
    We all hell's host o'erthrow;
And conquering them, through Jesu's blood
    We still to conquer go.

Him hath God exalted.
—Acts 5:31

Jesus, our Lord, once crucified, dead, and buried, now sits on the throne of glory. The highest place that heaven affords is His by undisputed right. It is sweet to remember that the exaltation of Christ in heaven is a representative exaltation. He is exalted at the Father's right hand, and though as Jehovah He had eminent glories in which finite creatures cannot share, yet as the Mediator, the honors that Jesus wears in heaven are the heritage of all the saints. It is delightful to reflect how close Christ's union is with His people. We are actually one with Him. We are members of His body, and His exaltation is our exaltation. He has a crown, and He gives us crowns, too. He will give us places of honor, even as He has overcome, and is set down with His Father on His throne. He is not content with having a throne to Himself. On His right hand, there must be His queen, arrayed *"in gold of Ophir"* (Ps. 45:9). He cannot be glorified without His bride. Look up, believer, to Jesus now. Let the eye of your faith behold Him with many crowns on His head. Remember that you will one day be like Him, when you will see Him as He is. You will not be as great as He is; you will not be as divine, but still you will, in a measure, share the same honors and enjoy the same happiness and the same dignity that He possesses. Be content to live unknown for a little while and to walk your weary way through the fields of poverty or up the hills of affliction. Soon you will reign with Christ, for He has *"made us kings and priests unto God"* (Rev. 1:6), and we will reign with Him forever and ever. Oh, wonderful thought for the children of God! We have Christ for our glorious representative in heaven's courts now, and soon He will come and receive us to Himself to be with Him there, to behold His glory, and to share His joy.

Thou shalt not be afraid for the terror by night.
—Psalm 91:5

What is this terror? It may be the cry of fire or the noise of thieves or imagined appearances or the shriek of sudden sickness or death. We live in the world of death and sorrow; therefore, we may look for trouble in the nighttime as well as during the glare of the broiling sun. Nor should this alarm us, for no matter what the terror is, the promise is that the believer will not be afraid. Why should he be fearful? Let us make it more personal: why should we be afraid? God our Father is here, and He will be here all through the lonely hours. He is an almighty Watcher, a sleepless Guardian, a faithful Friend. Nothing can happen without His direction, for even hell itself is under His control. Darkness is not dark to Him. He has promised to be a wall of fire around His people: who can break through such a barrier? Unbelievers may well be afraid, for they have an angry God above them, a guilty conscience within them, and a yawning hell below them. But we who rest in Jesus are saved from all these through rich mercy. If we give way to foolish fear, we will dishonor our profession of faith and lead others to doubt the reality of godliness. We ought to be afraid of being afraid, lest we vex the Holy Spirit by foolish distrust. Down, then, dismal foreboding and groundless apprehension. God has not forgotten to be gracious or shut up His tender mercies. It may be night in the soul, but there does not need to be any terror, for the God of love does not change. Children of light may walk through darkness, but they are not cast away. No, they are enabled to prove their adoption by trusting in their heavenly Father as hypocrites cannot do.

> Though the night be dark and dreary,
>   Darkness cannot hide from Thee;
> Thou art He, who, never weary,
>   Watchest where Your people be.

Nay, in all these things we are more than conquerors
through him that loved us.
—Romans 8:37

We go to Christ for forgiveness, and then too often look to the law for power to fight our sins. Paul thus rebuked us, *"O foolish Galatians, who hath bewitched you, that ye should not obey the truth?…This only would I learn of you, Received ye the Spirit by the works of the law, or by the hearing of faith? Are ye so foolish? having begun in the Spirit, are ye now made perfect by the flesh?"* (Galatians 3:1–3). Take your sins to Christ's cross, for the *"old man"* (Rom. 6:6) can only be crucified there; we are crucified with Him. The only weapon with which to fight sin is the spear that pierced the side of Jesus. If you want to overcome an angry temper, how do you go about it? It is very possible you have never tried the right way of going to Jesus with it. How did I receive salvation? I came to Jesus just as I was, and I trusted Him to save me. I must kill my angry temper in the same way. It is the only way in which I can ever kill it. I must go to the Cross with it, and say to Jesus, "Lord, I trust You to deliver me from it." This is the only way to give it a deathblow. Are you covetous? Do you feel the world entangle you? You may struggle against this evil as long as you please, but if it is your recurrent sin, you will never be delivered from it in any way but by the blood of Jesus. Take it to Christ. Tell Him, "Lord, I have trusted You, and Your name is Jesus, for You save Your people from their sins. Lord, this is one of my sins; save me from it!" Laws are nothing without Christ as the means of putting these sins to death. Your prayers, your repentance, and your tears—the whole of them put together—are worth nothing apart from Him. No one but Jesus can do helpless sinners any good—or helpless saints, either. You must be conquerors through Him who has loved you, if conquerors at all. Our laurels must grow among His olives in Gethsemane.

Lo, in the midst of the throne…stood a Lamb as it had been slain.
—Revelation 5:6

Why should our exalted Lord appear in His wounds in glory? The wounds of Jesus are His glories, His jewels, His sacred ornaments. To the eye of the believer, Jesus is more than beautiful; He is *"white and ruddy"* (Song 5:10)—white with innocence and ruddy with His own blood. We see Him as the lily of matchless purity and as the rose crimsoned with His own blood. Christ is lovely upon Olivet and Tabor, and by the sea, but oh, there never was such a matchless Christ as He who hung upon the cross! There we behold all His beauties in perfection, all His attributes developed, all His love drawn out, all His character expressed. Beloved, the wounds of Jesus are far fairer in our eyes than all the splendor and pomp of kings. The thorny crown is more than an imperial diadem. It is true that He no longer bears the scepter of reed, but there was a glory in it that never flashed from a scepter of gold. Jesus appears as a slain Lamb as He woos our souls and redeems them by His complete atonement. Nor are these the only ornaments of Christ. They are the trophies of His love and of His victory. He has divided *"the spoil with the strong"* (Isa. 53:12). He has redeemed for Himself a great multitude whom no man can number, and these scars are the memorials of the fight. If Christ thus loves to retain the thought of His sufferings for His people, how precious should his wounds be to us!

Behold how every wound of His
    A precious balm distills,
Which heals the scars that sin had made,
    And cures all mortal ills.

Those wounds are mouths that preach His grace;
    The ensigns of His love;
The seals of our expected bliss
    In paradise above.

And because of all this we make a sure covenant.
—Nehemiah 9:38

Many experiences in life may lead us, to our benefit, to renew our covenant with God. After recovery from sickness when, like Hezekiah, we have had a new term of years added to our lives, we may desire to do it. After any deliverance from trouble, when our joys bud forth anew, let us again visit the foot of the Cross and renew our consecration. Especially, let us do this after any sin that has grieved the Holy Spirit or brought dishonor to the cause of God. Let us, then, look to the blood that can make us whiter than snow and again offer ourselves to the Lord. We should not only let our troubles confirm our dedication to God, but also our prosperity should do the same. If we ever meet with occasions that deserve to be called "crowning mercies" then, surely, if He has honored us, we should honor our God. Let us bring forth anew all the jewels of the divine regalia that have been stored in the jewel boxes of our hearts, and let our God sit on the throne of our love, arrayed in royal apparel. If we would learn to profit by our prosperity, we would not need so much adversity. If we would gather from a kiss all the good it might confer upon us, we would not so often smart under the rod. Have we lately received some blessing that we little expected? Has the Lord put our feet in a large room? Can we sing of mercies multiplied? Then this is the day to put our hand on the horns of the altar, and say, "Bind me here, my God; bind me here with cords, even forever." Inasmuch as we need the fulfillment of new promises from God, let us offer renewed prayers that our old vows may not be dishonored. Let us this morning make with Him *"a sure covenant,"* because of the pains of Jesus that for the last month we have been considering with gratitude.

The flowers appear on the earth; the time of the singing of birds is come, and the voice of the turtle is heard in our land.
—Song of Solomon 2:12

The season of spring is sweet. The long, dreary winter helps us to appreciate spring's gentle warmth, and its promise of summer enhances its present delights. After periods of depression of spirit, it is delightful once again to see the light of the Sun of Righteousness. Then our slumbering graces rise from their lethargy like the crocus and the daffodil from their beds of earth. Our hearts are made merry with delightful notes of gratitude, far more melodious than the warbling of birds. The comforting assurance of peace, infinitely more appealing than the turtledove's note, is heard within the soul. Now is the time for the soul to seek communion with her Beloved. Now she must rise from her native sordidness and come away from her old associations. If we do not hoist the sail when the breeze is favorable, we will be to blame. Times of refreshing should not pass over us and leave us unchanged. When Jesus Himself visits us in tenderness and entreats us to arise, can we be so foolish as to refuse His request? He has risen so that He may draw us after Him. By His Holy Spirit, He now has revived us so that we may, in newness of life, ascend into the heavenlies and hold communion with Him. Let our wintry state suffice for coldness and indifference; when the Lord creates a spring within, let our sap flow with vigor and our branches blossom with high resolve. O Lord, if it is not springtime in my chilly heart, I pray that You would make it so, for I am thoroughly weary of living at a distance from You. When will You bring the long and dreary winter to an end? Come, Holy Spirit, and renew my soul. Renew me, restore me, and have mercy on me. This very night I earnestly implore the Lord to take pity on His servant and send me a happy revival of spiritual life.

Rise up, my love, my fair one, and come away.
—Song of Solomon 2:10

I hear the voice of my Beloved! He speaks to me. Fair weather is smiling upon the face of the earth, and He would not have me spiritually asleep while nature is all around me awaking from her winter's rest. He bids me, *"Rise up,"* and well He may, for I have long enough been lying among the campfires of worldliness. He is risen, and I am risen in Him. Why then should I cleave to the dust? From lower loves, desires, pursuits, and aspirations, I would rise toward Him. He calls me by the sweet title of *"My love,"* and counts me fair; this is a good argument for my rising. If He has exalted me and thinks I am beautiful, how can I linger in the tents of Kedar and find congenial associates among the sons of men? He bids me, *"Come away."* Further and further from everything selfish, groveling, worldly, sinful, He calls me; yes, from the outwardly religious world that does not know Him and has no sympathy with the mystery of the higher life, He calls me. *"Come away"* has no harsh sound in it to my ear, for what is there to hold me in this wilderness of vanity and sin? O my Lord, if only I could come away, but I am taken among the thorns and cannot escape from them as I want to. I would, if it were possible, have neither eyes, nor ears, nor heart for sin. You call me to Yourself by saying, *"Come away,"* and this is a melodious call indeed. To come to You is to come home from exile, to come to land out of the raging storm, to come to rest after long labor, to come to the goal of my desires and the summit of my wishes. But Lord, how can a stone rise, or how can a lump of clay come away from the horrible pit? Oh, raise me; draw me. Your grace can do it. Send forth Your Holy Spirit to kindle sacred flames of love in my heart, and I will continue to rise until I leave life and time behind me, and indeed *"come away."*

If any man hear my voice, and open the door, I will come in to him.
—Revelation 3:20

What is your desire this evening? Is it set on heavenly things? Do you long to enjoy the high doctrine of eternal love? Do you desire liberty in very close communion with God? Do you aspire to know the heights, depths, lengths, and breadths of God? Then you must draw near to Jesus. You must get a clear view of Him in His preciousness and completeness. You must see Him in His work, in His offices, and in His person. He who understands Christ receives an anointing from the Holy One, by which He knows all things. Christ is the great master key of all the chambers of God. There is no treasury of God that will not open and yield up all its wealth to the soul that lives near to Jesus. Are you saying, "Oh, that He would dwell in my heart. If only He would make my heart His dwelling place forever"? Open the door, beloved, and He will come into your soul. He has been knocking for a long time, and all with the purpose that He might dine with you and you with Him. He dines with you because you have invited Him into your heart, and you dine with Him because He brings the provision. He could not commune with you if it were not in your heart, you providing the house; and you could not fellowship with Him if He did not bring provision with Him, because you have a bare cupboard. Fling wide, then, the entrance to your soul. He will come with the love that you long to feel. He will come with the joy into which you cannot work your poor depressed spirit. He will bring the peace that now you do not have. He will come with His flagons of wine and sweet apples of love and cheer you until you have no other sickness but that of "love o'erpowering, love divine." Only open the door to Him, drive out His enemies, give Him the keys of your heart, and He will dwell there forever. Oh, wondrous love, that brings such a Guest to dwell in such a heart!

This do in remembrance of me.
—1 Corinthians 11:24

The implication from today's text seems to be that Christians may forget Christ! There could be no need for this loving exhortation if there were not a fearful supposition that our memories might prove treacherous. Nor is this a bare supposition. It is, alas, too well confirmed in our experience, not as a possibility, but as a lamentable fact! It appears almost impossible that those who have been redeemed by the blood of the dying Lamb, who have been loved with an everlasting love by the eternal Son of God, could forget that gracious Savior. But, if startling to the ear, it is, alas, too apparent to the eye to allow us to deny the crime. Forget Him who never forgot us! Forget Him who poured His blood forth for our sins! Forget Him who loved us even to the death! Can it be possible? Yes, it is not only possible, but conscience confesses that it is too sadly a fault with all of us, that we permit Him to be as a wayfaring man tarrying but for a night. He whom we should make the abiding tenant of our memories is but a visitor therein. The Cross, where one would think that memory would linger and inattentiveness would be an unknown intruder, is desecrated by the feet of forgetfulness. Does not your conscience say that this is true? Do you not find yourselves forgetful of Jesus? Some creature steals away your heart, and you are unmindful of Him on whom your affection ought to be set. Some earthly business engrosses your attention when you should fix your eye steadily on the Cross. It is the incessant turmoil of the world and the constant attraction of earthly things that take away the soul from Christ. While memory too well preserves a poisonous weed, it permits the Rose of Sharon to wither. Let us charge ourselves to bind a heavenly forget-me-not about our hearts for Jesus our Beloved, and, whatever else we let slip, let us hold fast to Him.

Blessed is he that watcheth.
—Revelation 16:15

I die daily" (1 Cor. 15:31), said the apostle Paul. This was the life of the early Christians. They went everywhere with their lives in their hands. In this day, we are not called to pass through the same fearful persecutions. If we were, the Lord would give us grace to bear the test; but the tests of the Christian life, at the present moment, though outwardly not as terrible, are yet more likely to overcome us than even those of the fiery age. If we have to bear the ridicule of the world, that is not so hard. Its flattery, its soft words, its oily speeches, its fawning, and its hypocrisy are far worse. Our danger is that we would grow rich and become proud, that we would give ourselves up to the trends of this present evil world and lose our faith. If wealth is not our trial, worldly care is just as dangerous. If we cannot be torn in pieces by the roaring lion, we may be hugged to death by the bear. The devil does not care which it is, as long as he destroys our love for Christ and our confidence in Him. I fear that the Christian church is far more likely to lose her integrity in these soft and silken days than in those rougher times. We must be awake now, for we travel on enchanted ground, and we are most likely to fall asleep, to our own undoing, unless our faith in Jesus is a reality and our love for Jesus a vehement flame. Many in these days of easy profession are likely to prove to be tares, and not wheat; hypocrites with fair masks on their faces, but not the true-born children of the living God. Christian, do not think that these are times in which you can dispense with watchfulness or with holy ardor. You need these things more than ever, and may God the eternal Spirit display His omnipotence in you so that you may be able to say, in all these softer things, as well as in the rougher, *"We are more than conquerors through him that loved us"* (Rom. 8:37).

God, even our own God.
—Psalm 67:6

It is strange how little use we make of the spiritual blessings that God gives us, but it is stranger still how little use we make of God Himself. Though He is *"our own God,"* we apply ourselves but little to Him and ask but little of Him. How seldom do we ask counsel at the hands of the Lord! How often do we go about our business without seeking His guidance! In our troubles how constantly do we strive to bear our burdens ourselves, instead of casting them on the Lord, so that He may sustain us! This is not because we may not, for the Lord seems to say, "I am yours, soul, come and make use of Me as you will. You may freely come to My store, and the more often, the more welcome." It is our own fault if we do not avail ourselves of the riches of our God. Then, since you have such a Friend, and He invites you, draw from Him daily. Never be in need while you have God to go to. Never fear or faint while you have God to help you. Go to your Treasure and take whatever you need. There is all that you can desire. Learn the divine skill of making God all things to you. He can supply you with all, or, better still, He can be all to you. Let me urge you, then, to make use of your God. Make use of Him in prayer. Go to Him often, because He is *your* God. Oh, will you fail to use so great a privilege? Fly to Him, and tell Him all your needs. Use Him constantly—by faith—at all times. If some dark circumstance has clouded your way, use your God as a light. If some strong enemy has attacked you, find in Jehovah a shield, for *"God is a sun and shield"* (Ps. 84:11) to His people. If you have lost your way in the mazes of life, use Him as a guide, for He will direct you. Whatever you are, and wherever you are, remember that God is just what you need and just where you need. He can do all you need.

The LORD is King for ever and ever.
—Psalm 10:16

Jesus Christ makes no despotic claim of divine right, for He is really and truly the Lord's anointed! *"It pleased the Father that in him should all fulness dwell"* (Col. 1:19). God has given to Him all power and all authority. As the Son of Man, He is now Head over all things to His church, and He reigns over heaven, earth, and hell with the keys of life and death. Certain princes have delighted to call themselves kings by the popular will, and certainly our Lord Jesus Christ is such in His church. If it could be put to the vote whether He should be King in the church, every believing heart would crown Him. Oh, that we could crown Him more gloriously than we do! We would consider no expense to be wasted that would glorify Christ. Suffering would be pleasure, and loss would be gain, if thereby we could surround His brow with brighter crowns and make Him more glorious in the eyes of men and angels. Yes, He shall reign. Long live the King! All hail to You, King Jesus! Go forth, virgin souls who love your Lord. Bow at His feet, and strew His way with the lilies of your love and the roses of your gratitude: "Bring forth the royal diadem, and crown Him Lord of all." Moreover, our Lord Jesus is King in Zion by right of conquest. He has taken and carried by storm the hearts of His people, and He has slain their enemies who held them in cruel bondage. In the Red Sea of His own blood, our Redeemer has drowned the Pharaoh of our sins. Will He not be King in Jeshurun? He has delivered us from the iron yoke and heavy curse of the law: shall not the Liberator be crowned? We are His portion, whom He has taken out of the hand of the Amorite with His sword and with His bow. Who will snatch His conquest from His hand? All hail, King Jesus! We gladly acknowledge Your gentle reign! Rule in our hearts forever, lovely Prince of Peace.

Remember the word unto thy servant, upon which
thou hast caused me to hope.
—Psalm 119:49

Whatever your special need may be, you may readily find some promise in the Bible suited to it. Are you faint and feeble because your way is rough, and you are weary? Here is the promise: *"He giveth power to the faint"* (Isa. 40:29). When you read such a promise, take it back to the great Promiser, and ask Him to fulfill His own Word. Are you seeking after Christ and thirsting for closer communion with Him? This promise shines like a star on you: *"Blessed are they which do hunger and thirst after righteousness: for they shall be filled"* (Matt. 5:6). Take that promise to the throne continually; do not plead anything else, but go to God over and over again with this: "Lord, You have said it; do as You have said." Are you distressed because of sin and burdened with the heavy load of your iniquities? Listen to these words: *"I, even I, am he that blotteth out thy transgressions for mine own sake, and will not remember thy sins"* (Isa. 43:25). You have no merit of your own to plead for His pardon, but plead His written promises, and He will perform them. Are you afraid lest you should not be able to hold on to the end, lest, after having thought yourself a child of God, you should prove a castaway? If that is your state, take this Word of grace to the throne and plead it: *"The mountains shall depart, and the hills be removed; but my kindness shall not depart from thee, neither shall the covenant of my peace be removed"* (Isa. 54:10). If you have lost the sweet sense of the Savior's presence and are seeking Him with a sorrowful heart, remember the promises: *"Return unto me, and I will return unto you"* (Mal. 3:7). *"For a small moment have I forsaken thee; but with great mercies will I gather thee"* (Isa. 54:7). Feast your faith on God's own Word, and whatever your fears or needs, return to the Bank of Faith with your Father's note, saying, *"Remember the word unto thy servant, upon which thou hast caused me to hope."*

APRIL 28

Evening

All the house of Israel are impudent and hardhearted.
—Ezekiel 3:7

Are there any exceptions? No, not one. Even the favored race is described as *"impudent and hardhearted."* If the best are so bad, then what must the worst be? Come, my heart; consider how much you have a share in this universal accusation, and while considering, be ready to accept your part of the guilt. The first charge is impudence, an arrogant spirit, a lack of holy shame, or an unhallowed boldness in evil. Before my conversion, I could sin and feel no compunction, hear of my guilt and yet remain unhumbled, and even confess my iniquity and manifest no inward humiliation on account of it. For a sinner to go to God's house and pretend to pray to Him and praise Him argues a brash disrespect of the worst kind! Alas, since the day of my new birth, I have doubted my Lord to His face, murmured unblushingly in His presence, worshipped before Him in a slovenly manner, and sinned without bewailing myself concerning it! If my head were not as hard as flint, I would have a far holier fear and a far deeper contrition of spirit. Woe is me! I am one of the impudent house of Israel. The second charge is hard-heartedness, and I must not venture to plead innocent here. Once I had nothing but a heart of stone, and although through grace I now have a new and fleshy heart, much of my former stubbornness remains. I am not affected by the death of Jesus as I should be; neither am I moved as much as I should be by the ruin of my fellowmen, the wickedness of the times, the chastisement of my heavenly Father, and my own failures. Oh, that my heart would melt at the recital of my Savior's sufferings and death! Would to God I were rid of this base millstone within me, this hateful body of death. Blessed be the name of the Lord! The disease is not incurable! The Savior's precious blood is the universal solvent, and it will effectively soften me, even me, until my heart melts as wax before the fire.

Thou art my hope in the day of evil.
—Jeremiah 17:17

The path of the Christian is not always bright with sunshine. He has his seasons of darkness and of storm. True, it is written in God's Word, *"Her ways are ways of pleasantness, and all her paths are peace"* (Prov. 3:17). It is a great truth that religion is calculated to give a man happiness below as well as bliss above. But experience tells us that if the course of the just be *"as the shining light, that shineth more and more unto the perfect day"* (Prov. 4:18), yet sometimes that light is eclipsed. At certain periods clouds cover the believer's sun, and he walks in darkness and sees no light. Many have rejoiced in the presence of God for a season. They have basked in the sunshine in the earlier stages of their Christian career; they have walked along the *"green pastures"* by the side of the *"still waters"* (Ps. 23:2), but suddenly they find the glorious sky is clouded. Instead of the Land of Goshen, they have to tread the sandy desert. In the place of sweet waters, they find troubled streams, bitter to their taste. They say, "Surely, if I were a child of God, this would not happen." Oh, do not say this, you who are walking in darkness. The best of God's saints must drink from the cup of bitterness; the dearest of His children must bear the cross. No Christian has enjoyed perpetual prosperity; no believer can always keep his harp from the willows. (See Psalm 137:2.) Perhaps the Lord allotted you at first a smooth and unclouded path, because you were weak and timid. He tempered the wind to the shorn lamb, but now that you are stronger in the spiritual life, you must enter on the riper and rougher experience of God's full-grown children. We need winds and tempests to exercise our faith, to tear off the rotten bough of self-dependence, and to root us more firmly in Christ. The day of evil reveals to us the value of our glorious hope.

The Lord taketh pleasure in his people.
—Psalm 149:4

How comprehensive is the love of Jesus! There is no part of His people's interests that He does not consider, and there is nothing that concerns their welfare that is not important to Him. Not merely does He think of you, believer, as an immortal being, but as a mortal being, too. Do not deny it or doubt it: *"The very hairs of your head are all numbered"* (Matt. 10:30). *"The steps of a good man are ordered by the Lord: and he delighteth in his way"* (Ps. 37:23). It would be a sad thing for us if this mantle of love did not cover all our concerns, for what mischief might be worked in us in that part of our business that did not come under our gracious Lord's inspection! Believer, rest assured that the heart of Jesus cares about your daily affairs. The breadth of His tender love is such that you may resort to Him in all matters; for in all your afflictions, He is afflicted, and as a father pities his children, so He pities you. The daily concerns of all His saints are borne in the broad heart of the Son of God. Oh, what a heart is His that does not merely understand His people but also comprehends the diverse and innumerable concerns of all those persons! Do you think, O Christian, that you can measure the love of Christ? Think of what His love has brought you: justification, adoption, sanctification, eternal life! The riches of His goodness are unsearchable; you will never be able to name them or even conceive them. Oh, the breadth of the love of Christ! Will such a love as this have half our hearts? Will it have a cold love in return? Will Jesus' marvelous lovingkindness and tender care meet with but faint response and delayed acknowledgment? Tune your harp, my soul, to a glad song of thanksgiving! Go to your rest rejoicing, for you are no desolate wanderer, but a beloved child, watched over, cared for, supplied, and defended by your Lord.

And all the children of Israel murmured.
—Numbers 14:2

There are complainers among Christians now, as there were in the camp of Israel of old. There are those who, when the rod falls, cry out against painful trials. They ask, "Why am I thus afflicted? What have I done to be chastened in this manner?" A word with you, O complainer! Why should you grumble against the actions of your heavenly Father? Can He treat you more harshly than you deserve? Consider what a rebel you were once, but He has pardoned you! Surely, if He in His wisdom sees fit now to chasten you, you should not complain. After all, are you smitten as harshly as your sins deserve? Consider the corruption that is in your heart, and then, will you wonder that so much of the rod is required to remove it? Weigh yourself, and discern how much dross is mingled with your gold. Do you think the fire is too hot to purge away as much dross as you have? Does not that proud, rebellious spirit of yours prove that your heart is not thoroughly sanctified? Are not those murmuring words contrary to the holy, submissive nature of God's children? Is not the correction needed? But if you will grumble against the chastening, take heed, for it will go hard with complainers. God always chastises His children twice if they do not bear the first stroke patiently. But know one thing: *"He doth not afflict willingly nor grieve the children of men"* (Lam. 3:33). All His corrections are sent in love, to purify you and to draw you nearer to Himself. Surely it must help you to bear the chastening with resignation if you are able to recognize your Father's hand. *"For whom the Lord loveth he chasteneth, and scourgeth every son whom he receiveth. If ye endure chastening, God dealeth with you as with sons"* (Heb. 12:6–7). *"Neither murmur ye, as some of them also murmured, and were destroyed of the destroyer"* (1 Cor. 10:10).

How precious also are thy thoughts unto me, O God!
—Psalm 139:17

Divine omniscience affords no comfort to the ungodly mind, but to the child of God it overflows with consolation. God is always thinking about us. He never turns aside His mind from us, and He always has us before His eyes. This is precisely as we would have it, for it would be dreadful to exist for a moment beyond the observation of our heavenly Father. His thoughts are always tender, loving, wise, prudent, and far-reaching. They bring to us countless benefits; therefore, it is a choice delight to remember them. The Lord has always thought about His people: hence, their election and the covenant of grace by which their salvation is secured. He always will think about them: hence, their final perseverance by which they will be brought safely to their final rest. In all our wanderings, the vigilant gaze of the eternal Watcher is always fixed upon us; we never roam beyond the Shepherd's eye. In our sorrows, He observes us incessantly, and not one of our pains escapes His attention. In our toils, He marks all our weariness and writes in His book all the struggles of His faithful ones. These thoughts of the Lord encompass us in all our paths and penetrate the innermost region of our being. Not a nerve or tissue, valve or vessel, of our bodily organization is uncared for; all the details of our little world are thought about by the great God. Dear reader, is this truth precious to you? Then hold to it. Never be led astray by those philosophic fools who preach an impersonal God and talk of self-existent, self-governing matter. The Lord lives and thinks about us; this is a truth far too precious for us to be lightly robbed of it. The notice of a nobleman is valued so highly that he who has it counts his fortune made; but what is it to be thought of by the King of Kings! If the Lord thinks of us, all is well, and we may rejoice forevermore.

His cheeks are as a bed of spices, as sweet flowers.
—Song of Solomon 5:13

The flowery month is here! March winds and April showers have done their work, and the earth is all adorned in beauty. Come, my soul, and put on your holiday attire; go forth to gather garlands of heavenly thoughts. You know where to go, for you know well the *"bed of spices."* You have often smelled the perfume of *"sweet flowers."* You will go at once to your Well Beloved and find all loveliness and all joy in Him. That cheek—once so rudely smitten with a rod, often wet with tears of sympathy and then defiled with spittle—that cheek, as it smiles with mercy, is a fragrant aroma to my heart. You did not hide Your face from shame and spittle, O Lord Jesus; therefore, I will find my dearest delight in praising You. Those cheeks were furrowed by the plow of grief and crimsoned with red lines of blood from Your thorn-crowned temples. Such marks of limitless love cannot but charm my soul far more than great quantities of perfume. If I may not see the whole of His face, I would behold His cheeks, for the least glimpse of Him is exceedingly refreshing to my spiritual sense and yields a variety of delights. In Jesus I find not only fragrance, but *"a bed of spices"*; not one flower, but all manner of *"sweet flowers."* He is to me my Rose and my Lily, my heart's comfort and my healing balm. When He is with me, it is May all year round. My soul goes forth to wash its happy face in the morning dew of His grace and to comfort itself with the singing of the birds of His promises. Precious Lord Jesus, let me truly know the blessedness that dwells in abiding, unbroken fellowship with You. I am a poor worthless one, whose cheek You have deigned to kiss! Oh, let me kiss You in return with the kisses of my lips.

MAY 1

Evening

I am the rose of Sharon.
—Song of Solomon 2:1

Whatever beauty there may be in the natural world, Jesus Christ possesses all that in the spiritual world in a tenfold degree. Among flowers, the rose is considered to be the sweetest, but Jesus is infinitely more beautiful in the garden of the soul than the rose can be in the gardens of earth. He takes first place as the fairest among ten thousand. He is the sun, and all others are the stars; the heavens and the day are dark in comparison with Him, for the King in His beauty transcends all. *"I am the rose of Sharon."* This was the best and rarest of roses. Jesus is not *"the rose"* alone; He is *"the rose of Sharon"*—the best of the best. He is positively lovely and superlatively the loveliest. There is variety in His charms. The rose is delightful to the eye, and its scent is pleasant and refreshing. Similarly, each of the senses of the soul—whether taste, feeling, hearing, sight, or spiritual smell—find appropriate gratification in Jesus. Even the remembrance of His love is sweet. Take the rose of Sharon, and pull it leaf from leaf; set aside the leaves in the jar of memory, and you will find each leaf fragrant long afterward, filling the house with perfume. Christ satisfies the highest taste of the most educated spirit to the fullest degree. The greatest amateur in perfumes is quite satisfied with the rose. When the soul has arrived at its highest elevation of true taste, it will still be content with Christ; no, it will be all the better able to appreciate Him. Heaven itself possesses nothing that excels the rose of Sharon. What symbol can fully express His beauty? Human speech and earthborn things fail to tell of Him. Earth's choicest charms combined inadequately depict His abounding preciousness. Blessed rose, bloom in my heart forever!

I pray not that thou shouldest take them out of the world.
—John 17:15

A sweet and blessed event that will occur to all believers in God's own time is the going home to be with Jesus. In a few more years the Lord's soldiers, who are now fighting *"the good fight of faith"* (1 Tim. 6:12), will be finished with conflict and will have entered into the joy of their Lord. But although Christ prays that His people may eventually be with Him where He is, He does not ask that they may be taken at once away from this world to heaven. He wishes them to stay here. Yet how frequently does the wearied pilgrim offer up the prayer, *"Oh that I had wings like a dove! for then would I fly away, and be at rest"* (Ps. 55:6), but Christ does not pray like that. He leaves us in His Father's hands, until, like shocks of fully ripened corn, we will each be gathered into our Master's granary. Jesus does not plead for our instant removal by death, for to abide in the flesh is necessary for others if not profitable for ourselves. He asks that we may be kept from evil, but He never asks for us to be admitted to the inheritance in glory until we are of full age. Christians often want to die when they have any trouble. Ask them why, and they tell you, "Because we would be with the Lord." We fear it is not so much that they are longing to be with the Lord, but rather that they are desiring to get rid of their troubles; otherwise, they would feel the same wish to die at other times, when not under the pressure of trial. They want to go home, not so much for the Savior's company, as to be at rest. Now it is quite right to desire to depart if we can do it in the same spirit that Paul did, because to be with Christ is far better, but the wish to escape from trouble is a selfish one. Rather let your care and wish be to glorify God by your life here as long as He pleases, even though it is in the midst of toil, conflict, and suffering, and leave it to Him to say when it is enough.

These all died in faith.
—Hebrews 11:13

Behold the epitaph of all those blessed saints who passed away before the coming of our Lord! It does not matter how they died, whether of old age or by violent means. This one point in which they all agree is the worthiest to record: *"These all died in faith."* In faith they lived. It was their comfort, their guide, their motive, and their support; and, in the same spiritual grace, they died, ending their life-song in the sweet strain in which they had so long continued. They did not die resting in the flesh or on their own achievements. They never wavered from their first acceptance of God's will, but they held to the way of faith to the end. Faith is as precious to die by as to live by. Dying in faith has distinct reference to the past. They believed the promises that had gone before and were assured that their sins were blotted out through the mercy of God. Dying in faith has to do with the present. These saints were confident of their acceptance with God. They enjoyed the rays of His love and rested in His faithfulness. Dying in faith looks into the future. They fell *"asleep in Christ"* (1 Cor. 15:18), affirming that the Messiah would surely come, and that when He would in the last days appear on the earth, they would rise from their graves to behold Him. To them the pains of death were but the birth pangs of a better state. Take courage, my soul, as you read this epitaph. Your life's journey is one of faith through grace, and sight seldom cheers you; this has also been the pathway of the brightest and the best. Faith was the orbit in which these stars of the first magnitude moved during all the time of their shining here; you will be happy if that it is also your path. Look anew tonight to Jesus, the Author and Finisher of your faith, and thank Him for giving you the same precious faith that belonged to the souls who are now in glory.

In the world ye shall have tribulation.
—John 16:33

Are you asking the reason for your trials, believer? Look *upward* to your heavenly Father, and behold Him pure and holy. Do you know that you are one day to be like Him? Will you easily be conformed to His image? Will you not require much refining in the *"furnace of affliction"* (Isa. 48:10) to purify you? Will it be an easy thing to get rid of your corruption and make you perfect, *"even as your Father which is in heaven is perfect"* (Matt. 5:48)? Next, Christian, turn your eye *downward*. Do you know what foes you have beneath your feet? You were once a servant of Satan, and no king will willingly lose his subjects. Do you think that Satan will leave you alone? No, he will always be after you, for *"as a roaring lion, [he] walketh about, seeking whom he may devour"* (1 Pet. 5:8). Expect trouble, therefore, Christian, when you look beneath you. Then look *around* you. Where are you? You are in an enemy's country, a stranger and a sojourner. The world is not your friend. If it is, then you are not God's friend, for he who is the friend of the world is the enemy of God. Be assured that you will find enemies everywhere. When you sleep, think that you are resting on the battlefield; when you walk, suspect an ambush in every hedge. As mosquitoes are said to bite strangers more than natives, so will the trials of earth be sharpest to you. Last, look *within* you, into your own heart, and observe what is there. Sin and self are still within. Ah, if you had no devil to tempt you, no enemies to fight you, and no world to ensnare you, you would still find in yourself enough evil to be a painful trouble to you, for *"the heart is deceitful above all things, and desperately wicked"* (Jer. 17:9). Expect trouble, then, but do not despair because of it, for God is with you to help and to strengthen you. He has said, *"I will be with [you] in trouble; I will deliver [you], and honour [you]"* (Ps. 91:15).

A very present help.
—Psalm 46:1

Covenant blessings are not meant to be only looked at; they are intended to be appropriated. Even our Lord Jesus is given to us for our present use. Believer, do you make use of Christ as you should? When you are in trouble, why do you not tell Him all your grief? Does He not have a sympathizing heart, and can He not comfort and relieve you? No, you are going about to all your friends, except for your best Friend, and you are telling your tale everywhere except to the heart of your Lord. Are you burdened with this day's sins? Here is a fountain filled with blood: use it, saint; use it. Has a sense of guilt returned to you? The pardoning grace of Jesus may be proved again and again. Come to Him at once for cleansing. Do you deplore your weakness? He is your strength; why not lean on Him? Do you feel naked? Come here, soul; put on the robe of Jesus' righteousness. Do not stand looking at it, but wear it. Strip off your own righteousness and your own fears, too. Put on the fair white linen, for it was meant to wear. Do you feel sick? Pull the night-bell of prayer, and call up the Beloved Physician! He will give the medicine that will revive you. You are poor, but then you have *"a kinsman…, a mighty man of wealth"* (Ruth 2:1). Will you not go to Him and ask Him to give you of His abundance, when He has given you the promise that you will be a joint heir with Him? All that He is and all that He has, He has made available to you. There is nothing Christ dislikes more than for His people to make a display of Him and not to use Him. He loves to be employed by us. The more burdens we put on His shoulders, the more precious He will be to us.

Let us be simple with Him, then,
  Not backward, stiff, or cold,
As though our Bethlehem could be
  What Sinai was of old.

MAY 4

Shall a man make gods unto himself, and they are no gods?
—Jeremiah 16:20

One great recurrent sin of ancient Israel was idolatry; spiritual Israel is plagued with a tendency toward the same evil. Mammon still intrudes his golden calf, and the shrines of pride are not forsaken. Self in various forms struggles to subdue the chosen ones under its dominion, and the flesh sets up its altars wherever it can find space for them. Favorite children are often the cause of much sin in believers. The Lord is grieved when He sees us doting on them above measure. They will live to be as great a curse to us as Absalom was to David, or they will be taken from us to leave our homes desolate. If Christians desire to grow thorns to stuff their sleepless pillows, let them dote on their dear ones. It is truly said that *"they are no gods,"* for the objects of our foolish love are very doubtful blessings, the solace that they yield us now is dangerous, and the help that they can give us in the hour of trouble is little indeed. Why, then, are we so bewitched with vanities? We pity the poor heathen who adore a god of stone, yet we worship a god of gold. Where is the vast superiority between a god of flesh and one of wood? The principle, the sin, the folly is the same in either case, only that in ours the crime is more aggravated because we have more light, and sin in the face of it. The heathen bows to a false deity, but he has never known the true God. We commit two evils when we forsake the living God and turn to idols. May the Lord purge us all from this grievous iniquity!

> The dearest idol I have known,
>> Whate'er that idol be;
> Help me to tear it from Thy throne,
>> And worship only Thee.

Being born again, not of corruptible seed, but of incorruptible.
—1 Peter 1:23

Peter most earnestly exhorted the scattered saints to love each other *"with a pure heart fervently"* (1 Pet. 1:22). He wisely based his argument, not on the law or human nature or philosophy, but on that high and divine nature that God has implanted in His people. Just as some wise tutor of princes might labor to instill and foster in them a kingly spirit and dignified behavior, finding arguments in their position and descent, so, looking upon God's people as heirs of glory, princes of the royal blood, descendants of the King of Kings, earth's truest and oldest aristocracy, Peter said to them, "See that you love one another because of your noble birth, being born of incorruptible seed; because of your pedigree, being descended from God, the Creator of all things; and because of your immortal destiny, for you will never pass away, though the glory of the flesh will fade, and even its existence will cease." (See 1 Peter 2:22–25.) It would be well if, in the spirit of humility, we recognized the true dignity of our regenerated nature and lived up to it. What is a Christian? If you compare him with a king, he adds priestly sanctity to royal dignity. The king's royalty often lies only in his crown, but with a Christian it is infused into his inmost nature. He is as much above his fellows through his new birth as a man is above the beast that perishes. Surely he should carry himself, in all his dealings, as one who is not of the crowd, but chosen out of the world, distinguished by sovereign grace, described as *"a peculiar people"* (1 Pet. 2:9). Therefore, the Christian cannot grovel in the dust as others do or live after the manner of the world's citizens. Let the dignity of your nature and the brightness of your prospects, believers in Christ, constrain you to cleave to holiness and to *"abstain from all appearance of evil"* (1 Thess. 5:22).

I will be their God, and they shall be my people.
—2 Corinthians 6:16

What a sweet title: *"my people"*! What a cheering revelation: *"their God"*!
How much meaning is couched in those two words, *"my people"*! Here is a
distinctive point. The whole world is God's. The heaven, even the heaven
of heavens, is the Lord's, and He reigns among the children of men; but
of those whom He has chosen, whom He has purchased for Himself, He
says what He does not say of others—*"My people."* In this phrase there is
the idea of ownership. In a special manner *"the LORD's portion is his people;*
Jacob is the lot of his inheritance" (Deut. 32:9). All the nations on earth are
His. The whole world is in His power, yet His people, His chosen, are His
special possession. He has done more for them than others. He has bought
them with His blood and has brought them close to Himself. He has set
His great heart on them and has loved them with an everlasting love, a
love that many waters cannot quench, and that the revolutions of time will
never suffice in the least degree to diminish. Dear friends, can you, by faith,
see yourselves in that number? Can you look up to heaven and say, "My
Lord and my God. You are mine by that sweet relationship that entitles
me to call You 'Father.' You are mine by that hallowed fellowship that I
delight to hold with You when You are pleased to manifest Yourself to me
as You do not to the world"? Can you read the Book of Inspiration, and find
there the indentures of your salvation? Can you read your name written in
precious blood? Can you, by humble faith, lay hold of Jesus' garments, and
say, "My Christ"? If you can, then God says of you, and of others like you,
"My people." If God is your God, and Christ is your Christ, the Lord pays
special attention to you. You are the object of His choice, accepted in His
beloved Son.

He that handleth a matter wisely shall find good:
and whoso trusteth in the LORD, *happy is he.*
—Proverbs 16:20

Wisdom is man's true strength; under its guidance, he best accomplishes his life's goals. Handling matters wisely gives man the richest enjoyment and presents the noblest occupation for his talents. By walking in wisdom, a person finds good in the fullest sense. Without wisdom, a man is like a wild colt, running here and there, wasting strength that otherwise might be profitably employed. Wisdom is the compass by which man is to steer across the trackless expanse of life; without it he is a derelict vessel, the sport of winds and waves. A man must be prudent in such a world as this, or he will find no good; instead, he will encounter unnumbered difficulties. The pilgrim will sorely wound his feet among the briers of the forest of life if he does not choose his steps with the utmost caution. He who is in a wilderness infested with robbers must handle matters wisely if he desires to journey safely. If, trained by the great Teacher, we follow where He leads, we will find good, even while in this dark abode. There are heavenly fruits to be gathered on this side of Eden's arbors and songs of paradise to be sung amid the groves of earth. But where will this wisdom be found? Many have dreamed of it, but they have not possessed it. Where will we learn it? Let us listen to the voice of the Lord, for He has declared the secret. He has revealed to the sons of men wherein true wisdom lies, and we have it in the text, *"Whoso trusteth in the* LORD, *happy is he."* The true way to handle a matter wisely is to trust in the Lord. This is the sure guide to the most intricate mazes of life; follow it and find eternal bliss. He who trusts in the Lord has a diploma for wisdom granted by inspiration. He is happy now, and he will be even happier above. Lord, in this sweet evening, walk with me in the garden and teach me the wisdom of faith.

We dwell in him.
—1 John 4:13

Do you want a house for your soul? Do you ask, "What is the price?" It is something less than proud human nature would like to give. It is without money and without price. Would you like to pay a respectable rent? Would you love to do something to win Christ? Then you cannot have the house, for it is *"without price"* (Isa. 55:1). Will you take my Master's house on a lease for all eternity, with nothing to pay for it, nothing but the rent of loving and serving Him forever? Will you take Jesus and *"dwell in him"*? See, this house is furnished with all you need. It is filled with riches more than you will spend as long as you live. Here you can have intimate communion with Christ and feast on His love. Here are tables well-stored with food for you to live on forever. In it, when weary, you can find rest with Jesus. From it, you can look out and see heaven itself. Will you have the house? If you are homeless, you will say, "I would like to have the house; may I have it?" Yes, there is the key. The key is, "Come to Jesus." "But," you say, "I am too shabby for such a house." Never mind, for there are clothes inside. If you feel guilty and condemned, come; and though the house is too good for you, Christ will make you good enough for the house in time. He will wash you and cleanse you, and you will yet be able to sing, *"We dwell in him."* Believer, you are thrice blessed to have such a dwelling place! You are greatly privileged, for you have a *"strong habitation"* (Ps. 71:3) in which you are ever safe. Dwelling in Him, you have not only a perfect and secure house, but also an everlasting one. When this world will have melted like a dream, our house will live and stand more imperishable than marble, more solid than granite, self-existent as God, for it is God Himself—*"We dwell in him."*

All the days of my appointed time will I wait.
—Job 14:14

A little stay on earth will make heaven more heavenly. Nothing makes rest as sweet as work does; nothing renders security as pleasant as exposure to danger does. The bitter tonics of earth will give a relish to the new wine that sparkles in the golden bowls of glory. Our battered armor and scarred countenances will render more illustrious our victory above, when we are welcomed to the seats of those who have overcome the world. We would not have full fellowship with Christ if we did not for a while sojourn below, for He was baptized with a baptism of suffering among men; we must be baptized with the same if we wish to share His kingdom. Fellowship with Christ is so honorable that the worst sorrow is a light price by which to procure it. Another reason for our lingering here is for the good of others. We would not wish to enter heaven until our work is done, and it may be that we are yet ordained to minister light to souls trapped in the darkness of sin. Our prolonged stay here is doubtless for God's glory. A tried saint, like a well-cut diamond, glitters much in the King's crown. Nothing reflects as much honor on a workman as a protracted and severe trial of his work, and its triumphant endurance of the ordeal without giving way in any part. We are God's workmanship, in whom He will be glorified by our afflictions. It is for the honor of Jesus that we endure the trials of our faith with sacred joy. Let each man surrender his own longings to the glory of Jesus, and feel, "If my lying in the dust would elevate my Lord by as much as an inch, let me still lie among the pots of earth. If to live on earth forever would make my Lord more glorious, it would be my heaven to be shut out of heaven." Our time is fixed and settled by eternal decree. Let us not be anxious about it, but wait with patience until the gates of pearl open.

Great multitudes followed him, and he healed them all.
—Matthew 12:15

What an abundance of hideous sickness must have thrust itself under the eye of Jesus! Yet we do not read that He was disgusted by it; instead, He patiently waited on every case. What an unusual variety of evils must have met at His feet! What sickening ulcers and putrefying sores! Yet He was ready for every new shape of monstrous evil, and He was victor over it in every form. Let the arrow fly from what quarter it might; He quenched its fiery power. The heat of fever or the cold of dropsy; the lethargy of palsy or the rage of madness; the filth of leprosy or the darkness of blindness—all knew the power of His word and fled at His command. In every corner of the field He was triumphant over evil and received the respect of delivered captives. He came, He saw, He conquered everywhere. It is even so this morning. Whatever my own case may be, the beloved Physician can heal me. Whatever may be the state of others whom I may remember at this moment in prayer, I may have hope in Jesus that He will be able to heal them of their sins. My child, my friend, my dearest one, I can have hope for each, for all, when I remember the healing power of my Lord. On my own account, however severe my struggle with sins and infirmities, I may yet be of good cheer. He who walked on earth healing the sick still dispenses His grace and works wonders among the sons of men. Let me go to Him at once in earnest. Let me praise Him this morning, as I remember how He performed His spiritual cures, which bring Him most renown. It was by taking our sicknesses on Himself. *"With his stripes we are healed"* (Isa. 53:5). The church on earth is full of souls healed by our beloved Physician. The inhabitants of heaven itself confess that He healed them all. Come, then, my soul; tell about the virtue of His grace everywhere, and let it be *"to the* Lord *for a name, for an everlasting sign that shall not be cut off"* (Isa. 55:13).

Jesus saith unto him, Rise, take up thy bed, and walk.
—John 5:8

Like many others, the crippled man had been waiting for a miracle to happen and for a sign to be given. Wearily, he watched the pool, but no angel came or came for him; yet, thinking it was his only chance, he waited still. He did not know that there was One near him whose word could heal him in a moment. Many are in the same plight. They are waiting for some extraordinary emotion, remarkable impression, or heavenly vision. They wait in vain and watch for nothing. Even supposing that, in a few cases, remarkable signs are seen, yet these are rare, and no one has a right to look for them in his own situation— especially no one who feels his inability to avail himself of the moving of the water even if it did come. It is very sad to realize that tens of thousands are now waiting on the use of means, ordinances, vows, or resolutions, and they have waited in vain, utterly in vain, longer than one can imagine. Meanwhile these poor souls forget the present Savior, who invites them to look to Him and be saved. He could heal them immediately, but they prefer to wait for an angel or a miracle. To trust God is the sure way to every blessing, and He is worthy of the most implicit confidence; but unbelief makes them prefer the cold porches of Bethesda to the warm bosom of His love. Oh, that the Lord may turn His eye upon the multitudes who are in this situation tonight. May He forgive the slights that they put upon His divine power. In His sweet, constraining voice, may He call them to rise from their beds of despair and in the energy of faith to take up their beds and walk. O Lord, hear our prayers for everyone who is in this situation tonight. At this calm hour of sunset and before the day breaks, may they look and live. Dear reader, is there anything in this passage that speaks to you?

He that was healed wist not who it was.
—John 5:13

Years are short to the happy and healthy, but thirty-eight years of disease must have dragged into a long time for the poor, impotent man. When Jesus, therefore, healed him by a word, while he lay at the pool of Bethesda, he was delightfully aware of a change. Likewise, the sinner who has for weeks and months been paralyzed with despair, and has wearily sighed for salvation, is very conscious of the change when the Lord Jesus speaks the word of power and gives joy and peace in believing. The evil removed is too great to be removed without our discerning it, the life imparted is too remarkable to be possessed and remain inoperative, and the change is too marvelous not to be perceived. Yet the poor man was ignorant of the Author of his cure. He did not know the sacredness of His person, the offices that He sustained, or the mission that brought Him among men. Much ignorance of Jesus may remain in hearts that yet feel the power of His blood. We must not hastily condemn men for lack of knowledge; but where we can see the faith that saves the soul, we must believe that salvation has been bestowed. The Holy Spirit makes men penitents long before He makes them holy. He who believes what he knows will soon know more clearly what he believes. Ignorance is, however, an evil, for this poor man was much tantalized by the Pharisees and was quite unable to cope with them. It is good to be able to answer the opposition, but we cannot do so if we do not know the Lord Jesus clearly and with understanding. The cure of his ignorance, however, soon followed the cure of his infirmity, for he was visited by the Lord in the temple. After that gracious manifestation, he was found testifying that *"it was Jesus, which had made him whole"* (John 5:15). Lord, if You have saved me, show me Yourself, so that I may declare You to the sons of men.

Acquaint now thyself with him.
—Job 22:21

If we desire to properly acquaint ourselves with God and be at peace, we must know Him as He has revealed Himself—not only in the unity of His essence and existence, but also in the plurality of His persons. "*God said, Let us make man in our image*" (Gen. 1:26). Do not let man be content until he knows something of the "*us*" from whom his being was derived. Endeavor to know the Father; bury your head in His bosom in deep repentance, and confess that you are not worthy to be called His child. Receive the kiss of His love. Let the ring that is the token of His eternal faithfulness be on your finger. Sit at His table, and let your heart be made merry in His grace. Then press forward and seek to know much of the Son of God, who is the brightness of His Father's glory; yet, in unspeakable condescension of grace, He became Man for our sakes. Know Him in the unique complexity of His nature: eternal God, yet suffering, finite man. Follow Him as He walks the waters with the footsteps of deity and as He sits on the well in the weariness of humanity. Do not be satisfied unless you know much of Jesus Christ as your Friend, your Brother, your Husband, your All. Do not forget the Holy Spirit. Endeavor to obtain a clear view of His nature and character, His attributes, and His works. Behold that Spirit of the Lord, who first of all moved upon chaos and brought forth order; who now visits the chaos of your soul and creates the order of holiness. Behold Him as the Lord and Giver of spiritual life, the Illuminator, the Instructor, the Comforter, and the Sanctifier. Behold Him as, in holy power, He descends on the head of Jesus, and then afterward rests on you who are as the skirts of His garments. Such an intelligent, scriptural, and experiential belief in the Trinity in Unity is yours if you truly know God. Such knowledge brings peace indeed!

Who hath blessed us with all spiritual blessings.
—Ephesians 1:3

Christ bestows on His people all the goodness of the past, present, and the future. In the mysterious ages of the past, the Lord Jesus was His Father's first elect. In His election He gave us an interest, for we were *"chosen...in him before the foundation of the world"* (Eph. 1:4). He had from all eternity the privileges of Sonship, as His Father's Only Begotten and well-beloved Son. He has, in the riches of His grace, by adoption and regeneration, elevated us to sonship also, so that to us He has given *"power to become the sons of God"* (John 1:12). The eternal covenant, based on suretyship and confirmed by oath, is ours, for our strong consolation and security. In the everlasting settlements of predestinating wisdom and omnipotent decree, the eyes of the Lord Jesus were ever fixed on us. We may rest assured that in the whole roll of destiny there is not a line that lessens the interests of His redeemed. The great betrothal of the Prince of Glory is ours, for it is to us that He is betrothed, as the sacred nuptials will before long declare to an assembled universe. The marvelous incarnation of the God of heaven, with all the amazing condescension and humiliation that attended it, is ours. The bloody sweat, the scourge, and the cross are ours forever. Whatever blissful consequences flow from perfect obedience, finished atonement, resurrection, ascension, or intercession—all are ours by His own gift. He is now bearing our names on His breastplate; and in His authoritative pleadings at the throne, He remembers our persons and pleads our cause. He employs His dominion over principalities and powers and His absolute majesty in heaven for the benefit of those who trust in Him. His high estate is as much at our service as was His condition of abasement. He who gave Himself for us in the depths of woe and death does not withdraw the grant now that He is enthroned in the highest heavens.

MAY 9

Evening

Come, my beloved, let us go forth into the field;…
let us see if the vine flourish.
—Song of Solomon 7:11–12

The church was about to engage in earnest labor and desired her Lord's company in it. She did not say, "I will go," but *"Let us go."* It is a blessing to work when Jesus is at our side! It is the business of God's people to be trimmers of God's vines. Like our first parents, we are put into the garden of the Lord for usefulness; therefore, let us go forth into the field. Observe that the church, when she is thinking rightly, desires to enjoy communion with Christ in all her many labors. Some imagine that they cannot serve Christ actively and still have fellowship with Him. They are mistaken. True, it is very easy to fritter away our inward life in outward activities and complain to the Spouse, *"They made me the keeper of the vineyards; but mine own vineyard have I not kept"* (Song 1:6). There is no reason, however, why this should be the case except through our own folly and neglect. Certainly, a believer may do nothing, yet grow quite as lifeless in spiritual things as those who are the busiest. Mary was not praised for sitting still, but for sitting at Jesus' feet. Even so, Christians are not to be praised for neglecting duties under the pretense of having secret fellowship with Jesus. It is not sitting, but sitting at Jesus' feet that is commendable. Do not think that activity is in itself evil. It is a great blessing and a means of grace to us. Paul called it a grace given to him to be allowed to preach, and every form of Christian service may become a personal blessing to those engaged in it. Those who have the most fellowship with Christ are not recluses or hermits, who have much time to spare, but indefatigable laborers who are toiling for Jesus, and who, in their labors, have Him side by side with them, so that they are *"workers together"* (2 Cor. 6:1) with God. Let us remember that in anything we have to do for Jesus, we can do it and should do it in close communion with Him.

MAY 10

Morning

> *But now is Christ risen from the dead.*
> —1 Corinthians 15:20

The whole system of Christianity rests on the fact that Christ is risen from the dead, for *"If Christ be not risen, then is our preaching vain, and your faith is also vain....Ye are yet in your sins"* (1 Cor. 15:14, 17). The divinity of Christ finds its surest proof in His resurrection, since He was *"declared to be the Son of God with power, according to the spirit of holiness, by the resurrection from the dead"* (Rom. 1:4). It would not be unreasonable to doubt His deity if He had not risen. Moreover, Christ's sovereignty depends on His resurrection, *"For to this end Christ both died, and rose, and revived, that he might be Lord both of the dead and living"* (Rom. 14:9). Again, our justification, that choice blessing of the covenant, is linked with Christ's triumphant victory over death and the grave; for He *"was delivered for our offences, and was raised again for our justification"* (Rom. 4:25). Moreover, our very regeneration is connected with His resurrection, for we are *"begotten...again unto a lively hope by the resurrection of Jesus Christ from the dead"* (1 Pet. 1:3). And most certainly our ultimate resurrection rests here, for *"if the Spirit of him that raised up Jesus from the dead dwell in you, he that raised up Christ from the dead shall also quicken your mortal bodies by his Spirit that dwelleth in you"* (Rom. 8:11). If Christ is not risen, then we will not rise; but if He is risen, then they who are asleep in Christ have not perished, but in their flesh will surely behold their God. Thus, the silver thread of resurrection runs through all the believer's blessings, from his regeneration to his eternal glory, and it binds them together. How important, then, will this glorious fact be in his estimation, and how will he rejoice that beyond a doubt it is established that *"now is Christ risen from the dead."*

> The promise is fulfill'd,
>   Redemption's work is done,
> Justice with mercy's reconciled,
>   For God has raised His Son.

The only begotten of the Father, full of grace and truth.
—John 1:14

Believer, you can give your testimony that Christ is the *"only begotten of the Father,"* as well as *"the first begotten of the dead"* (Rev. 1:5). You can say, "He is divine to me, even if He is human to all the world. He has done for me what no one but God could do. He has subdued my stubborn will, melted my hardened heart, opened *'gates of brass, and cut the bars of iron in sunder'* (Ps. 107:16). He has turned my mourning into laughter and my desolation into joy. He has led my captivity captive and made my heart *'rejoice with joy unspeakable and full of glory'* (1 Pet. 1:8). Let others think as they will of Him, to me He must be the *'only begotten of the Father.'"* Blessed be His name! And He is full of grace. Oh, if it had not been for Him, I would never have been saved. He drew me when I struggled to escape from His grace; and, when at last I came to His mercy seat, trembling like a condemned criminal, He said, "Your sins, which are many, are all forgiven: be of good cheer." And He is full of truth. His promises have all been true; not one has failed. I bear witness that no servant ever had such a master as I have. No brother has had a kinsman as He has been to me. No spouse has had a husband as Christ has been to my soul. No sinner has had a better Savior; no mourner has had a better comforter than Christ has been to my spirit. I desire no one besides Him. In life, He is my life; in death, He will be the death of death. In poverty, Christ is my riches; in sickness, He makes my bed. In darkness, He is my star; in brightness, He is my sun. He is the manna of the camp in the wilderness, and He will be the new corn of the host when they come to Canaan. Jesus is all grace and no wrath to me, all truth and no falsehood. He is full of truth and grace, infinitely full. My soul, this night, with all your strength, bless *"the only begotten."*

MAY 11

Lo, I am with you always.
—Matthew 28:20

It is good to know that there is One who is always the same, One who is always with us. It is good there is a stable rock in the midst of the billows of the sea of life. O my soul, do not set your affections on rusting, moth-eaten, decaying treasures, but set your heart on Him who abides forever faithful to you. Do not build your house on the moving quicksand of a deceitful world, but ground your hopes on the Rock, that, amid descending rain and roaring floods, will stand immovably secure. My soul, I charge you: lay up your treasure in the only secure cabinet; store your jewels where you can never lose them. Put your all in Christ. Set all your affections on His person, all your hope in His merit, all your trust in His efficacious blood, and all your joy in His presence, so that you may laugh at loss and defy destruction. Remember that all the flowers in the world's garden eventually fade, and the day is coming when nothing will be left but the black, cold earth. Death's black extinguisher must soon put out your candle. Oh, how sweet to have sunlight when the candle is gone! The dark flood must soon roll between you and all you have. Then wed your heart to Him who will never leave you. Trust yourself with Him who will go with you through the black and surging current of death's stream, and who will land you safely on the celestial shore and make you sit with Him in heavenly places forever. Go, sorrowing son of affliction, and tell your secrets to the Friend who sticks *"closer than a brother"* (Prov. 18:24). Trust all your concerns to Him who never can be taken from you, who will never leave you, and who will never let you leave Him, even *"Jesus Christ the same yesterday, and to day, and for ever"* (Heb. 13:8). *"Lo, I am with you alway"* is enough for my soul to live on, no matter who else might forsake me.

Only be thou strong and very courageous.
—Joshua 1:7

Gods tender love for His servants makes Him concerned for the state of their emotions. He wants them to be of good courage. Some consider it a small thing for a believer to be troubled with doubts and fears, but God does not think so. From this text, it is clear that our Master would not have us entangled with fears. He wants us to be free of cares, doubts, and cowardice. Our Master takes our unbelief more seriously than we do. When we are despondent, we are subject to a grievous disease that should not be ignored, but should be taken immediately to the Beloved Physician. Our Lord does not want to see our countenance sad. It was a law of Ahasuerus that no one could come into the king's court dressed in mourning; this is not the law of the King of Kings, for we may come mourning as we are. Still, He would have us put on *"the garment of praise for the spirit of heaviness"* (Isa. 61:3), for there are many reasons to rejoice. The Christian should be of a courageous spirit, so that he may glorify the Lord by enduring trials in a heroic manner. If he is fearful and fainthearted, it will dishonor his God. Besides, what a bad example it is. This disease of doubtfulness and discouragement is an epidemic that soon spreads among the Lord's flock. One downcast believer makes twenty souls sad. Moreover, unless your courage is kept up, Satan will be too much for you. Let your spirit be joyful in God your Savior. *"The joy of the LORD is your strength"* (Neh. 8:10), and no fiend of hell will make headway against you. But cowardice throws down the banner. Moreover, labor is light to a man of cheerful spirit, and success waits on cheerfulness. The man who toils, rejoicing in his God and believing with all his heart, has guaranteed success. He who sows in hope will reap in joy; therefore, dear reader, *"be thou strong and very courageous."*

MAY 12
Morning

I will love him, and will manifest myself to him.
—John 14:21

The Lord Jesus gives special revelations of Himself to His people. Even if Scripture did not declare this, there are many children of God who could testify to the truth of it from their own experience. They have had manifestations of their Lord and Savior Jesus Christ in an unusual manner, such as no mere reading or hearing could afford. In the biographies of eminent saints, you will find many instances recorded in which Jesus has been pleased, in a very special manner, to speak to their souls and to unfold the wonders of His person. Their souls have been steeped in happiness that they have thought themselves to be in heaven, whereas they were not there, though they were very close to the threshold of it. When Jesus manifests Himself to His people, it is heaven on earth; it is paradise in embryo; it is bliss begun. Special manifestations of Christ exercise a holy influence on the believer's heart. One effect will be humility. If a man says, "I have had such-and-such spiritual communications. I am a great man," then he has never had any communion with Jesus at all, for God has *"respect unto the lowly: but the proud he knoweth afar off"* (Ps. 138:6). He does not need to come near them to know them, and He will never give them any visits of love. Another effect of a true manifestation of Christ will be happiness, for in God's presence, *"there are pleasures for evermore"* (Ps. 16:11). Holiness will be sure to follow. A man who has no holiness has never had this manifestation. Some men profess a great deal, but we must not believe anyone unless we see that his deeds match his words. *"Be not deceived; God is not mocked"* (Gal. 6:7). He will not bestow His favors on the wicked, for while He will not cast away a perfect man, neither will He respect an evildoer. Thus there will be three effects of nearness to Jesus: humility, happiness, and holiness. May God give them to you, Christian!

Fear not to go down into Egypt; for I will there make of thee
a great nation: I will go down with thee into Egypt;
and I will also surely bring thee up again.
—Genesis 46:3–4

Jacob must have shuddered at the thought of leaving the land of his father and having to live among heathen strangers. It was a new scene and likely to be a trying one. Who could venture among couriers of a foreign monarch without anxiety? Yet the way was evidently appointed for him; therefore, he resolved to go. This is frequently the position of believers now: they are called to perils and temptations altogether untried. At such seasons let them imitate Jacob's example by offering sacrifices of prayer to God and seeking His direction. Do not let them take a step until they have waited on the Lord for His blessing. Then they will have Jacob's companion to be their Friend and Helper. How blessed to feel assured that the Lord is with us in all our ways and condescends to go down into our humiliation and banishment with us! Even beyond the ocean our Father's love beams like the sun in its strength. We cannot hesitate to go where Jehovah promises His presence; even the valley of the shadow of death grows bright with the radiance of this assurance. Marching onward with faith in their God, believers will have Jacob's promise. They will be brought up again, whether it is from the troubles of life or the rooms of death. Jacob's seed came out of Egypt in due time, and so will all the faithful pass unscathed through the tribulation of life and the terror of death. Let us exercise Jacob's confidence. *"Fear not"* is the Lord's command and His divine encouragement to those who at His bidding are launching upon new seas. The divine presence and preservation forbid so much as one unbelieving fear. Without our God, we would fear to move; but when He commands us to go, it would be dangerous to delay. Reader, go forward, and do not fear.

Weeping may endure for a night, but joy cometh in the morning.
—Psalm 30:5

Christian, if you are in a night of trial, think of tomorrow. Encourage your heart with thoughts of the coming of your Lord. Be patient, for He comes with clouds descending. Be patient! The Husbandman waits until He reaps His harvest. Be patient, for you know who has said, *"Behold, I come quickly; and my reward is with me, to give every man according as his work shall be"* (Rev. 22:12). If you are distressed now, remember,

A few more rolling suns, at most,
Will land you on fair Canaan's coast.

Your head may be crowned with thorny troubles now, but it will wear a starry crown before long. Your hand may be filled with cares now, but it will sweep the strings of the harp of heaven soon. Your garments may be soiled with dust now, but they will be white soon. Wait a little longer. Oh, how despicable our troubles and trials will seem when we look back on them! Looking at them here in the present, they seem immense; but when we get to heaven, we will then

With transporting joys recount,
The labors of our feet.

Our trials will then seem light and momentary afflictions. Let us go on boldly. Even if the night is never so dark, the morning comes, which is more than they can say who are shut up in the darkness of hell. Do you know what it is thus to live on the future—to live on expectation—to anticipate heaven? Happy believer, what joy it is to have so sure and so comforting a hope! It may be all dark now, but it will soon be light; it may be all trial now, but it will soon be all happiness. What does it matter though *"weeping may endure for a night,"* when *"joy cometh in the morning"*?

*Thou art my portion, O L*ORD*.*
—Psalm 119:57

Look at your possessions, believer, and compare your portion with the lot of your fellowmen. Some make their living in the field. They are rich, and their harvests yield them a golden increase. But what are harvests compared with your God, who is the God of harvests? What are bursting granaries compared with Him, who is the Husbandman who feeds you with the bread of heaven? Some do their work in the city. Their wealth is abundant and flows to them in constant streams, until they become a very reservoir of gold. But what is gold compared with your God? You could not live on it; your spiritual life could not be sustained by it. Apply it to a troubled conscience, and could it reduce its pain? Apply it to a discouraged heart, and see if it could stop a single groan or lessen one's grief. But you have God, and in Him you have more than gold or riches could ever buy. Some obtain their livelihood through that which most men love—applause and fame; but ask yourself, is God not more important to you than that? What if thousands of trumpets loudly blared your praise? Would this prepare you to cross the Jordan or cheer you in the face of judgment? No, there are griefs in life that wealth cannot alleviate; and there is the deep need at your dying hour for which no riches can provide. But when you have God for your portion, you have more than all else put together. In Him every need is met, whether in life or in death. With God for your portion, you are rich indeed; for He will supply your needs, comfort your heart, assuage your grief, guide your steps, be with you in the dark valley, and then take you home to enjoy Him forever. *"I have enough"* (Gen. 33:9), Esau said; that statement is the best a worldly man can say. However, Jacob replied, *"God hath dealt graciously with me, and…I have* [all things, more than] *enough"* (v. 11), which is a note too high for carnal minds to understand.

Joint-heirs with Christ.
—Romans 8:17

The boundless realms of His Father's universe are Christ's by prescriptive right. As *"heir of all things"* (Heb. 1:2), He is the sole proprietor of the vast creation of God. He has admitted us to claim the whole as ours, by virtue of that deed of joint heirship that the Lord has ratified with His chosen people. The golden streets of paradise, the pearly gates, the river of life, the transcendent bliss, and the unutterable glory are, by our blessed Lord, allotted to us for our everlasting possession. He shares all that He has with His people. The royal crown He has placed on the head of His church, appointing her a kingdom, and calling her sons *"a royal priesthood"* (1 Pet. 2:9), a generation of *"kings and priests"* (Rev. 1:6). He uncrowned Himself that we might have a coronation of glory. He would not sit on His own throne until He had procured a place on it for all who overcome by His blood. Crown the head and the whole body shares the honor. Behold here the reward of every Christian conqueror! Christ's throne, crown, scepter, palace, treasure, robes, and heritage are yours. Far superior to the jealousy, selfishness, and greed—that bring no advantages to those who practice them—Christ deems His happiness completed by His people sharing it. *"The glory which thou gavest me I have given them"* (John 17:22). *"These things have I spoken unto you, that my joy might remain in you, and that your joy might be full"* (John 15:11). The smiles of His Father are all the sweeter to Him, because His people share them. The honors of His kingdom are more pleasing, because His people appear with Him in glory. More valuable to Him are His conquests, since they have taught His people to overcome. He delights in His throne, because on it there is a place for them. He rejoices in His royal robes, since over them His skirts are spread. He delights the more in His joy, because He calls them to enter into it.

MAY 14
Evening

He shall gather the lambs with his arm,
and carry them in his bosom.
—Isaiah 40:11

Who is He of whom such gracious words are spoken? He is the Good Shepherd. Why does He carry the lambs close to His heart? Because He has a tender heart, and any weakness at once melts His heart. The sighs, the ignorance, the feebleness of the little ones of His flock elicit His compassion. It is His office, as a faithful High Priest, to consider the weak. Besides, He purchased them with His blood, so they are His property. He must and will care for that which cost Him so dearly. Then He is responsible for each lamb, bound by covenant engagements not to lose one. Moreover, they are all a part of His glory and reward. But how may we understand the expression, "He will carry them"? Sometimes He carries them by not permitting them to endure many trials. Providence deals tenderly with them. Often they are "carried" by being filled with an unusual degree of love, so that they bear up and stand fast. Though their knowledge may not be deep, they have great sweetness in what they do know. Frequently He carries them by giving them a very simple faith, which takes the promise just as it stands, and believingly, they run straight to Jesus with every trouble. The simplicity of their faith gives them an unusual degree of confidence, which lifts them above the world. He carries the lambs in His bosom. Here is boundless affection. Would He put them next to His heart if He did not love them so much? Here is tender nearness; they are so near that they could not possibly be nearer. Here is hallowed familiarity; there are precious love-passages between Christ and His weak ones. Here is perfect safety; next to His heart, who can hurt them? The enemy must hurt the Shepherd first. Here is perfect rest and sweetest comfort. Surely we are not sufficiently aware of the infinite tenderness of Jesus!

All that believe are justified.
—Acts 13:39

The believer in Christ receives a present justification. Faith does not produce this fruit in the future, but now. So far as justification is the result of faith, it is given to the soul in the moment when it surrenders to Christ and accepts Him as its all in all. Are they who stand before the throne of God justified now?—so are we, as truly and as clearly justified as they who walk in white and sing melodious praises to celestial harps. The thief on the cross was justified the moment that he turned the eye of faith to Jesus. The aged Paul, after years of service, was not more justified than was the thief with no service at all. We are today *"accepted in the beloved"* (Eph. 1:6), today absolved from sin, today acquitted at the bar of God. Oh, soul-transporting thought! There are some clusters of Eshcol's vine that we will not be able to gather until we enter heaven, but this is a bough that runs over the wall. This is not as the corn of the land, which we can never eat until we cross the Jordan. This is part of the manna in the wilderness, a portion of our daily nourishment with which God supplies us on our journey. We are pardoned even now. Even now are our sins put away. Even now we stand in the sight of God accepted, as though we had never been guilty. *"There is therefore now no condemnation to them which are in Christ Jesus"* (Rom. 8:1). There is not a sin in the Book of God, even now, against one of His people. Who dares to lay anything to their charge? There is neither speck, nor spot, nor wrinkle, nor any such thing remaining on any one believer in the matter of justification in the sight of the Judge of all the earth. Let present privilege awaken us to present duty, and now, while life lasts, let us spend and be spent for our sweet Lord Jesus.

Made perfect.
—Hebrews 12:23

There are two kinds of perfection that the Christian needs: the perfection of justification in the person of Jesus and the perfection of sanctification brought about in him by the Holy Spirit. At present, corruption remains, even in the hearts of the regenerate; experience soon teaches us this. Within us are still lusts and evil imaginations. But I rejoice to know that the day is coming when God will finish the work that He has begun, and He will present my soul, not only perfect in Christ, but perfect through the Spirit, *"not having spot, or wrinkle, or any such thing; but that it should be holy and without blemish"* (Eph. 5:27). Can it be true that this poor, sinful heart of mine is to become holy even as God is holy? Can it be that this spirit, which often cries, *"O wretched man that I am! who shall deliver me from the body of this death?"* (Rom. 7:24), will get rid of sin and death—that I will have no evil things to harass my ears and no unholy thoughts to disturb my peace? Oh, happy hour! May it come quickly! When I cross the Jordan, the work of sanctification will be finished; but not until that moment will I even claim perfection in myself. Then my spirit will have its last baptism in the Holy Spirit's fire. I long to die to receive that last and final purification that will usher me into heaven. Not even an angel will be purer than I; for I will be able to say, "I am clean," in a double sense, through Jesus' blood and through the Spirit's work. Oh, how we should extol the power of the Holy Spirit in making us fit to stand before our Father in heaven! Yet do not let the hope of perfection hereafter make us content with imperfection now. If it does this, our hope cannot be genuine; for a good hope is a purifying thing, even now. The work of grace must be abiding in us now, or it cannot be perfected then. Let us pray to *"be filled with the Spirit"* (Eph. 5:18), so that we may increasingly bring forth the fruits of righteousness.

MAY 16
Morning

Who giveth us richly all things to enjoy.
—1 Timothy 6:17

Our Lord Jesus is always giving. Not for a solitary instant does He withdraw His hand. As long as there is a vessel of grace not yet full to the brim, the oil will not be withheld. He is a sun that always shines. He is manna always falling round the camp. He is a rock in the desert that ever sends out streams of life from His smitten side. The rain of His grace is always falling; the river of His bounty is always flowing, and the wellspring of His love is constantly overflowing. As the King can never die, so His grace can never fail. Daily we pluck His fruit, and daily His branches bend down to our hand with a fresh store of mercy. There are seven feast days in His weeks, and as many as are the days, so many are the banquets in His years. Who has ever returned from His door unblessed? Who has ever risen from His table unsatisfied, or from His heart unloved? His mercies are *"new every morning"* (Lam. 3:23) and fresh every evening. Who can know the number of His benefits or recount the list of His bounties? Every grain of sand that drops from the glass of time is but the tardy follower of a myriad of mercies. The wings of our hours are covered with the silver of His kindness and with the gold of His affection. The river of time bears from the mountains of eternity the golden sands of His favor. The countless stars are but as the standard bearers of a more innumerable host of blessings. *"Who can count the dust of Jacob, and the number of the fourth part of Israel?"* (Num. 23:10). How will my soul extol Him *"who daily loadeth us with benefits"* (Ps. 68:19), and *"who crowneth [us] with lovingkindness"* (Ps. 103:4)? Oh, that my praise could be as ceaseless as His bounty! O miserable tongue, how can you be silent? Wake up, I pray you, lest I call you no more my glory, but my shame. *"Awake, psaltery and harp: I myself will awake early"* (Ps. 108:2).

And he said, Thus saith the LORD, Make this valley full of ditches.
For thus saith the LORD, Ye shall not see wind, neither shall ye see
rain; yet that valley shall be filled with water, that ye may drink, both
ye, and your cattle, and your beasts.
—2 Kings 3:16–17

The armies of the three kings were famishing from a lack of water. God was about to send it, and in these words the prophet announced the coming blessing. Here was a case of human helplessness. All the valiant men could not procure a drop of water from the skies or find any in the wells of earth. In the same way, the people of the Lord are often at their wits' end; they see their own inadequacy and discover where their help is to be found. Still the people were to prepare by faith for the divine blessing; they were to dig the trenches in which the precious liquid would be held. The church must by her varied agencies, efforts, and prayers make herself ready to be blessed; she must make the pools, and the Lord will fill them. This must be done in faith, in the full assurance that the blessing is about to descend. Soon there was a wonderful bestowal of the needed blessing. The shower did not pour from the clouds as it did in Elijah's case, but, in a silent and mysterious manner, the pools were filled. The Lord has His own sovereign methods of action. He is not tied to manner and time as we are, but He does as He pleases among the sons of men. It is ours to receive from Him thankfully and not to dictate to Him. We must also notice the remarkable abundance of the supply: there was enough to meet everyone's needs. And so it is in the gospel blessing. All the needs of the congregation and of the entire church will be met by divine power in answer to prayer; above all this, victory will be speedily given to the armies of the Lord. What am I doing for Jesus? What trenches am I digging? O Lord, make me ready to receive the blessing that You are so willing to bestow.

So to walk, even as he walked.
—1 John 2:6

Why should Christians imitate Christ? They should do it for their own sakes. If they desire to be in a healthy state of soul, if they want to escape the sickness of sin and enjoy the vigor of growing grace, let Jesus be their model. For the sake of their own happiness, if they would enjoy holy and happy communion with Jesus, and if they would be lifted above the cares and troubles of this world, let them walk even as He walked. There is nothing that can assist you in walking toward heaven with good speed as much as wearing the image of Jesus on your heart to rule all its motions. It is when, by the power of the Holy Spirit, you are enabled to walk with Jesus in His very footsteps that you are happiest and most known to be the sons of God. Peter's position of being *"afar off"* (Luke 22:54) is both unsafe and uneasy. Next, for faith's sake, strive to be like Jesus. Ah, poor faith, you have been sorely shot at by cruel foes, but you have not been wounded half so dangerously by your enemies as by your friends. Who made those wounds in the fair hand of godliness? The one who professed faith but used the dagger of hypocrisy. The man with pretenses who enters the fold, being nothing but a wolf in sheep's clothing, worries the flock more than the lion outside. There is no weapon half so deadly as a Judas-kiss. Inconsistent Christians injure the Gospel more than the sneering critic or the infidel. But, especially for Christ's own sake, imitate His example. Christian, do you love your Savior? Is His name precious to you? Is His cause dear to you? Would you see the kingdoms of the world become His? Is it your desire that He would be glorified? Are you longing that souls should be won to Him? If so, imitate Jesus; be an *"epistle of Christ"* (2 Cor. 3:3), *"known and read of all men"* (v. 2).

Thou art my servant; I have chosen thee.
—Isaiah 41:9

If we have received the grace of God in our hearts, its practical effect has been to make us God's servants. We may be unfaithful servants—we certainly are unprofitable ones—yet, blessed be His name, we are His servants, wearing His badge, feeding at His table, and obeying His commands. We were once the servants of sin, but He who made us free has now taken us into His family and taught us obedience to His will. We do not serve our Master perfectly, but we would if we could. As we hear God's voice saying to us, *"Thou art my servant,"* we can answer with David, *"I am thy servant;...thou hast loosed my bonds"* (Ps. 116:16). But the Lord calls us not only His servants, but also His chosen ones: *"I have chosen thee."* We have not chosen Him first, but He has chosen us. If we are God's servants, we were not always so; the change must be ascribed to sovereign grace. The eye of sovereignty singled us out, and the voice of unchanging grace declared, *"I have loved thee with an everlasting love"* (Jer. 31:3). Long before time began or space was created, God had written on His heart the names of His elect people. He had predestined them to be conformed to the image of His Son and ordained them heirs of all the fullness of His love, His grace, and His glory. What comfort is here! Has the Lord loved us so long, and will He yet cast us away? He knew how stiff-necked we would be. He understood that our hearts were evil, yet He made the choice. Oh, our Savior is no fickle Lover! He does not feel enchanted for a while with some gleams of beauty from His church's eye, and then afterward cast her off because of her unfaithfulness. No, He married her in old eternity; and it is written of Jehovah, *"He hateth putting away"* (Mal. 2:16). The eternal choice is a bond on our gratitude and on His faithfulness, which neither can disown.

In him dwelleth all the fulness of the Godhead bodily.
And ye are complete in him.
—Colossians 2:9–10

All the attributes of Christ, as God and man, are at our disposal. All the fullness of the Godhead, whatever that marvelous term may include, is ours to make us complete. He cannot endow us with the attributes of deity; but He has done all that can be done, for He has made even His divine power and Godhead subservient to our salvation. His omnipotence, omniscience, omnipresence, immutability, and infallibility are all combined for our defense. Arise, believer, and behold the Lord Jesus yoking the whole of His divine Godhead to the chariot of salvation! How vast His grace, how firm His faithfulness, how unswerving His immutability, how infinite His power, how limitless His knowledge! These are all made the pillars of the temple of salvation by the Lord Jesus. And all, without shortening their infinity, are covenanted to us as our perpetual inheritance. Every drop of the fathomless love of the Savior's heart is ours; every sinew in the arm of might, every jewel in the crown of majesty, the immensity of divine knowledge, and the sternness of divine justice are all ours and will be employed for us. The whole of Christ, in His adorable character as the Son of God, is by Himself made over to us most richly to enjoy. His wisdom is our direction, His knowledge our instruction, His power our protection, His justice our surety, His love our comfort, His mercy our solace, and His immutability our trust. He holds back no reserves, but opens the recesses of the mount of God and invites us to dig in its mines for the hidden treasures. "All, all, all are yours," He says. "Be satisfied with My favor and enjoy the full goodness of the Lord." Oh, how sweet it is to behold Jesus and to call on Him with the certain confidence that in seeking the intervention of His love or power, we are but asking for that which He has already faithfully promised.

Afterward.
—Hebrews 12:11

How happy are tried Christians, *"afterward"!* There is no calm deeper than that which follows a storm. Who has not rejoiced in bright sunshine after a rain? Victory banquets are for well-exercised soldiers. After killing the lion, we eat the honey. After climbing the Hill of Difficulty, we sit down in the shade to rest. After traversing the Valley of Humiliation and fighting with the devil, we see the Shining One appear with the healing branch from the Tree of Life. Our sorrows, like the passing keels of the vessels on the sea, leave a silver line of holy light behind them *"afterward."* It is peace—sweet, deep peace—that follows the horrible turmoil that once reigned in our tormented, guilty souls. See, then, the happy estate of a Christian! He has his best things last, and, in this world, he receives his worst things first. But even his worst things are *"afterward"* good things; harsh plowings yield joyful harvests. Even now he grows rich by his losses, he rises by his falls, he lives by dying, and he becomes full by being emptied. If, then, his grievous afflictions yield him so much *"peaceable fruit"* (Heb. 12:11) in this life, what will the full vintage of joy be *"afterward"* in heaven? If his dark nights are as bright as the world's days, what will his days be? If even his starlight is more splendid than the sun, what must his sunlight be? If he can sing in a dungeon, how sweetly will he sing in heaven? If he can praise the Lord in the fires, how will he extol Him before the eternal throne? If evil is good to him now, what will the overflowing goodness of God be to him then? Oh, blessed *"afterward"!* Who would not be a Christian? Who would not bear the present cross for the crown that comes *"afterward"?* But herein is work for patience, for the rest is not for today, nor the triumph for the present, but *"afterward."* Wait, O soul, and *"let patience have her perfect work"* (James 1:4).

I have seen servants upon horses, and princes walking
as servants upon the earth.
—Ecclesiastes 10:7

Upstarts frequently usurp the highest places, while the truly great pine in obscurity. This is a riddle in providence whose solution will one day gladden the hearts of the upright; but it is so common a fact, that none of us should murmur if it should fall to our own lot. When our Lord was on earth, although He is the Prince of the kings of the earth, yet He walked the footpath of weariness and service as the Servant of servants: what wonder is it if His followers, who are princes of the blood, should also be looked down on as inferior and contemptible persons? The world is upside down; therefore, the first are last and the last first. See how the servile sons of Satan lord it in the earth! What a high horse they ride! How they lift up their horn on high! Haman is in the court, while Mordecai sits in the gate; David wanders on the mountains, while Saul reigns in state; Elijah is complaining in the cave, while Jezebel is boasting in the palace; yet who would wish to take the places of the proud rebels? And who, on the other hand, might not envy the despised saints? When the wheel turns, those who are lowest rise, and the highest sink. Patience, then, believer, eternity will right the wrongs of time. Let us not fall into the error of letting our passions and carnal appetites ride in triumph, while our nobler powers walk in the dust. Grace must reign as a prince, and make the members of the body instruments of righteousness. The Holy Spirit loves order, and He therefore sets our powers and faculties in due rank and place, giving the highest room to those spiritual faculties that link us with the great King. Let us not disturb the divine arrangement, but ask for grace that we may keep under our body and bring it into subjection. We were not new created to allow our passions to rule over us, but that we, as kings, may reign in Christ Jesus over the triple kingdom of spirit, soul, and body, to the glory of God the Father.

And [Elijah] requested for himself that he might die.
—1 Kings 19:4

It was a remarkable thing that Elijah—the man for whom God had ordained an infinitely better lot, who was never to die, who would be carried to heaven in a chariot of fire and be translated so that he would not see death—would thus pray, "O LORD, *take away my life; for I am not better than my fathers*" (1 Kings 19:4). We have here a memorable proof that God does not always answer prayer in-kind, though He always does in effect. He gave Elijah something better than what he asked for, and thus God really heard and answered Elijah's prayer. It was unusual that the lion-hearted Elijah would be so depressed by Jezebel's threat as to ask to die, and it was blessedly kind on the part of our heavenly Father that He did not take His despondent servant at his word. There is a limit to the doctrine of the prayer of faith. We are not to expect that God will give us everything for which we choose to ask. We know that sometimes we ask and do not receive, because we "*ask amiss*" (James 4:3). If we ask for what is not promised, if we contradict the spirit that the Lord would have us cultivate, if we ask contrary to His will or to the decrees of His providence, if we ask merely for the gratification of our own comfort and without an eye to His glory, we must not expect that we will receive. Yet, when we ask in faith, without doubting, if we do not receive the precise thing for which we asked, we will receive an equivalent, and more than an equivalent for it. As one remarked, "If the Lord does not pay in silver, He will in gold; and if He does not pay in gold, He will in diamonds." If He does not give you precisely what you ask for, He will give you what is tantamount to it, and what you will greatly rejoice to receive in place of what you asked for. Be then, dear reader, much in prayer, and make this evening a season of earnest intercession. But be careful what you ask for.

Marvellous lovingkindness.
—Psalm 17:7

When we give our hearts along with our charitable gifts, we give well, but we must often admit to failing in this respect. Not so our Master and our Lord. His favors are always performed with the love of His heart. He does not send to us the cold meat and the broken pieces from the table of His luxury, but He dips our morsels into His own dish and seasons our provisions with the spices of His fragrant affections. When He puts the golden tokens of His grace into our palms, He accompanies the gift with such a warm pressure of our hand that the manner of His giving is as precious as the gift itself. He will come into our houses on His errands of kindness, but He will not act as some austere visitors do in a poor man's cottage; instead, He sits by our sides, not despising our poverty or blaming our weaknesses. Beloved, with what smiles does He speak! What golden sentences drop from His gracious lips! What embraces of affection He bestows on us! If He had but given us pennies, the way of His giving would have gilded them; but as it is, the costly gifts are set in a golden basket by His pleasant carriage. It is impossible to doubt the sincerity of His charity, for there is a bleeding heart stamped on the face of all His benefactions. He gives *"liberally, and upbraideth not"* (James 1:5). Not one hint that we are burdensome to Him; not one cold look for His poor pensioners; but He rejoices in His mercy and presses us to His bosom while He is pouring out His life for us. There is a fragrance in His spikenard that nothing but His heart could produce; there is a sweetness in His honeycomb that could not be in it unless the very essence of His soul's affection had been mingled with it. Oh, the rare communion that such singular sincerity produces! May we continually taste and know the blessedness of it!

I drew them with cords of a man, with bands of love.
—Hosea 11:4

Our heavenly Father often draws us with the cords of love; but oh, how hesitant we are to run toward Him! How slowly we respond to His gentle impulses! He wants us to exercise a simpler faith in Him, but we have not yet attained Abraham's level of trust in God. We do not leave our worldly cares with God, but, like Martha, we burden ourselves with much serving. Our meager faith brings leanness to our souls; we do not open our mouths wide, even though God has promised to fill them. (See Psalm 81:10.) Does He not this evening invite us to trust Him? Can we not hear Him say, "Come, My child, and trust Me. The veil is rent. Enter into My presence and boldly approach the throne of My grace. I am worthy of your full confidence; cast your cares on Me. Shake off the dust of your cares, and put on your beautiful garments of joy"? But though we are called with tones of love for the blessed exercise of this comforting grace, we do not respond. At other times, He draws us to closer communion with Himself. We have been sitting on the doorstep of God's house; He invites us to come into the banqueting hall and dine with Him, but we decline the honor. There are secret rooms not yet opened to us; Jesus invites us to enter them, but we hold back. Shame on our cold hearts! We are but poor lovers of our sweet Lord Jesus, not fit to be His servants, much less to be His brides. Yet He has exalted us to be bone of His bone and flesh of His flesh, married to Him by a glorious marriage covenant. Herein is love! But it is a love that accepts no denial. If we do not obey the gentle invitations of His love, He will send affliction to drive us into closer intimacy with Himself. He will do whatever it takes to draw us closer to Him. What foolish children we are to refuse those bands of love and so bring upon our backs that scourge of small cords, which Jesus knows how to use to our benefit!

> *If so be ye have tasted that the Lord is gracious.*
> —1 Peter 2:3

If"—then this is not a matter to be taken for granted concerning every one of the human race. "*If*"—then there is a possibility and a probability that some may not have tasted that the Lord is gracious. "*If*"—then this is not a general but a special mercy; and it is necessary to inquire whether we know the grace of God by inward experience. There is no spiritual favor that may not be a matter for heart-searching. But while this should be a matter of earnest and prayerful inquiry, no one ought to be content while there is any such thing as an "*if*" about his having "*tasted that the Lord is gracious.*" A jealous and holy distrust of self may give rise to the question even in the believer's heart, but the continuance of such a doubt would be an evil indeed. We must not rest without a desperate struggle to clasp the Savior in the arms of faith, and say, "*I know whom I have believed, and am persuaded that he is able to keep that which I have committed unto him*" (2 Tim. 1:12). Do not rest, believer, until you have a full assurance of your interest in Jesus. Let nothing satisfy you until, by the infallible witness of the Holy Spirit bearing witness with your spirit, you are certified that you are a child of God (Rom. 8:16). Oh, do not trifle here; let no "perhaps" or "peradventure" or "if" or "maybe" satisfy your soul. Build on eternal truths, and truly build on them. Get "*the sure mercies of David*" (Isa. 55:3), and surely get them. Let your anchor be cast into that which is within the veil, and see to it that your soul is linked to the anchor by a cable that will not break. Advance beyond these dreary *ifs*. Abide no more in the wilderness of doubts and fears. Cross the Jordan of distrust, and enter the Canaan of peace, where the Canaanite still lingers, but where the land does not cease to flow "*with milk and honey*" (Lev. 20:24).

There is corn in Egypt.
—Genesis 42:2

Famine pinched all the nations, and it seemed inevitable that Jacob and his family would suffer great need. But the God of providence, who never forgets the objects of electing love, had stored a granary for His people by giving the Egyptians warning of the scarcity and leading them to store up the grain during their years of plenty. Little did Jacob expect deliverance from Egypt, but the corn in store for him was there. Believer, though all things are apparently against you, rest assured that God has made a reservation on your behalf; in the list of your griefs there is a saving clause. Somehow He will deliver you, and somewhere He will provide for you. The place from which your rescue will arise may be a very unexpected one, but help will assuredly come during your time of critical need, and you will magnify the name of the Lord. If men do not feed you, ravens will; if the earth does not yield wheat, heaven will drop manna. Therefore, be of good courage, and rest quietly in the Lord. God can make the sun rise in the west if He pleases, and He can make your source of distress the channel of delight. The corn in Egypt was all in the hands of the beloved Joseph; he opened or closed the granaries at will. And so the riches of providence are all in the absolute power of our Lord Jesus, who will dispense them liberally to His people. Joseph was abundantly ready to provide for his own family; and Jesus is unceasing in His faithful care for His children. Our business is to go after the help that is provided for us: we must not sit still in despondency, but rouse ourselves. Prayer will soon bring us into the presence of our royal Brother. Once we are before His throne, we have only to ask and we will receive. His provisions are not exhausted; there is corn still. His heart is not hard; He will give the corn to us. Lord, forgive our unbelief, and this evening cause us to draw largely from Your fullness and receive *"grace for grace"* (John 1:16).

He led them forth by the right way.
—Psalm 107:7

Uncertain experiences often lead the anxious believer to inquire, "Why is this happening to me?" I looked for light, but lo, darkness came; for peace, but found trouble. I said in my heart, my mountain stands firm; I will never be moved. Lord, you hide Your face, and I am troubled. It was but yesterday that I could read my title clear; today my evidences are unsure, and my hopes are clouded. Yesterday I could climb to Pisgah's top and view the distant landscape. I could rejoice with confidence in my future inheritance. Today my spirit has no hopes, but many fears; no joys, but much distress. Is this part of God's plan for me? Can this be the way in which God would bring me to heaven? Yes, it is even so. The eclipse of your faith, the darkness of your mind, the fainting of your hope—all these things are but part of God's method of making you ready for the great inheritance into which you will soon enter. These trials are for the testing and strengthening of your faith. They are waves that wash you further upon the rock; they are winds that waft your ship the more swiftly toward the desired haven. According to David's words, so it might be said of you, *"He bringeth them unto their desired haven"* (Ps. 107:30). By honor and dishonor, by evil report and by good report, by plenty and by poverty, by joy and by distress, by persecution and by peace, by all these things are the lives of your souls maintained, and by each of these are you helped on your way. Oh, believer, do not think that your sorrows are out of God's plan; they are necessary parts of it. *"We must through much tribulation enter into the kingdom of God"* (Acts 14:22). Learn, then, even to *"count it all joy when ye fall into divers temptations"* (James 1:2).

> O let my trembling soul be still,
> And wait Thy wise, Thy holy will!
> I cannot, Lord, Thy purpose see,
> Yet all is well since ruled by Thee.

Behold, thou art fair, my beloved.
—Song of Solomon 1:16

From every point of view, our Well Beloved is most fair. Our various experiences are meant by our heavenly Father to furnish fresh viewpoints from which we may see the loveliness of Jesus. How beneficial are our trials when they carry us aloft where we may gain clearer sights of Jesus than ordinary life could afford us! We have seen Him *"from the top of Amana, from the top of Shenir and Hermon"* (Song 4:8), and He has shone upon us as the sun in his strength; but we have also seen Him *"from the lions' dens, from the mountains of the leopards"* (v. 8), and He has lost none of His loveliness. From the languishing of a sick bed, from the borders of the grave, we have turned our eyes to our soul's Spouse, and He has never been otherwise than *"all fair"* (v. 7). Many of His saints have looked on Him from the gloom of dungeons and from the fiery flames of the stake, yet they have never uttered a bad word about Him; instead, they have died extolling His surpassing charms. Oh, noble and pleasant employment to be forever gazing at our sweet Lord Jesus! Is it not unspeakably delightful to view the Savior in all His offices and to perceive Him matchless in each—to shift the kaleidoscope, as it were, and to find fresh combinations of unequaled graces? In the manger and in eternity, on the cross and on His throne, in the Garden and in His kingdom, among thieves or in the midst of angels, He is everywhere *"altogether lovely"* (Song 5:16). Examine carefully every little act of His life and every trait of His character, and He is as lovely in the minute as in the majestic. Judge Him as you will, you cannot censure; weigh Him as you please, and He will not be found wanting. Eternity will not discover the shadow of a spot in our Beloved, but rather, as ages revolve, His hidden glories will shine forth with yet more inconceivable splendor. His unutterable loveliness will more and more fill all celestial minds with rapturous joy.

The LORD will perfect that which concerneth me.
—Psalm 138:8

Clearly the confidence that the psalmist expressed here was a divine confidence. He did not say, "I have grace enough to perfect that which concerns me. My faith is so steady that it will not stagger. My love is so warm that it will never grow cold. My resolution is so firm that nothing can move it." No, his dependence was on the Lord alone. If we indulge in any confidence that is not grounded on the Rock of ages, our confidence is worse than a dream. It will fall on us and cover us with its ruins, to our sorrow and confusion. All that nature spins, time will unravel, to the eternal confusion of all who are clothed therein. The psalmist was wise. He rested on nothing short of the Lord's work. It is the Lord who has begun the good work within us. It is He who has carried it on, and if He does not finish it, it will never be completed. If there is one stitch in the celestial garment of our righteousness that we are to insert ourselves, then we are lost; but this is our confidence: the Lord who began will perfect. He has done it all, must do it all, and will do it all. Our confidence must not be in what we have done or in what we have resolved to do, but entirely in what the Lord will do. Unbelief insinuates, "You will never be able to stand. Look at the evil of your heart; you can never conquer sin. Remember the sinful pleasures and temptations of the world that besiege you; you will certainly be allured by them and led astray." Ah, yes, we would indeed perish if left to our own strength. If we had to navigate our frail vessels alone over so rough a sea, we might as well give up the voyage in despair. But thanks be to God! He *"will perfect that which concerneth* [us]" and bring us to the *"desired haven"* (Ps. 107:30). We can never be too confident when we confide in Him alone and never carry too many concerns when we have this assurance of His.

Thou hast bought me no sweet cane with money.
—Isaiah 43:24

Worshippers at the temple were accustomed to bringing presents of sweet perfumes to be burned on the altar of God. Yet Israel, in the time of her backsliding, became stingy and brought only a few offerings of thankfulness to her Lord. This was an evidence of coldness of heart toward God and His house. Reader, does this ever occur with you? Might not the complaint of the text be occasionally, if not frequently, brought against you? Those who are poor in pocket, if rich in faith, will be accepted even though their gifts are small; but, poor reader, do you give in fair proportion to the Lord, or is the widow's mite kept back from the sacred treasury? The rich believer should be thankful for the gifts entrusted to him, but he should not forget his large responsibility, for where *"much is given…much* [will be] *required"* (Luke 12:48). But, rich reader, are you mindful of your obligations and giving to the Lord according to the benefits you have received? Jesus gave His blood for us; what will we give to Him? We are His, and all that we have is His, for He has purchased us for Himself. Can we act as if we were our own? Oh, for more consecration and more love! Blessed Jesus, how good it is of You to accept our sweet cane bought with money! Nothing is too costly as a tribute to Your unrivalled love, yet You receive with favor the smallest sincere token of affection! You receive our poor forget-me-nots and love-tokens as though they were intrinsically precious, though indeed they are but as the bunch of wildflowers that the child brings to his mother. May we never grow miserly toward You. From this hour, may we never hear You complain again of our withholding the gifts of our love. We will give You the firstfruits of our increase and pay tithes of all to You. Then we will confess *"of thine own have we given thee"* (1 Chron. 29:14).

Blessed be God, which hath not turned away my prayer.
—Psalm 66:20

In looking back on the character of our prayers, if we do it honestly, we will be filled with wonder that God has ever answered them. There may be some who think their prayers are worthy of acceptance—as the Pharisee did; but the true Christian, in a more enlightened retrospect, weeps over his prayers, and if he could retrace his steps, he would desire to pray more earnestly. Remember, Christian, how cold your prayers have been. Instead of wrestling in prayer as Jacob did, your petitions have been weak and few—far removed from that humble, believing, persevering faith that cries, *"I will not let thee go, except thou bless me"* (Gen. 32:26). Yet, wonderful to say, God has heard these cold prayers of yours, and not only heard, but answered them. Reflect also on how infrequent your prayers have been, unless you have been in trouble, and then, you have gone often to the mercy seat. But when deliverance has come, where has your constant supplication been? Yet, even though you have ceased to pray as you once did, God has not ceased to bless. When you have neglected the mercy seat, God has not deserted it, but the bright light of the Shechinah has always been visible between the wings of the cherubim. Oh, it is marvelous that the Lord would regard those intermittent spasms of pleading that come and go with our needs. What a God He is to hear the prayers of those who come to Him when they have pressing needs, but neglect Him when they have received an answer; who approach Him when they are forced to come, but who almost forget to address Him when mercies are plentiful and sorrows are few! Let His gracious kindness in hearing such prayers touch our hearts, so that we may from this point on be found *"praying always with all prayer and supplication in the Spirit"* (Eph. 6:18).

Only let your conversation be as it becometh the gospel of Christ.
—Philippians 1:27

The word *"conversation"* does not merely mean our talk, but the whole course of our lives and behavior in the world. The Greek word signifies the actions and the privileges of citizenship. Thus, as citizens of the New Jerusalem, we are commanded to let our actions be such as become the Gospel of Christ. What sort of conversation is this? In the first place, the Gospel is very simple. So Christians should be simple and plain in their habits. Our manner, our speech, our dress, and our whole behavior should reflect a simplicity that is the very soul of beauty. The Gospel is pre-eminently true. It is gold without dross, and the Christian's life will be lusterless and valueless without the jewel of truth. The Gospel is a very fearless Gospel. It boldly proclaims the truth, whether men like it or not. We must be equally faithful and unflinching. But the Gospel is also very gentle. Mark this spirit in its Founder: *"a bruised reed shall he not break"* (Isa. 42:3). Some people who profess to be Christians are sharper than a thornbush; such people are not like Jesus. Let us seek to win others by the gentleness of our words and actions. The Gospel is very loving. It is the message of the God of love for a lost and fallen race. Christ's last command to His disciples was, *"Love one another"* (John 13:34). Oh, for more real, hearty unity and love for all the saints and for more tender compassion toward the souls of the worst and vilest of men! We must not forget that the Gospel is holy. It never excuses sin: it pardons it, but only through the Atonement. If our lives are to resemble the Gospel, we must shun, not merely the grosser vices, but everything that would hinder our perfect conformity to Christ. For His sake, for our own sakes, and for the sakes of others, we must strive day by day to let our conversation be more in accordance with His Gospel.

Forsake me not, O LORD.
—Psalm 38:21

Frequently we pray that God would not forsake us in the hour of trial and temptation, but we too often forget that we need to use this prayer at all times. There is no moment of our lives, however holy, in which we can do without His constant upholding. Whether in light or in darkness, in communion or in temptation, we need the prayer, "'Forsake me not, O LORD.' Hold me up, and I will be safe." A little child, while learning to walk, always needs his mother's hand. The ship left by the pilot drifts at once from her course. We cannot do without continued aid from above. Let it, then, be your prayer today, "Do not forsake me, Father. Do not forsake Your child, lest he fall by the hand of the enemy. Shepherd, do not forsake Your lamb, lest he wander from the safety of the fold. Great Husbandman, do not forsake Your plant, lest it wither and die. 'Forsake me not, O LORD,' now; and forsake me not at any moment of my life. Do not forsake me in my joys, lest they absorb my heart. Do not forsake me in my sorrows, lest I murmur against You. Do not forsake me in the day of my repentance, lest I lose the hope of pardon and fall into despair. Do not forsake me in the day of my strongest faith, lest faith degenerate into presumption. Do not forsake me, for without You I am weak, but with You I am strong. Do not forsake me, for my path is dangerous and full of snares, and I cannot do without Your guidance. The hen does not forsake her brood; will You then cover me evermore with Your feathers and permit me to find my refuge under Your wings? 'Be not far from me; for trouble is near; for there is none to help' (Ps. 22:11). 'Leave me not, neither forsake me, O God of my salvation' (Ps. 27:9)."

O ever in our cleansed breast,
  Bid Thine Eternal Spirit rest;
And make our secret soul to be
  A temple pure and worthy Thee.

MAY 25
Evening

*And they rose up the same hour, and returned to Jerusalem...and
they told what things were done in the way,
and how he was known of them.*
—Luke 24:33, 35

When the two disciples had reached Emmaus and were refreshing themselves at the evening meal, the mysterious stranger who had so enchanted
them upon the road took bread and broke it. He made Himself known
to them, and then He vanished out of their sight. They had urged Him
to abide with them, because the day was nearly over; but now, although it
was much later, their love was a lamp, yes, even wings to their feet. They
forgot the darkness. Their weariness was all gone, and immediately they
journeyed back the sixty furlongs to tell the glad news of a risen Lord,
who had appeared to them by the way. They reached the Christians in
Jerusalem and were received by a burst of joyful news before they could tell
their own tale. These early Christians were all on fire to speak of Christ's
resurrection and to proclaim what they knew of the Lord. They shared
their experiences. This evening let their example impress us deeply. We,
too, must give our witness concerning Jesus. John's account of the empty
tomb needed to be supplemented by Peter's, and Mary could add something further still; combined, we have a full testimony from which nothing
can be left out. Each of us has unique gifts and special manifestations, but
the one objective God has in view is the perfecting of the whole body of
Christ. We must, therefore, bring our spiritual possessions, lay them at the
apostles' feet, and distribute unto all from what God has given to us. Hold
back no part of the precious truth, but speak what you know and testify to
what you have seen. Do not allow the labor involved, darkness, or possible
unbelief of your friends hinder you in any way. Get up, march to the place
of duty, and tell what great things God has shown to your soul.

Cast thy burden upon the LORD, *and he shall sustain thee.*
—Psalm 55:22

Care, even though exercised on legitimate objects, if carried to excess, has in it the nature of sin. The precept to avoid anxious care is earnestly instilled by our Savior, again and again, in His teachings. It is reiterated by the apostles, and it is one that cannot be neglected without involving transgression: for the very essence of anxious care is the imagining that we are wiser than God, and the thrusting of ourselves into His place to do for Him what He has undertaken to do for us. We attempt to think of that which we imagine He will forget. We labor to take on ourselves our weary burden, as if He were unable or unwilling to take it for us. Now this disobedience to His plain precept, this unbelief in His Word, this presumption in intruding on His province, is all sinful. Yet more than this, anxious care often leads to acts of sin. He who cannot calmly leave his affairs in God's hand, but will carry his own burden, is very likely to be tempted to use wrong means to help himself. This sin leads to a forsaking of God as our Counselor, resorting instead to human wisdom. This is going to the *"broken cisterns"* (Jer. 2:13) instead of to the *"fountain of living waters"* (v. 13)—a sin that was laid against ancient Israel. Anxiety makes us doubt God's lovingkindness, and thus our love for Him grows cold. We feel mistrust, and thus grieve the Spirit of God, so that our prayers become hindered, our consistent example marred, and our lives ones of self-seeking. Thus lack of confidence in God leads us to wander far from Him; but if through simple faith in His promise, we cast each burden as it comes upon Him, and are *"careful for nothing"* (Phil. 4:6) because He undertakes to care for us, it will keep us close to Him and strengthen us against much temptation. *"Thou wilt keep him in perfect peace, whose mind is stayed on thee: because he trusteth in thee"* (Isa. 26:3).

Continue in the faith.
—Acts 14:22

Perseverance is the badge of true saints. The Christian life is more than a beginning in the ways of God. It is also a continuance in the faith as long as life lasts. It is the same for a Christian as it was with the great Napoleon. He said, "Conquest has made me what I am, and conquest must maintain me." So, under God, dear friend in the Lord, conquest has made you what you are, and conquest must sustain you. Your motto must be, "Excelsior" [still higher]. A true conqueror, who will be crowned at the last, is the one who continues until war's trumpet is blown no more. Perseverance is, therefore, the target of all our spiritual enemies. The world does not object to your being a Christian for a time, if it can tempt you to cease your pilgrimage and settle down to buy and sell in Vanity Fair. The flesh will seek to ensnare you and to prevent your pressing on to glory. The flesh says, "It is weary work being a pilgrim; come, give it up. Am I always to be mortified? Am I never to be indulged? Give me at least a vacation from this constant warfare." Satan will make many fierce attacks on your perseverance; it will be the mark for all his arrows. He will strive to hinder you in service. He will insinuate that you are doing no good and that you need to rest. He will endeavor to make you weary of suffering. He will whisper, *"Curse God, and die"* (Job 2:9). Or he will attack your steadfastness by asking, "What is the good of being so zealous? Be quiet like the rest; sleep as the others are, and let your lamp go out as the other virgins do." Or he will attack your doctrinal sentiments by asking, "Why do you hold to these denominational creeds? Sensible people are becoming more liberal; they are removing the old landmarks. Get with the times." Therefore, Christian, wear your shield close to your armor, and cry mightily to God so that by His Spirit you may endure to the end.

So Mephibosheth dwelt in Jerusalem: for he did eat continually
at the king's table; and was lame on both his feet.
—2 Samuel 9:13

Mephibosheth was no great ornament to a royal table, yet he had a continual place at David's board, because the king could see in his face the features of the beloved Jonathan. Like Mephibosheth, we may cry unto the King of Glory, *"What is thy servant, that thou shouldest look upon such a dead dog as I am?"* (2 Sam. 9:8). But still, the Lord indulges us with most familiar communion with Himself, because He sees in our countenances the remembrance of His dearly beloved Jesus. The Lord's people are dear for Another's sake. Such is the love that the Father bears for His Only Begotten that for His sake He raises His lowly brethren from poverty and banishment to courtly companionship, noble rank, and royal provision. Their deformity will not rob them of their privileges. Lameness is no bar to sonship; the cripple is as much the heir as if he could run like Asahel, who *"was as light of foot as a wild roe"* (2 Sam. 2:18). Our right does not limp, though our might may. A king's table is a noble hiding place for lame legs, and at the gospel feast we learn to glory in infirmities, because the power of Christ rests on us. Yet grievous disability may mar the persons of the best-loved saints. Here is one feasted by David, and yet so lame in both his feet that he could not go up with the king when he fled from the city, and was therefore maligned and injured by his servant Ziba. Saints whose faith is weak, and whose knowledge is slender, are great losers; they are exposed to many enemies and cannot follow the king wherever he goes. This disease frequently arises from falls. Bad nursing in their spiritual infancy often causes converts to fall into a despondency from which they never recover, and sin in other cases brings broken bones. Lord, help the lame to leap like a deer and satisfy all Your people with the bread of Your table!

*What is thy servant, that thou shouldest look upon
such a dead dog as I am?*
—2 Samuel 9:8

If Mephibosheth was thus humbled by David's kindness, what will we be in the presence of our gracious Lord? The more grace we have, the less we will think of ourselves, for grace, like light, reveals our impurity. Eminent saints have scarcely known to what to compare themselves; their sense of unworthiness has been so clear and keen. "I am," said holy Rutherford, "a dry and withered branch, a piece of dead carcass, dry bones, and not able to step over a straw." In another place he wrote, "Except as to open outbreakings, I want nothing of what Judas and Cain had." The lowliest objects in nature appear to the humbled mind to have a preference above itself, because they have never contracted sin. A dog may be greedy, fierce, or filthy, but it has no conscience to violate, no Holy Spirit to resist. A dog may be a worthless animal, yet by a little kindness, it is soon won to love its master and is faithful to death. But we forget the goodness of the Lord and do not respond to His call. The term *"dead dog"* is the most expressive of all terms of contempt, but it is not too strong to use to express the self-abhorrence of instructed believers. They do not pretend to be modest; they mean what they say. They have weighed themselves in the balances of the sanctuary and realized the vanity of their natures. At best, we are but clay, animated dust, mere walking hills; but viewed as sinners, we are monsters indeed. Let it be published in heaven as a miracle that the Lord Jesus would set His heart's love upon such as we. Dust and ashes though we are, we must and will magnify the *"exceeding greatness of his power"* (Eph. 1:19). Could not His heart find rest in heaven? Must He come to these tents of Kedar for a spouse and choose a bride on whom the sun had looked? (See Song of Solomon 1:5–6.) O heavens and earth, break forth into song, and give all glory to our sweet Lord Jesus.

Whom he justified, them he also glorified.
—Romans 8:30

Here is a precious truth for you, believer. You may be poor, in pain, or unknown, but for your encouragement, review your calling and the consequences that flow from it, especially that blessed result spoken of in this morning's text. As surely as you are God's child today, so surely will all your trials soon be at an end, and you will be rich to all the intents of bliss. Wait awhile, and that weary head will wear the crown of glory, and that hand of labor will grasp the palm branch of victory. Do not lament your troubles, but rather rejoice that before long you will be where *"there shall be no more death, neither sorrow, nor crying, neither shall there be any more pain"* (Rev. 21:4). The chariots of fire are at your door, and a moment will suffice to bear you to the glorified. The everlasting song is almost on your lips. The portals of heaven stand open for you. Do not think that you can fail to enter into rest. If He has called you, nothing can separate you from His love. Distress cannot sever the bond; the fire of persecution cannot burn the link; the hammer of hell cannot break the chain. You are secure. That voice that called you at first will call you yet again from earth to heaven, from death's dark gloom to immortality's unuttered splendors. Rest assured, the heart of Him who has justified you beats with infinite love toward you. You will soon be with the glorified, where your portion is; you are waiting here only to be made ready for the inheritance; once that is done, the wings of angels will carry you far away to the mount of peace, joy, and blessedness, where,

> Far from a world of grief and sin,
>   With God eternally shut in,

you will rest forever and ever.

MAY 28

Evening

This I recall to my mind, therefore have I hope.
—Lamentations 3:21

Memory is frequently the slave of despair. Despondent minds call to remembrance every dark prediction from the past and focus on every gloomy aspect of the present; thus memory, clothed in sackcloth, presents to the mind a cup of mingled gall and wormwood. There is, however, no need for this. Wisdom can readily transform memory into an angel of comfort. That same recollection that in its left hand brings so many gloomy omens may be trained to bear in its right a wealth of hopeful signs. She need not wear a crown of iron. She may encircle her brow with a ribbon of gold, all spangled with stars. Thus it was in Jeremiah's experience. In the previous verse, memory had brought him to deep humiliation of soul: *"My soul hath them still in remembrance, and is humbled in me"* (v. 20). Now this same memory restored him to life and comfort. *"This I recall to my mind, therefore have I hope."* Like a two-edged sword, his memory first killed his pride with one edge, and then slew his despair with the other. As a general principle, if we desire to exercise our memories more wisely, we might, in our very darkest distress, strike a match that would instantaneously kindle the lamp of comfort. There is no need for God to create a new thing upon the earth in order to restore believers to joy. If they would prayerfully rake the ashes of the past, they would find light for the present; and if they would turn to the Book of Truth and the throne of grace, their candle would soon shine as before. May we remember the lovingkindness of the Lord and rehearse His deeds of grace. Let us open the volume of recollection that is so richly illuminated with memorials of mercy, and we will soon be happy. Thus memory may be, as Coleridge called it, "the bosom-spring of joy." When the Divine Comforter bends it to His service, memory may be chief among earthly comforters.

Thou lovest righteousness, and hatest wickedness.
—Psalm 45:7

Be ye angry, and sin not" (Eph. 4:26). There can hardly be goodness in a man if he is not angry at sin; he who loves truth must hate every false way. How our Lord Jesus hated it when the temptation came! Thrice it assailed Him in different forms, but He always met it with, *"Get thee behind me, Satan"* (Matt. 16:23; Mark 8:33; Luke 4:8). He hated sin in others—none the less fervently because He showed His hate more often in tears of pity than in words of rebuke. Yet what language could be more stern, more Elijah-like, than the words, *"Woe unto you, scribes and Pharisees, hypocrites! for ye devour widows' houses, and for a pretence make long prayer"* (Matt. 23:14). He hated wickedness, so much that He bled to wound it to the heart; He died that it might die. He was buried that He might bury it in His tomb, and He rose that He might forever trample it beneath His feet. Christ is in the Gospel, and that Gospel is opposed to wickedness in every shape. Wickedness arrays itself in fair garments and imitates the language of holiness; but the precepts of Jesus, like His famous scourge of small cords, chase it out of the temple and will not tolerate it in the church. So, too, in the heart where Jesus reigns, what war there is between Christ and Belial! And when our Redeemer will come to be our Judge, those thundering words, *"Depart from me, ye cursed"* (Matt. 25:41), which are, indeed, but a prolongation of His life's teaching concerning sin, will manifest His abhorrence of iniquity. As warm as His love is for sinners, so hot is His hatred of sin; as perfect as His righteousness is, so complete will be the destruction of every form of wickedness. O you glorious Champion of right and Destroyer of wrong, for this cause has God, even Your God, *"anointed thee with the oil of gladness above thy fellows"* (Ps. 45:7).

Cursed be the man before the LORD, that riseth up
and buildeth this city Jericho.
—Joshua 6:26

Since the man who rebuilt Jericho was cursed, much more damned are those who labor to restore false religions among us. In our fathers' days, the gigantic walls of unrighteousness fell by the power of their faith, the perseverance of their efforts, and the blast of their gospel trumpets. Now there are some who want to rebuild accursed, so-called religious systems on their old foundations. O Lord, be pleased to thwart these unrighteous endeavors, and pull down every stone upon which they build. It should be a serious business with us to be thoroughly purged of every error that may have a tendency to foster an ungodly spirit. Then, when we have made a clean sweep at home, we should seek in every way to oppose sin's all-too-rapid spread abroad in the church and in the world. This last can be done in secret through fervent prayer and in public through giving a strong testimony. With judicious boldness, we must warn those who are inclined to believe false teachings. We must instruct the young in gospel truth and alert them to the sinful practices of religion in past times. We must aid in spreading the light more thoroughly through the land, for false teachers, like owls, hate daylight. Are we doing all we can for Jesus and the Gospel? If not, our negligence plays into the hands of the enemy. What are we doing to distribute the Bible? Are we spreading abroad good, sound gospel writings? Luther once said, "The devil hates goose quills," and, undoubtedly, he has good reason: ready writers, by the Holy Spirit's blessing, have done the devil's kingdom much damage. If the thousands who read this brief word tonight will do all they can to hinder the rebuilding of this accursed Jericho, the Lord's glory will speed among the sons of men. Reader, what can you do? What will you do?

Take us the foxes, the little foxes, that spoil the vines.
—Song of Solomon 2:15

A little thorn may cause much suffering. A little cloud may hide the sun. *"Little foxes...spoil the vines,"* and little sins do mischief to the tender heart. These little sins burrow in the soul and make it so full of that which is hateful to Christ that He will hold no comfortable fellowship and communion with us. A great sin cannot destroy a Christian, but a little sin can make him miserable. Jesus will not walk with His people unless they drive out every known sin. He says, *"If ye keep my commandments, ye shall abide in my love; even as I have kept my Father's commandments, and abide in his love"* (John 15:10). Some Christians very seldom enjoy their Savior's presence. How is this? Surely it must be an affliction for a tender child to be separated from his father. Are you a child of God and yet satisfied to go on without seeing your Father's face? What! You are the spouse of Christ and yet content without His company! Surely you have fallen into a sad state, for the chaste spouse of Christ mourns like a dove without her mate, when he has left her. Ask, then, this question: what has driven Christ from you? He hides His face behind the wall of your sins. That wall may be built up of little pebbles, as easily as of great stones. The sea is composed of drops, and the rocks are composed of grains; the sea that separates you from Christ may be filled with the drops of your little sins, and the rock that has nearly wrecked your weak vessel may have been made by the daily working of the coral insects of your little sins. If you would live with Christ, walk with Christ, see Christ, and have fellowship with Christ, take heed of *"the little foxes, that spoil the vines: for our vines have tender grapes"* (Song 2:15). Jesus invites you to go with Him and take them. He will surely, like Samson, take the foxes at once and easily. Go with Him to the hunting.

Henceforth we should not serve sin.
—Romans 6:6

Christian, what do you have to do with sin? Has it not cost you enough already? Burned child, will you play with fire? When you have already been between the jaws of the lion, will you step into his den a second time? Have you not had enough of the old serpent? Did he not poison all your veins once, and will you play upon the hole of the asp and put your hand on the serpent's den a second time? Oh, do not be so foolish! Did sin ever bring you real pleasure? Did you find solid satisfaction in it? If so, go back to your old drudgery and wear the chain again, if it pleases you. But inasmuch as sin never gave you what it promised to bestow, but deluded you with lies, do not be snared a second time by the old fowler. Be free, and let the remembrance of your ancient bondage forbid you to enter the net again! It is contrary to the intentions of eternal love, which all have an eye to your purity and holiness; therefore, do not run counter to the purposes of your Lord. Another thought should restrain you from sin. Christians can never sin cheaply; they pay a heavy price for iniquity. Transgression destroys peace of mind, obscures fellowship with Jesus, hinders prayer, and brings darkness over the soul; therefore, do not be the slave of sin. There is yet a higher argument: each time you *"serve sin,"* you have crucified the Lord *"afresh, and put him to an open shame"* (Heb. 6:6). Can you bear that thought? Oh, if you have fallen into any special sin during this day, it may be that my Master has sent this warning this evening to bring you back before you have backslidden very far. Turn to Jesus anew; He has not forgotten His love for you. His grace is still the same. With weeping and repentance, come to His footstool, and you will be once more received into His heart. You will be set upon a rock again, and He will direct your steps.

The king also himself passed over the brook Kidron.
—2 Samuel 15:23

David passed that gloomy brook when flying with his mourning company from his traitor son. The man after God's own heart was not exempt from trouble; no, his life was full of it. He was both the Lord's anointed and the Lord's afflicted. Why then should we expect to escape? At sorrow's gates the noblest of our race have waited with ashes on their heads; why then should we complain as though some strange thing had happened to us? The King of Kings Himself was not favored with a more cheerful or royal road. He passed over the filthy ditch of Kidron, through which the filth of Jerusalem flowed. God had one Son without sin, but not a single child without the rod. It is a great joy to believe that Jesus has been tempted in all points like as we are. What is our Kidron this morning? Is it a faithless friend, a sad bereavement, a slanderous reproach, a dark foreboding? The King has passed over all these. Is it bodily pain, poverty, persecution, or contempt? Over each of these Kidrons the King has gone before us. *"In all* [our] *affliction he was afflicted"* (Isa. 63:9). The idea of strangeness in our trials must be banished at once and forever, for He who is the Head of all saints knows by experience the grief that we think so peculiar. All the citizens of Zion must be free of the honorable company of mourners, of which the Prince Immanuel is Head and Captain. Notwithstanding the abasement of David, he yet returned in triumph to his city, and David's Lord arose victorious from the grave. Let us, then, be of good courage, for we also will win the day. We will yet with joy draw water out of the wells of salvation, though now for a season we have to pass by the noxious streams of sin and sorrow. Courage, soldiers of the Cross, the King Himself triumphed after going over Kidron, and so will you.

Who healeth all thy diseases.
—Psalm 103:3

Humbling as is the statement, yet the fact is certain that we are all more or less suffering under the disease of sin. What a comfort it is to know that we have a Great Physician who is both willing and able to heal us! Let us think about Him for a while tonight. His cures are very speedy; there is life in a look at Him. His cures are radical; He strikes at the center of the disease. Hence, His cures are sure and certain. He never fails, and the disease never returns. There is no relapse where Christ heals. There is no fear that His patients will be merely patched up for a season; He makes them new people. He gives them a new heart also and puts a right spirit within them. He is well skilled in all diseases. Physicians generally have some specialty. Although they may know a little about almost all our aches and pains, there is usually one area of medicine that they have studied above all others. But Jesus Christ is thoroughly acquainted with the whole of human nature. He is as much at home with one sinner as with another; never yet has He met with an out-of-the-way case that was difficult for Him. He has had extraordinary complications of strange diseases to deal with, but He has known exactly with one glance of His eye how to treat the patient. He is the only universal Doctor; and the medicine He gives is the only true remedy, healing in every instance. Whatever our spiritual malady may be, we should go at once to this Divine Physician. There is no brokenness of heart that Jesus cannot bind up. His blood *"cleanseth us from all sin"* (1 John 1:7). If we think of the countless number who have been delivered from all sorts of diseases through the power and virtue of His touch, we will joyfully put ourselves in His hands. We trust Him, and sin dies; we love Him, and grace lives; we wait for Him, and grace is strengthened; we see Him as He is, and grace is perfected forever.

The evening and the morning were the first day.
—Genesis 1:5

Was it so even in the beginning? Did light and darkness divide the realm of time in the first day? Then little wonder is it if I also have changes in my circumstances from the sunshine of prosperity to the midnight of adversity. It will not always be the blaze of noon. Even in my soul's concerns, I must expect at seasons to mourn the absence of my former joys and seek my Beloved in the night. Nor am I alone in this, for all the Lord's beloved ones have had to sing the mingled song of judgment and of mercy, of trial and deliverance, of mourning and of delight. It is one of the arrangements of Divine Providence that day and night will not cease either in the spiritual or natural creation until we reach the land of which it is written, *"There shall be no night there"* (Rev. 21:25). What our heavenly Father ordains is wise and good. What, then, my soul, is it best for you to do? Learn first to be content with this divine order, and be willing, with Job, to receive evil from the hand of the Lord as well as good. Study next to make *"the outgoings of the morning and the evening to rejoice"* (Ps. 65:8). Praise the Lord for the sun of joy when it rises, and for the gloom of evening as it falls. There is beauty both in the sunrise and sunset. Sing of their beauty, and glorify the Lord. Like the nightingale, pour forth your notes at all hours. Believe that the night is as useful as the day. The dew of grace falls heavily in the night of sorrow. The stars of promise shine forth gloriously amid the darkness of grief. Continue your service under all changes. If in the day your watchword is *labor,* at night exchange it for *watch.* Every hour has its duty. Continue in your calling as the Lord's servant until He will suddenly appear in His glory. My soul, your evening of old age and death is drawing near. Do not dread it, for it is part of the day; and the Lord has said, "I will *'cover him all the day long'* (Deut. 33:12)."

JUNE 1

Evening

He will make her wilderness like Eden.
—Isaiah 51:3

I see a vision of a howling wilderness, a great and terrible desert like the Sahara. I see nothing in it to relieve the eye. Everywhere I look, I am wearied with a vision of hot, arid sand, strewn with ten thousand bleaching skeletons of wretched men who have died in anguish, having lost their way in the merciless wasteland. What an appalling sight! How horrible! It is a sea of sand without end and without an oasis, a cheerless graveyard for a forlorn race! But behold and wonder! Suddenly I see, springing up from the scorching sand, a plant of renown. As it grows, it buds. The bud expands. It is a rose, and at its side, a lily bows its modest head. Miracle of miracles! As the fragrance of these flowers is diffused, the wilderness is transformed into a fruitful field; all around, it blossoms exceedingly. The glory of Lebanon is given to it, the excellency of Carmel and Sharon. Do not call it the Sahara; call it Paradise. Do not speak of it any longer as the valley of death's shadow; for where the skeletons lay bleaching in the sun, behold a resurrection is proclaimed. The dead spring up and become a mighty army, full of eternal life. Jesus is that plant of renown, and His presence makes all things new. Each individual's salvation is no less than a miracle. Yonder I see you, dear reader, cast out, an unswaddled, unwashed infant, defiled with your own blood and left to be food for beasts of prey. But a jewel has been thrown into your heart by a divine hand, and for its sake, you have been pitied and tended by divine providence. You are washed and cleansed from your defilement. You are adopted into heaven's family. The fair seal of love is on your forehead, and the ring of faithfulness is on your hand. Now, you are a prince unto God, though once you were an orphan who had been cast away. Highly value the matchless power and grace that changes deserts into gardens and makes the barren heart sing for joy.

JUNE 2

Morning

For the flesh lusteth against the Spirit,
and the Spirit against the flesh.
—Galatians 5:17

In every believer's heart there is a constant struggle between the old nature and the new. The old nature is very active, and it loses no opportunity of plying all the weapons of its deadly armory against newborn grace; while, on the other hand, the new nature is ever on the watch to resist and destroy its enemy. Grace within us will employ prayer, faith, hope, and love to cast out the evil. It takes to it the *"whole armour of God"* (Eph. 6:11) and wrestles earnestly. These two opposing natures will never cease to struggle as long as we are in this world. Bunyan's pilgrim, Christian, battled with Apollyon for three hours, but Christian's battle with himself lasted all the way from the Wicket Gate to the river Jordan. The enemy is so securely entrenched within us that he can never be driven out while we are in this body. Although we are troubled, and often in sore conflict, we have an almighty Helper, even Jesus, the Captain of our salvation. He is ever with us and assures us that we will eventually be *"more than conquerors through him"* (Rom. 8:37). With such assistance the newborn nature is more than a match for its foes. Are you fighting with the adversary today? Are Satan, the world, and the flesh all against you? Do not be discouraged or dismayed. Fight on, for God Himself is with you! Jehovah-Nissi is your banner, and Jehovah-Rophi is the healer of your wounds. Fear not, for you will overcome. Who can defeat Omnipotence? Fight on, *"looking unto Jesus"* (Heb. 12:2). Though the conflict is long and stern, sweet will be the victory and glorious the promised reward.

> From strength to strength go on;
>   Wrestle, and fight, and pray,
> Tread all the powers of darkness down,
>   And win the well-fought day.

JUNE 2
Evening

Good Master.
—Matthew 19:16

If the young man in the Gospel used this title in speaking to our Lord, how much more aptly may I address Him this way! He is indeed my Master in both senses, a ruling Master and a teaching Master. I delight to run His errands and to sit at His feet. I am both His servant and His disciple, and I count it my highest honor to acknowledge both relationships. If He would ask me why I call Him *"good,"* I would have a ready answer. It is true that *"there is none good but one, that is, God"* (Matt. 19:17), but then He is God, and all the goodness of deity shines forth in Him. In my experience, I have found Him good, so good, indeed, that all the good I have has come to me through Him. He was good to me when I was dead in sin, for He raised me by His Spirit's power. He has been good to me in all my needs, trials, struggles, and sorrows. There could never be a better Master, for His service is freedom, and His rule is love. I wish I were one-thousandth part as good a servant. When He teaches me as my Rabbi, He is unspeakably good. His doctrine is divine, His manner is gracious, and His spirit is gentleness itself. No error mingles with His instruction; the golden truth that He brings forth is pure, and all His teachings lead to goodness, sanctifying as well as edifying the disciple. Angels find Him a good Master and delight to pay their homage at His footstool. The ancient saints proved Him to be a good Master, and each of them rejoiced to sing, "I am Your servant, Lord!" My own humble testimony must certainly be to the same effect. I will give this witness before my friends and neighbors, for possibly they may be led by my testimony to seek my Lord Jesus as their Master. Oh, that they would do so! They would never regret so wise a choice. If they would but take His easy yoke, they would find themselves in so royal a service that they would enlist in it forever.

*These were the potters, and those that dwelt among plants and hedges:
there they dwelt with the king for his work.*
—1 Chronicles 4:23

Potters were the very highest grade of workers, but the king needed potters; therefore, they were in royal service, although the material on which they worked was nothing but clay. We, too, may be engaged in the most menial part of the Lord's work, but it is a great privilege to do anything for our King; therefore, we will abide in our calling, hoping that, although we *"have lien among the pots, yet shall* [we] *be as the wings of a dove covered with silver, and her feathers with yellow gold"* (Ps. 68:13). The text tells us of those who *"dwelt among plants and hedges,"* having rough, rustic hedging and ditching work to do. They may have desired to live in the city, amid its life, society, and refinement, but they kept their appointed places, for they were doing the king's work. The place of our habitation is fixed, and we are not to leave it out of whim and caprice, but seek to serve the Lord in it, by being a blessing to those among whom we reside. These potters and gardeners had royal company, for *"they dwelt with the king."* Although they lived among hedges and plants, they dwelt with the king there. No lawful place or gracious occupation, however lowly, can exclude us from communion with our divine Lord. In visiting hovels, crowded rooming houses, workhouses, or jails, we may go with the King. In all works of faith we may count on Jesus' fellowship. It is when we are in His work that we may depend on His smile. You unknown workers who are occupied for your Lord amid the dirt and wretchedness of the lowest of the low, be of good cheer, for jewels have been found on dunghills before now, earthen pots have been filled with heavenly treasure, and bad weeds have been transformed into precious flowers. Dwell with the King for His work, and when He writes His chronicles, your name will be recorded.

He humbled himself.
—Philippians 2:8

Jesus is the great Teacher of true humility. Daily we need to learn of Him. See the Master taking a towel and washing His disciples' feet! Follower of Christ, will you not humble yourself? See Him as the Servant of servants, and surely you cannot be proud! Is not this sentence the summary of His biography: *"He humbled himself"*? While on earth, was He not always stripping off first one robe of honor and then another, until, naked, He was nailed to the cross? Did He not empty His inmost self, pouring out His lifeblood, giving up all for us, until they laid Him penniless in a borrowed grave? How low was our dear Redeemer brought! How then can we be proud? Stand at the foot of the cross, and count the purple drops by which you have been cleansed. Wear the crown of thorns. Observe His scourged shoulders, still gushing with the crimson stream of His blood. See His hands and feet given up to the rough iron, and His whole self to mockery and scorn. Notice the bitterness, the anguish, and the pain of inward grief showing themselves in His outward frame. Hear the chilling cry, *"My God, my God, why hast thou forsaken me?"* (Matt. 27:46). And if you do not lie prostrate on the ground before that cross, you have never seen it. If you are not humbled in the presence of Jesus, you do not know Him. You were so lost that nothing could save you but the sacrifice of God's only begotten Son. Think of that, and as Jesus stooped for you, bow yourself in lowliness at His feet. A sense of Christ's amazing love for us has a greater tendency to humble us than even a consciousness of our own guilt. May the Lord bring us in contemplation to Calvary. Then our position will no longer be that of a pompous man of pride, but we will assume the humble place of one who loves much because he has had much forgiven. Pride cannot live beneath the cross. Let us sit there and learn our lesson, and then rise and put it into practice.

The kindness and love of God our Saviour.
—Titus 3:4

How sweet it is to behold the Savior communing with His own beloved people! There can be nothing more delightful than, by the divine Spirit, to be led into this fertile field of delight. Let the mind for an instant consider the history of the Redeemer's love, and a thousand enchanting acts of affection will suggest themselves—all of which have had for their design the weaving of the heart into Christ, and the intertwining of the thoughts and emotions of the renewed soul with the mind of Jesus. When we meditate on this amazing love and behold the all-glorious Kinsman of the church, endowing her with all His ancient wealth, our souls may well faint for joy. Who is he who can endure such a weight of love? That partial sense of it, which the Holy Spirit is sometimes pleased to afford, is more than the soul can contain; how transporting must be a complete view of it! When the soul will have understanding to discern all the Savior's gifts, wisdom wherewith to estimate them, and time in which to meditate on them, such as the world to come will afford us, we will then commune with Jesus in a nearer manner than at present. But who can imagine the sweetness of such fellowship? It must be one of the things that has not entered into the heart of man, but which God has prepared for those who love Him. Oh, to burst open the door of our Joseph's granaries and see the plenty that He has stored up for us! This will overwhelm us with love. By faith we see, as in *"a glass, darkly"* (1 Cor. 13:12), the reflected image of His unbounded treasures, but when we will actually see the heavenly things themselves, with our own eyes, how deep will be the stream of fellowship in which our soul will bathe itself! Until then, our loudest sonnets will be reserved for our loving Benefactor, Jesus Christ our Lord, whose love for us is wonderful, surpassing human love.

JUNE 4

Received up into glory.
—1 Timothy 3:16

We have seen our beloved Lord in the days of His flesh, humiliated and painfully distressed; for He was *"despised and rejected of men; a man of sorrows, and acquainted with grief"* (Isa. 53:3). He whose brightness is as the morning wore the sackcloth of sorrow as His daily dress: shame and reproach were His clothing. Yet now, inasmuch as He has triumphed on the bloody tree over all the powers of darkness, our faith beholds our King returning *"from Edom, with dyed garments"* (Isa. 63:1), robed in the splendor of victory. How glorious must He have been in the eyes of angels, when a cloud received Him out of mortal sight, and He ascended to heaven! Now He wears the glory that He had with God before the earth ever was, and yet another glory above all—that which He has well earned in the fight against sin, death, and hell. As Victor, He wears the illustrious crown. Listen to how the song swells high! It is a new and sweeter song: *"Worthy is the Lamb that was slain"* (Rev. 5:12), for He has *"redeemed us to God by [His] blood"* (v. 9). He wears the glory of an Intercessor who can never fail, of a Prince who can never be defeated, of a Conqueror who has vanquished every foe, of a Lord who has the heart's allegiance of every subject. Jesus wears all the glory that the pomp of heaven can bestow upon Him, which ten thousand times ten thousand angels can minister to Him. You cannot with your utmost stretch of imagination conceive His exceeding greatness; yet there will be a further revelation of it when He will descend from heaven in great power, with all the holy angels: *"Then shall he sit upon the throne of his glory"* (Matt. 25:31). Oh, the splendor of that glory! It will delight His people's hearts. Nor will that be the end of our praise, for eternity will sound His praise, *"Thy throne, O God, is for ever and ever"* (Ps. 45:6)! Reader, if you wish to rejoice in Christ's glory in the future, He must be glorious in your sight right now. Is He so?

JUNE 5
Morning

The LORD *shut him in.*
—Genesis 7:16

Noah was shut in away from all the world by the hand of divine love. The door of election comes between us and the world in which the wicked one exists. We *"are not of the world, even as* [Jesus was] *not of the world"* (John 17:14). Into the sin, the gaiety, the pursuits of the multitude we cannot enter; we cannot play in the streets of Vanity Fair with the children of darkness, for our heavenly Father has shut us in. Noah was shut in with his God. *"Come thou and all thy house into the ark"* (Gen. 7:1) was the Lord's invitation, by which He clearly showed that He Himself intended to dwell in the ark with His servant and his family. Thus all the chosen dwell in God and God in them. Happy people to be enclosed in the same circle that contains God in the Trinity of His persons: Father, Son, and Spirit. Let us never be inattentive to that gracious call, "Come, My people, enter into your chambers, and shut your doors about you, and hide yourself as it were for a little moment until the indignation is gone." Noah was so shut in that no evil could reach him. Floods did but lift him heavenward, and winds did but waft him on his way. Outside of the ark all was ruin, but inside all was rest and peace. Without Christ we perish, but in Christ Jesus there is perfect safety. Noah was so shut in that he could not even desire to come out, and those who are in Christ Jesus are in Him forever. They will go no more out forever, for eternal faithfulness has shut them in, and infernal malice cannot drag them out. The Prince of the house of David *"shutteth, and no man openeth"* (Rev. 3:7). When once in the last days, as Master of the house, He will rise up and shut the door, it will be in vain for mere professors of faith to knock, and cry "Lord, Lord open unto us," for that same door that shuts in the wise virgins will shut out the foolish forever. Lord, shut me in by Your grace.

He that loveth not knoweth not God.
—1 John 4:8

The distinguishing mark of a Christian is his confidence in the love of Christ, and his commitment to love Christ in return. First, faith sets her seal upon the man by enabling the soul to say with the apostle, Christ *"loved me, and gave himself for me"* (Gal. 2:20). Then love adds its signature and stamps upon the heart gratitude and love for Jesus in return. *"We love him, because he first loved us"* (1 John 4:19). In those grand days of the early church, a heroic period of the Christian faith, this double mark was clearly seen in all believers in Jesus. They were people who knew the love of Christ and rested on it as a man leans on a staff whose dependability he has proven. The love that they felt toward the Lord was not a quiet emotion that they hid within themselves in a secret room in their souls. They did not speak of it only in their private meetings when they gathered on the first day of the week and sang hymns in honor of Christ Jesus, the Crucified One. Instead, it was a passion of such fervid, all-consuming energy that it was visible in all their actions, spoken of in their daily conversation, and unmistakably seen in their eyes, even in their casual glances. Love for Jesus was a flame that fed on the core and heart of their being; therefore, from its own force, it burned its way into the outer man and shone there. Zeal for the glory of King Jesus was the seal and mark of all genuine Christians. Because of their dependence on Christ's love, they dared much; because of their love for Christ, they did much, and it is the same now. The children of God are ruled in their inmost powers by love: the love of Christ drives them. They rejoice that divine love is set upon them. They feel it shed abroad in their hearts by the Holy Spirit, who is given to them. Then, by force of gratitude, they love the Savior with a pure, fervent heart. Reader, do you love Him? Before you sleep, give an honest answer to this weighty question!

JUNE 6

Morning

Behold, I am vile.
—Job 40:4

Here is an encouraging word for you, poor lost sinner. You think you must not come to God because you are vile. Now, there is not a saint living on earth who has not been made to feel that he is vile. If Job, Isaiah, and Paul were all obliged to say they were vile, oh, poor sinner, will you be ashamed to join in the same confession? If divine grace does not eradicate all sin from the believer, how do you hope to do it yourself? And if God loves His people while they are yet vile, do you think your vileness will prevent His loving you? Believe on Jesus, you outcast of the world's society! Jesus calls you, and such as you are. "Not the righteous, not the righteous; sinners, Jesus came to call." Even now say, "You have died for sinners; I am a sinner, Lord Jesus. Sprinkle Your blood on me." If you will confess your sin, you will find pardon. If, now, with all your heart, you will say, "I am vile; wash me," you will be washed now. If the Holy Spirit will enable you from your heart to cry,

> Just as I am, without one plea
> But that Thy blood was shed for me,
> And that thou bidd'st me come to Thee,
> O Lamb of God, I come!

you will rise from reading this morning's portion with all your sins pardoned; and though you awoke this morning with every sin that man has ever committed on your head, you will rest tonight *"accepted in the beloved"* (Eph. 1:6). Though once degraded with the rags of sin, you will be adorned with a robe of righteousness and appear white as the angels are. For *"now,"* mark it, *"Now is the accepted time; behold, now is the day of salvation"* (2 Cor. 6:2). If you believe on Him who justifies the ungodly, you are saved. Oh, may the Holy Spirit give you saving faith in Him who receives the vilest.

JUNE 6

Evening

Are they Israelites? so am I.
—2 Corinthians 11:22

We have a personal claim here, and one that needs proof. The apostle knew that his claim was indisputable, but many persons have no right to the title who still claim to belong to Israel. If we confidently declare, "I, too, am an Israelite," let us say it only after having searched our hearts in the presence of God. But if we can give proof that we are following Jesus, if we can say from the heart, "I trust Him wholly, trust Him only, trust Him simply, trust Him now, and trust Him forever," then the position that the saints of God hold belongs to us; we possess all their privileges. We may be the very least in Israel, *"less than the least of all saints"* (Eph. 3:8); yet since the mercies of God belong to the saints as saints, and not as advanced saints or well-taught saints, we may put in our plea, and say, "Are they Israelites? I am, too; therefore, the promises are mine, grace is mine, and glory will be mine." The claim, rightfully made, is one that will yield untold comfort. When God's people are rejoicing that they are His, what happiness it brings if I can say, "So am I!" When they speak of being pardoned, justified, and *"accepted in the beloved"* (Eph. 1:6), how joyful to respond, "Through the grace of God, so am I." But this claim has not only its enjoyments and privileges, but also its conditions and duties. We must share with God's people in cloudy times as well as in sunshine. When we hear them spoken of with contempt and ridicule for being Christians, we must come boldly forward and say, "I am a Christian, too." When we see them working for Christ, giving their time, their talents, their whole hearts to Jesus, we must be able to say, "I will give of myself as well." Let us prove our gratitude by our devotion and live as those who, having claimed a privilege, are willing to take the responsibility connected with it.

Ye that love the Lörd, *hate evil.*
—Psalm 97:10

Yöu have good reason to *"hate evil."* Consider what harm it has already brought you! Oh, what a world of mischief sin has brought into your heart! Sin blinded you so that you could not see the beauty of the Savior; it made you deaf so that you could not hear the Redeemer's tender invitations. Sin turned your feet into the way of death and poured poison into the very fountain of your being. It tainted your heart, and made it *"deceitful above all things, and desperately wicked"* (Jer. 17:9). Oh, what a creature you were when evil had done its utmost with you, before divine grace intervened! You were an heir of wrath even as others; you ran with the *"multitude to do evil"* (Exod. 23:2). Such were all of us; but Paul reminded us, *"Ye are washed, but ye are sanctified, but ye are justified in the name of the Lord Jesus, and by the Spirit of our God"* (1 Cor. 6:11). We have good reason, indeed, for hating evil when we look back and trace its deadly workings. Evil did such mischief to us that our souls would have been lost had not omnipotent love interfered to redeem us. Even now it is an active enemy, ever watching to do us harm and to drag us to perdition. Therefore *"hate evil,"* O Christians, unless you desire trouble. If you would strew your path with thorns and plant nettles on the pillow of your deathbed, then neglect to *"hate evil"*; but if you would live a happy life and die a peaceful death, then walk in all the ways of holiness, hating evil, even unto the end. If you truly love your Savior and would honor Him, then *"hate evil."* We know of no cure for the love of evil in a Christian like abundant communion with the Lord Jesus. Dwell with Him, and it will be impossible for you to be at peace with sin.

> Order my footsteps by Thy Word,
>   And make my heart sincere;
> Let sin have no dominion, Lord,
>   But keep my conscience clear.

Be zealous.
—Revelation 3:19

If you desire to see souls converted; if you want to hear the cry that *"the kingdoms of this world are become the kingdoms of our Lord"* (Rev. 11:15); if you would place crowns upon the head of the Savior and lift His throne high, then be filled with zeal. For, under God, the way of the world's conversion must be by the zeal of the church. Every Christlike characteristic will be utilized, but zeal will be employed first; prudence, knowledge, patience, and courage will follow in their places, but zeal must lead the way. It is not the extent of your knowledge, though that is useful; it is not the extent of your talent, though that is not to be despised; it is your zeal that will do great exploits. This zeal is the fruit of the Holy Spirit. It draws its vital force from the continued operations of the Holy Spirit in the soul. If our inner lives dwindle, if our hearts beat slowly before God, we will not know zeal. But if all is strong and vigorous within, then we cannot but feel a loving eagerness to see the kingdom of Christ come and His will done on earth, even as it is in heaven. A deep sense of gratitude will nourish Christian zeal. Looking to the hole of the pit from which we were rescued, we find abundant reasons why we should spend and be spent for God. And zeal is also stimulated by the thought of the eternal future. It looks with tearful eyes down to the flames of hell, and it cannot sleep. It looks up with longing for the glories of heaven, and it cannot but rouse itself. It feels that time is short compared with the work to be done; therefore, it devotes all that it has to the cause of its Lord. And it is always strengthened by the remembrance of Christ's example. He was clothed with zeal as with a cloak. How swift the chariot wheels of duty went with Him! He knew no loitering by the way. Let us prove that we are His disciples by manifesting the same spirit of zeal.

JUNE 8
Morning

There fell down many slain, because the war was of God.
—1 Chronicles 5:22

Warrior, fighting under the banner of the Lord Jesus, observe this verse with holy joy. If the war is of God, the victory is sure. The sons of Reuben, the Gadites, and the half tribe of Manasseh could barely muster forty-five thousand fighting men, yet in their war with the Hagarites, they killed a hundred thousand men, *"for they cried to God in the battle, and he was entreated of them; because they put their trust in him"* (1 Chron. 5:20). The Lord does not save by many or by few; it is ours to go forth in Jehovah's name if we are but a handful of men, for the Lord of Hosts is with us as our Captain. They did not neglect their weaponry; neither did they place their trust in it. We must use all appropriate means, but our confidence must rest in the Lord alone. He is the sword and the shield of His people. The great reason for their extraordinary success was that *"the war was of God."* In fighting sin without and within, with doctrinal or practical errors, with spiritual wickedness in high places or low places, with devils and the devil's allies, you are waging Jehovah's war. Unless He can be defeated, you do not need to fear defeat. Do not cower before superior numbers, shrink from difficulties or impossibilities, or flinch at wounds or death. Smite with the two-edged sword of the Spirit, and the slain will lie in heaps. *"The battle is the Lord's"* (1 Sam. 17:47), and He will deliver His enemies into our hands. With steadfast foot, strong hand, dauntless heart, and flaming zeal, rush to the conflict, and the hosts of evil will fly like chaff before the gale.

> Stand up! stand up for Jesus!
>   The strife will not be long;
> This day the noise of battle,
>   The next the victor's song:
> To him that overcometh,
>   A crown of life shall be;
> He with the King of Glory
>   Shall reign eternally.

JUNE 8
Evening

*Thou shalt see now whether my word shall
come to pass unto thee or not.*
—Numbers 11:23

God promised Moses that for the space of a whole month He would feed the vast host in the wilderness with flesh. Moses, suddenly overtaken by unbelief, looked to the outward means and was at a loss to know how the promise could be fulfilled. He looked to the creature instead of to the Creator. But does the Creator expect the creature to fulfill His promise for Him? No. He who makes the promise always fulfills it by His own unaided omnipotence. If He speaks, it is done—done by Himself. His promises do not depend for their fulfillment on the cooperation of the puny strength of man. We can see at once the mistake that Moses made. Yet how often we do the same! God has promised to supply our needs, and we look to the creature to do what God has promised to do; then, because we perceive the creature to be weak and feeble, we indulge in unbelief. Why do we look in that direction at all? Will you look to the North Pole to gather fruits ripened in the sun? In truth, that would be no more foolish than looking to the weak for strength or to the creature to do the Creator's work. Let us, then, put the question on the right footing. The visible means for the performance of the promise is not a sufficient basis for faith; the all-sufficiency of the invisible God is the only solid foundation for faith. He will most surely do as He has said He would. After clearly seeing that the burden lies with the Lord and not with the creature, will we dare to indulge in mistrust? The question of God comes home mightily to us: *"Is the LORD's hand waxed short?"* (Num. 11:23). May it happen, too, in His mercy, that with the question there may flash upon our souls that blessed declaration, *"Thou shalt see now whether my word shall come to pass unto thee or not."*

JUNE 9

Morning

The LORD hath done great things for us; whereof we are glad.
—Psalm 126:3

Some Christians are sadly prone to look on the dark side of everything and to dwell more on what they have gone through than on what God has done for them. Ask for their impression of the Christian life, and they will describe their continual conflicts, their deep afflictions, their sad adversities, and the sinfulness of their hearts, yet with scarcely any allusion to the mercy and help that God has granted to them. But a Christian whose soul is in a healthy state will come forward joyously and say, "I will speak, not about myself, but to the honor of my God. *'He brought me up also out of an horrible pit, out of the miry clay, and set my feet upon a rock, and established my goings. And he hath put a new song in my mouth, even praise unto our God'* (Ps. 40:2–3). *'The LORD hath done great things for* [me]; *whereof* [I am] *glad.'*" Such an abstract of experience as this is the very best that any child of God can present. It is true that we endure trials, but it is just as true that we are delivered out of them. It is true that we have our depravity, and mournfully do we know this, but it is quite as true that we have an all-sufficient Savior, who overcomes these corruptions and delivers us from their dominion. In looking back, it would be wrong to deny that we have been in the Slough of Despond and have crept along the Valley of Humiliation, but it would be equally wicked to forget that we have been through them safely and profitably; we have not remained in them, thanks to our almighty Helper and Leader, who has brought *"us out into a wealthy place"* (Ps. 66:12). The deeper our troubles, the louder our thanks to God, who has led us through all and preserved us until now. Our grief cannot mar the melody of our praise; we consider them to be the bass part of our lives' song, *"The LORD hath done great things for us; whereof we are glad."*

Search the scriptures.
—John 5:39

The Greek word for *search* signifies a strict, close, diligent, curious search, such as men make when they are seeking gold, or hunters demonstrate when they are earnestly pursuing game. We must not rest content with having given a superficial reading to a chapter or two, but with the candle of the Spirit, we must deliberately seek out the hidden meaning of the Word. Holy Scripture requires searching—much of it can be learned only by careful study. There is milk for babies, but also meat for strong men. The rabbis wisely say that a mountain of matter hangs on every word, yes, upon every verse of Scripture. Tertullian exclaimed, "I adore the fullness of the Scriptures." No man who merely skims the Book of God can profit thereby; we must dig and mine until we obtain the hidden treasure. The door of the Word opens only with the key of diligence. The Scriptures demand searching. They are the writings of God, bearing the divine stamp and sanction. Who will dare to treat them lightly? He who despises them despises the God who wrote them. God forbid that any of us should allow our Bibles to become swift witnesses against us on the Great Judgment Day. The Word of God will repay searching. God does not tell us to sift a mountain of chaff in order to find a grain of wheat in it here and there, but the Bible is winnowed corn. We have but to open the granary door and find it. Scripture grows upon the student. It is full of surprises. Under the teaching of the Holy Spirit, to the searching eye, it glows with splendor of revelation, like a vast temple paved with gold and roofed with rubies, emeralds, and all manner of gems. There is nothing like the truth of Scripture. Last, the Scriptures reveal Jesus: "*They are they which testify of me*" (John 5:39). No more powerful motive can be urged upon Bible readers than this: he who finds Jesus finds life, heaven, and all things. Happy is he who, searching the Bible, discovers his Savior.

We live unto the Lord.
—Romans 14:8

If God had willed it, each of us might have entered heaven at the moment of conversion. It was not absolutely necessary for our preparation for immortality that we should tarry here. It is possible for a person to be taken to heaven and to be found ready to be a partaker of the inheritance of the saints in light, though he has but just believed in Jesus. It is true that our sanctification is a long, continual process, and we will not be perfected until we lay aside our bodies and enter within the veil; but nevertheless, had the Lord so willed it, He might have changed us from imperfection to perfection, and have taken us to heaven at once. Why, then, are we here? Would God keep His children out of paradise a single moment longer than was necessary? Why is the army of the living God still on the battlefield when one charge might give them the victory? Why are His children still wandering here and there through a maze, when a solitary word from His lips would bring them into the center of their hopes in heaven? The answer is—they are here that they may *"live unto the Lord,"* and may bring others to know His love. We remain on earth as sowers to scatter good seed; as ploughmen to break up the fallow ground; as heralds publishing salvation. We are here as the *"salt of the earth"* (Matt. 5:13), to be a blessing to the world. We are here to glorify Christ in our daily lives. We are here as workers for Him, and as *"workers together with him"* (2 Cor. 6:1). Let us see that our lives answer their end. Let us live earnest, useful, holy lives, *"to the praise of the glory of his grace"* (Eph. 1:6). Meanwhile, we long to be with Him and daily sing,

> My heart is with Him on His throne,
>   And ill can brook delay;
> Each moment listening for the voice,
>   "Rise up, and come away."

They are they which testify of me.
—John 5:39

Jesus Christ is the Alpha and Omega of the Bible. He is the constant theme of its sacred pages; from first to last they testify of Him. At the creation we at once discern Him as one of the sacred Trinity. We catch a glimpse of Him in the promise of the woman's Seed. We see Him typified in the ark of Noah. We walk with Abraham, as He sees Messiah's day. We dwell in the tents of Isaac and Jacob, feeding on the gracious promise. We hear the venerable Israel talking of Shiloh, and in the numerous types of the law, we find the Redeemer abundantly foreshadowed. Prophets and kings, priests and preachers, all look one way—they all stand as the cherubs did over the ark, desiring to look within and to read the mystery of God's great propitiation. Even more clearly, in the New Testament, we find our Lord the one pervading subject. It is not an ingot here and there or some gold dust thinly scattered. Here you stand on a solid floor of gold; for the whole substance of the New Testament is Jesus crucified, and even its closing sentence is bejeweled with the Redeemer's name. We should always read Scripture in this light. We should consider the Word to be like a mirror into which Christ looks down from heaven. Then we, looking into it, see His face reflected as in a mirror. It is true that the reflection is dim, but still it is a blessed preparation for seeing Him as we will see Him face-to-face. The Bible contains Jesus Christ's letters to us, perfumed by His love. Its pages are the garments of our King, and they all smell of myrrh, aloes, and cassia. Scripture is the royal chariot in which Jesus rides, and it is paved with love for the daughters of Jerusalem. The Scriptures are the swaddling clothes of the holy child Jesus; unroll them and you find your Savior. The essence of the Word of God is Christ.

We love him, because he first loved us.
—1 John 4:19

There is no light in the planet but what proceeds from the sun; and there is no true love for Jesus in the heart but what comes from the Lord Jesus Himself. From this overflowing fountain of the infinite love of God, all our love for God must spring. This must ever be a great and certain truth: we love Him for no other reason than that He first loved us. Our love for Him is the fair offspring of His love for us. Cold admiration, when studying the works of God, anyone may have, but the warmth of love can be kindled in the heart only by God's Spirit. How great the wonder that such as we should ever have been brought to love Jesus at all! How marvelous that when we had rebelled against Him, He would, by a display of such amazing love, seek to draw us back. No, we never would have had a grain of love toward God unless it had been sown in us by the sweet seed of His love for us! Love, then, has for its parent the love of God shed abroad in the heart; but after it is thus divinely born, it must be divinely nourished. Love is an exotic plant. It is not one that will flourish naturally in human soil; it must be watered from above. Love for Jesus is a flower of a delicate nature, and if it received no nourishment but that which could be drawn from the rock of our hearts, it would soon wither. As love comes from heaven, so it must feed on heavenly bread. It cannot exist in the wilderness unless it is fed by manna from on high. Love must feed on love. The very soul and life of our love for God is His love for us.

> I love Thee, Lord, but with no love of mine,
>> For I have none to give;
> I love Thee, Lord; but all the love is Thine,
>> For by Thy love I live.
> I am as nothing, and rejoice to be
>> Emptied, and lost, and swallowed up in Thee.

JUNE 11
Evening

*There brake he the arrows of the bow, the shield,
and the sword, and the battle.*
—Psalm 76:3

Our Redeemer's glorious cry of *"It is finished"* (John 19:30) was the death knell of all the adversaries of His people. It signified the breaking of *"the arrows of the bow, the shield, and the sword, and the battle."* The Hero of Golgotha used His cross as an anvil and His woes as a hammer, dashing to pieces bundle after bundle of our sins, those poisoned *"arrows of the bow."* He trampled on every indictment and destroyed every accusation. What glorious blows the mighty Breaker gives with a hammer far weightier than the fabled weapon of Thor! The diabolical darts were reduced to fragments, and the infernal shields were broken like potters' vessels! Jesus drew the dreadful sword of satanic power from its sheath of hellish workmanship. He snapped it across His knee, as a man breaks a bundle of dry wood and casts it into the fire. Beloved, no sin of a believer can now be an arrow to wound him mortally. No condemnation can now be a sword to kill him, for the punishment of our sin was borne by Christ. A full atonement was made for all our iniquities by our blessed Substitute and Surety. Who can accuse us now? Who can condemn us? *"It is Christ that died, yea rather, that is risen again"* (Rom. 8:34). Jesus has emptied the quivers of hell, has quenched every fiery dart, and has broken off the head of every arrow of wrath. The ground is strewn with the splinters and relics of the weapons of hell's warfare, which are visible to us only to remind us of our former danger and of our great deliverance. Sin no longer has dominion over us. Jesus has made an end of it and put it away forever. O enemy, your efforts to destroy have come to an end. Talk of all the wondrous works of the Lord. Make mention of His name, and do not keep silent either by day or when the sun goes to its rest at night. Bless the Lord, O my soul.

JUNE 12
Morning

Thou art weighed in the balances, and art found wanting.
—Daniel 5:27

It is well frequently to weigh ourselves in the scale of God's Word. You will find it a holy exercise to read some psalm of David, and, as you meditate on each verse, to ask yourself, "Can I say this? Have I felt as David felt? Has my heart ever been broken on account of sin, as his was when he penned his penitential psalms? Has my soul been full of true confidence in the hour of difficulty, as his was when he sang of God's mercies in the cave of Adullam or in the holds of Engedi? Do I take the cup of salvation and call on the name of the Lord?" Then turn to the life of Christ, and as you read, ask yourselves how far you are conformed to His likeness. Endeavor to discover whether you have the meekness, the humility, the lovely spirit that He constantly taught and displayed. Take, then, the epistles, and see whether you can go with the apostle in what he said of his experience. Have you ever cried out as he did—*"O wretched man that I am! who shall deliver me from the body of this death"*? (Rom. 7:24). Have you ever felt his self-abasement? Have you seemed to yourself the chief of sinners, and less than the least of all saints? Have you known anything of his devotion? Could you join with him and say, *"For to me to live is Christ, and to die is gain"* (Phil. 1:21)? If we thus read God's Word as a test of our spiritual condition, we will have good reason to stop many times and say, "Lord, I feel I have never yet been here. Oh, bring me here! Give me true penitence, such as this of which I read. Give me real faith; give me warmer zeal; inflame me with more fervent love; grant me the grace of meekness; make me more like Jesus. Let me no longer be *'found wanting'* when weighed in the balances of the sanctuary, lest I be *'found wanting'* in the scales of judgment." *"Judge not, that ye be not judged"* (Matt. 7:1).

Who hath saved us, and called us with an holy calling.
—2 Timothy 1:9

The apostle used the perfect tense when he wrote, *"Who hath saved us,"* which indicates that the action had already been completed. Believers in Christ Jesus are saved. They are not looked on as persons who are in a hopeful state in which they may ultimately be saved, but they are already saved. Salvation is not a blessing to be enjoyed on the deathbed and to be sung of in a future state above; it is a matter promised to be obtained, received, and enjoyed now. The Christian is perfectly saved in God's purpose. God has ordained him unto salvation, and that purpose is complete. He is saved also because of the price that has been paid for him. *"It is finished"* (John 19:30) was the cry of the Savior before He died. The believer is also perfectly saved in His covenant Head, for as he fell in Adam, so he lives in Christ. This complete salvation is accompanied by a holy calling. Those whom the Savior saved on the cross are in due time effectively called by the power of God the Holy Spirit to holiness. They leave their sins, and they endeavor to be like Christ. They choose holiness, not out of any compulsion, but from the influence of a new nature, which leads them to rejoice in holiness just as naturally as before they delighted in sin. God neither chose them nor called them because they were holy, but He called them so that they might be holy, and holiness is the beauty produced by His workmanship in them. The Christlike qualities that we see in a believer are as much the work of God as the Atonement itself. Thus the fullness of the grace of God is brought out very sweetly. Salvation must be of grace, because the Lord is the Author of it. What motive but grace could move Him to save the guilty? Salvation must be of grace, because the Lord works in such a way that our righteousness is forever excluded. The believer's privilege is a present salvation; the evidence that he is called to it is his holy life.

Whosoever will, let him take the water of life freely.
—Revelation 22:17

Jesus says, *"Take...freely."* He wants no payment or preparation. He seeks no recommendation from our virtuous emotions. If you have no good feelings, if you are but willing, you are invited; therefore, come! If you have no belief and no repentance, come to Him, and He will give them to you. Come just as you are, and take *"freely,"* without money and without price. He gives Himself to needy ones. The drinking fountains at the corners of our streets are valuable fixtures, and we can hardly imagine anyone so foolish as to feel for his purse, when he stands before one of them, and to cry, "I cannot drink because I do not have five pounds in my pocket." However poor the man is, there is the fountain, and, just as he is, he may drink of it. Thirsty passengers, as they go by, whether they are dressed in finery or in rags, do not look for authorization to drink from the fountain; its being there is their permission for taking its water freely. The generosity of some good friends has put the refreshing crystal liquid there, and we take it and ask no questions. Perhaps the only persons who need go thirsty through the street where there is a drinking fountain are the fine ladies and gentlemen who are in their carriages. They are very thirsty, but they cannot think of being so vulgar as to get out to drink. It would demean them, they think, to drink at a common drinking fountain: so they ride by with parched lips. Oh, how many there are who are rich in their own good works and cannot therefore come to Christ! "I will not be saved," they say, "in the same way as the harlot or the swearer." What! go to heaven in the same way as a chimney sweep? Is there no pathway to glory but the path that led the thief there? I will not be saved that way. Such proud boasters must remain without the living water, but *"whosoever will, let him take the water of life freely."*

Remove far from me vanity and lies.
—Proverbs 30:8

O my God, be not far from me.
—Psalm 38:21

Here we have two great lessons—what to pray for and what to pray against. The happiest state of a Christian is the holiest state. As there is the most heat nearest to the sun, so there is the most happiness nearest to Christ. No Christian enjoys comfort when his eyes are fixed on empty pursuits; he finds no satisfaction unless his soul is made alive in the ways of God. The world may find happiness elsewhere, but he cannot. I do not blame ungodly men for rushing to their pleasures. Why should I? Let them have their fill. That is all they have to enjoy. A converted wife who despaired of her husband's salvation was always very kind to him, for she said, "I fear that this is the only world in which he will be happy; therefore, I have made up my mind to make him as happy in it as I can." Christians must seek their delights in a higher sphere than the empty frivolities or sinful enjoyments of the world. Vain pursuits are dangerous to renewed souls. We have heard of a philosopher who, while he looked up to the stars, fell into a pit; but how deeply do they fall who look down. Their fall is fatal. No Christian is safe when his soul is lazy and his God is far from him. Every Christian is always safe on the great matter of his standing in Christ, but he is not safe on his experience in holiness and communion with Jesus in this life. Satan does not often attack a Christian who is living near to God. It is when the Christian departs from God, becomes spiritually starved, and endeavors to feed on self-conceit that the devil discovers his advantage. He may sometimes stand foot-to-foot with the child of God who is active in his Master's service, but the battle is generally short. He who slips as he goes down into the Valley of Humiliation, every time he takes a false step invites Apollyon to assail him. Oh, for grace to walk humbly with our God!

JUNE 14

Delight thyself also in the LORD.
—Psalm 37:4

The teaching of these words must seem very surprising to those who are strangers to vital godliness, but to the sincere believer, it is only the communication of a recognized truth. The life of the believer is here described as a delight in God, and we are thus certified of the great fact that true faith overflows with happiness and joy. Ungodly persons and mere professors never look on faith as a joyful thing; to them it is service, duty, or necessity, but never pleasure or delight. If they attend to religion at all, it is either that they may gain thereby, or else because they dare not do otherwise. The thought of delight in religion is so strange to most men that no two words in their language stand further apart than *holiness* and *delight*. But believers who know Christ understand that delight and faith are so blessedly united that the gates of hell cannot prevail to separate them. They who love God with all their hearts find that His *"ways are ways of pleasantness, and all* [His] *paths are peace"* (Prov. 3:17). Such joys, such brimful delights, such overflowing blessedness do the saints discover in their Lord that so far from serving Him from custom, they would follow Him though all the world cast out His name as evil. We do not fear God because of any compulsion. Our faith is no fetter; our profession is no bondage. We are neither dragged to holiness, nor driven to duty. No, our piety is our pleasure, our hope is our happiness, and our duty is our delight. Delight and true religion are as allied as root and flower—as indivisible as truth and certainty. They are, in fact, two precious jewels glittering side by side in a setting of gold.

> 'Tis when we taste Thy love,
>   Our joys divinely grow,
> Unspeakable like those above,
>   And heaven begins below.

O Lord, to us belongeth confusion of face…because
we have sinned against thee.
—Daniel 9:8

A deep sense and clear sight of sin, its hideousness, and the punishment that it deserves should make us bow low before the throne. We have sinned as Christians. It should not be so! Favored as we have been, we have been ungrateful. Privileged beyond most, we have not brought forth fruit in proportion. Who is there, although he may long have been engaged in Christian warfare, that will not blush when he looks back upon the past? As for our days before we were saved, may they be forgiven and forgotten. Yet, since then, though we have not sinned as before, we have sinned against light and against love—light that has really penetrated our minds and love in which we have rejoiced. Oh, the atrocity of the sin of a pardoned soul! An unpardoned sinner sins cheaply compared with the sin of one of God's own elect, who has had communion with Christ and leaned his head on Jesus' bosom. Look at David. Many will talk about his sin, but I trust you will look at his repentance. Hear his broken bones as each one of them moans out its sorrowful confession! See his tears as they fall on the ground, and hear the deep sighs with which he accompanies the softened music of his harp! We have sinned. Let us, therefore, seek the spirit of repentance. Look again at Peter. We speak much of Peter's denying his Master. Remember, it is written, Peter *"wept bitterly"* (Matt. 26:75). Have we no denials of our Lord to be lamented with tears? These sins of ours, before and after conversion, would send us to the place of inextinguishable fire if it were not for the sovereign mercy that has made us different. It has snatched us like burning wood from the fire. My soul, bow down under a sense of your natural sinfulness, and worship your God. Admire the grace that saves you, the mercy that spares you, and the love that pardons you!

Morning

And Sarah said, God hath made me to laugh,
so that all that hear will laugh with me.
—Genesis 21:6

It was far above the power of nature, and even contrary to its laws, that the aged Sarah should be honored with a son. Likewise, it is beyond all ordinary rules that I, a poor, helpless, undone sinner, should find grace to bear about in my soul the indwelling Spirit of the Lord Jesus. I, who once despaired, as well I might, for my nature was as dry, withered, barren, and accursed as a howling wilderness, even I have been made to bring forth fruit unto holiness. Well may my mouth be filled with joyous laughter, because of the singular, surprising grace that I have received from the Lord, for I have found Jesus, the promised Seed, and He is mine forever! This day will I lift up psalms of triumph unto the Lord who has remembered my low estate, for *"my heart rejoiceth in the LORD, mine horn is exalted in the LORD: my mouth is enlarged over mine enemies; because I rejoice in thy salvation"* (1 Sam. 2:1). I would have all those who hear of my great deliverance from hell, and my most blessed visitation from on high, laugh for joy with me. I would surprise my family with my abundant peace. I would delight my friends with my ever increasing happiness. I would edify the church with my grateful confessions, and even impress the world with the cheerfulness of my daily conversation. Bunyan tells us that Mercy laughed in her sleep, and no wonder when she dreamed of Jesus; my joy will not stop short of hers while my Beloved is the theme of my daily thoughts. The Lord Jesus is a deep sea of joy; my soul will dive therein, will be swallowed up in the delights of His society. Sarah looked on her Isaac and laughed with excessive rapture, and all her friends laughed with her; and you, my soul, look on your Jesus and bid heaven and earth unite in your unspeakable joy.

He…openeth, and no man shutteth.
—Revelation 3:7

Jesus is the Keeper of the gates of paradise. Before every believing soul, He sets an open door, which no man or devil is able to close. What joy it will be to find that faith in Him is the golden key to the everlasting doors. My soul, do you carry this key in your heart, or are you trusting in some deceitful burglar, who will fail you in the end? Hear this parable of the preacher, and remember it. The great King has made a banquet, and He has proclaimed to all the world that no one will enter but those who bring with them the fairest flower that blooms. The spirits of men advance to the gate by thousands, and each one brings the flower that he esteems to be the queen of the garden; but they are all driven from the royal presence and cannot enter into the festive halls. Some bear in their hands the deadly nightshade of superstition or the flaunting poppies of false religions or the hemlock of self-righteousness, but these are not dear to the King. The bearers of these flowers are shut out of the pearly gates. My soul, have you gathered the rose of Sharon? Do you wear the lily of the valley in your bosom constantly? If so, when you come up to the gates of heaven, you will know its value, for you need only to show this choicest of flowers, and the Porter will open the heavenly door for you. He will not deny you admission for one moment, for the Porter always opens the door when He sees that rose. You will find your way with the rose of Sharon in your hand up to the throne of God Himself, for heaven itself possesses nothing that excels its radiant beauty. Of all the flowers that bloom in paradise, there is none that can rival the lily of the valley. My soul, by faith get Calvary's bloodred rose into your hand, by love wear it, by communion preserve it, by daily watchfulness make it your all in all, and you will be blessed beyond all bliss and happy beyond all dreams. Jesus, be mine forever. Be my God, my heaven, and my all.

And I give unto them eternal life; and they shall never perish.
—John 10:28

The Christian should never think or speak lightly of unbelief. For a child of God to mistrust His love, His truth, His faithfulness, must be greatly displeasing to Him. How can we ever grieve Him by doubting His upholding grace? Christian, it is contrary to every promise of God's precious Word that you should ever be forgotten or left to perish. If it could be so, how could He be true who has said, *"Can a woman forget her sucking child, that she should not have compassion on the son of her womb? yea, they may forget, yet will I not forget thee"* (Isa. 49:15). Of what value would be the promise—*"The mountains shall depart, and the hills be removed; but my kindness shall not depart from thee, neither shall the covenant of my peace be removed, saith the* LORD *that hath mercy on thee"* (Isa. 54:10)? Where would the truth be in Christ's words—*"I give unto [*"my sheep," John 10:27*] eternal life; and they shall never perish, neither shall any man pluck them out of my hand. My Father, which gave them me, is greater than all; and no man is able to pluck them out of my Father's hand"* (John 10:28–29). Where would the doctrines of grace be? They would be all disproved if one child of God would perish. Where would the veracity of God, His honor, His power, His grace, His covenant, His oath be, if any of those for whom Christ has died, and who have put their trust in Him, would nevertheless be cast away? Banish those unbelieving fears that so dishonor God. Arise, shake yourself from the dust, and put on your beautiful garments. Remember that it is sinful to doubt His Word wherein He has promised you that you will never perish. Let the eternal life within you express itself in confident rejoicing.

> The Gospel bears my spirit up:
>   A faithful and unchanging God
> Lays the foundation for my hope,
>   In oaths, and promises, and blood.

JUNE 16

Evening

The LORD is my light and my salvation; whom shall I fear? the LORD is the strength of my life; of whom shall I be afraid?
—Psalm 27:1

T*he LORD is my light and my salvation.*" Here is personal interest: "*my light*" and "*my salvation.*" The soul is assured of it and therefore declares it boldly. At the new birth, divine light is poured into the soul as the precursor of salvation; where there is not enough light to reveal our own darkness and to make us long for the Lord Jesus, there is no evidence of salvation. After conversion, our God is our joy, comfort, guide, teacher, and in every sense our light. He is light within, light around, light reflected from us, and light to be revealed to us. Notice that it is not said that the Lord merely gives light, but that He is light; nor that He gives salvation, but that He is salvation. He, then, who by faith lays hold upon God, has all covenant blessings in his possession. This truth established, the argument drawn from it is then put in the form of a question: "*Whom shall I fear?*" This question provides its own answer. The powers of darkness are not to be feared, for the Lord, our light, destroys them. The damnation of hell is not to be dreaded, for the Lord is our salvation. This is a very different challenge from that of boastful Goliath. It rests not on the conceited strength of the "*arm of flesh*" (2 Chron. 32:8), but on the real power of the omnipotent I AM. (See Exodus 3:14.) "*The Lord is the strength of my life.*" Here is a third glowing epithet; it shows that the writer's hope was fastened with a threefold cord that could not be broken. We may well accumulate terms of praise where the Lord lavishes deeds of grace. Our lives derive all their strength from God; if He deigns to make us strong, we cannot be weakened by all the schemes of the adversary. "*Of whom shall I be afraid?*" The bold question looks into the future as well as the present. "*If God be for us, who can be against us?*" (Rom. 8:31)—either now or in the time to come!

Help, Lord.
—Psalm 12:1

The prayer itself is remarkable, for it is short, but seasonable, concise, and suggestive. David mourned the scarcity of faithful men, and therefore lifted up his heart in supplication. When the creature failed, he flew to the Creator. He evidently felt his own weakness, or he would not have cried for help. At the same time, he intended honestly to exert himself for the cause of truth, for the word *"help"* is inapplicable where we ourselves do nothing. There is much directness, clearness of perception, and distinctness of utterance in this petition of two words—much more, indeed, than in the long rambling outpourings of certain professors. The psalmist runs directly to his God, with a well-considered prayer; he knows what he is seeking and where to seek it. Lord, teach us to pray in the same blessed manner. The occasions for the use of this prayer are frequent. In providential afflictions how suitable it is for tried believers who find all helpers failing them. Students, in doctrinal difficulties, may often obtain aid by lifting up this cry of *"Help, Lord,"* to the Holy Spirit, the great Teacher. Spiritual warriors in inward conflicts may send to the throne for reinforcements, and this will be a model for their request. Workers in heavenly labor may thus obtain grace in time of need. Seeking sinners, in doubts and alarms, may offer up the same weighty supplication; in fact, in all these cases, times, and places, this will serve the turn of needy souls. *"Help, Lord,"* will suit us living and dying, suffering or laboring, rejoicing or sorrowing. In Him our help is found. Let us not be slack to cry to Him. The answer to the prayer is certain, if it is sincerely offered through Jesus. The Lord's character assures us that He will not leave His people. His relationship as Father and Husband guarantees us His aid. His gift of Jesus is a pledge of every good thing, and His sure promise stands, *"Fear not; I will help thee"* (Isa. 41:13).

JUNE 17
Evening

Then Israel sang this song, Spring up, O well; sing ye unto it.
—Numbers 21:17

The well of Beer in the wilderness was famous because it was the subject of a promise: *"That is the well whereof the* Lord *spake unto Moses, Gather the people together, and I will give them water"* (Num. 21:16). The people needed water, and it was promised by their gracious God. We need fresh supplies of heavenly grace, and in the covenant the Lord has pledged Himself to give all we require. The well became the cause of a song. Before the water gushed forth, cheerful faith prompted the people to sing; and as they saw the crystal fount bubbling up, the music grew even more joyous. In like manner, we who believe the promise of God should rejoice in the prospect of divine revivals in our souls. As we experience them, our holy joy should overflow. Are we thirsting? Let us not complain, but sing. Spiritual thirst is bitter to bear, but we need not bear it. The promise indicates a well; let us be of good heart and look for it. In addition, the well was the center of prayer. *"Spring up, O well."* What God has promised to give, we must seek after, or we show that we have neither desire nor faith. This evening let us ask that the Scripture we have read and our devotional exercises may not be empty formalities; instead, may they be a channel of grace to our souls. Oh, that God the Holy Spirit would work in us with all His mighty power, filling us with all the fullness of God! Last, the well was the object of effort. *"The nobles of the people digged it…with their staves"* (v. 18). The Lord wants us to be active in obtaining grace. Our staves are ill adapted for digging in the sand, but we must use them to our utmost ability. Prayer must not be neglected; the assembling of ourselves together must not be forsaken; ordinances must not be slighted. The Lord will give us His peace most abundantly, but not as a reward for idleness. Let us, then, rouse ourselves to seek Him in whom are all our fresh springs.

Thy Redeemer.
—Isaiah 54:5

Jesus, the Redeemer, is altogether ours and ours forever. All the offices of Christ are held on our behalf. He is King for us, Priest for us, and Prophet for us. Whenever we read a new title of the Redeemer, let us appropriate Him as ours under that name as much as under any other. The shepherd's staff, the father's rod, the captain's sword, the priest's miter, the prince's scepter, the prophet's mantle—all are ours. Jesus has no dignity that He will not employ for our exaltation and no prerogative that He will not exercise for our defense. His fullness of Godhead is our unfailing, inexhaustible treasure-house. His manhood also, which He took on Him for us, is ours in all its perfection. To us our gracious Lord communicates the spotless virtue of a stainless character; to us He gives the meritorious efficacy of a devoted life; on us He bestows the reward procured by obedient submission and incessant service. He makes the unsullied garment of His life our covering beauty, the glittering virtues of His character our ornaments and jewels, and the superhuman meekness of His death our boast and glory. He bequeaths us His manger, from which to learn how God came down to man, and His Cross to teach us how man may go up to God. All His thoughts, emotions, actions, utterances, miracles, and intercessions were for us. He trod the road of sorrow on our behalf and has made over to us as His heavenly legacy the full results of all the labors of His life. He is now as much ours as heretofore; and He does not blush to acknowledge Himself our Lord Jesus Christ, though He is the blessed and only Potentate, the King of Kings, and Lord of Lords. Christ everywhere and every way is our Christ, forever and ever most richly to enjoy. O my soul, by the power of the Holy Spirit, call Him this morning, *"thy Redeemer."*

JUNE 18

Evening

I am come into my garden, my sister, my spouse.
—Song of Solomon 5:1

The heart of the believer is Christ's garden. He bought it with His precious blood, and He enters it and claims it as His own. A garden implies separation. It is not public property; it is not a wilderness. It is walled around or hedged in. Would that we could see the wall of separation between the church and the world made broader and stronger. It makes one sad to hear Christians saying, "Well, there is no harm in this; there is no harm in that," thus getting as near to the world as possible. Grace is at a low ebb in the soul that can even raise the question of how far it may go in worldly conformity. A garden is a place of beauty. It far surpasses the wild, uncultivated lands. The genuine Christian must seek to be more excellent in his life than the best moralist, because Christ's garden should produce the best flowers in all the world. Even the best is poor compared with what Christ deserves; let us not put Him off with withering, dwarfed plants. The rarest, richest, choicest lilies and roses should bloom in the place that Jesus calls His own. The garden is a place of growth. The saints are not to remain undeveloped, always mere buds and blossoms. We should *"grow in grace, and in the knowledge of our Lord and Saviour Jesus Christ"* (2 Pet. 3:18). Growth should be rapid where Jesus is the Gardener and where the Holy Spirit is the dew from above. A garden is a place of retirement. The Lord Jesus Christ would have us reserve our souls as a place in which He can manifest Himself in ways that He does not reveal Himself to the world. Oh, that Christians were more reserved, that they would keep their hearts more closely guarded for Christ! We often worry and trouble ourselves, like Martha, with much serving, so that we do not have the room for Christ that Mary had, and we do not sit at His feet as we should. May the Lord grant the sweet showers of His grace to water His garden this day.

And they were all filled with the Holy Ghost.
—Acts 2:4

The blessings of this day would be rich if all of us were *"filled with the Holy Ghost."* The consequences of this sacred filling of the soul would be impossible to overestimate. Life, comfort, light, purity, power, peace, and many other precious blessings are inseparable from the Spirit's benign presence. As sacred oil, He anoints the head of the believer, sets him apart to the priesthood of saints, and gives him grace to execute his office aright. As the only truly purifying water, He cleanses us from the power of sin and sanctifies us unto holiness, working in us *"to will and to do of his good pleasure"* (Phil. 2:13). As light, He manifested to us at first our lost estate, and now He reveals the Lord Jesus to us and in us and guides us in the way of righteousness. Enlightened by His pure celestial ray, we are no more darkness but light in the Lord. As fire, He both purges us from dross and sets our consecrated nature on a blaze. He is the sacrificial flame by which we are enabled to offer our whole souls as a *"living sacrifice"* (Rom. 12:1) unto God. As heavenly dew, He removes our barrenness and fertilizes our lives. Oh, that He would drop from above upon us at this early hour! Such morning dew would be a sweet beginning to the day. As the Dove, with wings of peaceful love, He broods over His church and over the souls of believers; and as the Comforter, He dispels the cares and doubts that mar the peace of His beloved. He descends on the chosen as on the Lord in Jordan, and bears witness to their sonship by working in them a filial spirit by which they cry, *"Abba, Father"* (Gal. 4:6). As the wind, He brings the breath of life to men; blowing where He pleases, He performs the quickening operations by which the spiritual creation is animated and sustained. Would to God that we might feel His presence this day and every day.

My beloved is mine, and I am his: he feedeth among the lilies. Until the day break, and the shadows flee away, turn, my beloved, and be thou like a roe or a young hart upon the mountains of Bether.
—Song of Solomon 2:16–17

Surely if there is a joyous verse in the Bible it is this: *"My beloved is mine, and I am his."* This thought is so peaceful, so full of assurance, so overrunning with happiness and contentment that it might well have been written by the same hand that penned the Twenty-third Psalm. Although the prospect is exceedingly fair and lovely—earth cannot show its superior—it is not entirely a sunlit landscape. There is a cloud in the sky that casts a shadow over the scene. Listen, *"Until the day break, and the shadows flee away."* There is a word, too, about the *"mountains of Bether,"* or the "mountains of division," and to our love, anything like division is bitterness. Beloved, this may be your present state of mind: you do not doubt your salvation; you know that Christ is yours, but you are not feasting with Him. You understand that you are of vital concern to Him, so that you have no shadow of a doubt of your being His and of His being yours, but still His left hand is not under your head, and His right hand does not embrace you. A shade of sadness is cast over your heart, perhaps by affliction, certainly by the temporary absence of your Lord, so even while exclaiming, *"I am his,"* you are forced to fall to your knees and to pray, *"Until the day break, and the shadows flee away, turn, my beloved."* "Where is He?" asks the soul. And the answer comes, *"He feedeth among the lilies."* If we would find Christ, we must be in communion with His people, and we must come to the ordinances with His saints. Oh, for an evening glimpse of Him! Oh, to dine with Him tonight!

JUNE 20

Morning

For, lo, I will command, and I will sift the house of Israel
among all nations, like as corn is sifted in a sieve, yet shall
not the least grain fall upon the earth.
—Amos 9:9

Every sifting comes by divine command and permission. Satan must ask permission before he can lay a finger on Job. Furthermore, in some sense, our siftings are directly the work of heaven, for the text says, "*I will sift the house of Israel.*" Satan, like a drudge, may hold the sieve, hoping to destroy the corn; but the overruling hand of the Master is accomplishing the purity of the grain by the very process that the enemy intended to be destructive. Precious, but much sifted, corn of the Lord's floor, be comforted by the blessed fact that the Lord directs both flail and sieve to His own glory, and to your eternal profit. The Lord Jesus will surely use the fan that is in His hand and will divide the precious from the vile. All are not Israel who are of Israel. The heap on the barn floor is not clean food; hence, the winnowing process must be performed. In the sieve true weight alone has power. Husks and chaff, being devoid of substance, must fly before the wind, and only solid corn will remain. Observe the complete safety of the Lord's wheat; even the least grain has a promise of preservation. God Himself sifts, and therefore it is stern and terrible work. He sifts them in all places, "*among all nations*"; He sifts them in the most effective manner, "*like as corn is sifted in a sieve*"; and yet for all this, not the smallest, lightest, or most shriveled grain is permitted to fall to the ground. Every individual believer is precious in the sight of the Lord. A shepherd would not lose one sheep or a jeweler one diamond or a mother one child or a man one limb of his body. Neither will the Lord lose one of His redeemed people. However little we may be, if we are the Lord's, we may rejoice that we are "*preserved in Jesus Christ*" (Jude 1).

JUNE 20

Evening

Straightway they forsook their nets, and followed him.
—Mark 1:18

When Simon and Andrew heard the call of Jesus, they obeyed at once without question. If we would always, promptly and with resolute zeal, put into practice what we hear on the spot or at the first suitable occasion, our attention to the means of grace and our reading of good books could not fail to enrich us spiritually. He will not lose his loaf who has taken care to eat it immediately. Neither can he be deprived of the benefit of a doctrine who has already acted on it. Most readers and hearers become motivated to change; but, sadly, the proposal is a blossom that has not been rooted; therefore, no fruit comes of it. They wait, they waver, and then they forget, until, like the ponds on nights of frost, when the sun shines by day, they are thawed only in time to be frozen again. That fatal tomorrow is bloodred with the death of fair resolutions; it is the slaughterhouse of the innocents. We are very concerned that this little book of evening devotions would not be fruitless, and we pray that readers may not be readers only, but *"doers of the word"* (James 1:22). The practice of truth is the most profitable reading of it. Should the reader be impressed with any duty while perusing these pages, let him hurry to fulfill it before the holy glow has departed from his soul. Let him leave his nets, and all that he has, rather than be found rebellious to the Master's call. Do not give place to the devil by delay! Move while opportunity and renewal are in happy conjunction. Do not be caught in your own nets, but break the cords of worldliness. Come away to where glory calls you. Happy is the writer who finds readers who are resolved to carry out his teachings; his harvest will be a hundredfold, and his Master will receive great honor. Would to God that such might be the reward from these brief meditations and hurried hints. Grant it, O Lord, to your servant!

Thou art fairer than the children of men.
—Psalm 45:2

The entire person of Jesus is but as one gem, and His life is all along but one impression of the seal. He is altogether complete; not only in His several parts, but as a gracious, all-glorious whole. His character is not a mass of fair colors mixed confusedly, nor a heap of precious stones laid carelessly one upon another. He is a picture of beauty and a breastplate of glory. In Him, all the things of good repute are in their proper places and assist in adorning each other. Not one feature in His glorious person attracts attention at the expense of others, but He is perfectly and altogether lovely. Oh, Jesus! Your power, Your grace, Your justice, Your tenderness, Your truth, Your majesty, and Your immutability make up such a man, or rather such a God-man, as neither heaven nor earth has seen elsewhere. Your infancy, Your eternity, Your sufferings, Your triumphs, Your death, and Your immortality are all woven in one gorgeous tapestry, without seam or rent. You are music without discord. You are many, and yet not divided. You are all things, and yet not diverse. As all the colors blend into one resplendent rainbow, so all the glories of heaven and earth meet in You and unite so wondrously that there is none like You in all things; if all the virtues of the most excellent were bound in one bundle, they could not rival You, mirror of all perfection. You have been anointed with the holy oil of myrrh and cassia, which Your God has reserved for You alone. As for Your fragrance, it is as the holy perfume, the like of which none other can ever mingle, even with the art of the apothecary; each spice is fragrant, but the compound is divine.

> Oh, sacred symmetry! Oh, rare connection
> Of many perfects, to make one perfection!
> Oh, heavenly music, where all parts do meet
> In one sweet strain, to make one perfect sweet!

JUNE 21
Evening

Nevertheless the foundation of God standeth sure.
—2 Timothy 2:19

The foundation on which our faith rests is this: *"God was in Christ, reconciling the world unto himself, not imputing their trespasses unto them"* (2 Cor. 5:19). The great fact on which genuine faith relies is that *"the Word was made flesh, and dwelt among us"* (John 1:14), and that *"Christ also hath once suffered for sins, the just for the unjust, that he might bring us to God"* (1 Pet. 3:18); *"Who his own self bare our sins in his own body on the tree"* (1 Pet. 2:24), for *"the chastisement of our peace was upon him; and with his stripes we are healed"* (Isa. 53:5). In one word, the great pillar of the Christian's hope is substitution. His hope is in the vicarious sacrifice of Christ for the guilty, Christ being made *"sin for us...that we might be made the righteousness of God in him"* (2 Cor. 5:21), Christ offering up a true and proper expiatory and substitutionary sacrifice in the room, place, and stead of as many as the Father gave to Him, who are known to God by name and who are recognized in their own hearts by their trusting in Jesus. This is the cardinal fact of the Gospel. If this foundation were removed, what could we do? But it stands as firm as the throne of God. We know it; we rest on it; we rejoice in it; and our delight is to hold it, to meditate on it, and to proclaim it, while we desire to be moved by gratitude for it in every part of our lives and conversation. In these days a direct attack has been made on the doctrine of the Atonement. Men cannot bear substitution. They gnash their teeth at the thought of the Lamb of God bearing the sin of man. But we, who know by experience the preciousness of this truth, will proclaim it confidently and unceasingly in defiance of them. We will neither dilute it nor change it, nor fritter it away in any shape or fashion. It will still be Christ, a sure Substitute, who bears human guilt and suffering in the stead of men. We cannot or dare not give it up, for it is our life. Despite every controversy, we feel that *"nevertheless the foundation of God standeth sure."*

He shall build the temple of the LORD; and he shall bear the glory.
—Zechariah 6:13

Christ Himself is the builder of His spiritual temple, and He has built it on the mountains of His unchangeable affection, His omnipotent grace, and His infallible truthfulness. But as it was in Solomon's temple, so in this; the materials need to be made ready. There are the cedars of Lebanon, but they are not framed for the building. They are not cut down, shaped, and made into those cedar planks, whose odorous beauty will *"make glad"* (Ps. 46:4) the courts of the Lord's house in paradise. There are also the rough stones still in the quarry; they must be hewn from that place and squared. All this is Christ's own work. Each individual believer is being prepared, polished, and made ready for his place in the temple; but Christ's own hand performs the preparatory work. Afflictions cannot sanctify, excepting as they are used by Him to this end. Our prayers and efforts cannot make us ready for heaven, apart from the hand of Jesus, who fashions our hearts aright. As in the building of Solomon's temple, *"there was neither hammer nor ax nor any tool of iron heard in the house"* (1 Kings 6:7), because all was brought perfectly ready for the exact spot it was to occupy. So it is with the temple that Jesus builds; the making ready is all done on earth. When we reach heaven, there will be no sanctifying us there, no squaring us with affliction, no planing us with suffering. No, we must be made ready here. Christ will do all that beforehand. And when He has done it, we will be ferried by a loving hand across the stream of death and brought to the heavenly Jerusalem, to abide as eternal pillars in the temple of our Lord.

> Beneath His eye and care,
>   The edifice shall rise,
> Majestic, strong, and fair,
>   And shine above the skies.

That those things which cannot be shaken may remain.
—Hebrews 12:27

Many things in our possession at the present moment can be shaken, and it ill becomes a Christian to set much store by them, for there is nothing stable under these rolling skies; change is written on all things. Yet we have certain *"things which cannot be shaken,"* and I invite you this evening to think about them. If the things that can be shaken would all be taken away, you may derive real comfort from the things that cannot be shaken, which will remain. Whatever your losses have been, or may be, you enjoy present salvation. You are standing at the foot of His cross, trusting alone in the merit of Jesus' precious blood. No rise or fall of the markets can interfere with your salvation in Him. No breaking of banks, no failures, no bankruptcies can touch that. You are a child of God this evening. God is your Father. No change of circumstances can ever rob you of that. Although by losses, you are brought to poverty and stripped bare, you can say, "He is my Father still. In my Father's house are many mansions; therefore, I will not be troubled." You have another permanent blessing, namely, the love of Jesus Christ. He who is God and Man loves you with all the strength of His affectionate nature—nothing can affect that. The fig tree may not blossom, and the flocks may *"be cut off from the fold"* (Hab. 3:17). These things do not matter to the one who can sing, *"My beloved is mine, and I am his"* (Song 2:16). We cannot lose our best portion and richest heritage. Whatever troubles come, let us act like adults. Let us show that we are not such little children as to be cast down by what may happen in this poor, fleeting state of time. Our country is Immanuel's land, and our hope is above the sky; therefore, calm as the summer's ocean, we will see the wreck of everything earthborn, yet rejoice in the God of our salvation.

Ephraim is a cake not turned.
—Hosea 7:8

A cake not turned is uncooked on one side; and so Ephraim was, in many respects, untouched by divine grace. Although there was some partial obedience, there was much rebellion left. My soul, I charge you, see whether this is your case. Are you thorough in the things of God? Has grace gone through the very center of your being so as to be felt in its divine operations in all your powers, actions, words, and thoughts? To be sanctified, spirit, soul, and body, should be your aim and prayer; and although sanctification may not be perfect in you anywhere in degree, yet it must be universal in its action; there must not be the appearance of holiness in one place and reigning sin in another; otherwise, you, too, will be a cake not turned. A cake not turned is soon burned on the side nearest the fire, and although no man can have too much religion, there are some who seem burned black with bigoted zeal for that part of truth that they have received, or are charred to a cinder with a boastful Pharisaic ostentation of those religious performances that suit their character. The assumed appearance of superior sanctity frequently accompanies a total absence of all vital godliness. The saint in public is a devil in private. He deals in flour by day and in soot by night. The cake that is burned on one side is dough on the other. If it is so with me, O Lord, turn me! Turn my unsanctified nature to the fire of Your love, and let it feel the sacred glow. Let my burned side cool a little, while I learn my own weakness and lack of heat when I am removed from Your heavenly flame. Let me not be found to be a double-minded person, but one entirely under the powerful influence of reigning grace; for well I know if I am left like a cake unturned, and am not on both sides the subject of Your grace, I must be consumed forever amid *"everlasting burnings"* (Isa. 33:14).

Waiting for the adoption.
—Romans 8:23

Even in this world, saints are God's children, but people cannot recognize them to be so unless they observe certain moral characteristics in them. The adoption is not manifested, and the children are not yet openly declared. Among the Romans a man might adopt a child and keep the matter private for a long time, but there was a second adoption that took place in public. Then the child was brought before the constituted authorities, and his former garments were removed. The father who was adopting the child gave him clothing suitable to the child's new station in life. *"Beloved, now are we the sons of God, and it doth not yet appear what we shall be"* (1 John 3:2). We are not yet arrayed in the apparel that befits the royal family of heaven. We are wearing in this flesh and blood just what we wore as the sons of Adam. But we know that when the *"firstborn among many brethren"* (Rom. 8:29) appears, *"we shall be like him; for we shall see him as he is"* (1 John 3:2). Can you not imagine that a child taken from the lowest ranks of society and adopted by a Roman senator would say to himself, "I long for the day when I will be publicly adopted. Then I will remove these coarse, plebeian garments and be robed as becomes my senatorial rank"? Because he is happy in what he has received, for that very reason, he longs to get the fullness of what is promised to him. So it is with us today. We are waiting until we will put on our proper garments and will be manifested as the children of God. We are young nobles and have not yet worn our crowns. We are young brides, and the marriage day has not yet come. But because of the love our Spouse shows us, we are led to long and sigh for the bridal morning. Our very happiness makes us long for more; our joy, like a swollen spring, wants to well up like a geyser, leaping to the skies, and it heaves and groans within our spirits for lack of space and room by which to manifest itself to men.

A certain woman of the company lifted up her voice, and said
unto him, Blessed is the womb that bare thee, and the paps which thou
hast sucked. But He said, Yea rather, blessed are they
that hear the word of God, and keep it.
—Luke 11:27–28

It is fondly imagined by some that it must have involved very special privileges to have been the mother of our Lord, because they supposed that she had the benefit of looking into His very heart in a way in which we cannot hope to do. There may be an appearance of plausibility in the supposition, but not much. We do not know that Mary knew more than others. What she did know she did well to lay up in her heart, but she does not appear from anything we read in the Gospels to have been a better instructed believer than any other of Christ's disciples. All that she knew we also may discover. Do you wonder that we should say so? Here is a text to prove it: *"The secret of the* Lord *is with them that fear him; and he will show them his covenant"* (Ps. 25:14). Remember the Master's words, *"Henceforth I call you not servants; for the servant knoweth not what his lord doeth: but I have called you friends; for all things that I have heard of my Father I have made known unto you"* (John 15:15). So blessedly does this divine Revealer of secrets tell us His heart that He keeps back nothing that is profitable to us. His own assurance is, *"If it were not so, I would have told you"* (John 14:2). Does He not this day manifest Himself unto us as He does not unto the world? It is even so; therefore, we will not ignorantly cry out, *"Blessed is the womb that bare thee,"* but we will intelligently bless God that, having heard the Word and kept it, we have first of all as true a communion with the Savior as the Virgin had, and in the second place as true an acquaintance with the secrets of His heart as she can be supposed to have obtained. Happy soul to be thus privileged!

JUNE 24

Evening

Shadrach, Meshach, and Abednego, answered and said…,
Be it known unto thee, O king, that we will not serve thy gods.
—Daniel 3:16, 18

The story of the bold courage and marvelous deliverance of the three Hebrew children, or rather champions, well illustrates firmness and steadfastness in upholding the truth while facing the teeth of tyranny and the very jaws of death. It motivates believers to imitate their example. Let young Christians especially learn, both in matters of faith in religion and matters of uprightness in business, never to sacrifice their consciences. Lose all rather than to lose your integrity, and when all else is gone, still hold fast to a clear conscience as the rarest jewel that can adorn the human heart. Do not be guided by a will-o'-the-wisp kind of policy, but by the North Star of divine authority. Follow the right path at all costs. When you see no present advantage, *"walk by faith, not by sight"* (2 Cor. 5:7). Honor God by trusting Him even when it comes to matters of loss for the sake of principle. See whether He will be your debtor! See if He does not even in this life prove His Word that *"godliness with contentment is great gain"* (1 Tim. 6:6), and that those who seek *"first the kingdom of God, and his righteousness [will have] all these things…added unto [them]"* (Matt. 6:33). Should it happen that, in the providence of God, you suffer a loss by following your conscience, you will find that if the Lord does not pay you back in the silver of earthly prosperity, He will fulfill His promise in the gold of spiritual joy. Remember that a man's life does not consist *"in the abundance of the things which he possesseth"* (Luke 12:15). To wear a guileless spirit, to have a heart void of offense, and to have the favor and smile of God are greater riches than the mines of Ophir could yield or the business of Tyre could earn. *"Better is a dinner of herbs where love is, than a stalled ox and hatred therewith"* (Prov. 15:17). An ounce of heartsease is worth a ton of gold.

Get thee up into the high mountain.
—Isaiah 40:9

Our knowledge of Christ is somewhat like climbing one of our Welsh mountains. When you are at the base you see but little: the mountain itself appears to be but one-half as high as it really is. Confined in a little valley, you discover scarcely anything but the rippling brooks as they descend into the stream at the foot of the mountain. Climb the first rising knoll, and the valley lengthens and widens beneath your feet. Go higher, and you see the country for four or five miles round, and you are delighted with the widening prospect. Climb higher still, and the scene enlarges, until at last, when you are on the summit, and look east, west, north, and south, you see almost all of England lying before you. Yonder is a forest in some distant county, perhaps two hundred miles away, and here the sea, and there a shining river and the smoking chimneys of a manufacturing town, or the masts of the ships in a busy port. All these things please and delight you, and you say, "I could not have imagined that so much could be seen at this elevation." Now, the Christian life is of the same order. When we first believe in Christ we see but little of Him. The higher we climb, the more we discover of His beauties. But who has ever gained the summit? Who has known all the heights and depths of the *"love of Christ, which passeth knowledge"* (Eph. 3:19)? Paul, when grown old, sitting gray-haired, shivering in a dungeon in Rome, could say with greater emphasis than we can, *"I know whom I have believed"* (2 Tim. 1:12), for each experience had been like the climbing of a hill, each trial had been like ascending another summit, and his death seemed like gaining the top of the mountain, from which he could see the whole of the faithfulness and the love of Him to whom he had committed his soul. Get up, dear friend, into the high mountain.

The dove found no rest for the sole of her foot.
—Genesis 8:9

Reader, can you find rest apart from the ark, Christ Jesus? Then be assured that your religion is vain. Are you satisfied with anything short of a conscious knowledge of your union and interest in Christ? Then woe to you. If you profess to be a Christian, yet find full satisfaction in worldly pleasures and pursuits, your profession is false. If your soul can stretch itself, find the bed long enough, and the coverlet wide enough to cover it in the chambers of sin, then you are a hypocrite. You are far from any right thoughts of Christ or perception of His preciousness. On the other hand, if you could indulge in sin without receiving any punishment, but you feel that sin in itself would be a punishment; and if you could have the whole world and live in it forever, but you feel that would be true misery, for your God is what your soul craves; then be of good courage: you are a child of God. With all your sins and imperfections, let this thought comfort you: if your soul finds no rest in sin, you are not as the sinner is! If you are still crying for and craving after something better, Christ has not forgotten you, for you have not quite forgotten Him. The believer cannot do without his Lord. Words are inadequate to express his thoughts of Him. We cannot live on the sands of the wilderness. We need the manna that drops from on high. Our skin bottles of creature confidence cannot yield us a drop of moisture, but we drink of the Rock that follows us, and that Rock is Christ. (See 1 Corinthians 10:4.) When you feed on Him, your soul can sing, "He has satisfied my '*mouth with good things; so that* [my] *youth is renewed like the eagle's*'" (Ps. 103:5). But if you do not have Him, your bursting wine vat and well-filled barn can give you no sort of satisfaction. Instead, lament over them in the words of wisdom, "*Vanity of vanities; all is vanity*" (Eccl. 1:2).

JUNE 26

Morning

Art thou also become like unto us?
—Isaiah 14:10

What must be the apostate's doom when his naked soul appears before God? How will he bear that voice, "Depart, you cursed; you have rejected Me, and I reject you. You have played the harlot and departed from Me. I also have banished you forever from My presence, and I will not have mercy on you." What will be this wretch's shame at the Last Great Day when, before assembled multitudes, the apostate will be unmasked? See the profane, and sinners who never professed religion, lifting themselves up from their beds of fire to point at him. "There he is," says one. "Will he preach the Gospel in hell?" "There he is," says another. "He rebuked me for cursing and was a hypocrite himself!" "Aha!" says another. "Here comes a psalm-singing Methodist—one who was always at his meetings; he is the man who boasted of his being sure of everlasting life, and here he is!" No greater eagerness will ever be seen among satanic tormentors than in that Day when devils drag the hypocrite's soul down to perdition. Bunyan pictured this with massive but awful grandeur of poetry when he spoke of the back way to hell. Seven devils bound the wretch with nine cords and dragged him from the road to heaven, in which he had professed to walk, and thrust him through the back door into hell. Mind that back way to hell, false professors of faith! *"Examine yourselves, whether ye be in the faith"* (2 Cor. 13:5). Look well to your state; see whether you are in Christ or not. It is the easiest thing in the world to give a lenient verdict when oneself is to be tried; but oh, be just and true here. Be just to all, but be rigorous with yourself. Remember, if it is not a rock on which you build, when the house will fall, great will be *"the fall of it"* (Matt. 7:27). May the Lord give you sincerity, constancy, and firmness; and in no day, however evil, may you be led to turn aside.

Having escaped the corruption that is in the world through lust.
—2 Peter 1:4

Banish forever all thoughts of indulging the flesh if you want to live in the power of your risen Lord. It is immoral for a man who is alive in Christ to dwell in the corruption of sin. *"Why seek ye the living among the dead?"* (Luke 24:5), asked the angel of the women who came to Jesus' tomb. Should the living dwell in a tomb? Should divine life be buried in the mausoleum of fleshly lust? How can we partake of the cup of the Lord and yet drink from the cup of Satan? Surely, believer, you are delivered from open lusts and sins. Have you also escaped from the more secret and deceptive traps of the satanic fowler? Have you come forth from the lust of pride? Have you escaped from slothfulness? Have you made a clean break from carnal security? Are you seeking day by day to live above worldliness, the pride of life, and the ensnaring vice of greed? Remember, it is for this that you have been enriched with the treasures of God. If you are indeed the chosen of God and beloved by Him, do not permit all the lavish treasure of grace to be wasted on you. Follow after holiness; it is the Christian's crown and glory. An unholy church is useless to the world and has no esteem among men. It is an abomination; it is hell's laughter and heaven's abhorrence. The worst evils that have ever come upon the world have been brought by an unholy church. O Christian, the vows of God are upon you. You are God's priest: act as such. You are God's king: reign over your lusts. You are God's chosen: do not associate with the devil. Heaven is your portion: live like a heavenly spirit, and you will prove that you have true faith in Jesus. There cannot be faith in the heart unless there is holiness in the life.

> Lord, I desire to live as one
> Who bears a blood-bought name,
> As one who fears but grieving Thee,
> And knows no other shame.

Only ye shall not go very far away.
—Exodus 8:28

This is a crafty word from the lips of the arch tyrant Pharaoh. If the poor, enslaved Israelites needed to go out of Egypt, then he bargained with them that it should not be very far away—not too far for them to escape the terror of his arms and the observation of his spies. After the same fashion, the world does not love the lack of conformity of nonconformists or the dissidence of dissenters. It would have us be more charitable and not carry matters with too severe a hand. Death to the world and burial with Christ are experiences that carnal minds treat with ridicule; therefore, the law that sets them forth is almost universally neglected, and even condemned. Worldly wisdom recommends the path of compromise and talks of "moderation." According to this carnal policy, purity is admitted to be very desirable, but we are warned against being too precise; truth is, of course, to be followed, but error is not to be severely denounced. "Yes," says the world, "be spiritually minded by all means, but do not deny yourself a little frivolous society, an occasional ball, and a Christmas visit to a theater. What's the good of crying down a thing when it is so fashionable, and everybody does it?" Multitudes of professors yield to this cunning advice, to their own eternal ruin. If we would follow the Lord wholly, we must go right away into the wilderness of separation and leave the Egypt of the carnal world behind us. We must leave its maxims, its pleasures, and its religion, too, and go far away to the place where the Lord calls His sanctified ones. When the town is on fire, our house cannot be too far from the flames. When the plague is abroad, a man cannot be too far from its haunts. The further from a viper the better, and the further from worldly conformity the better. To all true believers let the trumpet call be sounded, *"Come out from among them, and be ye separate"* (2 Cor. 6:17).

Let every man abide in the same calling wherein he was called.
—1 Corinthians 7:20

Some people have the foolish notion that the only way they can live for God is by becoming ministers, missionaries, or Bible teachers. Think of how many would be shut out from any opportunity of magnifying the Most High if this were the case! Beloved, it is not your calling; it is earnestness. It is not your position; it is grace that will enable us to glorify God. God is most surely glorified in that cobbler's stall, where the godly worker, as he plies the awl, sings of the Savior's love. He is glorified far more there than in many churches where official religiousness performs its scanty duties. The name of Jesus is glorified by the poor, unlearned peddler, as he drives his horse and blesses his God or speaks to his fellow laborer by the roadside, as much as by the popular clergyman who, throughout the country, like Boanerges, is thundering out the Gospel. God is glorified by our serving Him in our proper vocations. Take care, dear reader, that you do not forsake the path of duty by leaving your occupation, and take care that you do not dishonor your profession while in it. Think little of yourselves, but do not think too little of your calling. Every lawful trade may be sanctified by the Gospel to the noblest ends. Turn to the Bible, and you will find the most menial forms of labor connected either with the most daring deeds of faith or with persons whose lives have been illustrious for holiness. Therefore, do not be discontented with your calling. Whatever God has made your position or your work, abide in that, unless you are quite sure that He calls you to something else. Let your first care be to glorify God to the utmost of your power where you are. Fill your present sphere to His praise, and if He needs you in another place, He will show it to you. This evening, lay aside distressing ambition, and embrace peaceful contentment.

Looking unto Jesus.
—Hebrews 12:2

It is always the Holy Spirit's work to turn our eyes away from self to Jesus; but Satan's work is just the opposite of this, for he is constantly trying to make us pay attention to ourselves instead of to Christ. He insinuates, "Your sins are too great for pardon; you have no faith. You do not repent enough. You will never be able to continue to the end. You do not have the joy of His children. You have such a weak hold of Jesus." All these are thoughts about self, and we will never find comfort or assurance by looking within. But the Holy Spirit turns our eyes entirely away from self. He tells us that we are nothing, but that "Christ is all in all." Remember, therefore, that it is not your hold of Christ that saves you; it is Christ. It is not your joy in Christ that saves you; it is Christ. It is not even your faith in Christ, though that is the instrument, but it is Christ's blood and His merits that save you; therefore, do not look as much to your hand, with which you are grasping Christ, as to Christ. Do not look to your hope, but to Jesus, the Source of your hope. Do not look to your faith, but to *"Jesus, the author and finisher of* [your] *faith"* (Heb. 12:2). We will never find happiness by looking at our prayers, our actions, or our feelings. It is what Jesus is, not what we are, that gives rest to the soul. If we would at once overcome Satan and have peace with God, it must be by *"looking unto Jesus."* Keep your eyes simply on Him. Let His death, His sufferings, His merits, His glories, and His intercession be fresh on your mind. When you wake in the morning, look to Him. When you lie down at night, look to Him. Oh, do not let your hopes or fears come between you and Jesus. Follow hard after Him, and He will never fail you.

> My hope is built on nothing less
>   Than Jesus' blood and righteousness:
> I dare not trust the sweetest frame,
>   But wholly lean on Jesus' name.

But Aaron's rod swallowed up their rods.
—Exodus 7:12

This incident is an instructive example of the sure victory of the divine handiwork over all opposition. Whenever a divine principle is cast into the heart, though the devil may fashion a counterfeit and produce swarms of opponents, as surely as God is in the work, it will swallow up all its foes. If God's grace takes possession of a man, the world's magicians may throw down all their rods. Every rod may be as cunning and poisonous as a serpent, but Aaron's rod will swallow up their rods. The sweet attractions of the Cross will woo and win the man's heart, and he who once lived only for this deceitful earth will now have an eye for the upper spheres and a wing to mount into heavenly heights. When grace has won the day, the person who once was concerned only with earthly matters now seeks the world to come. The same fact is to be observed in the life of the believer. What a host of foes our faith has had to meet! Our old sins—the devil threw them down before us, and they turned to serpents. What a great number of sins there were! But the Cross of Jesus destroys them all. Faith in Christ makes short work of all our sins. Then the devil has launched forth another host of serpents in the form of worldly trials, temptations, and unbelief; but faith in Jesus is more than a match for them and overcomes them all. The same absorbing principle shines in the faithful service of God! When one has an enthusiastic love for Jesus, his difficulties are surmounted, his sacrifices become pleasures, and his sufferings are honors. But if religion is thus a consuming passion in the heart, it follows that there are many persons who profess religion but do not have it; for what they have will not bear this test. Examine yourself, dear reader, on this point. Aaron's rod proved its heaven-given power. Is your religion doing so? If Christ is anything, He must be everything. Do not rest until love and faith in Jesus are the master passions of your soul!

Them also which sleep in Jesus will God bring with him.
—1 Thessalonians 4:14

Let us not imagine that the soul sleeps anesthetized. *"To day shalt thou be with me in paradise"* (Luke 23:43) is the whisper of Christ to every dying saint. They *"sleep in Jesus,"* but their souls are before the throne of God, praising Him day and night in His temple, singing hallelujahs to Him who washed them from their sins in His blood. The body sleeps in its lonely bed of earth, beneath the coverlet of grass. But what is this sleep? The idea connected with sleep is "rest," and that is the thought that the Spirit of God would convey to us. Sleep makes each night a Sabbath for the day. Sleep shuts fast the door of the soul and bids all intruders tarry for a while, so that the life within may enter its summer garden of ease. The toilworn believer quietly sleeps, as does the weary child when he slumbers on his mother's breast. Oh, happy are those who *"die in the Lord...: they...rest from their labours; and their works do follow them"* (Rev. 14:13). Their quiet repose will never be broken until God rouses them to give them their full reward. Guarded by angel watchers, curtained by eternal mysteries, they sleep on, the inheritors of glory, until the fullness of time will bring the fullness of redemption. What an awaking will be theirs! They were laid in their last resting place, weary and worn, but as such they will not rise. They went to their rest with furrowed brows and the wasted features, but they wake up in beauty and glory. The shriveled seed, so destitute of form and comeliness, rises from the dust a beauteous flower. The winter of the grave gives way to the spring of redemption and the summer of glory. Blessed is death, since it, through the divine power, disrobes us of this workday garment, to clothe us with the wedding garment of incorruption. Blessed are those who *"sleep in Jesus."*

Howbeit in the business of the ambassadors of the princes of Babylon,
who sent unto him to inquire of the wonder that was done in the land,
God left him, to try him, that he might know
all that was in his heart.
—2 Chronicles 32:31

Hezekiah was growing so inwardly great and priding himself so much on the favor of God that self-righteousness crept in. Because of his carnal security, the grace of God was, in its more active operations, withdrawn for a time. This explains his difficulties with the Babylonians; for if the grace of God would leave the best Christian, there is enough of sin in his heart to make him the worst of transgressors. If left to yourselves, you who are warmest for Christ would cool down like Laodicea into sickening luke-warmness. (See Revelation 3:16.) You who are sound in the faith would be white with the leprosy of false doctrine. You who now walk before the Lord in excellency and integrity would reel to and fro and stagger with a drunkenness of evil passion. Like the moon, we borrow our light; bright as we are when grace shines on us, we are darkness itself when the Sun of Righteousness withdraws Himself. Therefore, let us cry to God never to leave us. Lord, do not take Your Holy Spirit from us! Do not withdraw Your indwelling grace! Have You not said, *"I the* Lord *do keep it; I will water it every moment: lest any hurt it, I will keep it night and day"* (Isa. 27:3)? Lord, keep us everywhere. Keep us when we are in the valley, so that we will not complain about Your humbling hand. Keep us when we are on the mountain, so that we will not become dizzy from being lifted up. Keep us in our youth, when our passions are strong; keep us in our old age, when becoming conceited by our wisdom, we might prove greater fools than the young and foolish. Keep us when we come to die, lest, at the very end, we would deny You! Keep us living, keep us dying, keep us laboring, keep us suffering, keep us fighting, keep us resting, keep us everywhere, for every-where we need You, O our God!

And the glory which thou gavest me I have given them.
—John 17:22

Behold the superlative liberality of the Lord Jesus, for He has given us His all. Although a tithe of His possessions would have made a universe of angels rich beyond all thought, yet He was not content until He had given us all that He had. It would have been surprising grace if He had allowed us to eat the crumbs of His bounty beneath the table of His mercy. But He will do nothing by halves; He makes us sit with Him and share the feast. Had He given us some small pension from His royal coffers, we would have had cause to love Him eternally; but no, He will have His bride as rich as Himself, and He will not have a glory or a grace in which she will not share. He has not been content with less than making us joint heirs with Himself, so that we might have equal possessions. He has emptied all His estate into the coffers of the church and has all things in common with His redeemed. There is not one room in His house the key of which He will withhold from His people. He gives them full liberty to take all that He has to be their own; He loves them to help themselves freely to His treasure and appropriate as much as they can possibly carry. The boundless fullness of His all-sufficiency is as free to the believer as the air he breathes. Christ has put the flagon of His love and grace to the believer's lip and has invited him to drink on forever. Could he drain it, he is welcome to do so; but since he cannot exhaust it, he is bidden to drink abundantly, for it is all his own. What truer proof of fellowship can heaven or earth afford?

> When I stand before the throne
>   Dressed in beauty not my own;
> When I see Thee as Thou art,
>   Love Thee with unsinning heart;
> Then, Lord, shall I fully know—
>   Not till then—how much I owe.

JUNE 30

Evening

*Ah Lord GOD! behold, thou hast made the heaven and the earth
by thy great power and stretched out arm, and there is
nothing too hard for thee.*
—Jeremiah 32:17

At the very time when the Chaldeans surrounded Jerusalem, when the sword, famine, and pestilence had desolated the land, Jeremiah was commanded by God to purchase a field and have the deed of transfer legally sealed and witnessed. This was a strange purchase for a rational man to make. Prudence could not justify it, for there was scarcely a chance that Jeremiah could ever enjoy the possession. But it was enough for Jeremiah that his God had commanded him, for he knew well that God will be justified by all His children. He reasoned in this manner: "Lord God, You can make this plot of ground of use to me. You can rid this land of these oppressors. You can make me sit under my vine and my fig tree on the property that I have bought, for You made the heavens and the earth. There is nothing too hard for You." This gave a majesty to the early saints, for they dared to do at God's command things that human reason would condemn. Whether it was Noah who built a ship on dry land; Abraham who offered up his only son; Moses who despised the treasures of Egypt; or Joshua who besieged Jericho in seven days, using no weapons except for the blasts of rams' horns—they all acted on God's command, contrary to the dictates of earthly reason. And the Lord gave them a rich reward as the result of their obedient faith. Would to God that we had in the religion of these modern times a more potent infusion of this heroic faith in God! If we would venture more on the revealed promises of God, we would enter a world of miracles to which as yet we are strangers. Let Jeremiah's place of confidence be ours. Nothing is too hard for the God who created the heavens and the earth!

JULY 1

Morning

In summer and in winter shall it be.
—Zechariah 14:8

The streams of living water that flow from Jerusalem are not dried up by the parching heat of sultry midsummer any more than they were frozen by the cold winds of blustering winter. Rejoice, O my soul, that you are spared to testify of the faithfulness of the Lord. The seasons change and you change, but your Lord abides evermore the same, and the streams of His love are as deep, as broad, and as full as ever. The pressures of business cares and scorching trials make me need the cooling influences of the river of His grace. I may go at once and drink to the full from the inexhaustible fountain, for in summer and in winter it pours forth its flood. The upper springs are never scanty, and, blessed be the name of the Lord, the lower springs cannot fail either. Elijah found Cherith dried up, but Jehovah was still the same God of providence. Job said his brethren were like deceitful brooks, but he found his God an overflowing river of consolation. The Nile is the great confidence of Egypt, but its floods are variable; our Lord is evermore the same. By turning the course of the Euphrates, Cyrus took the city of Babylon, but no power, human or infernal, can divert the current of divine grace. The tracks of ancient rivers have been found all dry and desolate, but the streams that take their rise on the mountains of divine sovereignty and infinite love will ever be full to the brim. Generations melt away, but the course of grace is unaltered. The river of God may sing with greater truth than the brook in the poem,

Men may come, and men may go,
But I go on forever.

How happy are you, my soul, to be led beside such still waters! Never wander to other streams, lest you hear the Lord's rebuke, "Why go to Egypt to drink from the muddy river?" (See Jeremiah 2:18.)

JULY 1

Evening

They heard the voice of the LORD God
walking in the garden in the cool of the day.
—Genesis 3:8

My soul, now that the *"cool of the day"* has come, go to a quiet place and listen to the voice of your God. He is always ready to speak with you when you are prepared to hear. If you find that communion with God is slow in coming, the problem is not on His part but altogether on your own. For He stands at the door and knocks, and if His people will only open to Him, He will rejoice to enter. Yet in what state is my heart, which is my Lord's garden? May I venture to hope that it is well trimmed and watered and is bringing forth fruit fit for Him? If not, He will have much about which to reprove me. Yet I still ask Him to come to me, for nothing can so certainly bring my heart into a right condition as the presence of the Sun of Righteousness, who brings *"healing in his wings"* (Mal. 4:2). Come, therefore, O Lord my God; my soul invites You earnestly and waits for You eagerly. Come to me, O Jesus, my Well Beloved, and plant fresh flowers in my garden, such as I see blooming in perfection in Your matchless character. Come, O my Father. You are the Husbandman; deal with me in Your tenderness and prudence. Come, O Holy Spirit, and let Your dew fall on my whole nature, as the herbs are now moistened with the evening dews. Oh, that God would speak to me! *"Speak, LORD; for thy servant heareth"* (1 Sam. 3:9). Oh, that He would walk with me! I am ready to give up my whole heart and mind to Him, and every other thought is hushed. I only ask what He delights to give. I am sure that He will, in His grace, have fellowship with me, for He has given me His Holy Spirit to be with me forever. Sweet is the cool twilight, when every star seems like the eye of heaven and the cool wind is as the breath of divine love. My Father, my Elder Brother, my sweet Comforter, speak now in lovingkindness, for You have *"opened mine ear, and I [am] not rebellious"* (Isa. 50:5).

Our heart shall rejoice in him.
—Psalm 33:21

Blessed is the fact that Christians can rejoice even in the deepest distress. Although trouble may surround them, they still sing; and, like many birds, they sing best in their cages. The waves may roll over them, but their souls soon rise to the surface and see the light of God's countenance. They have a buoyancy about them that keeps their heads always above the water and helps them to sing amid the tempest, "God is with me still." To whom will the glory be given? Oh, to Jesus—it is all by Jesus. Trouble does not necessarily bring consolation with it to the believer, but the presence of the Son of God in the fiery furnace with him fills his heart with joy. He is sick and suffering, but Jesus visits him and makes his bed for him. He is dying, and the cold chilly waters of Jordan are gathering about him up to the neck, but Jesus puts His arms around him and cries, "Fear not, beloved; to die is to be blessed; the waters of death have their source in heaven. They are not bitter; they are sweet as nectar, for they flow from the throne of God." As the departing saint wades through the stream, and the billows gather around him, and heart and flesh fail him, the same voice sounds in his ears, *"Fear thou not; for I am with thee: be not dismayed; for I am thy God"* (Isa. 41:10). As he nears the borders of the infinite unknown and is almost too afraid to enter the realm of shadows, Jesus says, *"Fear not, little flock; for it is your Father's good pleasure to give you the kingdom"* (Luke 12:32). Thus strengthened and consoled, the believer is not afraid to die. He is even willing to depart, for since he has seen Jesus as the Morning Star, he longs to gaze on Him as the sun in its strength. Truly, the presence of Jesus is all the heaven we desire. He is at once "the glory of our brightest days; the comfort of our nights."

Unto thee will I cry, O LORD my rock; be not silent to me: lest, if thou be silent to me, I become like them that go down into the pit.
—Psalm 28:1

A cry is a natural expression of sorrow and a suitable utterance when all other modes of appeal fail us; but the cry must be directed to the Lord alone, for to cry to man is to waste our entreaties on the air. When we consider the readiness of the Lord to hear, and His ability to aid, we will see good reason for directing all our appeals immediately to the God of our salvation. It will be useless to call to the rocks to *"fall on us, and hide us"* (Rev. 6:16) in the Day of Judgment; but our Rock attends to our cries. *"Be not silent to me."* Those who go through merely the motions of prayer may be content without answers to their prayers, but genuine suppliants cannot be. They are not satisfied with the ability of prayer to calm the mind and subdue the will; they must go further and obtain actual replies from heaven, or they cannot rest. They long to receive those replies at once; they dread even a little of God's silence. God's voice is often so terrible that it shakes the wilderness, but His silence is equally terrible to an eager suppliant. When God seems to close His ear, we must not close our mouths. Instead, we must cry with more earnestness. For when our note grows shrill with eagerness and grief, He will not deny us a hearing for long. What a dreadful situation we would be in if the Lord were to become forever silent to our prayers! *"Lest, if thou be silent to me, I become like them that go down into the pit."* Deprived of the God who answers prayer, we would be in a more pitiable plight than the dead in their graves and would soon sink to the same level as the lost in hell. We *must* have answers to prayer. Ours is an urgent case of dire necessity. Surely the Lord will speak peace to our agitated minds, for He never can find it in His heart to permit His own elect to perish.

The ill favoured and leanfleshed kine did eat up
the seven well favoured and fat kine.
—Genesis 41:4

Pharaoh's dream has too often been my waking experience. My days of sloth have ruinously destroyed all that I had achieved in times of zealous industry. My seasons of coldness have frozen all the genial glow of my periods of fervency and enthusiasm, and my fits of worldliness have thrown me back from my advances in the divine life. I need to beware of lean prayers, lean praises, lean duties, and lean experiences, for these will eat up the fat of my comfort and peace. If I neglect prayer for ever so short a time, I lose all the spirituality to which I had attained. If I draw no fresh supplies from heaven, the old corn in my granary is soon consumed by the famine that rages in my soul. When the caterpillars of indifference, the cankerworms of worldliness, and the palmerworms of self-indulgence lay my heart completely desolate and make my soul to languish, all my former fruitfulness and growth in grace avails me nothing at all. How anxious should I be to have no lean-fleshed days, no ill-favored hours! If every day I journeyed toward the goal of my desires, I would soon reach it, but backsliding leaves me still far off from the prize of my high calling and robs me of the advances that I had so laboriously made. The only way in which all my days can be like the "*fat kine*" is to feed them in the right meadow, to spend them with the Lord, in His service, in His company, in His fear, and in His way. Why should not every year be richer than the past, in love, usefulness, and joy? I am nearer the celestial hills; I have had more experience of my Lord and should be more like Him. O Lord, keep the curse of leanness of soul far from me. Do not let me have to cry, "*My leanness, my leanness, woe unto me!*" (Isa. 24:16), but may I be well-fed and nourished in Your house, so that I may praise Your name.

If we suffer [with Christ], we shall also reign with him.
—2 Timothy 2:12

We must not imagine that we are suffering for Christ and with Christ, if we are not in Christ. Beloved friend, are you trusting in Jesus alone? If not, no matter what you may have to mourn over on earth, you are not suffering with Christ. Such suffering offers no hope of reigning with Him in heaven. Neither are we to conclude that all of a Christian's sufferings are sufferings with Christ; to suffer with Christ, the Christian must be called by God to suffer. If we are rash and imprudent, and then run into situations for which neither providence nor grace has prepared us, we ought to consider whether we are sinning rather than communing with Jesus. If we let passion take the place of judgment and allow self-will to reign instead of scriptural authority, we are attempting to fight the Lord's battles with the devil's weapons. If we are injured in the fight, we must not be surprised. Again, when troubles come upon us as a result of sin, we must not imagine that we are suffering with Christ. When Miriam spoke evil of Moses, and the leprosy defiled her, she was not suffering for God. Moreover, suffering that God accepts must have God's glory as its purpose. If I suffer in order to make a name for myself or to win applause, I will receive no other reward than that of the hypocritical Pharisee. It is essential that love for Jesus and love for His elect always be the chief motive for all our patience. We must manifest the Spirit of Christ in meekness, gentleness, and forgiveness. Let us search our hearts to see if we truly suffer with Jesus. If we do thus suffer, what is *"our light affliction"* (2 Cor. 4:17) compared with reigning with Him? Oh, it is very blessed to be in the furnace of affliction with Christ, and it is such an honor to stand in the face of scorn and ridicule with Him. If there were no future reward, we might consider ourselves happy in this present honor. Yet when the reward is so eternal, so infinitely more than we had any right to expect, will we not take up the cross with zeal and go on our way rejoicing?

Sanctify them through thy truth.
—John 17:17

Sanctification begins in regeneration. The Spirit of God infuses into man that new living principle by which he becomes *"a new creature"* (2 Cor. 5:17) in Christ Jesus. This work, which begins in the new birth, is carried on in two ways: through mortification, whereby the lusts of the flesh are subdued and kept under; and through vivification, by which the life that God has put within us is made to be a *"well of water springing up into everlasting life"* (John 4:14). This is carried on every day in what is called *perseverance*, by which the Christian is preserved and continued in a gracious state and is made to *"abound to every good work"* (2 Cor. 9:8) unto the praise and glory of God; and it culminates or comes to perfection in glory, when the soul, being thoroughly purged, is caught up to dwell with holy beings at the right hand of the Majesty on high. But while the Spirit of God is thus the Author of sanctification, yet there is a visible agency employed that must not be forgotten. Jesus said, *"Sanctify them through thy truth: thy word is truth"* (John 17:17). The passages of Scripture that prove that the instrument of our sanctification is the Word of God are many. The Spirit of God brings to our minds the precepts and doctrines of truth and applies them with power. These are heard in the ear, and being received in the heart, they work in us *"both to will and to do of* [God's] *good pleasure"* (Phil. 2:13). The truth is the sanctifier, and if we do not hear or read the truth, we will not grow in sanctification. We only progress in sound living as we progress in sound understanding. *"Thy word is a lamp unto my feet, and a light unto my path"* (Ps. 119:105). Do not say of any error, "It is a mere matter of opinion." No man indulges an error of judgment without sooner or later tolerating an error in practice. Hold fast the truth, for by so holding the truth, you will be sanctified by the Spirit of God.

*He that hath clean hands, and a pure heart; who hath not lifted up
his soul unto vanity, nor sworn deceitfully.*
—Psalm 24:4

Outward practical holiness is a very precious evidence of grace. It is to be feared that many who profess Christ have perverted the doctrine of justification by faith in such a way as to treat good works with contempt. Such people will receive everlasting contempt on the Last Great Day. If our hands are not clean, let us wash them in Jesus' precious blood, so that we may lift up pure hands to God. *"Clean hands"* will not suffice unless they are connected with *"a pure heart."* True religion is a work of the heart. We may wash the outside of the cup and the plate as long as we please. However, if the inward parts are filthy, we are filthy altogether in the sight of God, for our hearts are more truly ourselves than are our hands. The very life of our being lies in the inner nature, and that is why we have an imperative need for inward purity. It is the pure in heart who will see God; all others are but blind bats. The man who is born for heaven *"hath not lifted up his soul unto vanity."* All men have their joys by which their souls are lifted up. The worldly person lifts up his soul to carnal delights, which are mere empty vanities. However, the believer loves more substantial things. Like Jehoshaphat, he is lifted up in the ways of the Lord. He who is content with husks will be counted among the swine. Does the world satisfy you? Then you have your reward and portion in this life; make much of it, for you will know no other joy. *"Nor sworn deceitfully."* Believers in Christ are people of honor still. The Christian's word is his only oath; however, it is as good as the oaths of twenty others. False speaking will shut anyone out of heaven, for a liar will not enter into God's house, no matter what his profession of faith or deeds may be. Reader, does today's text condemn you, or do you hope to *"ascend into the hill of the Lord"* (Ps. 24:3)?

Called to be saints.
—Romans 1:7

We are very apt to regard the apostolic saints as if they were saints in a more special manner than the other children of God. All are saints whom God has called by His grace and sanctified by His Spirit; but we are apt to look on the apostles as extraordinary beings, scarcely subject to the same weaknesses and temptations as ourselves. Yet in so doing we are forgetful of this truth, that the nearer a man lives to God the more intensely has he to mourn over his own evil heart; and the more his Master honors him in His service, the more also does the evil of the flesh vex and tease him day by day. The fact is, if we had seen the apostle Paul, we would have thought him remarkably like the rest of the chosen family. And if we had talked with him, we would have said, "We find that his experience and ours are much the same. He is more faithful, more holy, and more deeply taught than we are, but he has the selfsame trials to endure. In some respects, he is more sorely tried than we." Do not, then, look on the ancient saints as being exempt either from infirmities or sins, and do not regard them with that mystic reverence that will almost make us idolaters. Their holiness is attainable even by us. We are *called to be saints* by that same voice that constrained them to their high vocation. It is a Christian's duty to force his way into the inner circle of sainthood. And if these saints were superior to us in their attainments, as they certainly were, let us follow them; let us emulate their ardor and holiness. We have the same light that they had; the same grace is accessible to us. Why should we, then, rest satisfied until we have equaled them in heavenly character? They lived with Jesus, and they lived for Jesus; therefore, they grew to be like Jesus. Let us live by the same Spirit as they did, *"looking unto Jesus"* (Heb. 12:2), and our sainthood will soon be apparent.

Trust ye in the Lord for ever: for in the Lord Jehovah
is everlasting strength.
—Isaiah 26:4

Since we have such a God on whom to rely, let us rest on Him with all our weight. Let us resolutely drive out all unbelief and endeavor to get rid of doubts and fears, which disturb our comfort so much. There is no excuse for fear when God is the foundation of our trust. A loving parent would be extremely grieved if his child could not trust him. How ungenerous and unkind is our conduct when we put so little confidence in our heavenly Father, who has never failed us and never will. It would be a good thing if doubting were banished from the household of God. However, it is to be feared that old Unbelief is as nimble nowadays as when the psalmist asked, *"Is his mercy clean gone for ever? doth his promise fail for evermore?"* (Ps. 77:8). David had not spent much time experimenting with the mighty sword of the giant Goliath, yet he said, "There is none like it." (See 1 Samuel 21:9.) He had tested it once in the hour of his youthful victory, and it had proven itself to be of the right metal; therefore, he praised it from that time forward. In the same way, we should speak well of our God, for there is no one like Him in heaven or on earth. *"To whom then will ye liken me, or shall I be equal? saith the Holy One"* (Isa. 40:25). There is no rock like the rock of Jacob, as our enemies themselves will affirm. Instead of allowing doubts to live in our hearts, let us take the whole detestable crew, as Elijah did the prophets of Baal, and slay them at the brook (1 Kings 18:40). Let us kill them at the sacred stream that wells forth from our Savior's wounded side. We have been in many trials, but we have never yet been in a place where we could not find in our God all that we needed. Let us, then, be encouraged to *"trust…in the Lord for ever,"* assured that His *"everlasting strength"* will be, as it has been, our help and support.

Whoso hearkeneth unto me shall dwell safely,
and shall be quiet from fear of evil.
—Proverbs 1:33

Divine love is rendered conspicuous when it shines in the midst of judgments. Fair is that lone star that smiles through the rifts of the thunderclouds. Bright is the oasis that blooms in the wilderness of sand. So fair and so bright is love in the midst of wrath. When the Israelites provoked the Most High by their continued idolatry, He punished them by withholding both dew and rain, so that their land was visited by a sore famine. But while He did this, He took care that His own chosen ones would be secure. If all other brooks are dry, yet will there be one reserved for Elijah; and when that fails, God will still preserve for him a place of sustenance. No, not only for one, because the Lord did not have simply one "Elijah," but He had a remnant according to the election of grace, who were hidden by fifties in a cave; and though the whole land was subject to famine, yet these fifties in the cave were fed, and fed from Ahab's table, too, by His faithful, God-fearing steward, Obadiah. Let us from this draw the inference: come what may, God's people are safe. Let convulsions shake the solid earth, let the skies themselves be rent in twain, yet amid the wreck of worlds, the believer will be as secure as in the calmest hour of rest. If God cannot save His people under heaven, He will save them in heaven. If the world becomes too hot to hold them, then, heaven will be the place of their reception and their safety. Be confident, then, when you *"hear of wars and rumours of wars"* (Matt. 24:6). Let no agitation distress you, but be quiet from fear of evil. Whatever comes on the earth, you, beneath the broad wings of Jehovah, will be secure. Abide on His promises, and rest in His faithfulness. Bid defiance to the blackest future, for there is nothing in it direful for you. Your sole concern should be to show forth to the world the blessedness of listening to the voice of wisdom.

How many are mine iniquities and sins?
—Job 13:23

Have you ever really weighed and considered how great the sin of God's people is? Think how heinous your own sin is, and you will find that not only does a sin here and there tower up like a high, rugged mountain, but also your iniquities heap upon each other, as in the old Greek myth of the giants who piled Mount Pelion upon Mount Ossa, mountain upon mountain. What an accumulation of sin there is in the life of one of the most sanctified of God's children! If you were to try to multiply the sin of only one person by the multitude of the redeemed, *"which no man could number"* (Rev. 7:9), you would have some idea of the great mass of the guilt of the people for whom Jesus shed His blood. However, we can arrive at a more adequate idea of the magnitude of sin by considering the greatness of the remedy provided for it: the blood of Jesus Christ, God's only and well-beloved Son. God's Son! Angels cast their crowns before Him. All the choral symphonies of heaven surround His glorious throne; He is *"over all, God blessed forever. Amen"* (Rom. 9:5). Yet He took on Himself the form of a servant and was scourged and pierced, bruised and torn, and finally slain, since nothing but the blood of the incarnate Son of God could make atonement for our offenses. No human mind can adequately estimate the infinite value of the divine sacrifice. For as great as is the sin of God's people, the Atonement, which takes it away, is immeasurably greater. Therefore, even when sin swells like a black flood and the remembrance of the past is bitter, the believer can still stand before the blazing throne of the great and holy God and cry, *"Who is he that condemneth? It is Christ that died, yea rather, that is risen again"* (Rom. 8:34). While the recollection of his sin fills him with shame and sorrow, at the same time, he uses it to reveal the brightness of God's mercy. Guilt is the dark night in which the fair star of divine love shines with serene splendor.

Brethren, pray for us.
—1 Thessalonians 5:25

We reserved this one morning in the year to refresh the reader's memory on the subject of prayer for ministers, and we most earnestly implore every Christian household to grant the fervent request of the text first uttered by an apostle and now repeated by us. Brethren, our work is solemnly momentous, involving well-being or woe to thousands. We deal with souls for God on eternal business, and our word is either the aroma of life to life, or of death to death. A very heavy responsibility rests on us, and it will be no small mercy if at the last we are found clear of the blood of all men. As officers in Christ's army, we are the special target of the hatred of men and devils; they watch for our halting and labor to take us by the heels. Our sacred calling involves us in temptations from which you are exempt. Above all it too often draws us away from our personal enjoyment of truth into a ministerial and official consideration of it. We meet with many knotty cases, and our wits are confounded. We observe very sad backslidings, and our hearts are wounded; we see millions perishing, and our spirits sink. We wish to benefit you by our preaching. We desire to be a blessing to your children. We long to be useful both to saints and sinners; therefore, dear friends, intercede for us with our God. Miserable men are we if we miss the aid of your prayers, but happy are we if we live in your supplications. You do not look to us but to our Master for spiritual blessings, and yet how many times has He given those blessings through His ministers. Ask, then, again and again, that we may be the earthen vessels into which the Lord may put the treasure of the Gospel. We, the whole company of missionaries, ministers, city missionaries, and students, do in the name of Jesus beseech you, *"Brethren, pray for us."*

When I passed by thee,…I said unto thee…, Live.
—Ezekiel 16:6

Saved one, consider gratefully this command of mercy in our text. Note first that this command of God is majestic. We perceive a sinner with nothing in him but sin, and expecting nothing but wrath. However, the eternal Lord passes by in His glory. He looks, He pauses, and He pronounces the solitary but royal word, *"Live."* There speaks a God. Who but He could thus venture to deal with life and dispense it with a single syllable? Second, this command is manifold. When He says, *"Live,"* His command includes many things. It is judicial life. The sinner is ready to be condemned, but the mighty One says, *"Live,"* and so he rises pardoned and absolved. It is spiritual life. Before we knew Jesus, our eyes could not see Him, and our ears could not hear His voice. Yet Jehovah said, *"Live,"* and we were *"quickened, who were dead in trespasses and sins"* (Eph. 2:1). Moreover, it is glory life, which is the perfection of spiritual life. *"I said unto thee…, Live."* This last word rolls on through all the years of time until death comes, and in the midst of the shadows of death, the Lord's voice is still heard: *"Live."* On the morning of the resurrection to life, this same word will be echoed by the archangel: *"Live."* As holy spirits rise to heaven to be blessed forever in the glory of their God, it will be in the power of this very word, *"Live."* Third, it is an irresistible command. Saul of Tarsus was on the road to Damascus to arrest the children of the living God. He heard a voice from heaven and saw a light brighter than the sun, and he cried out, *"Lord, what wilt thou have me to do?"* (Acts 9:6). Fourth, it is a command of free grace. When sinners are saved, God saves them solely to glorify His free, unpurchased, unsought grace. Christians, recognize your position: you are debtors to grace. Since God has commanded you to live, show your gratitude by living earnest, Christlike lives.

JULY 8
Morning

Tell me, I pray thee, wherein thy great strength lieth.
—Judges 16:6

Where lies the secret strength of faith? It lies in the food it feeds on; for faith studies what the promise is—an emanation of divine grace, an overflowing of the great heart of God. And faith says, "My God could not have given this promise, except from love and grace; therefore, it is quite certain His Word will be fulfilled." Then faith thinks, "Who gave this promise?" It considers not so much its greatness, as, "Who is the author of it?" Faith remembers that it is God who cannot lie—God omnipotent, God immutable; and therefore concludes that the promise must be fulfilled. Faith advances forward in this firm conviction. She remembers why the promise was given—namely, for God's glory. She feels perfectly sure that God's glory is safe, that He will never stain His own armor or mar the luster of His own crown; therefore, the promise must and will stand. Then faith also considers the amazing work of Christ as being a clear proof of the Father's intention to fulfill His word. *"He that spared not his own Son, but delivered him up for us all, how shall he not with him also freely give us all things?"* (Rom. 8:32). Moreover, faith looks back on the past, for her battles have strengthened her, and her victories have given her courage. She remembers that God has never failed her; no, that He never once has failed any of His children. She recollects times of great peril, when deliverance came; hours of awful need, when strength was found to meet the demands of the day, and she cries, "No, I never will be led to think that He can change and leave His servant now. *'Hitherto hath the LORD helped us'* (1 Sam. 7:12), and He will help me still." Thus faith views each promise in its connection with the Promise-giver, and, because she does so, can with assurance say, *"Surely goodness and mercy shall follow me all the days of my life"* (Ps. 23:6).

*Lead me in thy truth, and teach me: for thou art the God
of my salvation; on thee do I wait all the day.*
—Psalm 25:5

When the believer has begun with trembling feet to walk in the way of the Lord, he still asks to be led onward like a little child upheld by his parent's helping hand, and he craves to be further instructed in the alphabet of truth. Experiential instruction is the refrain of David's prayer in Psalm 25:4–5. David knew much, but he felt his ignorance and still desired to be in the Lord's school. Four times in these two verses he applied for a scholarship in the college of grace. It would be a good thing if believers would inquire into the good old ways of God's truth and earnestly ask the Holy Spirit to give them sanctified understanding and teachable spirits, instead of following their own devices and cutting out new paths of thought for themselves. *"For thou art the God of my salvation."* The triune Jehovah is the Author and Perfecter of salvation for His people. Is He the God of your salvation? Do you find in the Father's election, in the Son's atonement, and in the Spirit's quickening, all the grounds of your eternal hopes? If so, you may use these means of grace as the basis for obtaining further blessings. If the Lord has ordained to save you, surely He will not refuse to instruct you in His ways. It is a happy thing when we can address the Lord with the confidence that David manifested in our text; it gives us great power in prayer and comfort in trial. *"On thee do I wait all the day."* Patience is the fair handmaiden and daughter of faith; we cheerfully wait when we are certain that we will not wait in vain. It is our duty and privilege to wait on the Lord in service, in worship, in expectancy, and in trust all the days of our lives. Our faith will be tried faith; and if it is true faith, it will bear continued trial without yielding. We will not grow weary of waiting on God if we will remember how long and how graciously He once waited for us.

Forget not all his benefits.
—Psalm 103:2

It is a delightful and profitable occupation to mark the hand of God in the lives of ancient saints and to observe His goodness in delivering them, His mercy in pardoning them, and His faithfulness in keeping His covenant with them. But would it not be even more interesting and profitable for us to notice the hand of God in our own lives? Should we not look on our own history as being at least as full of God, as full of His goodness and of His truth, as much a proof of His faithfulness and veracity, as the lives of any of the saints who have gone before? We do our Lord an injustice when we suppose that He wrought all His mighty acts and showed Himself strong for those in the early times, but does not perform wonders or *"bare his holy arm"* (Isa. 52:10) for the saints who are now on the earth. Let us review our own lives. Surely in these we may discover some happy incidents, refreshing to ourselves and glorifying to our God. Have you had no deliverances? Have you passed through no rivers, supported by the divine presence? Have you walked through no fires unharmed? Have you had no manifestations? Have you had no choice favors? The God who gave Solomon the desire of his heart, has He never listened to you and answered your requests? That God of lavish bounty of whom David sang, *"Who satisfieth thy mouth with good things"* (Ps. 103:5), has He never satiated you with fatness? Have you never been made to lie down in green pastures? Have you never been led by the still waters? Surely the goodness of God has been the same to us as to the saints of old. Let us, then, weave His mercies into a song. Let us take the pure gold of thankfulness and the jewels of praise and make them into another crown for the head of Jesus. Let our souls give forth music as sweet and as exhilarating as came from David's harp, while we praise the Lord whose mercy endures forever.

JULY 9
Evening

And God divided the light from the darkness.
—Genesis 1:4

A believer has two principles at work within him. In his natural state, he was subject to one principle alone, which was darkness. However, now light has entered, and the two principles are in disagreement. Note the apostle Paul's words in the seventh chapter of Romans: *"I find then a law, that, when I would do good, evil is present with me. For I delight in the law of God after the inward man: but I see another law in my members, warring against the law of my mind, and bringing me into captivity to the law of sin which is in my members"* (vv. 21–23). How is this state of things brought about? *"God divided the light from the darkness."* Darkness, by itself, is quiet and undisturbed; however, when the Lord sends in light, there is conflict, for the one is in opposition to the other. This conflict will not cease until the believer is altogether light in the Lord. Since there is this division within the individual Christian, there is certain to be division outside of him, as well. As soon as the Lord gives light to anyone, he proceeds to separate himself from the darkness around him. He withdraws from a merely worldly religion of outward ceremony, for nothing short of the Gospel of Christ will now satisfy him. He withdraws from those who are worldly and from frivolous amusements, and he seeks the company of believers, for *"we know that we have passed from death unto life, because we love the brethren"* (1 John 3:14). The light gathers light to itself, and the darkness gathers darkness to itself. What God has divided, let us never try to unite. As Christ went *"without the camp, bearing his reproach"* (Heb. 13:13), let us come out from among the ungodly and be God's own people. Christ was *"holy, harmless, undefiled, separate from sinners"* (Heb. 7:26). As He was, so are we to be—nonconformists to the world, dissenting from all sin, and distinguished from the rest of mankind by our likeness to our Master.

Fellowcitizens with the saints.
—Ephesians 2:19

What does it mean to be a citizen of heaven? It means that we are under heaven's government. Christ the King of heaven reigns in our hearts; our daily prayer is, *"Thy will be done in earth, as it is in heaven"* (Matt. 6:10). The proclamations issued from the throne of glory are freely received by us; the decrees of the Great King we cheerfully obey. Then, as citizens of the New Jerusalem, we share heaven's honors. The glory that belongs to beatified saints belongs to us, for we are already sons of God, already princes of the blood imperial; already we wear the spotless robe of Jesus' righteousness; already we have angels for our servants, saints for our companions, Christ for our Brother, God for our Father, and a crown of immortality for our reward. We share the honors of citizenship, for we have come to the general assembly and church of the firstborn whose names are written in heaven. As citizens, we have common rights to all the property of heaven. Ours are its gates of pearl and walls of chrysolite; ours the azure light of the city that needs no candle nor light of the sun; ours the river of the water of life, and the twelve manner of fruits that grow on the trees planted on the banks thereof; there is nothing in heaven that does not belong to us. *"Things present, or things to come"* (1 Cor. 3:22) are all ours. Also as citizens of heaven we enjoy its delights. Do they there rejoice over sinners who repent—prodigals who have returned? So do we. Do they chant the glories of triumphant grace? We do the same. Do they cast their crowns at Jesus' feet? Such honors as we have we cast there, too. Are they charmed by His smile? It is not less sweet to us who dwell below. Do they look forward, waiting for His second advent? We also look and long for His appearing. If, then, we are thus citizens of heaven, let our walk and actions be consistent with our high dignity.

JULY 10
Evening

And the evening and the morning were the first day.
—Genesis 1:5

The evening was *"darkness"* (Gen. 1:5) and the morning was *"light"* (v. 5). Yet the two together are called by the name that is given to the light alone—*"day."* This is rather remarkable, but it has an exact analogy in spiritual experience. There is darkness and light in every believer, yet the believer is not to be called a "sinner," even though there is sin in him. He is to be called a "saint," because he possesses some degree of holiness. This should be a very comforting thought to those who are mourning over their weaknesses, and who ask, "Can I be a child of God while there is so much darkness in me?" Yes, you can; for you, like the day, take your name not from the evening, but from the morning. You are spoken of in the Word of God as if you are even now perfectly holy, as you will be soon. You are called a child of light, even though there is still darkness in you. You are named after what is the predominate quality in the sight of God, which will one day be the only principle remaining in you. Observe that the evening comes first. Naturally, in the order of time, we are darkness first, and the gloom is often first in our mournful understanding, driving us to cry out in deep humiliation, *"God be merciful to me a sinner"* (Luke 18:13). The place of the morning is second; it dawns when grace overcomes nature. John Bunyan's saying, "That which is last, lasts forever," is a blessed adage. What is first yields in due season to what is last, but nothing comes after what is last. Therefore, although you are naturally darkness, when you become light in the Lord, no evening will follow. *"Thy sun shall no more go down"* (Isa. 60:20). The first day in this earthly life was an evening and a morning; but the second day, when we will be with God forever, will be a day with no evening. It will be one, sacred, high, eternal noon.

After that ye have suffered a while, make you perfect,
stablish, strengthen, settle you.
—1 Peter 5:10

You have seen the arch of heaven as it spans the plain: glorious are its colors and rare its hues. It is beautiful, but, alas, it passes away. The fair colors give way to fleecy clouds, and the sky is no longer brilliant with the tints of heaven. It is not established. How can it be? A glorious show made up of transitory sunbeams and passing raindrops, how can it last? The graces of the Christian character must not resemble the rainbow in its transitory beauty, but, on the contrary, must be established, settled, abiding. Seek, believer, that every good thing you have may be an abiding thing. May your character not be a writing on the sand, but an inscription on the rock! May your faith be no "baseless fabric of a vision," but may it be built of material able to endure that awful fire that will consume the *"wood, hay, [and] stubble"* (1 Cor. 3:12) of the hypocrite. May you be *"rooted and grounded in love"* (Eph. 3:17). May your convictions be deep, your love real, and your desires earnest. May your whole life be so settled and established that all the blasts of hell and all the storms of earth will never be able to remove you. But notice how this blessing of being *"stablished in the faith"* (Col. 2:7) is gained. The apostle's words point us to suffering as the means employed: *"After that ye have suffered a while."* It is of no use to hope that we will be well rooted if no rough winds pass over us. All those old gnarlings on the root of the oak tree and those strange twistings of the branches tell of the many storms that have swept over it, and they are also indicators of the depth into which the roots have forced their way. So the Christian is made strong and firmly rooted by all the trials and storms of life. Do not shrink, then, from the tempestuous winds of trial, but take comfort, believing that by their rough discipline God is fulfilling this benediction to you.

Tell ye your children of it, and let your children tell their children,
and their children another generation.
—Joel 1:3

In this simple way, by God's grace, a living testimony for truth is always to be kept alive in the land—the beloved of the Lord are to hand down their witness for the Gospel and the covenant to their heirs; these, in turn, are to hand it down to their descendants. This is our first duty. We are to begin with the family. He who does not begin his ministry at home is a bad preacher. The unsaved are to be sought by all means, and the *"highways and hedges"* (Luke 14:23) are to be searched, but home has a prior claim. Woe to those who reverse the order of the Lord's arrangement. Teaching our children God's ways is a personal duty; we cannot delegate it to Sunday school teachers or other friendly helpers. They can assist us, but they cannot deliver us from our sacred obligation; proxies and sponsors are wicked instruments under these conditions. Mothers and fathers must, like Abraham, instruct their households in the fear of God and talk with their offspring concerning the wondrous works of the Most High. Parental teaching is a natural duty. Who are best able to look to a child's well-being as those who are the authors of his physical being? To neglect the instruction of our offspring is worse than foolish. Family religion is necessary for the family itself, for the nation, and for the church of God. One of the most effective means of preventing unbelief and doctrinal error is the instruction of children in the faith. However, this means is all but being neglected. Parents must realize the importance of this matter. It is a pleasant duty to talk to our sons and daughters about Jesus, and even more so because it has often proven to be an accepted work. God has saved children through their parents' prayers and admonitions. May every house into which this book comes honor the Lord and receive His smile of approval.

Sanctified by God the Father.
—Jude 1

Sanctified in Christ Jesus" (1 Cor. 1:2). *"Through sanctification of the Spirit"* (1 Pet. 1:2). Mark the union of the three divine persons in all their gracious acts. How unwisely do those believers talk who make preferences in the persons of the Trinity; who think of Jesus as if He were the embodiment of everything lovely and gracious, while the Father they regard as severely just, but destitute of kindness. Equally wrong are those who magnify the decree of the Father, and the Atonement of the Son, so as to depreciate the work of the Spirit. In deeds of grace none of the persons of the Trinity act apart from the rest. They are as united in their deeds as in their essence. In their love toward the chosen, they are one, and in the actions that flow from that great central source, they are still undivided. Take special notice of this in the matter of sanctification. While we may without mistake speak of sanctification as the work of the Spirit, yet we must take heed that we do not view it as if the Father and the Son had no part therein. It is correct to speak of sanctification as the work of the Father, of the Son, and of the Spirit. Still does Jehovah say, *"Let us make man in our image, after our likeness"* (Gen. 1:26), and thus we are *"his workmanship, created in Christ Jesus unto good works, which God hath before ordained that we should walk in them"* (Eph. 2:10). See the value that God sets on real holiness, since the three persons in the Trinity are represented as working together to produce a church without *"spot, or wrinkle, or any such thing"* (Eph. 5:27). And you, believer, as the follower of Christ, must also set a high value on holiness— on purity of life and godliness of conversation. Value the blood of Christ as the foundation of your hope, but never speak disparagingly of the work of the Spirit that qualifies you for the *"inheritance of the saints in light"* (Col. 1:12). This day let us so live as to manifest the work of the triune God in us.

His heavenly kingdom.
—2 Timothy 4:18

The city of the great King—heaven—is a place of active service. Redeemed spirits serve Him day and night in His temple. They never cease to fulfill the good pleasure of their King. They always rest, as far as ease and freedom from care are concerned, and they never rest, in the sense of laziness or inactivity. Jerusalem the Golden is the place of communion with all the people of God. We will sit in eternal fellowship with Abraham, Isaac, and Jacob. We will have exalted conversation with the noble host of the elect, all of whom are reigning with Him who by His love and powerful arm has brought them safely home. We will not sing solos but will praise our King in chorus. Heaven is a place of realized victory. Christian, whenever you have achieved a victory over your lusts—whenever, after hard struggling, you have laid a temptation dead at your feet—you have had in that hour a foretaste of the joy that awaits you. The Lord will shortly tread Satan under your feet, and you will find yourself more than a conqueror through Him who loved you (Rom. 8:37). Paradise is a place of security. When you enjoy the *"full assurance of faith"* (Heb. 10:22), you have the pledge of that glorious security that will be yours when you are a perfect citizen of the heavenly Jerusalem. O my sweet home, Jerusalem, happy harbor of my soul! Thanks, even now, to Him whose love has taught me to long for you; but louder thanks in eternity, when I will possess you.

My soul has tasted of the grapes
And now it longs to go
Where my dear Lord His vineyard keeps
And all the clusters grow.

Upon the true and living vine,
My famish'd soul would feast,
And banquet on the fruit divine,
An everlasting guest.

God said to Jonah, Doest thou well to be angry?
—Jonah 4:9

Anger is not always or necessarily sinful, but it has such a tendency to run wild that whenever it displays itself, we should be quick to question its character with this inquiry, *"Doest thou well to be angry?"* It may be that we can answer, "Yes." Very frequently anger is the madman's firebrand, but sometimes it is Elijah's fire from heaven. We do well when we are angry with sin, because of the wrong that it commits against our good and gracious God; or with ourselves because we remain so foolish after so much divine instruction; or with others when the sole cause of anger is the evil that they do. He who is not angry at transgression becomes a partaker in it. Sin is a loathsome and hateful thing, and no renewed heart can patiently endure it. God Himself is angry with the wicked every day, and it is written in His Word, *"Ye that love the Lord, hate evil"* (Ps. 97:10). Far more frequently it is to be feared that our anger is not commendable or even justifiable, and then, we must answer, "No." Why should we be fretful with children, angry with servants, and irate with companions? Is such anger honorable to our Christian profession or glorifying to God? Is it not the old evil heart seeking to gain dominion, and should we not resist it with all the might of our newborn nature? Many false believers give way to temper as though it were useless to attempt resistance; but let the true believer remember that he must be a conqueror in every point, or else he cannot be crowned. If we cannot control our tempers, what has grace done for us? Someone told Mr. Jay that grace was often grafted on the stump of a crab apple tree. "Yes," said he, "but the fruit will not be crabs." We must not make natural infirmity an excuse for sin, but we must fly to the cross and pray to the Lord to crucify our tempers and renew us in gentleness and meekness after His own image.

JULY 13
Evening

When I cry unto thee, then shall mine enemies turn back:
this I know; for God is for me.
—Psalm 56:9

It is impossible for any human words to express the full meaning of this delightful statement, *"God is for me."* He was for us before the universe was made. He was for us when He gave His well-beloved Son for us. He was for us when He struck the Only Begotten and laid the full weight of His wrath on Him; He was for us—though He was "against" Him. He was for us when we were ruined in the Fall; He loved us despite all. He was for us when we were rebels, defying Him with clenched fists. He was for us when He led us to humbly seek His face. He has been for us in many struggles; we have been summoned to encounter a multitude of dangers, and we have been assailed by internal and external temptations. How could we have remained unharmed to this hour if He had not been for us? He is for us with the infinity of His being, the omnipotence of His love, and the infallibility of His wisdom. He is for us, arrayed in all His divine attributes. He is eternally and unchangeably for us. He will be for us when the blue skies are rolled up like a worn-out garment; He will be for us throughout eternity. Because He is for us, our prayers will always secure His help. *"When I cry unto thee, then shall mine enemies turn back."* This is not an uncertain hope, but a well-grounded assurance: *"this I know."* I will direct my prayer to God and will look to Him for the answer, assured that it will come and that my enemies will be defeated, *"for God is for me."* O believer, how happy you are with the King of Kings on your side! How safe you are with such a Protector! How sure is your cause, when it is pleaded by such an Advocate! *"If God be for us, who can be against us?"* (Rom. 8:31).

If thou lift up thy tool upon it, thou hast polluted it.
—Exodus 20:25

God's altar was to be built of unhewn stones, so that no trace of human skill or labor might be seen on it. Human wisdom delights to trim and arrange the doctrines of the cross into a system more artificial and more congenial with the depraved tastes of fallen nature; however, instead of improving the Gospel, carnal wisdom pollutes it, until it becomes another gospel, and not the truth of God at all. All alterations and amendments of the Lord's own Word are defilements and pollutions. The proud heart of man is very anxious to have a hand in the justification of the soul before God; preparations for Christ are dreamed of, humblings and repentings are trusted in, good works are cried up, natural ability is much vaunted, and by all means the attempt is made to lift up human tools on the divine altar. It were well if sinners would remember that so far from perfecting the Savior's work, their carnal confidences only pollute and dishonor it. The Lord alone must be exalted in the work of atonement, and not a single mark of man's chisel or hammer will be endured. There is an inherent blasphemy in seeking to add to what Christ Jesus in His dying moments declared to . be finished, or to improve that in which the Lord Jehovah finds perfect satisfaction. Trembling sinner, away with your tools. Fall on your knees in humble supplication. Accept the Lord Jesus to be the altar of your atonement, and rest in Him alone. Many professors of faith may take warning from this morning's text as to the doctrines in which they believe. There is among Christians far too much inclination to square and reconcile the truths of revelation; this is a form of irreverence and unbelief. Let us strive against it and receive truth as we find it, rejoicing that the doctrines of the Word are unhewn stones, and so are all the more suitable to build an altar for the Lord.

As it began to dawn…, came Mary Magdalene…to see the sepulchre.
—Matthew 28:1

Let us learn from Mary Magdalene how to obtain fellowship with the Lord Jesus. Notice how she sought Him. She sought the Savior very early in the morning. If you cannot wait for Christ and be patient in the hope of having fellowship with Him at some later time, you will never have fellowship at all; for the heart that is prepared for communion is a hungering and thirsting heart. She sought Him also with very great boldness. Other disciples fled from the sepulchre, *"for they trembled and were amazed"* (Mark 16:8); but Mary, it is said, *"stood"* (John 20:11) at the sepulchre. If you want to have Christ with you, seek Him boldly. Let nothing hold you back. Defy the world. Press on when others flee. Mary also sought Christ faithfully: she stood *"at the sepulchre"* (v. 11). Some find it hard to stand by a living Savior, but she stood by a dead one. Let us seek Christ as she did, cleaving to the very least thing that has to do with Him, remaining faithful even though all others might forsake Him. Note further that she sought Jesus earnestly: she stood *"weeping"* (v. 11). Her tears moved the Savior and made Him come forth and show Himself to her. If you desire Jesus' presence, weep for it! If you cannot be happy unless He comes and says to you, "You are My beloved," you will soon hear His voice. Last, she sought *only* the Savior. What did she care about angels? She turned away from them; her search was only for her Lord. If Christ is your one and only love, if your heart has cast out all rivals, you will not lack the comfort of His presence for long. Mary Magdalene sought Jesus in these ways because *"she loved much"* (Luke 7:47). Let us rouse ourselves to the same intensity of affection. If our hearts, like Mary's, are full of Christ, then our love, like hers, will be satisfied with nothing short of Himself. O Lord, reveal Yourself to us this evening!

The fire shall ever be burning upon the altar; it shall never go out.
—Leviticus 6:13

Keep the altar of private prayer burning. This is the very life of all piety. The sanctuary and family altars borrow their fires here; therefore, let this burn well. Secret devotion is the very essence, evidence, and barometer of vital and experimental religion. Burn here the fat of your sacrifices. Let your private seasons of prayer be, if possible, regular, frequent, and undisturbed. Effectual prayer avails much. Have you nothing to pray for? Let us suggest the church, the ministry, your own soul, your children, your relations, your neighbors, your country, and the cause of God and truth throughout the world. Let us examine ourselves on this important matter. Do we engage with lukewarmness in private devotion? Is the fire of devotion burning dimly in our hearts? Do the chariot wheels drag heavily? If so, let us be alarmed at this sign of decay. Let us go with weeping and ask for the Spirit of grace and of supplications. Let us set apart special seasons for extraordinary prayer. For if this fire would be smothered beneath the ashes of a worldly conformity, it will dim the fire on the family altar and lessen our influence both in the church and in the world. The text also applies to the altar of the heart. This is a golden altar indeed. God loves to see the hearts of His people glowing toward Himself. Let us give to God our hearts, all blazing with love, and seek His grace, so that the fire may never be quenched; for it will not burn if the Lord does not keep it burning. Many foes will attempt to extinguish it, but if the unseen hand behind the wall pour the sacred oil on it, it will blaze higher and higher. Let us use texts of Scripture as fuel for our heart's fire. They are live coals. Let us pay attention to sermons, but above all, let us be much alone with Jesus.

JULY 15
Evening

He appeared first to Mary Magdalene.
—Mark 16:9

Jesus probably *"appeared first to Mary Magdalene"* not only because of her great love and persevering seeking, but also because she had been a special example of Christ's delivering power. We can learn from Mary's experience that the greatness of our sin before conversion should not make us think that we cannot be especially favored with the very highest degree of fellowship with the Lord. Mary had left everything else to continually tend to the Savior's needs. He was her first and chief object. Many who were on Christ's side did not take up Christ's cross; she did. She spent her substance on meeting His needs. If we want to see much of Christ, let us serve Him. Who are they who sit most often under the banner of His love and drink most deeply from the cup of communion? I am sure that they are those who give most, serve best, and remain closest to the bleeding heart of their dear Lord. But notice *how* Christ revealed Himself to this sorrowing one. It was by a word: *"Mary"* (John 20:16). Mary needed only one word, spoken in Christ's voice, for her to recognize Him at once. Her heart acknowledged allegiance by another word, for it was too full to say anything else. That one word would naturally be the most fitting for the occasion. It implied obedience. She said, *"Master"* (v. 16). There is no state of mind in which this confession of allegiance will be too cold. No, when your spirit glows most with heavenly fire, then you will say, *"I am thy servant....Thou hast loosed my bonds"* (Ps. 116:16). If you can say, "Master," if you feel that His will is your will, then you are standing in a happy, holy place. If He had not said, *"Mary,"* she could not have said, *"Rabboni"* (John 20:16). See, then, from all this, how Christ honors those who honor Him, how love draws our Beloved, how just one word of His will turn our weeping to rejoicing, how His presence brings sunshine to our hearts.

They gathered [manna] every morning.
—Exodus 16:21

Labor to maintain a sense of your entire dependence on the Lord's goodwill and pleasure for the continuance of your richest enjoyments. Never try to live on the old manna or seek to find help in Egypt. All must come from Jesus, or you are ruined forever. Old anointings will not suffice to impart unction to your spirit; your head must have fresh oil poured upon it from the golden horn of the sanctuary, or it will cease from its glory. Today you may be on the summit of the mount of God, but He who has put you there must keep you there; otherwise, you will sink far more speedily than you ever dreamed. Your mountain only stands firm when He settles it in its place; if He hides His face, you will soon be troubled. If the Savior should see fit, there is not a window through which you see the light of heaven that He could not darken in an instant. Joshua ordered the sun to stand still, but Jesus can shroud it in total darkness. He can withdraw the joy of your heart, the light of your eyes, and the strength of your life. In His hand your comforts lie, and at His will they can depart from you. Our Lord is determined that we will feel and recognize this hourly dependence, for He permits us to pray only for *"daily bread"* (Matt. 6:11), and only promises that *"as [our] days, so shall [our] strength shall be"* (Deut. 33:25). Is it not best for us that it should be this way, so that we may often repair to His throne and constantly be reminded of His love? Oh, how rich is the grace that supplies us so continually and does not refrain itself because of our ingratitude! The golden shower never ceases; the cloud of blessing tarries evermore above our habitation. O Lord Jesus, we would bow at Your feet, conscious of our utter inability to do anything without You, and in every favor that we are privileged to receive, we would adore Your blessed name and acknowledge Your inexhaustible love.

Thou shalt arise, and have mercy upon Zion: for the time to favour her, yea, the set time, is come. For thy servants take pleasure in her stones, and favour the dust thereof.
—Psalm 102:13–14

A selfish man in trouble is exceedingly hard to comfort, because the springs of his comfort lie entirely within himself; when he is sad, all his springs are dry. But a Christian who is full of love and generosity has other springs from which to supply himself with comfort besides those that lie within. First, he can go to God and find abundant help there; he can discover reasons for comfort in things relating to the world at large, to his country, and, above all, to the church. David was exceedingly sorrowful in the psalm from which our text comes. He wrote, *"I am like an owl of the desert. I watch, and am as a sparrow alone upon the house top"* (Ps. 102:6–7). His only comfort was in the thought that God would *"arise, and have mercy upon Zion."* Even though David was sad, Zion would prosper. No matter how low his own condition was, Zion would arise. Christian, learn to comfort yourself in God's gracious dealings toward the church. Should not what is so dear to your Master also be dear above all else to you? Even though your way may be dark, can you not encourage your heart with the triumphs of His Cross and the advancement of His truth? Our own personal troubles will be forgotten when we look not only at what God has done and is doing for Zion, but also on the glorious things He will do for His church. Believer, try this prescription whenever you are sad of heart and heavy in spirit: forget yourself and your little concerns, and seek the welfare and prosperity of Zion. When you bend your knee in prayer to God, do not limit your petition to the narrow circle of your own life, tried though it might be. Send out earnest prayers for the church's prosperity. *"Pray for the peace of Jerusalem"* (Ps. 122:6), and your own soul will be refreshed.

Knowing, brethren beloved, your election of God.
—1 Thessalonians 1:4

Many persons want to know their election before they look to Christ, but they cannot learn it thus; it is only to be discovered by *"looking unto Jesus"* (Heb. 12:2). If you desire to be sure of your own election, assure your heart before God by asking the following questions: Do you feel yourself to be a lost, guilty sinner? Then go immediately to the cross of Christ and tell Jesus so. Tell Him that you have read in the Bible, *"Him that cometh to me I will in no wise cast out"* (John 6:37). Tell Him that He has said, *"This is a faithful saying, and worthy of all acceptation, that Christ Jesus came into the world to save sinners"* (1 Tim. 1:15). Look to Jesus and believe on Him, and you be confident of your election directly, for as surely as you believe, you are elect. If you will give yourself wholly up to Christ and trust Him, then, you are one of God's chosen ones; but if you stop and say, "I want to know first whether I am elect," you do not know what you are asking. Go to Jesus; although you are ever so guilty, go just as you are. Leave all curious inquiry about election alone. Go straight to Christ and hide in His wounds, and you will know your election. The assurance of the Holy Spirit will be given to you, so that you will be able to say, *"I know whom I have believed, and am persuaded that he is able to keep that which I have committed unto him"* (2 Tim. 1:12). Christ was at the everlasting council. He can tell you whether you were chosen or not, but you cannot find it out in any other way. Go and put your trust in Him, and His answer will be, *"I have loved thee with an everlasting love: therefore with lovingkindness have I drawn thee"* (Jer. 31:3). There will be no doubt about His having chosen *you*, when you have chosen *Him*.

> Sons we are through God's election,
> Who in Jesus Christ believe.

Let not one of them escape.
—1 Kings 18:40

When the prophet Elijah had received the answer to his prayer, and the fire from heaven had consumed the sacrifice in the presence of all the people, he called on the assembled Israelites to seize the priests of Baal. Then he sternly cried, *"Let not one of them escape."* He took them all down to the brook Kishon and slew them there. We must do the same with our sins. They are all doomed; not one must be preserved. Your favorite sin must die. Do not spare it, even though it cries and begs. Strike it down, even though it is as dear to you as Isaac was to Abraham. Strike, for God struck at sin when it was laid on His own Son. With stern, unflinching purpose, you must condemn to death the sin that was once the idol of your heart. Do you ask how you are to accomplish this? Jesus will be your power. Grace to overcome sin was given to you in the covenant of grace. You have strength to win the victory in the crusade against inward lusts, because Christ Jesus has promised to be with you *"even unto the end"* (Matt. 28:20). If you want to triumph over darkness, place yourself in the presence of the Sun of Righteousness. No place is as well suited for the discovery of sin and recovery from its power and guilt as the immediate presence of God. Job didn't know how to get rid of sin half as well as he did when the eyes of his faith rested on God. Then he abhorred himself and repented *"in dust and ashes"* (Job 42:6). The fine gold of the Christian often becomes dim. We need the sacred fire to consume the dross. Let us run to our God. He is a consuming fire, but He will not consume our spirits, only our sins. Let the goodness of God move us to a sacred jealousy and a holy revenge against our iniquities, which are hateful in His sight. Go forth to battle in His strength, and utterly destroy the accursed crew of sins—*"let not one of them escape."*

They shall go hindmost with their standards.
—Numbers 2:31

The camp of Dan brought up the rear when the armies of Israel were on the march. The Danites occupied the hindmost place, but what did their position matter, since they were as truly a part of the host as were the foremost tribes? They followed the same fiery, cloudy pillar; they ate of the same manna; drank of the same spiritual rock; and journeyed to the same inheritance. Come, my heart, cheer up. Although you are the last and the least, it is your privilege to be in the army and to fare as they fare who lead the way. Someone must be hindmost in honor and esteem; someone must do menial work for Jesus, and why should it not be I? In a poor village among an ignorant peasantry or in a back street among degraded sinners, I will work on, and "*go hindmost with* [my standard]." The Danites occupied a very useful place. Stragglers have to be picked up along the march, and lost property has to be gathered from the field. Fiery spirits may dash forward over untrodden paths to learn fresh truth and win more souls to Jesus, but some with more conservative spirits may be well engaged in reminding the church of her ancient faith and restoring her fainting sons. Every position has its duties, and the slowly moving children of God will find their particular state one in which they may be eminently a blessing to the whole host. The rear guard is a place of danger. There are foes behind us as well as before us. Attacks may come from any side. We read that Amalek fell on Israel and slew some of the rear guard. The experienced Christian will find much work for his weapons in aiding those poor, doubting, despondent, wavering souls who are hindmost in faith, knowledge, and joy. These must not be left unaided; therefore, it should be the business of well-taught saints to bear their standards among the rear guard. My soul, tenderly watch to help the hindmost this day.

JULY 18
Evening

*Neither shall one thrust another; they shall walk
every one in his path.*
—Joel 2:8

Locusts always keep their ranks. Although their number is legion, they do not crowd each other, throwing their columns into confusion. This remarkable fact of nature shows how thoroughly the Lord has infused the spirit of order into His universe. The smallest animate creatures are as much controlled by it as are the revolving planets or the angelic messengers. It would be wise for believers to be ruled by the same influence in their spiritual lives. First, regarding Christian graces, no one virtue should usurp the sphere of another or drain the lifeblood of the rest for its own support. Affection must not smother honesty, courage must not elbow meekness out of the field, modesty must not jostle energy, and patience must not slaughter resolution. Second, regarding our duties, one must not interfere with another; public usefulness must not injure private piety; church work must not push family worship into a corner. It is wrong to offer God one duty stained with the blood of another. Each thing is beautiful in its season, but not otherwise. It was to the Pharisee that Jesus said, *"These ought ye to have done, and not to leave the other undone"* (Matt. 23:23). Third, the same rule applies to our personal positions. We must take care to know our place, take it, and keep to it. We must minister as the Spirit has given us ability and not intrude on our fellow servant's domain. Our Lord Jesus taught us not to covet the high positions, but to be willing to be least among our brothers and sisters. May an envious, ambitious spirit be far from us. Let us feel the force of the Master's command and do as He instructs us, keeping rank with the rest of the host. Tonight, let us examine whether or not we are keeping the *"unity of the Spirit in the bond of peace"* (Eph. 4:3). Let our prayer be that, in all the churches of the Lord Jesus, peace and order may prevail.

The LORD our God hath showed us his glory.
—Deuteronomy 5:24

God's great design in all His works is the manifestation of His own glory. Any aim less than this would be unworthy of Him. But how will the glory of God be manifested to such fallen creatures as we are? Man's eye is not single; he always has a side-glance toward his own honor. He has too high an estimate of his own powers, and so he is not qualified to behold the glory of the Lord. It is clear, then, that self must stand out of the way, so that there may be room for God to be exalted. This is the reason that He often brings His people into problems and difficulties, so that, being made conscious of their own folly and weakness, they may be fitted to behold the majesty of God when He comes forth to work their deliverance. He whose life is one even, smooth path will see only a little of the glory of the Lord, for he has few occasions of self-emptying; hence, he has only a little fitness for being filled with the revelation of God. Those who navigate little streams and shallow creeks know little of the God of tempests, but those who "*do business in great waters*" (Ps. 107:23) see "*his wonders in the deep*" (v. 24). Among the huge Atlantic waves of bereavement, poverty, temptation, and reproach, we learn the power of Jehovah, because we feel the inadequacy of man. Thank God, then, if you have been led by a rough road. It is this that has given you your experience of God's greatness and lovingkindness. Your troubles have enriched you with a wealth of knowledge to be gained by no other means. Your trials have been the cleft of the rock in which Jehovah has set you, as He did His servant Moses, so that you might behold His glory as it passes by. Praise God that you have not been left to the darkness and ignorance that continued prosperity might have involved, but that in the great fight of affliction, you have been equipped for the outshinings of His glory in His wonderful dealings with you.

A bruised reed shall he not break,
and smoking flax shall he not quench.
—Matthew 12:20

What is weaker than a bruised reed or smoking flax? If a wild duck merely lands on a reed that grows in a swamp or marsh, the reed will snap. If someone's foot brushes against it, it will become bruised or broken. Every wind that flits across the river moves it back and forth. One can conceive of nothing more frail or brittle, or whose existence is more in jeopardy, than a bruised reed. Now consider smoking flax—what is it? It is true that it has a spark within it. However, it is almost smothered; an infant's breath might blow it out. Nothing has a more precarious existence than its flame. Weak things are being described in our text, yet Jesus says of them, "The smoking flax I will not quench; the bruised reed I will not break." Some of God's children have been made strong to do mighty works for Him. God has His Samsons here and there who can pull up Gaza's gates and carry them to the top of the hill. He has a few mighty believers who are lionlike, but the majority of His people are a timid, trembling race. They are like starlings, frightened at every passerby; they are a fearful little flock. If temptation comes, they are taken like birds in a snare; if trial threatens, they are ready to faint. Their frail little boat is tossed up and down by every wave; they drift along like a seabird on the crest of the billows. They are weak things, without strength, without wisdom, and without foresight. Yet, weak as they are, and *because* they are so weak, this promise is made especially to them. Herein is grace and graciousness! Herein is love and lovingkindness! How it reveals to us the compassion of Jesus—so gentle, tender, and considerate. We never need to shrink back from His touch. We never need to fear a harsh word from Him. Although He may well chide us for our weakness, He does not rebuke us. Bruised reeds will receive no blows from Him, and smoking flax will receive no quenching frowns.

The earnest of our inheritance.
—Ephesians 1:14

Oh, what enlightenment, what joys, what consolation, what delight of heart is experienced by that man who has learned to feed on Jesus, and on Jesus alone! Yet the realization that we have of Christ's preciousness is, in this life, imperfect at best. As an old writer says, "'Tis but a taste!" We *"have tasted that the Lord is gracious"* (1 Pet. 2:3), but we do not yet know *how* good and gracious He is, although what we know of His sweetness makes us long for more. We have enjoyed the firstfruits of the Spirit, and they have set us hungering and thirsting for the fullness of the heavenly vintage. We groan within ourselves, waiting for the adoption. Here we are like Israel in the wilderness, who had but one cluster from Eshcol; there we will be in the vineyard. Here we see the manna falling small, like coriander seed, but there we will eat the bread of heaven and the old corn of the kingdom. We are but beginners now in spiritual education. Although we have learned the first letters of the alphabet, we cannot read words yet, much less put sentences together. But as one says, "He who has been in heaven but five minutes knows more than the general assembly of divines on earth." We have many ungratified desires at present, but soon every wish will be satisfied. All our powers will find the sweetest employment in that eternal world of joy. O Christian, anticipate heaven for a few years. Within a very little time you will be rid of all your trials and your troubles. Your eyes now suffused with tears will weep no longer. You will gaze in indescribable rapture on the splendor of Him who sits on the throne. Even more, you will sit on His throne. The triumph of His glory will be shared by you. His crown, His joy, and His paradise will be yours, and you will be co-heir with Him who is the *"heir of all things"* (Heb. 1:2).

JULY 20
Evening

*And now what hast thou to do in the way of Egypt,
to drink the waters of Sihor?*
—Jeremiah 2:18

By many miracles, mercies, and extraordinary deliverances, Jehovah had proved Himself worthy of Israel's trust. Yet they broke down the hedges with which God had enclosed them as a sacred garden; they forsook their own true and living God and followed after false gods. The Lord constantly reproved them for their unfaithfulness, and our text contains one instance of God's reasoning with them. "Why are you going to Egypt to drink the waters of the muddy river?" It may be translated, "Why do you wander afar and leave your own cool stream from Lebanon? Why do you forsake Jerusalem and turn aside to Noph and Tahpanhes? Why are you so strangely set on mischief that you cannot be content with the good and healthful but want to follow after what is evil and deceitful?" Is there not in our text a word of reproof and warning to the Christian? O true believer, called by grace and washed in the precious blood of Jesus, you have tasted better drink than the muddy river of this world's pleasures can give you. You have had fellowship with Christ; you have obtained the joy of seeing Jesus and leaning your head upon His chest. Do the novelties, the songs, the honors, and the merriment of this earth bring you contentment after you have experienced these things? After you have you eaten the bread of angels, can you live on husks? Good Rutherford once said, "I have tasted of Christ's own manna, and I have lost my taste for the brown bread of this world's joys." The same thing should be true of you. If you are wandering after the waters of Egypt, return quickly to the one living Fountain. The waters of Sihor may be sweet to the Egyptians, but they will prove only bitter to you. This evening, Jesus asks you, "What do you have to do with them?" What will you answer Him?

JULY 21
Morning

The daughter of Jerusalem hath shaken her head at thee.
—Isaiah 37:22

Reassured by the Word of the Lord, the poor trembling citizens of Zion grew bold and shook their heads at Sennacherib's boastful threats. Strong faith enables the servants of God to look with calm contempt on their haughtiest foes. We know that our enemies are attempting impossibilities. They seek to destroy the eternal life, which cannot die while Jesus lives; to overthrow the citadel, against which the gates of hell will not prevail. They *"kick against the pricks"* (Acts 9:5) to their own wounding and rush upon the raised ornamentation of Jehovah's shield to their own hurt. We know their weaknesses. What are they but men? And what is man but a worm? They roar and swell like waves of the sea, foaming out their own shame. When the Lord arises, they will fly as chaff before the wind and be consumed as crackling thorns. Their utter powerlessness to do damage to the cause of God and His truth may make the weakest soldiers in Zion's ranks laugh them to scorn. Above all, we know that the Most High is with us, and when He dresses Himself in arms, where are His enemies? If He comes forth from His place, the *"potsherds of the earth"* (Isa. 45:9) will not long contend with their Maker. His *"rod of iron"* will *"dash them in pieces like a potter's vessel"* (Ps. 2:9), and their very *"remembrance shall perish from the earth"* (Job 18:17). Away, then, all fears! The kingdom is safe in the King's hands. Let us shout for joy, for the Lord reigns, and His foes will be like straw for the dunghill.

> As true as God's own Word is true;
> Nor earth, nor hell, with all their crew,
> Against us shall prevail.
> A jest, and byword, are they grown.
> God is with us; we are his own.
> Our victory cannot fail.

JULY 21

Evening

Why go I mourning?
—Psalm 42:9

Can you answer this question, believer? Can you find any reason why you are so often mourning instead of rejoicing? Why yield to gloomy apprehension? Who told you that the night would never end in day? Who told you that the sea of circumstances would ebb out until there was nothing left but long, muddy stretches of horrible poverty? Who told you that the "winter of your discontent" would proceed from frost to frost; from snow, ice, and hail to deeper snow and an even worse blizzard of despair? Do you not know that day follows night, that flood comes after ebb, that spring and summer follow winter? Then hope! Always hope, for God will not fail you. Do you not know that your God loves you in the midst of all your troubles? Mountains, when hidden in darkness, are as real as they are in daylight. In the same way, God's love is as true to you now as it was in your brightest moments. No father disciplines continuously. Your Lord hates the rod as much as you do; He only cares to use it for the reason that should make you willing to receive it, namely, that it is for your lasting good. You will yet climb Jacob's ladder with the angels and behold Him who sits at the top of it—your covenant God. You will yet, amid the splendors of eternity, forget the trials of time—or only remember them to bless the God who led you through them and worked your lasting good by them. Come and sing in the midst of tribulation. Rejoice even while you are passing through the furnace of affliction. Make the wilderness blossom like the rose. Cause the desert to ring with your exulting joys. These light afflictions will soon be over; then, forever with the Lord, your bliss will never diminish.

> Faint not nor fear, His arms are near,
>   He changes not, and you are dear;
> Only believe and you will see,
>   That Christ is all in all to thee.

I am married unto you.
—Jeremiah 3:14

Christ Jesus is joined with His people in the union of marriage. In love He espoused His church as a chaste virgin, long before she fell under the yoke of bondage. Full of burning affection, Christ toiled, like Jacob for Rachel, until the whole of her purchase-money had been paid. And now, having sought her by His Spirit, and brought her to know and love Him, Christ awaits the glorious hour when their mutual bliss will be consummated at the Marriage Supper of the Lamb. Not yet has the glorious Bridegroom presented His betrothed, perfected and complete, before the Majesty of heaven; not yet has she actually entered into the enjoyment of her privileges as His wife and queen. She is as yet a wanderer in a world of woe, a dweller *"in the tents of Kedar"* (Ps. 120:5); but she is even now the bride, the spouse of Jesus, dear to His heart, precious in His sight, written on His hands, and united with His person. On earth He exercises toward her all the affectionate offices of Husband. He makes rich provision for her needs, pays all her debts, and allows her to assume His name and to share in all His wealth. Nor will He ever act otherwise to her. The word *divorce* He will never mention, for He *"hateth putting away"* (Mal. 2:16). Death must sever the conjugal tie between the most loving mortals, but it cannot divide the links of this immortal marriage. In heaven they do not marry, but are as the angels of God; yet there is this one marvelous exception to the rule, for in heaven Christ and His church will celebrate their joyous nuptials. Because this affinity is more lasting, it is more intimate than earthly wedlock. Although the love of a husband may be so pure and fervent, it is but a faint picture of the flame that burns in the heart of Jesus. Surpassing all human union is that mystical cleaving unto the church, for which Christ left His Father and became one flesh with her.

Behold the man!
—John 19:5

If there is one place where our Lord Jesus most fully became the joy and comfort of His people, it is where He plunged deepest into the depths of woe. Come, gracious souls, and *"behold the man"* in the Garden of Gethsemane. See His heart brimming so full of love that He cannot hold it in—and so full of sorrow that it must find release. See the bloody sweat as it drips from every pore of His body and falls to the ground. *"Behold the man"* as they drive the nails into His hands and feet. Look up, repenting sinners, and see the sorrowful image of your suffering Lord on the cross. Notice how the ruby drops of blood stand on the crown of thorns and adorn, as if priceless gems, the diadem of the King of Misery. *"Behold the man"* when all His bones are out of joint, and He is poured out like water and brought into the dust of death. God forsook Him and hell surrounded Him. Look and see: did anyone else ever sorrow as He sorrowed? All you who pass by, draw near and look upon this spectacle of grief—unique, unparalleled, a wonder to men and angels. Behold the Emperor of Woe, who has no equal or rival in His agonies! Gaze on Him, you mourners, for if there is no consolation in a crucified Christ, there is no joy on earth or in heaven. If there is no hope in the ransom-price of His blood, there is no joy in the harps of heaven, and the right hand of God will never know any pleasures. If we would sit more often at the foot of the cross, we would be less troubled with our doubts and sorrows. If we see His sorrows, we will be ashamed to mention our sorrows. If we but gaze into His wounds, our wounds will be healed. If we want to live right, it must be by the contemplation of His death. If we want to rise to dignity, it must be by considering His humiliation and sorrow.

Even thou wast as one of them.
—Obadiah 1:11

Brotherly kindness was due from Edom to Israel in their time of need, but instead, the men of Esau joined forces with Israel's foes. Special stress in the sentence before us is laid on the word *"thou,"* as when Caesar cried to Brutus, "and *thou* Brutus." A bad action may be all the worse because of the person who has committed it. When we, who are the chosen favorites of heaven, sin, ours is a crying offense, because we are so highly favored. If an angel would lay his hand on us when we are doing evil, he would not need to use any other rebuke than the question, "What, you? What are you doing here?" Much forgiven, much delivered, much instructed, much enriched, much blessed—will we dare to put forth our hand unto evil? God forbid! A few minutes of confession may be beneficial to you, gentle reader, this morning. Have you never been as the wicked? At an evening party certain men laughed at uncleanness, and the joke was not altogether offensive to your ear; *"even thou wast as one of them."* When hard things were spoken concerning the ways of God, you were bashfully silent; and so, to onlookers, you were as one of them. When worldlings were bartering in the market and driving hard bargains, were you not as one of them? When they were pursuing vanity, were you not as greedy for gain as they were? Could any difference be discerned among you and them? Is there any difference? Here the truth hits close to home. Be honest with your own soul, and make sure that you are a *"new creature"* (2 Cor. 5:17) in Christ Jesus. Even when your faith is true, be vigilant in your Christian walk, lest any should again be able to say, *"Even thou wast as one of them."* You would not desire to share their eternal doom, so why be like them here? Do not join their practices, lest you be united with them in their ruin. Side with the afflicted people of God, and not with the world.

The blood of Jesus Christ his Son cleanseth us from all sin.
—1 John 1:7

"Cleanseth," says the text—not "shall cleanse." There are multitudes who think they can wait until they are on their deathbeds before they ask God's pardon for their sins. Oh, how infinitely better to have cleansing now than to depend on the bare possibility of forgiveness when the time comes for me to die! Others imagine that a sense of pardon is only obtainable after many years of Christian experience. But forgiveness of sin is a *present* thing—a privilege for this day, a joy for this very hour. The moment a sinner trusts in Jesus, he is fully forgiven. The text is written in the present tense, indicating continuance; it was "*cleanseth*" yesterday, it is "*cleanseth*" today, and it will be "*cleanseth*" tomorrow. It will always be so with you, Christian, until you cross the river. You may come to this fountain every hour, for it cleanses still. Notice, likewise, the completeness of the cleansing: "*The blood of Jesus Christ his Son cleanseth us from all sin*"—not only from "*sin*," but from "*all sin*." Reader, I cannot express the exceeding sweetness of this word "*all*," but I pray that God the Holy Spirit may give you a taste of it. Our sins against God are manifold. Yet whether the debt is little or great, the same receipt can discharge one as well as the other. The blood of Jesus Christ is as blessed and divine a payment for the transgressions of blaspheming Peter as it is for the shortcomings of loving John. Our iniquity is gone, all gone at once, and all gone forever. Blessed completeness! What a sweet theme for us to dwell on as we drift off to sleep.

Sins against a holy God;
  Sins against His righteous laws;
Sins against His love, His blood;
  Sins against His name and cause;
Sins immense as is the sea—
  From them all He cleanses me.

Stand still, and see the salvation of the LORD.
—Exodus 14:13

These words contain God's command to the believer when he is reduced to great straits and brought into extraordinary difficulties. He cannot retreat; he cannot go forward. He is shut up on the right hand and on the left. What is he to do now? The Master's word to him is, *"Stand still."* It will be well for him if at such times he listens only to his Master's word, for evil advisers come with their suggestions. Despair whispers, "Lie down and die; give it all up." But God would have us put on a cheerful courage, and even in our worst times, rejoice in His love and faithfulness. Cowardice says, "Retreat; go back to the world's way of doing things. You cannot play the Christian's part; it is too difficult. Relinquish your principles." However much Satan may urge this course upon you, you cannot follow it if you are a child of God. His divine command has bid you to *"go from strength to strength"* (Ps. 84:7), and so you will, and neither death nor hell will turn you away from your course. If for a while you are called to stand still, this is but to renew your strength for some greater advance in due time. Hastiness cries, "Do something! Stir yourself! To stand still and wait is sheer idleness." We must be doing something at once. We must do it, so we think, instead of looking to the Lord, who will not only do something but will do everything. Presumption boasts, "If the sea is before you, march into it and expect a miracle." But Faith listens neither to Presumption, nor to Despair, nor to Cowardice, nor to Hastiness, but it hears God say, *"Stand still"*; and immovable as a rock, it stands. *"Stand still."* Keep the posture of an upright man: ready for action, expecting further orders, cheerfully and patiently awaiting the directing voice. It will not be long before God will say to you, as distinctly as He told Moses to say it to the people of Israel, *"Go forward"* (Exod. 14:15).

JULY 24
Evening

His camp is very great.
—Joel 2:11

My soul, consider the mightiness of the Lord, who is your glory and defense. He is a man of war; Jehovah is His name. All the forces of heaven are at His command. Legions wait at His door; cherubim and seraphim, watchers and holy ones, principalities and powers—all are attentive to His will. If our eyes were not blinded by the limitations of our flesh, we would see horses of fire and chariots of fire surrounding the Lord's beloved. (See 2 Kings 6:17.) The powers of nature are all subject to the absolute control of the Creator: stormy winds and tempests, lightning and rain, snow and hail, and the soft dews and cheering sunshine come and go at His decree. He looses the bands of Orion and binds the sweet influences of the Pleiades (Job 38:31). Earth, sea, air, and the places under the earth are the barracks for Jehovah's great armies. Space is His camp, light is His banner, and flame is His sword. When He goes forth to war, famine ravages the land, pestilence smites the nations, hurricanes sweep the sea, tornadoes shake the mountains, and earthquakes make the solid ground tremble. As for animate creatures, they all acknowledge His dominion; from the *"great fish"* (Jonah 1:17) that swallowed the prophet down to all manner of flies that plagued the field of Zoan (Ps. 78:43, 45), all are His servants. The palmerworm, the caterpillar, and the cankerworm are squadrons of His great army, for His *"camp is very great."* My soul, see to it that you are at peace with this mighty King. Even more than that, be sure to enlist under His banner, for to war against Him is foolishness, but to serve Him is glory. Jesus, *"Emmanuel... God with us"* (Matt. 1:23), is ready to receive recruits for the army of the Lord. If I am not already enlisted, let me go to Him before I sleep and beg to be accepted through His merits. If I am already a soldier of the Cross, as I hope I am, let me be of good courage, for the enemy is powerless compared with my Lord, whose *"camp is very great."*

He left his garment in her hand, and fled, and got him out.
—Genesis 39:12

In contending with certain sins there remains no mode of victory but flight. The ancient naturalists wrote much of basilisks, whose eyes fascinated their victims and rendered them easy victims; likewise, the mere gaze of wickedness puts us in solemn danger. He who would be safe from acts of evil must run away from occasions of it. A covenant must be made with our eyes not even to look on the cause of temptation, for such sins need only a spark to begin, and a blaze follows in an instant. Who would wantonly enter the leper's prison and sleep amid its horrible corruption? Only he who desires to be leprous himself would thus court contagion. If the mariner knew how to avoid a storm, he would do anything rather than run the risk of weathering it. Cautious pilots have no desire to see how near to quicksand they can sail, or how often they may touch a rock without springing a leak. Their aim is to keep as far away as possible from danger and navigate in the middle of a safe channel. This day I may be exposed to great peril; let me have the serpent's wisdom to keep out of it and avoid it. The wings of a dove may be of more use to me today than the jaws of a lion. It is true that I may be an apparent loser by declining evil company, but I would rather lose my coat than my character. It is not necessary that I should be rich, but it is imperative upon me to be pure. No ties of friendship, no accumulation of beauty, no displays of talent, no shafts of ridicule must turn me from the wise resolve to flee from sin. I am to *"resist the devil, and he will flee from* [me]*"* (James 4:7); but the lusts of the flesh, I must flee, or they will surely overcome me. O God of holiness, preserve your Josephs, so that they will not be bewitched by vile suggestions. May the horrible trinity of the world, the flesh, and the devil never overcome us!

JULY 25
Evening

In their affliction they will seek me early.
—Hosea 5:15

Losses and adversities are frequently the means that the Great Shepherd uses to fetch home His wandering sheep. Like fierce dogs, they worry the wanderers back to the fold. Lions cannot be tamed if they are too well fed; their stomachs must be deprived, and they must be brought down from their great strength, before they will submit to the tamer's hand. We have often seen the Christian rendered obedient to the Lord's will by lack of bread and difficult trials. When *"rich, and increased with goods"* (Rev. 3:17), many believers carry their heads much too proudly and speak exceedingly boastfully. Like David, they flatter themselves, saying, "My mountain stands strong; *'I shall never be moved'* (Ps. 30:6–7)." When the Christian grows wealthy, is in good repute, and has good health and a happy family, he too often admits Mr. Carnal Security as a guest at his table. If he is a true child of God, a rod of correction will be prepared for him. Wait awhile, and you may see his wealth melt away as if it were only a dream. There goes a portion of his estate—how soon the acres change hands. That debt, that unpaid bill—how fast his losses roll in; where will they end? It is a blessed sign of divine life if, when these embarrassments occur one after another, he begins to be distressed about his backsliding and goes back to his God. Blessed are the waves that wash the seaman upon the rock of salvation! Losses in business are often sanctified to our souls' enrichment. If the chosen soul will not come to the Lord full-handed, he will come empty-handed. If God, in His grace, finds no other means of making us honor Him among men, He will cast us into the deep; if we fail to honor Him on the pinnacle of riches, He will bring us into the valley of poverty. Yet do not faint, heir of sorrow, when you are thus rebuked. Instead, recognize the loving hand that disciplines, and say, *"I will arise and go to my father"* (Luke 15:18).

Add to your faith virtue; and to virtue knowledge....Give diligence.
—2 Peter 1:5, 10

If you would enjoy the eminent grace of the full assurance of faith, under the blessed Spirit's influence and assistance, do what the Scripture tells you: *"Give diligence."* Take care that your faith is of the right kind—that it is not a mere belief of doctrine, but a simple faith, depending on Christ, and on Christ alone. Give diligent heed to your courage. Plead with God that He would give you the face of a lion, that you may, with a consciousness of right, go on boldly. Study the Scriptures well, and get knowledge; for a knowledge of doctrine will lead to the confirmation of your faith. Try to understand God's Word; let it *"dwell in you richly"* (Col. 3:16). When you have done this, *"Add to your...knowledge temperance"* (2 Pet. 1:5–6). Pay attention to your body: practice moderation without. Pay attention to your soul: practice moderation within. Restrain your lips, your life, your heart, and your thoughts. Add to this, by God's Holy Spirit, patience. Ask Him to give you the patience that endures affliction, which, when it is tried, will *"come forth as gold"* (Job 23:10). Adorn yourself with patience, so that you may not complain or be depressed in your afflictions. When that grace is won, look to godliness. Godliness is something more than religion. Make God's glory your purpose in life. Live in His sight, and dwell closely to Him. Seek fellowship with Him, and you will be godly. To godliness, add brotherly love. Have a love for all the saints; and add to that love a charity that opens its arms to all people and loves their souls. When you are adorned with these jewels, and just in proportion as you practice these heavenly virtues, will you come to know by clearest evidence *"your calling and election"* (2 Pet. 1:10). *"Give diligence,"* if you would find assurance, for lukewarmness and doubting very naturally go hand in hand.

JULY 26
Evening

That he may set him with princes.
—Psalm 113:8

Our spiritual privileges are of the highest order. *"With princes"* is the place of select society. *"Truly our fellowship is with the Father, and with his Son Jesus Christ"* (1 John 1:3). Speaking of select society, there is none like this! *"Ye are a chosen generation, a royal priesthood,…a peculiar people"* (1 Pet. 2:9). *"Ye are come unto…the general assembly and church of the firstborn, [whose names] are written in heaven"* (Heb. 12:22–23). The saints have an audience with the King; princes have admittance to royalty, while common people must stand afar off. The child of God has free access to the inner courts of heaven. *"For through him we both have access by one Spirit unto the Father"* (Eph. 2:18). *"Let us therefore come boldly,"* said the apostle, *"unto the throne of grace"* (Heb. 4:16). Among princes there is abundant wealth, but what is the abundance of princes compared to the riches of believers? *"For all things are yours;…and ye are Christ's; and Christ is God's"* (1 Cor. 3:21, 23). *"He that spared not his own Son, but delivered him up for us all, how shall he not with him also freely give us all things?"* (Rom. 8:32). Princes have special power. A prince of heaven's empire has great influence; he wields a scepter in his own domain. He sits on Jesus' throne, for He *"hath made us kings and priests unto God"* (Rev. 1:6). We *"shall reign for ever and ever"* (Rev. 22:5). We reign over the united kingdom of time and eternity. Princes also have special honor. We may look down upon all earthly dignity from the eminence upon which grace has placed us. For what is human grandeur to this: He *"hath raised us up together, and made us sit together in heavenly places in Christ Jesus"* (Eph. 2:6)? We share the honor of Christ. Compared to this, earthly splendors are not worth a thought. Communion with Jesus is a richer gem than any that ever glittered in a royal crown. Union with the Lord is a coronet of beauty outshining all the brilliance of imperial splendor.

Exceeding great and precious promises.
—2 Peter 1:4

If you would know the preciousness of the promises and enjoy them in your own heart, meditate much on them. There are promises that are like grapes in the winepress; if you will tread on them, the juice will flow. Thinking over the hallowed words will often be the prelude to their fulfillment. While you are meditating on them, the blessings that you are seeking will gradually come to you. Many Christians who have thirsted for the promise have found the favor that it ensured gently distilling into their souls even while they have been considering the divine record. They have rejoiced that they were led to lay the promises near their hearts. But besides meditating on the promises, seek in your soul to receive them as being the very words of God. Speak to your soul, saying, "If I were dealing with a man's promise, I would carefully consider the ability and the character of the man who had covenanted with me. So with the promise of God; my eye must not be focused as much on the greatness of the mercy—that may stagger me—as on the greatness of the Promiser—that will cheer me. My soul, it is God, even your God, God who cannot lie, who speaks to you. This word of His that you are now considering is as true as His own existence. He is an unchangeable God. He has not altered the words that have gone out of His mouth, nor has He called back one single comforting sentence. Nor does He lack any power. It is the God who made the heavens and the earth who has spoken thus. Nor can He fail in wisdom as to the time when He will bestow the favors, for He knows when it is best to give and when it is better to withhold. Therefore, seeing that it is the word of a God so true, so immutable, so powerful, so wise, I will and must believe the promise." If we meditate on the promises, and consider the Promiser, we will experience their sweetness and obtain their fulfillment.

Who shall lay any thing to the charge of God's elect?
—Romans 8:33

What a blessed challenge is the question of our text! How unanswerable it is! Every sin of the elect was laid on the great Champion of our salvation and was carried away by the Atonement. There is no sin in God's book against His people. He sees no sin in Jacob or iniquity in Israel; they are justified in Christ forever. When the guilt of sin was taken away, the punishment of sin was also removed. For the Christian, there is no stroke from God's angry hand—not so much as a single frown of punitive justice. The believer may be disciplined by his Father, but God the Judge has nothing to say to the Christian except, "I have absolved you; you are acquitted." For the Christian, there is no penal death in this world, much less any *"second death"* (Rev. 2:11). He has been completely freed from all the punishment, as well as the guilt, of sin. The power of sin has been removed, too. It may stand in our way and agitate us with perpetual warfare, but sin is a conquered foe to every soul who is in union with Jesus. There is no sin that a Christian cannot overcome if he will only rely on his God to do it. Those who wear the white robes in heaven *"overcame…by the blood of the Lamb"* (Rev. 12:11), and we may do the same. No lust is too mighty, no besetting sin too strongly entrenched; we can overcome through the power of Christ. Christian, believe that your sin is a condemned thing. It may kick and struggle, but it is doomed to die. God has written *"condemned"* across its forehead. Christ has crucified it, *"nailing it to his cross"* (Col. 2:14). Go now and put it to death. May the Lord help you to live to His praise. For sin—with all its guilt, shame, and fear—is gone.

> Here's pardon for transgressions past,
>   It matters not how black their cast;
> And, O my soul, with wonder view,
>   For sins to come here's pardon, too.

So foolish was I, and ignorant: I was as a beast before thee.
—Psalm 73:22

Remember this is the confession of the man after God's own heart; and in telling us his inner life, David wrote, *"So foolish was I, and ignorant."* The word *"foolish"* here means more than it signifies in everyday language. David, in the third verse of this psalm, wrote, *"I was envious at the foolish, when I saw the prosperity of the wicked,"* which shows that the folly he intended had sin in it. He put himself down as being *"foolish,"* and added a word that gave intensity to it, *"so foolish was I"* (emphasis added). How foolish, he could not tell. It was a sinful folly, a folly that was not to be excused by frailty, but to be condemned because of its perverseness and willful ignorance; for he had been envious of the present prosperity of the ungodly and forgetful of the dreadful end awaiting them. And are we better than David that we should call ourselves wise? Do we profess that we have attained perfection or that we have been so chastened that the rod has taken all our willfulness out of us? Ah, this is pride indeed! If David was foolish, how foolish would we be in our own esteem if we could but see ourselves! Look back, believer. Think of your doubting God when He has been so faithful to you. Think of your foolish outcry of "Not so, my Father," when He crossed His hands in affliction to give you the larger blessing. Think of the many times when you have read His providences in the dark, misinterpreted His dispensations, and groaned out, "All these things are against me," when they are all working together for your good! Think how often you have chosen sin because of its pleasure, when indeed, that pleasure was a root of bitterness to you! Surely, if we know our own hearts, we must plead guilty to the indictment of a sinful folly. Conscious of this "foolishness," we must make David's consequent resolve our own: *"Thou shalt guide me with thy counsel"* (Ps. 73:24).

Who went about doing good.
—Acts 10:38

These are few words, yet they are an exquisite depiction of the Lord Jesus Christ. There are not many lines, but they are the strokes of a master's pencil. Of the Savior, and only of the Savior, is our text true in the fullest, broadest, and most unqualified sense. He *"went about doing good."* From this description, it is evident that He did good personally. The writers of the Gospels constantly told us that He touched the leper with His own hand; that He anointed the eyes of the blind; and that in cases where He was asked only to speak a word of healing at a distance, He usually did not comply, but went Himself to the sickbed and personally worked the cure. His example is a lesson to us: if we want to do good, we should do it personally. Give charity with your own hands; a kind look or word will enhance the value of the gift. Speak to a friend about the state of his soul; your loving appeal will have more influence than a whole library of tracts. Our Lord's method of doing good also shows His incessant activity. He not only did good close to home, but He also *"went about"* on His errands of mercy. Throughout the whole land of Judea, scarcely a village or a hamlet was not gladdened by the sight of Him. How His example reproves the slow, loitering manner in which many Christians serve the Lord! Let us *"gird up the loins"* (1 Pet. 1:13) of our minds and *"be not weary in well doing"* (2 Thess. 3:13). Does not the text imply that Jesus Christ went out of His way to do good? He *"went about doing good."* He was never deterred by danger or difficulty. He sought out the objects of His gracious intentions. So must we. If old plans will not serve, we must try new ones. Fresh measures sometimes achieve more than regular methods. Christ's perseverance and unity of purpose are also implied in our text. The practical application of our theme for today may be summed up in these words: *"Christ...[left] us an example, that [we] should follow his steps"* (1 Pet. 2:21).

Nevertheless I am continually with thee.
—Psalm 73:23

N*evertheless"*—notwithstanding all the foolishness and ignorance that David had just been confessing to God, not one atom the less was it true and certain that David was saved, accepted, and blessed by the constant presence of God. Fully conscious of his own lost state, and of the deceitfulness and vileness of his nature, yet, by a glorious outburst of faith, he sang, *"Nevertheless I am continually with thee."* Believer, you are forced to enter into the psalmist's confession and acknowledgment; endeavor in the same spirit to say, "Nevertheless, since I belong to Christ, I am continually with God!" This means that I am continually on His mind; He is always thinking of me for my good. I am continually before His eye; the eye of the Lord never sleeps, but is perpetually watching over my welfare. I am continually in His hand, so that none will be able to pluck me from it. I am continually on His heart, worn there as a memorial, even as the high priest bore the names of the twelve tribes on his heart forever. You always think of me, O God. Your love continually reaches out to me. You are always making providence work for my good. You have set me as a signet on Your arm. Your love is as *"strong as death"* (Song 8:6). *"Many waters cannot quench* [it], *neither can the floods drown it"* (v. 7). Surprising grace! You see me in Christ, and, though in myself abhorred, You behold me as wearing Christ's garments, washed in His blood; thus, I stand accepted in Your presence. I am continually in Your favor—*"continually with thee."* Here is comfort for the tried and afflicted soul: vexed with the tempest within, look at the calm without. *"Nevertheless"*—Oh, say it in your heart, and take the peace it gives. *"Nevertheless I am continually with thee."*

JULY 29
Evening

All that the Father giveth me shall come to me.
—John 6:37

This declaration concerns, first, the doctrine of election. There are some whom the Father gave to Christ. It also concerns the doctrine of effectual calling. Those who are given must and will come. However obstinately they may set themselves against it, they will be brought out of darkness into God's marvelous light. Our text also teaches us the indispensable necessity of faith, for even those who are given to Christ are not saved until they come to Jesus. Even they must come, for there is no other way to heaven but by the Door, Christ Jesus. All whom the Father gives to our Redeemer must come to Him; therefore, no one can enter heaven unless he first comes to Christ. Oh, the power and majesty that rest in the words *"shall come"*! Christ does not say that they have the power to come or that they may come if they will, but that they *"shall come."* By His messengers, His Word, and His Spirit, the Lord Jesus sweetly and graciously compels men to come in, so that they may eat of His marriage supper. He does this, not by any violation of the free will of man, but by the power of His grace. I may exercise power over another man's will, yet that other man's will may be perfectly free, because the constraint is exercised in a manner that is harmonious with the laws of the human mind. Jehovah Jesus knows how—by irresistible arguments addressed to the understanding, by mighty reasons appealing to the affections, and by the mysterious influence of His Holy Spirit operating on all the powers and passions of the soul—to subdue the whole man. In this way, whereas the man was once rebellious, he now yields cheerfully to Christ's rule, conquered by sovereign love. How will those whom God has chosen be known? They will be known by this result: they willingly and joyfully accept Christ and come to Him with simple and genuine faith, resting on Him as all their salvation and all their desire. Reader, have you thus come to Jesus?

And when he thought thereon, he wept.
—Mark 14:72

It has been thought by some that as long as Peter lived, the fountain of his tears began to flow whenever he remembered his denying his Lord. It is not unlikely that it was so, for his sin was very great, and grace in him had afterward a perfect work. This same experience is common to all the redeemed family according to the degree in which the Spirit of God has removed the natural heart of stone. We, like Peter, remember our boastful promise: *"Though all men shall be offended because of thee, yet will I never be offended"* (Matt. 26:33). We eat our own words with the bitter herbs of repentance. When we think of what we vowed we would be, and of what we have been, we may weep whole showers of grief. He thought about his denying his Lord: the place in which he did it, the insignificant reason that led him into such heinous sin, the oaths and blasphemies with which he sought to confirm his falsehood, and the dreadful hardness of heart that drove him to do so again and yet again. Can we, when we are reminded of our sins, and their exceeding sinfulness, remain impassive and stubborn? Will we not make our house a place of weeping and cry to the Lord for renewed assurances of pardoning love? May we never take a dry-eyed look at sin, unless before long we have a tongue parched in the flames of hell. Peter also thought about his Master's look of love. The Lord followed up the cock's warning voice with an admonishing look of sorrow, pity, and love. That glance was never out of Peter's mind as long as he lived. It was far more effective than ten thousand sermons would have been without the Spirit. The penitent apostle would be sure to weep when he remembered the Savior's full forgiveness, which restored him to his former place. To think that we have offended so kind and good a Lord is more than sufficient reason for being constant weepers. Lord, smite our rocky hearts and make the waters flow.

Him that cometh to me I will in no wise cast out.
—John 6:37

No limit is set on the duration of this promise. It does not say, "I will not cast out a sinner at his first coming," but *"I will in no wise cast out."* The original words in the Greek may be translated, "I will not, not cast out" or "I will never, never cast out." This means that Christ will not reject a believer the first time he comes, and that, as He will not reject him at the first, so He will not reject him to the last. Suppose the believer sins after coming? *"If any man sin, we have an advocate with the Father, Jesus Christ the righteous"* (1 John 2:1). Suppose the believer backslides? *"I will heal their backsliding, I will love them freely: for mine anger is turned away from him"* (Hos. 14:4). Yet the believer may fall under temptation. *"God is faithful, who will not suffer you to be tempted above that ye are able; but will with the temptation also make a way to escape, that ye may be able to bear it"* (1 Cor. 10:13). The believer may also fall into sin, as David did. Yes, but He will purge him with hyssop, and he will be clean; He will wash him, and he will be whiter than snow (Ps. 51:7). *"I will cleanse them from all their iniquity"* (Jer. 33:8).

Once in Christ, in Christ forever,
Nothing from His love can sever.

"I give unto [My sheep] *eternal life,"* He says, *"and they shall never perish, neither shall any man pluck them out of my hand"* (John 10:28). What do you say to this, O trembling, feeble mind? Is it not a precious mercy that, when you come to Christ, you do not come to one who will treat you well for a little while and then send you away, but One who will receive you and make you His bride, so that you will be His forever? Do not receive *"the spirit of bondage again to fear,"* but receive *"the Spirit of adoption, whereby* [you will] *cry, Abba, Father"* (Rom. 8:15). Oh, the grace of these words: *"I will in no wise cast out"*!

JULY 31

I in them.
—John 17:23

If such is the union that exists between our souls and the person of our Lord, how deep and broad is the channel of our communion! This is no narrow pipe through which a thread-like stream may wind its way. It is a channel of amazing depth and breadth, along whose glorious length a ponderous volume of living water may roll its floods. Behold, He has set before us an open door; let us not be slow to enter. This city of communion has many pearly gates. Each gate is of one pearl and is thrown wide open so that we may enter, assured of being welcome. If there were but one small hole through which to talk with Jesus, it would be a high privilege to thrust a word of fellowship through the narrow door. How much we are blessed in having so large an entrance! Had the Lord Jesus been far away from us, with many stormy seas between, we would have longed to send a messenger to Him to carry Him our love and bring us tidings from His Father's house. But note His kindness: He has built His house next door to ours; no, even more, He lodges with us and tabernacles in our poor, humble hearts, so that He may have perpetual contact with us. Oh, how foolish we must be, if we do not live in habitual communion with Him! When the road is long, dangerous, and difficult, we do not need to wonder that friends seldom meet each other, but when they live together, will Jonathan forget his David? A wife may, when her husband is on a journey, endure many days without being able to talk with him, but she could never tolerate being separated from him if she knew he was in one of the rooms of their very own house. Why, believer, do you not sit at His banquet of wine? Seek your Lord, for He is near. Embrace Him, for He is your Brother. Hold Him fast, for He is your Husband. Press Him to your heart, for He is of your own flesh.

JULY 31

Evening

And these are the singers…: for they were employed
in that work day and night.
—1 Chronicles 9:33

It was good that the sacred songs in the temple never ceased. The singers continuously praised the Lord, whose mercy endures forever. As mercy did not cease to rule either by day or by night, neither did music quiet its holy ministry. My heart, there is a sweet lesson for you in the ceaseless song of Zion's temple. You, too, are a constant debtor. See to it that your gratitude, like love, never fails. God's praise is constant in heaven, which is to be your final dwelling place; learn to practice the eternal hallelujah. As the sun scatters its light around the earth, its beams awaken grateful believers to sing their morning hymns, so that, by the priesthood of the saints, perpetual praise is kept up at all hours. These praises wrap our globe in a cloak of thanksgiving and encircle it with a golden belt of song. The Lord always deserves to be praised for what He is in Himself, for His works of creation and providence, for His goodness toward His creatures, and especially for the incomparable act of redemption and all the marvelous blessings that flow from it. It is always beneficial to praise the Lord. It cheers the day and brightens the night; it lightens work and softens sorrow. It sheds a sanctifying radiance over earthly gladness that makes it less liable to blind us with its glare. Have we not something to sing about at this moment? Can we not weave a song out of our present joys, our past deliverances, or our future hopes? Earth yields her summer fruits: the hay is housed, the golden grain invites the sickle, and the sun, lingering long to shine upon a fruitful earth, shortens the interval of darkness, so that we may lengthen our hours of devout worship. Let us be stirred by our love for Jesus to close the day with a psalm of sanctified gladness.

AUGUST 1

Morning

Let me now go to the field, and glean ears of corn.
—Ruth 2:2

Downcast and troubled Christian, come and glean today in the broad field of promises. Here is an abundance of precious promises that exactly meet your needs. Take this one: *"A bruised reed shall he not break, and the smoking flax shall he not quench"* (Isa. 42:3). Does that fit your case? A helpless and weak reed; a bruised reed, out of which no music can come; a reed weaker than weakness itself; an insignificant reed, and yet, He will not break you. On the contrary, He will restore and strengthen you. You are like the smoking flax. No light or warmth can come from you, but He will not quench you. He will blow with His sweet breath of mercy until He fans you into a flame. Would you glean another ear? *"Come unto me, all ye that labour and are heavy laden, and I will give you rest"* (Matt. 11:28). What inviting words! Your heart is tender, and the Master knows it; therefore, He speaks so gently to you. Will you not obey Him and come to Him even now? Take another ear of corn: *"Fear not…; I will help thee, saith the LORD, and thy redeemer, the Holy One of Israel"* (Isa. 41:14). How can you fear with such a wonderful assurance as this? You may gather ten thousand golden ears such as these! *"I have blotted out, as a thick cloud, thy transgressions, and, as a cloud, thy sins"* (Isa. 44:22). Or this, *"Though your sins be as scarlet, they shall be as white as snow; though they be red like crimson, they shall be as wool"* (Isa. 1:18). Or this, *"The Spirit and the bride say, Come. And let him that…is athirst come. And whosoever will, let him take the water of life freely"* (Rev. 22:17). Our Master's field is very rich; behold the handfuls of available promises. See them there before you, poor timid believer! Gather them up, and make them your own; for Jesus invites you to take them. Do not be afraid; only believe! Grasp these sweet promises, thresh them out by meditation, and feed on them with joy.

AUGUST 1

Evening

Thou crownest the year with thy goodness.
—Psalm 65:11

All year round, every hour of every day, God is richly blessing us. Both when we are asleep and when we are awake, His mercy attends us. The sun may not shine, but our God never ceases to shine on His children with beams of love. Like a river, His lovingkindness is always flowing with a fullness as inexhaustible as His own nature. Like the atmosphere that constantly surrounds the earth and is always ready to support the life of man, the benevolence of God surrounds all His creatures. In it, as in their element, they live, move, and have their being. As the sun on summer days makes us glad with rays that are warmer and brighter than at other times; as rivers are at certain seasons swollen by the rain; and as the atmosphere itself is sometimes fresher, more invigorating, or milder than previously, so it is with the mercy of God. It has its golden hours, its days of surplus, when the Lord magnifies His grace before the sons of men. Among His blessings, the joyous days of harvest are a special season of abundant favor. It is the glory of autumn that the ripe gifts of providence are then abundantly bestowed. It is the season of realization, whereas all that came before was but hope and expectation. Great is the joy of harvest. Happy are the reapers who fill their arms with the generosity of heaven. The psalmist tells us that the harvest is the crowning of the year. Surely these crowning mercies call for crowning thanksgiving! Let us offer thanks by inward expressions of gratitude. Let our hearts be warmed. Let our spirits remember and meditate on the goodness of the Lord. Then let us praise Him, glorifying and magnifying His name, from whose bounty all this goodness flows. Let us glorify God by yielding our gifts to His purposes. A practical proof of our gratitude is a special thank offering to the Lord of the harvest.

AUGUST 2

Morning

Who worketh all things after the counsel of his own will.
—Ephesians 1:11

Our belief in God's wisdom supposes and necessitates that He has a settled purpose and plan in the work of salvation. What would Creation have been without His design? Is there a fish in the sea or a fowl in the air that was left to chance for its formation? No, in every bone, joint, muscle, sinew, gland, and blood vessel, you observe the presence of a God working everything according to the design of infinite wisdom. And will God be present in creation, ruling over all, and not in grace? Will the new creation have the fickle genius of free will to preside over it when divine counsel rules the old creation? Look at Providence! Who does not know that not even a sparrow falls to the ground without your Father's knowledge? Even the hairs of your head are all numbered. God weighs the mountains of our grief on scales, and the hills of our tribulation on balances. And will there be a God in providence and not in grace? Will the shell be ordained by wisdom and the kernel be left to blind chance? No, He knows the end from the beginning. He sees in its appointed place, not merely the Cornerstone, which He has laid in fair colors in the blood of His dear Son, but He beholds in their ordained position each of the chosen stones taken out of the quarry of nature and polished by His grace. He sees the whole from corner to cornice, from base to roof, from foundation to pinnacle. He has in His mind a clear knowledge of every stone that will be laid in its prepared space, how vast the edifice will be, and when the top-stone will be brought forth with shoutings of "Grace! Grace! unto it." At the last it will be clearly seen that in every chosen vessel of mercy, Jehovah did as He willed with His own; and that in every part of the work of grace, He accomplished His purposes and glorified His own name.

AUGUST 2

So she gleaned in the field until even.
—Ruth 2:17

Let me learn from Ruth, the gleaner. As she went out to gather ears of corn, so I must go out into the fields of prayer, meditation, doctrine, and the hearing of the Word, in order to gather spiritual food. The gleaner gathers her portion ear by ear; her gains are little by little. I must be content to search for single truths, if there is no greater abundance of them. Every ear helps to make a bundle, and every gospel lesson assists in making us *"wise unto salvation"* (2 Tim. 3:15). The gleaner keeps her eyes open. If she were to stumble along the fields while daydreaming, she would have no load to carry home in the evening. I must be watchful while engaging in religious disciplines, so that they will not become unprofitable to me. I fear I have lost much already. Oh, that I may rightly estimate my opportunities and glean with greater diligence! The gleaner stoops for all she finds, and so must I. Haughty spirits criticize and object, but humble minds glean and receive benefit. A humble heart is a great help toward profitably hearing the Gospel. The soul-saving *"engrafted word"* (James 1:21) is not received except with meekness. A stiff back makes for bad gleaning. Pride is a vile robber, not to be endured for a moment. What the gleaner gathers, she holds. If she were to drop one ear to find another, the result of her day's work would be meager. She is as careful to retain as to obtain, so that in the end her gains are great. How often do I forget all that I hear; a second truth pushes the first out of my head, and so my reading and hearing end in much ado about nothing! Do I have the proper conviction of the importance of storing up the truth? A hungry stomach makes the gleaner wise. If there is no corn in her hand, there will be no bread on her table. She labors under a sense of necessity; therefore, she walks nimbly, and her grasp is firm. I have an even greater need. Lord, help me to be convinced of this need, so that it may urge me onward to glean in fields that yield so plenteous a reward to diligence.

The Lamb is the light thereof.
—Revelation 21:23

Quietly contemplate the Lamb as the light of heaven. Light in Scripture is the symbol of joy. The joy of the saints in heaven is comprised of this: Jesus chose us, loved us, bought us, cleansed us, robed us, kept us, and glorified us. We are here entirely through the Lord Jesus. Each one of these thoughts is like a cluster of the grapes of Eshcol. Light is also the cause of beauty. Nothing of beauty is left when light is gone. Without light no radiance flashes from the sapphire, no peaceful ray proceeds from the pearl; thus, all the beauty of the saints above comes from Jesus. As planets, they reflect the light of the Sun of Righteousness; they live as beams proceeding from the central orb. If He withdrew, they would die; if His glory were veiled, their glory would expire. Light is also the symbol of knowledge. In heaven our knowledge will be perfect, but the Lord Jesus Himself will be the fountain of it. Dark providences, never understood before, will then be clearly seen, and all that puzzles us now will become plain to us in the light of the Lamb. Oh, what revelations there will be and what glorifying of the God of love! Light also means manifestation. Light manifests. In this world it does *"not yet appear what we shall be"* (1 John 3:2). God's people are a hidden people, but when Christ receives His people into heaven, He will touch them with the wand of His own love and change them into the image of His manifested glory. They were poor and wretched, but what a transformation! They were stained with sin, but one touch of His finger, and they are as bright as the sun and as clear as crystal. Oh, what a manifestation! All this proceeds from the exalted Lamb. Whatever there may be of radiant splendor, Jesus will be the center and soul of it all. Oh, to be present and to see Him in His own light, the King of Kings and Lord of Lords!

But as he went.
—Luke 8:42

The context of our text is that Jesus is moving through the crowd toward the house of Jairus, to raise the ruler's dead daughter. However, Jesus is so abounding in goodness that He works another miracle while traveling on the road. Even while this *"rod of Aaron"* (Num. 17:8) bears the blossom of a latent miracle, it yields the ripe almonds of a perfect work of mercy. It is enough for us, if we have one purpose, to go and accomplish it right away. It would be imprudent for us to expend our energies along the way. If we were rushing to rescue a drowning friend, we could not afford to exhaust our strength on another in similar danger. It is enough for a tree to yield one kind of fruit, and for a man to fulfill his own particular calling. But our Master knows no limitation of power or boundary of mission. He is so prolific in grace that, like the sun that shines as it turns in its orbit, His path is radiant with lovingkindness. He is a swift arrow of love that not only reaches its ordained target but also perfumes the air through which it flies. Power is always emanating from Jesus, as sweet scents waft from flowers; it always will be flowing from Him, as water from a sparkling fountain. What delightful encouragement this truth affords us! If our Lord is so ready to heal the sick and bless the needy, then do not be slow to put yourself in His path, so that He may smile on you. Do not be slack in asking, since He gives so abundantly. Pay close attention to His Word now, and at all times, so that Jesus may speak through it to your heart. Frequent the place where He may be found, in order to obtain His blessing. When He is present to heal, will He not heal you? Surely, He is present even now, for He always comes to hearts that need Him. Do you not need Him? He knows how much you need Him! Son of David, turn Your eyes and look upon the distress that is now before You, and make Your petitioner whole.

The people that do know their God shall be strong.
—Daniel 11:32

Every believer understands that to know God is the highest and best form of knowledge. This spiritual knowledge is a source of strength to the Christian. It strengthens his faith. Believers are constantly spoken of in the Scriptures as being persons who are enlightened and taught of the Lord; they are said to *"have an unction from the Holy One"* (1 John 2:20), and it is the Spirit's special office to lead them into all truth, and all this for the increase and the fostering of their faith. Knowledge strengthens love, as well as faith. Knowledge opens the door, and then, through that door, we see our Savior. To use another metaphor, knowledge paints the portrait of Jesus, and when we see that portrait, then, we love Him. We cannot love a Christ whom we do not know, at least, in some degree. If we know only a little of the virtues of Jesus, what He has done for us, and what He is doing now, we cannot love Him much; but the more we know Him, the more we will love Him. Knowledge also strengthens hope. How can we hope for a thing if we do not know of its existence? Hope may be the telescope, but until we receive instruction, our ignorance stands in front of the glass, and we can see nothing whatsoever. Knowledge removes the interposing object, and when we look through the bright glass, we discern the glory to be revealed and anticipate it with joyous confidence. Knowledge supplies us reasons for patience. How will we have patience unless we know something of the sympathy of Christ and understand the good that is to come out of the correction that our heavenly Father sends us? Nor is there one single grace of the Christian that, under God, will not be fostered and brought to perfection by holy knowledge. How important, then, is it that we should grow not only *"in grace,"* but also *"in the knowledge of our Lord and Savior Jesus Christ"* (2 Pet. 3:18).

AUGUST 4

*I smote you with [blight] and with mildew and with hail
in all the labours of your hands.*
—Haggai 2:17

How destructive hail is to standing crops, beating the precious grain to the ground! How grateful we ought to be when the corn is spared so terrible a ruin. Let us offer thanksgiving to the Lord. Even more to be dreaded are those mysterious destroyers—disease and mildew. These spoilers turn an ear of corn into a mass of blackness; they render it putrid or dry it up—all in a manner so beyond human control that the farmer is compelled to cry, "This is the hand of God!" Innumerable, minute fungi cause the damage. If it were not for the goodness of God, the rider on the black horse would soon scatter famine over the land. Infinite mercy spares the food of men; however, in view of the active agents that are ready to destroy the harvest, we are very wisely taught to pray, *"Give us this day our daily bread"* (Matt. 6:11). The curse is widespread; we are in constant need of blessing. When blight and mildew come, they are often chastisements from heaven, and men must learn to recognize and heed God's correction. Spiritually, mildew is not an uncommon evil. When our work is most promising, this blight appears. Perhaps we had hoped for many conversions, but instead were met by a general apathy, an abounding worldliness, or a cruel hardness of heart. There may be no obvious sin in those for whom we are laboring, but rather a deficiency of sincerity and decision that sadly disappoints our desires. From these experiences, we learn that we must depend on the Lord and pray that no blight may fall on our work. Spiritual pride or sloth may soon bring on us the dreadful evil, and only the Lord of the harvest can remove it. Mildew may even attack our own hearts, shriveling our prayers and devotion. May it please the great Husbandman to avert so serious a calamity. Shine, blessed Sun of Righteousness, and drive the blights away!

We know that all things work together for good
to them that love God.
—Romans 8:28

On some points a believer is absolutely sure. He knows, for instance, that God sits with the passengers of the vessel when it rocks the most. He believes that an invisible hand is always on the world's tiller, and that wherever providence may lead the vessel, Jehovah steers it. That reassuring knowledge prepares him for everything. He looks over the raging waters and sees the spirit of Jesus treading the billows. He hears a voice saying, *"It is I; be not afraid"* (Matt. 14:27). He knows, too, that God is always wise; knowing this, he is confident that there can be no accidents, no mistakes. Nothing can occur that should not happen. He can say, "If I would lose all that I have, it is better that I should lose it than keep it, if God so wills. The worst calamity is the wisest and the kindest thing that could happen to me if God ordains it." *"We know that all things work together for good to them that love God."* The Christian does not merely hold this as a theory, but he knows it as a matter of fact. Everything has worked for good so far. The poisonous drugs mixed in proper proportions have worked the cure; the sharp cuts of the scalpel have cleansed out the ulcerous flesh and facilitated the healing. Every event thus far has worked out the most divinely blessed results. And so, believing that God rules all, that He governs wisely, that He brings good out of evil, the believer's heart is assured, and he is enabled calmly to meet each trial as it comes. The believer can in the spirit of true resignation pray, "Send me what You will, my God, as long as it comes from You. A bad portion has never come from Your table to any of Your children." Do not say, my soul,

> From whence can God relieve my care?
> Remember that Omnipotence has servants everywhere.
> His method is sublime; His heart profoundly kind.
> God never is before His time and never is behind.

AUGUST 5

Shall your brethren go to war, and shall ye sit here?
—Numbers 32:6

Family relationships have their obligations. The Reubenites and Gadites would have been unbrotherly if they had claimed the land that had been conquered, but had left the rest of the people to fight for their own land (Joshua 1:12–16). We in the church have received much by means of the efforts and sufferings of the saints in years past. If we do not make some repayment to the church of Christ by giving her our best energies, we are unworthy to be enrolled in her ranks. Others are combating the errors of the age manfully or excavating perishing ones from amid the ruins of the Fall. If we fold our hands in idleness, we must be warned, lest the curse of Meroz falls upon us. (See Judges 5:23.) The Master of the vineyard says, *"Why stand ye here all the day idle?"* (Matt. 20:6). What is the idler's excuse? Personal service for Jesus becomes all the more the duty of everyone because it is cheerfully and abundantly offered by some. The efforts of devoted missionaries and fervent ministers shame us if we sit in laziness. Shrinking from trial is the temptation of those who are *"at ease in Zion"* (Amos 6:1). They would be happy to escape the cross, yet wear the crown. To them, the question of this evening's meditation is very applicable. If the most precious of God's servants are tried in the fire, can we expect to escape the crucible? If a diamond must be distressed while it is being cleaved, cut, and polished, are we to be made perfect without suffering? Do we expect the wind to cease from blowing simply because our ship is at sea? Why should we be treated better than our Lord? If the Firstborn felt the rod, why shouldn't His younger brothers and sisters? It is cowardly pride that would choose a soft pillow and bed for a soldier of the Cross. Far wiser is the person who first submits to the divine will and then grows to be pleased with it through the operations of grace. He will learn to gather lilies at the foot of the cross and, like Samson, to find honey in the lion. (See Judges 14:1–9.)

Watchman, what of the night?
—Isaiah 21:11

What enemies are abroad? Numerous errors abound, and new ones appear every hour. What heresy must I guard against? Sins creep from their lurking places when darkness reigns. I must climb the watchtower and be attentive in prayer. Our heavenly Protector foresees all the attacks that are about to be made on us, and when as yet the evil designed for us is but Satan's desire, Jesus prays for us that our faith will not fail, when Satan tries to "*sift* [us] *as wheat*" (Luke 22:31). Continue, O gracious Watchman, to forewarn us of our foes, and for Zion's sake do not hold Your peace. "*Watchman, what of the night?*" What weather is coming for the church? Are the clouds lowering, or is it all clear and fair overhead? We must care for the church of God with anxious love; and now that infidelity is threatening, let us observe the signs of the times and prepare for conflict. "*Watchman, what of the night?*" What stars are visible? What precious promises suit our present case? You sound the alarm; give us the consolation also. Christ, the North Star, is ever fixed in His place, and all the stars are secure in the right hand of their Lord. But watchman, when will the morning come? The Bridegroom tarries. Are there no signs of His coming forth as the Sun of Righteousness? Has not the morning star arisen as the pledge of day? When will the day dawn, and the shadows flee away? O Jesus, if You do not come in person to Your waiting church this day, then come in Spirit to my sighing heart, and make it sing for joy.

> Now all the earth is bright and glad
>> With the fresh morn;
> But all my heart is cold, and dark and sad:
> Sun of the soul, let me behold Thy dawn!
>> Come, Jesus, Lord,
> O quickly come, according to Thy word.

Let the whole earth be filled with his glory; Amen, and Amen.
—Psalm 72:19

This is an enormous request. To intercede for a whole city requires us to stretch our faith, and there are times when prayer for one person is enough to stagger us. But how far-reaching was the psalmist's intercession! How comprehensive! How sublime! *"Let the whole earth be filled with his glory."* This prayer does not exempt a single country, no matter how crushed it may be by the foot of superstition. It does not exclude a single nation, no matter how barbarous it may be. This prayer was spoken for the cannibal as well as for the civilized person—for all regions and races. It encompasses the entire circumference of the earth and omits no child of Adam. We must be up and doing for our Master, or we cannot honestly offer such a prayer. We are not praying this prayer with a sincere heart if we are not endeavoring, as God helps us, to extend the kingdom of our Master. Are there not some who neglect both intercession and work? Reader, is the prayer of our text also your prayer? Turn your eyes to Calvary. See the Lord of Life nailed to the cross, with the crown of thorns on His brow, with His bleeding head, hands, and feet. What! Can you look upon this miracle of miracles—the death of the Son of God—without feeling within your heart a marvelous adoration that language could never express? When you perceive that the blood has been applied to your conscience and know that He has blotted out your sins, you are not a true believer unless you fall to your knees and cry out, *"Let the whole earth be filled with his glory; Amen, and Amen."* How can you bow before the Crucified One in loving homage, then not wish to see your Monarch take His rightful place as Master of the world? Shame on you if you can pretend to love your Prince, but not desire to see Him as the Universal Ruler. Your piety is worthless unless it leads you to wish that the same mercy that has been extended to you may bless the whole world. Lord, it is harvesttime. Put in Your sickle and reap.

The upright love thee.
—Song of Solomon 1:4

Believers love Jesus with a deeper affection than they dare to give to any other being. They would sooner lose father and mother than part with Christ. They hold all earthly comforts with a loose hand, but they carry Him locked securely in their hearts. They voluntarily deny themselves for His sake, but they are not to be driven to deny Him. It is a meager love that the fire of persecution can dry up; the true believer's love is a deeper stream than this. Men have labored to divide the faithful from their Master, but their attempts have been fruitless in every age. Neither crowns of honor nor frowns of anger have untied this Gordian knot. This is no everyday attachment that the world's power may at length dissolve. Neither man nor devils have found a key that opens this lock. Never has the craft of Satan been more at fault than when he has exercised it in seeking to tear apart this union of two divinely welded hearts. It is written, and nothing can blot out the sentence, *"The upright love thee."* The intensity of the love of the upright, however, is not so much to be judged by what it appears as by what the upright long for. It is our daily lament that we cannot love enough. Would that our hearts were capable of holding more and reaching further. Like Samuel Rutherford, we sigh and cry, "Oh, for as much love as would go round about the earth, and over heaven—yea, the heaven of heavens, and ten thousand worlds—that I might let all out upon fair, fair, only fair Christ." Alas, our longest reach is but a span of love, and our affection is but a drop in a bucket compared with what He is due. Measure our love by our intentions, and it is high indeed; we trust that this is how our Lord judges it. Oh, that we could give all the love in all hearts in one great mass, a gathering together of all loves to Him who *"is altogether lovely"* (Song 5:16)!

Satan hindered us.
—1 Thessalonians 2:18

From the first hour that goodness came into conflict with evil, it has never ceased to be true in spiritual experience that Satan hinders us. From all points of the compass, all along the battle lines—in the front and in the rear—at the dawn of day and in the midnight hour, Satan hinders us. If we toil in a field, he seeks to break the plow. If we build a wall, he works to knock down the stones. If we desire to serve God in suffering or in conflict, Satan hinders us. He hinders us everywhere. He hindered us when we first came to Jesus Christ. We had fierce conflicts with Satan when we first looked to the cross and lived. Now that we are saved, he endeavors to hinder the perfection of our personal characters. You may be congratulating yourself, saying, "I have walked consistently this far; no one can challenge my integrity." Beware of boasting, for your character will yet be tested. Satan will direct his schemes against the very character quality for which you are the most famous. If you have been a firm believer up to this point, your faith will be attacked before long. If you have been as meek as Moses, expect to be tempted to speak unadvisedly. The birds will peck at your ripest fruit, and the wild boar will dash his tusks at your choicest vines. Satan is sure to hinder us when we are earnest in prayer. He impedes our prayers and weakens our faith so that, if possible, we may miss the blessing. Satan is no less vigilant in obstructing Christian ministry. There never has been a revival of religion without a revival of his opposition. As soon as Ezra and Nehemiah began to work, Sanballat and Tobiah were stirred up to hinder them. (See Nehemiah 1–6; 8, especially 4:7–8.) What are we to do about these attacks of the enemy? We are not to be alarmed when Satan hinders us, for it is proof that we are on the Lord's side and are doing the Lord's work. In His strength, we will win the victory and triumph over our adversary.

They…weave the spider's web.
—Isaiah 59:5

Look at a spider's web, and see in it a most suggestive picture of the hypocrite's religion. It is meant to catch its prey: the spider fattens himself on flies, and the Pharisee has his reward. Foolish persons are easily entrapped by the loud professions of pretenders, and even the more judicious cannot always escape. Philip baptized Simon Magus, whose guileful declaration of faith was soon exploded by the stern rebuke of Peter. Custom, reputation, praise, advancement, and other flies are the small game that hypocrites capture in their nets. A spider's web is a marvel of skill: look at it and admire the cunning hunter's wiles. Is not a deceiver's religion equally wonderful? How does he make so barefaced a lie appear to be the truth? How can he make his tinsel answer so well the purpose of gold? A spider's web comes all from the creature's own insides. The bee gathers its wax from flowers; the spider sucks no flowers, yet it spins out its material to any length. In the same way, a hypocrite finds his trust and hope within himself; his anchor is forged on his own anvil, and his cable is twisted by his own hands. He lays his own foundation and hews out the pillars of his own house, disdaining to be a debtor to the sovereign grace of God. But a spider's web is very frail. It is curiously wrought, but not enduringly manufactured. It is no match for the servant's broom or the traveler's staff. The hypocrite needs no battery of high-pressure hydraulics to blow his hope to pieces; a mere puff of wind will do it. Hypocritical cobwebs will soon come down when the broom of destruction begins its purifying work. This reminds us of one more thought: such cobwebs are not to be endured in the Lord's house. He will see to it that they and those who spin them will be destroyed forever. Oh, my soul, rest on something better than a spider's web. May the Lord Jesus be your eternal hiding place.

All things are possible to him that believeth.
—Mark 9:23

Many professing Christians are constantly filled with doubt and fear. They forlornly think that this state of affairs is inevitable for a believer. This kind of thinking is a mistake, for *"all things are possible to him that believeth."* It is possible for us to reach a state in which a doubt or a fear will be to us as a migratory bird—flitting across the soul but never lingering there. When you read of the exalted and sweet communion enjoyed by favored saints, you sigh and murmur in your heart, "It is a pity that these blessings are not for me." O spiritual climber, if you will only have faith, you will yet stand on the sunny pinnacle of the temple, for *"all things are possible to him that believeth."* You hear of the exploits that holy men and women have done for Jesus—what they have enjoyed of Him, how much they have been like Him, and how they have been able to endure great persecution for His sake—and you say, "I am but a worm; I can never attain to that." However, there is nothing that one saint was that you cannot be. There is no height of grace, no attainment of spirituality, no clearness of assurance, no post of duty that is not open to you if you have the power to believe. Lay aside your sackcloth and ashes, and rise to the dignity of your true position. You are little in God's kingdom because you allow this to be the case, not because there is any necessity for it. It is not fitting that you should grovel in the dust, O child of the King. Ascend! The golden throne of assurance is waiting for you. The crown of communion with Jesus is ready to adorn your head. Wrap yourself in scarlet and fine linen, and eat sumptuously every day. For, if you believe, you may eat the choicest of wheat. Your land will flow with milk and honey, and your soul will be satisfied as with the richest and most abundant food. Gather golden sheaves of grace, for they await you in the fields of faith. *"All things are possible to him that believeth."*

The city had no need of the sun, neither of the moon, to shine in it.
—Revelation 21:23

Yonder in the better world, the inhabitants are independent of all creature comforts. They have no need of clothing. Their white robes never wear out; neither will they ever be defiled. They require no medicine to heal diseases, for the inhabitants will never need to say, "I am sick." They do not need any sleep to refresh their bodies. They do not rest day or night, but without ever growing weary, they praise Him in His temple. They have no need of social relationships to bring them comfort. Whatever happiness they may derive from association with their fellow saints is not essential to their bliss, for their Lord's presence is enough for their largest desires. They have no need for teachers there. Undoubtedly, they talk with one another concerning the things of God, but they do not require this by way of instruction; they will all *"be taught of the Lord"* (Isa. 54:13). Ours are the alms at the king's gate, but they feast at the table itself. Here we lean on a friendly arm, but there they lean on their Beloved and on Him alone. Here we must have the help of our companions, but there they find all they need in Christ Jesus. Here we look to meat that perishes and to clothing that can be destroyed by moths, but there they find everything in God. We use a bucket to fetch water from the well, but there they drink from the Fountainhead and put their lips to the living water. Here the angels bring us blessings, but we will need no messengers from heaven then. They need no Gabriels there to bring them love notes from God, for there they will see Him face to face. Oh, what a blessed time that will be when we rest in the arms of God! What a glorious hour when God, and not His creatures; the Lord, and not His works, will be our daily joy! Our souls will then have attained the perfection of bliss.

AUGUST 9
Evening

He appeared first to Mary Magdalene,
out of whom he had cast seven devils.
—Mark 16:9

Mary of Magdala was the victim of a dreadful evil. She was not possessed by only one demon but by seven. These frightful inmates caused much pain and defilement to the poor body in which they had found a lodging. Hers was a hopeless, horrible case. She could not help herself, nor could any human help avail. Yet Jesus passed her way. Unsought by the poor demoniac, and probably even resisted by her, He uttered the word of power, and Mary of Magdala became a striking example of the healing power of Jesus. All seven demons left her, never to return—forcibly ejected by the Lord of all. What a blessed deliverance! What a happy change! She went from delirium to delight, from despair to peace, from hell to heaven! Mary immediately became a constant follower of Jesus, hanging on His every word, following His itinerant steps, sharing His difficult life. She also became His generous helper. She was the first among the group of healed and grateful women who followed Jesus to minister to Him out of her substance. When Jesus was lifted up in crucifixion, Mary stayed to share in His shame. We first find her looking at Him from afar, and then drawing near to the foot of the cross. She could not die on the cross with Jesus, but she stood as near to it as she could. When His blessed body was taken down, she watched to see how and where it was laid. She was the faithful and watchful believer—last at the tomb where Jesus slept in death, first at the grave from which He arose. Her holy faithfulness made her a favored witness of her beloved *"Rabboni"* (John 20:16)—who graciously called her by name and made her His messenger of good news to Peter and the other frightened disciples. Thus grace found her when she was a deranged demoniac and made her into a minister; grace cast demons out of her, granted her to see angels, delivered her from Satan, and united her forever to the Lord Jesus. May I also be such a miracle of grace!

Christ, who is our life.
—Colossians 3:4

Paul's marvelously rich expression indicates that Christ is the source of our lives. *"You hath he quickened, who were dead in trespasses and sins"* (Eph. 2:1). The same voice that brought Lazarus out of the tomb raised us to *"newness of life"* (Rom. 6:4). He is now the substance of our spiritual life. It is by His life that we live. He is in us, the hope of glory, the spring of our actions, the central thought that directs every other thought. Christ is the sustenance of our lives. What can the Christian feed on but Jesus' flesh and blood? *"This is the bread which cometh down from heaven, that a man may eat thereof, and not die"* (John 6:50). Oh, weary pilgrims in this wilderness of sin, you never get a morsel to satisfy the hunger of your spirits, unless you find it in Him! Christ is the solace of our lives. All our true joys come from Him; and in times of trouble, His presence is our consolation. There is nothing worth living for but Him; and His *"lovingkindness is better than life"* (Ps. 63:3)! Christ is the object of our lives. As the ship speeds toward the port, so the believer hurries toward the haven of his Savior's heart. As the arrow flies to its target, so the Christian flies toward the perfecting of his fellowship with Christ Jesus. As the soldier fights for his captain and is honored by his captain's victory, so the believer contends for Christ and receives his triumph out of the triumphs of his Master. For him *"to live is Christ"* (Phil. 1:21). Christ is the example of our lives. Where there is the same life within, there will, there must be to a great extent, the same developments without. If we live in close fellowship with the Lord Jesus, we will grow like Him. We will set Him before us as our divine Example, and we will seek to walk in His footsteps, until He becomes the crown of our lives in glory. Oh, how safe, how honored, how happy is the Christian, since Christ is his life!

The Son of man hath power on earth to forgive sins.
—Matthew 9:6

Note one of the Great Physician's mightiest skills: He has the power to forgive sin! While He lived here on earth—before the ransom had been paid, before His blood had been sprinkled on the mercy seat—He had the power to forgive sin. Therefore, does He not have the power to forgive sin now that He has died? What power must dwell in Him who, to the last penny, has faithfully discharged the debts of His people! He has boundless power now that He has accomplished what was needed to pay for our transgressions and has made an end of sin (Dan. 9:24). If you doubt this truth, think of Him rising from the dead. See Him in ascending splendor raised to the right hand of God. Hear Him interceding before the eternal Father, pointing to His wounds, urging the merit of His sacred suffering. What power to forgive He has! He *"hast ascended on high"* and *"hast received gifts for men"* (Ps. 68:18). He is exalted on high to give repentance and remission of sins (Acts 5:31). The most crimson of sins are removed by the crimson of His blood. At this moment, dear reader, whatever your sinfulness, Christ has power to pardon—power to pardon *you,* and millions like you. A word from Him will grant it. He has nothing more to accomplish in order to win your pardon; all the atoning work is done. He can, in answer to your tears, forgive your sins today and cause you to know that He has done so. At this very moment, He can breathe into your soul a peace with God *"which passeth all understanding"* (Phil. 4:7), which will spring from perfect forgiveness of your many iniquities. Do you believe this? I trust that you believe it. May you experience now the power of Jesus to forgive sin. Waste no time in appealing to the Physician of souls, but hurry to Him with words like these: "Jesus, Master, hear my cry! Save me; heal me with a word."

Fainting at Your feet I lie,
You my whisper'd plaint have heard.

Oh that I were as in months past.
—Job 29:2

Numbers of Christians can view the past with pleasure, but regard the present with dissatisfaction. They look back on the days that they have passed in communing with the Lord as being the sweetest and the best they have ever known, but the present is clad in a sable garb of gloom and dreariness. Once they lived near to Jesus, but now they feel that they have wandered from Him, and they say, *"Oh that I were as in months past."* They complain that they have lost their assurance, that they are not experiencing present peace of mind, that they have no enjoyment in the means of grace, that their consciences are not so tender, or that they no longer have as much zeal for God's glory. The causes of this mournful state of things are manifold. It may arise through a comparative neglect of prayer, for a neglected prayer life is the beginning of all spiritual decline. Or it may be the result of idolatry. The heart has been occupied with something else, more than with God; the affections have been set on the things of earth, instead of on the things of heaven. A jealous God will not be content with a divided heart. He must be loved first and best. He will withdraw the sunshine of His presence from a cold, wandering heart. Or the cause may be found in self-confidence and self-righteousness. Pride is busy in the heart, and self is exalted instead of lying low at the foot of the cross. Christian, if you are not now as you *"were...in months past,"* do not rest satisfied with wishing for a return of former happiness, but go at once to seek your Master and tell Him about your sad state. Ask for His grace and strength to help you to walk more closely with Him. Humble yourself before Him, and He will lift you up and cause you yet again to enjoy the light of His countenance. Do not sit down to sigh and lament. While the beloved Physician lives, there is hope; no, there is a certainty of recovery for the worst cases.

Everlasting consolation.
—2 Thessalonians 2:16

Consolation." There is music in this word. Like David's harp, it chases away the evil spirit of melancholy (1 Sam. 16:23). It was a distinguished honor to Barnabas to be called *"the son of consolation"* (Acts 4:36). Indeed, this word is one of the illustrious names of One greater than Barnabas, for the Lord Jesus is *"the consolation of Israel"* (Luke 2:25). *"Everlasting consolation"*—this is the best part of all, for an eternity of comfort is our crown and glory. What is this *"everlasting consolation"*? It includes a sense of pardoned sin. A Christian has received in his heart the witness of the Spirit that his iniquities are *"blotted out...as a cloud"* and his transgressions *"as a thick cloud"* (Isa. 44:22). If sin is pardoned, is that not an *"everlasting consolation"*? Next, the Lord gives His people an abiding sense of acceptance in Christ. The Christian knows that God looks upon him as standing in union with Jesus. Union with the risen Lord is a consolation of the most abiding kind; it is, in fact, everlasting. Even if sickness sidelines us, have we not seen hundreds of believers as happy in the weakness of disease as they would have been in bodily strength and robust health? Even if death's arrows pierce us to the heart, our comfort does not die. Have not our ears very often heard the songs of dying saints while they have rejoiced as the living love of God was poured out into their hearts? Yes, a sense of acceptance in the Beloved is an *"everlasting consolation."* Moreover, the Christian has a conviction of his security. God has promised to save those who trust in Christ. The Christian does trust in Christ. He believes that God will be as good as His Word and will save him. He believes that he is safe by virtue of his being bound up with the person and work of Jesus.

The LORD reigneth; let the earth rejoice.
—Psalm 97:1

There are no reasons for anxiety as long as today's blessed text is true. On earth, the Lord's power as readily controls the rage of the wicked as the rage of the sea. His love as easily refreshes the poor with mercy as the earth with showers. Majesty gleams in flashes of fire amid the tempest's horrors, and the glory of the Lord is seen in its grandeur in the fall of empires and the crash of thrones. In all our conflicts and tribulations, we may behold the hand of the divine King.

> God is God; He sees and hears
> All our troubles, all our tears.
> Soul, forget not, 'mid thy pains,
> God o'er all forever reigns.

In hell, evil spirits acknowledge, with misery, His undoubted supremacy. When they are permitted to roam abroad, it is with a chain at their heels. The bit is in the mouth of the behemoth, and the hook in the jaws of the leviathan. Death's darts are under the Lord's lock, and the grave's prisons have divine power as their warden. The terrible vengeance of the Judge of all the earth makes fiends cower and tremble, even as dogs fear the hunter's whip.

> Fear not death, nor Satan's thrusts,
> God defends who in Him trusts;
> Soul, remember, in thy pains,
> God o'er all forever reigns.

In heaven, none doubt the sovereignty of the King Eternal, but all fall on their faces to pay Him homage. Angels are His courtiers, the redeemed His favorites, and all delight to serve Him day and night. May we soon reach the city of the great King!

> For this life's long night of sadness
> He will give us peace and gladness.
> Soul, remember, in thy pains,
> God o'er all forever reigns.

AUGUST 12
Evening

The bow shall be seen in the cloud.
—Genesis 9:14

The rainbow, the symbol of God's covenant with Noah, is a type of the Lord Jesus, who is God's witness to the people. When may we expect to see the sign of the covenant? The rainbow can only be seen painted against the backdrop of clouds. When a sinner's conscience is dark with clouds, when he remembers his past sin, mourns over it, and repents before God, Jesus Christ is revealed to him as the covenant Rainbow, displaying all the glorious colors of the divine character as a testimony to the sinner's peace with God. When a believer's trials and temptations surround him, it is sweet for him to think about the Lord Jesus Christ—to remember how He lived, bled, rose, and is even now interceding for His people. God's Rainbow is placed over the cloud of our sins, our sorrows, and our afflictions, to prophesy deliverance. A cloud alone does not produce a rainbow; there must also be raindrops to reflect the light of the sun. In the same way, sorrow for sin must not only threaten to fall on us, but must really fall on us, if we are to see God's Rainbow. Note that Christ would not have been our Redeemer if the vengeance of God had been merely a threatening cloud. Punishment had to fall in terrible drops upon our Surety. Until there is *real* anguish in the sinner's conscience, Christ cannot be his Savior. Until the conviction that the sinner experiences becomes grievous, he cannot see Jesus. But there must also be a sun, for clouds and drops of rain do not create rainbows unless the sun also shines. Beloved, our God, who is as the sun to us, always shines, but we do not always see Him—clouds hide His face. Yet no matter what drops may be falling or what clouds may be threatening, if He shines, there will be a rainbow at once. It is said that when we see a rainbow, the rain showers are over. Certainly, when Christ comes, our troubles leave. When we see Jesus, our sins vanish and our doubts and fears subside. When Jesus walks the waters of the sea, how profound the calm is!

The cedars of Lebanon, which he hath planted.
—Psalm 104:16

Lebanon's cedars are symbolic of the Christian, in that they owe their planting entirely to the Lord. This is quite true of every child of God. He is not man-planted or self-planted, but God-planted. The mysterious hand of the divine Spirit dropped the living seed into a heart that He had Himself prepared for its reception. Every true heir of heaven acknowledges the great Husbandman as his planter. Moreover, the cedars of Lebanon are not dependent on man for their watering. They stand on the lofty rock, not moistened by human irrigation, yet our heavenly Father provides for them. Thus it is with the Christian who has learned to live by faith. He is independent of man, even in temporal things. For his continued maintenance, he looks to the Lord his God, and to Him alone. The dew of heaven is his portion, and the God of heaven is his fountain. Again, the cedars of Lebanon are not protected by any mortal power. They owe nothing to man for their preservation from stormy wind and tempest. They are God's trees, kept and preserved by Him, and by Him alone. It is precisely the same with the Christian. He is not a hothouse plant, sheltered from temptation; he stands in the most exposed position. He has no shelter, no protection, except this: the broad wings of the eternal God always cover the cedars that He Himself has planted. Like cedars, believers are full of sap having vitality enough to always be green, even amid winter's snows. Last, the flourishing and majestic condition of the cedar is to the praise of God only. The Lord, even the Lord alone, has been everything to the cedars; therefore, David very sweetly put it in one of the psalms, *"Praise the LORD...fruitful trees, and all cedars"* (Ps. 148:7, 9). In the believer there is nothing that can magnify man. He is planted, nourished, and protected by the Lord's own hand, and to Him let all the glory be ascribed!

AUGUST 13

And I will remember my covenant.
—Genesis 9:15

Note the form of this promise. God did not say, "When you look upon the rainbow, and *you* remember My covenant, then I will not destroy the earth." The promise does not depend on our memories, which are fickle and frail; instead, it gloriously rests on God's memory, which is infinite and unchanging. *"The bow shall be in the cloud; and I will look upon it, that I may remember the everlasting covenant"* (v. 16). It is not my remembering God and my laying hold of His covenant, but it is God's remembering me and His covenant's laying hold of me that is the basis of my safety. Glory to God! All the fortresses of salvation are secured by divine power. Even the minor towers, which we may think are left to man to defend, are guarded by almighty strength. Even the remembrance of the covenant is not left to our memories. We might forget, but our Lord cannot forget the saints whom He has engraved on the palms of His hands (Isa. 49:16). It is with us as it was with Israel in Egypt. The blood was put on the tops and the two sides of the doorframes. The Lord did not say, "When you see the blood, I will pass over you," but, "When I see the blood, I will pass over you." (See Exodus 12:22–23.) My looking to Jesus brings me joy and peace, but it is God's looking to Jesus that secures my salvation and that of all His elect. It is impossible for God to look at Christ, our bleeding Surety, and then to be angry with us for sins already punished in Jesus. No, it is not even left to us to be saved by remembering the covenant. There is no mismatched combination of linen and wool in Christ's sacrifice—not a single thread of mankind mars the fabric of salvation. Salvation is not of man or by man but of the Lord alone. We should remember the covenant, and we will do so, through divine grace. However, the hinge of our safety does not hang there. It is God's remembering us, not our remembering Him, that is our security. This is why the covenant is an *"everlasting covenant"* (Gen. 9:16).

AUGUST 14

Thou, LORD, hast made me glad through thy work.
—Psalm 92:4

Do you believe that your sins are forgiven and that Christ has made a full atonement for them? Then what a joyful Christian you ought to be! How you should live above the common trials and troubles of the world! Since sin is forgiven, can it matter what happens to you now? Luther said, "Smite, Lord, smite, for my sin is forgiven; if Thou hast but forgiven me, smite as hard as Thou wilt." In a similar spirit you may say, "Send sickness, poverty, losses, crosses, persecution; send what You will, for You have forgiven me, and my soul is glad." Christian, if you are thus saved, while you are glad, be grateful and loving. Cling to the cross that took your sin away; serve Him who served you. *"I beseech you therefore, brethren, by the mercies of God, that ye present your bodies a living sacrifice, holy, acceptable unto God, which is your reasonable service"* (Rom. 12:1). Do not let your zeal evaporate in some little exuberant outburst of song. Show your love in expressive ways. Love the brethren of Him who loved you. If there is a Mephibosheth anywhere who is lame or halt, help him for Jonathan's sake. If there is a poor tried believer, weep with him and bear his cross for the sake of Him who wept for you and carried your sins. Since you are thus forgiven freely for Christ's sake, go and tell to others the joyful news of pardoning mercy. Do not be content with this unspeakable blessing for yourself alone, but publish abroad the story of the Cross. Holy gladness and holy boldness will make you a good preacher, and all the world will be a pulpit for you to preach in. Cheerful holiness is the most forcible of sermons, but the Lord must give it to you. Seek it this morning before you go into the world. When it is the Lord's work in which we rejoice, we do not need to be afraid of being too glad.

I know their sorrows.
—Exodus 3:7

The child is comforted as he sings, "This my father knows." Will we not be comforted as we realize that our dear Friend and tender Soul-husband knows all about us? First, He is the Physician. If He knows all, there is no need for the patient to know. Calm down, you silly, fluttering heart; stop your prying, peeking, and mistrusting! What you do not know now, you will know later on. Meanwhile, Jesus, the beloved Physician, knows your soul in its adversity. Why does the patient need to analyze all the medicine or evaluate all the symptoms? This is the Physician's work, not mine. It is my business to trust and His to prescribe. If I cannot read His handwriting on the prescription, I will not become uneasy. I will rely on His unfailing skill to make everything clear in the results that are obtained, however mysteriously they are accomplished. Second, He is the Master, and His knowledge is to serve us instead of our own knowledge. We are to obey, not to judge: *"The servant knoweth not what his lord doeth"* (John 15:15). Should the architect explain his plans to every unskilled laborer on the project? If he knows his own intent, is that not enough? The clay on the potter's wheel cannot guess what shape it is being made into, but if the potter understands his art, what does it matter if the clay is ignorant? My Lord must no longer be cross-examined by one as ignorant as I. Third, He is the Head. All understanding centers in Him. Does an arm exercise judgment? Does a foot have comprehension? All the power to know lies in the head. Why should a member of the body have a brain of its own when the head fulfills every intellectual function for it? Therefore, when a believer is sick, he must place his comfort in the following truth: he may not be able to see the end result, but Jesus knows all. Sweet Lord, be our eyes, soul, and head at all times, and let us be content to know only what You choose to reveal.

Isaac went out to meditate in the field at the eventide.
—Genesis 24:63

Isaac spent his time in an admirable pursuit. If those who spend so many hours in idle company, light reading, and useless pastimes could learn wisdom, they would find more profitable society and more interesting engagements in meditation than in the vanities that now have such charms for them. We would all know more, live nearer to God, and grow in grace, if we were alone more. Meditation chews the cud and extracts the real nutriment from the mental food gathered elsewhere. When Jesus is the theme, meditation is sweet indeed. Isaac found Rebekah while engaged in private musings; many others have found their best beloved there. Isaac's choice of place was admirable as well. In the field we have a study hung round with texts for thought. From the cedar to the hyssop, from the soaring eagle down to the chirping grasshopper, from the blue expanse of heaven to a drop of dew, all things are full of teaching; and when the eye is divinely opened, that teaching flashes upon the mind far more vividly than from written books. Our little rooms are neither as healthy, as suggestive, as agreeable, or as inspiring as the fields. Let us count nothing common or unclean, but feel that all created things point to their Maker, and the field will at once be hallowed. Isaac's choice of time for meditation was also wise. The season of sunset as it draws a veil over the day befits that repose of the soul when earthly cares yield to the joys of heavenly communion. The glory of the setting sun excites our wonder, and the solemnity of approaching night awakens our awe. If the business of this day will permit it, it will be well, dear reader, if you can spare an hour to walk in the field at eventide; if not, the Lord is in the town, too, and will meet with you in your house or on the crowded street. Let your heart go forth to meet Him.

AUGUST 15

Evening

And I will give you an heart of flesh.
—Ezekiel 36:26

A "*heart of flesh*" is known, first, by its tenderness concerning sin. To have indulged an impure thought or to have allowed a wild desire to linger, even for a moment, is quite enough to make a heart of flesh grieve before the Lord. A heart of stone (v. 26) will claim that a great iniquity is nothing, but a heart of flesh will not.

> If to the right or left I stray,
>   That moment, Lord, reprove;
> And let me weep my life away,
>   For having grieved Your love.

Second, a heart of flesh is tender toward God's will. The carnal will is very arrogant; it is hard to subject it to God's will. However, when a heart of flesh is given, the will quivers like an aspen leaf with every breath of heaven and bows like a willow with every breeze of God's Spirit. The natural will is like cold, hard iron, which cannot be hammered into form. Yet the renewed will, like molten metal, is soon molded by the hand of grace. Third, in a heart of flesh, there is a tenderness of the affections. The hard heart does not love the Redeemer, but the renewed heart burns with affection for Him. The hard heart is selfish and coldly demands, "Why should I weep for sin? Why should I love the Lord?" In contrast, the heart of flesh says, "Lord, '*thou knowest that I love thee*' (John 21:15). Help me to love You more!" Many are the privileges of this renewed heart.

> 'Tis here the Spirit dwells,
>   'Tis here that Jesus rests.

The renewed heart is ready to receive every spiritual blessing, and every blessing comes to it. It yields every heavenly fruit to the honor and praise of God. Therefore, the Lord delights in it. A tender heart is the best defense against sin and the best preparation for heaven. A renewed heart stands on its watchtower looking for the coming of the Lord Jesus. Do you have a "*heart of flesh*"?

AUGUST 16

Morning

Give unto the LORD the glory due unto his name.
—Psalm 29:2

God's glory is the result of His nature and acts. He is glorious in His character, for there is such a store of everything that is holy, good, and lovely in God that He must be glorious. The actions that flow from His character are also glorious; while He intends that they should manifest to His creatures His goodness, mercy, and justice, He is equally concerned that the glory associated with them should be given only to Himself. Nor is there anything in ourselves in which we may glory, for who makes us different from another? And what do we have that we did not receive from the God of all grace? Then how careful we should be to walk humbly before the Lord! The moment we glorify ourselves, since there is room for one glory only in the universe, we set ourselves up as rivals of the Most High. Will the insect of an hour glorify itself against the sun that warmed it into life? Will pottery exalt itself above the one who fashioned it on the wheel? Will the dust of the desert strive with the whirlwind? Or the drops of the ocean struggle with the tempest? Give to the Lord, all righteous people. *"Give unto the LORD the glory due unto his name."* Yet it is, perhaps, one of the hardest struggles of the Christian life to learn this sentence—*"Not unto us, O LORD, not unto us, but unto thy name give glory"* (Ps. 115:1). It is a lesson that God is ever teaching us, and teaching us sometimes through the most painful discipline. Let a Christian begin to boast, *"I can do all things,"* without adding *"through Christ which strengtheneth me"* (Phil. 4:13), and before long he will have to groan, *"I can do nothing,"* and moan himself into the dust. When we do anything for the Lord, and He is pleased to accept our actions, let us lay our crown at His feet and exclaim, *"Not I, but the grace of God which was with me"* (1 Cor. 15:10)!

Ourselves also, which have the firstfruits of the Spirit.
—Romans 8:23

Present possession is declared in this verse. At this present moment, we have the *"firstfruits of the Spirit."* We have repentance, that gem of purest luster; faith, that priceless pearl; hope, that heavenly emerald; and love, that glorious ruby. We already have been made new creations in Christ Jesus by the effective working of God the Holy Spirit. Salvation is considered the firstfruits because it comes first. The sheaf used in the wave offering was the first of the harvest. (See Leviticus 23:10–12.) Similarly, the spiritual life and all the graces that adorn that life are the first operations of the Spirit of God in our souls. The firstfruits were the pledge of the harvest. As soon as an Israelite had plucked the first handful of ripe ears, he looked forward with glad anticipation to harvesting his crop. In the same way, beloved, when God gives us things that are *"pure," "lovely,"* and *"of good report"* (Phil. 4:8) as the work of the Holy Spirit, these are a foretaste of the coming glory. The firstfruits were always holy to the Lord, and our new nature, with all its powers, is a consecrated thing. The new life is not ours that we should ascribe its excellence to our own merits. It is Christ's image and creation and is ordained for His glory. The firstfruits were not the harvest itself, and the works of the Spirit in us at this moment are not the consummation—perfection is yet to come. We must not boast that we have attained perfection, and thereby think that the sheaf for the wave offering is the entire produce of the year. We must *"hunger and thirst after righteousness"* (Matt. 5:6) and long for the day of full redemption. Dear reader, this evening, open your mouth wide, and God will fill it (Ps. 81:10). Let the blessing that you presently possess stir up in you a sacred craving for more grace. Groan within yourself for higher degrees of consecration, and your Lord will grant them to you. He is *"able to do exceeding abundantly above all that we ask or think"* (Eph. 3:20).

The mercy of God.
—Psalm 52:8

Meditate a little on this mercy of the Lord. It is *tender* mercy. With gentle, loving touch, He heals the broken in heart and binds up their wounds. He is as gracious in the manner of His mercy as in the matter of it. It is *great* mercy. There is nothing little in God. His mercy is like Himself: it is infinite. You cannot measure it. His mercy is so great that it forgives great sins to great sinners, after great lengths of time, and then, it gives great favors and great privileges, and raises us up to great enjoyments in the great heaven of the great God. It is *undeserved* mercy, as indeed all true mercy must be, for deserved mercy is only a misnomer for justice. There was no right on the sinner's part to the kind consideration of the Most High. Had the rebel been doomed at once to eternal fire, he would have truly deserved the sentence. But if he was delivered from wrath, sovereign love alone was the reason, for there was no goodness in the sinner himself. It is *rich* mercy. Some things are great, but have little efficacy in them, but this mercy is an encouragement to drooping spirits; a golden ointment to bleeding wounds; a heavenly bandage to broken bones; a royal chariot for weary feet; and an embrace of love for trembling hearts. It is *manifold* mercy. As Bunyan said, "All the flowers in God's garden are double." There is no single mercy. You may think you have but one mercy, but you will find it to be a whole cluster of mercies. It is *abounding* mercy. Millions have received it, yet far from its being exhausted, it is as fresh, as full, and as free as ever. It is *unfailing* mercy. It will never leave you. If mercy is your friend, mercy will be with you in temptation to keep you from yielding; with you in trouble to prevent you from sinking; with you in living to be the light and life of your countenance; and with you in dying to be the joy of your soul when earthly comfort is ebbing fast.

AUGUST 17
Evening

This sickness is not unto death.
—John 11:4

From the above words of our Lord, we learn that there is a limit to sickness. There is an *"unto"* within which the ultimate end of sickness is restrained, and beyond which it cannot go. Lazarus had to experience death, but death was not the final outcome of his sickness. In all sickness, the Lord says to the waves of pain, "This far you may go, but no farther." (See Job 38:11.) His steadfast purpose is the instruction—not the destruction—of His people. Wisdom hangs a thermometer at the mouth of the furnace of affliction and regulates the furnace's heat. The limitation on sickness is, first of all, encouragingly comprehensive. The God of providence has limited the time, manner, intensity, repetition, and effects of all our sicknesses. Each throb is decreed, each sleepless hour predestined, each relapse ordained, each depression of spirit foreknown, and each sanctifying result eternally purposed. Nothing great or small escapes the ordaining hand of Him who numbers the hairs of our heads (Matt. 10:30). Second, the limitation on sickness is wisely adapted to our strength, to the intended purpose of the sickness, and to the grace apportioned. Affliction does not come haphazardly. The weight of every stroke of the rod is accurately measured. He who made no mistakes in balancing the clouds and setting the boundaries of the heavens commits no errors in measuring out the ingredients that make up the medicine of souls. We cannot suffer too much or be relieved too late. Third, the limitation is tenderly set. The knife of the heavenly Surgeon never cuts deeper than is absolutely necessary. *"He doth not afflict willingly nor grieve the children of men"* (Lam. 3:33). A mother's heart cries, "Spare my child!" but no mother is more compassionate than our gracious God. When we consider how obstinate we are, it is a wonder that we are not driven with a sharper bit. It is very comforting to know that He who has set the boundaries of our habitation has also set the boundaries of our tribulation.

AUGUST 18

Strangers are come into the sanctuaries of the LORD's house.
—Jeremiah 51:51

In this account the faces of the Lord's people were covered with shame, for it was a terrible thing that men would intrude into the Holy Place that was reserved for the priests alone. Everywhere about us we see similar reasons for sorrow. How many ungodly men are now being educated with the view of entering the ministry! What a crying sin is that solemn lie by which our whole population is nominally included in a national church! How fearful it is that ordinances should be pressed upon the unconverted, and that among the more enlightened churches of our land, there should be such laxity of discipline. If the thousands who will read this portion will all take this matter before the Lord Jesus this day, He will intercede and avert the evil that otherwise will come on His church. To adulterate the church is to pollute a well, to pour water on fire, to sow a fertile field with stones. May we all have grace to maintain in our own proper way the purity of the church, as being an assembly of believers, and not an unsaved community of unconverted men. Our zeal must, however, begin at home. Let us examine ourselves as to our right to eat at the Lord's Table. Let us see to it that we have on our wedding garment, lest we ourselves be intruders in the Lord's sanctuaries. *"Many are called, but few are chosen"* (Matt. 22:14); *"strait is the gate, and narrow is the way, which leadeth unto life"* (Matt. 7:14). Oh, for grace to come to Jesus aright, with the faith of God's elect. He who smote Uzzah (see 2 Samuel 6:3–7) for touching the ark is very jealous of His two ordinances. As a true believer, I may approach them freely; as a stranger, I must not touch them lest I die. To search one's heart is the duty of all who are baptized or come to the Lord's Table. *"Search me, O God, and know my heart: try me, and know my thoughts"* (Ps. 139:23).

AUGUST 18

Evening

And they gave him to drink wine mingled with myrrh:
but he received it not.
—Mark 15:23

A golden truth is hidden in the fact that the Savior refused the cup of wine and myrrh. The Son of God stood on the heights of heaven before He became man. As He looked down upon our globe, He measured the long descent to the utmost depths of human misery. He added up the sum total of all the agonies that the Atonement would require, but He did not weaken at all. He solemnly determined that, to offer a sufficient atoning sacrifice, He must go the whole way—from the highest to the lowest, from the throne of highest glory to the cross of deepest misery. The cup of wine and myrrh, with its tranquilizing influence, would have kept Him a little within the utmost limits of misery. Therefore, He refused it. He would not stop short of all He had undertaken to suffer for His people. How many of us have longed to relieve our grief, which would have been injurious to us! Reader, have you never prayed, with a petulant and willful eagerness, to be released from difficult service or suffering? Perhaps providence has taken away from you the desire of your eyes with one stroke. Answer this, Christian: if you were to be told, "If you so desire, your loved one will live, but God will be dishonored," could you renounce the temptation and say, "*Thy will be done*" (Matt. 26:42)? Oh, it is sweet to be able to say, "My Lord, if I do not need to suffer for other reasons, but if I can honor You more by suffering, and if the loss of everything earthly that belongs to me will bring You glory, then let it be so. I refuse the comfort, if it stands in the way of Your honor." If only we would thus walk in the footsteps of our Lord— cheerfully enduring trial for His sake, promptly and willingly putting aside thoughts of self and comfort when they would interfere with our finishing the work He has given us to do. Great grace is needed if we are to walk in Christ's footsteps, but great grace is also provided.

AUGUST 19
Morning

He shall stand and feed in the strength of the LORD.
—Micah 5:4

Christ's reign in His church is that of a Shepherd-King. He has supremacy, but it is the superiority of a wise and tender Shepherd over His needy and loving flock. He commands and receives obedience, but it is the willing obedience of the well-cared-for sheep, rendered joyfully to their beloved Shepherd, whose voice they know so well. He rules by the force of love and the energy of goodness. His reign is practical in its character. It is said, *"He shall stand and feed."* The great Head of the church is actively engaged in providing for His people. He does not sit down on the throne in an empty state or hold a scepter without wielding it in government. No! He stands and feeds. The word *"feed,"* in the original, is analogous to one in the Greek that means to "shepherdize," to do everything expected of a shepherd: to guide, to watch, to preserve, to restore, to tend, as well as to feed. His reign is continual in its duration. It is said, *"He shall stand and feed"*; not *"He will feed now and then, and leave His position"*; not *"He will one day grant a revival, and then the next day leave His church to barrenness."* His eyes never slumber, and His hands never rest. His heart never ceases to beat with love, and His shoulders are never weary of carrying His people's burdens. His reign is completely powerful in its action. He feeds in the strength of Jehovah. Wherever Christ is, there is God; and whatever Christ does is the act of the Most High. Oh, it is a joyful truth to consider that He who stands today representing the interests of His people is very God of very God, to whom every knee will bow! We are happy to belong to such a Shepherd, whose humanity communes with us, and whose divinity protects us. Let us worship and bow down before Him as *"the people of his pasture"* (Ps. 95:7).

Pull me out of the net that they have laid privily for me:
for thou art my strength.
—Psalm 31:4

Our spiritual enemies are of the same nature as the serpent in the Garden of Eden; they seek to ensnare us by subtlety. The prayer of our text supposes the possibility of the believer being caught like a bird. So deftly does the fowler do his work that simple ones are soon surrounded by the net. The text asks that the captive one be delivered even out of Satan's meshes. This is a legitimate prayer, and one that can be granted. From between the jaws of the lion, and out of the belly of hell, eternal love can rescue the saint. A quick yank may be needed to save a believer from the net of temptation, and a mighty pull may be needed to extricate him from the snare of malicious cunning, but the Lord is equal to every emergency. The most skillfully placed nets of the hunter will never be able to hold His chosen ones. Those who are so clever at laying nets, those who tempt others, will themselves be destroyed. *"For thou art my strength."* What inexpressible sweetness may be found in these few words! How joyfully we may encounter struggles, and how cheerfully we may endure sufferings, when we can take hold of divine strength. Divine power will tear apart all the works of our enemies, confound their schemes, and frustrate their deceitful tricks. Happy is the one who has such matchless might engaged on his behalf! Our own strength is of little service when overwhelmed in the nets of base cunning, but the Lord's strength is always available to us. We only have to invoke it, and we will find it close at hand. If, by faith, we are depending on the strength of the mighty God of Israel alone, we may use our holy reliance as a plea in supplication.

Lord, evermore Your face we seek:
Tempted we are, and poor, and weak;
Keep us with lowly hearts, and meek.
Let us not fall. Let us not fall.

The sweet psalmist of Israel.
—2 Samuel 23:1

Among all the saints whose lives are recorded in Holy Writ, David possessed an experience of the most striking, varied, and instructive character. In his history, we meet with trials and temptations not to be discovered, as a whole, in other saints of ancient times; hence, he is all the more suggestive a type of our Lord. David knew the trials of all ranks and conditions of men. Kings have their troubles, and David wore a crown. The peasant has his cares, and David handled a shepherd's crook. The wanderer has many hardships, and David abode in the caves of Engedi. The captain has his difficulties, and David found the sons of Zeruiah too hard for him. The psalmist was also tried by his friends. His counselor Ahithophel forsook him: *"Mine own familiar friend, in whom I trusted, which did eat of my bread, hath lifted up his heel against me"* (Ps. 41:9). His worst foes were those of his own household, and his children were his greatest affliction. The temptations of poverty and wealth, of honor and reproach, of health and weakness, all tried their power on him. He had temptations from without to disturb his peace, and from within to mar his joy. David no sooner escaped from one trial than he fell into another; he no sooner emerged from one season of despondency and alarm than he was again brought into the lowest depths, and all God's waves and billows rolled over him. It is probably this reason that David's psalms are so universally the delight of experienced Christians. Whatever our frame of mind, whether ecstasy or depression, David has exactly described our emotions. He was an able master of the human heart because he had been tutored in the best of all schools—the school of heartfelt, personal experience. As we are instructed in the same school, as we grow mature in grace and in years, we increasingly appreciate David's psalms and find them to be *"green pastures"* (Ps. 23:2). My soul, let David's experience cheer and counsel you this day.

And they fortified Jerusalem unto the broad wall.
—Nehemiah 3:8

Cities that are well fortified have broad walls, as Jerusalem had in her glory. The New Jerusalem must, in like manner, be surrounded and preserved by a broad wall of nonconformity to the world and separation from its customs and spirit. The tendency in these days is to break down the holy barrier and to make the distinction between the church and the world merely nominal. Christians no longer keep a strict watch over their attitudes and actions, questionable literature is read everywhere, frivolous pastimes are commonly indulged, and a general laxity threatens to deprive the Lord's own people of the sacred singularity that separates them from sinners. It will be an evil day for the church and the world when the proposed unification is complete, and the *"sons of God"* and the *"daughters of men"* (Gen. 6:2) are as one. Then another flood of wrath will be ushered in. Beloved reader, let it be your aim in heart, word, dress, and action to maintain the *"broad wall,"* remembering that friendship with this world means enmity against God. The broad wall afforded a pleasant meeting place for the inhabitants of Jerusalem, from which they could have an excellent view of the surrounding countryside. This reminds us of the Lord's exceedingly broad commandments, in which we walk at liberty in communion with Jesus, overlooking the scenes of earth and looking out toward the glories of heaven. Although we are separated from the world and deny ourselves all ungodliness and fleshly lusts, we are nevertheless not in prison, nor restricted within narrow bounds. No, we walk at liberty, because we keep His precepts. Come, reader, walk with God in His statutes this evening. As friend met friend upon the city wall, so meet your God in the way of holy prayer and meditation. You have a right to traverse the fortresses of salvation, for you are a freeman of the royal borough, a citizen of the capital of the universe.

He that watereth shall be watered also himself.
—Proverbs 11:25

Here we are taught the great lesson that to receive, we must give; that to accumulate, we must scatter; that to make ourselves happy, we must make others happy; and that in order to become spiritually vigorous, we must seek the spiritual good of others. In watering others, we are ourselves watered. How? Our efforts to be useful bring out our powers for usefulness. We have latent talents and dormant faculties that are brought to light by exercise. Our strength for labor is hidden even from ourselves, until we venture forth to fight the Lord's battles or to climb the mountains of difficulty. We do not know what tender sympathies we possess until we try to dry the widow's tears or soothe the orphan's grief. We often find in attempting to teach others that we gain instruction for ourselves. Oh, what gracious lessons some of us have learned at sickbeds! We went to teach the Scriptures, and we came away blushing that we knew so little of them. In our conversations with poor saints, we are taught the way of God more perfectly for ourselves and receive a deeper insight into divine truth. So that watering others makes us humble. We discover how much grace there is where we had not looked for it, and how much the poor saint may outstrip us in knowledge. Our own comfort is also increased by our working for others. We endeavor to cheer them, and the consolation gladdens our own heart. Like the two men in the snow, one rubbed the other's limbs to keep him from dying, and in so doing kept his own blood in circulation and saved his own life. The poor widow of Sarepta gave from her scanty store a supply for the prophet's needs, and from that day she never again knew what it was to be in need. *"Give, and it shall be given unto you; good measure, pressed down, and shaken together, and running over"* (Luke 6:38).

AUGUST 21
Evening

I said not unto the seed of Jacob, Seek ye me in vain.
—Isaiah 45:19

We may gain much comfort by considering what God has *not* said. What He has said is inexpressibly full of comfort and delight; what He has not said is hardly less rich in consolation. It was one of these "said nots" that preserved the kingdom of Israel in the days of Jeroboam, the son of Joash. *"The Lord said not that he would blot out the name of Israel from under heaven"* (2 Kings 14:27, emphasis added). In our text, we have an assurance that God will answer prayer, because He *"said not unto the seed of Jacob, Seek ye me in vain."* You who say bitter things against yourselves should remember that, no matter what your doubts and fears may say, if God has not cut you off from mercy, there is no room for despair. Even the voice of conscience is of little weight if it is not seconded by the voice of God. What God has said, tremble at! But do not allow false ideas to overwhelm you with despondency and sinful despair. Many timid people have been troubled by the suspicion that there may be something in God's decree that shuts them out from hope. Yet here is a complete refutation of that troublesome fear, for no true seeker can be decreed to wrath: *"I have not spoken in secret, in a dark place of the earth: I said not* [even in the secret of My unsearchable decree] *unto the seed of Jacob, Seek ye me in vain"* (Isa. 45:19). God has clearly revealed that He will hear the prayer of those who call on Him, and that declaration cannot be contravened. He has so firmly, so truthfully, so righteously spoken that there can be no room for doubt. He does not reveal His mind in unintelligible words, but He speaks plainly and positively, *"Ask, and ye shall receive"* (John 26:24). Trembling one, believe these sure truths—that prayer must and will be heard, and that never, even in the secrets of eternity, has the Lord said to any living soul, *"Seek ye me in vain."*

I charge you, O daughters of Jerusalem, if ye find my beloved,
that ye tell him, that I am sick of love.
—Song of Solomon 5:8

Such is the language of the believer panting after present fellowship with Jesus: he is sick for his Lord. Gracious souls are never perfectly at ease unless they are in a state of nearness to Christ, for when they are away from Him, they lose their peace. The nearer to Him, the nearer they are to the perfect calm of heaven; the nearer to Him, the fuller their heart is, not only of peace, but also of life, vigor, and joy, for these all depend on constant communion with Jesus. What the sun is to the day, what the moon is to the night, what the dew is to the flower, such is Jesus Christ to us. What bread is to the hungry, clothing to the naked, the shadow of a great rock to the traveler in a weary land, such is Jesus Christ to us; therefore, if we are not consciously one with Him, it is little wonder if our spirits cry in the words of the Song, *"I charge you, O daughters of Jerusalem, if ye find my beloved, that ye tell him, that I am sick of love."* This earnest longing after Jesus has a blessing attending it: *"Blessed are they which do hunger and thirst after righteousness"* (Matt. 5:6). Supremely blessed, therefore, are those who thirst after the Righteous One. Blessed is that hunger, since it comes from God. If I may not have the full-blown blessedness of being filled, I would seek the same blessedness in its sweet budding stages of emptiness and eagerness, until I am filled with Christ. If I may not feed on Jesus, it will be next door to heaven to hunger and thirst after Him. There is a blessedness about that hunger, since it sparkles among the beatitudes of our Lord. But the blessing involves a promise. Such hungry ones *"shall be filled"* (v. 6) with what they are desiring. If Christ thus causes us to long after Himself, He will certainly satisfy those longings; and when He does come to us, as come He will, oh, how sweet it will be!

The unsearchable riches of Christ.
—Ephesians 3:8

My Master has riches beyond the count of arithmetic, the measurement of reason, the dream of imagination, or the eloquence of words. They are *"unsearchable"*! You may look, study, and weigh, but Jesus is a greater Savior than you think He is when your thoughts are at their greatest. My Lord is more ready to pardon than you are to sin, more able to forgive than you are to transgress. My Master is more willing to supply your needs than you are to acknowledge them. Never tolerate low thoughts of my Lord Jesus. When you put the crown on His head, you will crown Him only with silver when He deserves gold. My Master has riches of happiness to bestow on you now. He can cause you to lie down in green pastures and lead you beside still waters. There is no music like the music of His flute when He is the Shepherd and you are the sheep, and you lie down at His feet. There is no love like His; neither earth nor heaven can match it. To know Christ and to *"be found in him"* (Phil. 3:9)—this is life, this is joy, this is *"marrow and fatness"* (Ps. 63:5), *"wines on the lees well refined"* (Isa. 25:6)! My Master does not treat His servants in a stingy way. He gives to them as a king gives to another king. He gives them two heavens—a heaven below in serving Him here, and a heaven above in delighting in Him forever. His *"unsearchable riches"* will be best known in eternity. He will give you all you need on your way to heaven. Your place of defense will be the stronghold of rocks; your bread will be given to you, and your waters will be sure (Isa. 33:16). It is there where you will hear the song of those who triumph, the shout of those who feast, and will have a face-to-face view of the glorious and beloved One. *"The unsearchable riches of Christ"*! This is the tune for the musicians of earth and the song for the harpists of heaven. Lord, teach us more and more of Jesus, and we will tell the good news to others.

The voice of weeping shall be no more heard.
—Isaiah 65:19

The glorified weep no more, for all outward causes of grief are gone. There are no broken friendships or blighted prospects in heaven. Poverty, famine, peril, persecution, and slander are unknown there. No pain distresses; no thought of death or bereavement saddens. They weep no more, for they are perfectly sanctified. No *"evil heart of unbelief"* (Heb. 3:12) prompts them to depart from the living God. They are without fault before His throne and are fully conformed to His image. Well may they cease to mourn who have ceased to sin. They weep no more, because all fear of change is past. They know that they are eternally secure. Sin is shut out, and they are shut in. They live in a city that will never be stormed. They bask in a sun that will never set. They drink from a river that will never run dry, and they pick fruit from a tree that will never wither. Countless cycles may revolve, but eternity will not be exhausted; while eternity endures, their immortality and blessedness will coexist with it. They are forever with the Lord. They weep no more, because every desire is fulfilled. They cannot wish for anything that they do not already have in their possession. Eye and ear, heart and hand, judgment, imagination, hope, desire, will, and all the faculties are completely satisfied. As imperfect as our present ideas are of the things that God has prepared for those who love Him, we know enough by the revelation of the Spirit to know that the saints above are supremely blessed. The joy of Christ, which is an infinite fullness of delight, is in them. They bathe themselves in the bottomless, shoreless sea of infinite beatitude. That same joyful rest remains for us. It may not be far distant. Before long the weeping willow will be exchanged for the palm branch of victory, and sorrow's dewdrops will be transformed into the pearls of everlasting bliss. *"Wherefore comfort one another with these words"* (1 Thess. 4:18).

That Christ may dwell in your hearts by faith.
—Ephesians 3:17

Beyond measure, it is desirable that we, as believers, should keep the person of Jesus constantly in mind, in order to ignite our love for Him and to increase our knowledge of Him. I wish that all my readers were enrolled as diligent scholars in Jesus' college, students of "Corpus Christi" or the body of Christ, resolved to attain a good degree in the learning of the Cross. In order to keep Jesus always near, the heart must be full of Him, welling up with His love, even to overflowing. Therefore, the apostle prayed, *"That Christ may dwell in your hearts."* See how near he wanted Jesus to be! You cannot get a subject closer to you than to have it in your very heart. *"That Christ may dwell"*—not that He may visit you sometimes, as a casual visitor comes into a house and stays for a night, but that He may *"dwell,"* that Jesus may become the Lord and Tenant of your inmost being, never to leave. Observe these words: *"That Christ may dwell in your hearts."* The heart is the best room of the house of mankind. Christ is not to dwell in your thoughts alone, but in your affections; not merely in the mind's meditations, but in the heart's emotions. We should earnestly desire an abiding love for Christ—not a love that flames up, then dies out into the darkness of a few embers; but a constant flame, fed by sacred fuel, like the fire that never went out on the altar of the tabernacle (Lev. 6:12–13). This cannot be accomplished except *"by faith."* Faith must be strong or love will not be fervent. The root of the flower must be healthy, or we cannot expect the bloom to be sweet. Faith is the lily's root, and love is the lily's bloom. Jesus cannot be in your heart's love unless you have a firm hold of Him by your heart's faith. Therefore, pray that you may always trust Christ so that you may always love Him. If love is cold, you may be sure that faith is drooping.

The breaker is come up before them.
—Micah 2:13

Because Jesus has gone before us, things are not the same as they would have been had He never passed that way. He has conquered every foe that obstructed the way. Cheer up now, you fainthearted warrior. Not only has Christ traveled the road, but He has slain your enemies. Do you dread sin? He has nailed it to His cross. Do you fear death? He has been the death of death. Are you afraid of hell? He has barred it against the advent of any of His children; they will never see the gulf of perdition. Whatever foes may be before the Christian, they are all overcome. There are lions, but their teeth are broken; there are serpents, but their fangs are extracted; there are rivers, but they are bridged or fordable; there are flames, but we wear that matchless garment that makes us invulnerable to fire. The sword that has been forged against us is already blunted. The instruments of war that the enemy is preparing have already lost their point. God has taken away in the person of Christ all the power that anything can have to hurt us. The army may safely march on, then, and you may go joyously along your journey, for all your enemies are conquered beforehand. What will you do but march on to take the prey? They are beaten; they are vanquished. All you have to do is to divide the spoil. You will, it is true, often engage in combat; but your fight will be with a vanquished foe. His head is broken. He may attempt to injure you, but his strength will not be sufficient for his malicious design. Your victory will be easy, and your treasure will be beyond counting.

> Proclaim aloud the Savior's fame,
>   Who bears the Breaker's wond'rous name;
> Sweet name; and it becomes Him well,
>   Who breaks down earth, sin, death, and hell.

If fire break out, and catch in thorns, so that the stacks of corn, or the
standing corn, or the field, be consumed therewith; he that kindled the
fire shall surely make restitution.
—Exodus 22:6

What restitution can someone make who scatters around the firebrands of error or the coals of licentiousness and sets men's souls ablaze with the fires of hell? The guilt is beyond estimate, and the results are irretrievable. If such an offender is forgiven, what grief it will cause him in retrospect, since he cannot undo the harm that he has done! An evil example may kindle a flame that years of amended character cannot quench. To burn men's food is bad enough, but how much worse it is to destroy the soul! It may be useful to us to reflect to what extent we may have been guilty of this in the past. It may also be helpful to inquire whether, even in the present, there may not be in us an evil that has a tendency to bring damage to the souls of our relatives, friends, or neighbors. The fire of strife is a terrible evil when it breaks out in a Christian church. Where converts are multiplied and God is glorified, jealousy and envy do the devil's work most effectively. Where the golden grain is being housed to reward the toil of the Great Boaz, the fire of enmity comes in and leaves little else but smoke and a heap of blackness. Woe to those by whom offenses come. May they never come through us. For although we cannot make restitution, we will certainly be the chief sufferers if we are the chief offenders. Those who feed the fire deserve just censure, but he who first kindles it is the most to blame. Discord usually first takes hold of the thorns—it is nurtured among the hypocrites and low-minded Christians in the church. Then it goes among the righteous, blown by the winds of hell. No one knows where it may end. Lord and Giver of peace, make us peacemakers. Never let us aid and abet men of strife or even unintentionally cause the least division among Your people.

His fruit was sweet to my taste.
—Song of Solomon 2:3

Faith, in the Scripture, is spoken of as pertaining to all the senses. It is sight: *"Look unto me, and be ye saved"* (Isa. 45:22). It is hearing: *"Hear, and your soul shall live"* (Isa. 55:3). Faith is smelling: *"All thy garments smell of myrrh, and aloes, and cassia"* (Ps. 45:8); *"thy name is as ointment poured forth"* (Song 1:3). Faith is spiritual touch. By this faith the woman came behind and touched the hem of Christ's garment, and by this we handle the things of the good word of life. Faith is equally the spirit's taste. *"How sweet are thy words unto my taste! yea, sweeter than honey to my mouth"* (Ps. 119:103). Jesus said, *"Except ye eat the flesh of the Son of man, and drink his blood, ye have no life in you"* (John 6:53). This taste is faith in one of its highest operations. One of the first performances of faith is hearing. We hear the voice of God, not with the outward ear alone, but with the inward ear. We hear it as God's Word, and we believe it to be so. That is the hearing of faith. Then our mind looks on the truth as it is presented to us; that is to say, we understand it; we perceive its meaning. That is the seeing of faith. Next we discover its preciousness. We begin to admire it, and find how fragrant it is. That is faith in its smell. Then we appropriate the mercies that are prepared for us in Christ; that is faith in its touch. Hence follow the enjoyments—peace, delight, and communion—which are faith in its taste. Any one of these acts of faith is saving. To hear Christ's voice as the sure voice of God in the soul will save us, but what gives true enjoyment is the aspect of faith wherein Christ, by holy taste, is received into us, and made, by inward and spiritual understanding of His sweetness and preciousness, to be the food of our souls. It is then we sit *"under his shadow with great delight"* (Song 2:3) and find *"his fruit sweet to [our] taste."*

If thou believest with all thine heart, thou mayest.
—Acts 8:37

These words may answer your conscience, devout reader, regarding participating in the ordinances of the church. Perhaps you say, "I am afraid to be baptized. It is such a solemn thing to declare that I am dead and buried with Christ. I do not feel at liberty to come to the Lord's Table. I am afraid of eating and drinking damnation on myself by *'not discerning the Lord's body'* (1 Cor. 11:29)." Poor fearful one, Jesus has given you liberty. Do not be afraid. If a stranger came to your house, he would stand at the door or wait in the hall. He would not dream of intruding unasked into your private rooms, for he is not at home. However, your child feels very free to roam around the house. A stranger may not intrude where a child may go. It is this way with the child of God. When the Holy Spirit has enabled you to feel the *"Spirit of adoption"* (Rom. 8:15), you may come to Christian ordinances without fear. The same rule holds true of the Christian's inward privileges. You think, poor seeker, that you are not allowed to *"rejoice with joy unspeakable and full of glory"* (1 Pet. 1:8). If you are permitted to get inside Christ's door or to sit at the end of His table, you will be well contented. Oh, but you will not have fewer privileges than the very greatest. God makes no distinction in His love for His children. A child is a child to Him. He will not make him a hired servant. His child will feast on the fatted calf; he will have music and dancing as much as if he had never gone astray. When Jesus comes into a person's heart, He issues a general license to be *"glad in the LORD"* (Ps. 32:11). No chains are worn in the court of King Jesus. Our admission into full privileges may be gradual, but it is sure. Perhaps you are saying, "I wish I could enjoy the promises and walk at liberty in my Lord's commands." *"If thou believest with all thine heart, thou mayest."* Loose the chains from your neck, *"O captive daughter of Zion"* (Isa. 52:2), for Jesus makes you free.

He hath commanded his covenant for ever.
—Psalm 111:9

The Lord's people delight in the covenant. It is an unfailing source of consolation to them as often as the Holy Spirit leads them into its banqueting house and waves its banner of love. They delight to contemplate the antiquity of that covenant, remembering that before the sun knew its place or planets followed their orbits, the interests of the saints were made secure in Christ Jesus. It is particularly pleasing to them to remember the sureness of the covenant, while meditating on *"the sure mercies of David"* (Isa. 55:3). They delight to celebrate it as signed, sealed, and ratified, in all things ordered well. It often makes their hearts swell with joy to think of its immutability, as a covenant that neither time nor eternity, life nor death, will ever be able to violate—a covenant as old as eternity and as everlasting as the Rock of ages. They rejoice also to feast on the fullness of this covenant, for they see in it all things provided for them. God is their portion, Christ their Companion, the Spirit their Comforter, earth their house, and heaven their home. They see in it an inheritance reserved and assigned to every soul possessing an interest in its ancient and eternal gift. Their eyes sparkled when they saw it as a gold mine in the Bible; but oh, how their souls were gladdened when they saw in the last will and testament of their divine Kinsman that it was bequeathed to them! More especially it is the pleasure of God's people to contemplate the graciousness of this covenant. They see that the law was made void because it was a covenant of works and depended on merit; but this they perceive to be enduring because grace is the basis, grace the condition, grace the strain, grace the bulwark, grace the foundation, grace the top-stone. The covenant is a treasury of wealth, a granary of food, a fountain of life, a storehouse of salvation, a charter of peace, and a haven of joy.

The people, when they beheld him, were greatly amazed,
and running to him saluted him.
—Mark 9:15

What a great difference there was between Moses and Jesus! After Moses had spent forty days with God on Mount Sinai, he underwent a kind of transfiguration, so that his face shone with great brightness. When he came down from the mountain, he put a veil over his face, for the people could not endure to look upon the glory. This was not the case with our Savior. He was transfigured with a greater glory than that of Moses. (See Mark 9:2–8.) Yet the Bible does not say that the people were blinded by the blaze of His countenance. Rather, they *"were greatly amazed, and running to him saluted him."* The glory of the law repels, but the greater glory of Jesus attracts. Although Jesus is holy and just, so much truth and grace is blended with His purity that sinners run to Him, amazed at His goodness and fascinated by His love. They greet Him, become His disciples, and take Him as their Lord and Master. Reader, it may be that you are even now being blinded by the dazzling brightness of the law of God. You feel its claims on your conscience, but you cannot obey it in your life. It is not that you find fault with the law. On the contrary, it commands your most profound respect. Yet you are not drawn to God by it at all. Instead, your heart is hard, and you are close to desperation over it. Poor heart, turn your eyes from Moses, with all his repelling splendor, and look to Jesus, resplendent with gentler glories. See the blood flowing from His wounds and His head crowned with thorns! He is the Son of God; therefore, He is greater than Moses. Yet He is also the Lord of love and is more tender than the lawgiver. He bore the wrath of God. In His death, He revealed more of God's justice than Sinai did when it was ablaze with God's glory. However, God's justice has been vindicated, and now it is the guardian of believers in Jesus. Sinner, look to the bleeding Savior. As you feel the attraction of His love, run to His arms, and you will be saved.

How long will it be ere they believe me?
—Numbers 14:11

Strive with all diligence to keep out that monster of unbelief. It so dishonors Christ, that He will withdraw His visible presence if we insult Him by indulging it. It is true it is a weed, the seeds of which we can never entirely extract from the soil, but we must aim at its root with zeal and perseverance. Among hateful things it is the most to be abhorred. Its injurious nature is so venomous that he who exercises it and he on whom it is exercised are both hurt by it. In your case, believer, it is most wicked, for the mercies of your Lord in the past increase your guilt in doubting Him now. When you distrust the Lord Jesus, He may well cry out, *"Behold, I am pressed under you, as a cart is pressed that is full of sheaves"* (Amos 2:13). This is crowning His head with thorns of the sharpest kind. It is very cruel for a well-beloved wife to mistrust a kind and faithful husband. The sin is needless, foolish, and unwarranted. Jesus has never given the slightest ground for suspicion, and it is hard to be doubted by those to whom our conduct is uniformly affectionate and true. Jesus is the Son of the Highest and has unbounded wealth; it is shameful to doubt Omnipotence and distrust His all-sufficiency. The cattle on a thousand hills will suffice for our hungriest feeding, and the granaries of heaven are not likely to be emptied by our eating. If Christ were only a cistern, we might soon exhaust His fullness, but who can drain a fountain? Myriads of spirits have drawn their supplies from Him, and not one of them has murmured at the scantiness of His resources. Banish this lying traitor, unbelief, for his only errand is to cut the bonds of communion and make us mourn an absent Savior. Bunyan said that unbelief has "as many lives as a cat." If that is so, let us kill one life now, and continue the work until the whole nine are gone. Down with you, traitor. My heart abhors you!

Into thine hand I commit my spirit: thou hast redeemed me,
O LORD God of truth.
—Psalm 31:5

Frequently, these words have been used by holy men and women in their hour of departure from this world. We will benefit from considering them this evening. The object of the faithful believer's concern in life and in death is not his body or his estate, but his spirit. His spirit is his most valuable treasure. If this is safe, all is well. What is the state of the body compared to the state of the spirit? The believer commits his spirit into the hands of God. It came from Him; it is His own. He has sustained it, and He is able to preserve it; it is most fitting that He should receive it. All things are safe in Jehovah's hands. What we entrust to the Lord will be secure, both now and in that Day of days toward which we are quickly moving. It is peaceful living and glorious dying to rest in the care of heaven. At all times, we should commit our all to Jesus' faithful hands. Then, even though life may hang by a thread and adversities may multiply as the sands of the sea, our spirits will dwell at ease and delight in *"quiet resting places"* (Isa. 32:18). *"Thou hast redeemed me, O LORD God of truth."* Redemption is a solid basis for confidence. David did not know Calvary as we do, but temporal redemption comforted him. Will not eternal redemption comfort us even more sweetly? Past times of deliverance are strong pleas for present assistance. What the Lord has done in the past, He will do again, for He never changes. He is faithful to His promises and gracious to His saints. He will not turn away from His people.

> Though You slay me I will trust,
>   Praise You even from the dust,
> Prove, and tell it as I prove,
>   Thine unutterable love.
>
> You may chasten and correct,
>   But You never can neglect;
> Since the ransom price is paid,
>   On Your love my hope is stay'd.

Oil for the light.
—Exodus 25:6

My soul, how much you need this oil, for your lamp will not continue to burn long without it. Your snuff will smoke and become an offense if light is gone, and gone it will be if oil is absent. You have no oil well springing up in your human nature; therefore, you must go to them who sell and buy for yourself, or like the foolish virgins, you will have to cry, *"Our lamps are gone out"* (Matt. 25:8). Even the consecrated lamps could not give light without oil. Although they shone in the tabernacle, they needed to be fed. Even though no rough winds blew on them, they needed to be trimmed, and your need is equally as great. Under the happiest of circumstances, you cannot give light for another hour unless the fresh oil of grace is given to you. Not every oil could be used in the Lord's service. Neither the petroleum that exudes so plentifully from the earth nor that which is produced by fish nor that extracted from nuts would be accepted. Only the best olive oil was selected. Pretended grace from natural goodness or imaginary grace from priestly hands or from outward ceremonies will never serve the true saint of God. He knows that the Lord would not be pleased with rivers of such oil. He goes to the olive press of Gethsemane and draws his supplies from Him who was crushed therein. The oil of gospel grace is free from impurities; hence, the light that is fed on it is clear and bright. Our churches are the Savior's golden candelabra, and if they are to be lights in this dark world, they must have much holy oil. Let us pray for ourselves, our ministers, and our churches that they may never lack oil for the light. Truth, holiness, joy, knowledge, and love are all beams of the sacred light, but we cannot exemplify them in our lives unless we receive oil from God the Holy Spirit in private.

Sing, O barren.
—Isaiah 54:1

W e have yielded some fruit for Christ, and we have a joyful hope that we are plants that His right hand has planted (Ps. 80:15). Yet there are times when we feel very barren. Our prayers are lifeless, our love is cold, and our faith is weak. Each grace in the garden of our hearts languishes and droops. We are like flowers in the hot sun that need a refreshing shower. What are we to do in such a condition? The verse from which our text comes is addressed to those in just such a state: "*Sing, O barren…; break forth into singing, and cry aloud*" (v. 1). But what can I sing about? I cannot talk about the present, and even the past looks full of barrenness. Oh, I can sing of Jesus Christ! I can talk of visits that the Redeemer has paid me in the past. Or I can praise the great love by which He loved His people when He came from the heights of heaven for their redemption. I will go to the cross again. Come, my soul. You were once "*heavy laden*" (Matt. 11:28), but you lost your burden there. Go to Calvary again. Perhaps the very cross that gave you life may also give you fruitfulness. What is my barrenness? It is the platform for His fruit-creating power. What is my desolation? It is the black setting for the sapphire of His everlasting love. I will go in poverty; I will go in helplessness; I will go in all my shame and backsliding. I will tell Him that I am still His child. In confidence in His faithful heart, even I, the barren one, will "*sing…and cry aloud.*" Sing, believer, for it will comfort your own heart and the hearts of other desolate ones. Sing on, for now that you are really ashamed of being barren, you will be fruitful soon. Now that God has made you unwilling to be without fruit, He will soon cover you with clusters. The experience of our barrenness is painful, but the Lord's visitations are delightful. A sense of our own poverty drives us to Christ. That is where we need to be, for in Him our fruit is found.

AUGUST 29
Morning

Have mercy upon me, O God.
—Psalm 51:1

When Dr. Carey was suffering from a serious illness, he was asked, "If this sickness should prove fatal, what passage would you select as the text for your funeral sermon?" He replied, "Oh, I feel that such a poor sinful creature is unworthy to have anything said about him, but if a funeral sermon must be preached, let it be from the words, *'Have mercy upon me, O God, according to thy lovingkindness: according unto the multitude of thy tender mercies blot out my transgressions'* (Ps. 51:1)." In the same spirit of humility he directed in his will that the following inscription, and nothing more, should be cut on his gravestone:

WILLIAM CAREY, BORN AUGUST 17, 1761; DIED
A wretched, poor, and helpless worm,
On Thy kind arms I fall.

Only on the footing of free grace can the most experienced and most honored of the saints approach their God. The best of men are conscious above all others that they are men at best. Empty boats float high, but heavily laden vessels are low in the water; mere professors of faith can boast, but true children of God cry for mercy, recognizing their unworthiness. We need the Lord's mercy on our good works, our prayers, our preaching, our almsgiving, and our holiest things. The blood was sprinkled not only on the doorposts of Israel's dwelling houses, but also on the sanctuary, the mercy seat, and the altar, because as sin intrudes into our holiest things, the blood of Jesus is needed to purify them from defilement. If mercy is needed to be exercised toward our duties, what will be said of our sins? How sweet to remember that inexhaustible mercy is waiting to be gracious to us, to restore our backslidings, and to make our broken bones rejoice!

All the days of his separation shall he eat nothing that is made of the vine tree, from the kernels even to the husk.
—Numbers 6:4

Among other vows, Nazarites took a vow that precluded them from drinking wine. (See Numbers 6:2–3.) To keep them from violating the obligation, they were forbidden to drink wine vinegar or strong liquor. To make the rule even clearer, they were not to touch the unfermented juice of grapes or even eat the fruit of grapes— either fresh or dried. In order to completely ensure the integrity of the vow, they were not allowed anything that had to do with the vine. They were, in fact, to avoid the *"appearance of evil"* (1 Thess. 5:22). Surely, their abstinence is a lesson to the Lord's separated ones, teaching them to move away from sin in every form— not merely to avoid sin's more obvious forms, but also its spirit and likeness. Being strict with oneself in regard to walking in God's ways is much despised in these days. However, rest assured, dear reader, that it is both the safest and the happiest way to live. He who yields a point or two to the world is in fearful peril; he who eats the grapes of Sodom will soon drink the wine of Gomorrah. A little crack in the seawall lets in the sea, and the gap quickly grows until a town is completely flooded. Worldly conformity, in any degree, is a snare to the soul and makes the soul increasingly liable to presumptuous sins. The Nazarite who drank grape juice could not be quite sure that it had not undergone a degree of fermentation. Consequently, he could not have a clear conscience that his vow was intact. In the same way, the yielding, compromising Christian cannot maintain a clear conscience; he senses that his inward monitor doubts his integrity. We do not need to wonder about things that are questionable. They are wrong for us. We must not toy with things that are tempting, but quickly flee from them. It is better to be sneered at as a Puritan than to be despised as a hypocrite. Walking before the Lord carefully may involve much self-denial, but it has pleasures of its own that are more than sufficient compensation.

Wait on the LORD.
—Psalm 27:14

It may seem to be an easy thing to wait, but it is one of the postures that a Christian soldier does not learn without years of teaching. Marching is much easier for God's warriors than standing still. There are hours of perplexity when the most willing spirit, anxiously desirous to serve the Lord, does not know what action to take. Then what will it do? Vex itself by despair? Fly back in cowardice, turn to the right hand in fear, or rush forward in presumption? No, it must simply wait. Wait in prayer, however. Call on God, and spread the case before Him. Tell Him your difficulty and plead His promise of aid. In dilemmas between one duty and another, it is sweet to be humble as a child and to wait with simplicity of soul on the Lord. It is sure to be well with us when we feel and know our own folly and are heartily willing to be guided by the will of God. But wait in faith. Express your unstaggering confidence in Him. Unfaithful, untrusting waiting is an insult to the Lord. Believe that if He keep you tarrying even until midnight, He will come at the right time. The vision will come and will not tarry. Wait in quiet patience, not rebelling because you are under affliction, but blessing your God for it. Never murmur as the children of Israel did against Moses. Never wish you could go back to the world again, but accept the situation as it is and put it as it stands, simply and with your whole heart, without any self-will, into the hand of your covenant God. Say, "Now, Lord, not my will, but Yours be done. I do not know what to do. I am brought to extremities, but I will wait until You divide the floods or drive back my foes. I will wait, even if You keep me waiting for many days, because my heart is fixed on You alone, O God. My spirit waits for You in the full conviction that You will yet be my joy and my salvation, my refuge and my strong tower."

Heal me, O Lord, and I shall be healed.
—Jeremiah 17:14

I have seen his ways, and will heal him.
—Isaiah 57:18

It is the sole prerogative of God to remove spiritual disease. Physical disease may be healed by men in an accessory way. However, even then, the honor is to be given to God, who gives healing power to medicine and grants the human body the power to ward off disease. As for spiritual sicknesses, these are the domain of the Great Physician alone. He claims them as His exclusive right: *"I kill, and I make alive; I wound, and I heal"* (Deut. 32:39). One of the Lord's preeminent titles is Jehovah-Rapha, *"The Lord that healeth thee"* (Exod. 15:26). "I will heal you of your wounds" is a promise that could not come from man, but only from the eternal God. For this reason, the psalmist cried to the Lord, *"O Lord, heal me; for my bones are vexed"* (Ps. 6:2), and, *"Heal my soul; for I have sinned against thee"* (Ps. 41:4). For this reason, also, the godly praise the name of the Lord, saying, "He heals all our diseases." (See Psalm 103:3.) He who made man can restore man, and He who was the Creator of our nature at the beginning can newly create it. What an incomparable comfort it is to know that in the person of Jesus *"dwelleth all the fulness of the Godhead bodily"* (Col. 2:9)! No matter what your disease may be, the Great Physician can heal you. He is God, and there is no limit to His power. Come, then, with the blind eye of darkened understanding. Come with the limping foot of wasted energy or the maimed hand of weak faith. Come with the fever of an angry temper or the chills of shivering despondency. Come just as you are, for He who is God can certainly cure you of your plague. No one can restrain the healing power that proceeds from Jesus our Lord. Legions of demons have been forced to acknowledge the power of the beloved Physician. Never once has He been baffled. All His patients have been cured in the past and will be cured in the future. You will be among them, my friend, if you will only rest in Him tonight.

On mine arm shall they trust.
—Isaiah 51:5

In seasons of severe trial, the Christian has nothing on earth that he can trust in; therefore, he is compelled to cast himself on God alone. When his vessel is on its beam's end, and no human deliverance can avail, he must simply and entirely trust himself to the providence and care of God. Happy storm that wrecks a man on such a rock as this! O blessed hurricane that drives the soul to God and God alone! There is no communing with our God sometimes because of the multitude of our friends. But when a man is so poor, so friendless, so helpless that he has nowhere else to turn, he flies into his Father's arms and is blessedly embraced! When he is burdened with troubles so pressing and so unique that he cannot tell them to anyone but to God, he may be thankful for them. He will learn more of his Lord, then, than at any other time. Oh, tempest-tossed believer, it is a happy trouble that drives you to your Father! Now that you have only your God to trust, see that you put your full confidence in Him. Do not dishonor your Lord and Master by unworthy doubts and fears; but be strong in faith, giving glory to God. Show the world that your God is worth ten thousand worlds to you. Show rich men how rich you are in your poverty when the Lord God is your Helper. Show the strong man how strong you are in your weakness when underneath you are the *"everlasting arms"* (Deut. 33:27). Now is the time for feats of faith and valiant exploits. Be strong and courageous, and the Lord your God will certainly, as surely as He built the heavens and the earth, glorify Himself in your weakness and magnify His might in the midst of your distress. The grandeur of the arch of heaven would be spoiled if the sky were supported by a single visible column, and your faith would lose its glory if it rested on anything discernible by the carnal eye. May the Holy Spirit help you to rest in Jesus this closing day of the month.

If we walk in the light, as he is in the light.
—1 John 1:7

W*alk…as he is in the light*"! Can we ever attain to this? Will we ever be able to walk as clearly in the light as He whom we call *"Our Father"* (Matt. 6:9), of whom it is written, *"God is light, and in him is no darkness at all"* (1 John 1:5)? Certainly, this is the model that it set before us, for the Savior Himself said, *"Be ye therefore perfect, even as your Father which is in heaven is perfect"* (Matt. 5:48). Although we may feel that we can never measure up to the perfection of God, we are still to seek it and never be satisfied until we obtain it. When the youthful artist grasps his pencil at the beginning of his training, he can hardly hope to equal Raphael or Michelangelo. However, if he did not have a noble *beau idéal* or archetype in his mind, he would create something only very average and ordinary. Yet what is meant by the statement that the Christian is to *"walk in the light, as* [God] *is in the light"*? I understand this statement to mean likeness, rather than degree. We are as truly in the light, as completely in the light, as sincerely in the light, as honestly in the light as God is, although we cannot be in the light in the same measure that He is. I cannot dwell in the sun; it is too bright a place for me to reside in. However, I can *walk* in the light of the sun. Similarly, although I cannot attain to the perfection of purity and truth that belongs to the Lord of Hosts by nature as the Infinitely Good One, I can *"set the* LORD *always before me"* (Ps. 16:8). I can strive, by the help of the indwelling Spirit, to conform to His image. That famous old commentator, John Trapp, said, "We may be in the light as God is in the light for *quality*, but not for *equality*." We are to have the light and to walk in it as truly as God has the light and walks in it. As for equality with God in His holiness and purity, that must be left until we cross the Jordan and enter into the perfection of the Most High. Note that the blessings of sacred fellowship and perfect cleansing are tied to walking in the light. (See 1 John 1:7.)

SEPTEMBER 1

Morning

Thou shalt guide me with thy counsel,
and afterward receive me to glory.
—Psalm 73:24

The psalmist felt his need of divine guidance. He had just been discovering the foolishness of his own heart, and lest he would be constantly led astray by it, he resolved that God's counsel would henceforth guide him. A sense of our own folly is a great step toward being wise, when it leads us to rely on the wisdom of the Lord. The blind man leans on his friend's arm and reaches home in safety. Likewise, we should give ourselves up implicitly to divine guidance, nothing doubting, assured that though we cannot see, it is always safe to trust the all-seeing God. *"Thou shalt"* is a blessed expression of confidence. He was sure that the Lord would not decline the condescending task. There is a word for you, believer; rest in it. Be assured that your God will be your counselor and friend. He will guide you and will direct all your ways. In His written Word you have this assurance in part fulfilled, for Holy Scripture is His counsel to you. We are happy to have God's Word always to guide us! What would the mariner be without his compass? And what would the Christian be without the Bible? This is the unerring chart, the map in which every shoal is described, and all the channels from the quicksands of destruction to the haven of salvation are mapped and marked by One who knows all the way. Bless You, O God, that we may trust You to guide us now, and guide us even to the end! After this guidance through life, the psalmist anticipated a divine reception at last—*"and afterward receive me to glory."* What a thought for you, believer! God Himself will receive you to glory—you! Though you are wandering, erring, straying, yet He will bring you safe at last to glory! This is your portion. Live on it this day, and if perplexities should surround you, go, in the strength of this text, straight to the throne.

SEPTEMBER 1

Trust in him at all times.
—Psalm 62:8

Faith is as much the rule of temporal life as it is of spiritual life. We ought to have faith in God for our earthly matters as well as for our heavenly concerns. It is only as we learn to trust in God to supply all our daily needs that we will live above the world. We are not to be idle, for that would show that we do not trust in God, who continually works, but in the devil, who is the father of idleness. We are not to be imprudent or rash, for that would be to trust chance rather than the living God, who is a God of economy and order. Acting in all prudence and uprightness, we are to rely simply and entirely on the Lord at all times. Let me commend to you a life of trusting in God in temporal things. By trusting in God, you will not have to repent for having used sinful means to grow rich. Serve God with integrity. If you achieve no success, at least no sin will be on your conscience. By trusting in God, you will not become guilty of self-contradiction. He who trusts only in his own abilities sails this way today and that way the next, like a boat tossed about by the fickle wind. However, he who trusts in the Lord is like a steamship, which cuts through the waves, defies the wind, and makes one bright, silvery, straightforward track to her desired haven. Be someone who has living principles within him. Never yield to the varying practices of worldly wisdom. Walk in the path of integrity with determined steps, and show that you are invincibly strong in the strength that confidence in God alone can provide. Thus you will be delivered from burdensome care. You will not be troubled by bad news. Your heart will be steadfast, *"trusting in the LORD"* (Ps. 112:7). How pleasant it is to float along the stream of providence! There is no more blessed way of living than living a life of dependence upon a covenant-keeping God. We have no cares, *"for he careth for [us]"* (1 Pet. 5:7). We have no troubles, because we cast our burdens upon the Lord.

Morning

But Simon's wife's mother lay sick of a fever,
and anon they tell him of her.
—Mark 1:30

This little peep into the house of the apostolic fisherman is very interesting. We see at once that household joys and cares are no hindrance to the full exercise of ministry. In fact, since they furnish an opportunity for personally witnessing the Lord's gracious work on one's own flesh and blood, they may even instruct the teacher better than any other earthly discipline. Papists and other Nonconformists may decry marriage, but true Christianity and household life go well together. Peter's house was probably a poor fisherman's hut, but the Lord of Glory entered it, lodged in it, and worked a miracle in it. If our little book is read this morning in some very humble cottage, let this fact encourage those who reside there to seek the company of King Jesus. God is in small homes more often than in rich palaces. Jesus is looking around your room now and is waiting to be gracious to you. Sickness had entered Simon's house; fever in a deadly form had prostrated his mother-in-law. As soon as Jesus came, they told Him of the sad affliction, and He hurried to the patient's bed. Do you have any sickness in your house this morning? You will find Jesus to be the best physician by far. Go to Him at once and tell Him all about the matter. Immediately lay the case before Him. It concerns one of His people; therefore, it will not be trivial to Him. Observe that the Savior restored the sick woman immediately. No one can heal as He does. We may not be certain that the Lord will remove all disease right away from those we love, but we do know that believing prayer for the sick is far more likely to be followed by restoration than anything else in the world. Where prayer does not avail, we must meekly bow to His will by whom life and death are determined. The tender heart of Jesus waits to hear our grief. Let us pour them into His patient ear.

Except ye see signs and wonders, ye will not believe.
—John 4:48

A craving for miracles was a symptom of the sickly state of men's minds in our Lord's day. They refused solid nourishment and longed for mere wonders. The Gospel that they so greatly needed, they did not want. The miracles that Jesus did not always choose to give, they eagerly demanded. Many people today must see signs and wonders, or they will not believe. Some have said in their hearts, "I must feel a deep terror in my soul regarding my sins, or I will never believe in Jesus." But what if you never feel it, as you probably never will? Will you go to hell just to spite God, because He will not deal with you as He deals with others? Some say to themselves, "If I had a dream, or if I could feel a sudden shock of something—I don't know what—then I would believe." In this way, undeserving mortals imagine that the Lord is to be dictated to by them! You are beggars at His gate, asking for mercy. Will you draw up rules and regulations as to how He should give that mercy? Do you think that He will submit to this? My Master has a generous spirit, but He has a true royal heart. He spurns all other rule and maintains His sovereignty of action. Dear reader, if the text describes your condition, why do you crave signs and wonders? Is the Gospel not its own sign and wonder? Is it not a miracle of miracles that *"God so loved the world, that he gave his only begotten Son, that whosoever believeth in him should not perish"* (John 3:16)? Surely, this precious offer, *"Whosoever will, let him take the water of life freely"* (Rev. 22:17), and this solemn promise, *"Him that cometh to me I will in no wise cast out"* (John 6:37), are better than signs and wonders! A truthful Savior should be believed. He is truth itself. Why do you ask for proof of the truthfulness of One who cannot lie? The demons themselves declared Him to be the Son of God. (See Mark 3:11.) Will you mistrust Him?

Thou whom my soul loveth.
—Song of Solomon 1:7

Ic is wonderful to be able, without any *if* or *but*, to say of the Lord Jesus— *"Thou whom my soul loveth."* Many can say of Jesus only that they *hope* they love Him; they *trust* they love Him; but only a poor and shallow experience will be content to stay here. No one should give any rest to his spirit until he feels quite sure about this vitally important matter. We should not be satisfied with a superficial hope that Jesus loves us or with a bare trust that we love Him. The old saints did not generally speak with *buts, ifs, hopes,* and *trusts,* but they spoke positively and plainly. *"I know whom I have believed"* (2 Tim. 1:12), Paul said. *"I know that my redeemer liveth"* (Job 19:25), said Job. Get positive knowledge of your love for Jesus, and do not be satisfied until you can speak of your interest in Him as a reality, which you have made certain by having received the witness of the Holy Spirit and His seal on your soul by faith. True love for Christ is in every case the Holy Spirit's work, and it must be wrought in the heart by Him. He is the Agent of it, but the logical reason for our love for Jesus lies in Himself. Why do we love Jesus? *"Because he first loved us"* (1 John 4:19). Why do we love Jesus? Because He *"gave himself for us"* (Titus 2:14). We have life through His death; we have peace through His blood. *"Though he was rich, yet for* [our] *sakes he became poor"* (2 Cor. 8:9). Why do we love Jesus? Because of the excellency of His person. We are filled with a sense of His beauty, an admiration of His charms, and a consciousness of His infinite perfection! His greatness, goodness, and loveliness, in one resplendent ray, combine to enchant the soul until it is so ravished that it exclaims, *"Yea, he is altogether lovely"* (Song 5:16). This is a blessed love, a love that binds the heart with chains that are softer than silk, yet firmer than stone!

SEPTEMBER 3

Evening

The Lord trieth the righteous.
—Psalm 11:5

All events are under God's control. Consequently, all the trials of our outward lives may be directly traced to the great First Cause. Out of the golden gate of God's ordinance, the armies of trial march forth in order, dressed in their iron armor and armed with weapons of war. All acts of God's providence are doors to trial. Even our mercies, like roses, have their thorns. Men may be drowned in seas of prosperity as well as in rivers of affliction. Our mountains are not too high and our valleys are not too low for temptations; trials lurk on all roads. Everywhere, above and beneath, we are surrounded and attacked by dangers. Yet no showers fall from the threatening clouds without permission; every drop has its order before it hurries to the earth. The trials that come from God are sent to prove and strengthen our Christlike qualities. Therefore, at the same time, they illustrate the power of divine grace, test the genuineness of these qualities, and add to their effectiveness. Our Lord places so high a value on His people's faith that, in His infinite wisdom and abounding love, He will not screen them from the trials by which faith is strengthened. You would never have possessed the precious faith that now supports you if the trial of your faith had not been a trial by fire. You are a tree that never would have rooted as well if the winds of adversity had not rocked you back and forth and made you take firm hold of the precious truths of covenant grace. Worldly ease is a great enemy to faith; it loosens the joints of holy valor and snaps the sinews of sacred courage. A hot-air balloon doesn't rise until the cords holding it to the earth are cut. Affliction does a similar service for believing souls. While the wheat sleeps comfortably in the husk, it is useless to man. It must be threshed out of its resting place before its value can be known. Thus it is good that Jehovah *"trieth the righteous,"* for their trials cause them to grow rich toward God.

SEPTEMBER 4
Morning

I will; be thou clean.
—Mark 1:41

Primeval darkness heard the Almighty command, *"Let there be light"* (Gen. 1:3), and immediately *"there was light"* (v. 3). The word of the Lord Jesus is equal in majesty to that ancient word of power. Redemption, like Creation, has its word of might. Jesus speaks, and it is done. Leprosy yielded to no human remedies, but it fled at once at the Lord's *"I will."* The disease exhibited no hopeful signs or tokens of recovery. Nature contributed nothing to its own healing, but the unaided word effected the entire work on the spot and forever. The sinner is in a plight more miserable than the leper. Let him imitate the leper's example and go to Jesus, *"beseeching him, and kneeling down to him"* (Mark 1:40). Let him exercise what little faith he has, even though it should go no further than, "Lord, *'if thou wilt, thou canst make me clean'* (v. 40)." There need be no doubt as to the result of the application. Jesus heals all who come and casts out none. In reading the narrative in which our morning's text occurs, it is worthy of devout notice that Jesus touched the leper. This unclean person had broken through the regulations of the ceremonial law and pressed into the house, but Jesus, far from chiding him, broke through the law Himself in order to meet him. Jesus made an interchange with the leper, for while He cleansed him, He contracted by that touch a Levitical defilement. Likewise, Jesus Christ was made sin for us, although in Himself He knew no sin, so that we might be made the righteousness of God in Him. Oh, that poor sinners would go to Jesus, believing in the power of His blessed substitutionary work, and they would soon learn the power of His gracious touch. That hand that multiplied the loaves, that saved sinking Peter, that upholds afflicted saints, that crowns believers, that same hand will touch every seeking sinner and in a moment make him clean. The love of Jesus is the source of salvation. He loves, He looks, He touches us, and we live!

SEPTEMBER 4

Evening

Just balances, just weights, a just ephah, and a just hin, shall ye have.
—Leviticus 19:36

Weights, scales, and measures are all to be set according to the standard of justice. Surely, no Christian needs to be reminded of this in his business, for if righteousness were banished from the rest of the world, it would find shelter in believing hearts. There are, however, other balances that weigh moral and spiritual things, and these often need examining. Are the balances in which we weigh our own and others' characters accurate? Do we not turn our own ounces of goodness into pounds, and other people's bushels of excellence into pecks? Pay attention to weights and measures, Christian. Are the scales in which we measure our trials and troubles according to standard? Paul, who suffered more than we do, called his afflictions *"light"* (2 Cor. 4:17). Yet we often think that our afflictions are heavy. Surely, something must be amiss with the weights! We must see to this matter, lest we be reported to the heavenly court for unjust dealing. Are the weights with which we measure our doctrinal beliefs fair? The doctrines of grace should have the same weight with us as the precepts of the Word—no more and no less. However, it is to be feared that, with many people, one scale or the other is unfairly weighted. It is important to give a just measure in truth. Christian, be careful in regard to this. The measures by which we estimate our obligations and responsibilities look rather small. When a rich man contributes no more to the cause of God than a poor man contributes, is that *"a just ephah, and a just hin"*? When min-isters are half starved because of our selfishness, is that honest dealing? When the poor are despised while ungodly rich men are held in admiration, is that a just balance? Reader, I might lengthen the list, but I prefer to leave it as your evening's work to discover and destroy all unrighteous balances, weights, and measures in your life.

SEPTEMBER 5

Woe is me, that I sojourn in Mesech,
that I dwell in the tents of Kedar!
—Psalm 120:5

As a Christian you have to live in the midst of an ungodly world, and it is of little use for you to cry *"Woe is me."* Jesus did not pray that you would be taken out of the world, and what He did not pray for, you do not need to desire. It is far better to meet the difficulty in the Lord's strength and to glorify Him in it. The enemy is always on watch to detect inconsistency in your conduct; therefore, be very holy. Remember that the eyes of all are on you, and that more is expected from you than from other men. Strive to give no occasion for blame. Let your goodness be the only fault they can discover in you. Like Daniel, compel them to say of you, *"We shall not find any occasion against this Daniel, except we find it against him concerning the law of his God"* (Dan. 6:5). Seek to be useful as well as consistent. Perhaps you think, "If I were in a more favorable position, I might serve the Lord's cause; but I cannot do any good where I am." But the worse the people are around you, the more they need your good example. If they are crooked, the more they need you to set them straight. If they are perverse, the more they need for you to turn their proud hearts to the truth. Where should the physician be but where there are many sick? Where is honor to be won by the soldier but in the hottest fire of the battle? And when weary of the strife and sin that meets you on every hand, consider that all the saints have endured the same trial. They were not carried on beds of down to heaven, and you must not expect to travel more easily than they. They had to hazard their lives to the death in the high places of the field, and you will not be crowned until you also have endured *"hardness, as a good soldier of Jesus Christ"* (2 Tim. 2:3). Therefore, *"stand fast in the faith, quit you* [conduct yourselves] *like men, be strong"* (1 Cor. 16:13).

SEPTEMBER 5

Hast thou entered into the springs of the sea?
—Job 38:16

Some things in nature must remain a mystery to the most intelligent and enterprising investigators. Human knowledge has bounds beyond which it cannot pass. Universal knowledge is for God alone. If this is the case in regard to things that are seen and temporal, I may rest assured that it is even more the case in spiritual and eternal matters. Why, then, have I been torturing my mind with speculations about destiny and will, predestination, and human responsibility? I am no more able to comprehend these deep and mysterious truths than I am to plumb the depths that lie beneath, from which the old ocean draws her watery stores. Why am I so curious to know the reasons for my Lord's providences, the motives of His actions, the purposes of His visitations? Will I ever be able to clasp the sun in my fist and hold the universe in my palm? Yet these things are as a drop in the bucket compared to what the Lord my God is able to do. Let me not strive to understand the infinite, but rather spend my strength in love. What I cannot gain by intellect, I can possess by affection. Let that satisfy me. I cannot penetrate the heart of the sea, but I can enjoy the healthful breezes that sweep over its surface, and I can sail over its blue waves, if I have favorable winds. If I could enter *"the springs of the sea,"* the feat would serve no useful purpose either for me or for others. It would not save a sinking ship or give back a drowned sailor to his weeping wife and children. My solving deep mysteries would not profit me a single bit. The least love for God, and the simplest act of obedience to Him, are better than the most profound knowledge. My Lord, I leave the infinite to You. I pray that You would put far from me any love for the Tree of Knowledge of Good and Evil that would keep me from the Tree of Life.

In the midst of a crooked and perverse nation,
among whom ye shine as lights in the world.
—Philippians 2:15

We use lights in order to see things more clearly. A Christian should so shine in his life that a person could not live with him a week without knowing the Gospel. His conversation should be such that all who are around him would clearly perceive whose he is and whom he serves. People should see the image of Jesus reflected in his daily actions. Lights are intended for guidance. We are to help those around us who are in the dark. We are to hold forth the Word of life to them. We are to point sinners to the Savior and the weary to a divine resting place. Men sometimes read their Bibles and fail to understand them. We should be ready, like Philip, to instruct the inquirer in the meaning of God's Word, the way of salvation, and the life of godliness. Lights are also used for warning. On our rocks and shoals a lighthouse is sure to be erected. Christians should know that there are many false lights shining everywhere in the world; therefore, the right light is needed. The wreckers of Satan are always abroad, tempting the ungodly to sin under the name of pleasure. They hoist the wrong light. It is our responsibility to put up the true light on every dangerous rock, to point out every sin, and tell what it leads to, so that we may be clear of the blood of all men, shining as lights in the world. Lights also have a very cheering influence, and so do Christians. A Christian should be a comforter, with kind words on his lips and sympathy in his heart; he should carry sunshine wherever he goes and diffuse happiness around him.

> Gracious Spirit, dwell with me;
>   I myself would gracious be,
> And with words that help and heal
>   Would your life in mine reveal,
> And with actions bold and meek
>   Would for Christ my Savior speak.

If ye be led of the Spirit, ye are not under the law.
—Galatians 5:18

He who evaluates his own character and standing from a legalistic point of view not only will despair when he comes to the end of his assessment, but—if he is wise—will also despair at the beginning of it. If we are to be judged on the basis of the law, no one will be acquitted. How blessed to know that we dwell in the domain of grace and not of the law! When we consider our condition before God, we are not to ask, "Am I, in myself, perfect before the law?" but, "Am I perfect in Christ Jesus?" These are very different matters. We do not need to inquire, "Am I without sin through my own merits?" but, "Have I been washed in the fountain provided for sin and uncleanness?" The question is not, "Am I, in myself, well pleasing to God?" but, "Am I *accepted in the beloved*' (Eph. 1:6)?" When the Christian views his merits from the top of Mount Sinai, he grows alarmed concerning his salvation. He says, "My faith has unbelief in it. It is not able to save me." It would be far better for him to read his merits by the light of Calvary. He should consider the object of his faith rather than his faith itself. Then he could say, "There is no failure in Him; therefore, I am safe." The Christian sighs, "My hope of heaven is marred and dimmed because I am full of anxiety about present things. How can I be accepted?" If he had regarded the ground of his hope, he would have seen that the promise of God stands sure. Whatever our doubts may be, the oath and promise never fail. (See Hebrews 6:17.) Believer, it is always safer for you to be led by the Spirit into gospel liberty than to wear the chains of legalism. Judge yourself by what Christ is rather than by what you are. Satan will try to destroy your peace by reminding you of your sinfulness and imperfections. You can meet his accusations only by faithfully adhering to the Gospel and refusing to wear the yoke of bondage.

And when they could not come nigh unto him for the press,
they uncovered the roof where he was: and when they had broken
it up, they let down the bed wherein the sick of the palsy lay.
—Mark 2:4

Faith is full of inventions. The house was full, a crowd blocked the door, but faith found a way of getting at the Lord and placing the palsied man before Him. If we cannot get sinners where Jesus is by ordinary methods, we must use extraordinary ones. It seems, according to Luke 5:19, that tiles from the roof had to be removed, which would make dust and cause a measure of danger to those below. But where the case is very urgent, we must not mind running some risks and shocking some proprieties. Jesus was there to heal, and come what may, faith ventured all so that her poor paralyzed charge might have his sins forgiven. Oh, that we had more daring faith among us! Cannot we, dear reader, seek it this morning for ourselves and for our fellow workers, and will we not try today to perform some gallant act for the love of souls and the glory of the Lord? The world is constantly inventing; genius serves all the purposes of human desire. Cannot faith invent, too, and reach, by some new means, the outcasts who lie perishing around us? It was the presence of Jesus that excited victorious courage in the four bearers of the palsied man. Is the Lord not among us now? Have we seen His face for ourselves this morning? Have we felt His healing power in our own souls? If so, then through door, through window, or through roof, let us, breaking through all impediments, labor to bring poor souls to Jesus. All means are good and decorous when faith and love are truly set on winning souls. If hunger for bread can break through stone walls, surely hunger for souls is not to be hindered in its efforts. O Lord, make us quick to suggest methods of reaching Your poor sin-sick ones, and make us bold to carry them out, regardless of the hazards.

There is sorrow on the sea; it cannot be quiet.
—Jeremiah 49:23

We don't know what sorrow there may be on the sea at this moment. We are safe in our quiet rooms, but far away on the salty sea, a hurricane may be cruelly seeking the lives of men. Hear how the fiends of death howl among the rigging, how every timber loosens as the waves beat like battering rams against the vessel! May God help you, poor drenched and wearied ones! My prayer goes up to the great Lord of sea and land, that He will calm the storm and bring you to your desired haven! However, I should do more than just pray. I should also try to help those hardy men who risk their lives so constantly. Have I ever done anything for them? What can I do? How often the tumultuous sea swallows up the sailor! Thousands of corpses lie in the deep, where pearls lie. There is death-sorrow on the sea, which is echoed in the long wail of widows and orphans. The salt of the sea is in the eyes of many mothers and wives. Remorseless billows, you have devoured the love of women and the support of households. What a resurrection there will be from the caverns of the deep when the sea gives up its dead (Rev. 20:13)! Until then, there will be sorrow on the sea. As if in sympathy with the woes of the earth, the sea is continually fretting along a thousand shores, wailing with a sorrowful cry like its own birds, booming with a hollow crash of unrest, raving with noisy discontent, chafing with hoarse wrath, or jangling with the voices of ten thousand murmuring pebbles. The roar of the sea may be joyous to a rejoicing spirit, but to the child of sorrow, the wide, wide ocean is even more forlorn than the wide, wide world. This world is not our rest, and the restless billows tell us so. There is a land where there is *"no more sea"* (Rev. 21:1). Our faces are steadfastly set toward it; we are going to the place of which the Lord has spoken. Until then, we cast our sorrows on the Lord, who walked on the sea long ago, and who makes a way for His people through its depths.

SEPTEMBER 8

Morning

From me is thy fruit found.
—Hosea 14:8

Our fruit is found from our union with God. The fruit of the branch is directly traceable to the root. Sever the connection, and the branch dies; thus, no fruit is produced. By virtue of our union with Christ, we bring forth fruit. Every bunch of grapes has first been in the root. It has passed through the stem, flowed through the sap vessels, and fashioned itself externally into fruit. But it was first in the stem. Likewise, every good work was first in Christ, and then is brought forth in us. Christian, prize this precious union with Christ, for it must be the source of all the fruitfulness that you can hope to know. If you were not joined to Jesus Christ, you would be a barren bough indeed. Our fruit comes from God's spiritual providence. When the dewdrops fall from heaven, when the cloud looks down from on high and is about to distill its liquid treasure, when the bright sun swells the berries of the cluster, each heavenly blessing may whisper to the tree and say, *"From me is thy fruit found."* The fruit owes much to the root—that is essential to fruitfulness—but it also owes much to external influences. How much we owe to God's gracious providence! He provides us constantly with quickening, teaching, consolation, strength, or whatever else we need. To this we owe all of our usefulness or virtue. Our fruit comes from God as a result of His wise husbandry. The gardener's sharp-edged knife promotes the fruitfulness of the tree by thinning the clusters and by cutting off superfluous shoots. So is it, Christian, with the pruning that the Lord gives to you. *"My Father is the husbandman. Every branch in me that beareth not fruit he taketh away: and every branch that beareth fruit, he purgeth it, that it may bring forth more fruit"* (John 15:1–2). Since our God is the Author of our spiritual graces, let us give to Him all the glory of our salvation.

SEPTEMBER 8

Evening

*The exceeding greatness of his power to us-ward who believe,
according to the working of his mighty power, which he wrought in
Christ, when he raised him from the dead.*
—Ephesians 1:19–20

In the resurrection of Christ, as in our salvation, nothing short of divine power was employed. What can we say of those who think that conversion is brought about by the free will of man and is due to his own good character? When we see the dead rise from their graves by their own power, then we can expect to see ungodly sinners turning to Christ of their own free will. The preached or read Word, in itself, does not bring this divine power. All quickening power proceeds from the Holy Spirit. The power that raised Christ from the dead was irresistible. All the soldiers and the high priests could not keep the body of Christ in the tomb. Death itself could not hold Jesus in its chains. The same irresistible power is employed in the believer when he is raised to *"newness of life"* (Rom. 6:4). No sin, no corruption, no demons in hell or sinners on earth can hold back the hand of God's grace when He intends to convert someone. If God omnipotently says, "You will," man cannot say, "I will not." The power that raised Christ from the dead was also glorious. It reflected honor upon God and brought dismay to the hosts of evil. God receives great glory in the conversion of every sinner. The power was everlasting. *"Christ being raised from the dead dieth no more; death hath no more dominion over him"* (Rom. 6:9). Therefore, since we have been raised from the dead in Christ, we do not go back to our dead works or old corruptions. Instead, we live for God. Because He lives, we live also. *"For ye are dead, and your life is hid with Christ in God"* (Col. 3:3). *"As Christ was raised up from the dead by the glory of the Father, even so we also should walk in newness of life"* (Rom. 6:4). Last, note that the new life is united to Jesus. The same power that raised the Head works life in the members. What a blessing to be *"quickened…together with Christ"* (Eph. 2:5)!

SEPTEMBER 9

Morning

I will answer thee, and show thee great and mighty things,
which thou knowest not.
—Jeremiah 33:3

There are different translations of these words. One version renders it, *"I will show thee great and fortified things"*; another, *"great and reserved things."* Now, there are reserved and special things in Christian experience: all the developments of spiritual life are not equally easy to attain. There are the common frames and feelings of repentance, faith, joy, and hope, which are enjoyed by the entire family; but there is an upper realm of rapture, of communion, and of conscious union with Christ that is far from being the common dwelling place of believers. Not all of us have John's high privilege of leaning on Jesus' bosom or of Paul's being caught up into the third heaven. There are heights in the knowledge of the things of God that the eagle's eye of acumen and philosophic thought has never seen. God alone can bear us there. But the chariot in which He takes us up, and the fiery steeds with which that chariot is dragged, are prevailing prayers. Prevailing prayer is victorious over the God of mercy: *"By his strength he had power with God: yea, he had power over the angel, and prevailed: he wept, and made supplication unto him: he found him in Bethel, and there he spake with us"* (Hosea 12:3–4). Prevailing prayer takes the Christian to Carmel and enables him to cover heaven with clouds of blessing and earth with floods of mercy. Prevailing prayer bears the Christian aloft and shows him the inheritance reserved. It elevates and transfigures us, until in the likeness of our Lord, as He is, so are we also in this world. If you would reach to something higher than the ordinary experience, look to the *"rock that is higher than* [you]*"* (Ps. 61:2), and gaze with the eyes of faith through the window of persistent prayer. When you open the window on your side, it will not be bolted on the other!

And round about the throne were four and twenty seats: and upon the seats I saw four and twenty elders sitting, clothed in white raiment.
—Revelation 4:4

These representatives of the saints in heaven are said to be around the throne. In the passage where Solomon spoke of the king sitting at his table (Song 1:12), some scholars translate *"table"* as "a round table." From this translation, some Bible expositors—without stretching the meaning of the text, I believe—have said that this imagery means there is an equality among the saints. This idea is conveyed by the equal nearness of the twenty-four elders. The condition of glorified spirits in heaven is that of nearness to Christ, clear vision of His glory, constant access to His court, and intimate fellowship with Him. There is no difference, in this respect, between one saint and another. All the people of God—apostles, martyrs, ministers, as well as private and obscure Christians—will be seated near the throne, where they will forever gaze upon their exalted Lord and be satisfied in His love. They will all be near to Christ, all be in ecstasy over His love, all be eating and drinking at the same table with Him, all be equally beloved as His favorites and friends, even if they will not all be equally rewarded as servants. Let believers on earth imitate the saints in heaven in their nearness to Christ. Let us on earth be as the elders are in heaven, sitting around the throne. May Christ be the object of our thoughts, the center of our lives. How can we endure to live at such a distance from our Beloved? Lord Jesus, draw us nearer to Yourself. Say to us, *"Abide in me, and I in you"* (John 15:4). Permit us to sing, *"His left hand is under my head, and his right hand doth embrace me"* (Song 2:6).

O lift me higher, nearer Thee,
 And as I rise more pure and meet,
O let my soul's humility
 Make me lie lower at Thy feet;
Less trusting self, the more I prove
 The blessed comfort of Thy love.

And he goeth up into a mountain, and calleth unto him whom he would: and they came unto him.
—Mark 3:13

Here was sovereignty. Impatient spirits may fret and fume because they are not called to the highest places in the ministry. But, reader, rejoice that Jesus calls whom He will. If He permits me to be a doorkeeper in His house, I will cheerfully bless Him for His grace in allowing me to do anything in His service. The call of Christ's servants comes from above. Jesus stands on the mountain, evermore above the world in holiness, earnestness, love, and power. Those whom He calls must go up the mountain to Him. They must seek to rise to His level by living in constant communion with Him. They may not be able to mount to classic honors or attain scholastic eminence, but they must, like Moses, go up into the mount of God and have close communion with the unseen God; otherwise, they will never be fitted to proclaim the gospel of peace. Jesus went apart to hold high fellowship with the Father, and we must enter into the same divine companionship if we would bless our fellowmen. No wonder the apostles were clothed with power when they came down fresh from the mountain where Jesus was. This morning we must endeavor to ascend the mount of communion, so that there we may be ordained to the lifework for which we are set apart. Let us not see the face of man today until we have seen Jesus. Time spent with Him is laid out at blessed interest. We, too, will cast out devils and work wonders if we go down into the world girded with that divine energy that Christ alone can give. It is of no use going to the Lord's battle until we are armed with heavenly weapons. We must see Jesus; this is essential. At the mercy seat we will linger until He manifests Himself to us as He does not unto the world, and until we can truthfully say, "We were with Him on the Holy Mount."

SEPTEMBER 10

Evening

Evening wolves.
—Habakkuk 1:8

While I was preparing *Evening by Evening*, the above phrase came to my mind so frequently that, in order to free myself from its unrelenting persistence, I determined to devote a page to it! The evening wolf, infuriated by a day of hunger, was fiercer and more ravenous than he would have been in the morning. This furious creature may represent our doubts and fears after a day of distractions, losses in business, and perhaps ridicule from our fellowmen. How our thoughts howl in our ears, "Where is your God now?" How voracious and greedy they are, swallowing up all suggestions of comfort and remaining as hungry as before. Great Shepherd, slay these *"evening wolves."* Cause Your sheep to lie down in green pastures, undisturbed by insatiable unbelief. The fiends of hell are like the *"evening wolves."* When the flock of Christ is in a cloudy and dark day, and its sun seems to be going down, they are quick to tear and devour. They will hardly ever attack a Christian in the daylight of faith; but in the gloom of soul conflict, they will assault him. O Lord, You have laid down Your life for the sheep. Preserve them from the fangs of the wolf. False teachers, who craftily and industriously hunt for the precious lives of the sheep, and devour them by their falsehoods, are as dangerous and detestable as *"evening wolves."* Darkness is their element, deceit is their character, and destruction is their end. We are most in danger from them when they wear sheepskin. (See Matthew 7:15.) Blessed is the one who is kept from them, for thousands are made the prey of *"grievous* [destructive] *wolves"* (Acts 20:29) that enter within the fold of the church. What a wonder of grace it is when fierce persecutors are converted! Then the wolf dwells with the lamb, and men of cruel, ungovernable dispositions become gentle and teachable. O Lord, convert many of these wolves. We pray for their salvation tonight.

> *Be ye separate.*
> —2 Corinthians 6:17

The Christian, while *in* the world, is not to be *of* the world. He should be distinguished from it in the great objectives of his life. For him, *"to live* [should be] *Christ"* (Phil. 1:21). Whether he eats, drinks, or whatever he does, he should *"do all to the glory of God"* (1 Cor. 10:31). You may store up treasures, but store them in heaven, *"where neither moth nor rust doth corrupt, and where thieves do not break through nor steal"* (Matt. 6:20). You may strive to be rich, but let it be your ambition to be *"rich in faith"* (James 2:5) and *"rich in good works"* (1 Tim. 6:18). You may have pleasure, but when you are merry, *"sing psalms"* (James 5:13) and make *"melody in your heart to the Lord"* (Eph. 5:19). In your spirit, as well as in your aim, you should differ from the world. Waiting humbly before God, always conscious of His presence, delighting in communion with Him, and seeking to know His will, you will prove that you are of heavenly race. You should be separate from the world in your actions. If a thing is right, though you lose by it, it must be done. If it is wrong, though you would gain by it, you must scorn the sin for your Master's sake. You must have no fellowship with the unfruitful works of darkness, but rather reprove them. *"Walk worthy"* (Eph. 4:1) of your high calling and dignity. Remember, Christian, you are a child of the King of Kings. Therefore, keep yourself unspotted from the world. Do not soil the fingers that are soon to sweep celestial strings; do not let your eyes, which are soon to see the King in His beauty, become the windows of lust. Do not let your feet, which are soon to walk the golden streets, be defiled in miry places. Do not let your heart, which before long will be filled with heaven, be filled with pride and bitterness.

> Then rise my soul and soar away above the thoughtless crowd;
> Above the pleasures of the gay and splendors of the proud;
> Up where eternal beauties bloom and pleasures all divine;
> Where wealth, that never can consume,
> And endless glories shine.

SEPTEMBER 11

Evening

Lead me, O Lord, in thy righteousness because of mine enemies.
—Psalm 5:8

The enmity of the world against the followers of Christ is very bitter. People will forgive a thousand faults in others, but they will magnify the most trivial offenses in the followers of Jesus. Instead of regretting this state of affairs, which will accomplish nothing, let us use it for our benefit. Since so many are waiting for us to stumble, let this circumstance be our special motivation to walk very carefully before God. If we live carelessly, the eagle-eyed world will soon see it. With its hundred tongues, it will spread the story, exaggerated and emblazoned by the zeal of slander. People will shout triumphantly, "Aha! We were right! See how these Christians act. They are all hypocrites!" In this way, much damage will be done to the cause of Christ, and His name will be gravely insulted. The Cross of Christ is, in itself, an offense to the world. Let us be careful not to add any offense of our own. The Cross is *"unto the Jews a stumblingblock"* (1 Cor. 1:23). Let us make sure that we do not put any stumbling blocks where there are enough already. It is *"unto the Greeks foolishness"* (v. 23). Let us not add our folly, and thereby give any excuse for the scorn with which the worldly-wise deride the Gospel. How vigilant we need to be over ourselves! How strict we must be with our consciences! In the presence of adversaries who will misrepresent our best deeds and impugn our motives when they cannot censure our actions, how circumspect we must be! Pilgrims travel as suspect persons through Vanity Fair. Not only are we under surveillance, but also there are more spies than we imagine. The espionage is everywhere, at home and abroad. If we fall into our enemies' hands, we may sooner expect generosity from a wolf or mercy from a fiend than anything like patience with our weaknesses from men who spice their infidelity toward God with scandals against His people. O Lord, lead us always, lest our enemies trip us up!

God is jealous.
—Nahum 1:2

Your Lord is very jealous of your love, believer. Did He choose you? He cannot bear that you should choose another. Did He buy you with His own blood? He cannot endure that you should think that you are your own or that you belong to this world. He loved you with such a love that He would not stop in heaven without you; He would sooner die than see you perish. He cannot endure anything standing between your heart's love and Himself. He is very jealous of your trust. He will not permit you to trust in an arm of flesh. He cannot bear that you should hew out broken cisterns, when the overflowing fountain is always free to you. When we lean on Him, He is glad; but when we transfer our dependence to another, when we rely on our own wisdom or the wisdom of a friend—worst of all, when we trust in any works of our own—He is displeased and will chasten us so that He may bring us to Himself. He is also very jealous of our company. There should be no one with whom we converse as much as with Jesus. To abide in Him only is true love; but to commune with the world, to find sufficient solace in our carnal comforts, or to prefer even the society of our fellow Christians to intimate time with Him, this is grievous to our jealous Lord. He is happy to have us abide in Him and enjoy constant fellowship with Him. Many of the trials that He sends us are for the purpose of weaning our hearts from the creature and fixing them more closely on Him. Let this jealousy, which would keep us near to Christ, also be a comfort to us; for if He loves us so much as to care thus about our love, we may be sure that He will not allow anything to harm us, and He will protect us from all our enemies. Oh, that we may have grace this day to keep our hearts in sacred chastity for our Beloved alone, with sacred jealousy shutting our eyes to all the fascinations of the world!

SEPTEMBER 12
Evening

I will sing of mercy and judgment.
—Psalm 101:1

Faith triumphs in trial. When reason is thrust into the inner prison, with her feet secured in the stocks, faith makes the dungeon walls ring with her joyful notes, as she cries, *"I will sing of mercy and judgment: unto thee, O Lord, will I sing"* (Ps. 101:1). Faith pulls the black mask from the face of trouble and discovers the angel underneath. Faith looks up at the cloud and sees that

'Tis big with mercy and will break
In blessings on her head.

There is a theme for a song even in the judgments of God toward us. First, the trial is not as heavy as it might have been. Second, the trouble is not as severe as we deserve to bear. Third, our affliction is not as crushing as the burden that others have to carry. Faith sees that even her worst sorrow is not given to her as a punishment. There is not a drop of God's wrath in it; it is all sent in love. Faith discerns love gleaming like a jewel on the breast of an angry God. Faith says of her grief, "This is a badge of honor, for the child must undergo the rod." Then she sings of the sweet result of her sorrows, because they are for her spiritual benefit. Faith says, *"Our light affliction, which is but for a moment, worketh for us a far more exceeding and eternal weight of glory"* (2 Cor. 4:17). Therefore, Faith rides on its black horse, conquering and going forth to conquer, trampling down carnal reason and fleshly-mindedness, and singing songs of victory amid the thickest of the fray.

All I meet I find assists me
In my path to heavenly joy:
Where, though trials now attend me,
Trials never more annoy.

Blest there with a weight of glory,
Still the path I'll ne'er forget,
But, exulting, cry, it led me
To my blessed Savior's seat.

Who passing through the valley of Baca make it a well;
the rain also filleth the pools.
—Psalm 84:6

This teaches us that the comfort obtained by one may often prove serviceable to another, just as wells would be used by the company who came after. We read a book full of consolation, which is like Jonathan's rod, dripping with honey. We think our brother has been here before us and dug this well for us as well as for himself. Many wells have been dug by one pilgrim for himself but have proved quite as useful to others. We notice this especially in the Psalms, such as the ones that say, "*Why art thou cast down, O my soul?*" (Ps. 42:5, 11; 43:5). Travelers have been delighted to see the footprint of a man on a barren shore, and we love to see the signposts of pilgrims while passing through the vale of tears. The pilgrims dig the well, but, strangely enough, it fills from the top instead of the bottom. We use the means, but the blessing does not spring from the means. We dig a well, but heaven fills it with rain. "*The horse is prepared against the day of battle: but safety is of the LORD*" (Prov. 21:31). The means are connected with the end, but they do not of themselves produce it. See here the rain fills the pools so that the wells become useful as reservoirs for the water. Labor is not lost, yet it does not supersede divine help. Grace may well be compared to rain for its purity, for its refreshing and vivifying influence, for its coming alone from above, and for the sovereignty with which it is given or withheld. May our readers have showers of blessing, and may the wells they have dug be filled with water! Oh, what are means and laws without the smile of heaven! They are as clouds without rain and pools without water. O God of love, open the windows of heaven and pour out a blessing on us!

This man receiveth sinners.
—Luke 15:2

Note the graciousness of the fact that Jesus receives sinners. This Man, who towers above all other men, who is *"holy, harmless [innocent], undefiled, separate from sinners"* (Heb. 7:26)—*this* Man receives sinners. This Man, who is none other than the eternal God, before whom angels cover their faces (Isa. 6:2)—*this* Man receives sinners. Only the language of angels could describe such a mighty example of humility for the sake of love. It is not remarkable that any of us would be willing to seek lost men, women, and children, because they are of our own race. However, that He, the offended God, against whom the transgression has been committed, would take upon Himself the form of a servant and bear the sin of many, and would then be willing to receive the vilest of the vile—that is marvelous! *"This man receiveth sinners,"* not so that they may remain sinners, but so that He may pardon their sins, justify them, cleanse their hearts by His purifying Word, and preserve their souls by the indwelling of the Holy Spirit. He receives them so that He may enable them to serve Him, to show forth His praise, and to have communion with Him. He receives sinners into His heart's love. He takes them from the dunghill and wears them as jewels in His crown. He plucks them as brands from the fire and preserves them as costly monuments of His mercy. None are so precious in Jesus' sight as the sinners for whom He died. Jesus does not receive sinners at some outdoor receiving area or courtyard where He charitably shows them hospitality, as men might do for beggars who pass by. Instead, He opens the golden gates of His royal heart and receives the sinner right into Himself! Yes, He admits the humble penitent into personal union with Himself and makes Him a member of His body—of His own flesh and bones. There was never such a reception as this! This fact is still very certain this evening: He is still receiving sinners. I pray that sinners will receive Him.

There were also with him other little ships.
—Mark 4:36

Jesus was the Lord High Admiral of the sea that night, and His presence preserved the whole convoy. It is well to sail with Jesus, even though it is in a little ship. When we sail in Christ's company, we may not have a guarantee of fair weather; for great storms may toss the vessel that carries the Lord Himself, and we must not expect to find the sea less boisterous around our little boat. If we go with Jesus, we must be content to fare as He fares; and when the waves are rough to Him, they will be rough to us. It is by tempest and tossing that we will come to land, as He did before us. When the storm swept over Galilee's dark lake, all faces gathered blackness, and all hearts dreaded shipwreck. When all creature-help was useless, the slumbering Savior arose and, with a word, transformed the riot of the tempest into the deep quiet of a calm. Then were the other little vessels at rest as well as the one that carried the Lord. Jesus is the star of the sea; although there may be sorrow on the sea, when Jesus is on it, there is joy, too. May our hearts make Jesus their anchor, their rudder, their lighthouse, their lifeboat, and their harbor. His church is the Admiral's flagship. Let us attend her movements and cheer her officers with our presence. He Himself is the great attraction. Let us follow ever in His wake, mark His signals, steer by His chart, and never fear while He is within reach of our call. Not one ship in the convoy will suffer wreck; the great Commodore will steer every boat in safety to the desired haven. By faith we will slip our cable for another day's cruise and sail forth with Jesus into a sea of tribulation. Winds and waves will not spare us, but they all obey Him; therefore, whatever squalls may occur without, faith will feel a blessed calm within. He is ever in the center of the weather-beaten company. Let us rejoice in Him. His vessel has reached the haven, and so will ours.

*I acknowledged my sin unto thee, and mine iniquity have I not hid. I
said, I will confess my transgressions unto the* LORD;
and thou forgavest the iniquity of my sin.
—Psalm 32:5

David's grief over his sin was bitter. Its effects were visible on his body:
his bones wasted away (Ps. 32:3), and his vigor was turned into the *"drought
of summer"* (v. 4). He could find no remedy until he had made a full confession of his sin before the throne of heavenly grace. He told us that, for a
time, he kept silent, and his heart became more and more filled with grief
(vv. 3–4). Like a mountain lake whose outlet is blocked up, his soul was
swollen with torrents of sorrow. He made excuses, and he tried to divert
his thoughts, but it was no use. His anguish gathered like a festering sore.
Since he would not use the scalpel of confession, his spirit was full of torment and knew no rest. At last it came to this: he must return to his God
in humble penitence or die outright. So he ran to the mercy seat and there
unrolled the volume of his iniquities before the all-seeing One, acknowl-
edging all the evil of his ways in language such as you read in the Fifty-first
Psalm and other penitential psalms. Having done this, a work so simple
and yet so difficult on his pride, he immediately received the sign of divine
forgiveness. The bones that had been broken were caused to rejoice, and
he came forth singing of the blessedness of the man whose transgression
is forgiven (v. 1). See the value of a grace-worked confession of sin! It is to
be prized above all cost, for in every case where there is genuine, gracious
confession, mercy is freely given. This is not because the repentance and
confession deserve mercy; the mercy is given for Christ's sake. May God
be blessed, for there is always healing for the broken heart. The fountain is
continuously flowing to cleanse us from our sins. Truly, O Lord, *"thou art a
God ready to pardon"* (Neh. 9:17)! Therefore, we will acknowledge our iniquities to You.

He shall not be afraid of evil tidings.
—Psalm 112:7

Christian, you should not dread the arrival of evil tidings. If you are distressed by them, how are you different from other men? Other men do not have your God to go to. They have never proved His faithfulness as you have done. It is no wonder if they are bowed down with alarm and cowed with fear, but you profess to be of another spirit. You have been *"begotten... again unto a lively hope"* (1 Pet. 1:3), and your heart lives in heaven and not on earthly things. Now, if you are seen to be distracted as other men, what is the value of that grace that you profess to have received? Where is the dignity of that new nature that you claim to possess? If you would be filled with alarm, as others are, you would, doubtless, be led into the sins so common to others under trying circumstances. The ungodly, when they are overtaken by evil tidings, rebel against God. They murmur and think that God deals harshly with them. Will you fall into that same sin? Will you provoke the Lord as they do? Moreover, unconverted men often run to wrong means in order to escape from difficulties, and you will be sure to do the same if your mind yields to the present pressure. Trust in the Lord, and *"wait patiently for him"* (Ps. 37:7). Your wisest course is to do as Moses did at the Red Sea, *"Stand still, and see the salvation of the LORD"* (Exod. 14:13). If you give way to fear when you hear of evil tidings, you will be unable to meet the trouble with that calm composure that strengthens for duty and sustains under adversity. How can you glorify God if you play the coward? Saints have often sung God's high praises in the fires, but will your doubt and despair, as if you had none to help you, magnify the Most High? Then take courage, and relying in sure confidence on the faithfulness of your covenant God, do not let *"your heart be troubled, neither let it be afraid"* (John 14:27).

SEPTEMBER 15

A people near unto him.
—Psalm 148:14

The dispensation of the old covenant was one of distance. Even when God appeared to His servant Moses, He said, *"Draw not nigh hither: put off thy shoes from off thy feet"* (Exod. 3:5). When He manifested Himself on Mount Sinai to His own chosen and separated people, one of the first commands He gave was, *"Set bounds about the mount"* (Exod. 19:23). In the sacred worship of both the tabernacle and the temple, the thought of distance was always prominent. Into the inner court, none but the priests might dare to intrude, while into the innermost place or the Holy of Holies, the high priest entered only once a year. It was as if the Lord in those early ages wanted to teach man that sin was so utterly loathsome to Him that He had to treat men as lepers put outside the camp. When He came nearest to them, He still made them feel the width of the separation between a holy God and an impure sinner. Yet when the Gospel came, we were placed on quite another footing. The word "Go" was exchanged for "Come," distance was succeeded by nearness, and we who formerly were afar off were brought near by the blood of Jesus Christ. Incarnate Deity has no wall of fire around Him. *"Come unto me, all ye that labour and are heavy laden, and I will give you rest"* (Matt. 11:28) is the joyful proclamation of God as He appears in human flesh. Now He does not teach the leper his leprosy by setting him at a distance, but by Himself suffering the penalty of the leper's defilement. What a state of safety and privilege this nearness to God through Jesus is! Do you know it by experience? If you know it, are you living in the power of it? This nearness is marvelous, yet it is to be followed by a dispensation of even greater nearness, when it will be said, *"The tabernacle of God is with men, and he will dwell with them"* (Rev. 21:3). Make the time of this greater nearness come quickly, O Lord!

Partakers of the divine nature.
—2 Peter 1:4

To be a partaker of the divine nature is not, of course, to become God. That cannot be. The essence of deity is not to be participated in by the creature. Between the creature and the Creator there must ever be a gulf fixed in respect of essence. But as the first man Adam was made in the image of God, so we, by the renewal of the Holy Spirit, are in a diviner sense made in the image of the Most High and are partakers of the divine nature. We are, by grace, made like God. *"God is love"* (1 John 4:16). We become love: *"Every one that loveth is born of God"* (v. 7). God is truth; we become true, and we love that which is true. God is good, and He makes us good by His grace, so that we become the *"pure in heart"* who *"shall see God"* (Matt. 5:8). Moreover, we become *"partakers of the divine nature"* in even a higher sense than this—in fact, in as lofty a sense as can be conceived, short of our being absolutely divine. Do we not become members of the body of the divine person of Christ? Yes, the same blood that flows in the head flows in the hand, and the same life that quickens Christ quickens His people, for *"Ye are dead, and your life is hid with Christ in God"* (Col. 3:3). As if this were not enough, we are married to Christ. He has betrothed us unto Himself in righteousness and in faithfulness, and he who is joined to the Lord is one spirit. Oh, marvelous mystery! We look into it, but who can understand it? One with Jesus—so one with Him that the branch is not more one with the vine than we are a part of the Lord, our Savior and our Redeemer! While we rejoice in this, let us remember that those who are made *"partakers of the divine nature"* will manifest their high and holy relationship in their fellowship with others. It will be evident by their daily walk and conversation that they have *"escaped the corruption that is in the world through lust"* (2 Pet. 1:4). Oh, for more divine holiness of life!

SEPTEMBER 16

Am I a sea, or a whale, that thou settest a watch over me?
—Job 7:12

This was a strange question for Job to ask of the Lord. He felt he was too insignificant to be so strictly watched and chastened, and he hoped that he was not so unruly as to need to be restrained. The inquiry was natural from one surrounded by such insupportable miseries. Nevertheless, the question is such that it leaves the questioner open to receiving a very humbling answer. It is true that man is not the ocean, but he is even more troublesome and unruly than the sea. The sea obediently respects its own boundaries. It does not go beyond its limit, even though its limit may be only a sandbar. Mighty as it is, it obeys the divine *"Hitherto"* (Job 38:11). Even when it is raging at the height of a storm, it respects God's word. However, self-willed man defies heaven and oppresses earth. There is no end to his rebellious rage. The sea, obedient to the moon, ebbs and flows with ceaseless regularity, and thus fulfills an active as well as a passive obedience. Yet man is restless beyond his domain. He sleeps far inside the lines of duty, being lazy when he should be active. He will neither come nor go at the divine command, but sullenly prefers to do what he should not do and to leave undone what is required of him. Every drop in the ocean, every beaded bubble, every bit of foam, and every shell and pebble feel the power of God's law, and they yield or move at once. If only our nature were but one thousandth as much conformed to the will of God! We call the sea fickle and false, but how constant it is! From our fathers' days, and from ancient days before them, the sea has remained where it was, beating on the same cliffs, to the same tune. We know where to find it. It does not forsake its bed, and its ceaseless boom does not change. Yet where is man—vain, fickle man? Can the wise man guess by what foolishness he will next be seduced from his obedience? We need more watching than the billowy sea, for we are far more rebellious. Lord, rule us for Your own glory. Amen.

Bring him unto me.
—Mark 9:19

Despairingly, the poor, disappointed father turned away from the disciples to their Master. His son was in the worst possible condition, and all means had failed. But the pitiful child was soon delivered from the evil one when the parent, in faith, obeyed the Lord Jesus' word, *"Bring him unto me."* Children are a precious gift from God, but much anxiety comes with them. They may be a great joy or a great bitterness to their parents. They may be filled with the Spirit of God or possessed with the spirit of evil. In all cases, the Word of God gives us one prescription for the curing of all their ills, *"Bring* [them] *unto me."* Oh, for more agonizing prayer on their behalf while they are yet babies! Sin is there, so let our prayers begin to attack it. Our cries for our offspring should precede those cries that announce their actual advent into a world of sin. In the days of their youth, we will see sad indicators of that dumb and deaf spirit that will neither pray aright, nor hear the voice of God in the soul. Still, Jesus commands, *"Bring* [them] *unto me."* When they are grown up, they may wallow in sin and display enmity against God. Then, when our hearts are breaking, we should remember the Great Physician's words, *"Bring* [them] *unto me."* We must never cease to pray until they cease to breathe. No case is hopeless while Jesus lives. The Lord sometimes allows His people to be driven into a corner so that they may know how necessary He is to them. Ungodly children, when they show us our own powerlessness against the depravity of their hearts, drive us to flee to the Strong One for strength, and this is a great blessing to us. Whatever our morning's need may be, let it, like a strong current, bear us to the ocean of divine love. Jesus can soon remove our sorrow. He delights to comfort us. Let us hasten to Him while He waits to meet us.

Encourage him.
—Deuteronomy 1:38

God uses His people to encourage one another. He did not say to the angel, "Gabriel, my servant Joshua is about to lead my people into Canaan. Go and encourage him." God never works needless miracles. If His purposes can be accomplished by ordinary means, He will not use miraculous methods. Gabriel would not have been half as well equipped for the work of encouraging Joshua as Moses was. A brother's sympathy is more precious than an angel's message. The angel, who was swift of wing, would have known the Master's commands but might not have been familiar with the people's character. The angel had never experienced the hardness of the road or seen the fiery serpents; neither had he led the stiff-necked multitude in the wilderness, as Moses had done. We should be glad that God usually works *for* man *by* man. It forms a bond of brotherhood. When we are mutually dependent on one another, we are more completely blended into one family. Beloved, take the text as God's message to you. Work to help others, and especially strive to encourage them. Speak in an encouraging way to the young person who is anxiously seeking God, and lovingly try to move stumbling blocks out of his way. When you find a spark of grace in his heart, kneel down and blow it into a flame. Allow the young believer to discover the roughness of the road by degrees, but tell him of the strength that dwells in God, of the sureness of the promise, and of the delights of communion with Christ. Aim to comfort the sorrowful and to encourage the despondent. *"Speak a word in season to him that is weary"* (Isa. 50:4), and encourage those who are fearful to go on their way with gladness. God encourages you by His promises; Christ encourages you as He points to the heaven He has won for you; and the Spirit encourages you as He works in you *"to will and to do of his good pleasure"* (Phil. 2:13). Imitate divine wisdom, and encourage others, according to this evening's text.

If we live in the Spirit, let us also walk in the Spirit.
—Galatians 5:25

The two most important things in our holy religion are the *life of faith* and the *walk of faith*. He who rightly understand these is not far from being a master in practicing theology, for they are vital points to a Christian. You will never find true faith unattended by true godliness; on the other hand, you will never discover a truly holy life that is not rooted in a living faith based on the righteousness of Christ. Woe unto those who seek after the one without the other! There are some who cultivate faith and forget holiness; these may be very high in orthodoxy, but they will be very deep in condemnation, for they *"hold the truth in unrighteousness"* (Rom. 1:18). There are others who have strained after holiness of life, but have denied the faith, like the Pharisees of old, whom the Master said were like white-washed tombs. We must have faith, for this is the foundation; we must have holiness of life, for this is the superstructure. Of what service is the mere foundation of a building to a man in the day of tempest? Can he hide himself there? He needs a house to cover him, as well as a foundation for that house. Even so we need the superstructure of spiritual life if we would have comfort in the day of doubt. But do not seek a holy life without faith, for that would be to erect a house that can afford no permanent shelter, because it has no foundation on a rock. Let faith and a holy life be put together, and, like the two abutments of an arch, they will make our piety enduring. Like light and heat streaming from the same sun, they are both full of blessing. Like the two pillars of the temple, they are for glory and for beauty. They are two streams from the fountain of grace, two lamps lit with holy fire, two olive trees watered by heavenly care. O Lord, give us this day life within, and it will reveal itself without to Your glory.

And they follow me.
—John 10:27

We should follow our Lord as unhesitatingly as sheep follow their shepherd, for He has a right to lead us wherever He pleases. We are not our own; we are *"bought with a price"* (1 Cor. 6:20). Therefore, let us recognize the rights of the redeeming blood. The soldier follows his captain, and the servant obeys his master. How much more should we follow our Redeemer, to whom we are purchased possessions. We are not true to our profession of faith as followers of Christ if we question the commands of our Leader and Commander. Submission is our duty; being argumentative is our folly. Our Lord might often say to us, as He did to Peter, *"What is that to thee? follow thou me"* (John 21:22). Wherever Jesus leads us, He goes before us. Even if we do not know where we are going, we know with whom we go. With such a Companion, we do not need to dread the perils of the road. The journey may be long, but His *"everlasting arms"* (Deut. 33:27) will carry us to the end. The presence of Jesus is the assurance of eternal salvation. Because He lives, we also will live. We should follow Christ in simplicity and faith, because the paths in which He leads us all end in glory and immortality. It is true that they may not be smooth paths. They may be covered with sharp, unyielding trials, but they lead to the *"city which hath foundations, whose builder and maker is God"* (Heb. 11:10). *"All the paths of the LORD are mercy and truth unto such as keep his covenant"* (Ps. 25:10). Let us put full trust in our Leader. We know that, come prosperity or adversity, health or sickness, popularity or contempt, His purpose will be worked out. That purpose will be pure, unmingled good for every heir of mercy. We will find that it is sweet to go up the exposed side of the hill with Christ. When rain and snow blow into our faces, His dear love will make us far more blessed than those who sit at home and warm their hands at the world's fire. Into the dens of lions or to the hills of leopards, we will follow our Beloved. Precious Jesus, draw us, and we will run after You.

Stand fast therefore in the liberty wherewith Christ
hath made us free.
—Galatians 5:1

This *"liberty"* makes us free to heaven's charter—the Bible. Here is a choice passage, believer: *"When thou passest through the waters, I will be with thee"* (Isa. 43:2). You are free to that. Here is another: *"The mountains shall depart, and the hills be removed; but my kindness shall not depart from thee"* (Isa. 54:10). You are free to that. You are a welcome guest at the table of the promises. Scripture is a never-failing treasury filled with boundless stores of grace. It is the bank of heaven; you may draw from it as much as you please, without permission or hindrance. Come in faith, and you are welcome to all covenant blessings. There is not a promise in the Word that will be withheld. In the depths of tribulations, let this freedom comfort you. Amid waves of distress, let it cheer you. When sorrow surrounds you, let it be your solace. This is your Father's love-token. You are free to it at all times. You are also free to the throne of grace. It is the believer's privilege to have access at all times to his heavenly Father. Whatever our desires, our difficulties, our needs, we are at liberty to spread all before Him. It does not matter how much we may have sinned; we may ask for and expect pardon. No matter how wealthy or how poor we are, we may plead His promise that He will provide all things that we need. We have permission to approach His throne at all times—in midnight's darkest hour or in noontide's most burning heat. Exercise your right, believer, and live up to your privilege. You are free to all that is treasured up in Christ: wisdom, righteousness, sanctification, and redemption. It does not matter what your need is, for there is fullness of supply in Christ, and it is there for you! Oh, what a freedom is yours—freedom from condemnation, freedom to the promises, freedom to the throne of grace, and, at last, freedom to enter heaven!

SEPTEMBER 19
Evening

For this child I prayed.
—1 Samuel 1:27

Devout souls delight to look on the mercies that they have obtained in answer to prayer, for they can see God's special love in them. When we can name our blessings *Samuel*, that is, "asked of God," they will be as dear to us as Hannah's child was to her. Hannah's husband had another wife, Peninnah, who had many children. However, her children came as common blessings unsought in prayer. Hannah's one, heaven-given child was far dearer, because he was the fruit of earnest pleadings. The cup of prayer puts sweetness into the medicine it brings. When we have prayed for the conversion of our children, how doubly sweet it is for us when they are saved, for we see our own petitions fulfilled in them! It is even better to rejoice over our children as the fruit of our intercession than as the fruit of our bodies. Have we sought the Lord for one of the *"best [spiritual] gifts"* (1 Cor. 12:31)? When it comes to us, it will be wrapped up in the gold cloth of God's faithfulness and truth, and thus will be doubly precious. Have we prayed for success in the Lord's work? How joyful the prosperity is that comes flying upon the wings of prayer! It is always best to receive blessings into our house in the legitimate way—by the door of prayer. Then they are blessings indeed, and not temptations. Even when prayer is not quickly answered, the blessings grow all the richer because of the delay. When Jesus was a boy, He was all the more lovely in the eyes of Mary when she found Him after having sought Him sorrowfully. (See Luke 2:42–51.) We should dedicate to God what we gain by prayer, as Hannah dedicated Samuel. The gift came from heaven; let it be given back to heaven. Prayer brought it, and gratitude sang over it. Now let devotion consecrate it. It will be a special occasion for saying, "I have only given to You what is already Yours." (See 1 Chronicles 29:14.) Reader, does prayer invigorate or weary you? Which is it?

The sword of the LORD, and of Gideon.
—Judges 7:20

Gideon ordered his men to do two things. Covering up a torch in an earthen pitcher, he told them, at an appointed signal, to break the pitcher and let the light shine. Then they were to sound the trumpet, crying, *"The sword of the LORD, and of Gideon!"* This is precisely what all Christians must do. First, you must shine; break the pitcher that conceals your light. Throw aside the bushel that has been hiding your candle and shine. Let your light shine before men; let your good works be such that, when men look on you, they will know that you have been with Jesus. Then there must be the sound, the blowing of the trumpet. There must be active exertions for the ingathering of sinners by proclaiming Christ crucified. Take the Gospel to them. Carry it to their door. Put it in their way. Do not allow them to escape it; blow the trumpet right against their ears. Remember that the true war cry of the church is Gideon's watchword, *"The sword of the LORD, and of Gideon!"* God must do it; it is His own work. But we are not to be idle. Instrumentality is to be used—*"The sword of the LORD, and of Gideon!"* If we only cry, *"The sword of the LORD!"* we will be guilty of an idle presumption; and if we shout, *"The sword of Gideon!"* alone, we will manifest idolatrous reliance on an arm of flesh: we must blend the two in practical harmony, *"The sword of the LORD, and of Gideon!"* We can do nothing of ourselves, but we can do everything by the help of our God. Let us, therefore, in His name determine to go out personally and serve with our flaming torch of holy example and with our trumpet tones of earnest declaration and testimony. God will be with us, our enemy will be put to confusion, and the Lord of Hosts will reign forever and ever.

SEPTEMBER 20
Evening

In the evening withhold not thine hand.
—Ecclesiastes 11:6

Opportunities are plentiful in the evening. People return to their homes after work, and the zealous soulwinner finds time to go about telling of the love of Jesus. Am I engaged in evening work for Jesus? If not, let me no longer withhold my hand from a service that requires abundant labor. Sinners are perishing for lack of knowledge. He who delays may find the hems of his clothes crimson with the blood of souls. (See Jeremiah 2:34.) Jesus submitted both of His hands to the nails when He died on the cross. How can I keep back one of mine from His blessed work? Night and day, He toiled and prayed for me. How can I give a single hour to pampering my flesh with luxurious ease? Get up, idle heart. Stretch out your hands to work, or lift them up in prayer. Heaven and hell are in earnest. Let me be earnest, also, and sow good seed this evening for the Lord my God. The evening of life also has a claim on us. Life is so short that a morning of humanity's vigor and an evening of decline are the sum of it. To some people, life seems long, but a nickel is a great sum of money to a poor man. Life is so brief that no one can afford to lose a day. It has been well said that if a great king were to present us with a huge pile of gold and tell us to take as much of it as we could count in a day, we would make a long day of it. We would begin early in the morning and not stop even when it was evening. Winning souls is a far nobler work. Then why do we withdraw from it so soon? Some people are spared for a long evening of vigorous old age. If that is the case with me, let me use the talents that I still retain and serve my blessed and faithful Lord to my last hour. By His grace, I will die in the harness. I will lay down my charge only when I lay down my body. Those who are elderly may instruct the young, comfort the fainthearted, and encourage the despondent. If evening has less vigorous heat, it should have more calm wisdom. Therefore, in the evening, I will not withhold my hand.

I will rejoice over them to do them good.
—Jeremiah 32:41

How encouraging to the believer is the delight that God has in His saints! We cannot see any reason in ourselves why the Lord should take pleasure in us. We cannot take delight in ourselves, for we often have to groan, being burdened. We are conscious of our sinfulness and deplore our unfaithfulness. We fear that God's people cannot take much delight in us, for they must perceive so many of our imperfections and our follies that they may rather lament our infirmities than admire our graces. But we love to dwell on this transcendent truth, this glorious mystery: as the bridegroom rejoices over the bride, so the Lord rejoices over us. We do not read anywhere that God delights in the cloud-capped mountains or the sparkling stars, but we do read that He delights *"in the habitable part of his earth,"* and that His delights are *"with the sons of men"* (Prov. 8:31). We do not find it written that even angels give His soul delight. Nor does He say, concerning cherubim and seraphim, *"Thou shalt be called Hephzibah,... for the LORD delighteth in thee"* (Isa. 62:4), but He does say all that to poor fallen creatures like ourselves, debased and depraved by sin, but saved, exalted, and glorified by His grace. In what strong language He expresses His delight in His people! Who could have conceived of the Eternal One as bursting forth into a song? Yet it is written, *"He will rejoice over thee with joy; he will rest in his love, he will joy over thee with singing"* (Zeph. 3:17). As He looked on the world He had made, He said, "It is very good"; but when He beheld those who are the purchase of Jesus' blood, His own chosen ones, it seemed as if the great heart of the Infinite could restrain itself no longer, but overflowed in divine exclamations of joy. Should we not utter our grateful response to such a marvelous declaration of His love and sing, *"I will rejoice in the LORD, I will joy in the God of my salvation"* (Hab. 3:18)?

Gather not my soul with sinners.
—Psalm 26:9

Fear made David pray this prayer, for something whispered to him, "Perhaps, after all, you may be gathered with the wicked." Although marred by unbelief, this kind of fear springs mainly from holy anxiety arising from the recollection of past sin. Even the pardoned man will inquire, "What if, in the end, my sins are remembered, and I am left off the list of the saved?" He remembers his present unfruitfulness—so little grace, so little love, so little holiness. Looking toward the future, he considers his weaknesses and the many temptations that surround him, and he fears that he may fall and become prey to the enemy. A sense of sin and present evil, as well as his prevailing corruptions, compel him to pray, in fear and trembling, *"Gather not my soul with sinners."* Reader, if you have prayed this prayer, and if your character is described in the psalm from which it is taken, you do not need to be afraid that you will be gathered with sinners. Do you have the two virtues that David had—walking in integrity outwardly and trusting in the Lord inwardly? Are you resting in Christ's sacrifice, and can you approach the altar of God with humble hope? If so, rest assured that you will never be gathered with the wicked, for that calamity is impossible. At the Judgment, like will be gathered with like. *"Gather ye together first the tares, and bind them in bundles to burn them: but gather the wheat into my barn"* (Matt. 13:30). Therefore, if you are like God's people, you will be with God's people. You cannot be gathered with the wicked, for you were too dearly bought. You are redeemed by the blood of Christ, and you are His forever. Where He is, His people must be. You are loved too much to be cast away with reprobates. Will one who is dear to Christ perish? Impossible! Hell cannot hold you. Heaven claims you. Trust in your Surety, and do not fear!

Let Israel rejoice in him.
—Psalm 149:2

Be glad of heart, believer, but take care that your gladness springs from the Lord. You have much cause for gladness in your God, for you can sing with David, *"God my exceeding joy"* (Ps. 43:4). Be glad that the Lord reigns, that Jehovah is King! Rejoice that He sits on the throne and rules all things! Every attribute of God should become a fresh ray in the sunlight of our gladness. Knowing that He is wise should make us glad, as we look at our own foolishness. Knowing that He is mighty should cause us to rejoice, as we tremble at our weakness. Knowing that He is everlasting should always be a theme of joy, as we consider that we wither as the grass. Knowing that He is unchanging should perpetually yield us a song, since we change every hour. Knowing that He is full of grace, that He is overflowing with it, and that this grace in covenant He has given to us; that it is ours to cleanse us, ours to keep us, ours to sanctify us, ours to perfect us, ours to bring us to glory—all this should tend to make us glad in Him. This gladness in God is like a deep river. We have only as yet touched its brink. We know a little of its clear, sweet, heavenly streams, but onward the depth is greater, and the current more impetuous in its joy. The Christian feels that he may delight himself not only in what God is, but also in all that God has done in the past. The Psalms show us that God's people in olden times were inclined to think much of God's actions, and to have a song concerning each of them. So let God's people now rehearse the deeds of the Lord! Let them tell of His mighty acts and *"sing unto the Lord, for he hath triumphed gloriously"* (Exod. 15:1). Nor let them ever cease to sing, for as new mercies flow to them day by day, so should their gladness in the Lord's loving acts in providence and in grace show itself in continued thanksgiving. Be glad, children of Zion, and rejoice in the Lord your God.

*When my heart is overwhelmed: lead me to the rock
that is higher than I.*
—Psalm 61:2

Most of us know what it means to be overwhelmed in heart. It is like being emptied, as when someone thoroughly washes and rinses a dish and then turns it upside down to dry. Or it is like being thrown on one's side and submerged, like a ship mastered by a storm. Discoveries of inward corruption will overwhelm our hearts, when the Lord permits the great depths of our depravity to become troubled and to cast up mire and dirt. Disappointment and heartbreak will also overwhelm us, when billow after billow rolls over us, and we are like a broken shell that is hurled to and fro by the surf. May God be blessed, for at such seasons we are not without an all-sufficient solace. Our God is the Harbor of weather-beaten sails, the Lodging of forlorn pilgrims. He is higher than we are—His mercy is higher than our sins, and His love is higher than our thoughts. It is pitiful to see men putting their trust in something lower than themselves. Yet our confidence is fixed on an exceedingly high and glorious Lord. He is a Rock, since He does not change; and He is a high Rock, because the storms that overwhelm us roll far beneath at His feet. He is not disturbed by them, but rules them at His will. If we get under the shelter of this great Rock, we may defy the hurricane. All is calm under the protection of this towering cliff. Sadly, such is the confusion into which the troubled mind is often thrown, that we need piloting to this divine shelter! That is why we have the prayer of our text. O Lord, our God, by Your Holy Spirit, teach us the way of faith and lead us into Your rest. The wind blows us out to sea, and the helm does not respond to our feeble hands. You, and You alone, can steer us safely over the bar between the sunken rocks and into the fair haven. How dependent we are on You—we need You to bring us to You. To be wisely directed and steered into safety and peace is Your gift, and Yours alone. This night, be pleased to deal well with Your servants.

SEPTEMBER 23

Accepted in the beloved.
—Ephesians 1:6

What a privilege! It includes our justification before God, but the term *acceptance* in the Greek means more than that. It signifies that we are the objects of divine pleasure, or even more, of divine delight. How marvelous that we—worms, mortals, sinners—should be the objects of divine love! But it is only *"in the beloved."* Some Christians seem to be accepted in their own experience; at least, that is their understanding. When their spirit is lively and their hopes bright, they think God accepts them, for they feel so high, so heavenly-minded, so drawn above the earth! But when their souls cleave to the dust, they are the victims of the fear that they are no longer accepted. If they could but see that all their high joys do not exalt them, and all their low times of despair do not really depress them in their Father's sight; instead, they stand accepted in One who never alters, in One who is always the beloved of God, always perfect, always without spot or wrinkle. How much happier they would be, and how much more they would honor the Savior, if they realized this truth! Rejoice, then, believer! You are *"accepted in the beloved."* You look within and say, "There is nothing acceptable here!" But look at Christ and see if there is not everything acceptable there. Your sins trouble you, but God has cast your sins behind His back, and you are accepted in the Righteous One. You have to fight with corruption and to wrestle with temptation, but you are already accepted in Him who has overcome the powers of evil. The devil tempts you, but be of good cheer. He cannot destroy you, for you are accepted in Him who has broken Satan's head. Know by full assurance your glorious standing. Even glorified souls are not more accepted than you are. They are only accepted in heaven *"in the beloved,"* and you are even now accepted in Christ after the same manner.

Jesus said unto him, If thou canst believe.
—Mark 9:23

A certain man had a demon-possessed son, who was afflicted with a spirit that made him mute. The father had witnessed the futile attempts of Jesus' disciples to heal his child (see Mark 9:18), and so he had little or no faith in Christ. Therefore, when Jesus told him to bring his son to Him, he answered, *"If thou canst do any thing, have compassion on us, and help us"* (v. 22). Now, there was an *"if"* in his question, but the poor fearful father had put the *"if"* in the wrong place. Without commanding the man to retract the *"if,"* Jesus Christ kindly put it in its rightful position. "Truly," He seemed to say, "there should be no 'if' about My power or My willingness. The 'if' lies somewhere else." He told the father, ***"If thou** canst believe, all things are possible to him that believeth"* (v. 23, emphasis added). When the man heard these words, his trust was strengthened, and he offered a humble prayer for an increase of faith. Instantly, Jesus spoke the word, and the demon was cast out, with an injunction never to return. There is a lesson from this incident that we need to learn. Like this man, we often realize that there should be an "if" somewhere, but we are perpetually blundering by putting it in the wrong place. We make "if" statements, such as the following: "If Jesus can help me…." "If He can give me grace to overcome temptation…." "If He can give me pardon…." "If He can make me successful…." If *He* can? No, if *you* can believe, He both can and will. You have misplaced your "if." If you can confidently trust in Him, then, as all things are possible for Christ, all things will be possible for you. Faith stands in God's power and is robed in God's majesty. It wears the royal apparel and rides on the King's horse, for faith is a grace that the King delights to honor. Equipping itself with the glorious might of the all-working Spirit, faith becomes, in the omnipotence of God, mighty to work, to dare, and to suffer. *"All things"*—without limit—*"are possible to him that believeth."* My soul, can you believe your Lord tonight?

SEPTEMBER 24

Morning

For I was ashamed to require of the king a band of soldiers and horsemen to help us against the enemy in the way: because we had spoken unto the king, saying, The hand of our God is upon all them for good that seek him; but his power and his wrath is against all them that forsake him.
—Ezra 8:22

For many reasons, a convoy would have been desirable for the pilgrim band, but a holy shamefacedness would not allow Ezra to seek one. He feared lest the heathen king would think his professions of faith in God to be mere hypocrisy or imagine that the God of Israel was not able to preserve His own worshippers. He could not bring his mind to lean on an arm of flesh in a matter so evidently of the Lord; therefore, the caravan set out with no visible protection, guarded by Him who is the sword and shield of His people. It is to be feared that few believers feel this holy jealousy for God. Even those who, in a measure, walk by faith occasionally mar the luster of their lives by craving aid from man. It is a most blessed thing to have no props and no buttresses, but to stand upright on the Rock of Ages, upheld by the Lord alone. Would any believers seek state endowments for their church if they remembered that the Lord is dishonored by their asking for Caesar's aid? As if the Lord could not supply the needs of His own cause! Would we run so hastily to friends and relatives for assistance if we remembered that the Lord is magnified by our implicit reliance on His solitary arm? My soul, wait only on God. "But," says one, "are not means to be used?" Assuredly they are; but our fault seldom lies in their neglect. Far more frequently it springs out of foolishly believing in them instead of believing in God. Few run too far in neglecting the creature's arm, but many sin greatly in making too much of it. Learn, dear reader, to glorify the Lord by leaving means untried, if by using them you would dishonor the name of the Lord.

I sleep, but my heart waketh.
—Song of Solomon 5:2

Paradoxes abound in Christian experience. Our text provides us with an example of one: the spouse was asleep, yet she was awake. The only one who can solve the believer's riddle is the one who has plowed with the heifer of his experience. (See Judges 14:11–18.) I would like to emphasize two points in this evening's text: a mournful sleepiness and a hopeful wakefulness. *"I sleep."* Through the sin that dwells in us, we may become lax in holy duties, slothful in religious disciplines, lackluster in spiritual joys, and altogether slack and careless. Yet this is a shameful condition for one in whom the quickening Spirit dwells; it is dangerous to the highest degree. Even wise virgins sometimes sleep, but it is high time for all to shake off the shackles of sloth. It is to be feared that many believers lose their strength, as Samson lost his hair, while sleeping on the lap of carnal security. With a world perishing around us, to sleep is cruel. With eternity so near-at-hand, it is madness. Yet none of us is as awake as we should be. A few thunderclaps would do us all good. It may be that, unless we soon rouse ourselves, we will have them in the form of war, pestilence, or personal losses and bereavements. Oh, that we might leave forever the bed of fleshly ease and go forth with flaming torches to meet the coming Bridegroom! *"My heart waketh."* This is a happy sign. Life has not been extinguished, although it has been sadly smothered. When our renewed hearts struggle against our natural heaviness, we should be grateful to sovereign grace for keeping a little vitality within *"the body of this death"* (Rom. 7:24). Jesus will hear our hearts, help our hearts, and visit our hearts, for the voice of the wakeful heart is really the voice of our Beloved, saying, *"Open to me"* (Song 5:2). Holy zeal will surely open the door.

> Oh, lovely attitude! He stands
> With melting heart and laden hands;
> My soul forsakes her every sin;
> And lets the heavenly stranger in.

Just, and the justifier of him which believeth in Jesus.
—Romans 3:26

Being justified by faith, we have peace with God" (Rom. 5:1). Conscience no longer accuses. Judgment now decides *for* the sinner instead of *against* him. Memory looks back on past sins with deep sorrow for the sin, yet with no dread of any penalty to come. Christ paid the debt of His people to the last jot and tittle and received the divine receipt. Unless God can be so unjust as to demand double payment for one debt, no soul for whom Jesus died as a substitute can ever be cast into hell. It seems to be one of the very principles of our enlightened nature to believe that God is just. We feel that it must be so, and this causes us terror at first; but is it not marvelous that this very same belief that God is just afterward becomes the pillar of our confidence and peace! If God is just, I, a sinner, alone and without a substitute, must be punished. But Jesus stands in my stead and is punished for me. Now, if God is just, I, a sinner, standing in Christ, can never be punished. God must change His nature before one soul for whom Jesus was a substitute can ever by any possibility suffer the penalty of the law. Therefore, Jesus having taken the place of the believer, having rendered a full equivalent to divine wrath for all that His people ought to have suffered as the result of sin, the believer can shout with glorious triumph, *"Who shall lay any thing to the charge of God's elect?"* (Rom. 8:33). Not God, for He has justified. Not Christ, for He has died, *"yea rather,…[has] risen again"* (v. 34). My hope lives, not because I am not a sinner, but because I am a sinner for whom Christ died. My trust is not that I am holy, but that being unholy, He is my righteousness. My faith does not rest on what I am or will be or feel or know, but in what Christ is, in what He has done, and in what He is now doing for me. On the lion of justice the fair maid of hope rides like a queen.

SEPTEMBER 25

Evening

Who of God is made unto us wisdom.
—1 Corinthians 1:30

Man's intellect seeks rest and, by nature, seeks it apart from the Lord Jesus Christ. Even when they are converted, intellectuals are apt to look upon the simplicities of the Cross of Christ with insufficient reverence and love. They are snared in the old net in which the Greeks were taken; they desire to mix philosophy with revelation. The temptation for someone of refined thought and high education is to depart from the simple truth of *"Christ crucified"* (1 Cor. 1:23) and to invent a more "intellectual" doctrine. This temptation led the early Christian churches into Gnosticism and seduced them with all sorts of heresies. This is the root of Neology and other fine things that, in days gone by, were fashionable in Germany, and are now so ensnaring to certain members of the clergy. Whoever you are, good reader, and whatever your education may be, if you are the Lord's, be assured that you will find no rest in philosophizing theology. You may receive this dogma of one great thinker or that dream of another profound reasoner; however, what the chaff is to the wheat, these ideas are to the pure Word of God. When it is best guided, all that reason can learn is merely the ABCs of truth. Even then, its findings lack certainty. In contrast, all the fullness of wisdom and knowledge is treasured up in Christ Jesus. All attempts on the part of Christians to be content with systems that Unitarian and theologically liberal thinkers would approve of will fail. True heirs of heaven must come back to the great but simple reality that *"Christ Jesus came into the world to save sinners"* (1 Tim. 1:15). Jesus satisfies the most elevated intellect when He is received in faith. Apart from Him, the minds of the redeemed will find no rest. *"The fear of the LORD is the beginning of knowledge"* (Prov. 1:7). *"A good understanding have all they that do his commandments"* (Ps. 111:10).

SEPTEMBER 26

Morning

I saw by night, and behold a man riding upon a red horse, and he
stood among the myrtle trees that were in the bottom.
—Zechariah 1:8

The vision in this chapter describes the condition of Israel in Zechariah's day. Being interpreted in its aspect toward us, it describes the church of God as we find it now in the world. The church is compared to a myrtle grove flourishing in a valley. It is hidden, unobserved, secret. It courts no honor and attracts no observation from the careless gazer. The church, like her Head, has a glory, but it is concealed from carnal eyes, for the time of her breaking forth in all her splendor is not yet come. The idea of tranquil security is also suggested to us, for the myrtle grove in the valley is still and calm, while the storm sweeps over the mountain summits. Tempests spend their force on the craggy peaks of the Alps, but down where the stream flows that makes glad the city of our God, the myrtles flourish by the still waters, all unshaken by the impetuous wind. How great is the inward tranquility of God's church! Even when opposed and persecuted, she has a peace that the world does not give, and which, therefore, it cannot take away. The peace of God that passes all understanding keeps the hearts and minds of God's people. Does not the metaphor forcibly picture the peaceful, perpetual growth of the saints? The myrtle sheds not its leaves; it is always green. And the church, in her worst time, still has a blessed verdure of grace about her; in fact, she has sometimes exhibited the healthiest growth when her winter has been sharpest. She has prospered most when her adversities have been the most severe. Hence the text hints at victory. The myrtle is the symbol of peace and a significant token of triumph. The brows of conquerors were bound with myrtle and with laurel. Is not the church always victorious? Are not Christians *"more than conquerors"* (Rom. 8:37) through Christ who loves them? Living in peace, do not the saints fall asleep in the arms of victory?

SEPTEMBER 26

Howl, fir tree, for the cedar is fallen.
—Zechariah 11:2

When the crash of a falling oak is heard in the forest, it is a sign that the woodsman is at work. Every tree in the forest may tremble, for fear that tomorrow the sharp edge of the ax will find it out. We are all like trees marked for the ax. The fall of one should remind us that, whether we are as great as the cedar or as humble as the fir, the appointed hour is quickly creeping up on every one of us. I trust that we have not become callous toward death by hearing about it often. May we never be like the birds in the church steeple, which build their nests when the funeral bells are tolling and sleep quietly when the solemn peals are startling the air. May we regard death as the weightiest of all events and be sobered by its approach. It is foolish to spend our time on frivolous matters while our eternal destiny hangs on a thread. The sword is out of its sheath—let us not trifle with it. The sword is polished, and the edge is sharp— let us not play with it. He who does not prepare for death is more than an ordinary fool; he is a madman. When the voice of God is heard among the trees of the garden, let fig tree, sycamore, elm, and cedar alike hear the sound of it. Be ready, servant of Christ, for your Master comes without delay. He will come when an ungodly world least expects Him. See to it that you are faithful in His work, for a grave will soon be dug for you. Be ready, parents. See to it that your children are brought up in the fear of God, for they will soon be without their fathers and mothers. Be ready, you who are engaged in business. Make sure that your affairs are in order and that you serve God with all your hearts. The days of your earthly service will soon be over, and you will be called to give account for what you did while in the body, whether good or evil. May we all prepare for the tribunal of the great King with a circumspection that will be rewarded with the gracious commendation, *"Well done, good and faithful servant"* (Matt. 25:23).

SEPTEMBER 27
Morning

Happy art thou, O Israel: who is like unto thee,
O people saved by the LORD!
—Deuteronomy 33:29

He who affirms that Christianity makes men miserable is himself an utter stranger to it. It would be strange, indeed, if it made us wretched, for see to what a position it exalts us! It makes us children of God. Do you suppose that God will give all the happiness to His enemies and reserve all the mourning for His own family? Will His foes have mirth and joy, and will His own children inherit sorrow and wretchedness? Will the sinner, who has no part in Christ, call himself rich in happiness, and will we go mourning as if we were penniless beggars? No, we will *"rejoice in the Lord alway[s]"* (Phil. 4:4), and glory in our inheritance, for we *"have not received the spirit of bondage again to fear; but [we] have received the Spirit of adoption, whereby we cry, Abba, Father"* (Rom. 8:15). The rod of chastisement must rest on us in our measure, but it works for us the comfortable fruits of righteousness; therefore, by the aid of the divine Comforter, we, the people saved by the Lord, will joy in the God of our salvation. We are married to Christ. Will our great Bridegroom permit His spouse to linger in constant grief? Our hearts are knit to Him. We are His members, and though for a while we may suffer as our Head once suffered, yet we are even now blessed with heavenly blessings in Him. We have the guarantee of our inheritance in the comforts of the Spirit, which are neither few nor small. Inheritors of joy forever, we have foretastes of our portion. There are streaks of the light of joy to herald our eternal rising sun. Our riches are beyond the sea. Our city with firm foundations lies on the other side the river. Gleams of glory from the spirit world cheer our hearts and urge us onward. Truly is it said of us, *"Happy art thou, O Israel: who is like unto thee, O people saved by the LORD!"*

SEPTEMBER 27

Evening

My beloved put in his hand by the hole of the door,
and my [heart was] moved for him.
—Song of Solomon 5:4

Knocking was not enough, for my heart was too full of sleep, too cold and ungrateful, for me to rise and open the door. Yet the touch of His grace has caused my soul to awaken. Oh, the longsuffering of my Beloved! He waited for me when He found Himself shut out, and me asleep on the bed of laziness! Oh, the greatness of His patience, to knock and knock again, and to add His voice to His knocking, urging me to open to Him! How could I have refused Him! You base heart—blush, and be ashamed! Yet the greatest kindness of all is that He becomes His own doorman and unlocks the door Himself. Most blessed is the hand that graciously lifts the latch and turns the key. Now I see that nothing but my Lord's own power can save me, for I am a corrupt mass of wickedness. The church's ordinances fail to help me, and even the Gospel has no effect on me, until He stretches out His hand to help. I also now perceive that His hand is effective where everything else is unsuccessful. He can open when nothing else will. May His name be blessed! I feel His gracious presence even now. Well may my heart be moved for Him, when I think of all that He has suffered for me, and of my unkind response. I have allowed my affections to wander. I have set up rivals. I have grieved Him. Sweetest and dearest of all beloveds, I have treated You as an unfaithful wife treats her husband. Oh, my cruel sins, my cruel self. What can I do? Tears are a poor representation of my repentance. My whole heart boils with indignation at myself. What a wretch I am, to treat my Lord, my All in All, my Exceeding Great Joy, as though He were a stranger. Jesus, You freely forgive, but that is not enough. Prevent my unfaithfulness in the future. Kiss away these tears; but then purge my heart and bind it to Yourself seven times over, so that it never wanders again.

The LORD looketh from heaven; he beholdeth all the sons of men.
—Psalm 33:13

Perhaps no figure of speech represents God in a more gracious light than when He is spoken of as stooping from His throne and coming down from heaven to attend to the needs and to behold the sorrows of mankind. We love Him, who, when Sodom and Gomorrah were full of iniquity, would not destroy those cities until He had made a personal visitation to them. We cannot help pouring out our hearts in affection for our Lord, who inclines His ear from the highest glory and puts it to the lips of the dying sinner, whose failing heart longs for reconciliation. How can we but love Him when we know that He numbers the very hairs of our heads, marks our path, and orders our ways? This great truth is especially brought near to our hearts when we remember how attentive He is, not merely to the temporal interests of His creatures, but to their spiritual concerns. Though a long distance lies between the finite creature and the infinite Creator, yet there are links uniting both. When you weep, do not think that God does not see your tears, for *"like as a father pitieth his children, so the LORD pitieth them that fear him"* (Ps. 103:13). Your sigh is able to move the heart of Jehovah; your whisper can incline His ear unto you; your prayer can stay His hand; your faith can move His arm. Do not think that God sits on high paying no attention to you. Remember that however poor and needy you are, the Lord thinks about you. *"For the eyes of the LORD run to and fro throughout the whole earth, to show himself strong in the behalf of them whose heart is perfect toward him"* (2 Chron. 16:9). Oh, then, repeat the truth that never tires: No God is like the God my soul desires. He, at whose voice heaven trembles, even He, great as He is, knows how to stoop to me.

Go again seven times.
—1 Kings 18:43

Success is certain when the Lord has promised it. You may have pleaded in prayer month after month, without any evidence of an answer. However, it is not possible that the Lord will be deaf to His people when they are in earnest about a matter that concerns His glory. Elijah the prophet continued to wrestle with God on Mount Carmel, even when he did not receive an immediate answer to his prayer. Never for a moment did he give in to fear that he would not be served in Jehovah's courts. Six times, Elijah's servant returned to him, unable to report any sign of progress. However, on each occasion, Elijah merely told him, "Go *again*." We must not even consider giving in to unbelief, but hold to our faith even to "*seventy times seven*" (Matt. 18:22). Faith sends expectant hope to look from the top of Mount Carmel. If nothing can be seen, she sends again and again. Far from being crushed by repeated disappointment, Faith is animated to intercede more fervently with her God. She is humbled, but not discouraged. Her groans are deeper, and her sighs more vehement, but she never relaxes her hold. It would be more agreeable to flesh and blood to have a speedy answer, but believing souls have learned to be submissive, and to find it good to wait *for* as well as *upon* the Lord. Delayed answers often cause the heart to search itself, and so lead to contrition and spiritual reformation. Deadly blows are thus struck at our corruption, and our hearts are cleansed of idolatry. The great danger is that people might give up and miss the blessing. Reader, do not fall into that sin, but continue in prayer and watching. At last the little cloud was seen, the sure forerunner of torrents of rain. It will be the same with you. The "*token for good*" (Ps. 86:17) will surely be given, and you will rise as a prevailing prince to enjoy the mercy you have sought. Elijah was a man of "*like passions as we are*" (James 5:17). His power with God did not lie in his own merits. If his believing prayer availed much, why not yours? Plead the precious blood with unceasing persistence, and you will receive what you ask for.

Behold, if the leprosy have covered all his flesh,
he shall pronounce him clean that hath the plague.
—Leviticus 13:13

This regulation appears to be strange, yet there was wisdom in it, for the throwing out of the disease proved that the constitution was sound. This morning it may be well for us to see the typical teaching of so unusual a rule. We, too, are lepers and may read the law of lepers as applicable to ourselves. When a man sees himself to be altogether lost and ruined, covered all over with the defilement of sin, with no part free from pollution; when he disclaims all righteousness of his own and pleads guilty before the Lord, then is he made clean through the blood of Jesus and the grace of God. Hidden, unfelt, unconfessed iniquity is the true leprosy; but when sin is seen and felt, it has received its deathblow, and the Lord looks with eyes of mercy on the soul afflicted with it. Nothing is more deadly than self-righteousness or more hopeful than contrition. We must confess that we are nothing else but sin, for no confession short of this will be the whole truth. If the Holy Spirit is at work within us, convincing us of sin, there will be no difficulty about making such an acknowledgment. It will spring spontaneously from our lips. What comfort this Scripture affords to those under a deep sense of sin! Sin that is mourned and confessed, however black and foul, will never shut a man out from the Lord Jesus. Whoever comes to Him, He *"will in no wise cast out"* (John 6:37). Though dishonest as the thief, though unchaste as the woman who was a sinner, though fierce as Saul of Tarsus, though cruel as Manasseh, though rebellious as the Prodigal, the great heart of love will look on the man who feels himself to have no soundness in himself and will pronounce him clean when he trusts in Jesus crucified. Come to Him, then, poor heavy-laden sinner.

Come needy, come guilty, come loathsome and bare.
You can't come too filthy; come just as you are.

I found him whom my soul loveth:
I held him, and would not let him go.
—Song of Solomon 3:4

Does Christ receive us when we come to Him, regardless of all our past sinfulness? Does He ever chide us for having tried all other refuges first? Is there no one on earth like Him? Is He the best of all the good, the fairest of all the fair? Oh, then let us praise Him! Daughters of Jerusalem, glorify Him with timbrel and harp! Cast down your idols, and lift up the Lord Jesus. Let the standards of haughtiness and pride be trampled underfoot, but let the Cross of Jesus, at which the world frowns and scoffs, be lifted on high. Oh, for a throne of ivory for our King Solomon! Let Him be set on high forever. Let my soul sit at His footstool, kiss His feet, and wash them with my tears. Oh, how precious Christ is! How can it be that my thoughts have not often turned to Him? How can I go elsewhere for joy or comfort when He is so full, so rich, so satisfying? Fellow believer, make a covenant with your heart that you will never depart from Him, and ask your Lord to ratify it. Ask Him to set you as a signet ring on His finger, and as a bracelet on His arm. Ask Him to fasten you around Himself, as a bride adorns herself with jewels, and as a bridegroom clothes himself with finery (Isa. 61:10). I want to live in Christ's heart. In the clefts of that rock, my soul would eternally abide. *"The sparrow hath found an house, and the swallow a nest for herself, where she may lay her young, even thine altars, O LORD of hosts, my King, and my God"* (Ps. 84:3). I want to make my nest, my home, in You. May the *"soul of thy turtledove"* (Ps. 74:19) never leave You again. May I nestle close to You, O Jesus, my true and only rest.

> When my precious Lord I find,
>   All my ardent passions glow;
> Him with cords of love I bind,
>   Hold and will not let Him go.

Sing forth the honour of his name: make his praise glorious.
—Psalm 66:2

It is not left to our own choice whether we will praise God or not. Praise is God's most righteous due; every Christian, as the recipient of His grace, is bound to praise God from day to day. It is true we have no authoritative rule for daily praise; we have no commandment prescribing certain hours of song and thanksgiving. But the law written on the heart teaches us that it is right to praise God, and the unwritten mandate comes to us with as much force as if it had been recorded on the tablets of stone or handed to us from the top of thundering Sinai. Yes, it is the Christian's duty to praise God. It is not only a pleasurable exercise, but also the absolute obligation of his life. Do not think that you who are always mourning are guiltless in this respect or imagine that you can discharge your duty to your God without songs of praise. You are bound by the bonds of His love to bless His name as long as you live, and His praise should *"continually be in [your] mouth"* (Ps. 34:1), for you are blessed, in order that you may bless Him. *"This people have I formed for myself; they shall show forth my praise"* (Isa. 43:21). If you do not praise God, you are not bringing forth the fruit that He, as the Divine Husbandman, has a right to expect at your hands. Do not let your harp hang on the willows, but take it down, and strive, with a grateful heart, to bring forth its loudest music. Arise and sing His praise. With every morning's dawn, lift up your notes of thanksgiving, and let every setting sun be followed with your songs. Cover the earth with your praises. Surround it with an atmosphere of melody, and God Himself will hearken from heaven and accept your music.

> E'en so I love Thee, and will love,
>   And in Thy praise will sing,
> Because Thou art my loving God,
>   And my redeeming King.

SEPTEMBER 30
Evening

A living dog is better than a dead lion.
—Ecclesiastes 9:4

Life is a precious thing. In its humblest form, it is superior to death. This truth is especially certain regarding spiritual things. It is better to be the least in the kingdom of heaven than to be the greatest outside of it. The lowest degree of grace is superior to the noblest development of the unregenerate nature. When the Holy Spirit implants divine life in the soul, it is a precious deposit, which none of the refinements of education can equal. The thief on the cross excels Caesar on his throne; Lazarus among the dogs (see Luke 16:19–31) is better than Cicero among the senators; and the most uneducated Christian is, in the sight of God, superior to Plato. Life is the badge of nobility in the realm of spiritual things. Those without it are only coarser or finer specimens of the same lifeless material, needing to be made alive, for they are *"dead in trespasses and sins"* (Eph. 2:1). A living, loving, gospel sermon, however unlearned in matter and unpolished in style, is better than the finest discourse devoid of anointing and power. A living dog keeps better watch than a dead lion and is of more service to his master. Similarly, the poorest spiritual preacher is infinitely to be preferred to the exquisite orator who has no wisdom but that of words, no energy but that of sound. The same holds true of our prayers and other religious exercises. If we are quickened in them by the Holy Spirit, they are acceptable to God through Jesus Christ, even though we may think that they are worthless. In contrast, our "grand performances," in which our hearts are absent, are—like dead lions—as decaying flesh in the sight of the living God. Oh, we need living groans, living sighs, living despondency, rather than lifeless songs and dead calm. Anything is better than death. The snarls of the dog of hell will at least keep us awake. Yet what greater curse can a person have than dead faith? Quicken us, quicken us, O Lord!

*Pleasant fruits, new and old, which I have
laid up for thee, O my beloved.*
—Song of Solomon 7:13

The spouse desires to give all that she produces to Jesus. Our hearts have *"all manner of pleasant fruits"* (Song 7:13) both *"new and old,"* and they are laid up for our Beloved. At this rich autumn season of fruit, let us survey our harvest. We have *"new"* fruits. We desire to feel new life, new joy, new gratitude. We wish to make new resolves and carry them out by new labors. Our hearts blossom with new prayers, and our souls pledge themselves to new efforts. But we have some *"old"* fruits, too. There is our first love. What a choice fruit! Jesus delights in it. There is our first faith. It is the simple faith by which, having nothing, we became possessors of all things. There is our joy when first we knew the Lord; let us revive it. We have our old remembrances of the promises. How faithful God has been! In sickness, how softly He made our beds! In deep waters, how placidly He lifted us up! In the flaming furnace, how graciously He delivered us. Old fruits, indeed! We have many of them, for His mercies have been more than the hairs of our heads. Old sins we must regret, but then we have had times of repentance that He has given us, by which we have wept our way to the cross and learned the merit of His blood. We have fruits, this morning, both new and old; but here is the point—they are all laid up for Jesus. Truly, those are the best and most acceptable services in which Jesus is the solitary aim of the soul, and His glory, without any addition whatever, is the end of all our efforts. Let our many fruits be laid up only for our Beloved. Let us display them when He is with us and not hold them up before the gaze of men. Jesus, we will turn the key in our garden door, and none will enter to rob You of one good fruit from the soil that You have watered with Your bloody sweat. Our all will be Yours, Yours only, O Jesus, our Beloved!

OCTOBER 1
Evening

The LORD will give grace and glory.
—Psalm 84:11

It is the nature of Jehovah to be bounteous. He delights in giving. His gifts are precious beyond measure and are as freely given as the light of the sun. He gives grace to His elect because He wills it, to His redeemed because of His covenant, to the called because of His promise, to believers because they seek it, to sinners because they need it. He gives grace abundantly, seasonably, constantly, readily, sovereignly—doubly enhancing the value of the blessing by the way in which He gives it. He freely gives grace, in all its forms, to His people. He generously and unceasingly pours into their souls comforting, preserving, sanctifying, directing, instructing, and assisting grace. He will always give grace bountifully, no matter what may happen to us. We may become sick, but the Lord will give grace. We may experience poverty, but grace will surely be provided. Death must come, but grace will light a candle at the darkest hour. Reader, how blessed it is, as the seasons come and go, and as the leaves begin to fall again, to enjoy such an unfading promise as this: *"The LORD will give grace and glory."* The little conjunction *"and"* in this verse is a diamond rivet that binds the present with the future, for grace and glory always go together. God has married them, and no one can divorce them. The Lord will never deny glory to someone when He has freely granted that person the right to live in His grace. Indeed, glory is nothing more than grace in its Sunday best, grace in full bloom, grace like autumn fruit—ripe and perfected. No one can tell how soon we may have glory! It may be that before this month of October has ended, we will see the Holy City. However, whether the interval is long or short, we will be glorified before long. The Lord will surely give glory to His chosen—the glory of heaven, the glory of eternity, the glory of Jesus, the glory of the Father. Glory is the exceptional promise of a faithful God!

Two golden links of one divine chain:
Who owns grace will surely glory gain.

The hope which is laid up for you in heaven.
—Colossians 1:5

Our hope in Christ for the future is the mainspring and the mainstay of our joy here. It will animate our hearts to think often of heaven, for all that we can desire is promised there. Here we are weary and toilworn, but yonder is the land of rest where the sweat of labor will no more moisten the worker's brow, and fatigue will be forever banished. To those who are weary and spent, the word *rest* is full of heaven. We are always in the field of battle. We are so tempted within, and so molested by foes without, that we have little or no peace. But in heaven we will enjoy the victory, when the banner will be waved aloft in triumph, the sword will be sheathed, and we will hear our Captain say, *"Well done, thou good and faithful servant"* (Matt. 25:21). We have suffered bereavement after bereavement, but we are going to the land of the immortal, where graves are unknown things. Here sin is a constant grief to us, but there we will be perfectly holy. By no means will anything that defiles enter into that kingdom. Hemlock cannot spring up in the furrows of celestial fields. Oh, is it not joy, that you are not to be in banishment forever, that you are not to dwell eternally in this wilderness, but will soon inherit Canaan? Nevertheless, let it never be said of us that we are dreaming about the future and forgetting the present. Let the future sanctify the present to its highest uses. Through the Spirit of God, the hope of heaven is the most potent force for the product of virtue. It is a fountain of joyous effort; it is the cornerstone of cheerful holiness. The man who has this hope in him goes about his work with vigor, for the joy of the Lord is his strength. He fights against temptation with ardor, for the hope of the next world repels the fiery darts of the adversary. He can labor without present reward, for he looks for a reward in the world to come.

A man greatly beloved.
—Daniel 10:11

Child of God, do you hesitate to claim this title? Has your unbelief made you forget that you are greatly beloved, too? You must have been greatly beloved to have been bought *"with the precious blood of Christ, as of a lamb without blemish and without spot"* (1 Pet. 1:19). When *"God... gave his only begotten Son"* (John 3:16) for you, did that not mean that you were greatly beloved? You lived in sin. Not only that, but you reveled in it. You must have been greatly beloved for God to have been so patient with you. You were called by grace and led to a Savior. You were made a child of God and an heir of heaven. Does all of that not prove God's very great and superabundant love for you? Since that time, whether your path has been rough with troubles or smooth with mercies, it has been full of proofs that you are greatly beloved. If the Lord has disciplined you, He has not done so in anger. If He has made you poor, you have still been rich in grace. The more unworthy you feel, the more evidence you have that nothing but inexpressible love could have led the Lord Jesus to save a soul such as yours. The more sinful you feel, the clearer is the demonstration of the abounding love of God in that He chose you, called you, and made you an heir of bliss. Now, since there is such love between God and us, let us live in the influence and sweetness of it, and use the privilege of our position. Let us not approach our Lord as though we were strangers or as though He were unwilling to hear us, for we are greatly beloved by our loving Father. *"He that spared not his own Son, but delivered him up for us all, how shall he not with him also freely give us all things?"* (Rom. 8:32). Come boldly, believer, for despite the whisperings of Satan and the doubts of your own heart, you are greatly beloved. Meditate on the exceeding greatness and faithfulness of divine love this evening, and go to sleep in peace.

OCTOBER 3

Morning

Are they not all ministering spirits, sent forth to minister for them
who shall be heirs of salvation?
—Hebrews 1:14

Angels are the unseen attendants of the saints of God. They bear us up in their hands, lest we dash our foot against a stone. Loyalty to their Lord leads them to take a deep interest in the children of His love. They rejoice over the return of the Prodigal to his father's house below, and they welcome the advent of the believer to the King's palace above. In olden times, the sons of God were favored with their visible appearance, and at this day, although unseen by us, heaven is still opened, and the angels of God ascend and descend on the Son of Man so that they may visit the heirs of salvation. Seraphim still fly with live coals from off the altar to touch the lips of men who are greatly beloved. If our eyes could be opened, we would see horses and chariots of fire around the servants of the Lord; for we have come to an innumerable company of angels, who are all watchers and protectors of the royal seed. Edmund Spenser's line is no poetic fiction, where he sings,

How oft do they with golden pinions cleave
The flitting skies, like flying pursuivant
Against foul fiends to aid us militant!

To what dignity are the chosen elevated when the brilliant courtiers of heaven become their willing servants! Into what communion are we raised since we have fellowship with spotless celestials! How well are we defended since all the twenty thousand chariots of God are armed for our deliverance! To whom do we owe all this? Let the Lord Jesus Christ be forever endeared to us, for through Him we are made to sit *"in heavenly places"* (Eph. 2:6) far above principalities and powers. He it is whose camp is *"round about them that fear him"* (Ps. 34:7). He is the true Michael whose foot is on the dragon. All hail, Jesus! To You, the Angel of Jehovah's presence, this family offers its morning vows.

He himself hath suffered being tempted.
—Hebrews 2:18

This is a well-known concept, yet it tastes sweet to the weary heart: Jesus was tempted in the same ways I am. You probably have heard this truth many times, but have you really grasped it? He was tempted to commit the very same sins into which we fall. Do not disassociate Jesus from our common humanity. You are going through a dark place, but Jesus has already gone through it. You are waging a fierce battle, but Jesus has stood toe-to-toe with the same enemy. Let us be encouraged. Christ carried the load before we did, and the bloodstained footsteps of the King of Glory may be seen along the road that we are now traveling. Yet there is something even sweeter than the knowledge that Jesus was tempted in the same way that we are: although Jesus was tempted, He never sinned; therefore, it is not necessary for us to sin. Jesus was a man, and if one Man endured these temptations and did not sin, then in His power, the members of His body may also refrain from sin. Some who are just beginning the Christian life think that they cannot be tempted without sinning. However, they are mistaken. There is no sin in *being* tempted, only in *yielding* to temptation. This truth is comforting for those who are being severely tempted. There is still more to encourage them if they will reflect on the fact that the Lord Jesus, though tempted, gloriously triumphed. As He overcame, His followers will also surely overcome, for Jesus is the representative Man for His people. The Head has triumphed, and the members share in the victory. Fears are needless, for Christ is with us, armed for our defense. Our place of safety is in the Savior. Perhaps we are being tempted right now in order to drive us nearer to Him. Blessed is any wind that blows us into the port of our Savior's love! Blessed are the wounds that make us seek the beloved Physician. You who are tempted, come to your tempted Savior. He can sympathize with your weaknesses. He will come to the aid of everyone who is tried and tempted.

OCTOBER 4

Morning

At evening time it shall be light.
—Zechariah 14:7

Often we look with foreboding to the time of old age, forgetful that at eventide it will be light. To many saints, old age is the choicest season in their lives. A balmier air fans the mariner's cheek as he nears the shore of immortality. Fewer waves ruffle his sea, and quiet reigns, deep, still, and solemn. From the altar of age the flashes of the fire of youth are gone, but the more real flame of earnest feeling remains. The pilgrims have reached Beulah land, that happy country, whose days are as the days of heaven on earth. Angels visit it, celestial gales blow over it, flowers of paradise grow in it, and the air is filled with seraphic music. Some dwell here for years, and others come to it but a few hours before their departure, but it is an Eden on earth. We may well long for the time when we will recline in its shady groves and be satisfied with hope until the time of fruition comes. The setting sun seems larger than when aloft in the sky, and a splendor of glory tinges all the clouds that surround its going down. Pain does not break the calm of the sweet twilight of age, for *"strength…made perfect in weakness"* (2 Cor. 12:9) bears up with patience under it all. Ripe fruits of choice experience are gathered as the rare repast of life's evening, and the soul prepares itself for rest. The Lord's people will also enjoy light in the hour of death. Unbelief laments as it sees the shadows fall, the night coming, and existence ending. "Ah, no," cries faith. "The night is far spent; the true day is at hand." Light is come, the light of immortality, the light of a Father's countenance. Gather up your feet in the bed; see the waiting bands of spirits! Angels carry you away. Farewell, beloved one. You wave your hand; you are gone. Ah, now it is light. The pearly gates are open. The golden streets shine in the jasper light. We cover our eyes, but you behold the unseen. Farewell, brother; you have light at eventide, such as we have not yet seen.

If any man sin, we have an advocate with the Father,
Jesus Christ the righteous.
—1 John 2:1

"I*f any man sin, we have an advocate.*" Yes, even though we may sin, we still have Him. John did not say, "If any man sins, he has forfeited his advocate" but, "*We have an advocate*"—sinners though we are. All the sins that a believer ever committed, or can commit, cannot destroy his right to have the Lord Jesus Christ as his Advocate. The name that our Lord is called in the text is significant. First, He is called "*Jesus.*" He is just the Advocate we need, for "*Jesus*" is the name of the One whose business and delight it is to save. "*Thou shalt call his name Jesus: for he shall save his people from their sins*" (Matt. 1:21). His sweetest name implies His success. Second, He is "*Christ.*" The word "*Christ*" in the Greek is *Christos*, meaning "anointed." This shows His authority to intercede on our behalf. The Christ has a right to intercede, for He is the Father's own appointed Advocate and elected Priest. If He were of our choosing, He might fail. However, if God has "*laid help upon one that is mighty*" (Ps. 89:19), we may safely lay our trouble where God has laid His help. He is Christ, and therefore He is authorized. He is Christ, and therefore He is qualified, for the anointing has fully equipped Him for His work. He can intercede in such as way that He moves the heart of God and prevails. What words of tenderness, what sentences of persuasion, will the Anointed One use when He stands up to intercede for me! One more part of His name remains: "*the righteous.*" This title reflects not only His character, but also His plea. "*Righteous*" is His character, and if the Righteous One is my Advocate, then my cause is good, or He would not have espoused it. It is also His plea, for He meets the charge of unrighteousness against me by the plea that He is righteous. He declares Himself as my substitute, and puts His obedience to my account. You have a Friend who is well suited to be your Advocate. He cannot do anything but succeed. Therefore, leave yourself entirely in His hands.

OCTOBER 5

Morning

He arose, and did eat and drink, and went in the strength of that
meat forty days and forty nights.
—1 Kings 19:8

All the strength supplied to us by our gracious God is meant for service, not for wantonness or boasting. When the prophet Elijah found the cake baked on the coals and the cruse of water placed at his head as he lay under the juniper tree, he was no gentleman to be gratified with dainty fare so that he might stretch himself at his ease; far from it. He was commissioned to go forty days and forty nights in the strength of it, journeying toward Horeb, the mount of God. When the Master invited the disciples to *"come and dine"* (John 21:12) with Him, after the feast was concluded, He said to Peter, *"Feed my sheep"* (vv. 16–17). He further said, *"Follow me"* (v. 19). This is true with us also. We eat the bread of heaven so that we may expend our strength in the Master's service. We come to the Passover and eat of the Paschal Lamb with loins girded and staff in hand, so as to start off at once when we have satisfied our hunger. Some Christians are for living *on* Christ, but are not so anxious to live *for* Christ. Earth should be a preparation for heaven, and heaven is the place where saints feast most and work most. They sit down at the table of our Lord, and they serve Him day and night in His temple. They eat of heavenly food and give perfect service. Believer, in the strength you daily gain from Christ, labor for Him. Some of us have yet to learn much concerning the design of our Lord in giving us His grace. We are not to retain the precious grains of truth as the Egyptian mummy held the wheat for ages, without giving it an opportunity to grow. We must sow it and water it. Why does the Lord send down the rain on the thirsty earth and give the genial sunshine? Is it not that these may all help the fruits of the earth to yield food for man? Even so, the Lord feeds and refreshes our souls so that afterward we may use our renewed strength in the promotion of His glory.

OCTOBER 5

Evening

He that believeth and is baptized shall be saved.
—Mark 16:16

Mr. MacDonald asked the inhabitants of the island of St. Kilda, Scotland, how a person must be saved. An old man replied, "We will be saved if we repent, forsake our sins, and turn to God." "Yes," said a middle-aged woman, "and with a true heart, too." "Aye," rejoined a third, "and with prayer." A fourth added, "It must be the prayer of the heart." "And we must be diligent, too," said a fifth, "in keeping the commandments." Each having contributed his thoughts, and feeling that a very decent creed had been put together, they all looked to the preacher and waited for his approval—but they had aroused his deepest pity. The carnal mind always maps out for itself a way in which self can work and become great. However, the Lord's way is quite the reverse. Believing and being baptized are not matters of merit to be gloried in. They are so simple that boasting is excluded. It is God's free grace that has won the victory. It may be that you are unsaved. If so, what is the reason? Do you think that the way of salvation prescribed in the text is doubtful? How can that be, when God has pledged His own Word for its certainty? Do you think it is too easy? Then why do you not obey it? Its ease leaves those who neglect it without excuse. To believe is simply to trust, to depend, to rely on Christ Jesus. To be baptized is to submit to the ordinance that our Lord fulfilled at the Jordan River (see Matthew 3:13–17), that the converted ones submitted to at Pentecost (see Acts 2:1–42), and that the jailer yielded obedience to on the very night of his conversion (see Acts 16:23–33). Baptism is an outward sign of inward faith. It does not save, but it demonstrates to us our death, burial, and resurrection with Jesus. Like the Lord's Supper, it is not to be neglected. Do you believe in Jesus? Then, dear friend, dismiss your fears, for you will be saved. Are you still an unbeliever? Then remember that there is only one Door. (See John 10:7–9.) If you will not enter by it, you will perish in your sins.

OCTOBER 6

Whosoever drinketh of the water that I shall give him
shall never thirst.
—John 4:14

He who is a believer in Jesus finds enough in his Lord to satisfy him now and to keep him content forevermore. The believer is not the man whose days are weary for lack of comfort or whose nights are long from absence of heart-cheering thoughts. He finds in Christ such a spring of joy, such a fountain of consolation, that he is content and happy. Put him in a dungeon, and he will find good company. Place him in a barren wilderness, and he will eat the bread of heaven. Drive him away from friendship, and he will meet the *"friend that sticketh closer than a brother"* (Prov. 18:24). Blast all his gourds, and he will find shadow beneath the Rock of Ages. Sap the foundation of his earthly hopes, and his heart will still be fixed, trusting in the Lord. The heart is as insatiable as the grave until Jesus enters it, and then, it is a cup full to overflowing. There is such a fullness in Christ that He alone is the believer's all. The true saint is so completely satisfied with the all-sufficiency of Jesus that he thirsts no more—unless it is for deeper draughts of the living Fountain. In that sweet manner, believer, you will thirst. It will not be a thirst of pain, but of loving desire; you will find it a sweet thing to be panting after a fuller enjoyment of Jesus' love. One, in days of yore, said, "I have often been sinking my bucket down into the well, but now my thirst after Jesus has become so insatiable that I long to put the well itself to my lips and drink right from it." Is this the feeling of your heart now, believer? Do you feel that all your desires are satisfied in Jesus and that you have no lack now, but to know more of Him and to have closer fellowship with Him? Then come continually to the Fountain, and *"take the water of life freely"* (Rev. 22:17). Jesus will never think you take too much, but will ever welcome you, saying, "Drink, yes, drink abundantly, beloved."

He had married an Ethiopian woman.
—Numbers 12:1

This was a strange choice for Moses. Yet how much stranger is the choice of Him who is a prophet *"like unto Moses"* (Deut. 34:10), but who is greater than he! (See Hebrews 3:1–3.) Our Lord, who is as fair as the lily, has entered into marriage with one who confesses herself to be *"black, because the sun hath looked upon me"* (Song 1:6). It is the marvel of angels that the love of Jesus is given to poor, lost, guilty men. Each believer, when filled with a sense of Jesus' love, must also be overwhelmed with astonishment that such love should be lavished on an object so utterly unworthy of it. Knowing, as we do, our secret guiltiness, unfaithfulness, and black-heartedness, we are overcome with grateful admiration for the incomparable freeness and sovereignty of grace. Jesus must have found the cause of His love in His own heart. He could not have found it in us, for it is not there. Even after our conversion, we have been *"black"* (Song 1:5), though grace has made us *"comely"* (v. 5). Rutherford said of himself what we must each subscribe to: "His relation to me is that I am sick, and He is the Physician of whom I stand in need. Alas! How often I play fast and loose with Christ! He binds, and I loose; He builds, and I cast down. I quarrel with Christ, and He agrees with me twenty times a day!" Most tender and faithful Husband of our souls, pursue Your gracious work of conforming us to Your image, until You can present us to Yourself without *"spot, or wrinkle, or any such thing"* (Eph. 5:27). Moses met with opposition because of his marriage. Both he and his spouse were the subjects of criticism and gossip. Do we wonder, then, if this vain world opposes Jesus and His spouse, especially when great sinners are converted? The Pharisee's ground of objection is always, *"This man receiveth sinners"* (Luke 15:2).

OCTOBER 7

Morning

Wherefore hast thou afflicted thy servant?
—Numbers 11:11

Our heavenly Father sends us frequent troubles to try our faith. If our faith is worth anything, it will stand the test. Gilt is afraid of fire, but gold is not. The artificial gem dreads to be touched by the diamond, but the true jewel fears no test. It is a weak faith that can trust God only when friends are true, the body is full of health, and business is profitable. True faith holds by the Lord's faithfulness when friends are gone, when the body is sick, when spirits are depressed, and when the light of our Father's countenance is hidden. A faith that can say, in the direst trouble, *"Though he slay me, yet will I trust in him"* (Job 13:15) is heaven-born faith. The Lord afflicts His servants to glorify Himself, for He is greatly glorified in the graces of His people, which are His own handiwork. When *"tribulation worketh patience; and patience, experience; and experience, hope"* (Rom. 5:3), the Lord is honored by these growing virtues. We would never know the music of the harp if the strings were left untouched or enjoy the juice of the grape if it were not trodden in the winepress or discover the sweet perfume of cinnamon if it were not pressed and beaten or feel the warmth of fire if the coals were not utterly consumed. The wisdom and power of the great Workman are discovered by the trials through which His vessels of mercy are permitted to pass. Present afflictions tend also to heighten future joy. There must be shadows in the picture to bring out the beauty of the light. Could we be so supremely blessed in heaven if we had not known the curse of sin and the sorrow of earth? Will not peace be sweeter after conflict, and rest more welcome after toil? Will not the remembrance of past sufferings enhance the bliss of the glorified? There are many other comforting answers to the question with which we opened our brief meditation. Let us ponder these thoughts all day long.

Now on whom dost thou trust?
—Isaiah 36:5

Reader, this is an important question. Listen to the Christian's answer, and see if it is yours. *"On whom dost thou trust?"* "I trust," says the Christian, "in a triune God. I trust the Father, believing that He has chosen me from *'before the foundation of the world'* (Eph. 1:4). I trust Him to provide for me in providence, to teach me, to guide me, to correct me, if need be, and to bring me home to His own house, where there are *'many mansions'* (John 14:2). I trust the Son. He is 'very God of very God,' the Man Christ Jesus. I trust in Him to take away all my sins by His own sacrifice, and to adorn me with His perfect righteousness. I trust Him to be my Intercessor, to present my prayers and desires before His Father's throne. I trust Him to be my Advocate at the Last Great Day, to plead my cause, and to justify me. I trust Him for who He is, what He has done, and what He has promised to do. I trust the Holy Spirit. He has begun to deliver me from my innate sins, and I trust Him to drive them all out. I trust Him to curb my temper, to subdue my will, to enlighten my understanding, to check my passions, to comfort my despondency, to help my weaknesses, and to illuminate my darkness. I trust Him to dwell in me as my life; to reign in me as my King; to sanctify me wholly, spirit, soul, and body; and to take me to dwell with the *'saints in light'* (Col. 1:12) forever." Oh, blessed trust! It is blessed to trust Him whose power will never be exhausted, whose love will never wane, whose kindness will never change, whose faithfulness will never fail, whose wisdom will never be baffled, and whose perfect goodness can never be diminished! Blessed are you, reader, if you have this trust! With it, you will enjoy sweet peace now, and glory in the next life. The foundation of your trust will never be removed.

Launch out into the deep, and let down your nets for a draught.
—Luke 5:4

We learn from this narrative the necessity of human involvement. The draught of fish was miraculous, yet neither the fisherman nor his boat nor his fishing tackle were ignored. All were used to catch the fish. Likewise, in the saving of souls, God uses many different means. While the present economy of grace will stand, God is pleased by the foolishness of preaching to save those who believe. When God works without instruments, undoubtedly, He is glorified; but He Himself has selected this plan by which He is most magnified in the earth. Means, by themselves, are utterly unavailing. *"Master, we have toiled all the night, and have taken nothing"* (Luke 5:5). What was the reason for this? Were they not fishermen plying their special calling? Verily, they were no raw hands; they understood the work. Had they gone about the toil unskillfully? No. Had they lacked industry? No, they had toiled. Had they lacked perseverance? No, they had toiled all night. Was there a deficiency of fish in the sea? Certainly not, for as soon as the Master came, they swam to the net in shoals. What, then, is the reason? It is because there is no power in the means, by themselves, apart from the presence of Jesus. We can do nothing without Him. But with Christ we can do all things. Christ's presence confers success. Jesus sat in Peter's boat, and His will, by a mysterious influence, drew the fish to the net. When Jesus is lifted up in His church, His presence is the church's power—the shout of a king is in the midst of her. *"I, if I be lifted up, will draw all men unto me"* (John 12:32).

Let us go out this morning on our work of soul-fishing, looking up in faith and around us in solemn concern. Let us toil until night comes, and we will not labor in vain. He who bids us let down the net will fill it with fish.

OCTOBER 8

Evening

Praying in the Holy Ghost.
—Jude 20

This is the great characteristic of true prayer: "*in the Holy Ghost.*" The seed of acceptable devotion must come from heaven's storehouse. Only the prayer that comes from God can go to God. We must shoot the Lord's arrows back to Him. The desire that He writes on our hearts will move His heart and bring down a blessing; but the desires of the flesh have no power with Him. "*Praying in the Holy Ghost*" means praying with fervency. Cold prayers ask the Lord not to hear them. Those who do not intercede with fervency do not intercede at all. One may as well speak of lukewarm fire as of lukewarm prayer. It is essential that prayer be red-hot. Second, it means praying with perseverance. The true suppliant gathers force as he proceeds, and grows more fervent when God delays to answer. The longer the door of the gate is closed, the more vehemently he knocks. The longer the angel lingers, the more resolved he is that he will not let the angel go without receiving the blessing. (See Genesis 32:24–30.) Tearful, agonizing, unconquerable persistence is beautiful in God's sight. Third, it means praying humbly, for the Holy Spirit never puffs us up with pride. His role is to convict us of sin, and thus to cause us to bow down in contrition and brokenness of spirit. We will never sing "*Gloria in excelsis*" unless we also pray to God *de profundis.* That is, we will never see "glory in the highest" unless we cry to God "out of the depths." Fourth, it means praying with love. Prayer should be perfumed with love, saturated with love—love for our fellow saints and love for Christ. Last, it means offering prayers that are full of faith. A man prevails only as he believes. The Holy Spirit is the author of faith. He also strengthens faith, so that we may pray believing God's promise. May this blessed combination of excellent graces, as priceless and sweet as the spices of the merchant, be fragrant within us, because the Holy Spirit is in our hearts! Most blessed Comforter, help our weaknesses in prayer by exerting Your mighty power within us.

Able to keep you from falling.
—Jude 24

In one sense the path to heaven is very safe, but in other respects, there is no road as dangerous. It is surrounded with difficulties. One false step—and how easy it is to take that if grace is absent—and down we go. What a slippery path some of us have to tread! How many times have we exclaimed with the psalmist, *"My feet were almost gone; my steps had well nigh slipped"* (Ps. 73:2). If we were strong, surefooted mountaineers, this would not matter so much; but in ourselves, how weak we are! On the best roads we soon falter; on the smoothest paths we quickly stumble. These feeble knees of ours can scarcely support our tottering weight. A straw may throw us, and a pebble can wound us. We are mere children tremblingly taking our first steps in the walk of faith. Our heavenly Father holds us by the arms, or we would soon be down. Oh, if we are kept from falling, how must we bless the patient power that watches over us day by day! Think how prone we are to sin, how apt to choose danger, how strong our tendency to cast ourselves down, and these reflections will make us sing more sweetly than we have ever done: "Glory be to Him, who is *'able to keep* [us] *from falling.'"* We have many foes who try to push us down. The road is rough, and we are weak. In addition, enemies lurk in ambush who rush out when we least expect them. They labor to trip us up or hurl us down the nearest precipice. Only an almighty arm can preserve us from these unseen foes who are seeking to destroy us. Such an arm is engaged for our defense. He is faithful who has promised. He is able to keep us from falling, so that with a deep sense of our utter weakness, we may cherish a firm belief in our perfect safety. We may say, with joyful confidence,

> Against me earth and hell combine,
>   But on my side is power divine;
> Jesus is all, and He is mine!

But he answered her not a word.
—Matthew 15:23

Those who are genuinely seeking salvation in Christ, but who have not yet obtained the blessing, may take comfort from the story from which our text is taken. The Savior did not immediately give the woman the blessing she sought, even though she had great faith in Him. He intended to give it, but He waited a while. *"He answered her not a word."* Were her prayers not good? Never in the world were there better prayers than hers. Was her case not needy? It was sorrowfully needy. Did she not feel her need sufficiently? She felt it overwhelmingly. Was she not earnest enough? She was intensely so. Did she have no faith? She had such a high degree of it that even Jesus marveled, and said, *"O woman, great is thy faith"* (Matt. 15:28). We may see, then, that although it is true that faith brings peace, it does not always bring it instantaneously. There may be certain reasons that call for the trial of faith, rather than the reward of faith. Genuine faith may be in the soul like a hidden seed, not yet having budded and blossomed into joy and peace. A painful silence from the Savior is the grievous trial of many seeking souls, but heavier still is the affliction of a harsh, cutting reply such as this: *"It is not meet to take the children's bread, and cast it to dogs"* (v. 26). Many people find immediate delight in waiting on the Lord, but this is not the case with all. Some, like the jailer, are turned from darkness to light in a moment (see Acts 16:23–33), but others are plants of slower growth. A deeper sense of sin may be given to you instead of a sense of pardon. In such a case, you will need patience to bear the heavy blow. Poor heart, even though, in a spiritual sense, Christ may beat and bruise you, or even slay you, trust Him. (See Job 13:15.) Though He may give you an angry word, believe in the love of His heart. Do not, I beg you, give up seeking or trusting my Master because you have not yet obtained the conscious joy that you long for. Cast yourself on Him, and perseveringly depend on Him, even when you cannot joyfully hope.

Faultless before the presence of his glory.
—Jude 24

Ponder this wondrous word *"faultless"*! We are far from it now, but since our Lord never stops short of perfection in His work of love, we will reach it one day. The Savior who will keep His people to the end will also present them at last to Himself as *"a glorious church, not having spot, or wrinkle, or any such thing; but that is should be holy and without blemish"* (Eph. 5:27). All the jewels in the Savior's crown are of first quality and without a single flaw. All the maids of honor who attend the Lamb's wife are pure virgins without spot or stain. But how will Jesus make us faultless? He will wash us from our sins in His own blood until we are white and fair as God's purest angel. We will be clothed in His righteousness—that righteousness that makes the saint who wears it positively faultless, yes, perfect in the sight of God. We will be without blame and without reproof even in His eyes. His law will not only have no charge against us, but also will be magnified in us. Moreover, the work of the Holy Spirit within us will be altogether complete. He will make us so perfectly holy that we will have no lingering tendency to sin. Judgment, memory, will, every power and passion will be emancipated from the slavery of evil. We will be holy even as God is holy, and in His presence we will dwell forever. Saints will not be out of place in heaven. Their beauty will be as great as that of the place prepared for them. Oh, the rapture of that hour when the everlasting doors will be lifted up, and we, being made ready for the inheritance, will dwell with the saints in light. Sin gone, Satan shut out, temptation past forever, and ourselves *"faultless"* before God—this will be heaven indeed! Let us be joyful now as we rehearse the song of eternal praise so soon to roll forth in full chorus from all the blood-washed host. Let us copy David's praise before the ark as a prelude to our ecstasies before the throne.

And I will deliver thee out of the hand of the wicked,
and I will redeem thee out of the hand of the terrible.
—Jeremiah 15:21

Note the glorious personality of this promise: *"I will…I will."* The Lord Jehovah Himself intervenes to deliver and redeem His people. He pledges Himself personally to rescue them. His own arm will do it, that He may have the glory. Not a word is said of any effort of our own that may be needed to assist the Lord. Neither our strength nor our weaknesses are taken into account. The lone *"I,"* like the sun in the heavens, shines out, resplendent in all-sufficiency. Why, then, do we calculate our forces and consult with flesh and blood—to our grievous wounding? Jehovah has power enough without borrowing from our puny strength. *"Peace, be still"* (Mark 4:39), you unbelieving thoughts, and know that the Lord reigns. There is no hint in the text about secondary means and causes. The Lord says nothing of friends and helpers. He undertakes the work alone, and feels no need of human strength to aid Him. All our looking around for the help of companions and relatives is useless. They will be to us as broken reeds if we lean on them. (See Isaiah 36:6.) They are often unwilling to help when they are able, and unable when they are willing. Since the promise comes from God alone, we would do well to wait only on Him. When we do so, our expectation never fails us. Who are the wicked that we should fear them? The Lord will utterly consume them; they are to be pitied rather than feared. As for terrible oppressors, they are only terrors to those who have no God to run to. For when the Lord is on our side, whom will we fear? If we run back into sin in order to please the wicked, we have reason to be alarmed. However, if we hold fast to our integrity, the rage of tyrants will be overruled for our good. When the fish swallowed Jonah, he encountered a morsel that he could not digest. Similarly, when the world devours the church, it is glad to be rid of it again. In all times of fiery trial, let us secure our souls through patient endurance.

Let us lift up our heart with our hands unto God in the heavens.
—Lamentations 3:41

The act of prayer teaches us our unworthiness, which is a very beneficial lesson for such proud beings as we are. If God gave us favors without constraining us to pray for them, we would never know how poor we are. A true prayer is an inventory of needs, a catalogue of necessities, a revelation of hidden poverty. While it is an application to divine wealth, it is a confession of human emptiness. The healthiest state of a Christian is to be always empty and poor in self, constantly depending on the Lord for supplies, rich in Jesus, weak as water personally, but mighty through God to do great exploits. Hence, the use of prayer, because, while it adores God, it lays the creature where it should be, in the very dust. Prayer is in itself, apart from the answer that it brings, a great benefit to the Christian. As the runner gains strength for the race by daily exercise, so for the great race of life we acquire energy by the hallowed labor of prayer. Prayer plumes the wings of God's young eaglets so that they may learn to mount above the clouds. Prayer girds the loins of God's warriors and sends them forth to combat with their sinews braced and muscles firm. An earnest pleader comes out of his prayer time, even as the sun rises from the chambers of the east, rejoicing like a strong man to run his race. Prayer is that uplifted hand of Moses that routs the Amalekites more than the sword of Joshua. It is the arrow shot from the chamber of the prophet foreboding defeat to the Syrians. Prayer girds human weakness with divine strength, turns human folly into heavenly wisdom, and gives to troubled mortals the peace of God. We cannot think of anything that prayer cannot do! We thank You, great God, for the mercy seat, a choice proof of Your marvelous lovingkindness. Help us to use it aright throughout this day!

Whom he did predestinate, them he also called.
—Romans 8:30

In 2 Timothy 1:9, we read, *"Who hath saved us, and called us with an holy calling."* In this verse, we find the first standard by which we may test our calling. It is *"an holy calling, not according to our works, but according to his own purpose and grace"* (v. 9). This calling forbids all trust in our own works, and directs us to Christ alone for salvation. Then, after we are saved, it purges us from *"dead works to serve the living God"* (Heb. 9:14). *"As he which hath called you is holy, so be ye holy"* (1 Pet. 1:15). If you are living in sin, you are not called. If you are truly Christ's, you will say, "Nothing pains me as much as sin; I desire to be rid of it. Lord, help me to be holy." Is this the longing of your heart? Is this the tenor of your life toward God and His divine will? Second, in Philippians 3:14, we are told of *"the high calling of God in Christ Jesus."* Is your calling a *"high calling"*? Has it ennobled your heart and set it on heavenly things? Has it elevated your hopes, your tastes, your desires? Has it raised the general tendency of your life, so that you spend it with God and for God? We find a third test in Hebrews 3:1: *"Partakers of the heavenly calling."* A *"heavenly calling"* means that the call must be from heaven. If man alone calls you, you are not called. Is your calling of God? Is it a call to heaven as well as from heaven? Unless you are a stranger on this earth, and heaven is your true home, you have not been called with a *"heavenly calling."* Those who have been called declare that they look for a *"city which hath foundations, whose builder and maker is God"* (Heb. 11:10), and that they themselves are *"strangers and pilgrims on the earth"* (v. 13). Is your calling *"holy," "high,"* and *"heavenly"*? Then, beloved, you have been called by God, for such is the calling by which God calls His people.

I will meditate in thy precepts.
—Psalm 119:15

There are times when solitude is better than society, and silence is wiser than speech. We would be better Christians if we spent more time alone, waiting on God and gathering, through meditation on His Word, spiritual strength for labor in His service. We ought to meditate on the things of God, because we thus get the real nutrition out of them. Truth is something like the cluster of the vine. If we would have wine from it, we must bruise it; we must press and squeeze it many times. The bruiser's feet must come down joyfully on the bunches; otherwise, the juice will not flow. They must tread the grapes well, or else much of the precious liquid will be wasted. So we must, by meditation, tread the clusters of truth, if we would get the wine of consolation from it. Our bodies are not supported by merely taking food into the mouth. The process that really supplies the muscle, nerve, sinew, and the bone is the process of digestion. It is by digestion that the outward food becomes assimilated with the inner life. Our souls are not nourished merely by listening for a while to this, and then to that, and then to the other part of divine truth. Hearing, reading, marking, and learning all require inward digesting to complete their usefulness, and the inward digesting of the truth lies for the most part in meditating on it. Why is it that some Christians, although they hear many sermons, make slow advances in the divine life? Because they neglect their prayer time and do not thoughtfully meditate on God's Word. They love the wheat, but they do not grind it. They want the corn, but they will not go forth into the fields to gather it. The fruit hangs on the tree, but they will not pluck it; the water flows at their feet, but they will not stoop to drink it. Lord, deliver us from such folly, and be this our resolve this morning, "*I will meditate in thy precepts.*"

OCTOBER 12

Evening

The Comforter, which is the Holy Ghost.
—John 14:26

We live in an age that is distinctively the dispensation of the Holy Spirit. Jesus comforts us, not by His physical presence, as He will do in the future, but by the indwelling and constant abiding of the Holy Spirit, who is the Comforter of the church. The Holy Spirit's role is to console the hearts of God's people. He convicts us of sin, and He illuminates and instructs us. However, the main part of His work lies in bringing joy to the hearts of the renewed, in strengthening the weak, and in lifting up all those who are bowed down. He does this by revealing Jesus to them. The Holy Spirit consoles, but Christ is the Consolation. If I may use this metaphor, the Holy Spirit is the Physician, but Jesus is the Medicine. The Holy Spirit heals the wound, but He does so by applying the holy ointment of Christ's name and grace. He does not draw from what is His, but from the things of Christ. So if we give to the Holy Spirit the name Paraclete (from the Greek word *parakletos*, meaning "comforter"), as we sometimes do, then our hearts may confer on our blessed Lord Jesus the title of Paraclesis. If the Holy Spirit is the Comforter, Jesus is the Comfort. Now, when the Christian has such rich provision for his needs, why should he be sad and despondent? The Holy Spirit has graciously pledged to be your Comforter. Do you imagine, O weak and trembling believer, that He will be negligent of His sacred trust? Do you suppose that He has undertaken what He cannot or will not perform? If it is His special work to strengthen and comfort you, do you suppose that He has forgotten His business or that He will fail in the loving duty that He performs on your behalf? Do not think so harshly of the tender and blessed Spirit, whose name is *"Comforter."* He delights to give *"the oil of joy for mourning, the garment of praise for the spirit of heaviness"* (Isa. 61:3). Trust in Him, and He will surely comfort you until the *"house of mourning"* (Eccl. 7:2) is closed forever, and the Marriage Feast (Rev. 19:9) has begun.

Godly sorrow worketh repentance.
—2 Corinthians 7:10

Genuine, spiritual mourning for sin is the work of the Spirit of God. Repentance is too choice a flower to grow in nature's garden. Pearls grow naturally in oysters, but penitence never shows itself in sinners unless divine grace works it in them. If you have one particle of real hatred for sin, God must have given it to you, for human nature's thorns never produced a single fig. *"That which is born of the flesh is flesh"* (John 3:6). True repentance has a distinct reference to the Savior. When we repent of sin, we must have one eye on sin and another on the cross. It will be better still if we fix both our eyes on Christ and see our transgressions only in the light of His love. True sorrow for sin is eminently practical. No man may say he hates sin if he lives in it. Repentance makes us see the evil of sin, not merely as a theory, but experientially—as a burned child dreads fire. We will be as much afraid of it as a man who has recently been stopped and robbed is afraid of the thief on the highway. We will shun it—shun it in everything—not only in great things, but also in little things, as men shun little vipers as well as great snakes. True mourning for sin will make us very jealous over our tongues, lest we should say a wrong word. We will be very watchful over our daily actions, lest in anything we offend. Each night we will close the day with painful confessions of our shortcomings, and each morning we will awaken with anxious prayers that this day God would hold us up so that we may not sin against Him. Sincere repentance is continual. Believers repent until their dying day. Their sadness over sin is not intermittent. Every other sorrow yields to time, but this dear sorrow grows with our growth, and it is so sweet as well as bitter that we thank God we are permitted to enjoy and to suffer it until we enter our eternal rest.

Love is strong as death.
—Song of Solomon 8:6

Whose love can this be that is as mighty as the destroyer of the human race, the conqueror of monarchs? Would it not sound like satire if it were applied to my poor, weak, and scarcely living love for Jesus my Lord? I do love Him, and perhaps, by His grace, I could even die for Him. However, as for my love, in itself, it can scarcely endure a scoff or a jeer, much less a cruel death. Surely, it is my Beloved's love that is spoken of in the text—the love of Jesus, the matchless Lover of souls. His love was indeed stronger than the most terrible death, for it endured the trial of the cross triumphantly. It was a lingering death, but love survived the torment. It was a shameful death, but love despised the shame. It was a punitive death, but love bore our iniquities. It was a forsaken, lonely death, from which the eternal Father hid His face, but love endured the curse and gloried over all. There has never been such love, or such a death. It was a desperate duel, but love won the victory. What then, my heart? Are no emotions stirred within you at the contemplation of such heavenly affection? Yes, my Lord, I long, I yearn, to feel Your love flaming like a furnace within me. Come and ignite the fervor of my spirit.

> For every drop of crimson blood
>   Thus shed to make me live,
> O wherefore, wherefore have not I
>   A thousand lives to give?

Why should I despair of loving Jesus with a love as *"strong as death"*? He deserves it, and I desire it. The martyrs felt such love, and they were only flesh and blood. Why not I? They mourned their weaknesses, yet *"out of weakness were made strong"* (Heb. 11:34). Grace gave them their unflinching constancy. The same grace is available for me. Jesus, Lover of my soul, pour out Your love, *"love...strong as death,"* into my heart this evening.

OCTOBER 14
Morning

I count all things but loss for the excellency of the knowledge
of Christ Jesus my Lord.
—Philippians 3:8

Spiritual knowledge of Christ will be a personal knowledge. I cannot know Jesus through another person's acquaintance with Him. No, I must know Him myself. I must know Him on my own account. It will be an intelligent knowledge. I must know Him, not as the visionary dreams of Him, but as the Word reveals Him. I must know His natures, both divine and human. I must know His offices, His attributes, His works, His shame, and His glory. I must meditate on Him until I *"comprehend with all saints what is the breadth, and length, and depth, and height; and…know the love of Christ, which passeth knowledge"* (Eph. 3:18–19). It will be an affectionate knowledge of Him. Indeed, if I know Him at all, I must love Him. An ounce of heart knowledge is worth a ton of head learning. Our knowledge of Him will be a satisfying knowledge. When I know my Savior, my mind will be full to the brim. I will feel that I have that which my spirit longed for. Jesus said, *"I am the bread of life: he that cometh to me shall never hunger"* (John 6:35). At the same time, it will be an exciting knowledge. The more I know of my Beloved, the more I will want to know. The higher I climb, the loftier will be the summits that invite my eager footsteps. I will want all the more as I get more. Like the miser's treasure, my gold will make me covet more. In conclusion, this knowledge of Christ Jesus will be a most happy one. In fact, it will be so elevating that sometimes it will completely bear me up above all trials, doubts, and sorrows. It will, while I enjoy it, make me something more than a *"man that is born of a woman [who] is of few days, and full of trouble"* (Job 14:1). It will fling about me the immortality of the ever-living Savior and gird me with the golden girdle of His eternal joy. Come, my soul, sit at Jesus' feet and learn of Him all this day.

OCTOBER 14

Evening

And be not conformed to this world.
—Romans 12:2

If a Christian can possibly be saved while he conforms to this world, it will only be by fire. Such a bare salvation is almost as much to be dreaded as desired. Reader, would you wish to leave this world in the darkness of despondency, and enter heaven as a shipwrecked sailor climbs the cliffs of his native country in order to reach home? Then be worldly. Be mixed up with those who love money but not God. (See Matthew 6:24.) Refuse to go outside the camp bearing Christ's reproach. (See Hebrews 13:11–13.) Or do you want to have a heaven below as well as a heaven above? Do you want to *comprehend with all saints what is the…depth, and height; and to know the love of Christ, which passeth knowledge* (Eph. 3:18–19)? Do you want to receive an abundant entrance into the joy of your Lord? Then *come out from among them, and be ye separate, saith the Lord, and touch not the unclean thing* (2 Cor. 6:17). Do you want to attain the *full assurance of faith* (Heb. 10:22)? You cannot attain it while you commune with sinners. Do you want to flame with fervent love for God? Your love will be dampened by the drenchings of godless society. You may be a babe in grace, but you cannot become a great Christian, you cannot be a *perfect man* (Eph. 4:13) in Christ Jesus, while you yield to the principles and business practices of worldly people. It is harmful for an heir of heaven to be a great friend of the heirs of hell. It looks bad when a courtier is too friendly with his king's enemies. Even small inconsistencies are dangerous. Little thorns make great blisters, little moths destroy fine garments, and a little frivolousness and disobedience will rob faith of a thousand joys. If you are a believer, but are compromising your faith, you do not know what you lose by your conformity to the world. It cuts the tendons of your strength, and makes you creep when you should be running. Therefore, for your own comfort's sake, and for the sake of your growth in grace, if you are a Christian, be a Christian, and be a marked and distinct one.

But who may abide the day of his coming?
—Malachi 3:2

His first coming was without external pomp or show of power. Yet, in truth, there were few who could abide its testing might. Herod and all Jerusalem were stirred at the news of the wondrous birth. Those who supposed themselves to be waiting for Him showed the fallacy of their professions by rejecting Him when He came. His life on earth was a winnowing fan, which tried the great heap of religious profession, and few could abide the process. But what will His second advent be? What sinner can endure to think of it? *"He shall smite the earth with the rod of his mouth, and with the breath of his lips shall he slay the wicked"* (Isa. 11:4). When in His humiliation He said to the soldiers, *"I am he"* (John 18:5), they fell backward. What will be the terror of His enemies when He will more fully reveal Himself as the "I am"? His death shook earth and darkened heaven. What will be the dreadful splendor of that day in which, as the living Savior, He summons the living and the dead before Him? Oh, that the terrors of the Lord would persuade men to forsake their sins and *"kiss the Son, lest he be angry"* (Ps. 2:12)! Though a lamb, He is yet the *"Lion of the tribe of Juda"* (Rev. 5:5), rending the prey in pieces; though *"a bruised reed shall he not break"* (Isa. 42:3), He will break His enemies *"with a rod of iron"* and *"dash them in pieces like a potter's vessel"* (Ps. 2:9). None of His foes will bear up before the tempest of His wrath or hide themselves from the sweeping hail of His indignation. His beloved blood-washed people, though, look for His appearing with joy and hope to abide it without fear. To them He sits as a refiner even now, and when He has tried them, they will *"come forth as gold"* (Job 23:10). Let us search ourselves this morning and make our calling and election sure, so that the coming of the Lord may cause no dark foreboding in our minds. Oh, for grace to cast away all hypocrisy and to be found sincere and without rebuke in the day of His appearing!

But the firstling of an ass thou shalt redeem with a lamb: and if thou
redeem him not, then shalt thou break his neck.
—Exodus 34:20

Every firstborn animal belonged to the Lord. However, since the donkey was unclean, it could not be presented in sacrifice. Then what was to be done with it? Could it be freed from the universal law? By no means. God allowed no exceptions. The donkey was His due, but He would not accept it. He would not nullify the claim, yet He could not be pleased with the victim. No way of escape remained but redemption—the animal could be saved only by the substitution of a lamb in its place. If it was not redeemed, it had to die. This Old Testament law provides us with an important lesson. That unclean animal is yourself. You are justly the property of the Lord who made you and preserves you. Yet you are so sinful that God will not, cannot, accept you. Therefore, it has come to this: the Lamb of God must take your place, or you must die eternally. Let all the world know of your gratitude to that spotless Lamb who has already bled for you, and thus redeemed you from the fatal curse of the law. The Israelite must sometimes have questioned which should die, the donkey or the lamb. Would not a good man pause to evaluate and compare? Assuredly, there is no comparison between the value of the soul of man and the life of the Lord Jesus. However, the Lamb died, and man the donkey was spared. Admire the boundless love of God to you and others of the human race. Imagine—worms are bought with the blood of the Son of the Highest; dust and ashes are redeemed with a price far above silver and gold! What a doom would have been ours if abundant redemption had not been provided! The breaking of the neck of the donkey was only a momentary penalty. Yet who can measure the *"wrath to come"* (Matt. 3:7), for which no limit can be imagined? Immeasurably precious is the glorious Lamb, who has redeemed us from such a fate.

Jesus saith unto them, Come and dine.
—John 21:12

In these words, the believer is invited to a holy nearness to Jesus. *"Come and dine"* implies the same table and the same meat; yes, and sometimes it means to sit side by side and lean our head on the Savior's bosom. It is being brought into the banquet room where the banner of redeeming love waves. *"Come and dine"* gives us a vision of union with Jesus, because the only food that we can feast on when we dine with Jesus is Himself. Oh, what union this is! It is a depth that reason cannot fathom, that we thus feed on Jesus. *"He that eateth my flesh, and drinketh my blood, dwelleth in me, and I in him"* (John 6:56). It is also an invitation to enjoy fellowship with the saints. Christians may differ on a variety of points, but they all have one spiritual appetite. If we cannot all feel alike, we can all feed alike on the Bread of Life sent down from heaven. At the table of fellowship with Jesus, we are one bread and one cup. As the loving cup goes around, we pledge our love and unity to one another heartily. Get nearer to Jesus, and you will find yourself linked more and more in spirit to all who are like yourself, supported by the same heavenly manna. If we were closer to Jesus, we would be closer to one another. We likewise see in these words the source of strength for every Christian. To look at Christ is to live, but for strength to serve Him you must *"come and dine."* We labor under much unnecessary weakness on account of neglecting this percept of the Master. None of us needs to put himself on a low-calorie diet; on the contrary, we should fatten ourselves on the marrow and fatness of the Gospel, so that we may accumulate strength from it and urge every power to its full tension in the Master's service. Thus, if you would realize nearness to Jesus, union with Jesus, love for His people, and strength from Jesus, *"come and dine"* with Him by faith.

With thee is the fountain of life.
—Psalm 36:9

There are times in our spiritual experience when human counsel or sympathy, or Christian ordinances, fail to comfort or help us. Why does our gracious God permit this? Perhaps it is because we have been living too much without Him. Therefore, He has taken away everything upon which we have been in the habit of depending, so that He may drive us to Himself. It is a blessed thing to live at the fountainhead. While our water bottles are full, we are content, like Hagar and Ishmael, to go into the wilderness. (See Genesis 21:14.) However, when they are dry, nothing will satisfy us but the knowledge that *"thou God seest me"* (Gen. 16:13). We are like the Prodigal Son. We love pig troughs but forget our Father's house. Remember, we can make pig troughs and husks even out of religious practices. Such practices are blessed things, but when we substitute them for God, they are of no value. Anything becomes an idol when it keeps us away from God. Even the bronze serpent is to be despised as *"Nehushtan"* (2 Kings 18:4) if we worship it instead of God. The Prodigal was never safer than when he was driven to the arms of his father, because he could find sustenance nowhere else. The Lord may allow a famine in the land in order to prompt us to seek Him all the more. The best position for a Christian to be in is to live wholly and directly on God's grace—remaining where he stood when he first came to Christ: *"Having nothing, and yet possessing all things"* (2 Cor. 6:10). Let us never for a moment think that our standing is in our sanctification, our self-denial, our graces, or our feelings. Let us recognize that we are saved because Christ offered a full atonement, for we are *"complete in him"* (Col. 2:10). Having nothing of our own to trust in, we rest on the merits of Jesus. His sacrifice and holy life furnish us with our only sure ground of confidence. Beloved, when we are brought into a thirsty condition, we are sure to turn to the *"fountain of life"* with eagerness.

And David said in his heart, I shall now perish one day
by the hand of Saul.
—1 Samuel 27:1

The thought of David's heart at this time was a false thought. He certainly had no ground for thinking that God's anointing him by Samuel was intended to be left as an empty, meaningless act. Never on any occasion had the Lord deserted His servant. He had been placed in perilous positions often, but not one instance had occurred in which divine intervention had not delivered him. The trials to which he had been exposed had been varied; they had not assumed one form only, but many. Yet, in every case, He who sent the trial had also graciously ordained a way of escape. David could not put his finger on any entry in his diary and say of it, "Here is evidence that the Lord will forsake me," for the entire tenor of his life had proved the very reverse. He should have realized from what God had done for him that God would be his defender still. But do we not doubt God's help in this same way? Is it not mistrust without a cause? Have we ever had the shadow of a reason to doubt our Father's goodness? Have not His lovingkindnesses been marvelous? Has He once failed to justify our trust? Ah, no! Our God has not left us at any time. We have had dark nights, but the star of love has shone forth amid the blackness. We have been in stern conflicts, but He has held aloft the shield of our defense over our heads. We have gone through many trials, but never to our detriment, always to our advantage. The conclusion from our past experiences is that He who has been with us in six troubles will not forsake us in the seventh. What we have known of our faithful God proves that He will keep us to the end. Let us not, then, reason contrary to evidence. How can we ever be so ungenerous as to doubt our God? Lord, throw down the Jezebel of our unbelief, and let the dogs devour it.

He shall gather the lambs with his arm.
—Isaiah 40:11

Our Good Shepherd has a variety of sheep in His flock. Some are strong in the Lord, while others are weak in faith. However, He cares for all His sheep impartially. The weakest lamb is as dear to Him as the most advanced of the flock. Lambs tend to lag behind, wander, and grow weary. Yet the Shepherd protects them from the dangers of these tendencies with His arm of power. He finds newborn souls, like young lambs, ready to perish, and He nourishes them until they are strong. He finds weak minds ready to faint and die, and He comforts them and renews their strength. He gathers all the little ones, for it is not the will of our heavenly Father that any of them should perish. What a quick eye He must have to see them all, what a tender heart to care for them all, what a far-reaching and powerful arm to gather them all! During His lifetime on earth, He was a great gatherer of the weak. Now that He dwells in heaven, His loving heart yearns toward the meek and contrite, the timid and feeble, and the fearful and fainting here below. How gently He gathered me—to Himself, to His truth, to His blood, to His love, to His church! With great grace, He compelled me to come to Himself. Since my conversion, He has frequently restored me from my wanderings, and again embraced me within the circle of His everlasting arms. Best of all, He does all this Himself, personally. He does not delegate the task of love, but graciously takes it upon Himself to rescue and preserve even the most unworthy servant. How will I love Him enough or serve Him worthily? I would gladly make His name *"great unto the ends of the earth"* (Mic. 5:4). Yet what can my feebleness do for Him? Great Shepherd, add to Your mercies one other: a heart to love You more truly, as I should.

Thy paths drop fatness.
—Psalm 65:11

Many are *"the paths of the LORD"* (Ps. 25:10) that *"drop fatness,"* but a special one is the path of prayer. No believer who spends much time in prayer will have any need to cry, *"My leanness, my leanness, woe unto me!"* (Isa. 24:16). Starving souls live at a distance from the mercy seat and become like parched fields in times of drought. Prevalence with God in wrestling prayer is sure to make the believer strong—if not happy. The nearest place to the gate of heaven is the throne of heavenly grace. Spend much time alone with Jesus, and you will have much assurance; spend little time alone with Him, and your religion will be shallow, polluted with many doubts and fears, not sparkling with the joy of the Lord. Since the soul-enriching path of prayer is open to the very weakest saint; since no high attainments are required; since you are not bidden to come because you are an advanced saint, but freely invited if you are a saint at all; see to it, dear reader, that you are often in the place of private devotion. Spend much time on your knees, for so Elijah drew the rain down on famished Israel's fields. There is another special path dripping with fatness to those who walk therein: it is the secret walk of communion. Oh, the delights of fellowship with Jesus! Earth has no words that can set forth the holy calm of a soul leaning on Jesus' breast. Few Christians understand it. They live in the lowlands and seldom climb to the mountaintop. They live in the outer court. They do not enter the holy place. They do not take up the privilege of priesthood. At a distance they see the sacrifice, but they do not sit down with the priest to eat of it and to enjoy the fat of the burnt offering. But, reader, always sit under the shadow of Jesus. Come up to that palm tree and take hold of the branches of it. Let your Beloved be to you as the apple tree in the woods, and you will be satisfied as with marrow and fatness. Jesus, visit us with Your salvation!

Behold, to obey is better than sacrifice.
—1 Samuel 15:22

Saul had been commanded to slay all the Amalekites and their cattle. Instead of doing so, he preserved the king and allowed the Israelites to take the best of the oxen and sheep. When called to account for this, he declared that he had done it with the idea of offering sacrifices to God. However, Samuel immediately countered him with this certain truth: sacrifices are no excuse for an act of direct rebellion. The text for this evening is worthy to be printed in letters of gold, and to be hung up before the eyes of the present idolatrous generation. They are very fond of the fineries of worshipping their own wills, yet they utterly neglect the laws of God. Always remember that to keep strictly in the path of your Savior's commands is better than any outward form of religion. Listening to His precepts with an attentive ear is better than bringing the *"fat of rams"* (1 Sam. 15:22), or any other precious thing, to place on His altar. If you are failing to keep the least of Christ's commands to His disciples, I urge you not to be disobedient any longer. All the pretensions you make of attachment to your Master, and all the devout actions that you may perform, are no recompense for disobedience. *"To obey,"* even in the slightest thing, *"is better than sacrifice"*—no matter how elaborate it is. We are not to rely on Gregorian chant, sumptuous robes, incense, or banners in our desire to please God. The first thing that God requires of His child is obedience. Even though you might give your body to be burned, and all your goods to feed the poor, if you do not listen to the Lord's precepts, all your formalities will be of no profit to you. It is a blessed thing to be as teachable as a little child. However, it is a much more blessed thing, when one has been taught the lesson, to carry it out to the letter. How many people decorate their churches and adorn their clergymen, but refuse to obey the Word of the Lord! Do not be like one of them.

Babes in Christ.
—1 Corinthians 3:1

Are you mourning, believer, because you are so weak in the divine life, because your faith is so little, your love so feeble? Cheer up, for you have reason for gratitude. Remember that in some things you are equal to the greatest and most mature Christian. You are as much bought with blood as he is. You are as much an adopted child of God as any other believer. An infant is as truly a child of its parents as is the full-grown man. You are as completely justified, for your justification is not a thing of degrees. Your little faith has made you completely clean. You have as much right to the precious things of the covenant as the most advanced believers, for your right to covenant mercies does not lie in your growth, but in the covenant itself. Your faith in Jesus is not the measure but the token of your inheritance in Him. You are as rich as the richest, if not in enjoyment, in real possession. The smallest star that gleams is set in heaven. The faintest ray of light has affinity with the great orb of day. In the family register of glory the small and the great are written with the same pen. You are as dear to your Father's heart as the greatest in the family. Jesus is very tender over you. You are like the smoking flax. A rougher spirit would say, "Put out that smoking flax. It fills the room with an offensive odor!" But *the smoking flax shall he not quench*" (Isa. 42:3). You are like a bruised reed; and any less tender hand than that of the Chief Musician would tread on you or throw you away, but He will never break the bruised reed (v. 3). Instead of being downcast because of what you are, you should triumph in Christ. Am I but little in Israel? Yet in Christ I am made to sit in heavenly places. Am I poor in faith? Still in Jesus I am heir of all things. Though I have nothing about which to boast, if the root of the matter is in me, I can and will rejoice in the Lord and glory in the God of my salvation.

OCTOBER 19

Evening

God my maker, who giveth songs in the night.
—Job 35:10

Anyone can sing in the day. When the cup is full, man draws inspiration from it. When wealth flows around him in abundance, anyone can praise the God who gives a plenteous harvest or sends home a ship loaded with goods. It is easy enough for an aeolian harp to whisper music when the wind is blowing. The difficulty is in getting the music to swell when no wind is stirring. It is easy to sing when we can read the notes by daylight. Yet the one who can sing when there is not a ray of light to read by—who sings from his heart—is skillful. No one can compose a song in the night by his own ability. He may attempt it, but he will find that it must be divinely inspired. If everything is going well, I can weave songs wherever I go, forming them out of the flowers that grow on my path. However, put me in a desert, where nothing green grows, and then how will I create a hymn of praise to God? How can a mortal man make a crown for the Lord where there are no jewels? If my voice is clear, and my body is full of health, I can sing God's praises. Yet silence my tongue, and put me on a sickbed, and then how will I sing God's high praises, unless He Himself gives me the song? No, it is not in man's power to sing when everything is going badly, unless a coal from the altar touches his lips. (See Isaiah 6:5–7.) Habakkuk sang a divine song when he said, in the night, *"Although the fig tree shall not blossom, neither shall fruit be in the vines; the labour of the olive shall fail, and the fields shall yield no meat; the flock shall be cut off from the fold, and there shall be no herd in the stalls: yet I will rejoice in the LORD, I will joy in the God of my salvation"* (Hab. 3:17–18). Therefore, since our Maker gives *"songs in the night,"* let us wait on Him for the music. O Chief Musician, let us not remain songless when affliction is upon us. Tune our lips to the melody of thanksgiving.

OCTOBER 20
Morning

Grow up into him in all things.
—Ephesians 4:15

Many Christians remain stunted and dwarfed in spiritual things, so as to present the same appearance year after year. No advanced and refined feelings are manifest in them. They exist but do not *"grow up into him in all things."* Should we rest content with being in the green blade when we might advance to the ear and eventually ripen into the full corn in the ear? Should we be satisfied to believe in Christ, and to say, "I am safe," without wishing to know in our own experience more of the fullness that is to be found in Him? It should not be so. We should, as good traders in heaven's market, covet to be enriched in the knowledge of Jesus. It is all very well to keep other men's vineyards, but we must not neglect our own spiritual growth and ripening. Why should it always be wintertime in our hearts? We must have our seed time, it is true, but, oh, for a springtime—yes, a summer season that gives promise of an early harvest! If we would ripen in grace, we must live near to Jesus—in His presence—ripened by the sunshine of His smiles. We must hold sweet communion with Him. We must leave the distant view of His face and come near, as John did, and pillow our head on His breast. Then will we find ourselves advancing in holiness, in love, in faith, in hope—yes, in every precious gift. As the sun rises first on the mountaintops and gilds them with its light, it presents one of the most charming sights to the eye of the traveler. So is it one of the most delightful contemplations in the world to notice the glow of the Spirit's light on the head of some saint, who has risen in spiritual stature, like Saul, above his fellows. Like the mighty snowcapped Alps, he reflects first among the chosen the beams of the Sun of Righteousness. Then he bears the sheen of His brilliant glory high aloft for all to see, and seeing it, he brings glory to His Father who is in heaven.

Keep not back.
—Isaiah 43:6

Although this message was given to the *"south"* (Isa. 43:6), referring to the children of Israel, we may benefit by considering it an exhortation to us, also. We are naturally unlearned in all good things, and it is a lesson of grace to learn to go forward in the ways of God. Reader, if you are unconverted, do you desire to trust in the Lord Jesus? Then *"keep not back."* Love invites you, the promises secure your success, and the precious blood of Jesus prepares the way. Do not let sins or fears hinder you, but come to Jesus just as you are. Do you long to pray? Do you want to pour out your heart before the Lord? *"Keep not back."* The mercy seat is prepared for those who need mercy. A sinner's cries will prevail with God. You are invited—not only so, you are commanded—to pray. Therefore, come with boldness to the throne of grace. Dear friend, are you already saved? Then *"keep not back"* from fellowshipping with the Lord's people. Do not neglect the ordinances of baptism and the Lord's Supper. You may have a timid disposition. However, you must strive against it, so that it will not lead you into disobedience. A sweet promise is given to those who confess Christ. By no means miss it, lest you come under the condemnation of those who deny Him. If you have talents, *"keep not back"* from using them. Do not hoard your wealth. Do not waste your time. Do not let your abilities rust or your influence go unused. Jesus did not hold back. Imitate Him by being foremost in self-denial and self-sacrifice. *"Keep not back"* from close communion with God, from boldly taking hold of covenant blessings, from advancing in the Christian life, from looking into the precious mysteries of the love of Christ. Beloved friend, do not be guilty of keeping others back by your coldness, harshness, or suspicions. For Jesus' sake, go forward yourself, and encourage others to do the same. Hell and the joint forces of superstition and unfaithfulness are on the frontlines of the fight. O soldiers of the Cross, *"keep not back."*

The love of Christ constraineth us.
—2 Corinthians 5:14

How much do you owe to my Lord? Has He ever done anything for you? Has He forgiven your sins? Has He covered you with a robe of righteousness? Has He set your feet on a rock? Has He established your goings? Has He prepared heaven for you? Has He prepared you for heaven? Has He written your name in His book of life? Has He given you countless blessings? Has He laid up for you a store of mercies, which *"eye hath not seen, nor ear heard"* (1 Cor. 2:9)? Then do something for Jesus worthy of His love. Do not give a mere wordy offering to a dying Redeemer. How will you feel when your Master comes, if you have to confess that you did nothing for Him, but kept your love shut up like a stagnant pool, neither flowing forth to His poor or to His work? Let such love as that be gone! What do men think of a love that never shows itself in action? Why, they say, *"Open rebuke is better than secret love"* (Prov. 27:5). Who will accept a love so weak that it does not motivate you to a single deed of self-denial, of generosity, of heroism, or zeal? Think how He has loved you and given Himself for you! Do you know the power of that love? Then let it be like a rushing, mighty wind to your soul to sweep out the clouds of your worldliness and clear away the mists of sin. May the words "For Christ's sake" be the tongue of fire that will sit upon you. May they be the divine rapture, the heavenly inspiration to bear you aloft from earth, the divine spirit that will make you bold as lions and swift as eagles in your Lord's service. Love should give wings to the feet of service and strength to the arms of labor. Fixed on God with a constancy that is not to be shaken, resolute to honor Him with a determination that is not to be turned aside, and pressing on with an ardor never to be wearied, let us manifest the constraints of love for Jesus. May the divine lodestone draw us heavenward toward itself.

Why are ye troubled? and why do thoughts arise in your hearts?
—Luke 24:38

Why sayest thou, O Jacob, and speakest, O Israel, My way is hid from the Lord, and my judgment is passed over from my God?" (Isa. 40:27). The Lord cares for all things, and the humblest creatures share in His universal providence; but His particular providence is over His saints. *"The angel of the Lord encampeth round about them that fear him"* (Ps. 34:7). *"Precious shall their blood be in his sight"* (Ps. 72:14). *"Precious in the sight of the Lord is the death of his saints"* (Ps. 116:15). *"We know that all things work together for good to them that love God, to them that are the called according to his purpose"* (Rom. 8:28). Let this fact encourage and comfort you: while He is the *"Saviour of all men"* (1 Tim. 4:10), He is the Savior *"specially of those that believe"* (v. 10). You are His special care, His regal treasure that He guards as the *"apple of his eye"* (Deut. 32:10), His vineyard over which He watches day and night. *"The very hairs of your head are all numbered"* (Matt. 10:30). Let the thought of His special love for you be a spiritual painkiller, a dear soother of your troubles. *"I will never leave thee, nor forsake thee"* (Heb. 13:5). God speaks that promise to you as much as He did to any saint of old. *"Fear not,...I am thy shield, and thy exceeding great reward"* (Gen. 15:1). We lose much comfort by our habit of reading His promises as if they were only for the church as a whole, instead of applying them directly to ourselves. Believer, grasp the divine Word with a personal, appropriating faith. Hear Jesus say to you, *"I have prayed for thee, that thy faith fail not"* (Luke 22:32). See Him walking on the waters of your trouble, for He is there, and He is saying, *"Be of good cheer; it is I; be not afraid"* (Matt. 14:27). Oh, those sweet words of Christ! May the Holy Spirit enable you to think of them as words spoken to you. Forget others for a while, and accept the voice of Jesus as addressed to you. Say, "Jesus whispers comfort. I cannot refuse it. I will sit *'under his shadow with great delight'* (Song 2:3)."

OCTOBER 22

I will heal their backsliding, I will love them freely.
—Hosea 14:4

This sentence is a body of divinity in miniature. He who understands its meaning is a theologian, and he who can dive into its fullness is a true master in Israel. It is a condensation of the glorious message of salvation that was delivered to us in Christ Jesus our Redeemer. The meaning hinges on the word "*freely.*" This is the glorious, suitable, divine way by which love streams from heaven to earth, a spontaneous love flowing forth to those who neither deserved it, purchased it, or sought after it. It is, indeed, the only way in which God can love us as we are. The text is a deathblow to all sorts of fitness: "*I will love them freely.*" Now, if there were any suitability necessary in us, then He would not love us freely; at the least, this would be a mitigation and a drawback to the freeness of it. But it stands, "*I will love [you] freely.*" We complain, "Lord, my heart is so hard." He responds, "*I will love [you] freely.*" We say, "But I do not feel my need of You as I wish I could. I do not feel that softening of spirit that I should desire." And He answers, "I will not love you because you feel your need. *'I will love [you] freely.*'" Remember, the softening of spirit is not a condition, for there are no conditions. The covenant of grace has no stipulations whatsoever. We, without any worthiness, may venture on the promise of God that was made to us in Christ Jesus, when He said, "*He that believeth on him is not condemned*" (John 3:18). It is a blessing to know that the grace of God is free to us at all times, without preparation, without suitability, without money, and without price! "*I will love them freely.*" These words invite backsliders to return: indeed, the text was especially written for such—"*I will heal their backsliding, I will love them freely.*" Backslider, surely the generosity of the promise will at once break your heart, and you will return and seek your injured Father's face.

OCTOBER 22
Evening

He shall take of mine, and shall show it unto you.
—John 16:15

There are times when all the promises and doctrines of the Bible are of no benefit, unless a gracious hand applies them to us. We are thirsty, but we are too faint to crawl to the brook to drink. When a soldier is wounded in battle, it is of little use for him to know that there are those at the hospital who can bind up his wounds, and that there are medicines that can ease all the pain he is suffering. What he needs is to be carried to the hospital, and to have the remedies applied to his wounds. It is the same way with our souls. To meet this need, there is One, *"even the Spirit of truth"* (John 14:17), who takes of the things of Jesus and applies them to us. Do not think that Christ has placed His joys on heavenly shelves, and that we have to climb up to them ourselves. No, He draws near and pours His peace into our hearts. O Christian, if you are laboring under deep distresses tonight, your Father does not give you promises and then leave you to draw them up from the Word like buckets from a well. The promises He has written in the Word, He will write anew on your heart. He will manifest His love to you and, by His blessed Spirit, dispel your cares and troubles. O mourner, know that it is God's prerogative to wipe every tear from the eyes of His people. The Good Samaritan did not say to the wounded man, "Here are the oil and wine." He actually poured the oil and wine into the man's wounds. In the same way, Jesus does not only give you the sweet wine of the promise, but He also holds the golden chalice to your lips and pours the lifeblood into your mouth. The poor, sick, weary pilgrim is not merely strengthened to walk, but he is also carried on eagles' wings. What a glorious Gospel we have, which provides everything for the helpless, which draws near to us when we cannot reach for it, which brings us grace even before we seek it! There is as much glory in the way the gift is given as in the gift itself. Happy are those who have the Holy Spirit to bring Jesus to them.

OCTOBER 23

Morning

Will ye also go away?
—John 6:67

Many have forsaken Christ and have walked no more with Him. But what reason do you have to make a change? Has there been any reason for it in the past? Has not Jesus proved Himself all-sufficient? He appeals to you this morning: *"Have I been a wilderness unto [you]?"* (Jer. 2:31). When your soul has simply trusted Jesus, have you ever been confounded? Have you not up until now found your Lord to be a compassionate and generous friend to you, and has not simple faith in Him given you all the peace your spirit could desire? Can you so much as dream of a better friend than He has been to you? Then do not change the old and tried for the new and false. As for the present, can that compel you to leave Christ? When we are troubled by this world or with severe trials within the church, we find it a most blessed thing to pillow our head on the bosom of our Savior. This is the joy we have today—that we are saved in Him. If this joy is satisfying, why would we think of changing? Who barters gold for dross? We will not reject the sun until we find a better light or leave our Lord until a brighter lover will appear. Since this can never be, we will hold Him with an immortal grasp and bind His name as a seal on our arm. As for the future, can you suggest anything that can arise that will render it necessary for you to mutiny or to desert the old flag to serve under another captain? We think not. If life is long, He does not change. If we are poor, what could be better than to have Christ who can make us rich? When we are sick, what more do we need than Jesus to make our bed in our sickness? When we die, is it not written that *"neither death, nor life, nor angels, nor principalities, nor powers, nor things present, nor things to come, nor height, nor depth, nor any other creature, shall be able to separate us from the love of God, which is in Christ Jesus our Lord"* (Rom. 8:38–39)? We say with Peter, *"Lord, to whom shall we go?"* (John 6:68).

OCTOBER 23

Evening

Why sleep ye? rise and pray, lest ye enter into temptation.
—Luke 22:46

When is the Christian most liable to sleep? Is it not when his temporal circumstances are prosperous? Have you not found this to be the case? When you had daily troubles to take to the throne of grace, were you not more wakeful than you are now? Easy roads make sleepy travelers. Another dangerous time is when all is going well in spiritual matters. In Bunyan's *The Pilgrim's Progress*, Christian did not go to sleep when lions were in the way, when he was wading through the river, or when he was fighting with Apollyon. However, when he climbed halfway up the hill Difficulty and came to a delightful arbor, he sat down and immediately fell asleep, to his great sorrow and loss. The Enchanted Ground is a place of warm breezes, laden with fragrant scents and soft influences, all tending to lull pilgrims to sleep. Remember Bunyan's description: "Then they came at an arbor, warm, and promising much refreshing to the pilgrims; for it was finely wrought above-head, beautified with greens, furnished with benches and settles. It also had in it a soft couch, whereon the weary might lean....This arbor was called The Slothful's Friend, and was made on purpose to allure, if it might be, some of the pilgrims there to take up their rest when weary." Depend upon this truth: it is in easy places that men shut their eyes and wander into the dreamy land of forgetfulness. Erskine wisely remarked, "I like a roaring devil better than a sleeping devil." There is no temptation half as dangerous as not being tempted. The distressed soul does not sleep. It is after we enter into peaceful confidence and full assurance that we are in danger of slumbering. The disciples fell asleep after they had seen Jesus transfigured on the mountaintop. Take note, joyous Christian, that good circumstances are near neighbors to temptations. Be as happy as you wish, but also be watchful.

OCTOBER 24

Morning

The trees of the Lord are full of sap.
—Psalm 104:16

Without sap the tree cannot flourish or even exist. Vitality is essential to a Christian. There must be life—a vital principle infused into us by God the Holy Spirit, or we cannot be trees of the Lord. The mere name of being a Christian is but a dead thing. We must be filled with the spirit of divine life. This life is mysterious. We do not understand the circulation of the sap, by what force it rises, and by what power it descends again. So the life within us is a sacred mystery. Regeneration is wrought by the Holy Spirit entering into a believer and becoming his life. This divine life afterward feeds on the flesh and blood of Christ and is thus sustained by divine food, but where it comes and where it goes—who will explain it to us? What a secret thing the sap is! The roots go searching through the soil, but we cannot see them suck out the various gases or transmute the mineral into the vegetable. This work is done down in the dark. Our root is Christ Jesus, and our life is hidden in Him. This is the secret of the Lord. The primary source of the Christian life is as secret as the life itself. How permanently active is the sap in the cedar! In the Christian, the divine life is always full of energy—not always in fruit-bearing, but in inward operations. The believer's graces are not all in constant motion, but his life never ceases to palpitate within. He is not always working for God, but his heart is always living on Him. As the sap manifests itself in producing the foliage and fruit of the tree, so it must be with a truly healthy Christian. His grace is externally manifested in his walk and conversation. If you talk with him, he cannot help speaking about Jesus. If you notice his actions, you will see that he has been with Jesus. He has so much sap within that it must fill his conduct and conversation with life.

He…began to wash the disciples' feet.
—John 13:5

The Lord Jesus loves His people so much that, every day, He is still doing for them much that is analogous to washing their soiled feet. He accepts their poorest actions, feels their deepest sorrows, hears their slenderest wishes, and forgives all their transgressions. He is still their Servant, as well as their Friend and Master. He not only performs majestic deeds for them as their High Priest, such as wearing the turban on His head and the precious jewels glittering on His breastplate, and standing up to plead for them, but He also humbly and patiently goes among His people with basin and towel. He does this when, day by day, He removes our constant weaknesses and sins from us. Last night, when you prayed, you mournfully confessed that much of your conduct was not worthy of your profession of faith. Even tonight, you must mourn afresh that you have fallen again into the same folly and sin from which special grace delivered you long ago. Yet Jesus will have great patience with you. He will hear your confession of sin, and will say, "*I will; be thou clean*" (Matt. 8:3). He will again apply the "*blood of sprinkling*" (Heb. 12:24), speak peace to your conscience, and remove every spot. It is a great act of eternal love when Christ once for all absolves the sinner and puts him into the family of God. However, what gracious patience the Savior has when, with much longsuffering, He bears the often-recurring sins of His wayward disciple, day by day and hour by hour washing away the multiplied transgressions of His erring yet beloved child! To dry up a flood of rebellion is a marvelous thing. Yet to endure the constant dripping of repeated offenses—to bear with a perpetual trying of His patience—this is divine indeed! While we find comfort and peace in our Lord's daily cleansing, its real influence on us will be to increase our watchfulness and activate our desire for holiness. Is this the case with you?

OCTOBER 25

Morning

For the truth's sake, which dwelleth in us,
and shall be with us for ever.
—2 John 2

Once the truth of God obtains an entrance into the human heart and subdues the whole person to itself, no power—human or infernal—can dislodge it. We entertain it not as a guest, but as the master of the house. This is a Christian necessity; he is no Christian who does not thus believe. Those who feel the vital power of the Gospel and know the might of the Holy Spirit, as He opens, applies, and seals the Lord's Word, would sooner be torn to pieces than be torn away from the Gospel of their salvation. What a thousand mercies are wrapped up in the assurance that the truth will be with us forever; will be our living support, our dying comfort, our rising song, our eternal glory. This is the Christian's privilege; without it our faith would be of little worth. Some truths we outgrow and leave behind, for they are but rudiments and lessons for beginners. But we cannot deal this way with divine truth, for though it is sweet food for babies, it is in the highest sense strong meat for men. The truth that we are sinners is painfully with us to humble us and make us watchful. The more blessed truth, that whoever believes on the Lord Jesus will be saved, abides with us as our hope and joy. Experience, far from loosening our hold of the doctrines of grace, has knit us to them more and more firmly. Our grounds and motives for believing are now stronger and more numerous than ever. We have reason to expect that it will be so until in death we clasp the Savior in our arms. Wherever this abiding love of truth can be discovered, we are bound to exercise our love. No narrow circle can contain our gracious sympathies; wide as the election of grace must be our communion of heart. Much error may be mingled with truth received. Let us war against the error, but still love the brother for the measure of truth that we see in him. Above all, let us love and spread the truth ourselves!

*She…gleaned in the field after the reapers: and her hap was to
light on a part of the field belonging unto Boaz,
who was of the kindred of Elimelech.*
—Ruth 2:3

H*er hap was.*" The situation seemed to come about from nothing but chance, yet it was the direct result of divine guidance. Ruth had gone out to the field to do humble but honorable work with her mother-in-law's blessing, and under the care of her mother-in-law's God, and the providence of God was guiding her every step. Little did she know that among the sheaves she would find a husband, that he would make her the joint owner of all those broad acres, and that she, a poor foreigner, would become one of the ancestors of the great Messiah. God is very good to those who trust in Him, and He often surprises them with unlooked-for blessings. Little do we know what may happen to us tomorrow, but this sweet fact may encourage us: no good thing will be withheld from us. (See Psalm 84:11.) Chance is banished from the faith of Christians, for they see the hand of God in everything. The trivial events of today or tomorrow may involve consequences of the highest importance. O Lord, deal as graciously with Your servants as You did with Ruth. What a blessing it would be if, while wandering in the field of meditation tonight, we happened to come upon the place where our next Kinsman (see Ruth 2:20) will reveal Himself to us! O Spirit of God, guide us to Him. We would rather glean in His field than carry away the whole harvest from any other. Oh, for the footsteps of His flock, which may conduct us to the green pastures where He dwells! This is a weary world when Jesus is away. We could better do without sun and moon than without Him. Yet how divinely beautiful all things become in the glory of His presence! Our souls know the virtue that dwells in Jesus, and can never be content without Him. We will wait in prayer tonight until we happen to come upon a part of the field belonging to Jesus, in which He will manifest Himself to us.

Ye looked for much, and, lo, it came to little; and when ye brought it home, I did blow upon it. Why? saith the LORD of hosts. Because of mine house that is waste, and ye run every man unto his own house.
—Haggai 1:9

Churlish souls limit their contributions to the ministry and missionary endeavors and call such savings good economy. Little do they dream that they are impoverishing themselves. Their excuse is that they must care for their own families, and they forget that to neglect the house of God is the sure way to bring ruin on their own houses. Our God has a method in providence by which He can bless our endeavors beyond our expectations or can defeat our plans to our confusion and dismay. By a turn of His hand, He can steer our vessel in a profitable channel or run it aground in poverty and bankruptcy. It is the teaching of Scripture that the Lord enriches the liberal and leaves the miserly to find out that withholding leads to poverty. In a very wide sphere of observation, I have noticed that the most generous Christians of my acquaintance have always been the happiest, and almost invariably the most prosperous. I have seen the liberal giver rise to wealth of which he never dreamed, and I have as often seen the stingy, ungenerous person descend to poverty by the very penny-pinching by which he thought to succeed. Men trust good stewards with larger and larger sums, and so it frequently is with the Lord. He gives by cartloads to those who give by bushels. Where wealth is not bestowed, the Lord turns the little into much through the contentment that the sanctified heart feels in proportion to the dedication with which the tithe has been given to the Lord. Selfishness looks first at home, but godliness seeks *"first the kingdom of God, and his righteousness"* (Matt. 6:33). In the long run, selfishness is loss, and godliness is great gain. It takes faith to act toward our God with an open hand, but surely He deserves it of us. All that we can do is a very poor acknowledgment of our amazing indebtedness to His goodness!

OCTOBER 26

All the rivers run into the sea; yet the sea is not full; unto the place from whence the rivers come, thither they return again.
—Ecclesiastes 1:7

Everything that is of this earth is on the move. Time knows nothing of rest. The solid earth is a rolling ball, and the great sun itself is a star obediently fulfilling its course around a greater luminary. Tides move the sea, winds stir the airy ocean, and erosion wears away the rock. Change and death rule everywhere. The sea is not a miser's storehouse for a wealth of waters, for as by one force the waters flow into it, by another they are lifted from it. Men are born, only to die. Everything is hurry, worry, and *"vexation of spirit"* (Eccl. 1:14). Friend of the unchanging Jesus, what a joy it is to reflect on your changeless heritage. Your sea of bliss will be full forever, since God Himself will pour eternal rivers of pleasure into it. We seek an abiding city beyond the skies, and we will not be disappointed. The text for this evening may well teach us gratitude. Father Ocean is a great receiver, but he is a generous distributor. What the rivers bring him, he returns to the earth in the form of clouds and rain. The person who takes everything but returns nothing is out of harmony with the universe. To give to others is to sow seed for ourselves. He who is a good steward, willing to use his substance for the Lord, will be entrusted with more. Friend of Jesus, are you giving back to Him according to the benefit you have received? Much has been given to you. What is your fruit? Have you done everything you can? Can you do more? To be selfish is to be wicked. Suppose the ocean gave up none of its watery treasure. It would bring ruin upon the human race. God forbid that any of us would follow the ungenerous and destructive policy of living for ourselves. Jesus did not please Himself. All fullness dwells in Him, but *"of his fulness have all we received"* (John 1:16). May we have Jesus' nature, so that, from this time forward, we may not live for ourselves!

It is a faithful saying.
—2 Timothy 2:11

Paul had four of these *"faithful"* sayings. The first occurs in 1 Timothy 1:15, *"This is a faithful saying, and worthy of all acceptation, that Christ Jesus came into the world to save sinners."* The next is in 1 Timothy 4:8–9, *"Godliness is profitable unto all things, having promise of the life that now is, and of that which is to come. This is a faithful saying and worthy of all acceptation."* The third is in 2 Timothy 2:11–12, *"It is a faithful saying:...If we suffer, we shall also reign with him."* The fourth is in Titus 3:8, *"This is a faithful saying,...that they which have believed in God might be careful to maintain good works."* We may trace a connection among these faithful sayings. The first one lays the foundation of our eternal salvation in the free grace of God, as shown to us in the mission of the great Redeemer. The next affirms the double blessedness that we obtain through this salvation—the blessings of the upper and lower springs—of time and of eternity. The third shows one of the duties to which the chosen people are called. We are ordained to suffer for Christ with the promise that *"if we suffer, we shall also reign with him"* (2 Tim. 2:12). The last sets forth the active form of Christian service, bidding us to diligently maintain good works. Thus we have the root of salvation in free grace; next, the privileges of that salvation in the life which now is, and in that which is to come; and we also have the two great branches of suffering with Christ and serving with Christ, loaded with the fruits of the Spirit. Treasure up these faithful sayings. Let them be the guides of your life, your comfort, and your instruction. The apostle of the Gentiles proved them to be faithful; they are faithful still. Not one word will fall to the ground. They are worthy of acceptance. Let us accept them now and prove their faithfulness. Let these four faithful sayings be written on the four corners of your house.

We are all as an unclean thing.
—Isaiah 64:6

The believer is a new creation. He belongs to a holy generation, a special people. The Spirit of God is in him, and, in all respects, he is far removed from the natural man. Yet, for all that, the Christian is still a sinner. He is a sinner because of the imperfection of his nature, and will continue to be so to the end of his earthly life. The blackened fingers of sin leave smudges on our whitest robes. Sin mars our repentance before the great Potter has finished it on the wheel. Selfishness defiles our tears, and unbelief tampers with our faith. The best thing we ever did independent of the merit of Jesus only swelled the number of our sins. For even when we have been purest in our own sight, we, like the heavens, have not been pure in God's sight. (See Job 15:15.) Since He charged His angels with folly, how much more must He charge us with it, even in our most angelic frames of mind. The song that ascends to heaven and seeks to emulate angelic tunes has human discords in it. The prayer that moves the arm of God is still a bruised and battered prayer, and only moves His arm because the sinless One, the great Mediator, has stepped in to take away the sin of our supplication. The most golden faith or the purest degree of sanctification that a Christian ever attained on earth still has so much alloy in it that it is only worthy of the flames, considered in itself. Every night that we look in the mirror, we see a sinner, and we need to confess, *"We are all as an unclean thing, and all our righteousnesses are as filthy rags"* (Isa. 64:6). Oh, how precious the blood of Christ is to hearts such as ours! How priceless a gift His perfect righteousness is! How bright our hope of perfect holiness in the next world is! Although sin dwells in us, even now, its power is broken; it has no dominion. It is like a broken-backed snake. We are in bitter conflict with it, but we are dealing with a vanquished enemy. In a little while, we will enter victoriously into the city where nothing defiles. (See Revelation 21:27.)

I have chosen you out of the world.
—John 15:19

Here is distinguishing grace and discriminating regard, for some are made the special objects of divine affection. Do not be afraid to dwell on this high doctrine of election. When your mind is heaviest and most depressed, you will find this assuring tenet to be a bottle of soothing medicine. Those who doubt the doctrines of grace or who cast them into the shade miss the richest clusters of Eshcol; they lose the well-refined wines or the richest delicacies full of marrow. There is no balm in Gilead comparable to it. If the honey in Jonathan's wood, when but touched, enlightened the eyes, this is honey that will enlighten your heart to love and learn the mysteries of the kingdom of God. Eat, and do not worry about being too full. Live on this choice dainty, and do not fear that it will be too delicate a diet. Meat from the King's table will hurt none of His courtiers. Desire to have your mind enlarged so that you may comprehend more and more the eternal, everlasting, discriminating love of God. When you have mounted as high as election, tarry on its sister mount, the covenant of grace. Covenant engagements are the defense of stupendous rocks behind which we lie entrenched; covenant engagements with the Surety, Christ Jesus, are the quiet resting places of trembling spirits.

> His oath, His covenant, His blood,
>   Support me in the raging flood;
> When every earthly prop gives way,
>   This still is all my strength and stay.

If Jesus undertook to bring me to glory, and if the Father promised that He would give me to the Son to be a part of the infinite reward of the travail of His soul, then, my soul, until God Himself is unfaithful, until Jesus ceases to be the Truth, you are safe. When David danced before the ark, he told Michal that election made him do so. Come, my soul, and rejoice before the God of grace; leap for joy of heart.

His head is as the most fine gold, his locks are bushy,
and black as a raven.
—Song of Solomon 5:11

Comparisons fail to describe the Lord Jesus, but the spouse used the best analogies she could. The *"head"* of Jesus signifies His deity, for *"the head of Christ is God"* (1 Cor. 11:3). *"Most fine [pure] gold"* is the best conceivable metaphor. However, it is all too poor to describe One so precious, so pure, so dear, so glorious. Jesus is not a grain of gold, but a vast globe of it, a priceless mass of treasure that earth and heaven cannot excel. Created beings are mere iron and clay. They will all perish like *"wood, hay, [and] stubble"* (1 Cor. 3:12). Yet the ever living Head of the creation of God will shine on forever and ever. There is no mixture in Him, or even the smallest taint of alloy. He is forever infinitely holy and altogether divine. The "bushy locks" depict His manly vigor. There is nothing effeminate in our Beloved. He is the manliest of men—bold as a lion, industrious as an ox, swift as an eagle. Every conceivable and inconceivable beauty may be found in Him, though once He was *"despised and rejected of men"* (Isa. 53:3).

> His head the finest gold;
> With secret sweet perfume,
> His curled locks hang all as black
> As any raven's plume.

The glory of His head is not cut off—He is eternally crowned with peerless majesty. The *"black"* hair indicates youthful freshness, for Jesus has the dew of His youth upon Him. Others grow weak with age, but He is forever a Priest, as was Melchizedek. Others come and go, but He abides as God upon His throne, *"world without end"* (Eph. 3:21). Let us behold Him tonight and adore Him. Angels are gazing upon Him. His redeemed must not turn their eyes away from Him. Where else is there such a Beloved? Oh, for an hour's fellowship with Him! Away, you intruding cares! Jesus draws me, and I run after Him.

After this manner therefore pray ye: Our Father which art in heaven.
—Matthew 6:9

This prayer begins where all true prayer must begin, with the spirit of adoption, *"Our Father."* There is no acceptable prayer until we can say, *"I will arise and go to my father"* (Luke 15:18). This childlike spirit soon perceives the grandeur of the Father *"in heaven"* and ascends to devout adoration, *"Hallowed be thy name"* (Matt. 6:9). The child lisping, "Abba, Father," grows into the cherub crying, "Holy, Holy, Holy." There is but a single step from rapturous worship to the glowing missionary spirit, which is a sure outgrowth of filial love and reverent adoration, *"Thy kingdom come. Thy will be done in earth, as it is in heaven"* (v. 10). Next follows the heartfelt expression of dependence on God, *"Give us this day our daily bread"* (v. 11). Being further illuminated by the Spirit, the one who prays discovers that he is not only dependent, but also sinful, hence he entreats for mercy, *"Forgive us our debts, as we forgive our debtors"* (v. 12). The man who is really forgiven is anxious not to offend again; the possession of justification leads to an anxious desire for sanctification. *"Forgive us our debts"* (v. 12)—that is justification. *"Lead us not into temptation, but deliver us from evil"* (v. 13)—that is sanctification in its negative and positive forms. Being pardoned, having the righteousness of Christ imputed, and knowing his acceptance with God, the one who prays humbly supplicates for holy perseverance, *"Lead us not into temptation"* (v. 13). As the result of all this, there follows a triumphant ascription of praise, *"Thine is the kingdom, and the power, and the glory, for ever. Amen"* (v. 13). We rejoice that our King reigns in providence and will reign in grace, from the river even to the ends of the earth, and of His dominion there will be no end. Thus, this short model prayer conducts the soul from a sense of adoption to fellowship with our reigning Lord. Lord, teach us thus to pray.

But their eyes were holden that they should not know him.
—Luke 24:16

The disciples ought to have known Jesus. They had heard His voice so often, and gazed upon His marred face so frequently, that it is amazing they did not perceive Him. Yet is this not the case with you, also? You have not seen Jesus lately. You have been to His Table, but you have not met Him there. You may be in the midst of dark trouble this evening, and though He plainly says, *"It is I; be not afraid"* (Matt. 14:27), you still cannot discern Him. Our eyes are *"holden."* We know His voice; we have looked into His face; we have leaned our heads upon His chest. However, although Christ is very near to us, we say, "If only I knew where I might find Him!" We should know Jesus, for the Scriptures reflect His image. Yet how possible it is for us to open that precious Book and to have no glimpse of the Well Beloved! Dear child of God, is this your situation? Jesus *"feedeth among the lilies"* (Song 2:16) of the Word, and you walk among those lilies, yet you do not see Him. He is accustomed to walking through the glades of Scripture, and communing with His people, as the Father did with Adam in the cool of the day. Yet you are in the garden of Scripture, and you cannot see Him, though He is always there. Why do we not see Him? In our case, as in the disciples' case, this lack of vision must be ascribed to unbelief. They evidently did not expect to see Jesus, and therefore they did not recognize Him. To a great extent, in spiritual things, we get what we expect from the Lord. Faith alone can bring us to see Jesus. Make this your prayer: "Lord, open my eyes, that I may see my Savior present with me." It is a blessed thing to want to see Him, but it is far better to gaze on Him! To those who seek Him, He is kind. However, to those who find Him, He is precious beyond expression!

I will praise thee, O Lord.
—Psalm 9:1

Praise should always follow answered prayer, just as the mist of earth's gratitude rises when the sun of heaven's love warms the ground. Has the Lord been gracious to you and inclined His ear to the voice of your supplication? Then praise Him as long as you live. Let the ripe fruit drop on the fertile soil from which it drew its life. Do not deny a song to Him who has answered your prayer and given you the desire of your heart. To be silent over God's mercies is to incur the guilt of ingratitude. It is to act as basely as the nine lepers, who, after they had been cured of their leprosy, did not return to give thanks to the healing Lord. To forget to praise God is to refuse to benefit ourselves. Praise, like prayer, is one great means of promoting the growth of the spiritual life. It helps to remove our burdens, to excite our hopes, to increase our faith. It is a healthful and invigorating exercise that quickens the pulse of the believer and strengthens him for fresh enterprises in his Master's service. To bless God for mercies received is also the way to benefit our fellowmen: *"The humble shall hear thereof, and be glad"* (Ps. 34:2). Others who have been in similar circumstances will take comfort if we can say, *"O magnify the Lord with me, and let us exalt his name together....This poor man cried, and the Lord heard him"* (vv. 3, 6). Weak hearts will be strengthened, and drooping saints will be revived as they listen to our *"songs of deliverance"* (Ps. 32:7). Their doubts and fears will be rebuked, as we teach and admonish *"one another in psalms and hymns and spiritual songs"* (Col. 3:16). They too will *"sing in the ways of the Lord"* (Ps. 138:5) when they hear us magnify His holy name. Praise is the most heavenly of Christian duties. The angels do not pray, but they do not cease to praise both day and night; and the redeemed, clothed in white robes, with palm branches in their hands, are never weary of singing the new song, *"Worthy is the Lamb"* (Rev. 5:12).

Thou that dwellest in the gardens, the companions hearken
to thy voice: cause me to hear it.
—Song of Solomon 8:13

My sweet Lord Jesus remembers well the Garden of Gethsemane. Although He has left that Garden, He now dwells in the garden of His church. There He reveals Himself to those who keep His blessed company. The voice of love with which He speaks to His beloved is more musical than the harps of heaven. There is a depth of melodious love within it that leaves all human music far behind. Tens of thousands on earth, and millions above, are favored with its harmonious tones. Some whom I well know, and whom I greatly envy, are at this moment listening to the beloved voice. If only I were a partaker of their joys! It is true that some of them are poor, others are bedridden, and still others are near the gates of death. Yet, O my Lord, I would cheerfully starve with them, languish with them, or die with them, if I might only hear Your voice. Once I did hear it often, but I have grieved Your Spirit. Return to me in compassion, and once again say to me, *"I am thy salvation"* (Ps. 35:3). No other voice can satisfy me. I know Your voice, and cannot be deceived by another. I beg You, let me hear it. O my Beloved, I do not know what You will say, and I do not ask with any conditions. Only let me hear You speak. If it is a rebuke, I will bless You for it. Cleansing my dull ears may require an operation that is very grievous to the flesh. Yet whatever the cost, I do not turn from my one consuming desire: cause me to hear Your voice. Pierce my ears anew; pierce my ears with Your harshest notes. Only do not permit me to continue deaf to Your calls. Tonight, Lord, grant Your unworthy one his desire, for I am Yours, and You have bought me with Your blood. You have opened my eyes to see You, and the sight has saved me. Now, Lord, open my ears. I have read Your heart. Now let me hear Your voice.

Renew a right spirit within me.
—Psalm 51:10

Abacklider, if there is a spark of life left in him, will groan after restoration. In this renewal, the same exercise of grace is required as at our conversion. We needed repentance then, and we certainly need it now. At first, we needed faith so that we might come to Christ. Now, only the same grace can bring us to Jesus. Then, we needed a word from the Most High, a word from the lips of the loving One, to end our fears; we will soon discover, when under a sense of present sin, that we need it now. No one can be renewed without as real and true a manifestation of the Holy Spirit's energy as he felt at first, because the work is as great, and flesh and blood are as much in the way now as they ever were. Let your personal weakness, Christian, be an argument to make you pray earnestly to your God for help. Remember that David, when he felt himself to be powerless, did not fold his arms or close his lips; instead, he hastened to the mercy seat with this prayer: *"Renew a right spirit within me."* Do not let the doctrine that you, unaided, can do nothing make you sleep; but let it be a goad in your side to drive you with an extreme earnestness to Israel's strong Helper. Oh, that you may have grace to plead with God, as though you pleaded for your very life. "Lord, *'renew a right spirit within me.'"* He who sincerely prays to God to do this will prove his honesty by using the means through which God works. Be much in prayer; live much on the Word of God. Kill the lusts that have driven your Lord from you; be careful to watch over the future uprisings of sin. The Lord has His own appointed ways. Sit by the wayside, and you will be ready when He passes by. Continue in all those blessed ordinances that will foster and nourish your dying graces. Knowing that all the power must proceed from Him, do not cease to cry, *"Renew a right spirit within me."*

OCTOBER 31

Evening

I did know thee in the wilderness, in the land of great drought.
—Hosea 13:5

Yes, Lord, You did indeed know me in my fallen state, and even then, You chose me for Yourself. When I was loathsome, and abhorred myself, You received me as Your child and met my urgent needs. May Your name be blessed forever for this free, rich, abounding mercy. Since then, my inward experience has often been a wilderness. Yet You have still acknowledged me as Your beloved, and have poured streams of love and grace into me, to bring me joy and to make me fruitful. Yes, when my outward circumstances have been at their worst, and I have wandered in a land of drought, Your sweet presence has comforted me. Men have abandoned me when I have faced scorn, but You have known my soul in adversity, for no affliction dims the luster of Your love. Most gracious Lord, I magnify You for all Your faithfulness to me in trying circumstances. I deplore that I have at any time forgotten You and been prideful—since I have owed everything to Your gentleness and love. Have mercy on Your servant in this thing! My soul, since Jesus acknowledged you in your low estate, be sure that you acknowledge both Himself and His cause now that you are prosperous. Do not be not lifted up by your worldly successes, so that you are ashamed of the truth or of the poor church with which you have been associated. Follow Jesus into the wilderness. Bear the cross with Him when the heat of persecution grows hot. He acknowledged you, O my soul, in your poverty and shame. Never be so treacherous as to be ashamed of Him. Oh, for more shame at the thought of being ashamed of my Best Beloved! Jesus, my soul clings to You.

> I'll turn to You in days of light,
>   As well as nights of care,
> You brightest amid all that's bright!
>   You fairest of the fair!

NOVEMBER 1
Morning

The church in thy house.
—Philemon 2

Is there a church in your house? Are parents, children, and friends all members of it, or are some still unconverted? Let us pause here and let the question be asked of each one: Am I a member of the church in this house? How a father's heart would leap for joy and a mother's eyes fill with holy tears if all were saved from the eldest to the youngest! Let us pray for this great mercy until the Lord grants it to us. Probably it had been the dearest object of Philemon's desires to have all his household saved, but it was not at first granted him in its fullness. He had a wicked servant, Onesimus, who, having wronged him, ran away from his service. His master's prayers followed him, though, and, at last, as God would have it, Onesimus was led to hear Paul preach. His heart was touched, and he returned to Philemon, not only to be a faithful servant, but a beloved brother, adding another member to the church in Philemon's house. Is there an unconverted member of the household absent this morning? Make special supplication that such may, on his return home, gladden all hearts with good news of what grace has done! Is there an unconverted person present? Let him partake in the same earnest entreaty. If there is such a church in your house, order it well, and let all act as in the sight of God. Move in the common affairs of life with studied holiness, diligence, kindness, and integrity. More is expected of a church than of an ordinary household. Family worship must, in such a case, be heartier and more devout. Internal love must be warmer and unbroken, and external conduct must be more sanctified and Christlike. We do not need to fear that the smallness of our number will remove us from the list of churches, for the Holy Spirit has here enrolled a family-church in the inspired book of remembrance. As a church, let us now draw near to the great Head of the one universal church, and let us ask Him to give us grace to shine before men to the glory of His name.

NOVEMBER 1

Evening

*And knew not until the flood came, and took them all away; so shall
also the coming of the Son of man be.*
—Matthew 24:39

The doom was universal. Neither rich nor poor escaped. The learned and the illiterate, the admired and the hated, the religious and the profane, the old and the young, all sank in one common ruin. Some had undoubtedly ridiculed the patriarch Noah. Where are their lighthearted jests now? Others had threatened him for his zeal, which they had considered madness. Where are their boasting and harsh words now? The critic who judged the old man's work was drowned in the same sea that covered his sneering companions. Those who spoke patronizingly of the good man's faithfulness to his convictions, but did not share in them, sank to rise no more. All the workers who had helped to build the wondrous ark for pay were also lost. The flood swept them all away; it did not make a single exception. Similarly, for those who are outside of Christ, final destruction is sure. No rank, possession, or character will suffice to save a single soul who has not believed in the Lord Jesus. My soul, take note of this widespread judgment, and tremble at it. The general apathy of the people was astonishing! They were all *"eating and drinking, marrying and giving in marriage"* (Matt. 24:38), until the terrible morning dawned. There was not one wise man on earth outside the ark. Folly duped the whole race, folly in regard to self-preservation—the most foolish of all follies; folly in doubting the true God—the most malignant of foolishness. It is strange, is it not? All men are negligent of their souls until grace gives them reason. Then they leave their madness and act like rational beings—but not until then. May God be blessed, for all who were in the ark were safe. No ruin entered there. From the huge elephant down to the tiny mouse, all were safe. The timid hare was equally as secure as the courageous lion; the helpless coney was as safe as the industrious ox. Everyone who is in Jesus is safe. Are you in Him this evening?

I am the LORD, I change not.
—Malachi 3:6

It is well for us that, amid all the variableness of life, there is One whom change cannot affect, One whose heart can never alter, and One on whose brow mutability can make no furrows. Everything else has changed or is changing. The sun itself grows dim with age. The world is growing old. The folding up of worn-out garments has begun. The heavens and earth must soon pass away; they will perish and will become old as does a garment. But there is only One who has immortality, of whose years there is no end, and in whose person there is no change. The delight that the mariner feels when, after having been tossed about for many days, he steps again on the solid shore is the satisfaction of a Christian when, amid all the changes of this stormy life, he rests the foot of his faith on this truth: *"I am the LORD, I change not."* The stability that the anchor gives the ship when it has at last obtained a holdfast is like that which the Christian's hope affords him when it fixes itself on this glorious truth. With God *"is no variableness, neither shadow of turning"* (James 1:17). Whatever His attributes were of old, they are now. His power, His wisdom, His justice, and His truth are all unchanged. He has always been the refuge of His people, their *"strong hold in the day of trouble"* (Nah. 1:7), and He is their sure Helper still. He is unchanged in His love. He has loved His people with *"an everlasting love"* (Jer. 31:3). He loves them now as much as He ever did, and when all earthly things will have melted in the last conflict, His love will still wear the *"dew of [its] youth"* (Ps. 110:3). Precious is the assurance that He does not change! The wheel of providence revolves, but its axle is eternal love.

> Death and change are busy ever,
>> Man decays, and ages move;
> But His mercy waneth never;
>> God is wisdom, God is love.

Horror hath taken hold upon me because of the wicked
that forsake thy law.
—Psalm 119:53

Do you experience a holy shuddering at the sins of others? If not, you lack inward holiness. David's cheeks were wet with rivers of water because of the prevailing unholiness. Jeremiah desired eyes like fountains, so that he might mourn the iniquities of Israel. Lot was oppressed by the conversation of the men of Sodom. In Ezekiel's vision, those upon whom the mark was put were those who sighed and cried for the abominations of Jerusalem. It cannot but grieve the godly to see what pains men take to go to hell. They know the evil of sin experientially, and they are alarmed to see others flying like moths into its blaze. Sin makes the righteous shudder because it violates holy law, which is in every person's highest interest to keep. It pulls down the pillars of the commonwealth. Sin in others horrifies the believer, because it reminds him of the baseness of his own heart. When he sees a transgressor, he cries, along with the saint mentioned by Bernard, "He fell today, and I may fall tomorrow." To the believer, sin is horrible because it crucified the Savior. He sees the nails and the spear in every iniquity. How can a saved soul not look with abhorrence on cursed sin, which killed Christ? My heart, is this how you feel about sin? It is an awful thing to insult God to His face. The good God deserves better treatment, the great God claims it, and the just God will have it, or repay His adversary to his face. An awakened heart trembles at the audacity of sin, and stands alarmed at the contemplation of its punishment. What a monstrous thing rebellion is! What dreadful doom is prepared for the ungodly! My soul, never laugh at sin's foolishness, lest you come to smile at sin itself. Sin is your enemy, and your Lord's enemy. Regard it with abhorrence, for only thus can you evidence the possession of *"holiness, without which no man shall see the Lord"* (Heb. 12:14).

NOVEMBER 3
Morning

Behold, he prayeth.
—Acts 9:11

Prayers are instantly noticed in heaven. The moment Saul began to pray, the Lord heard him. Here is comfort for the distressed but praying soul. Often a poor, brokenhearted one bends his knees, but can only utter his wailing in the language of sighs and tears. Yet that groan has made all the harps of heaven thrill with music; that tear has been caught by God and is treasured in heaven. *"Put thou my tears into thy bottle"* (Ps. 56:8) implies that they are caught as they flow. The suppliant, whose fears prevent his words, will be well understood by the Most High. He may only look up with misty eyes, but "prayer is the falling of a tear." Tears are the diamonds of heaven; sighs are a part of the music of Jehovah's court and are numbered with "the sublimest strains that reach the Majesty on high." Do not think that your prayer, however weak or trembling, will be unregarded. Jacob's ladder is lofty, but our prayers will lean on the Angel of the covenant and so climb its starry rounds. Our God not only hears prayer but also loves to hear it. *"He forgetteth not the cry of the humble"* (Ps. 9:12) True, He does not regard high looks and lofty words and does not care for the pomp and pageantry of kings. He does not listen to the swell of martial music. He does not regard the triumph and pride of man. But wherever there is a heart that is full of sorrow, lips that are quivering with agony, a deep groan, or a penitential sigh, the heart of Jehovah is open. He marks it down in the registry of His memory. He puts our prayers, like rose leaves, between the pages of His book of remembrance, and when the volume is opened at last, there will be a precious fragrance springing up from it.

> Faith asks no signal from the skies,
> To show that prayers accepted rise,
> Our Priest is in His holy place,
> And answers from the throne of grace.

NOVEMBER 3
Evening

Their prayer came up to his holy dwelling place, even unto heaven.
—2 Chronicles 30:27

Prayer is the never-failing resource of the Christian, for any situation, in every plight. When you cannot use your sword, you may take up the weapon of all-prayer. Your gunpowder may be damp, your bowstring may be relaxed, but the weapon of all-prayer is never out of order. Leviathan laughs at the javelin, but he trembles at prayer. Sword and spear need furbishing, but prayer never rusts, and when we think it is the bluntest, it cuts the best. Prayer is an open door that no one can shut. Devils may surround you on all sides, but the way upward is always open. As long as that road is unobstructed, you will not fall into the enemy's hands. We can never be taken by blockade, escalade, mine, or storm, as long as heavenly help can come down to us by Jacob's ladder, to relieve us in our times of need. Prayer is never out of season: in summer and in winter, its merchandize is precious. Prayer gains an audience with heaven in the dead of night, in the midst of business, in the heat of noonday, and in the shades of evening. In every condition, whether poverty, sickness, obscurity, slander, or doubt, your covenant God will welcome your prayer and answer it from His holy place. Prayer is never futile. True prayer is always true power. You may not always receive what you ask for, but you will always have your real needs supplied. When God does not answer His children according to the letter, He does so according to the spirit. If you ask for coarse meal, will you become angry when He gives you the finest flour? If you seek bodily health, should you complain if, instead of physical healing, He causes your sickness to work for the healing of your spiritual maladies? Is it not better to have the cross sanctified than removed? This evening, do not forget to offer your petition and request, for the Lord is ready to grant your desires.

NOVEMBER 4

Morning

For my strength is made perfect in weakness.
—2 Corinthians 12:9

A primary qualification for serving God with any amount of success, and for doing God's work well and triumphantly, is a sense of our own weakness. When God's warrior marches forth to battle, strong in his own might, and boasts, "I know that I will conquer. My own right arm and my conquering sword will bring me victory," defeat is not far away. God will not go forth with that man who marches in his own strength. He who counts on victory has calculated wrongly, for it is *"not by might, nor by power, but by my spirit, saith the Lord of hosts"* (Zech. 4:6). Those who go forth to fight, boasting of their prowess, will return with their colorful banners trailed in the dust and their armor stained with disgrace. Those who serve God must serve Him in His own way, and in His strength, or He will never accept their service. What man does unaided by divine strength, God can never own. The mere fruits of the earth He casts away. He will reap only that corn whose seed was sown from heaven, watered by grace, and ripened by the sun of divine love. God will empty out all that you have before He will put His own into you. He will first clean out your granaries before He will fill them with the finest of the wheat. The river of God is full of water, but not one drop of it flows from earthly springs. God will have no strength used in His battles but the strength that He Himself imparts. Are you mourning over your own weakness? Take courage, for there must be a consciousness of weakness before the Lord will give you victory. Your emptiness is but the preparation for your being filled, and your casting down is but the making ready for your lifting up.

> When I am weak then am I strong,
> Grace is my shield and Christ my song.

NOVEMBER 4

In thy light shall we see light.
—Psalm 36:9

No words can explain the love of Christ to the heart until Jesus Himself speaks within. All descriptions are empty and fall flat unless the Holy Spirit fills them with life and power. Until Immanuel reveals Himself within, the soul does not see Him. If you wanted to see the sun, would you gather together various lamps and candles, and then go out and try to view it using their light? No, the wise person knows that the sun must reveal itself, and that only by its own blaze can that mighty lamp be seen. It is the same way with Christ. *"Blessed art thou, Simon Barjona,"* He said to Peter, *"for flesh and blood hath not revealed it unto thee"* (Matt. 16:17). You may refine flesh and blood by any educational process you select; you may elevate mental faculties to the highest degree of intellectual power; yet neither of these methods can reveal Christ. The Spirit of God must come with power, overshadowing a person with His wings. Then, in that mysterious "Holy of Holies," the Lord Jesus will display Himself to the sanctified eye—as He will not do for the shortsighted sons of men. Christ must be His own mirror. The great mass of this bleary-eyed world can see nothing of the transcendent glories of Immanuel. He stands before them without *"form nor comeliness"* (Isa. 53:2), *"a root out of a dry ground"* (v. 2), rejected by the vain, and despised by the proud. Jesus is understood only where the Spirit has touched the eyes with balm, quickened the heart with divine life, and educated the soul to a heavenly taste. *"Unto you therefore which believe he is precious"* (1 Pet. 2:7). To you, He is the *"chief corner stone"* (Eph. 2:20), the Rock of your salvation, your all in all. Yet to others, He is *"a stone of stumbling, and a rock of offence"* (1 Pet. 2:8). Happy are those to whom our Lord manifests Himself, for His promise to them is that He will make His home with them. O Lord Jesus, our hearts are open. Come in, never to leave. Show Yourself to us now! Favor us with a glimpse of Your all-conquering charms.

No weapon that is formed against thee shall prosper.
—Isaiah 54:17

This day is notable in English history for two great deliverances wrought by God for us. On this day in 1605, the Gun Powder Plot, the conspiracy to destroy our Houses of Parliament, was discovered.

> While for our princes they prepare
> In caverns deep a burning snare,
> He shot from heaven a piercing ray,
> And the dark treachery brought to day.

Second, today is the anniversary of the landing of King William III at Torbay in 1688, by which a Protestant monarchy and religious liberty were secured. This day ought to be celebrated, not by the unrestrained celebrations of youth, but by the songs of saints. Our Puritan forefathers most devoutly made it a special time of thanksgiving. There is still in existence a record of the annual sermons preached by Matthew Henry on this day. Our Protestant feeling, and our love of liberty, should make us regard its anniversary with holy gratitude. Let our hearts and lips exclaim, *"We have heard with our ears, O God, our fathers have told us, what work thou didst in their days, in the times of old"* (Ps. 44:1). You have made this nation the home of the Gospel; and when the foe has risen against her, You have shielded her. Help us to offer repeated songs for repeated deliverances. Grant us more and more a hatred of the spirit of the Antichrist, and hasten on the day of its entire extinction. Until then, we believe the promise, *"No weapon that is formed against thee shall prosper."* On this day, should it not be laid on the heart of every lover of the Gospel of Jesus to plead for the overturning of false doctrines and the extension of divine truth? Would it not be good to search our own hearts and eradicate any of the lumber of self-righteousness that may lie concealed therein?

NOVEMBER 5
Evening

Be thankful unto him, and bless his name.
—Psalm 100:4

Our Lord wants all His people to be rich in high and happy thoughts concerning His blessed person. Jesus is not content to have His brethren think poorly of Him. It is His pleasure that His espoused ones be delighted with His beauty. We are not to regard Him as a bare necessary, like bread and water, but as a luxurious delicacy, as a rare and exquisite delight. To this end, He has revealed Himself as the *"pearl of great price"* (Matt. 13:46) in its peerless beauty, as the *"bundle of myrrh"* (Song 1:13) in its refreshing fragrance, as the *"rose of Sharon"* (Song 2:1) in its lasting perfume, and as the *"lily"* (v. 1) in its spotless purity. To help yourself think high thoughts of Christ, remember the estimation that Christ is held in beyond the skies, where things are measured by the right standards. Think how God esteems the Only Begotten, His *"unspeakable gift"* (2 Cor. 9:15) to us. Consider what the angels think of Him, as they consider it their highest honor to veil their faces as they worship Him. Consider what the blood-washed saints think of Him, as day without night they sing His well-deserved praises. High thoughts of Christ will enable us to act consistently in our relationship with Him. The more exaltedly we see Christ enthroned, and the more humble we are when bowing before the foot of the throne, the more truly we will be prepared to act properly toward Him. Our Lord Jesus desires us to think well of Him, so that we may submit cheerfully to His authority. High thoughts of Him increase our love. Love and esteem go together. Therefore, believer, think much of your Master's excellencies. Study Him in His original glory, before He took your nature upon Himself. Think of the mighty love that drew Him from His throne to die on the cross! Admire Him as He conquers all the powers of hell! See Him risen, crowned, glorified! Bow before Him as *"Wonderful, Counsellor, The mighty God"* (Isa. 9:6), for only thus will your love for Him be what it should be.

NOVEMBER 6

I will pour water upon him that is thirsty.
—Isaiah 44:3

When a believer has fallen into a low, sad state of feeling, he often tries to lift himself out of it by chastening himself with dark and doleful fears. This is not the way to rise from the dust, but to continue in it. You might as well chain the eagle's wing to make it mount as to doubt in order to increase your grace. It is not the law, but the Gospel that saves the seeking soul at first; and it is not a legal bondage, but gospel liberty that can restore the fainting believer afterward. Slavish fear does not bring the backslider back to God, but the sweet wooings of love allure him to Jesus' bosom. Are you thirsting for the living God this morning and unhappy because you cannot find Him to the delight of your heart? Have you lost the joy of religion, and is this your prayer, *"Restore unto me the joy of thy salvation"* (Ps. 51:12)? Are you conscious also that you are barren like the dry ground and that you are not bringing forth the *"fruit unto God"* (Rom. 7:4) that He has a right to expect of you? Are you aware that you are not as useful in the church or in the world as your heart desires to be? Then here is exactly the promise that you need, *"I will pour water upon him that is thirsty."* You will receive the grace you so much require, and you will have it to the utmost extent of your needs. Water refreshes the thirsty: you will be refreshed, and your desires will be gratified. Water quickens sleeping vegetable life; your life will be quickened by fresh grace. Water swells the buds and makes the fruits ripen; you will have grace that will make you fruitful in the ways of God. Whatever good quality there is in divine grace, you will enjoy it to the full. All the riches of divine grace you will receive in abundance. You will be, as it were, drenched with it. As sometimes the meadows become flooded by the bursting rivers and the fields are turned into pools, so will you be; the thirsty land will be transformed into springs of water.

*This is the blood of the testament which God
hath enjoined unto you.*
—Hebrews 9:20

There is a strange power about the word *blood*, and the sight of it is always affecting. A kind heart cannot bear to see a sparrow bleed, and unless it has become accustomed to it, it turns away with horror at the slaughter of an animal. As for the blood of men, it is a consecrated thing. It is murder to shed it in wrath, and it is a terrible crime to squander it in war. Is the reason for this solemnity the fact that *"the blood is the life"* (Deut. 12:23), and that the pouring out of blood is a sign of death? I think so. When we contemplate the blood of the Son of God, our awe is increased even more, and we shudder when we think of the guilt of sin and the terrible penalty that the Sin-bearer endured. Blood, always precious, is priceless when it streams from Immanuel's side. The blood of Jesus seals the covenant of grace and makes it forever sure. Covenants of old were made by sacrifice, and the everlasting covenant was ratified in the same manner. Oh, the delight of being saved on the sure foundation of divine pledges that cannot be dishonored! Salvation by the works of the law is a frail and broken vessel whose shipwreck is sure. However, the covenant vessel fears no storms, for the blood insures that it will stay intact. The blood of Jesus made His testament valid. Wills have no power unless the testators die. In this light, the soldier's spear that pierced the Savior's side is a blessed aid to faith, since it proved that our Lord was really dead. There can be no doubt about that matter; therefore, we may boldly take hold of the legacies He has left for His people. Happy are those who see their title to heavenly blessings assured them by a dying Savior. But does this blood have nothing to say to us? Does it not call us to sanctify ourselves to Him by whom we have been redeemed? Does it not call us to *"newness of life"* (Rom. 6:4) and stir us to entire consecration to the Lord? Oh, that the power of the blood might be known and felt in us this night!

Behold, I have graven thee upon the palms of my hands.
—Isaiah 49:16

No doubt a part of the wonder that is concentrated in the word *"behold"* is increased by the unbelieving lamentation of this earlier sentence, *"Zion said, The Lord hath forsaken me, and my Lord hath forgotten me"* (Isa. 49:14). How amazed the divine mind seems to be at this wicked unbelief! What can be more astounding than the unfounded doubts and fears of God's favored people? The Lord's loving word of rebuke should make us blush. He cries, "How can I have forgotten you, when *'I have graven you on the palms of my hands'*? How dare you doubt My constant remembrance, when the memorial is set on My very flesh?" O unbelief, how strange a marvel you are! We do not know which to wonder at most: the faithfulness of God or the unbelief of His people. He keeps His promise a thousand times, and yet the next trial makes us doubt Him. He never fails. He is never a dry well. He is never as a setting sun, a passing meteor, or a melting vapor; yet we are as continually vexed with anxieties, molested with suspicions, and disturbed with fears, as if our God were the mirage of the desert. *"Behold"* is a word intended to incite admiration. Here, indeed, we have a theme for marveling. Heaven and earth may well be astonished that rebels should obtain so great a nearness to the heart of infinite love as to be written on the palms of His hands. *"I have graven thee."* It does not say, *"Thy name."* The name is there, but that is not all: *"I have graven thee."* See the fullness of this! I have graven your person, your image, your case, your circumstances, your sins, your temptations, your weaknesses, your needs, your works. I have graven you, everything about you, all that concerns you. I have put you altogether there. Will you ever say again that your God has forsaken you when He has *"graven [you] upon the palms of [His] hands"*?

And ye shall be witnesses unto me.
—Acts 1:8

In order to learn how to discharge your duty as a witness for Christ, look at His example. He was always witnessing: by the well of Samaria, in the temple at Jerusalem, by the Sea of Galilee, or at the top of a mountain. He witnessed night and day. His mighty prayers were as vocal to God as His daily services. He witnessed under all circumstances. Scribes and Pharisees could not silence Him. Even before Pilate, He *"witnessed a good confession"* (1 Tim. 6:13). He witnessed so clearly and distinctly that there was no mistake in Him. Christian, make your life a clear testimony. Be like a brook of which you can see every stone at the bottom—not like a muddy creek, of which you can see only the surface. Be clear and transparent, so that your heart's love for God and man may be visible to all. You do not need to say, "I am true." Instead, *be* true. Do not boast of integrity. Rather, *be* upright. Then your testimony will be such that people cannot help seeing it. Never suppress your witness out of a fear of man, who is weak. Your lips have been warmed with a coal from the altar. (See Isaiah 6:6–7.) Let them speak as heaven-touched lips should. *"In the morning sow thy seed, and in the evening withhold not thine hand"* (Eccl. 11:6). Do not watch the clouds or consult the wind. In season and out of season, witness for the Savior. If it happens that, for Christ's sake and the Gospel's sake, you must endure suffering in any form, do not shrink from it, but rejoice in the honor thus conferred on you, that you are counted worthy to suffer with your Lord. Rejoice also in this: your suffering, losses, and persecution will be a platform from which you can witness for Christ Jesus even more vigorously, and with greater power. Study your great Exemplar, and be filled with His Spirit. Remember that you need much teaching, much upholding, much grace, and much humility, if your witnessing is to be to your Master's glory.

As ye have therefore received Christ Jesus the Lord.
—Colossians 2:6

The life of faith is represented as receiving—an act that implies the very opposite of anything involving merit. It is simply the acceptance of a gift. As the earth drinks in the rain, as the sea receives the streams, as night accepts light from the stars, so we, giving nothing, partake freely of the grace of God. By nature, the saints are not wells or streams; they are only cisterns into which the living water flows. They are empty vessels into which God pours His salvation. The idea of receiving implies a sense of realization, making the matter a reality. One cannot very well receive a shadow; we receive that which is substantial. So is it in the life of faith. Christ becomes real to us. While we are without faith, Jesus is a mere name to us—a person who lived a long time ago, so long ago that His life is only history to us now! By an act of faith, Jesus becomes a real person in the consciousness of our hearts. But receiving also means grasping or gaining possession. The thing that I receive becomes my own. I take hold for myself what is given. When I receive Jesus, He becomes my Savior, so much mine that neither life nor death will be able to rob me of Him. All this is to receive Christ—to take Him as God's free gift, to realize Him in my heart, and to appropriate Him as mine. Salvation may be described as the blind receiving sight, the deaf receiving hearing, the dead receiving life; but we have received not only these blessings, but also Christ Jesus Himself! It is true that He gave us life from the dead. He gave us pardon of sin and imputed righteousness. These are all precious things, but we are not content with them; we have received Christ Himself! The Son of God has been poured into us, and we have received Him and taken hold of Him. What a heartful Jesus must be, for heaven itself cannot contain Him!

NOVEMBER 8
Evening

The Master saith, Where is the guestchamber, where I shall eat the
passover with my disciples?
—Mark 14:14

Jerusalem at the time of the Passover was one great inn. Each householder had invited his own friends, but no one had invited the Savior, and He had no dwelling of His own. It was by His own supernatural power that He found an upper room in which to keep the Feast. This is the case even to this day. Jesus is not received among the sons of men, except where, by His supernatural power and grace, He makes the heart anew. All doors are wide open to the prince of darkness, but Jesus must clear a way for Himself, or else lodge in the streets. It was through the mysterious power exerted by our Lord that the householder raised no objections, but immediately, cheerfully, and joyfully opened his guest room. Who he was, and what he was, we do not know. However, he readily accepted the honor that the Redeemer proposed to confer on him. Today, we discover who are the Lord's chosen, and who are not, in much the same way. For when the Gospel comes to some, they fight against it and will not have it. Yet when people receive it, welcoming it, this is a sure indication that there is a secret work going on in their souls, and that God has chosen them for eternal life. Are you willing, dear reader, to receive Christ? Then there is no difficulty blocking the way. Christ will be your guest. His own power is working in you, making you willing. What an honor it is to entertain the Son of God! The heaven of heavens cannot contain Him, yet He graciously finds a home within our hearts! We are not worthy for Him to come under our roof, but what an unutterable privilege it is when He graciously enters! For then He makes a banquet and causes us to feast with Him on royal delicacies. We sit at a banquet where the food is immortal and gives immortality to those who feed on it. Blessed among the sons of Adam is he who entertains the angels' Lord.

As ye have therefore received Christ Jesus the Lord,
so walk ye in him.
—Colossians 2:6

If we have received Christ Himself in our inmost hearts, our new lives will manifest their intimate acquaintance with Him by a walk of faith in Him. Walking implies action. Our religion is not to be confined to our private prayer times. We must carry out into practical actions that which we believe. If a person walks in Christ, then he acts as Christ would act. Since Christ is in him as his hope, his love, his joy, his life, he is the reflection of the image of Jesus. People say of that person, "He is like his Master; he lives like Jesus Christ." Walking signifies progress. "*So walk ye in him.*" Proceed from grace to grace. Run forward until you reach the uttermost degree of knowledge that a person can attain concerning our Beloved. Walking implies continuance. There must be a perpetual abiding in Christ. How many Christians think that in the morning and evening they ought to come into the company of Jesus, but then they give their hearts to the world all day? But this is poor living. We should always be with Him, treading in His steps and doing His will. Walking also implies habit. When we speak of a man's walk and conversation, we mean his habits and the constant character of his life. Now, if we sometimes enjoy Christ, and then forget Him; sometimes call Him ours, and immediately lose our hold, that is not a habit. We do not walk in Him. We must keep close to Him, cling to Him, never let Him go; we should live and have our being in Him. "*As ye have therefore received Christ Jesus the Lord, so walk ye in him.*" Persevere in the same way in which you began. As at the first Christ Jesus was the trust of your faith, the source of your life, the principle of your action, and the joy of your spirit, so let Him be the same until life's end—the same when you walk through the valley of the shadow of death and enter into the joy and the rest that remains for the people of God. Holy Spirit, enable us to obey this heavenly precept.

His place of defence shall be the munitions of rocks: bread shall be given him; his waters shall be sure.
—Isaiah 33:16

O Christian, do you doubt whether God will fulfill His promise? Can the *"munitions of rocks"* be taken by storm? Can the storehouses of heaven fail? Do you think that your heavenly Father will forget you, even though He knows that you need food and clothing? When not one sparrow falls to the ground without your Father's knowledge, and the *"very hairs of your head are all numbered"* (Matt. 10:30), will you mistrust and doubt Him? Perhaps your affliction will continue until you dare to trust your God, and then it will end. There are a great many believers who have undergone trials and been very distressed, until at last they have been driven in sheer desperation to exercise faith in God—and the moment of their faith has been the instant of their deliverance. They have seen whether or not God would keep His promise. Oh, I urge you, do not doubt Him any longer! Do not please Satan, and do not distress yourself, by indulging in unbelieving thoughts about God any longer. Do not think it is a light matter to doubt Jehovah. Remember, it is a sin, and not a little sin, either; it is criminal in the highest degree. The angels never doubted Him, and neither did the demons. We alone, out of all the beings that God has made, dishonor Him by unbelief, and tarnish His honor by mistrust. Shame on us for this! Our God is not deserving of such low-minded suspicion. In the past, we have proven Him to be true and faithful to His Word. With the many examples of His love and kindness that we have received, and are daily receiving, from His hands, it is disgraceful and inexcusable for us to allow a doubt to stay within our hearts. From this time on, may we wage constant war against doubts about our God, which are enemies to our peace, and to His honor. With an unwavering faith, may we believe that what He has promised, He will also perform. *"Lord, I believe; help thou mine unbelief"* (Mark 9:24).

The eternal God is thy refuge.
—Deuteronomy 33:27

The word *"refuge"* may be translated "mansion" or "abiding place," which gives the thought that God is our abode, our home. There is a fullness and sweetness in the metaphor, for dear to our hearts are our homes, although they may be the humblest cottages. Far dearer is our blessed God, *"for in him we live, and move, and have our being"* (Acts 17:28). It is at home that we feel safe. We shut the world out and dwell in quiet security. So when we are with our God, we *"fear no evil"* (Ps. 23:4). He is our shelter and retreat, our abiding refuge. At home, we rest, and it is there we find repose after the fatigue and toil of the day. And so our hearts find rest in God when, wearied with life's conflicts, we turn to Him, and our souls dwell at ease. At home, also, we let our hearts loose; we are not afraid of being misunderstood, nor of our words being misconstrued. So when we are with God, we can commune freely with Him, laying open all our hidden desires; for if the *"secret of the* LORD *is with them that fear him"* (Ps. 25:14), the secrets of them that fear Him ought to be, and must be, with their Lord. Home, too, is the place of our truest and purest happiness. It is in God that our hearts find their deepest delight. We have joy in Him that far surpasses all other joy. It is also for home that we work and labor. The thought of it gives strength to bear the daily burdens and quickens the fingers to perform the task; in this sense, we may also say that God is our home. Love for Him strengthens us. We think of Him in the person of His dear Son, and a glimpse of the suffering face of the Redeemer constrains us to labor in His cause. We feel that we must work, for we have friends and loved ones yet to be saved, and we have our Father's heart to make glad by bringing home His wandering ones. We would fill the sacred family among whom we dwell with holy mirth. Happy are those who have the God of Jacob for their refuge!

It is enough for the disciple that he be as his master.
—Matthew 10:25

No one can dispute this statement, for it would be improper for the servant to be exalted above his Master. When our Lord was on earth, what was the treatment He received? Were His claims acknowledged, His instructions followed, and His perfections worshipped by those whom He came to bless? No, He was *"despised and rejected of men"* (Isa. 53:3). His place was outside the camp. (See Hebrews 13:11–13.) Crossbearing was His occupation. Did the world give Him comfort and rest? *"Foxes have holes, and the birds of the air have nests; but the Son of man hath not where to lay his head"* (Matt. 8:20). That inhospitable country afforded Him no shelter: it cast Him out and crucified Him. If you are a follower of Jesus, and maintain a consistent, Christlike walk and conversation, you must expect to be treated in the same way in regard to the part of your spiritual life that, in its outward development, comes under the observation of men. They will treat it as they treated the Savior—they will despise it. Do not imagine that worldly people will admire you, or that the holier and more Christlike you are, the more peaceably people will act toward you. They did not prize the polished gem, so why should they value the jewel in the rough? *"If they have called the master of the house Beelzebub, how much more shall they call them of his household?"* (Matt. 10:25). If we were more like Christ, we would be more hated by His enemies. It would be a sad dishonor for a child of God to be the world's favorite. It is a very bad sign to hear a wicked world clap its hands and shout "Well done!" to the Christian. The believer may begin to examine his character, and wonder whether he has not been doing something wrong, when the unrighteous give him their approval. Let us be true to our Master and have no friendship with a blind and base world that scorns and rejects Him. Far be it from us to seek a crown of honor where our Lord found a crown of thorns.

Underneath are the everlasting arms.
—Deuteronomy 33:27

God, the eternal God, is Himself our support at all times, especially when we are sinking in deep trouble. There are seasons when the Christian sinks very low in humiliation. Under a deep sense of his great sinfulness, he is humbled before God until he scarcely knows how to pray, because he appears, in his own sight, so worthless. Well, child of God, remember that when you are at your worst and lowest point, *"underneath [you] are the everlasting arms."* Sin may drag you low, but Christ's great atonement is still under all. You may have descended into deep distress, but you cannot have fallen so low as *"the uttermost"* (Heb. 7:25), and to the uttermost He saves. Again, the Christian sometimes sinks very deeply in sore trials from without. Every earthly prop is cut away. What then? Still underneath him are *"the everlasting arms."* He cannot fall so deep in distress and affliction without the covenant grace of an ever-faithful God still encircling him. The Christian may be sinking under trouble from within through fierce conflict, but even then he cannot be brought so low as to be beyond the reach of the *"everlasting arms."* They are underneath him, and, while thus sustained, all Satan's efforts to harm him avail nothing. This assurance of support is a comfort to any weary but earnest worker in the service of God. It implies a promise of strength for each day, grace for each need, and power for each duty. Further, when death comes, the promise will still hold good. When we stand in the midst of Jordan, we will be able to say with David, *"I will fear no evil: for thou art with me"* (Ps. 23:4). We will descend into the grave, but we will go no lower, for the eternal arms prevent our further fall. All through life, and at its close, we will be upheld by the *"everlasting arms"*— arms that neither flag nor lose their strength, for *"the everlasting God, the* Lord, *the Creator of the ends of the earth, fainteth not, neither is weary"* (Isa. 40:28).

He shall choose our inheritance for us.
—Psalm 47:4

Believer, if your earthly inheritance is a modest one, you should be satisfied with your portion, for you may rest assured that it is the best one for you. Unerring wisdom ordained your circumstances and selected for you the safest and best conditions. Suppose a ship of large tonnage were to be sailed up a river that had a sandbank in one part of it. If someone were to ask, "Why does the captain steer through the deep part of the channel and deviate so much from sailing in a straight line?" the captain's answer would be, "Because I would not get my ship into the harbor at all if I did not keep to the deep channel." Likewise, it may be that you would run aground and suffer shipwreck if your Divine Captain did not steer you into the depths of affliction, where waves of trouble follow each other in quick succession. Some plants die if they have too much sunshine. It may be that you are planted where you receive only a little. You are put there by the loving Farmer, because only in this situation will you bring forth *"fruit to perfection"* (Luke 8:14). Remember this: if any other condition had been better for you than the one you are in, divine love would have put you there. You have been placed by God in the most suitable circumstances. If you could choose your own situation, you would soon cry out, "Lord, choose my inheritance for me, for by my self-will I am *'pierced…through with many sorrows'* (1 Tim. 6:10)." Be content with what you have, since the Lord has ordered all things for your good. Take up your own daily cross. It is the burden best suited for your shoulder, and will prove most effective in making you perfect *"in every good word and work"* (2 Thess. 2:17), to the glory of God. Down, meddlesome self and proud impatience! It is not for you, but only for the Lord of Love, to choose!

> Trials must and will befall—
> But with humble faith to see
> Love inscribed upon them all;
> This is happiness to me.

The trial of your faith.
—1 Peter 1:7

Untried faith may be true faith, but it is sure to be little faith, and it is likely to remain stunted as long as it is without trials. Faith never prospers as well as when all things are against her. Tempests are her trainers, and lightning is her illuminator. When calm reigns on the sea, spread the sails as you will, but the ship will not move to its harbor; for on a slumbering ocean, the keel sleeps, too. But let the howling winds rush forth, and let the waters lift up themselves. Though the vessel may rock, her deck may be washed with waves, and her mast may creak under the pressure of the full and swelling sail, it is then that she makes headway toward her desired haven. No flowers wear as lovely a blue as those that grow at the foot of the frozen glacier. No stars gleam as brightly as those that glisten in the polar sky. No water tastes as sweet as that which springs amid the desert sand; and no faith is as precious as that which lives and triumphs in adversity. Tried faith brings experience. You could not have believed your own weakness had you not been compelled to pass through the rivers; and you would never have known God's strength had you not been supported amid the flooding waters. Faith increases in solidity, assurance, and intensity the more it is exercised with tribulation. Faith is precious, and its trial is precious, too. Let not this, however, discourage those who are young in faith. You will have trials enough without seeking them; the full portion will be measured out to you in due season. Meanwhile, if you cannot yet claim the results of long experience, thank God for what grace you have. Praise Him for that degree of holy confidence that you have already attained. Walk according to that rule, and you will yet have more and more of the blessings of God, until your faith will remove mountains and conquer impossibilities.

NOVEMBER 12
Evening

*And it came to pass in those days, that he went out into a mountain
to pray, and continued all night in prayer to God.*
—Luke 6:12

If anyone might have lived without prayer, it was our spotless, perfect Lord. Yet no one ever prayed as much as He! Such was His love for His Father, that He cherished being in frequent communion with Him. Such was His love for His people, that He desired to intercede for them often. The prominent prayerfulness of Jesus is a lesson for us. He has given us an example, so that we may follow in His steps. The time of prayer that He chose—night—was admirable. It was the hour of silence, when the crowd would not disturb Him; the time of inaction, when all but He had stopped working; the season when sleep made people forget their troubles and cease coming to Him for help. While others found rest in sleep, He refreshed Himself with prayer. The place of prayer was also well selected. He was alone where no one would intrude, where no one could observe Him. Thus He was free from the pretentiousness of the Pharisees and the interruptions of the public. Those dark and silent hills were a fitting place of prayer for the Son of God. Heaven and earth in midnight stillness heard the groans and sighs of the mysterious Being in whom both worlds were blended. The duration of His supplication is remarkable. The long watches were not too long for Him. The cold wind did not chill His devotions. The grim darkness did not darken His faith, nor the loneliness inhibit His persistence. We are not able to watch with Him for one hour, but He watched for us during entire nights. The occasion of Jesus' night of prayer is notable. It was after His enemies had been enraged, and therefore prayer was His refuge and solace. It was also before He chose the twelve apostles, and so prayer was the entranceway to His ministry, the herald of His new work. Should we not learn from Jesus to resort to special prayer when we are under particular trial or when we contemplate fresh endeavors for the Master's glory? Lord Jesus, *"teach us to pray"* (Luke 11:1).

NOVEMBER 13

Morning

The branch cannot bear fruit of itself.
—John 15:4

How did you begin to bear fruit? It was when you came to Jesus and cast yourselves on His great atonement and rested on His finished righteousness. Ah, what fruit you had then! Do you remember those early days? Then indeed the vine flourished, the tender grape appeared, the pomegranates budded forth, and the beds of spices gave forth their smell. Have you declined since then? If you have, we charge you to remember that time of love and repent; do your first works. Be most engaged in those experiences that have proven to draw you nearest to Christ, because it is from Him that all your fruit proceeds. Any holy exercise that will bring you to Him will help you to bear fruit. The sun is, no doubt, a great aid in creating fruit among the trees of the orchard. Jesus is even more so among the trees of His garden of grace. When have you been the most fruitless? Has it not been when you have lived farthest from the Lord Jesus Christ, when you have slackened in prayer, and when you have departed from the simplicity of your faith? Has it not been when your graces have engrossed your attention instead of your Lord, when you have said, "My mountain stands firm. I will never be moved," and have forgotten where your strength dwells? Has it not been then that your fruit has ceased? Some of us have been taught by terrible humility of the heart before the Lord that we are nothing apart from Christ. When we have seen the utter barrenness and death of all creature-power, we have cried in anguish, "From Him all my fruit must be found, for no fruit can ever come from me." We are taught, by past experience, that the more simply we depend on the grace of God in Christ and wait on the Holy Spirit, the more we will bring forth fruit unto God. Oh, to trust Jesus for fruit as well as for life!

Men ought always to pray.
—Luke 18:1

If "*men*" should always pray, and not lose heart (Luke 18:1), how much more should Christian men pray! Jesus has sent His church into the world on the same mission on which He Himself came, and this mission includes intercession. He has made us "*priests unto God*" (Rev. 1:6), and we are to intercede for the world. Creation is mute, but the church is to find a voice for it. It is the church's high privilege to pray with God's acceptance. The door of grace is always open for her petitions, and they never return empty-handed. The veil was torn for her, the blood was sprinkled on the altar for her, and God constantly invites her to ask what she desires. Will she refuse a privilege that even angels might envy? Is she not the bride of Christ? May she not go in to her King at every hour? Will she allow the precious privilege to go unused? The church is always in need of prayer. There are always some in her midst who are declining, or falling into open sin. There are lambs to be prayed for, that they may be carried in Christ's arms; there are the strong to be prayed for, lest they grow presumptuous, and the weak, lest they become despairing. If we maintained prayer meetings twenty-four hours a day, every day of the year, we might never be without a special subject for supplication. Are we ever without the sick and the poor, the afflicted and the wavering? Are we ever without those who seek the conversion of relatives, the reclaiming of backsliders, or the salvation of the wicked? No, with congregations constantly gathering, with ministers always preaching, with millions of sinners lying "*dead in trespasses and sins*" (Eph. 2:1), in a country over which the darkness of false religion is certainly descending, in a world full of idols, cruelty, and wickedness, if the church does not pray, how will she excuse her disgraceful neglect of the commission of her loving Lord? Let the church be constant in supplication, and let every individual believer cast his mite of prayer into the treasury.

I will cut off the remnant of Baal from this place, and…them that
worship the host of heaven upon the housetops; and them that swear
by the LORD, *and that swear by Malcham.*
—Zephaniah 1:4-5

Such persons thought themselves safe because they were with both parties. They went with the followers of Jehovah and bowed at the same time to Malcham. But duplicity is abominable with God, and His soul hates hypocrisy. The idolater who distinctly gives himself to his false god has one sin less than he who brings his polluted and detestable sacrifice to the temple of the Lord while his heart is with the world and the sins thereof. To hold with the hare and run with the hounds is a coward's policy. In the common matters of daily life, a double-minded man is despised, but in religion he is loathsome to the last degree. The penalty pronounced in the verse before us is terrible, but it is well deserved. How should divine justice spare the sinner, who knows the right, approves it, and professes to follow it, and all the while loves evil and gives it dominion in his heart? My soul, search yourself this morning, and see whether you are guilty of double-dealing. You profess to be a follower of Jesus, but do you truly love Him? Is your heart right with God? Are you of the family of old Father Honest, or are you a relative of Mr. Stretch-the-Truth? A good name is of little value if I am indeed dead in trespasses and sins. To have one foot on the land of truth and another on the sea of falsehood will involve a terrible fall and total ruin. Christ will be all or nothing. God fills the whole universe; therefore, there is no room for another god. If He reigns in my heart, there will be no space for another reigning power. Do I rest alone on Jesus crucified and live alone for Him? Is it my desire to do so? Is my heart set on doing so? Then, blessed be the mighty grace that has led me to salvation. If this is not the case, O Lord, pardon my sad offense and unite my heart to fear Your name.

NOVEMBER 14

Evening

And Laban said, It must not be so done in our country,
to give the younger before the firstborn.
—Genesis 29:26

We do not excuse Laban for his dishonesty, but we do not hesitate to learn from the custom that he quoted as his excuse. There are some things that must be taken in order, and if we want to gain the second, we must secure the first. The second may be more lovely in our eyes, but the rule of the heavenly country must stand, and the elder must be married first. For instance, many believers desire the *"beautiful and well favoured"* (Gen. 29:17) Rachel of *"joy and peace in believing"* (Rom. 15:13), but they must first be wedded to the *"tender eyed"* (Gen. 29:17) Leah of repentance. Everyone falls in love with happiness, and many would cheerfully serve twice seven years to enjoy it. However, according to the rule of the Lord's kingdom, the Leah of real holiness must be beloved to our souls before the Rachel of true happiness can be attained. Heaven does not come first but second, and only by persevering to the end can we gain a share in it. The cross must be carried before the crown can be worn. We must follow our Lord in His humiliation, or we will never rest with Him in glory. My soul, are you so vain as to hope to break through the heavenly rule? Do you hope for reward without labor, or honor without toil? Dismiss that idle expectation, and be content to take the difficult things for the sake of the sweet love of Jesus, which will compensate you for everything. In such a spirit, laboring and suffering, you will find that bitter things grow sweet, and hard things easy. Like Jacob, your years of service will seem to you but a few days, because of the love you have for Jesus. Then, when the dear hour of the Wedding Feast has come, all your toils will be as though they had never been. An hour with Jesus will make up for ages of pain and labor.

> Jesus, to win Yourself so fair,
>   Your cross I will with gladness bear:
> Since so the rules of heaven ordain,
>   The first I'll wed the next to gain.

NOVEMBER 15

The LORD's portion is his people.
—Deuteronomy 32:9

How are they His? By His own sovereign choice. He chose them and set His love on them. He did this altogether apart from any goodness in them at the time, or any goodness that He foresaw in them. He had mercy on whom He would have mercy and ordained a chosen company unto eternal life; therefore, they are His by His unconstrained election. They are His not only by choice, but also by purchase. He has bought and paid for them to the last cent; hence, there can be no dispute about His title. The Lord's portion has been fully redeemed, *"not...with corruptible things, as silver and gold,...but with the precious blood of Christ"* (1 Pet. 1:18–19). There is no mortgage on His estate; no suits can be raised by opposing claimants. The price was paid in open court, and the church is the Lord's property forever. See the bloodmark on all the chosen, invisible to human eye, but known to Christ, for *"the Lord knoweth them that are his"* (2 Tim. 2:19). He does not forget any of those whom He has redeemed from among men. He counts the sheep for whom He laid down His life and remembers well the church for which He gave Himself. They are also His by conquest. What a battle He had in us before we would be won! How long He laid siege to our hearts! How often He sent us terms of capitulation, but we barred our gates and fenced our walls against Him. Do we not remember that glorious hour when He carried our hearts by storm? When He placed His cross against the wall and scaled our ramparts, planting on our strongholds the bloodred flag of His omnipotent mercy? Yes, we are, indeed, the conquered captives of His omnipotent love. Thus chosen, purchased, and subdued, the rights of our divine Possessor are inalienable. We rejoice that we can never be our own, and we desire, day by day, to do His will and to show forth His glory.

Strengthen, O God, that which thou hast wrought for us.
—Psalm 68:28

It is our wisdom, as well as our necessity, to petition God continually to strengthen what He has worked in us. Many Christians have neglected to do this, and thus they may blame themselves when they experience trials and afflictions of spirit that arise from unbelief. It is true that Satan seeks to flood the fair garden of the heart and to make it a scene of desolation. However, it is also true that many Christians leave open the floodgates themselves, and let in the dreadful deluge through carelessness and lack of prayer to their strong Helper. We often forget that the Author of our faith must also be the Preserver of it. The lamp that was burning in the temple was never allowed to go out. It had to be replenished daily with fresh oil. Likewise, our faith can only live by being sustained with the oil of grace, and we can only obtain this grace from God Himself. We will prove to be foolish virgins if we do not secure the needed sustenance for our lamps. (See Matthew 25:1–13.) He who built the world also upholds it, or it would fall in one tremendous crash. He who made us Christians must maintain us by His Spirit, or our ruin will be speedy and final. Let us, then, evening by evening, go to our Lord for the grace and strength we need. We have a strong argument to plead, for it is His own work of grace that we ask Him to strengthen—*"That which thou hast wrought for us."* Do you think that He will fail to protect and sustain that work? Only let your faith take hold of His strength, and all the powers of darkness, led on by the master fiend of hell, cannot cast a cloud or shadow over your joy and peace. Why faint when you may be strong? Why suffer defeat when you may conquer? Oh, take your wavering faith and drooping graces to Him who can revive and replenish them! Earnestly pray, *"Strengthen, O God, that which thou hast wrought for us."*

The LORD is my portion, saith my soul.
—Lamentations 3:24

This verse does not say, "The Lord is partly my portion" or "The Lord is in my portion," but He Himself makes up the sum total of my soul's inheritance. Within the circumference of that circle lies all that we possess or desire. "*The LORD is my portion*"—not His grace merely or His love or His covenant, but Jehovah Himself! He has chosen us for His portion, and we have chosen Him for ours. It is true that the Lord must first choose our inheritance for us, or else we will never choose it for ourselves; but if we are really called according to the purpose of electing love, we can sing

> Lov'd of my God for Him again
> With love intense I burn;
> Chosen of Him ere time began,
> I choose Him in return.

The Lord is our all-sufficient portion. God fills Himself; and if God is all-sufficient in Himself, He must be all-sufficient for us. It is not easy to satisfy man's desires. When he dreams that he is satisfied, immediately he awakens to the perception that there is something yet beyond, and the greed in his heart cries, "Give! Give!" But all that we can wish for is to be found in our divine portion, so that we ask, "*Whom have I in heaven but thee? and there is none upon earth that I desire beside thee*" (Ps. 73:25). Well may we delight in the Lord who makes us to drink of the river of His pleasures. Our faith stretches her wings and mounts like an eagle into the heaven of divine love as to her proper dwelling place. "*The lines are fallen unto me in pleasant places; yea, I have a goodly heritage*" (Ps. 16:6). Let us rejoice in the Lord always. Let us show the world that we are a happy and blessed people, and thus cause them to exclaim, "We will go with you, for we have heard that God is with you."

Thine eyes shall see the king in his beauty.
—Isaiah 33:17

The more you know about Christ, the less you will be satisfied with superficial views of Him. The more deeply you study His transactions in the eternal covenant, His guarantees on your behalf as the eternal Surety, and the fullness of His grace, which shines in all His offices, the more you will truly *"see the king in his beauty."* Give yourself to such contemplation. Long more and more to see Jesus. Meditation and contemplation are often like windows of agate and gates of carbuncle, through which we see the Redeemer. Meditation puts the telescope to the eye and enables us to see Jesus better than we could have seen Him if we had lived in the days when He was on earth. If only our conduct were more heavenly, and that we were more taken up with the person, work, and beauty of our incarnate Lord! If we meditated more on Jesus, the beauty of the King would gleam upon us with more resplendence. Beloved, when it is time for us to die, it is very probable that we will have a sight of our glorious King such as we have never had before. Many saints, in dying, have looked up from amid the stormy waters and seen Jesus walking on the waves of the sea. They have heard Him say, *"It is I; be not afraid"* (Matt. 14:27). Ah, yes, when the house begins to shake, and the clay falls away, we see Christ through the openings; and between the rafters, the sunlight of heaven comes streaming in. Yet if we want to see the *"king in his beauty"* face-to-face, we must go to heaven for the sight, or the King must come here in person. Oh, that He would come on the *"wings of the wind"* (2 Sam. 22:11)! He is our Husband, and we are widowed by His absence. He is our dear and fair Brother, and we are lonely without Him. Thick veils and clouds hang between our souls and their true life. When will the *"day break, and the shadows flee away"* (Song 2:17)? Oh, long-expected day, begin!

To whom be glory for ever. Amen.
—Romans 11:36

To whom be glory for ever." This should be the single desire of the Christian. All other wishes must be subservient to this one. The Christian may wish for prosperity in his business, but only so far as it may help him to promote this cause—"To Him be glory forever." He may desire to attain more gifts and more graces, but it should only be for God's glory. You are not acting as you should when you are moved by any other motive than a single eye to your Lord's glory. As a Christian, you are *of* God, and *through* God; then live *to* God. Let nothing ever set your heart beating so mightily as love for Him. Let this ambition fire your soul. May this be the foundation of every enterprise on which you enter and your sustaining motive whenever your zeal would grow cold. Make God your only object. Depend on it. Where self begins, sorrow begins. But if God is my supreme delight and only purpose,

> To me 'tis equal whether love ordain
> My life or death—appoint me ease or pain.

Let your desire for God's glory be a growing desire. You blessed Him in your youth; do not be content with such praises as you gave Him then. Has God prospered you in business? Give Him more as He has given you more. Has God given you experience? Praise Him by stronger faith than you exercised at first. Does your knowledge grow? Then sing more sweetly. Do you enjoy happier times than you once had? Have you been restored from sickness, and has your sorrow been turned into peace and joy? Then give Him more music. Put more coals and more sweet frankincense into the censer of your praise. Practically in your life give Him honor, putting the "Amen" to this doxology to your great and gracious Lord by your own individual service and increasing holiness.

He that cleaveth wood shall be endangered thereby.
—Ecclesiastes 10:9

Oppressors may have their way with the poor and needy as easily as they can split logs of wood. However, they had better beware, for they are involved in a dangerous business—a splinter from a tree has often killed a woodsman. Jesus is persecuted in every injured saint, and He is mighty to avenge His beloved ones. Success in treading down the poor and needy is a thing to be feared, for if there is no danger to persecutors on earth, there will be great danger in the next world. Splitting wood is a common, everyday task, yet it has its dangers. Similarly, reader, there are dangers connected with your calling and daily life, which it would benefit you to be aware of. I do not refer to hazards relating to floods, wars, disease, and sudden death, but to spiritual perils. Your occupation may be as humble as log splitting, yet the devil can tempt you in it. You may be a household servant, a farm laborer, or a mechanic, and you may be greatly screened from temptations to the more obvious vices, yet some secret sin may do you harm. Those who stay at home and do not associate with the rough world may still be endangered by their very seclusion. The person who thinks he is safe is not safe anywhere. Pride may enter a poor man's heart; greed may reign in a laborer's soul; uncleanness may venture into the quietest home; and anger, envy, and malice may insinuate themselves into the most rural dwelling. We may sin even in speaking a few words to a servant. A little purchase at a shop may be the first link in a chain of temptations. Merely looking out a window may be the beginning of evil. O Lord, how vulnerable we are! How will we be protected? Guarding ourselves is too hard a job for us. Only You are able to preserve us in such a world of evils. Spread Your wings over us, and we, like little chicks, will crouch down beneath You and feel safe!

A spring shut up, a fountain sealed.
—Song of Solomon 4:12

In this metaphor, which has reference to the inner life of a believer, we have very plainly the idea of secrecy. It is *"a spring shut up."* Just as there were springs in the East, over which an edifice was built, so that none could reach them except those who knew the secret entrance, so is the heart of a believer when it is renewed by grace. There is a mysterious life within that no human skill can touch. It is a secret that no other man knows; no, the very man who is the possessor of it cannot tell it to his neighbor. The text includes not only secrecy, but separation. It is not the common spring, of which every passerby may drink; it is one kept and preserved from all others. It is a fountain bearing a particular mark—a king's royal seal, so that all can perceive that it is not a common fountain, but a fountain owned by a proprietor and placed especially by itself. So is it with the spiritual life. The chosen of God were separated in the eternal decree. They were separated by God in the day of redemption, and they are separated by the possession of a life that others do not have. It is impossible for them to feel at home with the world or to delight in its pleasures. There is also the idea of sacredness. The *"spring shut up"* is preserved for the use of some special person, and such is the Christian's heart. It is a spring kept for Jesus. Every Christian should feel that he has God's seal on him. He should be able to say with Paul, *"From henceforth let no man trouble me: for I bear in my body the marks of the Lord Jesus"* (Gal. 6:17). Another prominent idea is that of security. Oh, how sure and safe is the inner life of the believer! If all the powers of earth and hell could combine against it, that immortal principle must still exist, for He who gave it pledged His life for its preservation. And who is He that will harm you, when God is your protector?

Thou art from everlasting.
—Psalm 93:2

Christ is *"everlasting."* Of Him we may sing, with David, *"Thy throne, O God, is for ever and ever"* (Ps. 45:6). Rejoice, believer, in *"Jesus Christ the same yesterday, and to day, and for ever"* (Heb. 13:8). Jesus always was. The Babe born in Bethlehem was united to the Word, who was *"in the beginning"* (John 1:2), and by whom *"all things were made"* (v. 3). The title by which Christ revealed Himself to John in Patmos was, *"Him which is, and which was, and which is to come"* (Rev. 1:4). If He were not God *"from everlasting,"* we could not love Him so devoutly. We could not feel that He had any share in the eternal love that is the fountain of all covenant blessings. Yet since He was from all eternity with the Father, we trace the stream of divine love to Himself equally with His Father and the blessed Spirit. As our Lord always *was*, He also *is* eternally. Jesus is not dead: *"He ever liveth to make intercession for [us]"* (Heb. 7:25). Go to Him in all your times of need, for He is waiting to bless you still. Moreover, Jesus our Lord always *will be*. If God spares your life so that you have a full life span of *"threescore years and ten"* (Ps. 90:10), you will find that His cleansing fountain is still open, and that His precious blood has not lost its power. You will find that the Priest who filled the healing fountain with His own blood, lives to purge you from all iniquity. When only your last battle remains to be fought, you will find that the hand of your conquering Captain has not grown weak. The living Savior will encourage the dying saint. When you enter heaven, you will find Him there bearing the dew of His youth. Through eternity, the Lord Jesus will still remain the perennial spring of joy, life, and glory to His people. May you draw living waters from this sacred well! Jesus always was, always is, and always will be. He is eternal in all His attributes, in all His offices, in all His might, and in His willingness to bless, comfort, guard, and crown His chosen people.

Avoid foolish questions.
—Titus 3:9

Our days are few and are far better spent in doing good than in disputing over matters which are, at best, of minor importance. In the past, men have done a world of mischief by their incessant discussion of subjects of no practical importance. Our churches suffer as well from petty wars over obscure points and unimportant questions. After everything has been said that can be said, neither party is any wiser; therefore, the discussion no more promotes knowledge than love, and it is foolish to sow in so barren a field. Questions on points wherein Scripture is silent, on mysteries that belong to God alone, on prophecies of doubtful interpretation, and on mere modes of observing human ceremonials are all foolish, and wise men avoid them. Our business is neither to ask nor answer foolish questions, but to avoid them altogether. If we observe the apostle's precept to *"be careful to maintain good works"* (Titus 3:8), we will find ourselves far too occupied with profitable business to take much interest in unworthy, contentious, needless strivings. There are, however, some questions that are the reverse of foolish ones, questions that we must not avoid, but fairly and honestly meet, such as these: Do I believe in the Lord Jesus Christ? Am I renewed in the spirit of my mind? Am I walking not after the flesh, but after the Spirit? Am I growing in grace? Does my conversation adorn the doctrine of God my Savior? Am I looking for the coming of the Lord and watching as a servant who expects his master should? What more can I do for Jesus? Such inquiries as these urgently demand our attention. If we have been at all given to quibbling, let us now turn our critical abilities to a service so much more profitable. Let us be peacemakers and endeavor to lead others, both by our precept and example, to *"avoid foolish questions."*

Oh that I knew where I might find him!
—Job 23:3

In Job's extreme need, he cried out to the Lord. The greatest desire of an afflicted child of God is to see his Father's face once more. His first prayer is not, "Oh, that I might be healed of the disease that now festers in every part of my body!" or even, "Oh, that I might see my children restored from the jaws of the grave, and my property returned from the hand of the spoiler!" Instead, his first and foremost cry is, *"Oh that I knew where I might find him'* who is my God, that I might come even to His throne!" God's children run home when the storm comes on. It is the heaven-born instinct of the godly to seek shelter from all trouble beneath the wings of Jehovah. "He who has made God his refuge" might serve as the title of a true believer. A hypocrite, when afflicted by God, resents the infliction and, like a slave, wants to run from the Master who has scourged him. This is not the case with the true heir of heaven. He kisses the hand that struck him, and seeks shelter from the rod in the arms of the God who frowned on him. Job's desire to commune with God was intensified by the failure of all other sources of comfort. The patriarch turned away from his sorry friends and looked up to the heavenly throne, just as a traveler turns from his empty water bottle and hurries to the well. He bids farewell to earthborn hopes, and cries, "If only I knew where I might find my God!" Nothing teaches us the preciousness of the Creator as much as when we discover the emptiness of everything else. Turning away with bitter scorn from earth's hives, where we find no honey but many sharp stings, we rejoice in Him whose faithful Word is sweeter than honey or the honeycomb. In every trouble, we should first seek to realize God's presence with us. If we can only enjoy His smile, we can bear our daily cross with a willing heart, for His dear sake.

O Lord, thou hast pleaded the causes of my soul;
thou hast redeemed my life.
—Lamentations 3:58

Notice how positively the prophet spoke. He did not say, "I hope, I trust, I sometimes think that God has pleaded the causes of my soul." Instead, he spoke of it as a matter of fact not to be disputed. *"Thou hast pleaded the causes of my soul."* Let us, by the aid of the gracious Comforter, shake off those doubts and fears that so often mar our peace and comfort. May this be our prayer: that we may be done with the harsh, croaking voice of surmise and suspicion and be able to speak with the clear, melodious voice of full assurance. Notice how gratefully the prophet spoke, ascribing all the glory to God alone! There was not a word concerning himself or his own pleadings. He did not ascribe his deliverance in any measure to any man, much less to his own merit; but he said, *"Thou"*—*"O Lord, thou hast pleaded the causes of my soul; thou hast redeemed my life."* A grateful spirit should be cultivated by the Christian; especially after deliverances we should prepare a song for our God. Earth should be a temple filled with the songs of grateful saints, and every day should be a smoking censor, filled with the sweet incense of thanksgiving. How joyful Jeremiah seemed to be while he recorded the Lord's mercy! How triumphantly he lifted up the strain! He had been in the low dungeon, and even now, he is considered to be the weeping prophet; yet in the very book that is called Lamentations, clear as the song of Miriam when she dashed her fingers against the tabor, shrill as the note of Deborah when she met Barak with shouts of victory, we hear the voice of Jeremiah going up to heaven—*"Thou hast pleaded the causes of my soul; thou hast redeemed my life."* Children of God, seek after a vital experience of the Lord's lovingkindness. When you have it, speak positively of it, sing gratefully, and shout triumphantly.

*The conies are but a feeble folk, yet make they
their houses in the rocks.*
—Proverbs 30:26

Conscious of their own natural defenselessness, the coneys resort to burrows in the rocks, and are secure from their enemies. My heart, be willing to glean a lesson from these *"feeble folk."* You are as weak and as exposed to peril as the timid coney. Therefore, be as wise to seek a shelter. My best security is within the fortifications of an unchangeable Jehovah, where His unalterable promises stand like giant walls of rock. It will be well with you if you can always hide in the bulwarks of His glorious attributes, all of which are guarantees of safety for those who put their trust in Him. May the name of the Lord be blessed, for I have done so, and have found myself like David in Adullam (see 1 Samuel 22:1)—safe from the cruelty of my enemy. I do not now have to discover the blessedness of the man who puts his trust in the Lord. For, long ago, when Satan and my sins pursued me, I fled to the cleft of the Rock Christ Jesus, and in His torn side I found a delightful resting place. My heart, run to Him anew tonight, no matter what your present grief may be. Jesus feels for you; Jesus comforts you; Jesus will help you. No monarch in his impenetrable fortress is more secure than the coney in his rocky burrow. The captain of ten thousand chariots is not one bit better protected than the little dweller in the cleft of the mountain. In Jesus, the weak are strong, and the defenseless are safe. They could not be stronger if they were giants, or safer if they were in heaven. Faith gives to men on earth the protection of the God of heaven. They could not wish for anything more. The coneys cannot build a castle, but they avail themselves of what is already there. Similarly, I cannot make myself a refuge, but Jesus has provided it, His Father has given it, and His Spirit has revealed it. I enter it again tonight and am safe from every foe.

Grieve not the holy Spirit of God.
—Ephesians 4:30

All that the believer has must come from Christ, but it comes solely through the channel of the Spirit of grace. Moreover, as all blessings thus flow to you through the Holy Spirit, so also no good thing can come out of you in holy thought, devout worship, or gracious actions, apart from the sanctifying operation of the same Spirit. Even if the good seed is sown in you, it lies dormant unless He works *"in you both to will and to do of his good pleasure"* (Phil. 2:13). Do you desire to speak for Jesus—how can you unless the Holy Spirit touches your tongue? Do you desire to pray? Alas, what dull work it is unless the *"Spirit itself maketh intercession for [you]"* (Rom. 8:26)! Do you desire to subdue sin? Would you be holy? Would you imitate your Master? Do you desire to rise to superlative heights of spirituality? Are you wanting to be made like the angels of God, full of zeal and ardor for the Master's cause? You cannot without the Spirit—*"Without me ye can do nothing"* (John 15:5). Branch of the vine, you can have no fruit without the sap! Child of God, you have no life within you apart from the life that God gives you through His Spirit! Then let us not grieve Him or provoke Him to anger by our sins. Let us not quench Him in one of His faintest motions in our souls. Let us foster every suggestion and be ready to obey every prompting. If the Holy Spirit is indeed so mighty, let us attempt nothing without Him. Let us begin no project and carry on no enterprise and conclude no transaction without imploring His blessing. Let us give Him the due homage of feeling our entire weakness apart from Him, and then, depending alone on Him, have this as our prayer, "Open my heart and my whole self to Your incoming. Uphold me with Your free Spirit when I will have received that Spirit in my inmost being."

Lazarus was one of them that sat at the table with him.
—John 12:2

Lazarus is to be envied. It would have been good to have been Martha, and to have served Jesus. However, it would have been even better to have been Lazarus, and to have communed with Him. There are times for each purpose, and each is fitting in its season. Yet none of the trees of the garden yield clusters like the vine of fellowship. To sit with Jesus, to hear His words, to take note of His actions, and to receive His smiles, is such a blessing that it must have made Lazarus as happy as the angels. When it has been our happy circumstance to feast with our Beloved in His banquet hall, we would not have given half a sigh for all the kingdoms of the world, if such a breath could have bought them. Lazarus is also to be imitated. It would have been a strange thing if Lazarus had not been at the table where Jesus was, for he had been dead, and Jesus had raised him. For the one who had been raised to have been absent when the Lord who gave him life was at his house, would have been ungrateful, indeed. We, too, were once dead and, like Lazarus, were stinking in the grave of sin. Yet Jesus raised us, and by His life we live. Can we be content to live at a distance from Him? Do we neglect to remember Him at His table, where He graciously feasts with His brethren? Oh, this is cruel! We must repent and do as He has commanded us. His least wish should be law to us. To have lived without constant communion with the One of whom the Jews said, *"Behold how he loved him!"* (John 11:36), would have been disgraceful for Lazarus. Is it excusable in us, whom Jesus has loved *"with an everlasting love"* (Jer. 31:3)? To have been cold to Him who wept over his lifeless corpse would have demonstrated a great callousness in Lazarus. What does it show about us, over whom the Savior has not only wept, but also bled? Come, beloved, let us return to our heavenly Bridegroom and ask for His Spirit, so that we may have more intimate fellowship with Him. From this time forward, let us sit at the table with Him.

Israel served for a wife, and for a wife he kept sheep.
—Hosea 12:12

Jacob, while reasoning with Laban, described his own toil in this way, "*This twenty years have I been with thee....That which was torn of beasts I brought not unto thee; I bare the loss of it; of my hand didst thou require it, whether stolen by day, or stolen by night. Thus I was; in the day the drought consumed me, and the frost by night; and my sleep departed from mine eyes*" (Gen. 31:38–39). Even more toilsome than this was the life of our Savior here below. He watched over all His sheep until He gave as His last account, "*Of them which thou gavest me have I lost none*" (John 18:9). His hair was wet with dew, and His locks with the drops of the night. Sleep departed from His eyes, for all night He was in prayer, wrestling for His people. One night Peter must be pleaded for; then another claims His tearful intercession. No shepherd sitting beneath the cold skies, looking up at the stars, could ever utter such complaints because of the hardness of his toil as Jesus Christ might have done, if He had chosen to do so, because of the difficulty of His service in order to procure His spouse.

> Cold mountains and the midnight air,
>   Witnessed the fervor of His prayer;
> The desert His temptations knew,
>   His conflict and His victory, too.

It is sweet to dwell on the spiritual parallel of Laban having required all the sheep at Jacob's hand. If they were attacked and destroyed by beasts, Jacob must make it good; if any of them died, he must stand as surety for the whole. Was not the toil of Jesus for His church the toil of one who was under suretyship obligations to bring every believing one safe to the hand of Him who had committed them to His charge? Look on toiling Jacob, and you see a representation of Him of whom we read, "*He shall feed his flock like a shepherd*" (Isa. 40:11).

The power of his resurrection.
—Philippians 3:10

The doctrine of a risen Savior is exceedingly precious. The Resurrection is the cornerstone of the entire building of Christianity. It is the keystone of the arch of our salvation. It would take a volume to describe all the streams of living water that flow from this one sacred source, the resurrection of our dear Lord and Savior Jesus Christ. However, both to know that He has risen, and to have fellowship with Him in His resurrection—communing with the risen Savior by possessing a risen life, seeing Him leave the tomb by leaving the tomb of worldliness ourselves—is even more precious. The doctrine is the basis of the experience; but as the flower is lovelier than the root, so is the experience of fellowship with the risen Savior lovelier than the doctrine itself. I want you to believe that Christ rose from the dead in such a way that you can sing of His resurrection, and derive all the consolation that it is possible for you to extract from this well-ascertained and well-witnessed fact. However, I urge you not to be content with facts alone. Though you cannot, as the disciples did, see Him visibly, I urge you to aspire to see Christ Jesus by the eyes of faith. Though, like Mary Magdalene, you may not *"touch"* (John 20:17) Him, may you be privileged to converse with Him, and to know that He is risen—you yourselves being risen in Him to *"newness of life"* (Rom. 6:4). To know a crucified Savior as having crucified all my sins, is a high degree of knowledge. Yet to know a risen Savior as having justified me, and to realize that He has bestowed on me new life, since He has granted it to me to be a new creation through His own newness of life—this is a noble experience. Short of it, no one ought to rest satisfied. May you *"know him, and the power of his resurrection"* (Phil. 3:10). Why should those who are made alive with Jesus wear the grave clothes of worldliness and unbelief? Rise, for the Lord is risen.

Fellowship with him.
—1 John 1:6

When we were united by faith to Christ, we were brought into such complete fellowship with Him that we were made one with Him. His interests and ours became mutual and identical. We have fellowship with Christ in His love. What He loves, we love. He loves the saints; so do we. He loves sinners; so do we. He loves the poor perishing race of man and longs to see earth's deserts transformed into the garden of the Lord; so do we. We have fellowship with Him in His desires. He desires the glory of God; we also labor for the same. He desires that the saints may be with Him where He is; we desire to be with Him there, too. He desires to drive out sin; behold, we fight under His banner. He desires that His Father's name may be loved and adored by all His creatures; we pray daily, "*Thy kingdom come. Thy will be done in earth, as it is in heaven*" (Matt. 6:10). We have fellowship with Christ in His sufferings. We are not nailed to the cross, nor do we die a cruel death; but when He is reproached, we are reproached. It is a very sweet thing to be blamed for His sake, to be despised for following the Master, to have the world against us. "*The disciple is not above his master, nor the servant above his lord*" (Matt. 10:24). In our measure we commune with Him in His labors, ministering to people by the word of truth and by deeds of love. Our meat and our drink, like His, "*is to do the will of him that sent [us], and to finish his work*" (John 4:34). We also have fellowship with Christ in His joys. We are happy in His happiness, and we rejoice in His exaltation. Have you ever tasted that joy, believer? There is no purer or more thrilling delight to be known this side of heaven than that of having Christ's joy fulfilled in us so that our joy may be full. His glory awaits us to complete our fellowship, for His church will sit with Him on His throne, as His well-beloved bride and queen.

Get thee up into the high mountain.
—Isaiah 40:9

Each believer should be thirsting *"for God, for the living God"* (Ps. 42:2), and longing to climb the hill of the Lord, to see Him face-to-face. We should not rest content in the mists of the valley when the summit of Mount Tabor awaits us. My soul thirsts to drink deeply of the cup that is reserved for those who reach the summit of the mountain, whose heads are wet with the dew of heaven. How pure is the dew of the hills, how fresh is the mountain air, how rich is the fare of those who dwell on high, whose windows look into the New Jerusalem! Many believers are content to live like men in the coal mines, who do not see the sun. They eat dust like the serpent, when they could taste the heavenly food of angels. They are content to wear miners' clothes, when they could put on royal robes. Tears mar their faces, when they could anoint them with heavenly oil. I am convinced that many believers languish in the dungeon when they could walk on the palace roof and view the *"goodly mountain, and Lebanon"* (Deut. 3:25). Rouse yourself, O believer, from your low condition! Cast away your sloth, your lethargy, your coldness, or whatever interferes with your spotless and pure love for Christ, your soul's Husband. Make Him the source, the center, and the circumference of your soul's entire range of delight. What beguiles you into such folly that you remain in a pit when you may sit on a throne? Do not live in the lowlands of bondage now that mountain liberty has been conferred on you. Do not be satisfied any longer with your dwarfish attainments, but press forward to more sublime and heavenly things. Aspire to a higher, nobler, and fuller life. Upward to heaven! Nearer to God!

When will You come to me, Lord?
Oh, come, my Lord most dear!
Come near, come nearer, nearer still,
I'm blessed when You are near.

The glorious LORD *will be unto us a place*
of broad rivers and streams.
—Isaiah 33:21

Broad *rivers and streams"* produce fertility and abundance in the land. Places near broad rivers are remarkable for the variety of their plants and their plentiful harvests. God is all this to His church. Having God, she has abundance. What can she ask for that He will not give her? What need can she mention that He will not supply? *"In this mountain shall the* LORD *of hosts make unto all people a feast of fat things"* (Isa. 25:6). Do you want the bread of life? It drops like manna from the sky. Do you want refreshing streams? The rock follows you, and that Rock is Christ. If you suffer any lack, it is your own fault. If you are suffering any deficiency, you are not deficient in Him, but in your own hearts. Broad rivers and streams also point to commerce. Our glorious Lord is to us a place of heavenly merchandise. Through our Redeemer, we have commerce with the past; the wealth of Calvary, the treasures of the covenant, the riches of the ancient days of election, and the stores of eternity all come to us down the broad stream of our gracious Lord. We have commerce, too, with the future. What boats, laden to the water's edge, come to us from the Millennium! What visions we have of the days of heaven on earth! Through our glorious Lord, we have commerce with angels and communion with the bright spirits washed in His blood, who sing before the throne. Better still, we have fellowship with the Infinite One. Broad rivers and streams are especially intended to set forth the idea of security. Rivers were a defense in the past. Beloved, what a defense God is to His church! The devil cannot cross this broad river of God. How he wishes he could turn the current, but do not fear, for God abides immutably the same. Satan may worry, but he cannot destroy us. No boat with oars will invade our river; neither will stately ships pass thereby.

Yet a little sleep, a little slumber, a little folding of the hands to sleep:
so shall thy poverty come as one that travelleth;
and thy want as an armed man.
—Proverbs 24:33–34

The worst of sluggards only ask for a *"little slumber."* They would be indignant if they were accused of thorough idleness. *"A little folding of the hands to sleep"* is all they crave, and they have a crowd of reasons to show that this indulgence is a very proper one. Yet by these "littles," the day goes by. The time for labor is all gone, and the field is grown over with thorns. It is by little procrastinations that people ruin their souls. They have no intention of delaying for years. They think a few months will bring a more convenient season. Tomorrow they will attend to serious things; but the present hour is so busy, and so altogether unsuitable, that they beg to be excused. Like sands from an hourglass, time slips by. Life is wasted one drop at a time, and seasons of grace are lost by "little slumbers." Oh, to be wise, to catch the hurrying hour, to use the moments that are flying by! May the Lord teach us this sacred wisdom. Otherwise, a poverty of the worst sort awaits us—eternal poverty—in which we will desire just one drop of water, though we will beg for it in vain. Like a traveler steadily pursuing his journey, poverty overtakes the lazy, and ruin overthrows the undecided. Each hour brings the dreaded pursuer nearer. He does not pause along the way, for he is on his master's business and must not delay. As an armed man enters with authority and power, poverty will come to the idle, and death to the unrepentant, and there will be no escape. Oh, if only men would be wise in good season, and would seek the Lord Jesus diligently before the solemn Day dawns. Then it will be too late to plow and sow, too late to repent and believe. In harvest, it is useless to mourn that seedtime was neglected. Faith and holy decision are sill timely. May we obtain them this night.

To preach deliverance to the captives.
—Luke 4:18

No one but Jesus can give deliverance to the captives. Real liberty comes only from Him. It is a liberty righteously bestowed; for the Son, who is Heir of all things, has a right to make men free. The saints honor the justice of God, which now secures their salvation. It is a liberty that has been dearly purchased. Christ speaks it by His power, but He bought it by His blood. He makes you free, but it is by His own bonds. You go clear, because He bore your burden for you. You are set at liberty, because He has suffered in your place. But, though dearly purchased, He freely gives it. Jesus asks nothing of us as a preparation for this liberty. He finds us sitting in sackcloth and ashes and invites us to put on the beautiful array of freedom. He saves us just as we are, and all without our help or merit. When Jesus sets free, the liberty is perpetually given; no chains can bind again. Let the Master say to me, "Captive, I have delivered you," and it is done forever. Satan may plot to enslave us, but if the Lord is on our side, whom will we fear? The world, with its temptations, may seek to ensnare us, but mightier is He who is for us than all they who are against us. *"If God be for us, who can be against us?"* (Rom. 8:31). The schemes of our own deceitful hearts may harass and annoy us, but *"he which hath begun a good work"* (Phil. 1:6) in us will carry it on and perfect it to the end. The foes of God and the enemies of man may gather their hosts together and come with concentrated fury against us, but if God acquits, *"who is he that condemneth?"* (Rom. 8:34). The eagle that mounts to his rocky nest, and afterward outsoars the clouds, is not any freer than the soul that Christ has delivered. If we are no more under the law, but free from its curse, let our liberty be practically exhibited in our serving God with gratitude and delight. *"I am thy servant, and the son of thine handmaid: thou hast loosed my bonds"* (Ps. 116:16). *"Lord, what wilt thou have me to do?"* (Acts 9:6).

For he saith to Moses, I will have mercy on whom I will have mercy,
and I will have compassion on whom I will have compassion.
—Romans 9:15

With these words, the Lord clearly claims the right to give or withhold His mercy, according to His own sovereign will. As the prerogative of life and death is vested in the monarch, so the Judge of all the earth has a right to spare or condemn the guilty, as seems best in His sight. By their sins, men have forfeited all their claims on God. They deserve to perish for their sins, and if they all do so, they have no grounds for complaint. If the Lord steps in to save any, He may do so if the purposes of justice are not thwarted. However, if He judges that it is best to allow the condemned to suffer the righteous sentence, they may not arraign Him at their own court of opinion. Foolish and impudent are the discourses that say that all men have a right to be placed on the same footing. Ignorant, if not worse, are the contentions against discriminating grace, which are only the rebellion of proud human nature against the crown and scepter of Jehovah. When we understand our own utter ruin, that we are deserving of punishment, and the justice of the divine verdict against sin, we no longer quibble at the truth that the Lord is not obligated to save us. We do not complain if He chooses to save others, as though He were doing us an injury. Instead, we feel that if He graciously looks upon us, it will be His own free act of goodness, undeserved on our part, for which we will forever bless His name. How will those who are the subjects of divine election sufficiently adore the grace of God? They have no room for boasting, for sovereignty most effectively excludes it. The Lord's will alone is glorified, and the very notion of human merit is cast out to everlasting contempt. There is no more humbling doctrine in Scripture than that of election, none that promotes more gratitude, and, consequently, none more sanctifying. Believers should not be afraid of it, but rejoice in it with adoration.

Whatsoever thy hand findeth to do, do it with thy might.
—Ecclesiastes 9:10

Whatsoever thy hand findeth to do" refers to works that are possible. There are many things that our hearts find to do that we will never do. It is well it is in our hearts, but if we would be eminently useful, we must not be content with forming schemes in our hearts and talking about them. We must practically carry out whatever our hands find to do. One good deed is worth more than a thousand brilliant theories. Let us not wait for large opportunities or for different kinds of work, but do the things that we find to do day by day. We have no other time in which to live. The past is gone; the future has not arrived. We will never have any time but the present. Then do not wait until your experience has ripened into maturity before you attempt to serve God. Endeavor now to bring forth fruit. Serve God now, but be careful as to the way in which you perform what you find to do—*"do it with thy might."* Do it promptly. Do not fritter away your life in thinking of what you intend to do tomorrow, as if that could make up for the idleness of today. No man ever served God by doing things tomorrow. If we honor Christ and are blessed, it is by the things that we do today. Whatever you do for Christ, throw your whole soul into it. Do not give Christ a little shoddy labor, done as a matter of course now and then. When you serve Him, do it with your heart, soul, and strength. But where is the might of a Christian? It is not in himself, for he is perfect weakness. His strength lies in the Lord of Hosts. Then let us seek His help; let us proceed with prayer and faith, and when we have done what our *"hand findeth to do,"* let us wait on the Lord for His blessing. What we do thus will be well done and will not fail in its purpose.

They shall rejoice, and shall see the plummet in the hand of Zerubbabel.
—Zechariah 4:10

Small things" (Zech. 4:10) marked the beginning of the work in the "*hand of Zerubbabel*," the work of rebuilding the temple in Jerusalem. Yet no one could despise these "*small things*," for the Lord had raised up one who would persevere until the capstone could be brought forth with shouts (v. 7). The "*plummet*" or plumb line was in good hands. Spiritually, this is a comfort to every believer in the Lord Jesus. Even if the work of grace is very small in its beginnings, the plumb line is in good hands, for a Master Builder greater than Solomon has undertaken the building of the heavenly temple. He "*shall not fail nor be discouraged*" (Isa. 42:4) until the topmost pinnacle is raised. If the plumb line were in the hand of a mere human being, we might worry about the building. However, "*the pleasure of the* Lord *shall prosper*" (Isa. 53:10) in Jesus' hand. The work of rebuilding the temple did not proceed irregularly, and without care, for the overseer's hand carried a good instrument. If the walls had been constructed hurriedly, without due supervision, they might not have been built completely upright. Yet the plumb line was used by the chosen overseer. Similarly, Jesus is continuously watching over the construction of His spiritual temple, so that it may be built securely and well. We are for haste, but Jesus is for judgment. He will use the plumb line, and what is out of line must come down, every stone of it. This is why many promising works have failed and many glittering professions of faith have fallen by the wayside. It is not for us to judge the Lord's church, since Jesus has a steady hand and a true eye, and can use the plumb line well. Do we not rejoice that judgment is left to Him? The "*plummet*" was in active use—it was in the builder's hand, a sure indication that he meant to push forward with the work to completion. O Lord Jesus, how we would indeed be glad if we could see You at Your great work. O Zion the beautiful, your walls are still in ruins! Rise, glorious Builder, and make her ruins rejoice at Your coming.

Joshua the high priest standing before the angel of the LORD.
—Zechariah 3:1

In Joshua, the high priest, we see a picture of each and every child of God who has been *"made nigh by the blood of Christ"* (Eph. 2:13) and has been taught to minister in holy things and enter into that which is within the veil. Jesus has made us *"kings and priests unto God"* (Rev. 1:6), and even here on earth, we exercise the priesthood of consecrated living and hallowed service. But this high priest is said to be *"standing before the angel of the LORD,"* that is, standing to minister. This should be the perpetual position of every true believer. Every place is now God's temple, and His people can as truly serve Him in their daily employment as in His house. They are always to be ministering, offering the spiritual sacrifice of prayer and praise and presenting themselves a *"living sacrifice"* (Rom. 12:1). But notice where it is that Joshua stands to minister; it is before the angel of Jehovah. It is only through a mediator that we poor, defiled ones can ever become priests unto God. I present what I have before the messenger, the Angel of the covenant, the Lord Jesus. Through Him, my prayers find acceptance wrapped up in His prayers; my praises become sweet as they are bound up with bundles of myrrh, aloe, and cassia from Christ's own garden. If I can bring Him nothing but my tears, He will put them with His own tears in His own bottle, for He once wept. If I can bring Him nothing but my groans and sighs, He will accept these as an acceptable sacrifice, for He once was broken in heart, and sighed heavily in spirit. I myself, standing in Him, am *"accepted in the beloved"* (Eph. 1:6); and all my polluted works, though in themselves only objects of divine abhorrence, are received so that God smells a sweet savor. He is content, and I am blessed. See, then, the position of the Christian—a *"priest standing before the angel of the LORD."*

The forgiveness of sins, according to the riches of his grace.
—Ephesians 1:7

Can there be a sweeter word in any language than the word *"forgiveness,"* when it spoken in a guilty sinner's ear? It is like the silver notes of jubilee to the captive Israelite. May the dear star of pardon, which shines into the cells of the condemned, and gives the perishing a gleam of hope amid the midnight of despair, be forever blessed! Is it possible that sin, sin such as mine, can be forgiven—forgiven altogether and forever? Hell is my portion as a sinner. There is no possibility of my escaping from it while sin remains upon me. Can the load of guilt be lifted, the crimson stain removed? Can the impenetrable stones of my prison ever be loosed from their mortises, or the doors be lifted from their hinges? Jesus tells me that I can be blameless. Forever blessed is the revelation of atoning love, which tells me not only that pardon is possible, but also that it is secured to all who rest in Jesus. I have believed in the appointed propitiation, even Jesus, who was crucified. Therefore my sins are, at this moment and forever, forgiven by virtue of His substitutionary pains and death. What joy this forgiveness brings! How blissful it is to be a perfectly pardoned soul! I dedicate all that I am to Him who, out of His own love—unearned by me—became my Surety and worked redemption for me through His blood. What riches of grace free forgiveness exhibits! To forgive at all, to forgive fully, to forgive freely, to forgive forever—there is a constellation of wonders in this forgiveness. When I think about how great my sins were, how dear the precious drops of blood were that cleansed me from them, and how gracious the method was by which pardon was sealed for me, I am overcome with marveling, worshipping affection. I bow before the throne that absolves me, and I clasp the cross that delivers me. For the rest of my life, I will serve the Incarnate God, through whom I am a pardoned soul tonight.

*For I rejoiced greatly, when the brethren came and testified of the
truth that is in thee, even as thou walkest in the truth.*
—3 John 3

The truth was in Gaius, and Gaius walked in the truth. If the first had
not been the case, the second could never have occurred; and if the second
could not have been said of him, the first would have been a mere pretense.
Truth must enter into the soul, penetrate and saturate it, or else it is of
no value. Doctrines held as a matter of creed are like bread in the hand,
which ministers no nourishment to the frame. But doctrine accepted by
the heart is as digested food, which, by assimilation, sustains and builds up
the body. In us truth must be a living force, an active energy, an indwelling
reality, a part of the essence of our being. If it is in us, we cannot part with
it. A man may lose his clothes or his limbs, but his inward parts are vital
and cannot be torn away without absolute loss of life. A Christian can die,
but he cannot deny the truth. Now it is a rule of nature that the inward
affects the outward, as light shines from the center of the lantern through
the glass. When, therefore, the truth is kindled within, its brightness soon
shines forth in the outward life and conversation. It is said that the food of
certain worms colors the cocoons of silk that they spin. In the same way,
the nutriment on which a man's inward nature lives gives a tinge to every
word and deed proceeding from him. To walk in the truth signifies a life
of integrity, holiness, faithfulness, and simplicity—the natural product of
those principles of truth that the Gospel teaches and that the Spirit of God
enables us to receive. We may judge of the secrets of the soul by their manifestation in the man's conversation. Be it ours today, O gracious Spirit, to
be ruled and governed by Your divine authority, so that nothing false or
sinful may reign in our hearts, lest it extend its malignant influence to our
daily walk among men.

Seeking the wealth of his people.
—Esther 10:3

Mordecai was a true patriot. Therefore, when he was exalted to the highest position under King Ahasuerus, he used his position to promote the prosperity of Israel. In this, he was a type of Jesus, who, upon His throne of glory, does not seek His own interests, but expends His power for His people. It would be a good thing if every Christian were a Mordecai to the church, striving, according to his ability, for its prosperity. Some believers have been placed in positions of affluence and influence. Let them honor their Lord in the high places of the earth, and testify for Jesus before great men. Others have what is far better, namely, close fellowship with the King of Kings. Let them be sure to plead daily for the weak among the Lord's people—the doubting, the tempted, and the comfortless. It will be to their honor if they intercede much for those who are in darkness and who do not dare to draw near to the mercy seat. Believers who are knowledgeable in the things of God may serve their Master greatly if they use their talents for the general good, and impart their wealth of heavenly learning to others by teaching them the things of God. Even the least person in the body of Christ may *seek* the welfare of his people. His desire, if he can give no more, will be acceptable. The most Christlike, as well as the happiest, way for a believer to live is to cease from living for himself. He who blesses others cannot fail to be blessed himself. On the other hand, seeking our own personal greatness is a wicked and unhappy way of life. Its way will be grievous, and its end will be fatal. Now is the time to ask you, my friend, whether you are, to the best of your ability, seeking the wealth of the church in your neighborhood. I trust you are not doing it harm by bitterness and scandal, or weakening it by neglect. Friend, unite with the Lord's poor, bear their cross, do them all the good you can, and you will not miss your reward.

*Thou shalt not go up and down as a talebearer among
thy people….Thou shalt in any wise rebuke thy neighbour,
and not suffer sin upon him.*
—Leviticus 19:16–17

Talebearing emits a threefold poison: it injures the teller, the hearer, and the person concerning whom the tale is told. Whether the report is true or false, we are forbidden by this precept of God's Word to spread it. The reputations of the Lord's people should be very precious in our sight, and we should be ashamed to help the devil to dishonor the church and the name of the Lord. Some tongues need a bridle rather than a spur. Many glory in pulling down their brethren, as if thereby they raised themselves. Noah's wise sons cast a mantle over their father, and he who exposed him earned a fearful curse. We may ourselves one of these dark days need forbearance and silence from our brethren, so let us render it cheerfully to those who require it now. Let this be our family rule and our personal bond: Speak no evil of any man.

The Holy Spirit, however, permits us to censure sin and prescribes the way in which we are to do it. It must be done by rebuking our brother to his face, not by railing behind his back. This course is manly, brotherly, Christlike, and under God's blessing will be useful. Does the flesh shrink from it? Then we must lay greater stress on our consciences and keep ourselves to the work, lest by accepting our friend's sin, we ourselves become partakers of it. Hundreds have been saved from gross sins by the timely, wise, affectionate warnings of faithful ministers and friends. Our Lord Jesus has given us a gracious example of how to deal with erring friends in His warning given to Peter, the prayer with which He preceded it, and the gentle way in which He bore with Peter's boastful denial that he needed such a caution.

Spices for anointing oil.
—Exodus 35:8

Much use was made of anointing oil under the law, and what it represents is of primary importance under the Gospel. The Holy Spirit, who anoints us for all holy service, is indispensable to us if we want to serve the Lord acceptably. Without His aid, our religious service is just an empty offering, and our inward experience is dead. Whenever the ministry of the church lacks anointing, it becomes a miserable thing—and when individual Christians lack anointing, their prayers, praises, meditations, and efforts aren't any better. A holy anointing is the life and soul of piety. Its absence is the most grievous of all calamities. Going before the Lord without anointing is the equivalent of a common Levite in Old Testament times thrusting himself into the office of priest. In such a situation, his ministering would have been sin rather than service. May we never undertake holy service without sacred anointing. Sacred anointing comes upon us from our glorious Head. From His anointing, we who are as the *"skirts of his garments"* (Ps. 133:2) partake of a plentiful anointing. Choice spices were skillfully mixed to form the anointing oil, to show us how rich all the influences of the Holy Spirit are. All good things are found in the divine Comforter. Matchless comfort, infallible instruction, immortal quickening, spiritual energy, and divine sanctification all lie compounded with other excellencies in that sacred ointment, the heavenly anointing oil of the Holy Spirit. It imparts a delightful fragrance to the character and person of the one on whom it is poured. Nothing like it can be found in all the treasuries of the rich or the secrets of the wise. It cannot be imitated. It comes from God alone, and is freely given through Jesus Christ to every waiting soul. Let us seek it, for we may have it—we may have it this very evening! O Lord, anoint Your servants.

*And Amaziah said to the man of God, But what shall we do
for the hundred talents which I have given to the army of Israel? And
the man of God answered, The LORD is able
to give thee much more than this.*
—2 Chronicles 25:9

This seemed to be a very important question to the king of Judah, and possibly it is of even more weight with the tried and tempted Christian. To lose money is at no times pleasant, and when a principle is involved, the flesh is not always ready to make the sacrifice. "Why lose that which may be so useful to us? May not the truth itself be bought at too costly a price? What will we do without it? Remember the children and our small income!" All these things and a thousand more would tempt the Christian to put forth his hand to unrighteous gain or keep him from carrying out his conscientious convictions, when they involve serious loss. All men cannot view these matters in the light of faith; and even with the followers of Jesus, the doctrine of "we must live" has quite sufficient weight. "The Lord is able to give you much more than this" is a very satisfactory answer to the anxious question. Our Father holds the purse strings, and what we lose for His sake, He can repay a thousandfold. It is ours to obey His will, and we may rest assured that He will provide for us. The Lord will be no man's debtor at the last. Saints know that a grain of heart's rest is of more value than a ton of gold. He who wraps a threadbare coat about a good conscience has gained a spiritual wealth far more desirable than any he has lost. God's smile and a dungeon are enough for a true heart; His frown and a palace would be hell to a gracious spirit. Let the worst come to the worst, let all talents go, and we still have not lost our treasure, for that is above, where Christ sits at the right hand of God. Meanwhile, even now, the Lord makes the meek to *"inherit the earth"* (Matt. 5:5), and *"no good thing will he withhold from them that walk uprightly"* (Ps. 84:11).

Michael and his angels fought against the dragon;
and the dragon fought and his angels.
—Revelation 12:7

War will always rage between the two great kingdoms until one or the other is crushed. Peace between good and evil is an impossibility. In fact, the very pretense of it would mean the triumph of the powers of darkness. The archangel Michael will always fight. His holy soul is distressed with sin, and will not endure it. Jesus will always be the dragon's foe—not in a quiet sense, but actively, vigorously, and with full determination to exterminate evil. All His servants, whether angels in heaven or messengers on earth, will and must fight. Believers are born to be warriors. At the cross, they enter into covenant never to make a truce with evil. They are warlike—firm in defense and fierce in attack. The duty of every soldier in the army of the Lord is to fight against the dragon daily, with all his heart, soul, and strength. The dragon and his angels will not decline to fight. They are incessant in their onslaughts, sparing no weapon, fair or foul. We are foolish to expect to serve God without opposition from the enemy. The more zealous we are, the surer we are to be assailed by the followers of hell. The church may become lazy, but this is not the case with her great antagonist. His restless spirit never allows the war to pause. He hates the woman's seed (see Genesis 3:15) and would gladly devour the church if he could. The servants of Satan have much of the old dragon's energy and are usually active. War rages everywhere, and to dream of peace is dangerous and futile. Glory be to God, we know the outcome of the war! The great dragon will be cast out and destroyed forever, while Jesus and those who are with Him will receive the crown. Tonight, let us sharpen our swords and ask the Holy Spirit to strengthen our arms for the conflict. Never was there a more important battle; never was there a more glorious crown. Every soldier to his post, warriors of the Cross, and may the Lord *"bruise Satan under your feet shortly"* (Rom. 16:20)!

DECEMBER 1
Morning

Thou hast made summer and winter.
—Psalm 74:17

My soul, begin this wintry month with your God. The cold snows and the piercing winds both remind you that He keeps His covenant with day and night, and they tend to assure you that He will also keep that glorious covenant that He has made with you in the person of Christ Jesus. He who is true to His word in the revolutions of the seasons of this poor, sin-polluted world will not prove unfaithful in His dealings with His own well-beloved Son. Winter in the soul is by no means a comfortable season, and if it is on you just now, it will be very painful to you. But there is this comfort: namely, that the Lord makes it. He sends the sharp blasts of adversity to nip the buds of expectation. He scatters the frost like ashes over the once verdant meadows of our joy. He casts forth His ice like morsels freezing the streams of our delight. He does it all. He is the great King of winter, and He rules in the realms of frost; therefore, you cannot complain. Losses, crosses, heaviness, sickness, poverty, and a thousand other ills are of the Lord's sending, and they come to us with wise design. Frost kills deadly insects and limits raging diseases; it breaks up the clods and sweetens the soul. Oh, that such good results would always follow our winters of affliction! How we prize the fire just now! How pleasant is its cheerful glow! Let us prize our Lord in the same manner, who is the constant source of warmth and comfort in every time of trouble. Let us draw near to Him and find joy and peace in believing. Let us wrap ourselves in the warm garments of His promises and go forth to labors that are appropriate to the season. To be like the sluggard who will not plough because of the cold will result in severe consequences, for he will have to beg even in the summer and will have nothing.

DECEMBER 1

Oh that men would praise the Lord *for his goodness, and for his*
wonderful works to the children of men!
—Psalm 107:8

If we complained less and praised more, we would be happier, and God would be more glorified. Let us daily praise God for common mercies— common as we frequently call them, yet so priceless that, when deprived of them, we are ready to perish. Let us bless God for the eyes with which we behold the sun, for the health and strength to walk around, for the bread we eat, for the clothing we wear. Let us praise Him that we are not cast out among the hopeless or confined among the guilty. Let us thank Him for liberty, for friends, for family, and for comforts. Let us praise Him, in fact, for everything that we receive from His bounteous hand; for we deserve little, yet we are abundantly endowed. But, beloved, the sweetest and the loudest note in our songs of praise should be of redeeming love. God's redeeming acts toward His chosen are forever the favorite themes of their praise. If we know what redemption means, let us not withhold our sonnets of thanksgiving. We have been redeemed from the power of our corruptions, uplifted from the depth of sin in which we were naturally plunged. We have been led to the cross of Christ. Our shackles of guilt have been broken; we are no longer slaves, but children of the living God. We can anticipate the time when we will be presented before the throne without *"spot, or wrinkle, or any such thing"* (Eph. 5:27). Even now by faith we wave the palm branch and wrap ourselves about with the fair linen that is to be our everlasting array. Will we not unceasingly give thanks to the Lord our Redeemer? Child of God, can you be silent? Awake, awake, inheritors of glory, and lead your *"captivity captive"* (Ps. 68:18), as you cry with David, *"Bless the* Lord, *O my soul: and all that is within me, bless his holy name"* (Ps. 103:1). Let the new month begin with new songs.

Thou art all fair, my love.
—Song of Solomon 4:7

The Lord's admiration of His church is wonderful, and His description of her beauty is glowing. She is not merely fair, but *"all fair."* He views her in Himself, washed in His sin-atoning blood and clothed in His meritorious righteousness. He considers her to be full of comeliness and beauty. No wonder that such is the case, since it is but His own perfect excellency that He admires. The holiness, glory, and perfection of His church are His own glorious garments on the back of His own well-beloved spouse. She is not simply pure or well-proportioned; she is positively lovely and fair! She has actual merit! Her deformities of sin are removed. In addition, she has, through her Lord, obtained a meritorious righteousness by which an actual beauty is conferred on her. Believers have a positive righteousness given to them when they become *"accepted in the beloved"* (Eph. 1:6). Nor is the church merely lovely; she is superlatively so. Her Lord calls her *"fairest among women"* (Song 1:8). She has real worth and excellence that cannot be rivaled by all the nobility and royalty of the world. If Jesus could exchange His elect bride for all the queens and empresses of earth, or even for the angels in heaven, He would not, for He puts her first and foremost—*"fairest among women."* Like the moon, she far outshines the stars. Nor is this an opinion that He is ashamed of, for He invites all people to hear it. He sets a *"behold"* before it, a special note of exclamation, inviting and arresting attention. *"Behold, thou art fair, my love; behold, thou art fair"* (Song 4:1). He publishes His opinion abroad even now, and one day from the throne of His glory, He will declare the truth of it before the assembled universe. *"Come, ye blessed of my Father"* (Matt. 25:34) will be His solemn affirmation of the loveliness of His elect.

Behold, all is vanity.
—Ecclesiastes 1:14

Nothing can satisfy the entire man but the Lord's love and the Lord's own self. Saints have tried to anchor in other harbors, but they have been driven out of such deadly refuges. Solomon, the wisest of men, was permitted to make experiments for us all, and to do for us what we must not dare to do for ourselves. Here is his testimony in his own words: *"So I was great, and increased more than all that were before me in Jerusalem: also my wisdom remained with me. And whatsoever mine eyes desired I kept not from them, I withheld not my heart from any joy; for my heart rejoiced in all my labour: and this was my portion of all my labour. Then I looked on all the works that my hands had wrought, and on the labour that I had laboured to do: and, behold, all was vanity and vexation of spirit, and there was no profit under the sun"* (Eccl. 2:9–11). *"Vanity of vanities; all is vanity"* (Eccl. 1:2). What! The whole of it is vanity? O favored monarch, is there nothing in all your wealth? Nothing in that wide dominion reaching from the river even to the sea? Nothing in your glorious palaces? Nothing in the house of the forest of Lebanon? Is there nothing in all your music and dancing, and wine and luxury? "Nothing," he answers, "but weariness of spirit." This was his verdict when he had traveled the whole globe of pleasure. To embrace our Lord Jesus, to dwell in His love, and to be fully assured of union with Him—this is all in all. Dear reader, you do not need to try other forms of life in order to see whether they are better than the Christian's. If you roam the world over, you will see no sights like the sight of the Savior's face. If you could have all the comforts of life, but you lost your Savior, you would be wretched. But if you win Christ, then even if you rotted away in a dungeon, you would find it a paradise. If you lived in obscurity or died from starvation, you would still be satisfied with favor and be full of the goodness of the Lord.

There is no spot in thee.
—Song of Solomon 4:7

Having pronounced His church positively full of beauty, our Lord confirms His praise by a precious negative, *"There is no spot in thee."* It is as if the thought occurred to the Bridegroom that the critical world would insinuate that He had only mentioned her comely parts and had purposely omitted those features that were deformed or defiled. He sums up all by declaring her universally and entirely fair and utterly devoid of stain. A spot may soon be removed; it is the very least thing that can disfigure beauty. But even from this little blemish, the believer is delivered in his Lord's sight. If He had said there is no hideous scar, no horrible deformity, no deadly ulcer, we might have marveled even then; but when He testifies that she is free from the slightest spot, all these other forms of defilement are included, and the depth of wonder is increased. If He had but promised to remove all spots by and by, we would have had eternal reason for joy; but when He speaks of it as already done, who can restrain the most intense emotions of satisfaction and delight? My soul, here is *"marrow and fatness"* (Ps. 63:5) for you; eat your full, and be satisfied with royal delicacies. Christ Jesus has no quarrel with His spouse. She often wanders from Him and grieves His Holy Spirit, but He does not allow her faults to affect His love. He sometimes chides, but it is always in the tenderest manner, with the kindest intentions: it is *"my love"* (Song 4:1), even then. There is no remembrance of our wrongdoing. He does not cherish evil thoughts of us, but He pardons and loves as well after the offense as before it. His forgiveness is beneficial to us, for if Jesus were as mindful of injuries as we are, how could He commune with us? Many times a believer will put himself out of sorts with the Lord for some slight turn in providence, but our precious Husband knows our silly hearts too well to take any offense at our bad manners.

DECEMBER 3

Evening

The LORD mighty in battle.
—Psalm 24:8

God is glorious in the eyes of His people, seeing that He has worked such wonders for them, in them, and by them. For them, the Lord Jesus on Calvary dispelled every foe, breaking all the weapons of the enemy in pieces by His finished work of satisfactory obedience. By His triumphant resurrection and ascension, He completely overturned the hopes of hell, leading *"captivity captive"* (Ps. 68:18), making an open show of our enemies, triumphing over them by His Cross. Every arrow of guilt that Satan might have shot at us is broken, for *"who shall lay any thing to the charge of God's elect"* (Rom. 8:33)? Vain are the sharp swords of infernal malice and the perpetual battles of the serpent's seed, for in the midst of the church, the lame take the prey, and the feeblest warriors are crowned. The saved may well adore their Lord for His conquests in them, since the arrows of their natural hatred are snapped, and the weapons of their rebellion are broken. What victories grace has won in our evil hearts! How glorious Jesus is when the will is subdued and sin is dethroned! As for our remaining corruptions, they will sustain an equally sure defeat; every temptation, doubt, and fear will be utterly destroyed. In the Salem of our peaceful hearts, the name of Jesus is great beyond comparison. He has won our love, and He will wear it. Secure in His love, we may expect to be victorious. *"We are more than conquerors through him that loved us"* (v. 37). By our faith, zeal, and holiness, we will cast down the powers of darkness that are in the world. We will win sinners to Jesus, we will overturn false systems, and we will convert nations; for God is with us, and none will stand before us. This evening let the Christian warrior chant the war song and prepare for tomorrow's fight. *"Greater is he that is in [us], than he that is in the world"* (1 John 4:4).

DECEMBER 4

Morning

I have much people in this city.
—Acts 18:10

Today's text should be a great encouragement to try to do good, since God has among the vilest of the vile, the most reprobate, the most debauched and drunken, an elect people who must be saved. When you take the Word to them, you do so because God has ordained you to be the messenger of life to their souls, and they must receive it, for so the decree of predestination runs. They are as much redeemed by blood as the saints before the eternal throne. They are Christ's property, and yet, perhaps, they are lovers of the tavern and haters of holiness; but if Jesus Christ purchased them, He will have them. God is not unfaithful to forget the price that His Son has paid. He will not suffer His substitution to be in any case an ineffective, dead thing. Tens of thousands of redeemed ones are not regenerated yet, but regenerated they must be. This is our comfort when we go forth to them with the quickening Word of God. Even more, these ungodly ones are prayed for by Christ before the throne. *"Neither pray I for these alone,"* said the great Intercessor, *"but for them also which shall believe on me through their word"* (John 17:20). Poor, ignorant souls, they know nothing about prayer for themselves, but Jesus prays for them. Their names are on His breastplate, and before long, they must bow their stubborn knee, breathing the penitential sigh before the throne of grace. *"The time of figs [is] not yet"* (Mark 11:13). The predestined moment has not struck; but, when it comes, they will obey, for God will have His own. They must, for the Spirit is not to be resisted when He comes forth with fullness of power. They must become the willing servants of the living God. My people *"shall be willing in the day of [My] power"* (Ps. 110:3). *"He shall see of the travail of his soul, and shall...justify many"* (Isa. 53:11). *"I will divide him a portion with the great, and he shall divide the spoil with the strong"* (v. 12).

*Even we ourselves groan within ourselves, waiting
for the adoption, to wit, the redemption of our body.*
—Romans 8:23

This groaning is universal among the saints; we all feel it to a greater or lesser extent. It is not the groan of murmuring or complaint; it is the note of desire rather than of distress. Having received a down payment, we desire the whole of our portion. We are yearning for the day when our entire personhood—in its trinity of spirit, soul, and body—may be set free from the last vestige of the Fall. We long to put off corruption, weakness, and dishonor and to wrap ourselves in incorruption, in immortality, in glory, in the spiritual body that the Lord Jesus will bestow upon His people. We long for the manifestation of our adoption as the children of God. We groan, but it is *"within ourselves."* It is not the hypocrite's groan, by which he would make men believe that he is a saint because he is wretched. Our sighs are sacred things, too hallowed for us to express. We keep our longings to our Lord alone. Then the apostle said that we are *"waiting,"* by which we learn that we are not to be petulant, like Jonah or Elijah, when they said, "Let me die." Neither are we to whimper and sigh for the end of life because we are tired of work. Nor should we wish to escape from our present sufferings until the will of the Lord is done. We are to groan for glorification, but we are to wait patiently for it, knowing that what the Lord appoints is best. Waiting implies being ready. We are to stand at the door, expecting the Beloved to open it and take us away to Himself. This *"groaning"* is a test. You may judge a man by what he groans after. Some men groan after wealth—they worship money. Some groan continually under the troubles of life; they are merely impatient. But the man who sighs after God, who is uneasy until he is made like Christ, that is the blessed man. May God help us to groan for the coming of the Lord and the resurrection that He will bring to us.

Ask, and it shall be given you.
—Matthew 7:7

I know of a place in England where a ration of bread was served to every passerby who chose to ask for it. Whoever the traveler was, he had only to knock at the door of St. Cross Hospital, and there was a portion of bread for him. Jesus Christ so loves sinners that He has built a St. Cross Hospital, so that whenever a sinner is hungry, he has only to knock and have his needs supplied. No, He has done better. He has attached to this Hospital of the Cross a bath; whenever a soul is black and filthy, he has but to go there and be washed. The fountain is always full, always efficacious. No sinner ever went into it and found that it could not wash away his stains. Sins that were scarlet and crimson have all disappeared, and the sinner has been made whiter than snow. As if this were not enough, there is attached to this Hospital of the Cross a wardrobe, and a sinner making application simply as a sinner may be clothed from head to foot. If he wishes to be a soldier, he may not merely have clothes for ordinary wear, but armor, which will cover him from the sole of his foot to the crown of his head. If he asks for a sword, he will have that given to him, and a shield, too. Nothing that is good for him will be denied him. He will have spending money as long as he lives, and he will have an eternal heritage of glorious treasure when he enters into the joy of his Lord. If all these things are to be had by merely knocking at mercy's door, O my soul, knock hard this morning. Ask largely of your generous Lord. Do not leave the throne of grace until all your needs have been spread before the Lord, and until by faith you have a comforting assurance that they will all be supplied. No bashfulness should hold you back when Jesus invites. No unbelief should hinder when Jesus promises. No coldheartedness should restrain when such blessings are to be obtained.

DECEMBER 5

Evening

And the Lord showed me four carpenters.
—Zechariah 1:20

In the vision described in this chapter, the prophet saw four terrible horns. They were pushing this way and that way, dashing down the strongest and the mightiest. The prophet asked, *"What be these?"* (Zech. 1:19). The answer was, *"These are the horns which have scattered Judah, Israel, and Jerusalem"* (v. 19). He saw before him a representation of those powers that had oppressed the church of God. There were four horns, for the church is attacked from all quarters. Well might the prophet have felt dismayed, but suddenly there appeared before him four carpenters. He asked, *"What come these to do?"* (v. 21). These are the men whom God has found to break those horns in pieces. God will always find men for His work, and He will find them at the right time. The prophet did not see the carpenters first, when there was nothing to do; he first saw the horns, then the carpenters. Moreover, the Lord finds enough men. He did not find three carpenters, but four; there were four horns, so there needed to be four workmen. God finds the right men—not four men with pens to write, not four architects to draw plans, but four carpenters to do rough work. Rest assured, you who tremble for the ark of God, that when the *"horns"* grow troublesome, the *"carpenters"* will be found. You do not need to fret concerning the weakness of the church of God at any moment; there may be growing up in obscurity the valiant reformer who will shake the nations. Church fathers like John Chrysostom or Augustine may come forth from our lowliest schools or from the thickest darkness of London's poverty. The Lord knows where to find His servants. He has in ambush a multitude of mighty men. At His word they will move to the battle; *"for the battle is the Lord's"* (1 Sam. 17:47), and He will win for Himself the victory. Let us remain faithful to Christ, and He, in the right time, will raise up for us a defense, whether it is in the day of our personal need or in the season of peril to His church.

DECEMBER 6

As is the heavenly, such are they also that are heavenly.
—1 Corinthians 15:48

The Head and members of the body of Christ are of one nature, and not like that monstrous image that Nebuchadnezzar saw in his dream. Its head was of fine gold, but the belly and thighs were of brass, the legs of iron, and the feet were part iron and part clay. Christ's mystical body is no absurd combination of opposites. The members were mortal; therefore, Jesus died. The glorified Head is immortal; therefore, the body is immortal, too, for thus the record stands, *"Because I live, ye shall live also"* (John 14:19). As is our loving Head, such is the body, and every member in particular. A chosen Head and chosen members; an accepted Head and accepted members; a living Head and living members. If the Head is pure gold, all the parts of the body are of pure gold also. Thus is there a double union of nature as a basis for the closest communion. Pause here, devout reader, and see if you can, without ecstatic amazement, contemplate the infinite condescension of the Son of God in thus exalting your wretchedness into blessed union with His glory. You are so lowly that in remembrance of your mortality, you may say to corruption, "You are my father," and to the worm, "You are my sister." Yet in Christ, you are so honored that you can say to the Almighty, "Abba, Father," and to the Incarnate God, "You are my brother and my husband." Surely if relationships to ancient and noble families make men think highly of themselves, we have much more reason to glory over them all. Let the poorest and most despised believer lay hold of this privilege. May a senseless laziness not make him negligent to trace his pedigree. Let him allow no foolish attachment to present vanities to occupy his thoughts to the exclusion of this glorious, heavenly honor of union with Christ.

DECEMBER 6
Evening

Girt about the paps with a golden girdle.
—Revelation 1:13

O*ne like unto the Son of man*" (Rev. 1:13) appeared to John on Patmos, and the beloved disciple noted that He wore a *"girdle"* of gold—a girdle, for Jesus never was unprepared while on earth. He always stood ready for service. Now before the eternal throne, He continues His holy ministry; but as a priest, He is girded with *"the curious girdle of the ephod"* (Exod. 28:8). We are blessed that He has not ceased to fulfill His offices of love for us, since this is one of our choicest safeguards that He *"ever liveth to make intercession for* [us]" (Heb. 7:25). Jesus is never an idler; His garments are never loose, as though His ministry were over. He diligently carries on the cause of His people. A *"golden girdle"* manifests the superiority of His service, the royalty of His person, the dignity of His state, and the glory of His reward. No longer does He cry out of the dust, but He intercedes with authority. He is a King as well as a Priest. Our cause is safe enough in the hands of our enthroned Melchizedek. Our Lord presents all His people with an example. We must never unbind our girdles. This is not the time for lying down at ease; it is the season of service and warfare. We need to bind the girdle of truth more and more tightly around our loins. It is a *"golden girdle,"* so it will be our richest ornament. We greatly need it, for a heart that is not well braced up with the truth as it is in Jesus, and with the fidelity that is worked by the Spirit, will be easily entangled with the things of this life and tripped up by the snares of temptation. It is in vain that we possess the Scriptures unless we bind them around us like a girdle, surrounding our entire nature, keeping each part of our character in order, and giving substance to our whole man. If in heaven Jesus does not unbind His girdle, much less may we who are still on the earth. *"Stand therefore, having your loins girt about with truth"* (Eph. 6:14).

DECEMBER 7

Morning

Base things of the world…hath God chosen.
—1 Corinthians 1:28

Walk the streets by moonlight, if you dare, and you will see sinners then. Watch when the night is dark, the wind is howling, and the burglar is hiding in the doorway, and you will see sinners then. Go to the jail and walk through the wards; you will observe men with heavy overhanging brows, men whom you would not like to meet at night, and you will find sinners there. Go to the reformatories, and note those who have revealed a rampant juvenile depravity, and you will see sinners there. Go across the seas to the place where a man will gnaw a bone on which is reeking human flesh, and there is a sinner there. Go where you will, for you need not ransack the earth to find sinners, for they are common enough. You may find them in every street of every city, town, village, and hamlet. It is for such that Jesus died. If you will select the grossest specimen of humanity, if he is but born of woman, I would have hope for him yet, because Jesus Christ *"is come to seek and to save that which was lost"* (Luke 19:10). Electing love has selected some of the worst to be made the best. Pebbles from the brook Grace turn into jewels for the royal crown. He transforms worthless dross into pure gold. Redeeming love has set apart many of the worst of mankind to be the reward of the Savior's passion. Effectual grace calls forth many of the vilest of the vile to sit at the table of mercy; therefore, let none despair. Reader, by that love looking out of Jesus' tearful eyes; by that love streaming from those bleeding wounds; by that faithful love, that strong, pure, impartial, and abiding love; by the heart of the Savior's compassion, we charge you not to turn away as though it were nothing to you. Believe on Him, and you will be saved. Trust your soul with Him, and He will bring you to His Father's right hand in glory everlasting.

I am made all things to all men, that I might by all means save some.
—1 Corinthians 9:22

Paul's great objective was not merely to instruct and to improve, but to save. Anything short of this goal would have disappointed him. He desired that people would be renewed in heart, forgiven, saved, and sanctified. Have our Christian labors been aimed at anything below this great point? Then let us amend our ways, for of what avail will it be at the Last Great Day to have taught and moralized men if they appear before God unsaved? Our skirts will be bloodred if through life we have sought inferior purposes and forgotten that people need to be saved. Paul knew the ruin of man's natural state. He did not try to educate men, but to save them. He saw men sinking to hell, and he did not talk about refining them, but of their being saved from the *"wrath to come"* (Matt. 3:7). To bring about their salvation, he gave himself up with untiring zeal to preaching the Gospel, to warning and beseeching men to be reconciled to God. His prayers were importunate, and his labors were incessant. To save souls was his consuming passion, his ambition, his calling. He became a servant to all men, toiling for his race, feeling a sorrow within him if he did not preach the Gospel. He laid aside his preferences to prevent prejudice; he submitted his will in things indifferent, and if men would but receive the Gospel, he raised no questions about forms or ceremonies. The Gospel was the one all-important business with him. If he might save some, he would be content. This was the crown for which he strove, the sole and sufficient reward of all his labors and self-denials. Dear reader, have you and I lived to win souls at this noble rate? Are we possessed with the same all-absorbing desire? If not, why not? Jesus died for sinners; can we not live for them? Where is our tenderness? Where is our love for Christ, if we do not seek His honor in the salvation of men? Oh, that the Lord would saturate us through and through with an undying zeal for the souls of men.

DECEMBER 8

Morning

Thou hast a few names even in Sardis which have not defiled their garments; and they shall walk with me in white: for they are worthy.
—Revelation 3:4

We may understand this to refer to justification. *"They shall walk with me in white"*; that is, they will enjoy a constant sense of their own justification by faith; they will understand that the righteousness of Christ is imputed to them, that they have all been washed and made whiter than the newly fallen snow. Again, it refers to joy and gladness, for white robes were holiday attire among the Jews. They who have not defiled their garments will have their faces always bright. They will understand what Solomon meant when he said *"Go thy way, eat thy bread with joy, and drink thy wine with a merry heart; for God now accepteth thy works. Let thy garments be always white"* (Eccl. 9:7–8). He who is accepted by God will wear white garments of joy and gladness, while he walks in sweet communion with the Lord Jesus. Why are there so many doubts, so much misery, and mourning? It is because so many believers defile their garments with sin and error and, thus, they lose the joy of their salvation and the comfortable fellowship of the Lord Jesus. They do not walk in white here on earth. The promise also refers to walking in white before the throne of God. Those who have not defiled their garments here will most certainly walk in white up yonder, where the white-robed hosts sing perpetual hallelujahs to the Most High. They will possess inconceivable joy, happiness beyond a dream, bliss that imagination cannot know, blessedness that even the stretch of desire has not reached. The *"undefiled in the way"* (Ps. 119:1) will have all this—not by merit or of works, but by grace. They will walk with Christ in white, for He has made them *"worthy."* In His sweet company, they will drink of the living fountains of waters.

Thou, O God, hast prepared of thy goodness for the poor.
—Psalm 68:10

All God's gifts are prepared gifts laid up in store for needs that are foreseen. God anticipates our needs. Out of the fullness that He has treasured up in Christ Jesus, He provides of His goodness for the poor. You may trust Him for all the necessities that can occur, for He has infallibly foreknown every one of them. He can say of us in all conditions, "I knew that you would be in this situation." A man makes a journey across the desert, and when he has gone a day's distance and stops to rest, he discovers that he needs many comforts and necessaries that he has not brought in his luggage. "Ah!" says he, "I did not foresee this: if I had to take this journey again, I would bring things with me that are necessary for my comfort." But God has noticed with His all-seeing eyes all the requirements of His poor, wandering children; and when those needs occur, He has supplies ready. It is goodness that He has prepared for the poor in heart, goodness and goodness only. *"My grace is sufficient for thee"* (2 Cor. 12:9). *"As thy days, so shall thy strength be"* (Deut. 33:25). Reader, is your heart heavy this evening? God knew it would be. The comfort that your heart needs is treasured in the sweet assurance of the text. You are poor and needy, but He has thought about you. He has in store for you the exact blessing that you require. Plead the promise, believe it, and obtain its fulfillment. Do you feel that you never were so consciously vile as you are now? Behold, the crimson fountain is open still, with all its former effectiveness to wash your sin away. You will never come into such a position that Christ cannot help you. No trouble will ever arrive in your spiritual affairs in which Jesus Christ will not be equal to the emergency, for your history has all been foreknown and provided for in Jesus.

Therefore will the LORD wait, that he may be gracious unto you.
—Isaiah 30:18

God often delays in answering prayer. We have several instances of this in sacred Scripture. Jacob did not get the blessing from the angel until near the dawn of day; he had to wrestle all night for it. The poor woman of Syrophenicia was not answered a word for a long while. Paul sought the Lord three times, asking that the *"thorn in the flesh"* (2 Cor. 12:7) might be taken from him. He received no assurance that it would be taken away; instead, he was given a promise that God's grace would be sufficient for him. If you have been knocking at the gate of mercy and have received no answer, shall I tell you why the mighty Maker has not opened the door and let you in? Our Father has reasons known only to Himself for thus keeping us waiting. Sometimes it is to show His power and His sovereignty so that men may know that Jehovah has a right to give or to withhold. More frequently the delay is for our profit. Perhaps you are kept waiting in order that your desires may be more fervent. God knows that delay will quicken and increase desire, and that if He keeps you waiting, you will see your need more clearly and will seek more earnestly. He also knows that you will prize the mercy all the more for its long delay. There may also be something wrong in you that needs to be removed before the joy of the Lord is given. Perhaps your views of the gospel plan are confused, or you may be placing some reliance on yourself, instead of trusting simply and entirely on the Lord Jesus. Or God makes you wait for a while so that He may the more fully display the riches of His grace to you at last. Your prayers are all filed in heaven, and if not immediately answered, they are certainly not forgotten. In a little while, they will be fulfilled to your delight and satisfaction. Do not let despair make you silent, but continue faithfully in earnest supplication.

My people shall dwell in…quiet resting places.
—Isaiah 32:18

Peace and rest do not belong to the unregenerate. They are the special possession of the Lord's people, and for them alone. The God of Peace gives perfect peace to those whose hearts are fixed on Him. Before man fell, God gave him the flowery bowers of Eden as his quiet resting place; sadly, sin soon blighted the fair abode of innocence. In the day of universal wrath, when the flood swept away a guilty race, the chosen family were quietly secured in the resting place of the ark, which floated them from the old condemned world into the new earth of the rainbow and the covenant, herein typifying Jesus, the Ark of our salvation. Israel rested safely beneath the blood-sprinkled habitations of Egypt when the destroying angel smote the firstborn; in the wilderness, the shadow of the pillar of cloud and the flowing rock gave the weary pilgrims sweet repose. At this hour we rest in the promises of our faithful God, knowing that His words are full of truth and power. We rest in the doctrines of His Word, which are consolation itself. We rest in the covenant of His grace, which is a haven of delight. We are more highly favored than David in Adullam (see 1 Samuel 22:1) or Jonah beneath his gourd, for none can invade or destroy our shelter. The person of Jesus is the quiet resting place of His people. When we draw near to Him in the breaking of the bread, the hearing of the Word, the searching of the Scriptures, prayer, or praise, we find any form of approach to Him to be the return of peace to our spirits.

I hear the words of love, I gaze upon the blood,
   I see the mighty sacrifice, and I have peace with God.
'Tis everlasting peace, sure as Jehovah's name,
   'Tis stable as His steadfast throne, for evermore the same.
    The clouds may go and come,
And storms may sweep my sky,
   This blood-sealed friendship changes not,
The cross is ever nigh.

So shall we ever be with the Lord.
—1 Thessalonians 4:17

Even the sweetest visits from Christ are brief and transitory. One moment our eyes see Him, and we *"rejoice with joy unspeakable and full of glory"* (1 Pet. 1:8), but in a little while, we do not see Him, for our Beloved withdraws Himself from us. Like a roe or a young deer, He leaps over the mountains. He is gone to the land of spices and feeds no more among the lilies.

> If today He deigns to bless us
>> With a sense of pardoned sin,
> He tomorrow may distress us,
>> Make us feel the plague within.

Oh, how sweet the prospect of the time when we will not behold Him at a distance, but see Him face-to-face! When He will not be as a wayfaring man tarrying but for a night, but will eternally enfold us in the heart of His glory! We will not see Him for a little season, but

> Millions of years our wondering eyes,
>> Shall o'er our Savior's beauties rove;
> And myriad ages we'll adore,
>> The wonders of His love.

In heaven there will be no interruptions from care or sin. No weeping will dim our eyes, and no earthly business will distract our happy thoughts. We will have nothing to hinder us from gazing forever with unwearied eyes on the Sun of Righteousness. Oh, if it is so sweet to see Him now and then, how sweet to gaze on that blessed face forever and never have a cloud rolling between or never have to turn one's eyes away to look on a world of weariness and woe! Blessed day, when will you dawn? Rise, unsetting sun! The joys of the tangible world may leave us as soon as they will, for this will make glorious amends. If to die is but to enter into uninterrupted fellowship with Jesus, then death is indeed gain, and the black drop is swallowed up in a sea of victory.

Whose heart the Lord opened.
—Acts 16:14

There are many points of interest in Lydia's conversion. It was brought about by providential circumstances. She was a *"seller of purple"* (Acts 16:4) in the city of Thyatira; however, just at the right time for hearing Paul, we find her at Philippi. Providence, the handmaiden of grace, led her to the right spot. Again, grace was preparing her soul for the blessing—grace preparing for grace. She did not know the Savior, but as a Jewish woman, she knew many truths that were excellent stepping-stones to a knowledge of Jesus. Her conversion took place as she used the means of grace. On the Sabbath she went when prayer was customarily made, and there prayer was heard. Never neglect the means of grace. God may bless us when we are not in His house, but we have greater reason to hope that He will when we are in communion with His saints. Observe the words, *"Whose heart the Lord opened."* She did not open her own heart. Her prayers did not do it; Paul did not do it. In order for us to receive the things that bring about our peace with God, the Lord Himself must open our hearts. He alone can put the key into the hole of the door, open it, and gain admittance for Himself. He is the heart's Master as He is the heart's Maker. The first outward evidence of the opened heart was obedience. As soon as Lydia had believed in Jesus, she was baptized. It is a sweet sign of a humble and broken heart when a child of God is willing to obey a command that is not essential to his salvation, that he does not feel forced to comply with out of a selfish fear of condemnation, but that is a simple act of obedience and communion with his Master. The next evidence was love, manifesting itself in acts of grateful kindness to the apostles. Love for the saints has always been a mark of the true convert. Those who do nothing for Christ or His church give but sorry evidence of an "opened" heart. Lord, give me an opened heart forever.

DECEMBER 11
Morning

Faithful is he that calleth you, who also will do it.
—1 Thessalonians 5:24

Heaven is a place where we will never sin and where we will cease our constant watch against an indefatigable enemy, because there will be no tempter to ensnare our feet. There the wicked cease from troubling, and the weary are at rest. Heaven is the *"inheritance incorruptible, and undefiled"* (1 Pet. 1:4). It is the land of perfect holiness and therefore of complete security. But do not the saints even on earth sometimes taste the joys of blissful security? The doctrine of God's Word is that all who are in union with the Lamb are safe; that all the righteous will hold on their way; and that those who have committed their souls to the keeping of Christ will find Him a faithful and immutable Preserver. Sustained by such a doctrine, we can enjoy security even on earth—not that high and glorious security that renders us free from every slip, but that holy security that arises from the sure promise of Jesus that none who believe in Him will ever perish, but will be with Him where He is. Believer, let us often reflect with joy on the doctrine of the perseverance of the saints and honor the faithfulness of our God by a holy confidence in Him. May our God bring home to you a sense of your safety in Christ Jesus! May He assure you that your name is graven on His hand and whisper in your ear the promise, *"Fear not: for I am with thee"* (Isa. 43:5). Look on Him, the great Surety of the covenant, as faithful and true, and, therefore, bound and engaged to present you, the weakest of the family, with all the chosen race, before the throne of God. In such a sweet contemplation, you will drink the juice of the spiced wine of the Lord's pomegranate and taste the dainty fruits of paradise. You will have a taste of the enjoyments that delight the souls of the perfect saints above, if you can believe with unstaggering faith that *"faithful is he that calleth you, who also will do it."*

Ye serve the Lord Christ.
—Colossians 3:24

To what choice group of officials was this word spoken? To kings who proudly boast a divine right? No, too often they serve themselves or Satan and forget the God whose mercy permits them to wear their mock majesty for their little hour. Did the apostle, then, speak to those so-called "right reverend fathers in God," the bishops or the venerable archdeacons? No, indeed. Paul knew nothing of these mere inventions of man. Not even to pastors and teachers or to the wealthy and esteemed among believers was this word spoken, but to servants, yes, and to slaves. Among the toiling multitudes— the journeymen, the day laborers, the domestic servants, the drudges of the kitchen— the apostle found, as we find still, some of the Lord's chosen. To them he said, "*Whatsoever ye do, do it heartily, as to the Lord, and not unto men; knowing that of the Lord ye shall receive the reward of the inheritance: for ye serve the Lord Christ*" (Col. 3:23–24). This saying ennobles the weary routine of earthly employment and shines a halo around the most humble occupations. To wash feet may be servile, but to wash His feet is royal work. To untie shoelaces is a poor job, but to untie the great Master's shoe is a princely privilege. The shop, the barn, and the kitchen become temples when men and women do all to the glory of God! Divine service is not a thing of a few hours and a few places, but all life becomes holiness unto the Lord. Every place and thing may be as consecrated as the tabernacle and its golden candlestick.

Teach me, my God and King, in all things Thee to see;
   And what I do in anything to do it as to Thee.
All may of Thee partake, nothing can be so mean,
   Which with this tincture, for Thy sake,
Will not grow bright and clean.
   A servant with this clause makes drudgery divine;
Who sweeps a room, as for Thy laws,
   Makes that and the action fine.

His ways are everlasting.
—Habakkuk 3:6

What God has done at one time, He will do yet again. Man's ways are changeable, but God's ways are everlasting. There are many reasons for this most comforting truth. Among them are the following: the Lord's ways are the result of wise deliberation. He orders all things according to the *"counsel of his own will"* (Eph. 1:11). Human action is frequently the hasty result of passion or fear and is followed by regret and alteration. But nothing can take the Almighty by surprise or happen otherwise than He has foreseen. His ways are the outgrowth of an immutable character, and in them the fixed and settled attributes of God are clearly to be seen. Unless the eternal One Himself can undergo change, His ways, which are Himself in action, must remain forever the same. Is He eternally just, gracious, faithful, wise, and tender? Then His ways must ever be distinguished for the same excellence. Human beings act according to their nature. When those natures change, their conduct varies also; but since God cannot know the *"shadow of turning"* (James 1:17), His ways will abide everlastingly the same. Moreover there is no reason from without that could reverse the divine ways, since they are the embodiment of irresistible might. Habbakuk said that God divided the earth with rivers; that mountains saw Him and trembled; that the deep lifted up its hands; and that the sun and moon stood still when Jehovah marched forth for the salvation of His people (Hab. 3:9–12). Who can stay His hand or say to Him, "What are You doing?" But it is not might alone that gives stability. God's ways are the manifestation of the eternal principles of right and, therefore, can never pass away. Wrong breeds decay and involves ruin, but the true and the good have a vitality that ages cannot diminish. This morning let us go to our heavenly Father with confidence, remembering that Jesus Christ is the *"same yesterday, and to day, and for ever"* (Heb. 13:8), and the Lord is ever gracious to His people.

DECEMBER 12

Evening

They have dealt treacherously against the LORD.
—Hosea 5:7

Believer, here is a sorrowful truth: you are the beloved of the Lord, redeemed by blood, called by grace, preserved in Christ Jesus, *"accepted in the beloved"* (Eph. 1:6), and on your way to heaven, yet you *"have dealt treacherously"* with God, your best Friend; treacherously with Jesus, whose you are; and treacherously with the Holy Spirit, by whom you have been quickened unto life eternal! How treacherous you have been in the matter of vows and promises! Do you remember your first love, that happy time— the springtime of your spiritual life? Oh, how closely you clung to your Master then! You said, "He will never charge me with indifference. My feet will never grow slow in the way of His service. I will not permit my heart to wander after other loves. In Him is every store of inexpressible sweetness. I give all up for my Lord Jesus' sake." Has it been so? Sadly, if conscience speaks, it will say, "He who promised so well has performed most poorly. Prayer has often been neglected. It has been short, but not sweet; brief, but not fervent. Communion with Christ has been forgotten. Instead of a heavenly mind, there have been carnal cares, worldly vanities, and evil thoughts. Instead of service, there has been disobedience; instead of fervency, lukewarmness; instead of patience, petulance; instead of faith, confidence in an *"arm of flesh"* (2 Chron. 32:8). As a soldier of the Cross, there has been cowardice, disobedience, and desertion to a very shameful degree. You *"have dealt treacherously."* Treachery to Jesus! What words will be used in denouncing it? Words avail little. Let our penitent thoughts denounce the sin that is so surely in us. We have been treacherous to Your wounds, O Jesus! Forgive us, and let us not sin again. How shameful to be treacherous to Him who never forgets us, but who this day stands with our names engraved on His breastplate before the eternal throne.

Salt without prescribing how much.
—Ezra 7:22

Salt was used in every offering made by fire to the Lord. From its preserving and purifying properties, it was the grateful symbol of divine grace in the soul. It is worthy of our attention that when Artaxerxes gave salt to Ezra the priest, he set no limit to the quantity (Ezra 6:9); we may be quite certain that when the King of Kings distributes grace among His royal priesthood, the supply is not cut short by Him. Often we are restricted in ourselves, but never in the Lord. He who chooses to gather much manna will find that he may have as much as he desires. There is no famine in Jerusalem such that the citizens must limit the portions of their bread and water. Some things in the economy of grace are measured; for instance, our vinegar and gall are given to us with such exactness that we never have a single drop too much, but of the salt of grace no restriction is made: *"Whatsoever thou wilt ask of God, God will give it thee"* (John 11:22). Parents need to lock up the fruit cupboard and the candy jars, but there is no need to keep the salt shaker under lock and key, for few children will eat too greedily from that. A man may have too much money or too much honor, but he cannot have too much grace. Jeshurun *"waxed fat, and kicked"* (Deut. 32:15) against God, but there is no fear of a man's becoming too full of grace. It is impossible to have too much grace. More wealth brings more care, but more grace brings more joy. Increased wisdom is increased sorrow, but abundance of the Spirit is fullness of joy. Believer, go to the throne for a large supply of heavenly salt. It will season your afflictions, which are unsavory without salt. It will preserve your heart, which corrupts if salt is absent, and it will kill your sins even as salt kills reptiles. You need much. Seek much, and you will have much.

I will make thy windows of agates.
—Isaiah 54:12

The church is most instructively symbolized by a building erected by heavenly power and designed by divine skill. Such a spiritual house must not be dark, for the Israelites had light in their dwellings; therefore, there must be windows to let the light in and to allow the inhabitants to gaze outside. These windows are precious as agates. The ways in which the church beholds her Lord and heaven, and spiritual truth in general, are to be held in the highest esteem. Agates are not the most transparent of gems. They are but semi-transparent at best. "Our knowledge of that life is small; our eye of faith is dim." Faith is one of these precious agate windows, but it is often so misty and cloudy that we see but dimly, and we mistake much that we do see. Yet if we cannot gaze through windows of diamonds and know even as we are known (see 1 Corinthians 13:12), it is a glorious thing to behold the One who is *"altogether lovely"* (Song 5:16), even though the glass is as hazy as the agate. Experience is another of these dim but precious windows, yielding to us a subdued religious light, in which we see the sufferings of the Man of Sorrows through our own afflictions. Our weak eyes could not endure windows of transparent glass to let in the Master's glory, but when they are dimmed with weeping, the beams of the Sun of Righteousness are tempered. Then they shine through the windows of agate with a soft radiance that is inexpressibly soothing to tempted souls. Sanctification, as it conforms us to our Lord, is another agate window. Only as we become heavenly can we comprehend heavenly things. The pure in heart see a pure God. Those who are like Jesus see Him as He is. Because we are so little like Him, the window is but agate; because we are somewhat like Him, it is agate. We thank God for what we have, and we long for more. When will we see God and Jesus, and heaven and truth, face-to-face?

They go from strength to strength.
—Psalm 84:7

Th<small>ey go from strength to strength.</small>" There are various renderings of these words, but all of them contain the idea of progress. Our own good translation of the King James Version is enough for us this morning. "*They go from strength to strength.*" That is, they grow stronger and stronger. Usually, if we are walking, we go from strength to weakness. We start fresh and in good order for our journey, but as time passes, the road is rough, and the sun is hot; we sit down by the wayside, and then again painfully pursue our weary way. But the Christian pilgrim, having obtained fresh supplies of grace, is as vigorous after years of toilsome travel and struggle as when he first set out. He may not be quite so elated and buoyant or perhaps quite so hot and hasty in his zeal as he once was, but he is much stronger in all that constitutes real power. He travels, if more slowly, far more surely. Some gray-haired veterans have been as firm and as zealous in their grasp of truth as they were in their younger days; however, it must be confessed that it is often otherwise, "*because iniquity shall abound, the love of many shall wax cold*" (Matt. 24:12). But this is their own sin and not the fault of the promise that still holds good: "*The youths shall faint and be weary, and the young men shall utterly fall: but they that wait upon the LORD shall renew their strength; they shall mount up with wings as eagles; they shall run, and not be weary; and they shall walk, and not faint*" (Isa. 40:30–31). Fretful spirits sit down and trouble themselves about the future. "Alas!" they say, "we go from affliction to affliction." Very true, you of little faith, but then you go "*from strength to strength*" also! You will never find a bundle of affliction that does not have sufficient grace bound up in the midst of it. God will give the strength of mature manhood with the burden allotted to full-grown shoulders.

I am crucified with Christ.
—Galatians 2:20

In what He did, the Lord Jesus Christ acted as a great public representative, and His dying on the cross was the virtual dying of all His people. Through Him, all His saints rendered unto justice what was due and made an atonement to divine vengeance for all their sins. Paul, the apostle to the Gentiles, delighted to think that as one of Christ's chosen people, he died upon the cross in Christ. He did more than believe this doctrinally. He accepted it confidently, resting his hope upon it. He believed that by virtue of Christ's death, he had satisfied divine justice and had found reconciliation with God. Beloved, what a blessed thing it is when the soul can, as it were, stretch itself upon the cross of Christ and feel, "I am dead. The law has slain me; therefore, I am free from its power. In my Surety I have borne the curse, and in my Substitute the whole that the law could do, by way of condemnation, has been executed upon me, for I am crucified with Christ!" But Paul meant even more than this. He not only believed in Christ's death and trusted in it, but also actually felt its power in himself in causing the crucifixion of his old corrupt nature. When he saw the pleasures of sin, he said, "I cannot enjoy these. I am dead to them." Such is the experience of every true Christian. Having received Christ, he is to this world as one who is utterly dead. Yet, while conscious of death to the world, he can, at the same time, exclaim with the apostle, "Nevertheless I live." He is fully alive to God. The Christian's life is a matchless riddle. No earthly-minded person can comprehend it; even the believer himself cannot understand it. Dead, yet alive! Crucified with Christ, yet at the same time risen with Christ in newness of life! Union with the suffering, bleeding Savior and death to the world and sin are soul-cheering things. Oh, for more enjoyment of them!

Orpah kissed her mother in law; but Ruth clave unto her.
—Ruth 1:14

Both Orpah and Ruth had affection for Naomi. That is why they set out with her on her return to the land of Judah. But the hour of testing came. Naomi most unselfishly set before each of them the trials that awaited them. If they cared for ease and comfort, she encouraged them to return to their Moabite friends. At first both of them declared that they would cast in their lot with the Lord's people; but on further consideration, Orpah, with much grief and a respectful kiss, left her mother-in-law and her people and her God. She went back to her idolatrous friends. Ruth, however, with all her heart gave herself up to the God of her mother-in-law. It is one thing to love the ways of the Lord when all is fair, and quite another to cleave to them under all discouragement and difficulties. The kiss of outward profession is very cheap and easy, but the practical cleaving to the Lord, which must show itself in holy decision for truth and holiness, is not so small a matter. How does the case stand with us? Are our hearts fixed on Jesus? Is the sacrifice bound with cords to the horns of the altar? Have we counted the cost, and are we solemnly ready to suffer all worldly loss for the Master's sake? The future gain will be an abundant recompense, for Egypt's treasures are not to be compared with the glory to be revealed. Orpah is heard of no more; in glorious ease and idolatrous pleasure her life melts into the gloom of death. But Ruth lives in history and in heaven, for grace has placed her in the noble line from which came the King of Kings. Blessed among women will those be who for Christ's sake can renounce all; but forgotten and worse than forgotten will those be who in the hour of temptation do violence to conscience and turn back to the world. Oh, that this morning we may not be content with the form of devotion, which may be no better than Orpah's kiss, but may the Holy Spirit work in us a cleaving of our whole hearts to our Lord Jesus.

And lay thy foundations with sapphires.
—Isaiah 54:11

Not only that which is seen of the church of God, but also that which is unseen, is fair and precious. Foundations are out of sight. As long as they are firm, it is not expected that they should be valuable. But in Jehovah's work, everything is from Him; nothing is worthless or defective. The deep foundations of the work of grace are as precious sapphires; no human mind is able to measure their glory. We build on the covenant of grace, which is firmer than diamonds and as enduring as jewels on which age spends itself in vain. Sapphire foundations are eternal, and the covenant lasts throughout the lifetime of the Almighty. Another foundation is the person of the Lord Jesus, which is as clear, spotless, everlasting, and beautiful as the sapphire. It blends the deep blue of earth's ever-rolling ocean and the azure of its all-embracing sky. Once, as our Lord stood covered with His own blood, He might have been compared to the ruby; but now we see Him radiant with the soft blue of love, an abundant, everlasting, and deep love. Our eternal hopes are built on the justice and the faithfulness of God, which are as clear and cloudless as the sapphire. We are not saved by a compromise, by mercy defeating justice or law suspending its operations; no, we defy the eagle's eye to detect a flaw in the groundwork of our confidence—our foundation is of sapphire, and it will endure the fire. The Lord Himself has laid the foundation of His people's hopes. It is a matter for grave inquiry whether our hopes are built on such a basis. Good works and ceremonies are not a foundation of sapphires, but of *"wood, hay,* [and] *stubble"* (1 Cor. 3:12); neither are they laid by God, but by our own conceit. Foundations will all be tried before long. Woe unto him whose lofty tower comes down with a crash, because it is based on quicksand. He who is built on sapphires may await storm or fire with calmness, for he will withstand the test.

Come unto me.
—Matthew 11:28

The cry of the Christian religion is the gentle word, *"Come."* The Jewish law harshly said, "Go, take heed to your steps as to the path in which you will walk. Break the commandments, and you will perish; keep them, and you will live." The law was a dispensation of terror, which drove men before it like a scourge. The Gospel draws with bands of love. Jesus is the Good Shepherd going before His sheep, inviting them to follow Him, and always leading them onward with the sweet word, *"Come."* The law repels; the Gospel attracts. The law shows the distance there is between God and man; the Gospel bridges that awful chasm and brings the sinner across it. From the first moment of your spiritual life until you are ushered into glory, the language of Christ to you will be, *"Come unto me."* As a mother puts out her finger and coaxes her little child to walk by saying, "Come," even so does Jesus. He will always be ahead of you, bidding you to follow Him as the soldier follows his captain. He will always go before you to pave your way and clear your path, and you will hear His animating voice calling you after Him all through life. While you face the solemn hour of death, His sweet words with which He will usher you into the heavenly world will be: *"Come, ye blessed of my Father"* (Matt. 25:34). Further, this is not only Christ's cry to you, but, if you are a believer, this is your cry to Christ: "Come! Come!" You will be longing for His second coming. You will be saying, "Come quickly. *'Even so, come, Lord Jesus'* (Rev. 22:20)." You will be panting for nearer and closer communion with Him. As His voice calls to you, "Come," your response to Him will be, "Come, Lord, and abide with me. Come, and occupy alone the throne of my heart. Reign there without a rival, and consecrate me entirely to Your service."

DECEMBER 16

Evening

Yea, thou heardest not; yea, thou knewest not; yea,
from that time that thine ear was not opened.
—Isaiah 48:8

It is painful to remember that, to a certain degree, this accusation may be laid at the door of believers, who too often are in a measure spiritually insensitive. We may well bewail ourselves that we do not hear the voice of God as we ought. *"Yea, thou heardest not."* There are gentle motions of the Holy Spirit in the soul that are unheeded by us. There are whisperings of divine command and of heavenly love that are alike unobserved by our leaden intellects. Alas! We have been carelessly ignorant—*"Yea, thou knewest not."* There are matters within that we should have seen, corruptions that have made headway into our lives unnoticed; sweet affections that are being blighted like flowers in the frost, untended by us; glimpses of the divine face that might be perceived if we did not wall up the windows of our soul. But we *"have not known"* (Isa. 44:18). As we think of it, we are humbled in the deepest self-abasement. How we must adore the grace of God as we learn from the context that all this folly and ignorance, on our part, was foreknown by God, and, notwithstanding that foreknowledge, He yet has been pleased to deal with us in a merciful way! Admire the marvelous sovereign grace that could have chosen us in the sight of all this! Wonder at the price that was paid for us when Christ knew what we would be! He who hung on the cross foresaw us as unbelieving, backsliding, coldhearted, indifferent, careless, lax in prayer, yet He said, *"I am the LORD thy God, the Holy One of Israel, thy Saviour....Since thou wast precious in my sight, thou hast been honourable, and I have loved thee: therefore will I give men for thee, and people for thy life"* (Isa. 43:3–4)! O redemption, how wondrously resplendent you shine when we think how black we are! O Holy Spirit, from this point on, give us a hearing ear and an understanding heart!

I remember thee.
—Jeremiah 2:2

Let us note that Christ delights to think about His church and to look on her beauty. As the bird returns often to its nest and the wayfarer hurries to his home, so does the mind continually pursue the object of its choice. We cannot look too often on the face that we love; we desire always to have our precious things in our sight. It is even so with our Lord Jesus. From all eternity His *"delights were with the sons of men"* (Prov. 8:31). His thoughts rolled onward to the time when His elect would be born into the world. He viewed them in the mirror of His foreknowledge. *"In thy book,"* David wrote, *"all my members were written, which in continuance were fashioned, when as yet there was none of them"* (Ps. 139:16). When the world was set on its pillars, He was there, and He set the bounds of the people according to the number of the children of Israel. Many times before His incarnation, He descended to earth in the likeness of a man: on the plains of Mamre, by the brook of Jabbok, beneath the walls of Jericho, and in the fiery furnace of Babylon, the Son of Man visited His people. Because His soul delighted in them, He could not rest away from them, for His heart longed after them. Never were they absent from His heart, for He had written their names on His hands and engraved them on His side. As the breastplate containing the names of the tribes of Israel was the most brilliant ornament worn by the high priest, so the names of Christ's elect were His most precious jewels, and they glittered on His heart.

We may often forget to meditate on the perfections of our Lord, but He never ceases to remember us. Let us chide ourselves for past forgetfulness, and pray for grace always to bear Him in fondest remembrance. Lord, paint on the eyes of my soul the image of Your Son.

*I am the door: by me if any man enter in, he shall be saved, and shall
go in and out, and find pasture.*
—John 10:9

Jesus, the great I Am, is the entrance into the true church, and the way
of access to God Himself. He gives four choice privileges to the man who
comes to God by Him. First, he will be saved. The fugitive manslayer went
through the gate of the city of refuge and was safe. Noah entered the door
of the ark and was secure. None can be lost who take Jesus to their souls
as the door of faith. Entrance through Jesus into peace is the guarantee of
entrance by the same door into heaven. Jesus is the only door, an open door,
a wide door, a safe door. Blessed is he who rests all his hope of admission
to glory on the crucified Redeemer. Second, he will go in. He will be privileged to go in among the divine family, sharing the children's bread and
participating in all their honors and enjoyments. He will go into the rooms
of communion, to the banquets of love, to the treasures of the covenant,
to the storehouses of the promises. He will go in to the King of Kings in
the power of the Holy Spirit, and the secret of the Lord will be with him.
Next, he will go out. This blessing is much forgotten. We go out into the
world to labor and suffer, but what a mercy to go in the name and power of
Jesus! We are called to bear witness to the truth, to cheer the disconsolate,
to warn the careless, to win souls, and to glorify God. The angel said to
Gideon, *"Go in this thy might"* (Judg. 6:14); likewise, the Lord wants us to
proceed as His messengers in His name and strength. Fourth, he will find
pasture. He who knows Jesus will never want. Going in and out will both
be helpful to him: in fellowship with God he will grow, and in watering
others he will be watered. Having made Jesus his all, he will find all in
Jesus. His soul will *"be like a watered garden, and like a spring of water, whose
waters fail not"* (Isa. 58:11).

Rend your heart, and not your garments.
—Joel 2:13

Tearing one's garments and other outward signs of religious emotion are easily manifested and are frequently hypocritical. To feel true repentance is far more difficult; consequently, it is far less common. Men will attend to the most multiplied and minute ceremonial regulations, for such things are pleasing to the flesh. True religion, however, is too humbling, too heart-searching, too thorough for the tastes of carnal men. They prefer something more ostentatious, flimsy, and worldly. Outward observances are temporarily comfortable; eye and ear are pleased, self-conceit is fed, and self-righteousness is puffed up. But they are ultimately misleading, for at the point of death, and on the Judgment Day, the soul needs something more substantial than ceremonies and rituals to lean on. Apart from vital godliness, all religion is utterly vain. Offered without a sincere heart, every form of worship is a solemn sham and an impudent mockery of the majesty of heaven. Heartrending is a divine operation and is solemnly felt. It is a secret grief that is personally experienced, not in mere form, but as a deep, soul-moving work of the Holy Spirit on the inmost heart of each believer. It is not a matter to be merely talked about and believed in, but keenly and sensitively felt in every living child of the living God. It is powerfully humiliating and completely sin-purging; but then, it is sweetly preparative for those gracious consolations that proud spirits are unable to receive. It is distinctly discriminating, for it belongs to the elect of God, and to them alone. The text commands us to rend our hearts, but they are naturally hard as marble. How, then, can this be done? We must take them to Calvary. A dying Savior's voice rent the rocks once, and it is as powerful now. Blessed Spirit, let us hear the death cries of Jesus, and our hearts will be rent even as men tear their clothes in the times of great sorrow.

DECEMBER 18
Evening

Be thou diligent to know the state of thy flocks,
and look well to thy herds.
—Proverbs 27:23

Every wise businessman will periodically take stock of his company. He will update his accounts, examine his inventory, and evaluate whether his trade is prospering or declining. Every man who is wise in the kingdom of heaven will cry, *"Search me, O God, and know my heart: try me"* (Ps. 139:23). He will frequently set apart special seasons for self-examination, to discover whether things are right between God and his soul. The God whom we worship is a great heart-searcher. In times past, His servants knew Him as the Lord who searches the heart and examines the minds of His children. (See Jeremiah 17:10.) Let me encourage you in His name to diligently search and solemnly investigate your spiritual condition, lest you come short of the promised rest. That which every wise man does, that which God Himself does with us all, I exhort you to do with yourself this evening. Let the oldest saint look well to the fundamentals of his faith, for gray heads may cover black hearts. Do not let the young believer despise the word of warning, for the greenness of youth may be joined to the rottenness of hypocrisy. Every now and then a cedar falls into our midst. The enemy still continues to sow tares among the wheat. It is not my aim to introduce doubts and fears into your mind; instead, I hope that the rough wind of self-examination may help to drive them away. It is not security, but carnal security, that we want to kill; not confidence, but fleshly confidence, that we want to overthrow; not peace, but false peace, that we want to destroy. By the precious blood of Christ, which was not shed to make you a hypocrite, but so that sincere souls might show forth His praise, I beg you, search and look, lest in the end it will be said of you, *"Mene, Mene...Tekel; thou art weighed in the balances, and art found wanting"* (Dan. 5:25, 27).

The lot is cast into the lap; but the whole
disposing thereof is of the Lord.
—Proverbs 16:33

If the disposal of the lot is the Lord's, whose is the arrangement of our whole lives? If the simple casting of a lot is guided by Him, how much more the events of our entire lives, especially when we are told by our blessed Savior, "*The very hairs of your head are all numbered*" (Matt. 10:30). Not a sparrow falls to the ground apart from your Father's will (v. 29). It would bring a holy calm over your mind, dear friend, if you were always to remember this. It would relieve your mind from anxiety, so that you would be better able to walk in patience, quiet, and cheerfulness as a Christian should. When a man is anxious, he cannot pray with faith. When he is troubled about the world, he cannot serve his Master; his thoughts are serving himself. If you would "*seek...first the kingdom of God, and his right-eousness*" (Matt. 6:33), all things would then be added unto you. You are meddling with Christ's business and neglecting your own when you fret about your lot and circumstances. You have been trying "providing" work and forgetting that it is yours to obey. Be wise and attend to the obeying; let Christ manage the providing. Come and survey your Father's store-house, and ask whether He will let you starve while He has laid up so great an abundance in His garner. Look at His heart of mercy. See if that can ever prove unkind! Look at His inscrutable wisdom. See if that will ever be at fault. Above all, look to Jesus Christ, your Intercessor, and ask yourself, while He pleads, can your Father deal ungraciously with you? If He remembers even sparrows, will He forget one of the least of His poor children? "*Cast thy burden upon the Lord, and he shall sustain thee: he shall never suffer the righteous to be moved*" (Ps. 55:22).

My soul, rest happy in thy low estate,
  Nor hope nor wish to be esteem'd or great;
To take the impress of the Will Divine,
  Be that thy glory, and those riches thine.

And there was no more sea.
—Revelation 21:1

Scarcely could we rejoice at the thought of losing the glorious old ocean: the new heavens and the new earth are none the fairer to our imagination, if, indeed, literally there is to be no great and wide sea, with its gleaming waves and shelly shores. Is not the text to be read as a metaphor, tinged with the prejudice with which the Oriental mind universally regarded the sea in the olden times? A real, physical world without a sea is mournful to imagine. It would be an iron ring without the sapphire which made it precious. There must be a spiritual meaning here. In the new dispensation there will be no division—the sea separates nations and divides peoples from each other. To John in Patmos the deep waters were like prison walls, shutting him out from his brothers and his work. There will be no such barriers in the world to come. Leagues of rolling billows lie between us and many relatives whom tonight we prayerfully remember, but in the bright world to which we go, there will be unbroken fellowship for all the redeemed family. In this sense there will be no more sea. The sea is the emblem of change; with its ebbs and flows—its glassy smoothness and its mountainous billows, its gentle murmurs and its tumultuous roarings—it is never the same for long. Slave of the fickle winds and the changeful moon, its instability is proverbial. In this mortal state we have too much of this. Earth is constant only in her inconstancy. But in the heavenly state, all mournful change will be unknown, and with it all fear of storm to wreck our hopes and drown our joys. The sea of glass glows with a glory unbroken by a wave. No tempest howls along the peaceful shores of paradise. Soon we will reach that happy land where partings, changes, and storms will be ended! Jesus will carry us there. Are we in Him or not? This is the grand question.

Yea, I have loved thee with an everlasting love.
—Jeremiah 31:3

Sometimes the Lord Jesus tells His church His love thoughts. R. Erskine states: "He does not think it enough behind her back to tell it, but in her very presence, He says, *'Thou art all fair, my love'* (Song 4:7). It is true that this is not His ordinary method. He is a wise lover and knows when to keep back the intimation of love and when to let it out, but there are times when He will make no secret of it—times when He will put it beyond all dispute in the souls of His people." The Holy Spirit is often pleased, in a most gracious manner, to witness with our spirits of the love of Jesus. He takes of the things of Christ and reveals them to us. (See John 16:13–15.) No voice is heard from the clouds, and no vision is seen in the night, but we have a testimony more sure than either of these. If an angel should fly from heaven and inform the saint personally of the Savior's love for him, the evidence would not be one bit more satisfactory than that which is borne in the heart by the Holy Spirit. Ask those of the Lord's people who have lived the nearest to the gates of heaven, and they will tell you that they have had seasons when the love of Christ toward them has been a fact so clear and sure that they could no more doubt it than they could question their own existence. Yes, beloved believer, you and I have had times of refreshing from the presence of the Lord, and then, our faith has mounted to the topmost heights of assurance. We have had confidence to lean our heads on the bosom of our Lord. We have no more questioned our Master's affection for us than John did when he was in that same blessed posture. No, we have not even been moved to ask the dark question, "Lord, is it I that will betray You?" That thought has been put far from us. He has kissed us with the kisses of His mouth and killed our doubts by the closeness of His embrace. His love has been sweeter than wine to our souls.

Call the labourers, and give them their hire.
—Matthew 20:8

God is a good employer. He pays His servants while they work as well as when they have finished working. One of His payments is an easy conscience. If you have spoken faithfully of Jesus to one person, when you go to bed at night you feel happy in thinking, "Today, I have discharged my conscience of that man's blood." There is a great comfort in doing something for Jesus. Oh, what happiness it brings to place jewels in His crown and to allow Him to see the results of His saving work! There is also great reward in watching the first budding of conviction in a soul. To say of a girl in your class, "She is tenderhearted. I hope that her sensitivity reflects the Lord's work within"; to go home and pray over the boy who said something that made you think he must know more of divine truth than you had feared—oh, the joy of hope! As for the joy of success, it is unspeakable! This joy, overwhelming as it is, is a hungry thing—you long for more of it. To be a soulwinner is the happiest thing in the world. With every soul you bring to Christ, you get a new heaven on earth. Who can conceive the bliss that awaits us above? Oh, how sweet is that sentence, *"Enter thou into the joy of thy lord"* (Matt. 25:21)! Do you know what the joy of Christ is over a saved sinner? This is the very joy that we are to possess in heaven. Yes, when He mounts the throne, you will mount with Him. When the heavens ring with, "Well done, well done," you will partake in the reward. You have toiled with Him, and you have suffered with Him; now, you will reign with Him. You have sown with Him, and you will reap with Him. Your face was covered with sweat like His, and your soul was grieved as His soul was for the sins of men. Now your face will be bright with heaven's splendor as is His countenance, and your soul will be filled with blissful joy even as His soul is.

DECEMBER 21

He hath made with me an everlasting covenant.
—2 Samuel 23:5

This covenant is divine in its origin. *"He hath made with me an everlasting covenant."* Oh, that great word *"He"*! Stop, my soul. God, the everlasting Father, has positively made a covenant with you—yes, that God who spoke the world into existence by a word! He, stooping from His majesty, takes hold of your hand and makes a covenant with you. Is not the stupendous condescension of this act enough to ravish our hearts forever if we could really understand it? *"He hath made with me an everlasting covenant."* A king has not made a covenant with me—that would be something; but the Prince of the kings of the earth, Shaddai, the Lord All-sufficient, the Jehovah of ages, the everlasting Elohim, *"He hath made with me an everlasting covenant."* But notice, it is particular in its application. *"He hath made with **me** an everlasting covenant"* (emphasis added). Here lies the sweetness of it to each believer. It is nothing to me that He made peace for the world; I need to know whether He has made peace for me! It is little that He has made a covenant; I want to know whether He has made a covenant with me. Blessed is the assurance that He has made a covenant with me! If God the Holy Spirit gives me assurance, then His salvation is mine, His heart is mine, He Himself is mine—He is my God. This covenant is everlasting in its duration. An everlasting covenant means a covenant that had no beginning and that will never, never end. How sweet, amid all the uncertainties of life, to know that the *"foundation of God standeth sure"* (2 Tim. 2:19), and to have God's own promise, *"My covenant will I not break, nor alter the thing that is gone out of my lips"* (Ps. 89:34). Like dying David, I will sing of this, even though all the affairs and members of my house may not be in the place that my heart desires before God.

*I clothed thee also with broidered work, and shod thee
with badgers' skin, and I girded thee about with fine linen,
and I covered thee with silk.*
—Ezekiel 16:10

See the matchless generosity with which the Lord provides for His people. They are clothed such that divine skill is seen producing an unrivalled embroidered work, in which every attribute takes its part and every divine beauty is revealed. There is no art like the art displayed in our salvation and no cunning workmanship like that beheld in the righteousness of the saints. Justification has engaged learned writers in all ages of the church, and it will be the theme of admiration in eternity. God has indeed "curiously wrought it." With all this elaboration, there is mingled utility and durability, comparable to our being shod with badgers' skins. The animal mentioned here is unknown, but its skin covered the tabernacle and formed one of the finest and strongest leathers known. The righteousness that is of God by faith endures forever, and he who is shod with this divine preparation will tread the desert safely. He may even set his foot *"upon the lion and adder"* (Ps. 91:12). Purity and dignity of our holy vesture are brought out in the fine linen. When the Lord sanctifies His people, they are clad as priests in pure white. The snow itself does not excel them. In the eyes of men and angels, they are fair to look upon; even in the Lord's eyes, they are without spot. Meanwhile the royal apparel is delicate and rich as silk. No expense is spared, no beauty is withheld, and no daintiness is denied. What then? Is there no inference from this? Surely there is gratitude to be felt and joy to be expressed. Come, my heart. Do not refuse your evening hallelujah! Tune your pipes! Touch your chords!

> Strangely, my soul, art thou arrayed
> By the Great Sacred Three!
> In sweetest harmony of praise
> Let all thy powers agree.

I will strengthen thee.
—Isaiah 41:10

God has a strong reserve with which to discharge this engagement, for He is able to do all things. Believer, until you can drain dry the ocean of omnipotence, until you can break into pieces the towering mountains of almighty strength, you never need to fear. Do not think that the strength of man will ever be able to overcome the power of God. While the earth's huge pillars stand, you have enough reason to abide firm in your faith. The same God who directs the earth in its orbit, who feeds the burning furnace of the sun, and trims the lamps of heaven has promised to supply you with daily strength. While He is able to uphold the universe, do not think that He will prove unable to fulfill His own promises. Remember what He did in the days of old, in the former generations. Remember how He spoke, and it was done; how He commanded, and it stood fast. Will He who created the world grow weary? He hangs the world on nothing; will He who does this be unable to support His children? Will He be unfaithful to His word for lack of power? Who is it that restrains the tempest? Does He not ride on the wings of the wind, make the clouds His chariots, and hold the ocean in the hollow of His hand? How can He fail you? When He has put such a faithful promise as this on record, will you for a moment indulge the thought that He has outpromised Himself and gone beyond His power to fulfill? Ah, no! You can doubt no longer. You who are my God and my strength, I can believe that this promise will be fulfilled, for the boundless reservoir of Your grace can never be exhausted, and the overflowing storehouse of Your strength can never be emptied by Your friends or pilfered by Your enemies.

Now let the feeble all be strong,
    And make Jehovah's arm their song.

The spot of his children.
—Deuteronomy 32:5

What is the secret *"spot"* that infallibly denotes the child of God? It would be vain presumption to decide this based on our own judgment, but God's Word reveals it to us. We may walk confidently where we have divine revelation as our guide. Now, we are told concerning our Lord, *"As many as received him, to them gave he power to become the sons of God, even to them that believe on his name"* (John 1:12). Then, if I have received Christ Jesus into my heart, I am a child of God. That reception is described in the same verse as believing on the name of Jesus Christ. If, then, I believe on Jesus Christ's name—that is, simply from my heart, I trust myself with the crucified, but now exalted, Redeemer—I am a member of the family of the Most High. Whatever else I may not have, if I have this, I have the privilege to become a child of God. Our Lord Jesus puts it another way: *"My sheep hear my voice, and I know them, and they follow me"* (John 10:27). Here is the matter in a nutshell. Christ appears as a Shepherd to His own sheep, not to others. As soon as He appears, His own sheep recognize Him. They trust Him and are prepared to follow Him. He knows them, and they know Him. There is a mutual knowledge, and there is a constant connection between them. Thus the one mark, the sure mark, the infallible mark of regeneration and adoption, is a hearty faith in the appointed Redeemer. Reader, are you in doubt? Are you uncertain whether you bear the secret mark of God's children? Then do not let an hour go by until you have said, *"Search me, O God, and know my heart"* (Ps. 139:23). Do not handle this matter lightly, I beg you! If you must trifle anywhere, let it be about some secondary matter: your health, if you will, or the deeds of your estate. But about your soul, your never-dying soul and its eternal destiny, I beseech you to be in earnest. Be certain about where you will spend eternity!

Friend, go up higher.
—Luke 14:10

When the life of grace first begins in the soul, we do indeed draw near to God, but it is with great fear and trembling. The soul, conscious of its guilt and humbled thereby, is in awe over the solemnity of its position. It is cast to the earth by a sense of the grandeur of Jehovah, in whose presence it stands. With unfeigned bashfulness, it takes the lowest room. But later, as the Christian grows in grace, although he will never forget the solemnity of his position and will never lose that holy awe that must encompass a gracious man when he is in the presence of the God who can create or can destroy, his fear has all its terror taken out of it. It becomes a holy reverence and no longer an overshadowing dread. He is called up higher to greater access to God in Christ Jesus. Then the man of God, walking amid the splendors of deity and veiling his face like the glorious cherubim with those twin wings—the blood and righteousness of Jesus Christ—will approach the throne reverently and bowed in spirit. Seeing there a God of love, of goodness, and of mercy, he will realize the covenant character of God rather than His absolute deity. He will see in God His goodness rather than His greatness and more of His love than of His majesty. Then, the soul, bowing still as humbly as before, will enjoy a more sacred liberty of intercession. While prostrate before the glory of the Infinite God, it will be sustained by the refreshing consciousness of being in the presence of boundless mercy and infinite love, and by the realization of its acceptance *"in the beloved"* (Eph. 1:6). Thus the believer is invited to come up higher and is enabled to exercise the privilege of rejoicing in God and drawing near to Him in holy confidence, saying, *"Abba, Father"* (Rom. 8:15).

> So may we go from strength to strength,
>   And daily grow in grace,
> Till in Thine image raised at length,
>   We see Thee face to face.

The night also is thine.
—Psalm 74:16

Lord, You do not abdicate Your throne when the sun goes down, nor do You leave the world all through these long wintry nights to be the prey of evil. Your eyes watch us as the stars, and Your arms surround us as the zodiac encircles the sky. The dews of benevolent sleep and all the influences of the moon are in Your hand. The alarms and solemnities of night are the same with You. This is very sweet to me when watching through the midnight hours or when tossing to and fro in anguish. There are precious fruits put forth by the moon as well as by the sun. May my Lord make me to be a favored partaker in them. The night of affliction is as much under the arrangement and control of the Lord of Love as the bright summer days when all is bliss. Jesus is in the tempest. His love wraps the night about itself as a mantle, but to the eye of faith, the sable robe is hardly a disguise. From the first watch of the night to the break of day, the eternal Watcher observes His saints. He overrules the shades and dews of midnight for His people's highest good. We believe in no rival deities of good and evil contending for mastery, but we hear the voice of Jehovah saying, "I create light, and I create darkness. I, the Lord, do all these things." Gloomy seasons of religious indifference and social sin are not exempted from the divine purpose. When the altars of truth are defiled, and the ways of God forsaken, the Lord's servants weep with bitter sorrow. But they do not need to despair, for the darkest times are governed by the Lord, and they will come to their end at His command. What may seem defeat to us may be victory to Him.

> Though enwrapt in gloomy night,
> We perceive no ray of light;
> Since the Lord Himself is here,
> 'Tis not meet that we should fear.

Though he was rich, yet for your sakes he became poor.
—2 Corinthians 8:9

The Lord Jesus Christ was eternally rich, glorious, and exalted, but *"though he was rich, yet for your sakes he became poor."* The rich saint cannot be true in his communion with his poor brethren unless he gives of his substance to meet their needs. Likewise, the same rule applies to the Head and the members of the body of Christ. It is impossible that our divine Lord could have had fellowship with us unless He had imparted to us of His own abundant wealth and had become poor to make us rich. Had He remained on His throne of glory, and had we continued in the ruins of the Fall without receiving His salvation, communion would have been impossible on both sides. Our position by the Fall, apart from the covenant of grace, made it as impossible for fallen man to communicate with God as it is for Belial to be in agreement with Christ. In order, therefore, that communion might be achieved, it was necessary that the rich Kinsman would bestow His estate to His poor relatives, that the righteous Savior would give to His sinning brethren of His own perfection, and that we, the poor and guilty, would receive of His fullness *"grace for grace"* (John 1:16). Thus, in giving and receiving, the One might descend from the heights and the other ascend from the depths, and so be able to embrace each other in true and hearty fellowship. Poverty must be enriched by Him in whom are infinite treasures before it can proceed to commune; guilt must lose itself in imputed and imparted righteousness before the soul can walk in fellowship with purity. Jesus must clothe His people in His own garments, or He cannot admit them into His palace of glory. He must wash them in His own blood, or else they will be too defiled for the embrace of His fellowship. Believer, herein is love! For your sake the Lord Jesus *"became poor"* so that He might lift you up into communion with Himself.

The glory of the LORD shall be revealed,
and all flesh shall see it together.
—Isaiah 40:5

We anticipate the happy day when the whole world will be converted to Christ; when the gods of the heathen will be cast *"to the moles and to the bats"* (Isa. 2:20); when the crescent of Mohammed will wane, never again to cast its baleful rays upon the nations; when kings will bow down before the Prince of Peace, and all nations will call their Redeemer blessed. Some despair of this. They look at the world as a vessel breaking up and going to pieces, never to float again. We know that the world and all that is in it will one day be burned up; afterward, we look for new heavens and a new earth. We cannot read our Bibles without the conviction that "Jesus shall reign where'er the sun / Does his successive journeys run." We are not discouraged by the length of His delays; we are not disheartened by the long period that He allots to the church in which to struggle with little success and much defeat. We believe that God will never permit this world, which has once seen Christ's blood shed upon it, to always be the devil's stronghold. Christ came here to deliver this world from the detested sway of the powers of darkness. What a shout that will be when men and angels unite to cry, *"Alleluia: for the Lord God omnipotent reigneth"* (Rev. 19:6)! What satisfaction it will be in that day to have had a share in the fight, to have helped to break the arrows of the bow, and to have aided in winning the victory for our Lord! Happy are they who trust themselves with this conquering Lord and who fight side by side with Him, doing their little in His name and by His strength! How unhappy are those on the side of evil! It is a losing side, and it is a matter wherein to lose is to lose and to be lost forever. On whose side are you?

Behold, a virgin shall conceive, and bear a son,
and shall call his name Immanuel.
—Isaiah 7:14

Let us go today to Bethlehem, and, in company with wondering shepherds and adoring Magi, let us see Him who was born King of the Jews; for we, by faith, can claim an interest in Him and can sing, "*Unto us a child is born, unto us a son is given*" (Isa. 9:6). Jesus is Jehovah incarnate, our Lord and our God, yet our Brother and Friend. Let us adore and admire Him. Let us notice at the very first glance His miraculous conception. It was a thing unheard of before, and unparalleled since, that a virgin should conceive and bear a son. "*The LORD hath created a new thing in the earth, a woman shall compass a man*" (Jer. 31:22). The first promise involved the seed of the woman—not the offspring of the man. Since adventuresome woman led the way in the sin that brought forth Paradise lost, she, and she alone, ushers in the One who could regain paradise. Our Savior, although truly Man, was, as to His human nature, the Holy One of God. By the power of the Holy Spirit, He was born of the virgin without the taint of original sin, which belongs to all those who are born of the flesh. Let us reverently bow before the holy Child, whose innocence restores to manhood its ancient glory. Let us pray that He may be formed in us, "*the hope of glory*" (Col. 1:27). Do not fail to note His humble parentage. Our morning portion describes His mother as simply "*a virgin,*" not a princess, prophetess, or a matron of a large estate. True, her lineage was not to be despised, for the blood of kings ran in her veins; nor was her mind a weak and untaught one, for she could sing most sweetly a song of praise. Yet how humble her position, how poor the man to whom she stood betrothed, and how miserable the accommodation afforded to the newborn King! Thus has poverty become consecrated, and men of low estate are exalted to honor. Every believer is a portrait of Christ, but a poor saint is the same well-drawn picture hung in the same frame of poverty that surrounds the Master's image.

We esteem every day alike, but still, as the seasons and the general custom suggest thoughts of Jesus, let us joyfully remember our dear

Redeemer's glorious birth. To a renewed soul, every day should be the birthday of the Savior. Amid all that is humiliating, there is much that is honorable in the circumstances of the birth of our Immanuel. Whose birth was ever ushered in by a long train of prophecy or longed for by such a multitude of hearts? Who but He can boast of a forerunner who marked Him as the coming Man? When did angels indulge in midnight songs or did God ever hang a new star in the sky before? To whose cradle did rich and poor make so willing a pilgrimage and offer such hearty, unsought acts of worship? Well may earth rejoice; well may all men cease their labors to celebrate the great birthday of Jesus. Bethlehem, house of bread, we see in you our hopes forever gratified. 'Tis He, the Savior, long foretold, who will usher in the age of gold. Let gladness rule the hour. Let holy songs and sweet heart-music accompany our souls in their raptures of delight.

The golden name, Immanuel, is inexpressibly delightful. It is a word fit for the lips of cherubim for its majesty, but, because of its marvelous condescension, none but men can utter it. He is not so with seraphs as He is with us. Immanuel, *"God with us"* (Matt. 1:23)—in our nature, in our sorrow, in our lifework, in our punishment, in our grave, and now with us, or rather, we with Him, in resurrection, ascension, triumph, and Second Advent splendor. The babe of Bethlehem appears to be manifestly with us in weakness and in poverty. Let us not forget that He is equally with us in His glory and honor. Faith clasps the child, and love kisses Him with the kisses of her lips. Oh, for true spiritual fellowship with Immanuel all this day!

DECEMBER 25

Evening

And it was so, when the days of their feasting were gone about,
that Job sent and sanctified them, and rose up early in the morning,
and offered burnt offerings according to the number of them all:
for Job said, It may be that my sons have sinned,
and cursed God in their hearts. Thus did Job continually.
—Job 1:5

What the patriarch Job did early in the morning, after the family festivities, would be good for the believer to do for himself before he rests tonight. Amid the cheerfulness of family gatherings, it is easy to slide into sinful frivolities and to forget our avowed character as Christians. It should not be so, but it is. Our days of celebrating are very seldom days of sanctified enjoyment; too frequently, they degenerate into unholy levity. There is a joy that is as pure and sanctifying as though one bathed in the rivers of Eden.

Holy gratitude should be as purifying an element as grief. Unfortunately, for our poor hearts, the fact is that the *"house of mourning"* (Eccl. 7:2) is better than the *"house of feasting"* (v. 2). Come, believer, in what have you sinned today? Have you been forgetful of your high calling? Have you been as those who speak idle words and have loose tongues? Then confess the sin, and fly to the Sacrifice. The Sacrifice sanctifies. The precious blood of the slain Lamb removes the guilt and purges away the defilement of our sins of ignorance and carelessness.

Behold the Lamb of God, which taketh away the sin of the world.
(John 1:29)

The best ending for a Christmas Day would be to wash anew in the cleansing fountain. Believer, come to this sacrifice continually; if it is good to do so tonight, it is good every night. To live at the altar is the privilege of the royal priesthood. As great as it is, sin is nevertheless no cause for despair, since believers may yet again draw near to the sin-atoning Sacrifice, and have their consciences purged from dead works.

> Gladly I close this festive day,
> Grasping the altar's hallow'd horn;
> My slips and faults are washed away,
> The Lamb has all my trespass borne.

DECEMBER 26

Morning

Lo, I am with you alway.
—Matthew 28:20

The Lord Jesus is in the midst of His church. He walks among the golden candlesticks. His promise is, *"Lo, I am with you alway."* He is as surely with us now as He was with the disciples at the lake, when they saw coals of fire, and fish laid thereon and bread. Not in the flesh, but still in real truth, Jesus is with us. And a blessed truth it is, for where Jesus is, love becomes inflamed. Of all the things in the world that can set the heart burning, there is nothing like the presence of Jesus! A glimpse of Him so overcomes us that we are ready to say, "Turn Your eyes away from me, for they have overcome me." Even the smell of the aloes, the myrrh, and the cassia, which comes from His perfumed garments, causes the sick and the faint to grow strong. Let there be but a moment's leaning of the head on that gracious breast, and a reception of His divine love into our poor cold hearts, and we are no longer cold. Instead, we glow like angels, equal to every labor and capable of every suffering. If we know that Jesus is with us, every power will be developed, and every grace will be strengthened. We will cast ourselves into the Lord's service with heart, soul, and strength; therefore, the presence of Christ is to be desired above all things. His presence will be most realized by those who are most like Him. If you desire to see Christ, you must grow in conformity to Him. Bring yourself, by the power of the Spirit, into union with Christ's desires, motives, and plans of action, and you are likely to be favored with His company. Remember that His presence may be felt. His promise is as true as ever. He delights to be with us. If He does not come, it is because we hinder Him by our indifference. He will reveal Himself to our earnest prayers. He graciously permits Himself to be detained by our entreaties and by our tears, for these are the golden chains that bind Jesus to His people.

The last Adam.
—1 Corinthians 15:45

Jesus is the Head of His elect. In Adam, every heir of flesh and blood has a personal interest because Adam is the covenant head and representative of the race as considered under the law of works. Under the law of grace, every redeemed soul is one with the Lord from heaven, since He is the Second Adam, the Sponsor and Substitute of the elect in the new covenant of love. The apostle Paul declared that Levi was in the loins of Abraham when Melchisedec met him. It is a certain truth that the believer was in the loins of Jesus Christ, the Mediator, when, in old eternity, the covenant settlements of grace were decreed, ratified, and made sure forever. Thus, whatever Christ has done, He has done for the whole body of His church. We were crucified and *"buried with him"* (Col. 2:12), and to make it still more wonderful, we are risen with Him and even ascended with Him to *"sit together in heavenly places"* (Eph. 2:6). It is thus that the church has fulfilled the law and is *"accepted in the beloved"* (Eph. 1:6). It is thus that she is regarded with pleasure by the just Jehovah, for He views her in Jesus and does not look on her as separate from her covenant Head. As the anointed Redeemer of Israel, Christ Jesus has nothing separate from His church, but all that He has, He holds for her. Adam's righteousness was ours as long as he maintained it, and his sin was ours the moment that he committed it. In the same manner, all that the Second Adam is or does is ours as well as His, seeing that He is our Representative. Here is the foundation of the covenant of grace. This gracious system of representation and substitution—that moved Justin Martyr to cry out, "O blessed change, O sweet permutation!"—is the very groundwork of the Gospel of our salvation, and it is to be received with strong faith and rapturous joy.

And the Lord shall guide thee continually.
—Isaiah 58:11

T*he Lord shall guide thee."* Not an angel, but Jehovah will guide you. He said He would not go through the wilderness before His people, that an angel would go before them to lead them in the way; but Moses said, *"If thy presence go not with me, carry us not up hence"* (Exod. 33:15). Christian, God has not left you in your earthly pilgrimage to an angel's guidance: He Himself leads the way. You may not see the cloudy, fiery pillar, but Jehovah will never forsake you. Notice the word *"shall"*—*"The Lord shall guide thee."* How certain this makes it! How sure it is that God will not forsake us! His precious shalls and wills are better than men's promises. *"I will never leave thee, nor forsake thee"* (Heb. 13:5). Then notice the adverb "continually." We are not merely to be guided sometimes, but we are to have a perpetual monitor. We are not occasionally to be left to our own understanding, and so to wander; but we are continually to hear the guiding voice of the Great Shepherd. If we follow close at His heels, we will not err. We will be led by a right way to a city to dwell in. If you have to change your position in life; if you have to move to distant shores; if it happens that you are cast into poverty or uplifted suddenly into a more responsible position than the one you now occupy; if you are thrown among strangers or cast among foes, do not fear, for *"the Lord shall guide thee continually."* If you live close to God and your heart is kept warm by His holy love, there are no dilemmas out of which you will not be delivered. You cannot go wrong when you follow in the company of God. Like Enoch, walk with God, and you cannot mistake your road. You have infallible wisdom to direct you, immutable love to comfort you, and eternal power to defend you. *Jehovah*—pay attention to that word—Jehovah will guide you continually.

DECEMBER 27

Evening

Can the rush grow up without mire?
—Job 8:11

The rush plant is spongy and hollow, and so is a hypocrite. There is no substance or stability in him. The rush is shaken to and fro in every wind, just as formalists yield to every influence. For this reason the rush is not broken by the tempest; neither are hypocrites troubled with persecution. I would not willingly be a deceiver or be deceived; perhaps the text for this day may help me to examine myself to see whether or not I am a hypocrite. The rush by nature lives in water, and it owes its very existence to the mire and moisture wherein it has taken root. If the marsh becomes dry, the rush withers very quickly. Its greenness is absolutely dependent on circumstances; a present abundance of water makes it flourish, and a drought destroys it right away. Is this my case? Do I serve God only when I am in good company, or when religion is profitable and respectable? Do I love the Lord only when temporal comforts are received from His hands? If so, I am a base hypocrite; and like the withering rush, I will perish when death deprives me of outward joys. But can I honestly assert that when bodily comforts have been few and my surroundings have been rather adverse to grace than at all helpful to it, I have still held fast my integrity? Then I have hope that there is a genuine, vital godliness in me.

The rush cannot grow without moisture, but plants that belong to the Lord can and do flourish, even in the year of drought. A godly man often grows best when his worldly circumstances decay. He who follows Christ for gain is a Judas. Those who follow for loaves and fish are children of the devil, but those who walk with Him out of love for Himself are His own beloved ones. Lord, let me find my life in You, and not in the mire of this world's favor or gain.

I came not to send peace, but a sword.
—Matthew 10:34

The Christian is sure to make enemies. It will be one of his goals to make none; but if, in doing right and believing the truth, he loses every earthly friend, he will count it but a small loss, since his great Friend in heaven will be friendlier and will reveal Himself to him more graciously than anyone else ever could. You who have taken up His cross, do you not know what your Master said? *"I am come to set a man at variance against his father, and the daughter against her mother,…and a man's foes shall be they of his own household"* (Matt. 10:35–36). Christ is the great Peacemaker; but before peace, He brings war. Where the light comes, the darkness must retire. Where truth is, lies must flee; or, if falsehoods remain, there must be a stern conflict, for the truth cannot and will not lower its standard, and lies must be trodden underfoot. If you follow Christ, you will have all the dogs of the world yelping at your heels. If you wish to live so as to stand the test of the Last Judgment, depend on this: the world will not speak well of you. He who has the friendship of the world is an enemy to God; but if you are true and faithful to the Most High, men will resent your unflinching fidelity, since it is a testimony against their iniquities. Fearless of all consequences, you must do right. You will need the courage of a lion unhesitatingly to pursue a course that will turn your best friend into your fiercest foe; but, for the love of Jesus, you must be courageous. To risk reputation and affection for the truth's sake is such a deed that to do it constantly you will need a degree of moral principle that only the Spirit of God can work in you. Do not turn your back like a coward, but act like a man. Boldly follow in your Master's steps, for He has walked this rough way before you. Better a brief warfare and eternal rest than false peace and everlasting torment.

The life which I now live in the flesh I live
by the faith of the Son of God.
—Galatians 2:20

When the Lord in mercy passed by and saw us in our blood, He first of all said, "Live." He did this first, because life is one of the absolutely essential things in spiritual matters. Until it is given, we are incapable of partaking in the things of the kingdom. Now the life that grace confers on the saints at the moment of their quickening is none other than the life of Christ. Like the sap from the stem, faith runs into us—the branches—and it establishes a living connection between our souls and Jesus. Faith is the grace that perceives this union, having proceeded from it as its firstfruit. It is the neck that joins the body of the church to its all-glorious Head.

Oh, Faith, thou bond of union with the Lord,
    Is not this office thine? And thy fit name,
In the economy of gospel types,
    And symbols apposite—the Church's neck;
Identifying her in will and work
    With Him ascended?

Faith lays hold of the Lord Jesus with a firm and determined grasp. It knows His excellence and worth, and no temptation can induce it to repose its trust elsewhere. Christ Jesus is so delighted with this heavenly grace that He never ceases to strengthen and sustain it by the loving embrace and all-sufficient support of His eternal arms. Here, then, is established a living, sensible, and delightful union that casts forth streams of love, confidence, sympathy, pleasure, and joy, whereof both the bride and Bridegroom love to drink. When the soul can evidently perceive this oneness between itself and Christ, the pulse may be felt as beating for both, and the one blood as flowing through the veins of each. Then is the heart as near heaven as it can be on earth and is prepared for the enjoyment of the most sublime and spiritual kind of fellowship.

What think ye of Christ?
—Matthew 22:42

The great test of your soul's health is, What do you think of Christ? Is He to you *"fairer than the children of men"* (Ps. 45:2), *"chiefest among ten thousand"* (Song 5:10), the *"altogether lovely"* (v. 16)? Wherever Christ is thus esteemed, all the faculties of the spiritual man exercise themselves with energy. I will judge your faith by this barometer: does Christ stand high or low with you? If you have thought little of Christ, if you have been content to live without His presence, if you have cared little for His honor, if you have been neglectful of His laws, then I know that your soul is sick. May God grant that it will not be sick unto death! But if the first thought of your spirit has been, How can I honor Jesus? and if the daily desire of your soul has been, *"Oh that I knew where I might find him!"* (Job 23:3), I tell you that you may have a thousand infirmities and even scarcely know whether you are a child of God at all, yet I am persuaded, beyond a doubt, that you are safe, since Jesus is great in your esteem. I do not care about your rags; what do you think of His royal apparel? I do not care about your wounds, though they bleed in torrents; what do you think of His wounds? Are they like glittering rubies in your estimation? I think no less of you, though you lie like Lazarus on the dunghill, and dogs lick your sores. I do not judge you by your poverty; what do you think of the King in His beauty? Has He a glorious high throne in your heart? Would you set Him higher if you could? Would you be willing to die if you could but add another trumpet to the melody that proclaims His praise? Then it is well with you. Whatever you may think of yourself, if Christ is greater to you, you will be with Him before long.

Though all the world my choice deride,
   Yet Jesus shall my portion be;
For I am pleased with none beside,
   The fairest of the fair is He.

Hitherto hath the LORD helped us.
—1 Samuel 7:12

The word *"hitherto"* seems like a hand pointing in the direction of the past. Whether for twenty years or seventy, *"hitherto hath the LORD helped us"*! Through poverty, through wealth, through sickness, through health, at home, abroad, on the land, on the sea, in honor, in dishonor, in perplexity, in joy, in trial, in triumph, in prayer, in temptation, *"hitherto hath the LORD helped us"*! We delight to look down a long avenue of trees. It is delightful to gaze from end to end of the long vista, a sort of verdant temple, with its branching pillars and its arches of leaves; in the same way, look down the long aisles of your years, at the green boughs of mercy overhead, and the strong pillars of lovingkindness and faithfulness that bear up your joys. Are there no birds in the branches singing? Surely there must be many, and they all sing of mercy received *"hitherto."* But the word also points forward. For when a man gets up to a certain mark and writes "hitherto," he is not yet at the end; there is still a distance to be traversed. More trials, more joys; more temptations, more triumphs; more prayers, more answers; more toils, more strength; more fights, more victories; and then come sickness, old age, disease, and death. Is it over now? No! There is still more awakening in Jesus' likeness, thrones, harps, songs, psalms, white raiment, the face of Jesus, the society of saints, the glory of God, the fullness of eternity, the infinity of bliss. Oh, be of good courage, believer, and with grateful confidence raise your Ebenezer, for He who has helped you *"hitherto"* will help you all your journey through. When read in heaven's light, how glorious and marvelous a prospect will your *"hitherto"* unfold to your grateful eyes!

Knowest thou not that it will be bitterness in the latter end?
—2 Samuel 2:26

If you are merely a professor of faith but not a possessor of faith in Christ Jesus, the following lines are a true depiction of your end. You are a respectable attendant at a place of worship; you go because others go, not because your heart is right with God. This is your beginning. I will suppose that for the next twenty or thirty years, you will be spared to go on as you do now, professing religion by an outward attendance on the means of grace, but having no heart in the matter. Tread softly, for I must show you the deathbed of such a one as yourself. Let us gaze upon him gently. A clammy sweat is on his brow, and he wakes up crying, "O God, it is hard to die. Did you send for my minister?" "Yes, he is coming." The minister comes. "Sir, I fear that I am dying!" "Have you any hope?" "I cannot say that I have. I fear to stand before my God; oh, pray for me!" The prayer is offered for him with sincere earnestness, and the way of salvation is for the ten-thousandth time put before him, but before he has grasped the rope, I see him sink. I may put my finger on those cold eyelids, for they will never see anything here again. But where is the man, and where are the man's true eyes? It is written, *"In hell he lift up his eyes, being in torments"* (Luke 16:23). Oh, why did he not lift up his eyes before? Because he was so accustomed to hearing the Gospel that his soul slept under it. Alas! If you lift up your eyes there, how bitter will be your wailing. Let the Savior's own words reveal the woe: *"Father Abraham, have mercy on me, and send Lazarus, that he may dip the tip of his finger in water, and cool my tongue; for I am tormented in this flame"* (v. 24). There is a frightful meaning in those words. May you never have to understand its truth by the red light of Jehovah's wrath!

DECEMBER 30
Evening

Better is the end of a thing than the beginning thereof.
—Ecclesiastes 7:8

Look at our Lord and Master, and see His beginning. He was *"despised and rejected of men; a man of sorrows, and acquainted with grief"* (Isa. 53:3). Would you see the end? He sits at His Father's right hand, expectant, waiting until His enemies are made His footstool (Ps. 110:1). *"As he is, so are we in this world"* (1 John 4:17). You must bear the cross, or you will never wear the crown; you must wade through the mire, or you will never walk the golden pavement. Cheer up, then, poor Christian. *"Better is the end of a thing than the beginning thereof."* See that creeping worm; how contemptible is its appearance! It is the beginning of a thing. Notice that insect with gorgeous wings, playing in the sunbeams, sipping at the flower bells, full of happiness and life; that is the end thereof. That caterpillar is you, until you are wrapped up in the chrysalis of death; but when Christ appears, you will *"be like him; for [you] shall see him as he is"* (1 John 3:2). Be content to be like Him, so that like Him you may *"be satisfied, when [you] awake, with [His] likeness"* (Ps. 17:15). That rough-looking diamond is put on the wheel of the lapidary. He cuts it on all sides. It loses much—much that seemed costly to itself. The king is crowned; the diadem is put on the monarch's head with the trumpet's joyful sound. A glittering ray flashes from that coronet, and it beams from that very diamond that was so recently sorely vexed by the lapidary. You may venture to compare yourself to such a diamond, for you are one of God's people; this is the time of the cutting process. Let faith and *"patience have [their] perfect work"* (James 1:4), for in the day when the crown will be set on the head of the *"King eternal, immortal, invisible"* (1 Tim. 1:17), one ray of glory will stream from you. *"They shall be mine, saith the LORD of hosts, in that day when I make up my jewels"* (Mal. 3:17). *"Better is the end of a thing than the beginning thereof."*

The harvest is past, the summer is ended, and we are not saved.
—Jeremiah 8:20

N*ot saved*"! Dear reader, is this your mournful plight? You have been warned of the judgment to come, encouraged to escape for your life, yet at this moment, you are not saved! You know the way of salvation. You read it in the Bible, you hear it from the pulpit, and it is explained to you by friends; yet you neglect it and, therefore, are not saved. You will be without excuse when the Lord will *"judge the quick and the dead"* (2 Tim. 4:1). The Holy Spirit has given more or less of a blessing upon the Word that has been preached in your hearing. Times of refreshing have come from the divine presence, yet you are without Christ. All these hopeful seasons have come and gone—your summer and your harvest have passed—yet you are not saved. Years have followed one another into eternity, and your last year will soon be here. Youth has gone, and adulthood is going, yet you are not saved. Let me ask you: will you ever be saved? Is there any likelihood of it? Already the most propitious seasons have left you unsaved. Will other occasions alter your condition? Means—the best of means, used perseveringly and with the utmost affection—have failed with you. What more can be done for you? Affliction and prosperity have both failed to impress you. Tears and prayers and sermons have been wasted on your barren heart. Are not the probabilities dead against your ever being saved? Is it not more than likely that you will abide as you are until death forever bars the door of hope? Do you recoil from the supposition? Yet it is a most reasonable one. He who is not washed in the cleansing waters will, in all probability, go to his end filthy. The convenient time has not come yet. Why should it ever come? It is logical to fear that it never will arrive, and that like Felix (see Acts 24:24–25), you will find no convenient season to be saved—until you are in hell! Oh, think about what hell is and of the frightening probability that you will soon be cast into it! Reader, suppose you would die unsaved. No words can describe your doom. Write out your terrible state in tears and blood; talk of it with groans and gnashing of teeth. You will be punished with everlasting destruction from the glory of the Lord and from the glory of His power. A brother's voice would gladly startle you into earnestness. Be wise. Be wise in time, and before another year begins. Believe in Jesus, who is able to save *"to the uttermost"* (Heb. 7:25). Consecrate these last hours of this year to solitary thought, and if deep repentance is bred in you, it will be well; if it leads to a humble faith in Jesus, it will be best of all. See to it that this year does not pass away with your still having an unforgiven spirit. Do not let the New Year's midnight peals sound upon a joyless spirit! Believe now and live. *"Escape for thy life; look not behind thee, neither stay thou in all the plain; escape to the mountain, lest thou be consumed"* (Gen. 19:17).

In the last day, that great day of the feast, Jesus stood and cried,
saying, If any man thirst, let him come unto me, and drink.
—John 7:37

Patience had *"her perfect work"* (James 1:4) in the Lord Jesus, and until the last day of the feast, He pleaded with the Jews. Even as on this last day of the year, He pleads with us and waits to be gracious to us. Admirable indeed is the longsuffering of the Savior in bearing with some of us year after year, notwithstanding our provocations, rebellions, and resistance of His Holy Spirit. Wonder of wonders that we are still in the land of mercy!

Pity expressed herself most plainly, for Jesus *"cried,"* which implies not only the loudness of His voice, but the tenderness of His tones. He entreats us to be reconciled. *"As though God did beseech you by us: we pray you in Christ's stead"* (2 Cor. 5:20), said the apostle Paul. What earnest, pathetic terms are these! How deep must be the love that makes the Lord weep over sinners, and like a mother coax His children to His bosom! Surely at the call of such a cry our willing hearts will come.

Provision is made most plenteously; all is provided that man can need to quench his soul's thirst. The Atonement brings peace to his conscience; the Gospel brings the richest instruction; the person of Jesus is the noblest object of affection to his heart; the truth as it is in Jesus supplies the purest nutriment to the whole man. Thirst is terrible, but Jesus can remove it. Though the soul were utterly famished, Jesus could restore it.

Proclamation is made most freely, so that every thirsty one is welcome. No other distinction is made but that of thirst. Whether it is the thirst of avarice, ambition, pleasure, knowledge, or rest, he who suffers from it is invited. The thirst may be bad in itself, and be no sign of grace, but rather a mark of inordinate sin longing to be gratified with deeper draughts of lust; but it is not goodness in the creature that brings him the invitation. The Lord Jesus sends it freely, and without respect of persons.

Personality is declared most fully. The sinner must come to Jesus, not to works, ordinances, or doctrines, but to a personal Redeemer, who His own self bare our sins in His own body on the tree. The bleeding, dying, rising Savior is the only star of hope to a sinner. Oh, for grace to come now and drink, before the sun sets on the year's last day!

No waiting or preparation is so much as hinted at. Drinking represents a reception for which no suitability is required. A fool, a thief, or a harlot can drink; and so sinfulness of character is no bar to the invitation to believe in Jesus. We want no golden cup, no bejeweled chalice, in which to convey the water to the thirsty; the mouth of poverty is welcome to stoop down and drink deeply of the flowing flood. Blistered, leprous, filthy lips may touch the stream of divine love; they cannot pollute it, but will themselves be purified. Jesus is the fount of hope. Dear reader, hear the dear Redeemer's loving voice as He cries to each of us, *"If any man thirst, let him come unto me, and drink."*

ABOUT THE AUTHOR

Charles Haddon Spurgeon was born on June 19, 1834, at Kelvedon, Essex, England, the firstborn of eight surviving children. His parents were committed Christians, and his father was a preacher. Spurgeon was converted in 1850 at the age of fifteen. He began to help the poor and to hand out tracts, and he was known as "The Boy Preacher."

He preached his first sermon at the age of sixteen. At age eighteen, he became the pastor of Waterbeach Baptist Chapel, preaching in a barn. By 1854, he was well-known as a preacher and was asked to become the pastor of New Park Street Chapel in London. In 1856, Spurgeon married Susannah Thompson; they had twin sons, both of whom later entered the ministry.

Spurgeon's compelling sermons and lively preaching style drew multitudes of people, and many came to Christ. Soon the crowds had grown so large that they blocked the narrow streets near the church. Services eventually had to be held in rented halls, and he often preached to congregations of more than ten thousand. The Metropolitan Tabernacle was built in 1861 to accommodate the large numbers of people.

Spurgeon published over thirty-five hundred sermons, which were so popular that they sold by the ton. At one point his sermons sold twenty-five thousand copies every week. An 1870 edition of the English magazine Vanity Fair called him an "original and powerful preacher...honest, resolute, sincere; lively, entertaining." The prime minister of England, members of the royal family, and Florence Nightingale, among others, went to hear him preach. Spurgeon preached to an estimated ten million people throughout his lifetime. Not surprisingly, he is called the "Prince of Preachers."

In addition to his powerful preaching, Spurgeon founded and supported charitable outreaches, including educational institutions. His pastors' college, which is still in existence today, taught nearly nine hundred students in Spurgeon's time. He also founded the famous Stockwell Orphanage.

Charles Spurgeon died in 1892, and his death was mourned by many.